Drawing from a stunning collection of bibliographic Corwin presents a welcome and timely volume on SIM's long history. He sheds significant light on the evolution of the Faith Missions Movement from the late 19th century until today. No recent work comes close to matching the insights Corwin's book provides on the topic. Evangelicals will benefit greatly from this mission history as it discusses SIM's shortcomings, particularly with regard to issues of race and diversity, alongside the things it did right. It also masterfully reveals a template for how such shortcomings can be righted, and how the global gospel harvest force can be more fully unleashed. Through the geographically diverse mergers that have taken place over the years, it is clear that God has placed SIM in a privileged position to both facilitate and accelerate the wonderful God-ordained pattern of missions from anywhere to everywhere. It is a pleasure to endorse *By Prayer to the Nations: A Short History of SIM*.

Ayman S. Ibrahim, Ph.D.
Bill and Connie Jenkins Associate Professor of Islamic Studies
Director, Jenkins Center for the Christian Understanding of Islam
The Southern Baptist Theological Seminary, Louisville, Kentucky

Engaging, at times poignant, this abbreviated history of the various streams of missionaries and the agencies that today comprise SIM deserves a place of great significance in the library of historical evangelical faith missions. In a series of compelling, well-told stories Corwin recounts the multiple people and streams that merged together into a single organization. This is a must-read for everyone who wants to understand not only SIM and its various forebearers, but also the faith missions movement over the course of the past century.

Scott Moreau, D.Miss.
Academic Dean, Wheaton College Graduate School
Professor of Intercultural Studies

Missiologist Gary Corwin has done the greater mission community a marvelous service by providing this extensive and definitive work on one of the premier global missions that has been making a positive impact for well over a century. Not only does it provide historical facts, persons, and events, but a helpful bonus is the detailed sections that candidly deal with the major issues SIM has navigated through in its long history. Here is the inside story of a forward moving mission.

Marvin Newell, D.Miss.
Senior Vice President, Missio Nexus

Why write a history book in an age when we are constantly interrupted and tempted to see what is happening right now in the world—all with a device in our pocket? We can find out anything . . . only the reality is, we cannot!

It is a great service to the kingdom of God and the body of Christ that Gary Corwin—along with many of his co-workers and dear friends—has put together *By Prayer to the Nations* . . . If you want to learn about long-range ministry, what it takes to stick it out and learn from your failures, you need this book. If you want to learn more about how real, faithful, committed believers live out faith, sacrifice, the gospel, church, leadership, training, and courage—all in the midst of cross-cultural situations more and more of us face globally, you need this book.

Greg H Parsons, Ph.D.
Global Director
Frontier Ventures

Today we celebrate the advent of "global Christianity," the prospect of hundreds of millions of Christ followers throughout Asia, Africa, the Americas, and other regions. Less recognized are the origins of this astonishing global movement—the pioneering missionaries and agencies to whom virtually every church network can be traced. These missionary bands are the unsung heroes of church history, men and women who have selflessly planted the gospel seed over the last century or more. Corwin's *By Prayer to the Nations: A Short History of SIM* chronicles one of the most consequential of these missionary streams, along with the tributaries that fed it. His masterful compilation is but a tantalizing precursor, I suspect, to the celestial story-fest that awaits!

Steve Richardson
President, Pioneers USA

Gary Corwin has written a compelling and inspiring history of SIM that tells the story of the mission as it emerged from the faith mission movement of the late 19th century and now grapples with changing realities and complexities of the early 21st century. Packed full of details, it weaves together the unique faith stories of different agencies that, over time, came together in the SIM we know today. The book stands as a tribute to those who have sacrificed much because they were convinced that no one should live and die without hearing God's good news.

Stephen Roy, Ph.D.
President, Emmanuel Bible College, Kitchener, Ontario, Canada
Chair, SIM Board of Governors, 2008–2016

BY PRAYER TO THE NATIONS

BY PRAYER TO THE NATIONS

A Short History of SIM

GARY R. CORWIN

credo
house publishers

N: 978-1-625860-82-8

d interior design by Frank Gutbrod
ing: "You Are Worthy," by Chuck Guth
abeth Banks

d States of America

To the men and women from widely diverse
backgrounds who have for more than a century established,
embraced, and extended outposts of the kingdom of God
in the world through the work of SIM.

CONTENTS

FOREWORD

Malcolm McGregor

For well over a century, an amazing work of God has been accomplished through the dedication and sacrifice of many people in SIM. This work has deeply impacted the lives of people all over the world. Having played a very small part in this story in over 18 years of leadership (eight years as the UK / N. Europe Director and ten years as the International Director), I have been reflecting on the following convictions that have helped SIM maintain its focus and direction:

Faith and Courage
This was demonstrated in the lives of the founders of SIM who stepped into Sub-Saharan Africa, South Africa, South America, and Asia—places where the name of Jesus was not known at that time. This same faith and courage continue to be evident today—the 2014 Ebola crisis in West Africa is but one example.

Sacrifice
Stories of sacrifice run through the pages of this book and through the history of SIM. Stories of gaining through losing, life through death, and work accomplished through taking up the cross of Jesus and following him.

Dependence on God
At various times in its history SIM's back has been against the wall. Again and again we have seen God step into tough situations to do more that we could ever ask or imagine.

Prayer
By Prayer is the motto of SIM—through prayer we acknowledge our reliance on God and seek direction and resources to accomplish his work. SIM people are people of prayer.

The Gospel in All Its Power
SIM believes that the Gospel demands both proclamation and action, rooted in an unshakeable conviction that the greatest human need that exists in a person's life is to know God.

The Central Role of the Church
The establishment of local, viable, biblically centered, growing churches that are equipped for mission has always been at the heart of the vision of SIM.

Leadership Development and Leadership Transitions

Organisations need good leaders if they are to prosper and the training of godly leaders means investment. SIM places a strong emphasis on this and its ability to transition well from one generation of leaders to another is evidence of this.

International and Global

The increasing cultural diversity in SIM has been a wonderful blessing to the organisation. God is at work through his global church and its vitality and spiritual energy have influenced SIM for good. It is a joy to see the founding values of SIM being rediscovered by the many cultures that now make up the organisation.

Deep Theological Convictions

In the midst of times of significant theological drift in some churches and organisations, SIM has consistently affirmed its commitment to biblical truth to underpin its vision and mission. Yet it has also been able to draw people into fellowship and service from across denominational lines who share our statement of faith.

Kingdom Mindset

An organisation can so easily develop a culture of self-preservation, turn inward and take its eyes off the vision. SIM seeks to live and act on Kingdom values where the vision and mission is bigger than the organisation itself. God has shown his faithfulness to SIM as this has been lived out in practice.

Sound Financial Policies

The funding of SIM and its ministries is, and always has been, "by faith" but this is built on sound and prudent financial policies and accountability. SIM has been blessed throughout its history with men and women of God who have demonstrated great wisdom and skill in this area.

Open to Change—Constantly Looking to God for Direction

The pain of change is often greater than the pain of staying the same yet every organisation needs to be open and willing to face this pain if effective change is to take place. SIM proactively, creatively and appropriately embraces change so that the unchanging Gospel can continue to be made known.

As you read through this unique history you will recognise these principles directing and guiding the organisation from its founding to where it is today. The recent appointment of a Nigerian, Dr. Joshua Bogunjoko, as the International Director of SIM is evidence of the exciting change that has taken place in the profile of the church worldwide and in the cause of mission—a change in which God has graciously allowed SIM to play its part. To Him him be the glory.

Malcolm McGregor (2014)

FOREWORD

Tibebe Esthete, Ph.D.

By *Prayer to the Nations: A Short History of SIM* by Gary R. Corwin presents a riveting account of the SIM—a farsighted and well-organized mission enterprise with global ramifications. The book allows us to look deeply into the rich history and complex journey of SIM, which was birthed in the context of the faith mission movement of the late nineteenth century. Tracing its roots from the visions of its various founders, the author maps out the fascinating voyage of the SIM from an "inland" endeavor in the missionally unchartered interior of West Africa, to engagement throughout most of Africa, and in much of the Middle East, Asia and Latin America, amply showing how one small step of faith and obedience can lead far beyond the founders' dreams. I myself am most grateful that I came to faith through the ministry of the SIM, namely, through the International Evangelical Church in Addis Ababa.

The book is rich in texture as it addresses a wide array of topics and themes such as evangelism, church planting, partnership, indigenization, mission theology and practice, racism, encounters with Islam, and mission strategies in rural and urban contexts, to offer just a partial list. It also ably weaves together a wide variety of primary sources ranging from reports, diaries, letters, and other archival materials. Its contribution is further enhanced by the insightful supplements provided at the end of most of the chapters and the extensive bibliographical sources supplied at the end of the book.

The book cogently shows that the missionary enterprise is not a straight and one-way trajectory. This is validated by the adaptability and the various innovative approaches that SIM embraced throughout its history to make its mission relevant across changing times, regional and cultural contexts, and with due regard and sensitivity to demographic variables. Without a doubt, *By Prayer to the Nations* is an excellent resource for students, researchers in the field of missiology/mission history, and for anyone wanting to know more of the intriguingly impressive journey of the SIM, a faithful, reflective, and pulsating force for the gospel in the world.

Tibebe Eshete
Assistant Professor, History Department
Michigan State University

PREFACE

"A history of missions is the history of answered prayer."
—Samuel Zwemer

Concerning This Book's Title

By *Prayer to the Nations: A Short History of SIM*[1] is the title of this book because Zwemer is absolutely right and because "By Prayer" has been both a motto and an aspiration for SIM from its early days. Whether we have always been as faithful in our practice as we should be, I will leave to the judgment of our heavenly Father; but there is much evidence that we have at least tried.

While it is likely that Rowland Bingham commonly used the phrase and was the inspiration for its wider use, the first formal use of "By Prayer" as a motto can be dated to 16 December 1935 when it was used at the bottom of the first SIM lapel pin. The motto comes from 2 Corinthians 1:11 (KJV) which reads "Ye also helping together by prayer for us."[2]

Photos Preface 1–3. "By Prayer" pins through the decades.
Pin for 1935, 1967, and 1989.[3]

In his introduction to the 2017 *SIM Prayer Guide*, Dr. Joshua Bogunjoko, SIM International Director, reflects on the motto "By Prayer" this way:

> How gratifying to see that SIM continues to live up to and live in to this motto that was first made plain in 1935. By Prayer is not a slogan pasted on the outside of our literature; it is a conviction bound on the inside of our hearts. By Prayer is not a clever sound bite; it is a humble posture. By Prayer is not

compartmentalized as one duty of ministry; it shapes every aspect of every ministry. By Prayer is not an empty ritual; it is an activity that in itself expresses love and compassion for others.

By prayer we view our calling. By prayer we respond to new and existing open doors to proclaim the crucified and risen Christ in communities where He is least known. Prayer reveals barriers, and, by prayer alone, we cross them.

Preface to the Draft Edition
(*Service and Sacrifice: A Short History of SIM from 19th Century Roots to 21st Century Reach*, SIM, 2015)

SIM International Director Malcolm McGregor invited me in 2011 to update the only "institutional" history of SIM then extant, *Root From Dry Ground*, last published in 1991. This small book of 67 pages contains only six pages added to that edition about the missions (Andes Evangelical Mission [AEM] and International Christian Fellowship [ICF]) that merged with SIM in 1982 and 1989 respectively. The most recent merger with Africa Evangelical Fellowship (AEF) in 1998, of course, was not included.

The more I reflected on this, the more I was convinced that a more complete short history was long overdue. While significant historical work has been done over the years on many pieces of the SIM story, no overall history of the mission existed. That, then, is what this project became. Both Malcolm McGregor and the current international director, Joshua Bogunjoko, have been very supportive of this project and patient with its author who attempted to complete the project while remaining faithful to other commitments.

The nature of this history is not likely to please many serious academic historians very much. I aspired to be one once, before my love affair with applied missiology took over, so I know where this work falls short. First of all, it suffers the common failing of all "short" histories in leaving way too much unsaid. In addition, it is not built upon primary research. It is not even built upon exhaustive use of all available secondary sources. It also makes excessive use of long quotations and includes whole sections written by others—sometimes as original writing and sometimes as writing adapted by this author for length and readability. Necessary permissions were secured for material not possessed by SIM.

The principal reason behind the long quotations is to allow the reader to hear the story as much as possible from contemporary voices. That's not to say that additional commentary is not proffered, but that the primary voice, like the long history of decision making in SIM, comes from those as close to the action as possible.

The target audience for this book is twofold: It is first of all, for those thousands of individuals who either are invested or are considering investment, emotionally or otherwise, in the success of SIM in fulfilling its calling in mission. Whether they are goers, givers, those who pray, or interested onlookers—or are considering engaging in any of those roles—this book is published with them in mind.

The secondary audience this book is intended for are the academics, whether secular or religious social scientists of many sorts; graduate students or advanced scholars in the history of missions, missiology, and related subjects; or institutions catering to these groups. I hope that some of the things alluded to in this volume will spark interest in fuller exploration of particular subjects. The bibliography that is included, courtesy of Dr. Tim Geysbeek and SIM's International Archives, is designed to tempt others in just this way.

Finally, let me just say how much I am indebted to my good friend and colleague, Dr. Tim Geysbeek, for excellent writing, bibliographic work, and the merger chart that he provided. My debt goes also to Tim and the staff of the SIM Archives led by Sue McKinney, for pulling together huge amounts of material for my use. This is the fodder out of which this book is crafted. Any shortcomings in the book, however, are mine alone. I am convinced that the first regular edition of this book will be much better than this first draft, benefiting by constructive feedback that will undoubtedly come concerning key people and events it missed, incorrect details, and the relative attention given to subjects covered. I welcome such feedback and trust that future editions will reflect significant improvement as a result.

Preface to This Edition
(*By Prayer to the Nations: A Short History of SIM*, **Credo House Publishers, 2018**)
The wish for constructive feedback that was alluded to in the preface to the draft edition of this book was more than fulfilled. The 350 copies of the draft edition that went out around the world starting from Chiang Mai, Thailand, in March 2015 reaped a treasure trove of excellent material advising on, correcting, and adding to what is found in the draft edition. I have sometimes joked with friends that I received back everything I had hoped for, plus about 100 percent more. Unfortunately, it is not possible to employ all of it in this current edition. This is after all *A Short History of SIM*, and the draft edition was already almost four hundred pages. Much is being added, however, and what is not being added here will be part of the book feedback collection placed in the SIM Archives for use by future researchers and writers, perhaps one of whom will tackle the still needed *Comprehensive History of SIM* in five volumes.[4]

In addition to numerous corrections and other improvements made to the draft edition, there are several additions that should be mentioned: These include significant material on ministries of compassion, SIM governance over the last 25 years, a master list of directors of SIM and related missions, the formation of denominations, and the history of MECO (Middle East Christian Outreach) - the most recent group to unite its ministry efforts with those of SIM. In addition there have been a number of illuminating supplements and sidebars added, as well as an index and a much-improved firsthand take on the Life Challenge merger with SIM.

My sincere thanks to all that have contributed to make the first regular edition of this short history a much-improved product over the draft edition. Credo House Publishers has certainly been a huge help in this process. I sincerely thank its publisher, Tim Beals, and editor, Elizabeth Banks, who have been so insightful, helpful, and patient in guiding this manuscript through the publication process. Tami Geysbeek kindly proofread one of the last drafts of the manuscript. Special thanks must once again go to Dr. Tim Geysbeek, without whose excellent writing, proofing, and ferreting out of photos and details this volume would be greatly impoverished. There are too many others to mention, to whom a debt of gratitude is also certainly owed. I know their contributions have been a labor of love, as has mine, but it has been a very substantial labor and I am grateful. This book is being sent forth with great hope that it will be a blessing to many and bring much glory to God. As always, however, responsibility for whatever failings it still exhibits is solely mine.

Coram Deo,
Gary R. Corwin
21 November 2017

"To live coram Deo *is to live one's entire life in the presence of God, under the authority of God, to the glory of God."*
—R. C. Sproul

ILLUSTRATIONS

Photos

Note: all photos, unless otherwise indicated, are courtesy of the SIM International Archives and Records.

Epilogue

Appendices

MAPS

ACRONYMS

ACLA	Africa Christian Literature Advancement
ACROSS	Action of Christian Resource Organizations Serving Sudan
ACTEA	Accrediting Council for Theological Education in Africa
AEA	Association of Evangelicals in Africa
AEAM	Association of Evangelicals in Africa and Madagascar
AEC-B	Africa Evangelical Church of Botswana
AEC-M	Africa Evangelical Church of Malawi
AEC-SA	Africa Evangelical Church of South Africa
AEF	Africa Evangelical Fellowship
AEM	Andes Evangelical Mission
AFM	Abyssinian Frontiers Mission
ALM	Arabic Literature Mission
AMS	African Missionary Society (renamed Evangelical Missionary Society)
ASTMH	American Society of Tropical Medicine and Hygiene
BCA	Bible Church of Africa (Ghana)
BIM	Bolivian Indian Mission
BOG	Board of Governors
BSM	British Syrian Mission
CALL	Christian Arabic Literature League
CCWM	Congress on the Church's World Mission
CEG	Challenge Enterprises of Ghana
CGM	Cape General Mission
CIGM	Ceylon and Indian General Mission
CIM	China Inland Mission
C & MA	Christian and Missionary Alliance
CMS	Church Missionary Society
C-SEA	Central/Southeast Asia Area
CSM	Central Soudan Mission
CSM	Community Services Ministries
DMG	Deutsche Missionsgemeinschaft
DRC	Dutch Reformed Church
ECFA	Evangelical Council for Financial Accountability
ECOL	Evangelical Church of Liberia

ECSA	Evangelical Church of South Africa
ECWA	Association of the Evangelical Churches of West Africa, later renamed Evangelical Church of West African, and now Evangelical Church Winning All
ECZ	Evangelical Church of Zambia
EE-BF	Église Evangélique (Burkina Faso)
EEGHV	Eglise Evangélique Gourmantché en Haute Volta
EEIT	L'église Évangélique Indépendante du Togo
EERN	Église Évangelique de la République du Niger
EESN	Église Évangélique Salama du Niger
EF	Evangel Fellowship
EFMA	Evangelical Foreign Mission Association
EFSA	Evangelical Fellowship of South Africa
EGM	Egypt General Mission
EHA	Emmanuel Hospital Association
EJAC	Evangelical Joint Accounting Committee
EKHC	Ethiopia Kale Heywet Church
ELWA	Eternal Love Winning Africa
EMB	Egypt Mission Band
EMM	Eastern Mennonite Mission
EMS	Evangelical Missionary Society
ESL	English as a Second Language
ETS	ECWA Theological Seminary
ETU	Ebola Treatment Unit
EVD	Ebola Virus Disease
IC	International Council
ICETE	International Council for Evangelical Theological Education
ICF	International Christian Fellowship
IEP	Iglesia Evangélica Peruara (Evangelical Peruvian Church)
IFMA	Interdenominational Foreign Mission Association (today's Missio Nexus)
IRC	International Resource Center
KHC	Kale Heywet Church
LCWE	Lausanne Congress on World Evangelization
LEM	Lebanon Evangelical Mission
LES	Lebanese Evangelical Society
MECO	Middle East Christian Outreach
MEGM	Middle East General Mission
MIDP	Maradi Integrated Development Project
MSF	Médecins Sans Frontières/Doctors Without Borders
NEF	Nigerian Evangelical Fellowship

NLFA   New Life For All
NMP   Nile Mission Press
OCLA   Oficiana de Conexión de Latina America (Latin America Service Center)
PBS   Pastors' Book Set
PCFC   Pakistan Christian Fellowship of Churches
PEA   Portuguese East Africa (today's Mozambique)
PIVM   Poona and Indian Village Mission
RMP   Roodepoort Mission Press
SAGM   South Africa General Mission
SEAEM   South East Africa Evangelistic Mission
SIC   Sudan Interior Church
SIM   Sudan Interior Mission, and/or the merged missions
SIMCOME   SIM Consultation on Muslim Evangelism
SIMIAR   SIM International Archives and Records
SIMTIA   SIM Theological Initiative in Africa
SUM   Sudan United Mission
TECMW   *The Evangelical Christian and Missionary Witness*
TEE   Theological Education by Extension
UBC   United Baptist Church (Zimbabwe)
UCE   Unión Christiana Evangélica or Evangelical Christian Union (Bolivia)
UEEB   Union des Eglises Evangéliques du Bénin
UEEPN   Union des Église Évangéliques Protestants du Niger
UIEA   União de Igiejas Evangelicas de Angola
                (Union of the Evangelical Church of Angola)
UMSG   Urban Ministries Support Group
VNL   Voice of New Life
VTV   Vision Through Vision
WABA   West African Broadcasting Association
WAO   West Africa Office
WKHC   Wolaitta Kale Heywet Church

INTRODUCTION:
SHARED ROOTS IN THE FAITH
MISSIONS MOVEMENT

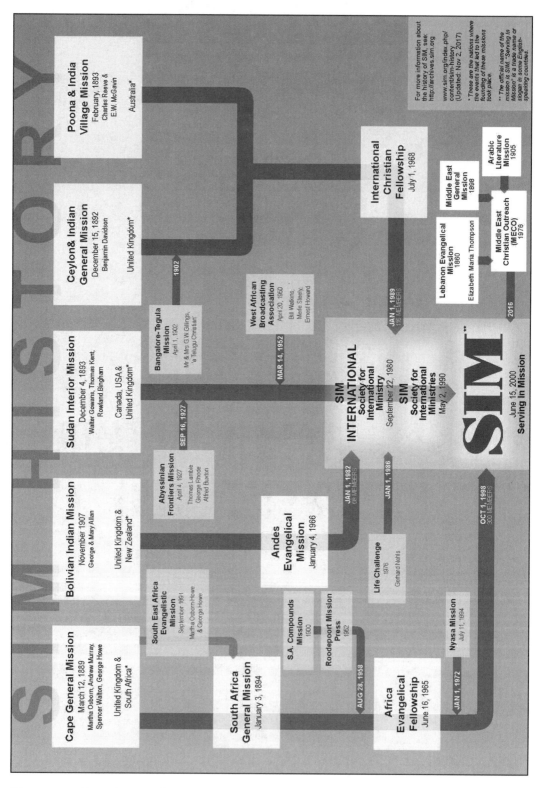

Photo 1.1. SIM History Chart. *Designer: Nigel Head (SIM UK)*

CHAPTER I

THE FAITH MISSIONS STORY

t is not possible to understand the history of SIM without at least some understanding of the late nineteenth century faith missions movement of which it was a part. All four of the primary mission streams that make up SIM today have deep roots going back to the early expansion phase of that movement. We will say much more about each of these mission streams as we proceed to tell the SIM story, but for now it will suffice to say that each of these streams—the Sudan Interior Mission, the Andes Evangelical Mission, International Christian Fellowship, and Africa Evangelical Fellowship—share the common roots and basic characteristics that have defined faith missions since Hudson Taylor and the China Inland Mission set a model for the movement in 1865.

What are those common characteristics? At least three major ones come to mind. First, and from this writer's point of view the most important, they shared a common burden for the least reached—those peoples with least access to the saving gospel of the Lord Jesus Christ. This led many of them to those "interior" or "inland" areas that had been largely neglected by the denominational missions that had followed the coast-hugging patterns of the European expansion of the time. Hence a number of them, like the China Inland Mission and the Sudan Interior Mission, incorporated reference to those least reached areas in their names. Ralph Winter dubbed this phenomenon and the period from 1865 until about 1980, the "Inland Era" of modern missions,[1] although as we shall see, many other neglected areas were also addressed. We will say much more about this burden for the least reached in the next section.

Secondly, they shared a common fountainhead. They were interdenominational in their approach and drew members from across the spectrum of denominations and nondenominations who shared their evangelical commitments. For many, as Klaus Fiedler points out, it was this interdenominational emphasis, rather than any claim to superior faith, that most clearly defined the faith missions. This can be seen in how the association that grew out of the faith missions movement named itself in 1917 (Interdenominational Foreign Mission Association). Fiedler summarizes the situation this way:

> The term "faith missions" was not coined by the faith missions themselves. They did not claim that other missions worked without faith, nor did they claim to have more faith than the missions that had started their work decades earlier. It was others who took one of the faith missions' innovative

concepts—the "faith principle" of financial support—and referred to them under that name. This was only partially correct, because "faith support" is not the most important characteristic of these missions. The most important characteristic is indeed brought out by the name they often use for themselves: "interdenominational" missions.[2]

A point sometimes missed is that the faith missions movement actually preceded the time when liberal theology was rapidly increasing in its influence, a time when an evangelical consensus still dominated the religious scene in the English-speaking world. It is true, however, that growth of the faith missions movement did accelerate greatly during the post–World War I period when faith in the finished work of Christ on the cross was losing some of its dominance theologically, particularly in many of the mainline denominations.

It is worth noting that the leaders who emerged in each of the missions that would become part of SIM came from a variety of nations and denominations. Cape General Mission (CGM) was founded in 1889 by Martha Osborn, Spencer Walton, and Andrew Murray. Murray, of the Dutch Reformed Church of South Africa, a well-known author and evangelist who founded a university and seminary, always considered missions "the supreme end of the church."[3] After Martha Osborn married George Howe, they formed the South East Africa Evangelistic Mission (SEAEM) in 1891. CGM and SEAEM merged in 1894 to become the South Africa General Mission (SAGM). Because their ministry had spread into other African countries in the decades that followed, they changed their name to Africa Evangelical Fellowship (AEF) in 1965.

Soudan Interior Mission (SIM) began in 1893. Canadians Walter Gowans (Presbyterian), Rowland Bingham (Baptist), and American Thomas Kent (Congregationalist) had a vision to evangelize the sixty or more million unreached people of the African Soudan (primarily sub-Saharan Sahel region). Unable to interest established missions—most of which said reaching the Soudan was impossible—they set out on their own.

Malaria overtook all three. Gowans and Kent respectively died of dysentery and fever in 1894, and Bingham returned to Canada one year later. On his second attempt in 1900, he again came down with malaria and was forced to go back home. Unable to return to Africa, Bingham sent out a third team one year later. They successfully established a base about three hundred miles (483 km) inland at Patigi in 1902. From there, the work of Sudan Interior Mission in Africa began. (Bingham started to write "Sudan" rather than "Soudan" by 1900.)

In 1892, the Ceylon and India General Mission (CIGM) was founded. A year later, they began work among Ceylon's Sinhalese Buddhists and Tamil Hindus. The mission, founded by Scottish businessman Benjamin Davidson, expanded from Ceylon into South India. Eventually CIGM's ministry reached across the subcontinent and to the Philippines.

Also in 1893, Charles F. Reeve and E. W. McGavin left their homes in Australia for India. They were influenced by a Eurasian Christian (Eurasian is equivalent to Aryan, that implies the Brahman ruling class), who went to Australia in search of missionaries for his home area, and by J. Hudson Taylor. Reeve and McGavin answered the challenge and set sail under the name Poona and Indian Village Mission (PIVM). In 1968, these two south Asian organizations merged to become the International Christian Fellowship (ICF).

In 1893 British Keswick evangelists visited South America and published a report called *South America: The Neglected Continent*. New Zealand Presbyterians George Allan and Mary Stirling read it and felt God calling them. In 1907, following marriage and ministry together in Argentina, they founded the Bolivian Indian Mission (BIM). They entered Bolivia two years later to minister to the Quechua Indians. Allan's BIM grew in the years that followed to become the Andes Evangelical Mission (AEM) in 1966.

The members of these missions included men and women, both married and unmarried, and most of them lay people from various vocational backgrounds.[4] Though there were certainly exceptions, they generally lacked both ordination and the higher levels of university education common in most of the denominational missions. Training at a Bible institute or Bible college was most commonly the norm.

Finally, they shared a common approach in their principles and practices of operation. Though not as important as their interdenominational nature as discussed above, this included what nevertheless became perhaps the most enduring characteristic of faith missions in the minds of many—their approach to finance:

> One of the most distinctive features of faith missions is their financial philosophy, which, operating in faith that God will provide, generally does not guarantee salaries for missionaries. Faith missions will generally refrain from directly soliciting funds, but application of this philosophy ranges from a policy of simply stating a need, to not publicly revealing the needs of missionaries.[5]

While all faith missions have evolved in these matters over the years, the mission streams that became part of SIM generally followed a policy of providing full financial information without directly soliciting funds. Rowland Bingham, however, caused something of a stir by 1942 as correspondence with others in the Interdenominational Foreign Mission Association (IFMA) (today's Missio Nexus) shows. He had, by the latter years of his life at least, become somewhat more aggressive in his fund-raising communications to the angst of some of his IFMA mission colleagues.[6]

Other important principles and practices that they shared from the beginning included commitment to a clear evangelical statement of faith (often adapted or borrowed from the China Inland Mission), the empowerment of laity and women in mission (though not always with full equality), and the primacy of evangelism (though ministry to human need and church development were also assumed and fostered). There is more to be said on all these matters in the context of the development over time of faith missions generally, and of each of the missions that now constitute SIM.

One other thing they shared throughout most of their history was their Anglophone orientation and the connections that naturally developed from them. Their sending bases were almost exclusively in their earliest years, and predominantly for many years since, in the countries of the English-speaking world. And, with one important exception (SAGM), all of their first generations of missionaries were white. In more recent decades, SIM's geographic and ethnic orientation has been changing at an accelerating pace, though the English language remains the primary though less exclusive vehicle for internal communications within SIM.

In addition to the basic characteristics that the early faith missions shared, they also shared several sources of influence that were very important in shaping what they would become. These included the influence of missionary statesmen and evangelistic entrepreneurs like Grattan and Fanny Guinness, A. J. Gordon, A. T. Pierson, A. B. Simpson, and D. L. Moody; as well as the premillennial missiology, missionary training endeavors, and the Keswick brand of "deeper life" or "full surrender" teaching which they imbibed.

While it is beyond our scope here to trace all the interconnections between these individuals, their beliefs and endeavors, and the faith missions movement in general,[7] here is but a smattering that connects them to the missions that now constitute SIM:[8]

- The Irish couple, Fanny and Grattan Guinness, were truly remarkable people to whom the vast majority of faith missions could trace some connection.
- Encouraged by Hudson Taylor, the Guinness' founded the East London Training Institute in 1873, the first interdenominational mission training institute, which became the prototype for others. Fanny managed the institute and was the mission writer, while Grattan was the evangelist and teacher.
- A. B. Simpson, who later founded the Christian and Missionary Alliance (C & MA), was converted under the ministry of Grattan Guinness in Canada in 1858.
- All three Soudan Interior Mission founders (Gowans, Kent, and Bingham) studied at Simpson's New York Missionary Training Institute that was established in 1883.
- In 1889 Grattan Guinness convinced A. J. Gordon to start the Boston Missionary Training Institute, and assisted Emma Dryer to organize what would become the Moody Bible Institute, the products of which were hundreds of recruits over the years for SIM missions.

- A. T. Pierson played a key role in launching the Student Volunteer Movement (SVM) at Moody's Northfield Conference in 1886. It is likely that Pierson coined the SVM watchword, "The Evangelization of the World in This Generation."
- In 1890, two years after his immigration from Britain, Bingham met John Salmon, founder of the C & MA in Canada.
- Bingham left the Salvation Army, under which he had been converted, and served as Salmon's assistant pastor during 1892–1893.
- A. J. Gordon lectured in Toronto on "The Holy Spirit and Missions" and won Bingham to the cause of world mission.
- Grattan Guinness, A. J. Gordon, A. T. Pierson, and A. B. Simpson all contributed articles through one or more of these periodicals that Bingham edited from 1904 until his death in 1942: *The Faithful Witness* (1904–1905), *The Missionary Witness* (1905–1911), *The Evangelical Christian and Missionary Witness* (1911–1931), and *The Evangelical Christian* (1931-1942).

Our outline of interconnections leaves us short on detail concerning the influence of the two worldviews that had powerful input in faith mission circles at the time: Keswick "full surrender" teaching and premillennial missiology. To these we now turn. The Keswick influence was especially pronounced in a direct way on George and Mary Allan. British Keswick evangelists visited South America in 1893 and published a report called *South America: The Neglected Continent*. It was in reading it that the young New Zealanders, George Allan and Mary Stirling, were led to South America where they ministered, married, and in 1907 founded BIM.

Keswick influence was also readily apparent in Sudan Interior Mission circles through the involvement of its first and longtime General Director, Rowland Bingham. Ever the entrepreneur, he founded Canadian Keswick at Muskoka in 1924, and used the venue for many years as a recruitment and training center for the mission. Less direct, but still powerfully important in influencing all the SIM missions, and faith missions more broadly, was the Keswick "deeper life" teaching itself, and its emphasis on "full surrender." Though impossible to quantify accurately, there is little doubt that it was a significant influence that led a great many young people into missions, particularly prior to World War II.

For some like A. B. Simpson, "full surrender" meant living in "victory over sin." Those who were "genuinely sanctified" did not need to take medicine because the atonement provided for spiritual and physical healing.[9] SIM's first missionaries to Africa believed in this doctrine.[10] Gowans and Kent had been students of Simpson before they went to Africa, and Bingham's mentor in Toronto was John Salmon who became the founder of Simpson's C & MA in Canada. Gowans and Kent died, in part, because they did not believe in taking certain medicine such as quinine.[11] Bingham started to encourage the use of quinine in the early 1900s, and publicly rejected Simpson's views about divine healing on the eve of World War I.[12]

Two of the four major missions that merged with SIM showed strong sympathies for divine healing in their formative years. The most vocal was CIGM whose missionaries published pro faith healing articles in its mission's periodical and republished some of Simpson's articles. In 1914, CIGM founder-director Benjamin Davidson went to the C & MA convention in Maine that Simpson was leading; he spoke at a divine healing meeting and assisted in an anointing service. By 1930, however, less than a decade after he resigned from CIGM, the mission was publishing articles that told of missionaries using prayer and medicine to heal.[13] Some members of SAGM, likely influenced at least in part by SAGM president Andrew Murray, also believed in divine healing. Missionaries started to question this doctrine after John Copeland died of malaria in Matabeleland (later, Zimbabwe) in 1897 because he "steadily refused" to take medicine.[14] PIVM and BIM rejected divine healing. While they acknowledged God could heal if he so desired, they chose to demonstrate God's power through preaching and medicine.[15]

A premillenial eschatology and accompanying missiology took center stage in evangelical Christian circles during the late nineteenth and early twentieth centuries, the same period in which the faith missions movement blossomed. The faith missions movement was not the vehicle, however, but rather a beneficiary, as we shall see.

Postmillenial eschatology and accompanying missiology had been largely unchallenged during the eighteenth and early nineteenth centuries, but began a weakening trajectory at the time of the American Civil War. Based on "an optimistic world-view that counted on an evolution of world history into the fullness of God's kingdom,"[16] the downward trajectory continued until it reached its nadir in the period after the horrors of the First World War.

The change to a predominantly premillennial eschatology, meanwhile, was not brought about by faith missions, but took place as key individuals and institutions close to them led the way. People like D. L. Moody, A. T. Pierson, A. J. Gordon, A. B. Simpson, Grattan and Fanny Guinness and others were becoming convinced during this period, often through the testimony of unnamed laymen or one another, and their own study of the Bible, that this understanding was correct. The impact this had on the faith missions movement came primarily through two avenues: first, the institutions that these individuals operated—Bible colleges, Bible conferences, etc. and their wide ministries of preaching, teaching, and writing—meant that vast numbers of believers were also being influenced. And that was significant because premillennial eschatology (both historic and futuristic types) emphasized that the gospel must first be preached among all nations, and then the end would come (Mark 13:10). The second avenue then was the premillennial missiology itself, that King Jesus would return when that was accomplished, and that "when in God's providence the whole world had become accessible, it was the church's duty—with a tremendous missionary effort—to work for the fulfillment of this last sign and 'to bring the king back.'"[17]

Before leaving this subject it should be noted that faith missions eschatology has never been uniform. There have always been amillennial, postmillennial, and premillennial views represented. Nor is the balance of views necessarily the same today as it was during the early years of the faith missions movement.[18] What is certain, however, is that the ascendancy of premillennial eschatology and accompanying missiology during this period provided a significant support to the early faith missions movement.

THE BURDEN OF THE LEAST REACHED

What we are calling the burden of the least reached was common among almost all of the early faith missions. For the missions that became part of SIM their burdens included focus on the Quechua and Aymara Indians of the high Andes, the teeming millions of south India, and the many African peoples and south Asian emigrants of southern Africa. But nowhere was this burden more explicitly articulated or dramatically lived out than for the three founders of the Sudan Interior Mission. As worthy representatives of this aspect for the entire faith mission movement, we turn now to their story, which they spoke of as "the burden of the Sudan."[1]

How the Burden Began

In 1893 Mrs. Margaret Gowans, originally from Scotland and living in Toronto, Canada, was a woman who had a great interest in the work of missions and prayed much for it.

Photo 2.1. *Margaret Gowans, Walter Gowans' mother and spiritual mentor*

There is no doubt that much of her passion and burning for mission was passed on to her family—her daughter Miss Annie Gowans was a member of A. B. Simpson's International Missionary Alliance (IMA) in China,[2] and she believed God had led her son Walter to work as a missionary in the Sudan.[3] "Sudan," more widely known in the nineteenth century by its more French derivative as "Soudan," is an Arabic word that means "land of the black people." The Sudan was known in North America, Europe, and the Middle East at that time as the Sahel that stretched from east to west Africa, and was situated between the Sahara and the upper Congo River.[4] Margaret Gowans required very little convincing that the Sudan, which encompassed an area larger than India and had a population of sixty to ninety million without a single Christian missionary, was the place God wanted her son to go. In particular, her son wanted to go to the region in West Africa around Lake Chad, to an area known today as northeast Nigeria.

More and more interest in missionary work was growing in North America and a number of missionary colleges were founded. Dr. A. B. Simpson (founder of what became the Christian and Missionary Alliance) established one such college in 1883 for the purpose of training men and women to be evangelists at home and missionaries overseas.

It was at this college, the New York Missionary Training Institute in New York City, that the three young men studied—Thomas Kent (b. 1870) and Walter Gowans (b. 1868) in the early 1890s and Rowland V. Bingham (b. 1872) in 1895. No doubt the passion and vision for mission and the Sudan was instilled or increased for each of them while they were there.

The men had offered themselves to mission boards in North America: Gowans to the IMA (part of today's C & MA),[5] Kent to the "Gospel Mission" or "Union" which was likely the newly-formed Gospel Missionary Union (today's Avant),[6] and one of the men to the Southern

Photo 2.2. *Albert B. Simpson, who profoundly influenced Gowans, Kent, and Bingham*

Baptist's Foreign Mission Board (today's International Mission Board).[7] The IMA told Gowans his plan was "unwise" given his lack of experience and funding. The Union, having only just been founded, was organizationally weak and not prepared to decide whether to accept them before they departed for Africa.

Photo 2.3. *Walter Gowans, Thomas Kent, and Rowland Bingham, the Sudan Interior Mission's first missionaries to Africa*

After they crossed over to Britain, they continued to see if any mission society there could be induced to send them to the the Central Soudan. (The Central Soudan was then known as a large region that surrounded Lake Chad, including what is known today as northern Nigeria.) They may have contacted the Church Missionary Society (CMS) and Wesleyan Methodist Missionary Society.[8] The three men did not accept overtures from the Central Soudan Mission (CSM) to join them, however, because they were just as independently minded as the CSM's director, Herman Harris.[9] The boards, overall, refused to accept them as missionaries because of the cost and lack of European-based stations along the way that were needed to maintain communication links and supply provisions.[10]

Mrs. Gowans shared her son's vision and difficulties with Rowland V. Bingham who had been seeking God's will for his own life, and as a result he felt compelled to visit Walter Gowans in Britain and go to Africa with him. The thought of a land with not one Christian nor missionary haunted Rowland Bingham. Images of cannibals and slaves pushed away sleep and Mrs. Gowans' words, "Are you prepared to go if God calls you?" echoed over and over as he turned over in his bed. Was he, Rowland Bingham, willing to go to the Sudan, which was such a deadly place for white people. It is interesting to note that an African Anglican Bishop, Samuel Ajayi Crowther, had earlier stationed several African CMS missionaries along the Niger River on the southern border of the Central Sudan. Young conservative English missionaries, however, disbanded his mission, relieved most of his missionaries, and drove him to resign in 1891.[11]

Finally, after much reflection and prayer, and at the age of 20, Bingham committed himself to serving not only in Africa, but in Africa's Sudan interior.

Bingham wrote of Gowans' mother:

> It was the impassioned pleading of a quiet little Scotch lady that linked my life up with the Sudan. She had invited me to her home for lunch from a meeting where I had been speaking in the city of Toronto. There, in the quietness of her parlour she told the story of her home, and unburdened her heart.[12]

The Burden Spurs Action in the 1890s

The efforts of Gowans and his companions were aimed at penetrating to the interior, hence the name "Sudan Interior Mission."

Neither Gowans nor Bingham had enough money to proceed to Africa, but a few friends rallied around and gave them gifts. When Tom Kent learned that Rowland Bingham was going to join Walter Gowans in the United Kingdom, and that they were bound for Africa, he wrote to tell them that he was coming to England to join them. At the same time, Gowans and Bingham were convinced that they should ask Tom Kent to join them. Here is Bingham's account of what happened:

> At the same time we each wrote this decision to a mutual friend, Mr. Thomas Kent in America, who had offered to join us if desired. It confirmed our faith when shortly after a letter arrived from Tom Kent stating that following a time of waiting on God, he felt impelled to come on to Britain to join us, whatever our decision. These letters were in the mail at the same time, each announcing his decision without knowing the conviction of the others.[13]

In the summer of 1893, therefore, God drew three lives together with one common call—to carry the gospel to the Central Sudan.[14]

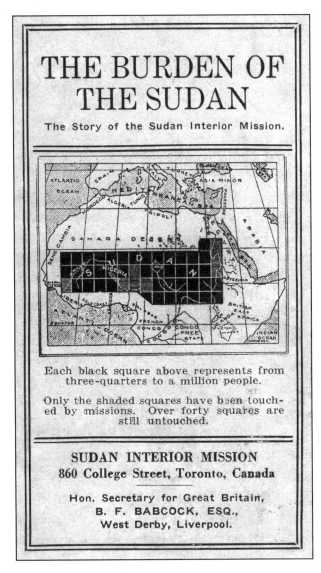

Map 2.1. *"The Burden of the Sudan," 1918*

Gowans, Kent, and Bingham made strenuous efforts to raise interest and support in Britain to take the gospel to the Sudan, but as in America, were unsuccessful. Finally driven to the conclusion that none of the regular mission boards would accept or send them, the decision was reached in Southport, England, after much prayer, that it was incumbent on them to obey the command of the Lord to go, board or no board.[15] They felt they still had to answer to the One who had commissioned them to go and whose command they believed to be sovereign.[16]

On 4 December 1893,[17] a ship anchored off Lagos with three young men on board, the oldest, Gowans, being only 25. But each man burned with a desire to establish a Christian witness among sixty to ninety million unreached people who lived in the Sudan in sub-Saharan Africa.

In Lagos they met the missionaries of the three Societies laboring there. The missionaries in Lagos prophesied dire calamity and said they were undertaking the impossible. Bryan Roe, the Superintendent of the Methodist Mission, warned them saying: "Young men, you will never see the Sudan; your children will never see the Sudan; your grandchildren may."[18]

The three of them had very little money with which to journey from Lagos into the great interior of the Central Sudan. They realized their resources were altogether inadequate for the long journey through the unknown. They then decided to spend a week in prayer and proposed to dispose of any keepsakes or nonessential articles. The next mail that reached them brought $500. Rowland Bingham wrote:

Keeping well in Lagos was a very real problem. We did not understand the terrible climate. Expedition after expedition of white men was wiped out. Of a party of six missionaries who had landed in Lagos ten days after our arrival, four died before they reached their destination on the lower Niger, a fifth one was invalided home, and one solitary survivor walked into the mission station. That station witnessed the death of the remaining member of the party within twelve months.[19]

Confusion has arisen from time to time over the original name given by the founders to the mission, but a letter sent by Walter Gowans to Mr. J. C. Hindle of Southport, England, in January 1894 states, "We have decided to call the mission THE SOUDAN INTERIOR MISSION." There is also a postcard with the postmark 7 March 1894 sent by Mr. Hindle to Walter Gowans' mother. The oval stamp bears the name THE SOUDAN INTERIOR MISSION. He comments that the stamp shows the name chosen for the mission by the three missionaries. (For the stamp, see Photo F.1, page 356).[20]

Gowans, Kent, and Bingham would have known of the difficult task they faced and the supreme sacrifice others had made to try and enter the Sudan, but were spiritually prepared to face the challenge. In England they were told, and again after they arrived in Africa, that the Central Sudan was a closed field. They were not however, as Bingham records, prepared to accept this:

Mr. Gowans used to say that the Sudan was a closed field simply because the Church had never in any adequate sense put her hand to the door to open it. We expressed our conviction in a little Sudan battle song, which we recall today not as having any poetic value, but as expressive of the faith with which the little band was actuated. One verse ran:

For many years have Christians gazed, and then stood still aghast, and said the dangers were too great, this field was closed fast. But Jesus' power shall break the bars, and burst the gates of brass. The dark Sudan shall hear the name of Jesus.[21]

Years later, SIM adopted Charles Wesley's "Faith, Mighty Faith," as its mission song. This refrain, which was also a favorite of "Holy Ann" Preston who Helen Bingham popularized in her book *An Irish Saint: The Life Story of Ann Preston known as "Holy Ann,"* goes as follows: "Faith, mighty faith, the promise sees, and looks to God alone; Laughs at impossibilities, and cries, 'It shall be done.'"[22]

After only being in Lagos for about three weeks, Bingham became ill and a doctor who saw him did not give him any hope of recovery. However, Gowans and Kent prayed over and anointed him. Bishop Joseph Hill and his Church Missionary Society team that had just arrived in Lagos also prayed for him. Bingham recovered, but only a short time later Bishop Hill and his wife Lucy both died, on successive days, followed by several members of his team.[23]

Bingham stayed at the coast to recover from his illness, purchase supplies, and maintain contact with friends overseas. Gowans and Kent began their journey inland that February 1894. They departed with several African employees including an English-speaking Kru Christian from Liberia named Tom Coffee. After Gowans and Kent departed for the interior, Coffee became a key intermediary with local officials and someone who Gowans wrote was "very faithful to me" for having stayed with him during war, sickness, and other difficult times after his other workers abandoned him.[24] (For more information about Coffee, see chapter 16, pages 206-207).

A little more than three hundred miles (483 km) from Lagos, after having crossed the Niger River, they reached the great walled city of Bida. Then in June, Kent returned to Lagos for more supplies. He arrived very ill. But after being nursed back to health, he set out again in August to join Gowans. But they were never to meet. Gowans, meanwhile, had continued his journey northward from Bida. An army that engaged in slave raiding conquered the city of Birnin Gwari where Gowans and his entourage had camped. He was allowed to go free, with Coffee who stayed with him, but by the time he reached Zaria he was very ill. Here a party of three European travelers with the Hausa Association found him and decided to send him back to the coast. Porters carried him in a hammock, but he died of dysentery in Girku, just 45 miles south of Zaria, on 16 or 17 November 1894.[25] In the meantime Kent, on his return trip, took ill with malaria at Bida. Two missionaries from the Central Soudan Mission cared for him during the last days of his life and buried him on 8 December 1894.[26]

Bingham visited Mrs. Gowans in August 1895 after returning from Africa to give her a few of her son's personal belongings. She met him with extended hands and through her tears said to him: "Well, Mr. Bingham, I would rather have had Walter go out to the Sudan and die there, all alone, than have him home today, disobeying his Lord."[27]

Professor Yusufu Turaki writes:

This dramatic account of the experience of the SIM Pioneers on the West Coast of Africa is heart-breaking, but one cannot help but hold his breath at the triumph of martyrdom and sacrifice for a cause. In spite of all dangers, nothing deterred them. They were only feeble humans against the formidable and impregnable natural barriers. They left North America and England for the Sudan without any name, except for the heart that burned for the Sudan. Three individuals whose souls and hearts were knit together by a common burden ventured into pioneering missions to the Sudan.[28]

SUPPLEMENT 2.1

Walter Gowans[29]

Photo 2.4. *Walter Gowans, the first "leader" of SIM*

For those who know something of the history of the Sudan Interior Mission piece of SIM (now unofficially "Serving in Mission") the name of Rowland Bingham is the one that usually comes to mind. And this is understandable, as he was one of its three founders and served as General Director until his death in 1942. But another of the founders, Walter Gowans, a young Canadian of Scottish background, was actually looked upon as the group's leader when Bingham, Gowans, and Thomas Kent set out in 1893 for the Islam-dominated "Central Soudan."

Although the initial leader of this youthful band (all three in their early 20s), the actual missionary career of Gowans, and for Kent as well, lasted less than a year. Gowans and Kent left Bingham convalescing from illness on the coast and began their trek inland on 24 February 1894. They had been told upon their arrival in Lagos, that they would never see the Soudan, nor would their children, but that perhaps their grandchildren might. They proved the prophecy wrong about seeing the Central Soudan, but the estimation of the perils involved was not mistaken.

In spite of the brevity of his missionary career, Gowans penned some words that are both inspiring and revealing about Gowans the man. What follows are several quotations from his diary and from a letter he wrote to the Young People's Society of the St. James Square Presbyterian Church in Toronto, with which he had a strong connection. Also included are brief headings that attempt to capture the essence of their application for us today:

Burden for the least reached

As most of you are aware, I anticipate going to the Soudan—a pioneer for Christ. The Soudan, with a population of from 60 to 90 million, is, of all foreign fields, the most destitute of the gospel, being almost entirely without a representative for Christ.

Love for the lost more than for life

Our success in this enterprise means nothing less than the opening of the country for the Gospel; our failure, at the most, nothing more than the death of two or three deluded fanatics. . . . After all, is it not worth a venture? Sixty million are at stake? Is it not worth even risking our lives for so many?

Faith over fear

It is said that God has closed the door to the Soudan. Beloved! God closes no door to the Gospel. It is not God, it is the enemy who closes the door. With God no door is closed. We have simply to march forward in the name of Jesus, and in the faith of God, and the doors must and will fly open every time.
Hallelujah!

Maintaining an eternal perspective

Diary for 9 August 1894: *I am 3 days from Zaria. I would have been at Kano long ago were it not for the repeated delays caused by the war on the road. Written in view of my approaching end which has often lately seemed so near but just now seems almost imminent, and I want to write while I have the power to do it. . . .*

I have no regret for undertaking this venture and in this manner my life has not been thrown away. My only regrets are for my poor Mother, and for her sake I would have chosen to live. . . .

Don't mourn for me, darling dearest Mother. If the suffering was great remember it is all over now and think of the glory I am enjoying and rejoice that "your boy" was permitted to have a hand in the redemption of the Soudan.

Gowans did indeed die shortly after writing these words, but he also certainly did "have a hand in the redemption of the Soudan." That which he and his colleagues began is now a network of churches that claim more than 6 million worshipers in Nigeria alone, and is part of an energetic reproducing Gospel movement that stretches across the globe.

CHAPTER 3

THE COMMON CONTEXT, CHARACTERISTICS, AND CHALLENGES

The story of SIM is rich in the history of its four major mission streams and their founders who shared a common context as well as a number of common characteristics and challenges. Because their common context included their beginnings during the high watermark of late nineteenth-century European conquest and their maturation during the period of its decline and demise, over the first half and more of the twentieth century, the impact of that setting on mission cannot be ignored.

In the same way, the common characteristics of their founders, visions, and organizations are a reflection of the common influences they shared from the state of religion in their day. This included the motivational impact of the modernist theological challenge; the articulate voices of key evangelical leaders on the state of the church and the needs of the world; and the impact of revival and the newer evangelical mission fountainheads—the Bible conferences and the Bible and mission training institutes.

Finally, the common challenges they faced were both numerous and daunting: the challenge of seeking to penetrate difficult places with the gospel of Jesus Christ, and discerning how far to try and how fast to go; the organizational challenge of starting a missionary endeavor from scratch; the challenge of deadly opposition from climate, disease, and powerful human antagonists; and the challenge of mobilizing sufficient prayer and support to maintain the endeavor. In spite of these common difficulties, each of the four missions managed, by the Lord's grace, to find a way to overcome those challenges step by step over more than a century of labor in the task. What follows is reflection on how that happened.

As mentioned in the introduction, the faith missions that ultimately came together under the banner of SIM shared something beyond their common characteristics as faith missions in the model of Hudson Taylor and the China Inland Mission. They shared an Anglophone organizational orientation as a result of their common roots in Anglophone countries.

A side effect of this orientation was that they also shared, during their first half-century and more, many of the intrinsic strengths and weaknesses inherent in the

Anglophone colonial experience. The one major exception to this in SIM was the Andes Evangelical Mission (AEM) experience, as British colonial endeavors missed the South American regions where AEM and its predecessor, Bolivian Indian Mission, operated. Even here, however, their Anglophone sending church roots (New Zealand primarily in the early years) meant that certain mindsets and views of the world were not completely lost, even as they had to cope with predominantly Spanish and Catholic colonial legacies.

Brian Stanley has done much to capture and analyze the nature of the Anglophone colonial experience and its interaction with, and influence on, the missionary experience of the time. His summary of that interaction in *The Bible and the Flag: Protestant Missions & British Imperialism in the Nineteenth & Twentieth Centuries*, is worth noting:

> The missionaries who have been the subject of this book had a clear and compelling grasp of the "imperial" demands of the gospel. Their vision was frequently clouded by national and racial pride, and in certain essential respects was distorted by the mechanistic world-view which they had inherited from Enlightenment thought. As a result, they sometimes failed to apply the ethical demands of the kingdom of God as rigorously to their own nation as they did to the non-Western societies to which they were sent. Their relationship to the diverse forces of the British imperialism was complex and ambiguous. If it was fundamentally misguided, their error was not that they were indifferent to the cause of justice for the oppressed, but that their perceptions of the demands of justice were too easily moulded to fit the contours of prevailing Western ideologies. In this respect, our predecessors reflect our own fallibility more closely that we care to admit.[1]

In a book edited by Stanley, Adrian Hastings makes a significant point about how the competing interests of nationalism and missionary endeavor were worked out in the British colonial enterprise. He points out that it was the British alone who maintained an evenhanded open door policy with regard to foreign religious workers:

> Of the colonial powers, Britain alone was generally happy to accept missionaries of any nation into its colonies, even at the episcopal level: the mixed religious condition of Britain itself, the sheer size of its empire, the strength of liberal opinion at home to criticize apparent discrimination, but above all a prudent realization that the cause of empire could best be served by religious neutrality had all helped bring this about.[2]

This, of course, goes a long way toward explaining the internationalism (especially of the Anglophone variety) that characterized the mission streams that constitute SIM today. It is interesting to note, however, as Hastings also points out, that by the beginning of the twentieth century it was only those evangelical Anglo-American agencies like those that constitute SIM today that maintained this broad denominational and national perspective:

> If the Church Missionary Society's early recruitment of Germans was a remarkable exception, representing what Paul Jenkins has called "the Protestant internationalism" of the early nineteenth century, it did not last beyond 1860. Apart from American-British faith missions, Protestant missionary activity at the beginning of the twentieth century was as intensely national as it was denominational.[3]

Perhaps at least part of the reason they shared this common approach is that they were influenced by what W. Harold Fuller calls "a common circle of Christian leaders."[4] Included in this group were those like H. Grattan Guinness, Samuel H. Kellogg, A. T. Pierson, A. B. Simpson, and J. Hudson Taylor who were highly internationalized in their own right and shared the same basic commitments of Word-centered obedience and dependence on divine enablement.

As some of the other common characteristics, both theological and experiential, are covered elsewhere, we shall turn now to some of the common challenges they faced. There are many nuances to these, but the main categories of challenge would number at least three: (1) connecting with and nurturing sending constituencies adequately enough to provide the appropriately gifted personnel, finances, and prayer necessary to keep the mission going; (2) maintaining adequate levels of leadership to provide strategic vision, ministry oversight, and care for members; and (3) dealing with the external challenges presented by high-powered political (both colonial and indigenous) and religious antagonists.

All three of these challenges remained with these missions throughout their history, and remain with the combined SIM today. The first, though never easy, grew easier during the first half of the twentieth century as the fundamentalist/modernist divide created many more distinctively evangelical churches, training institutions, conferences for Christian nurture, etc. where the faith missions were provided a wonderful platform for recruitment, raising support, etc. The trust level of the missions was very high in those days, but declined along with that of other institutions in the second half of the twentieth century making constituency relations increasingly challenging. Expectations were becoming more specific and pronounced regarding communication, accountability, direct involvement, missionary care, etc., at the same time that many churches were pursuing a vision of short-term missions and a philosophy that said we can do it better and more cheaply ourselves without the involvement of the agencies. The increased expectations of the churches, combined with less trust and enthusiastic support toward agencies has no doubt played a part in catalyzing many mergers where the economies of scale make meeting constituency expectations less onerous and more cost effective.

On the second challenge of maintaining adequate levels of leadership to provide strategic vision, ministry oversight, and care for members, this was very spotty in the early years and generally meant that only the more entrepreneurial and self-motivated personalities would tend to volunteer in the first place or survive the experience. As time passed and things became marginally easier, the number of workers grew, but the need for levels of leadership that could guide and care for them also grew. The reader is encouraged to read Appendix G by Dr. Ian Hay, entitled "A Time Line Depicting Changes in SIM Organizational Structure from 1893–1993," as it provides valuable insight into how this issue evolved and was treated over time.

The third challenge of dealing with powerful political opposition and religious antagonists has never been easy, but at the same time it has often been an area where the glory of God and the power of faith in Him has shined most brightly. It has taken many forms through the years, from the Catholic hierarchy in South America encouraging the population to throw stones at the missionaries and evangelical believers, to British colonial administration in Nigeria forbidding passage and withholding permission for missionary work in the Muslim north, to Orthodox Church leaders seeking to persuade the Ethiopian government to end all evangelical ministry in the south, to Fascist and Communist regimes in Ethiopia expelling missionaries, to Imams and Hindu priests threatening new converts in south Asia, and on the list could go. In many of these cases, the resistances have been overcome with spectacular results of gospel transformation having been achieved. The reader is encouraged to read Supplement 8.2, pages 115-116, on Ethiopian Reversals for an encouraging taste of what this has looked like.

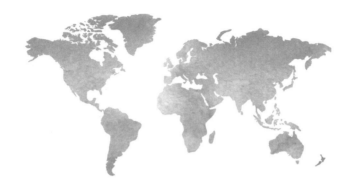

PART I
THE PRE-MERGER MISSIONS

CHAPTER 4

THE SUDAN INTERIOR MISSION STORY

The Formal Establishment of SIM

On his return to Canada in 1895 following the death of his two friends, Bingham accepted a call to a church in Newburgh, New York, in the USA, where he emphasized the need for missionary work, especially the cause of the "Sudan." The greatest response, however, came in the city of Toronto, Canada. Knowing how essential it was to have a mission to further the cause, he was able to form a missionary council there on 27 May 1898, and shortly afterward resigned from his pastorate to become secretary of this new council.

Photo 4.1. *"Mrs. R. V. Bingham & and her two daughters, 1908."*
Helen Bingham was born in Aberfoye, Ontario, in 1872, and married Rowland just three days before the mission was founded in 1898. She was the person primarily responsible for raising their daughters Winifred and Meredith because Rowland traveled so much. She actively supported her husband, serving on the boards of SIM Canada, Canadian Keswick, and Evangelical Publishers, working as an editor of *The Evangelical Christian* that her husband edited, and doing critical administrative work for SIM (especially when her husband was traveling). One contemporary wrote that while she was "in second place to her husband," she was "not subservient." An example of a time when they differed was when Rowland "determined" to move the entire staff of *The Evangelical Christian* to New York. According to one insider, the "collective wisdom of the staff and the firm remonstrances of Mrs. Bingham, who also refused to entertain the suggestion of moving, prevailed in the end." Helen became well-known, in her own right, for publishing *An Irish Saint: The Life Story of Ann Preston ("Holy Ann")*. First published in 1907, it has been republished more than 30 times in a few languages, and far exceeded the sales of any of the books her husband published. As a lasting tribute to her, Rowland wrote that she has shared in

all the trials and triumphs as a true helpmate. . . . I know of no one who has sacrificed more for its [SIM's] success than she. But for her loyal support, wise counsel, undimmed faith, sacrificial service and able cooperation, we question whether there would be any Sudan Interior Mission today.[1]

The work that had begun informally with Gowans, Kent, and Bingham, known as the "Soudan Interior Mission," was now officially established as the "Africa Industrial Mission." The name was modified to "Africa Evangelistic Mission" in 1905. The name then changed to "Sudan United Mission" when it merged in 1906, but this amalgamation only lasted a year. The mission finally took "Sudan Interior Mission," the name its co-founders had chosen the previous decade. (For a discussion about the early name changes, see Appendix F.) The Sudan Interior Mission changed its official name to "SIM International" in 1980, with "Society for International Ministry" as its byline.[2] The mission revised its name to SIM in 1990, using the byline "Society for International Ministries" for English-speaking countries,[3] and changed its slogan to "Serving in Mission" in 2000.[4]

SIM's Beginnings in Nigeria

In 1900 Bingham set out again with two other young men. When they landed at Lagos they found the missionaries more than ever out of sympathy with their plans. Within three weeks Bingham took seriously ill with malaria and was ordered home by a doctor. His two companions assured him they would carry on, but discouraged by the bleak picture painted by the Lagos missionaries, they followed him on the next ship.

Within six months of Bingham's return to Canada there were four men prepared to consider going to Africa. They were E. A. Anthony, Charles Robinson, Albert Taylor and Alexander W. Banfield. A third attempt was made by this party of four who sailed from England in 1901. Upon reaching Nigeria they went up the Niger River to Lokoja. After searching for a suitable mission site, they traveled by boat further along the Niger to Eboji and established the first mission station near Bida at Patigi. Patigi is about 385 miles (617 km) up the Niger River, well beyond its confluence with the Kaduna River. This was made possible with the help of the British-based Royal Niger Company that provided supplies for them to go to Patigi, an important town among the three hundred thousand Nupe people. Only those familiar with the geography of Nigeria can appreciate how arduous and dangerous this journey would have been over a hundred years ago.

In 1901, Bingham started to encourage SIM's missionaries to take quinine after he heard a leading epidemiologist in England explain that quinine, which came from the bark of South American cinchona trees, could cure malaria. In doing so, he moderated his earlier resistance to using quinine based on the radical version of divine healing that he, Kent, and Gowans held when they went to Africa eight years earlier.[5] However, because malaria continues to adapt and become resistant to medical treatments it remains a deadly threat.

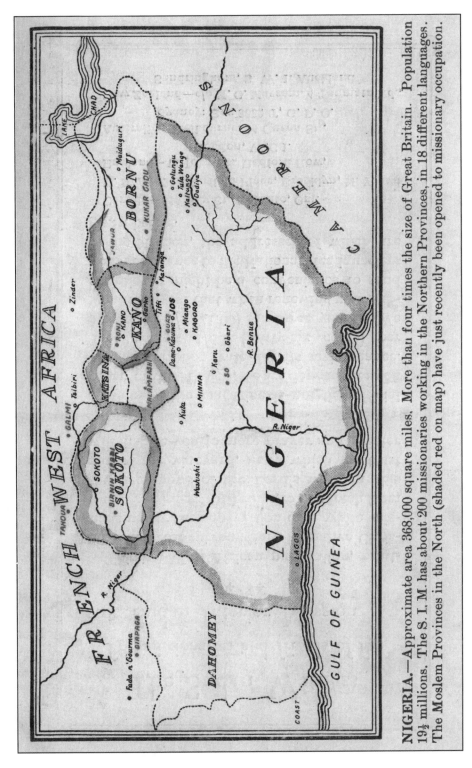

Map 4.1. *SIM's stations in Nigeria, 1937.*

Map credit: Sudan Witness 12, no. 5 (1937), back cover.

A. W. Banfield reported that he had concentrated on studying the language at Patigi in Nupeland, and in less than 12 months was able to hold gospel services. He later wrote:

At once I applied myself diligently and strenuously to Nupe, spoken by a million people in the middle Niger. For the first two years I never read a book or paper of any kind in English, except for my Bible. I determined to get this language at all costs. I lived in it; I thought in it; I dreamed in it. So great was my passion to learn it that I even put it before my health and life. At no time, during my years of language work, did I ever have as a teacher a Nupe man who knew a word of English. I struggled for and hunted out every word I learned. I never forgot a word.[6]

He soon began to translate the Word of God into the Nupe language, and compiled his own dictionary. When he returned for furlough, or what SIM now calls "home assignment," he already had the manuscript of the four gospels completed which the British and Foreign Bible Society published.

Banfield also set up a printing press, later called Niger Press, and built a home in Shonga after he joined the United Missionary Society. He printed a great number of books on his hand press. In spite of great difficulties, he eventually translated the whole Bible into Nupe, which the British and Foreign Bible Society printed in England. All his other books were printed on his own press. Among these is the Nupe hymnbook that was used for several years. He printed a Nupe grammar and two dictionaries, one from English to Nupe and the other from Nupe to English. Among so many others was a book especially popular among the Nupe, simply called *Old Testament Stories*.[8]

This area proved to be very resistant to the gospel. The strongest opposition to the work of the mission in Patigi and the surrounding Nupe area came from highly resistant Muslims who gave Banfield a great deal of trouble. However, the respect he had among the people of Shonga is indicated by the name they gave him—"the White Nupe."[9]

"Dr." Andrew Stirrett from Toronto, Canada, joined the team in 1902. Before being accepted by the mission he had sold his drug business and left his property, stocks, and bonds to the mission before setting out for Liverpool, England, to study tropical medicine.

When he completed his course he booked his passage for

Photo 4.2. *Alex Banfield teaching in Patigi, Nigeria, 1902.*

A Muslim named Nda Lemung, to Banfield's right, was the first person converted to Christianity in SIM's ministry.[7]

West Africa and wrote to the mission headquarters to ask the superintendent there whether he was accepted or rejected. Finally he was accepted on probation (they had been reluctant to accept him because of his age—he was 37 years old). They also held

some reservation about his sincerity when he willingly handed over so much property to the mission, so kept it in trust until his return after four years when he willingly signed over the whole estate to the mission.[11]

Photo 4.3. *Andrew Stirrett preaching in the Jos market*

Before leaving Liverpool, Andrew Stirrett armed himself with a letter from the representative of the Royal Niger Company for their agent in Nigeria. The letter gave permission for the company boat to take him up the river to Patigi. It was here that the first missionary party had settled as a base of operation and were praying for a wedge to overcome the restrictions that prevented them from working farther into the interior. They were

Photo 4.4. *Dr. Francis "Daisy" Wakefield, SIM's first medical doctor.*

Andrew Stirrett was a pharmacist, but is commonly regarded in SIM as its first doctor. SIM's first medical doctor (M.D.) was Dr. Francis "Daisy" Wakefield from Kendal, England. She joined SIM after having learned Arabic in North Africa for three years and studied Hausa in Northern Nigeria under the auspices of the Church Missionary Society (CMS). She left CMS to join SIM in 1911. Based in Piako, Wakefield undoubtedly did considerable medical work there and many other places. In one instance, she raised the ire of mission and government officials for bringing to the attention of the International Missionary Council in the United Kingdom the case of a Nigerian evangelist working with SIM missionaries who the British authorities had detained. She left SIM at the beginning of World War I, worked at a CMS hospital in the Anglo-Egyptian Sudan after the war, and then went to Algeria as an independent missionary for several years where she worked among the Tuareg and translated some books of the Bible into *Tamasheq*.[10]

Photo credit: R. V. Bingham, "Lady Doctor joins the Sudan Interior Mission," The Evangelical Christian and Missionary Witness 8, no. 1 (January 1912): 26.

particularly desirous of pushing into the Muslim and pagan areas in the northern part of Nigeria.

On his arrival at Forcados on the coast, the company's local boat came alongside the steamer that Stirrett had traveled on. He lost no time getting in touch with the agent and showing his letter of permission for passage up the river. In a land where white men are few and far between, and where one might expect real camaraderie when fellow Anglo-Saxons meet, he was shocked with the rejection he received. Here was a state of affairs he had not anticipated—of being refused passage on the steamer and being left in the hot, steamy jungle of mangrove swamp and untold perils, while fellow "white men" would leave him to his own devices.

On urging his letter once more upon the agent, he was finally told quite plainly that knowledge of his coming had preceded him but that he could not, and would not, be accommodated. Andrew Stirrett was generally mild to the point of not even realizing the affront that had been put upon him, but even he felt perturbed at the circumstances under which he had been placed. He had an unfailing source of help, however, and he was not long in availing himself of it. To quote him, "There I was at the mouth of the river, stranded. Stranded, but not forsaken." And as he stood at the railing lifting his heart to God, his fingers idly tearing up the now useless letter, he heard the hearty chug-chug of a large river boat, and opening his eyes, saw coming around a sweep of land a heavy launch with the government flag at its prow.

As it swept up in a wide arc and tied up at the foot of the steamer's gangplank, Stirrett breathed a hurried prayer and hastened to the captain who was even then clambering up the steep side of the ship. They met at the top of the ladder, and he was not long in putting forward his request. Again we quote the words of the man who was soon to be known as the "Paul of Nigeria":

> "Well," said the captain to me, "I have no cabin for you, but if you can rough it on the deck we can take you." I was used to roughing it, so the bargain was made. I soon got my things out of the hold and into the launch, the *Sarauta* (Hausa for ruling or governing), and we immediately got away. Before long we passed the slower Niger Company boat which had refused me passage. We beat it by one and a half or two days to Patigi. Hallelujah! How good the Saviour is and was to me, His unworthy servant![12]

The journey up the river took four days—four hot, steaming, sweating days—which was the start of 45 years serving the Lord in Nigeria. Political circumstances at the time did not, however, make the new endeavor an easy one.

In 1903, after the British defeated the century-old Sokoto Caliphate in most of what is now northern Nigeria, the colonial government absorbed most of the caliphate's Fulani and Hausa rulers into a new colonial administrative structure. Many existing institutions and ruling families, directed by British administrators who changed some key provisions in customary law and gradually abolished slavery, became the means through which Great Britain administered the region. The preferences of the Muslim emirs governing northern Nigeria were mostly respected, and missions were by and large prevented from working directly in the Hausa and Fulfulde-speaking heartland of northern Nigeria.

When the SIM missionaries discovered that the British colonial administration was not going to permit direct evangelization of the Muslim Hausa in northern Nigeria, the goal of the mission's original founders was temporarily revised. As historian Barbara Cooper points out, "...they put their energies into evangelizing non-Muslim groups outside the Hausa-speaking heartland and producing Hausa-language materials that could be carried into the central emirates by traders and colporteurs."[13]

But there were other factors influencing this new focus as well. The work of Dr. Stirrett and Rev. Banfield at Patigi, Bida, and subsequently Wushishi proved to be very difficult and unfruitful as they were strong Muslim towns. This lack of response caused the missionaries to consider turning their attention to other places.

Dr. Bingham relates how, on one occasion, he walked hundreds of miles with Stirrett: "During that whole time we never knew a day's march so long but that ere he went to rest Stirrett would insist on gathering any kind of a motley crowd to tell out the story of the gospel."[14]

Thomas Titcombe, more commonly known as Tommy, joined the mission in 1908.[15] After two or three weeks spent at Patigi with Stirrett, the doctor announced it was time to open a new station. An ethnic group living several days journey away had appealed for help, so Stirrett sent Titcombe to the Yagba-Yoruba in Yorubaland. The Yagba were predominantly traditional (non-Muslim) and quite responsive to the gospel.

The first SIM baptisms, which led to the formation of its first church, took place at Ogga near Egbe, Nigeria, in 1909. Ten men and three women were baptized. This event essentially marked the beginning of the Evangelical Churches of West Africa (ECWA) which was formally established in 1954, and that is today known as Evangelical Church Winning All.[16]

After Banfield had served among the Nupe at Shonga for 12 years, the United Missionary Society released him to the British and Foreign Bible Society. He moved to Lagos to serve as secretary of the society for West Africa. There he became an advisor on all of the society's translation projects, a post that he held for 15 years. The Shonga years had been most successful linguistically. During this period the whole Bible had been translated into Nupe, and a great deal of other Christian literature had been made available through his efforts to the Nupe people.

In 1914 Titcombe arranged his first Bible conference. More than one hundred converts who had been examined with the greatest care publicly followed their profession of faith in Christ with baptism.

In 1915 Dr. Bingham went to Nigeria for nine months to visit all the places where the mission was working. By this time the work had spread, with the help of more missionaries and African converts, to a large number of towns and districts going as far north as the Jos Plateau. A retreat center for missionaries was built on the outskirts of a village called Miango, situated on the plateau. Even today SIM missionaries, ECWA church members, and other Christians use what is popularly known as the Miango Rest Home to restore their strength on an annual holiday and for conferences, as the plateau is cool and a very refreshing part of the country.[17]

The mission continued to spread into many regions, covering more territory than any other mission. At times the challenge was great and there were many dangers. In order for them to reach the Tangale they had to pass through an area occupied by 10 other ethnic groups, and in 1915 it was a region entirely without missionaries. The carriers for Bingham and Stirrett were not happy when they heard reports about one cannibal group they had to pass through, but together they all faced it and finally passed through safely.[18]

The men, women, and children of one group were said to live in complete nakedness. There was more than rumour in the story of their fierceness and cannibalism. They marked with a stone the place where they buried the skulls of the victims they had killed and eaten, and there were plenty of such stones around. As they left that area Stirrett and Bingham knelt and prayed that God would send at least two missionaries to that faraway place. When Bingham arrived home, he appealed strongly for those ten peoples without a missionary, and especially for two men for the Tangale. God answered in a remarkable way and two men responded, Rev. John S. Hall and C. Gordon Beacham. Within a year these two men were on their way, and in 1917 they settled down in the midst of those people at Kaltungo.[19]

How C. Gordon Beacham joined the mission is a remarkable story. Dr. Herbert Mackenzie, pastor of a church in Cleveland, Ohio, had accompanied Dr. Bingham on his tour to Nigeria in 1915. Later, when Dr. Mackenzie was holding his Annual Missionary Day, he invited Dr. Bingham to be the guest speaker. On that occasion Dr. Bingham spoke about the Tangales and of their lifestyle and urgent need of the gospel. When Dr. Bingham had finished speaking Pastor Mackenzie rose and said:

> Before we bring our offerings for missions this morning there is one thing more important and that is the offering of life. Who will place his life upon the altar for service? Who will go anywhere in the world that Christ calls?[20]

Beacham responded, in spite of the fact that he had a handicapped brother and a widowed mother and that he was the main support for the family. The previous week he mentioned to his mother about the possibility of going into the Lord's work. Her reply was, "Gordon, I gave you to the Lord for this work when you were born, and of course you'll go." The handicapped brother also offered to go wherever the Lord should lead him.

C. Gordon Beacham and John Hall immediately started to learn the language. Reducing it to writing, they were so successful that within 12 months they had translated their first gospel in the Tangale language.[21]

Meanwhile, back in Yorubaland, Titcombe usually saw people with sores while preaching from place to place. This encouraged him to embark on health-care services. He was quick to notice that this was another avenue to winning souls. Formation of the SIM Hospital in Egbe gradually began. Tommy Titcombe married Ethel McIntosh in 1915; this union brought about a turning point in the history of the hospital.[22]

When Tommy and Ethel arrived in Egbe after their honeymoon and two days before Christmas 1915, they didn't realize how exciting Christmas Day was going to be. As they were getting ready to go to the five o'clock service that morning, a messenger came running from the town beckoning Ethel to come quickly. There was a woman who had just given birth to twins. She had had four babies and all had died. At that time the Yagba people believed that a woman who gave birth to twins was less than human, and they wouldn't let them live in the village any longer. They believed one of the twins must be an evil spirit, and they were waiting for the medicine man to come and kill both of them. Consequently, Ethel was able to save the twins from being killed and the woman from being driven into the forest, though there was considerable resistance from the people.

The first twins (Reuben and Ruth) were saved on that day without any evil befalling them. As the people believed in the gospel, the practice was gradually abolished from among the Yagba people. Perhaps because Ethel wanted to save more twins, she decided to start a small maternity room in their house. In 1925 they started building a maternity unit and clinic, with the support and hard labour of Christian converts. The building was completed in 1926.

Because of the interest and financial contribution of SIM toward the upkeep of the Niger Press, the Rev. Banfield invited SIM to take over the press. But SIM declined on the grounds that it would serve the interests of all the missions on the field in a better way if the press were under the direction of an independent corporation to serve all missions on equal terms. SIM suggested that Evangelical Publishers be contacted. In July 1917 Banfield handed Niger Press over to the Evangelical Publishers, a corporation founded and run by Dr. Bingham and affiliated with Sudan Interior Mission. Based in Toronto, Canada, Evangelical Publishers agreed to maintain the high ideals for which Niger Press stood.[23]

New equipment was sent out to upgrade Niger Press in 1918. They also sent Mr. and Mrs. Ernie George, who had wide experience in the printing business, to manage it. In 1919 the press was moved from Shonga to a new building in Minna. This was a very big task to move so much machinery and paper, but the move enabled the press to expand and cope with the growing need for printed material.[24]

With regard to advancing into the predominately Muslim north, SIM faced the same situation as the Church Missionary Society. The government refused to allow the missions to proceed north. The British government's system of granting missions "spheres of influence" restricted SIM's activities in the same way that the Catholic mission's work had been curtailed since the beginning of the twentieth century. However, things with the colonial government by the late 1920s were beginning to change. Because the government was now prepared to pay for primary education, it became much more dynamically interested in the content and the organization of missionary education.[25]

When SIM decided to move its headquarters from Minna to Jos in 1928, Niger Press was also moved to Jos. On occasions the press was forced to close for perhaps a month during the harmattan season (when seasonal conditions brought dry sand-laden winds down from the Sahara) because the dry air and dust made the rollers crack and turn hard, making it extremely difficult to print.[26]

Two years later, while Bingham was in Nigeria just three months after the Great Depression started, Bingham sent a cable overseas that read: DISREGARDING SEVERE SHORTAGE WHOLE MISSIONARY BODY UNANIMOUSLY URGE UNDELAYED SENDING EVERY APPROVED WORKER FOR CONTINUOUS ADVANCE CHALLENGE HOME COUNCILS AND CONSTITUENCY EXERCISE SAME SACRIFICIAL FAITH.

From the earliest days when a missionary entered a new district, time was spent learning a local language and converting it into written script. Work then focused on translating portions of Scripture into the language of the people. This was no small task as the languages indigenous to Nigeria number over four hundred.[27] SIM also played a major role in literacy development with the opening of bookshops to sell Bibles and Christian literature. The rise of the literature ministry also brought into being *African Challenge* in the early 1950s, a popular gospel magazine that made a substantial impact in much of West Africa.[28]

SIM established the Igbaja Training Centre in 1941, with 18 students under the leadership of Rev. William Crouch. In 1951 A. J. Classen, principal of the theological

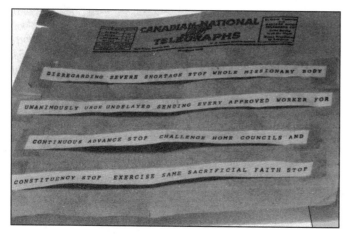

Photo 4.5. 4 *February 1930 depression-era cable.*
Even though times were difficult in an era when missions were beginning to withdraw personnel and curb expansion, SIM continued to press forward into areas that were not reached.
Source: Ian M. Hay, "Stewardship in Times of Recession," SIMNOW 58 (Spring 1992): 2–3.

college, could see the need for more mature and better-trained ministers for the church. Advanced training seemed necessary to meet the challenge of a more progressive and better-educated laity in the church. Plans were made in 1955, therefore, to establish post-secondary theological training. A student could earn a B.Th. degree if they finished their studies at Toronto Bible College for one year. The first class of 13 students enrolled in Igbaja Seminary or the Igbaja Teacher Training College in January 1956; this later became known as ECWA Theological Seminary. Initially the seminary offered a three-year program. In 1960 the curriculum was reorganized and the seminary began to offer two programs: the intermediate program—a three-year course leading to a diploma in theology—and an advanced program—a four-year course leading to an advanced diploma in theology.[29]

After the sudden death of Dr. Bingham on 8 December 1942, C. Gordon Beacham became acting general director. He was succeeded by Rev. Guy W. Playfair who became the next general director a year and a half later. He saw the almost unbelievable expansion of the mission through the course of his tenure that ended in 1957. New fields were entered and new projects were initiated, including the establishment of an eye hospital, four leprosaria, three general hospitals, a nursing home, and numerous clinics and treatment centers. SIM was greatly involved in medical work, in dispensaries, clinics, and hospitals throughout the country.[30]

By 1950, the Egbe people had started to develop and manifest a very positive response to the medical services. As a result, it was becoming more and more difficult to cope with the increasing number of patients. The work of Olutoju, who was a trained nurse, was a great help, but it became clear that there was an immediate need for more trained personnel. Rev. and Mrs. Titcombe had worked hard to help sustain the hospital through several visits following their departure in 1930. It was undoubtedly hard for them, as neither of them had formal medical training, but each had developed solid nursing skills over time.

Rev. Titcombe had been in consultation with Dr. George Campion since 1949, when Campion was in his final year of medical training in Canada. He agreed to go to Egbe after he completed his studies. The arrival of Dr. Campion and his wife Esther in 1951 were key to the final transition of the hospital into one of the biggest, most popular, and most successful hospitals in the present Kogi State and in Nigeria at large.[31]

Tommy and Ethel's decision to return home was "sad news" for the Egbe people. But Tommy was getting old, and he departed from Egbe for the last time in 1958 at the age of 77.[32]

To give some indication of how the work expanded and was blessed, the following statistics were given for 1959 from the Egbe Hospital: 67 beds; 6,088 new patients; 50,087 attendances; 1,161 patients admitted; 811 operations; 22,705 laboratory examinations; 332 babies delivered; and 134 who professed to accept Christ as Saviour. There was also an excellent Nurses' Training School at the hospital with 43 in attendance.[33] In recent years SIM, in partnership with ECWA and Samaritan's Purse/World Medical Mission, has improved the hospital and surrounding buildings, restored water and electricity, resupplied the hospital with new equipment, and recruited more Nigerians and missionary health-care workers, administrators, and maintenance personnel.[34]

ECWA is the denomination associated with SIM in Nigeria and other countries that was established in Nigeria in 1954. In the early 1950s, consideration was given to having the churches registered with the Nigerian government, which took place in 1952. This led to attention being given to drawing up a constitution and registering the churches as an indigenous denomination. Constitutional matters were discussed in January 1954 at Kagoro. The name chosen, the "Association of the Evangelical Churches of West Africa," came be be known by the acronym ECWA. (ECWA became the Evangelical Church of West Africa in 1989, and Evangelical Church Winning All by 2011.)[35] The first General Church Assembly that met in May 1954 confirmed this name. In 1957 a meeting of the General Church Assembly of ECWA was held in Kwoi, when R. J. Davis, the field director of the SIM work, announced that the Evangelical Churches of West Africa was now a legal entity and recognized as such by the government of Nigeria.

It is interesting to add that what became the Evangelical Missionary Society, the indigenous mission society of ECWA, actually preceded the formal establishment of the denomination by more than a decade. Passing along a missionary vision for the unreached was clearly an early hallmark of SIM work in both Nigeria (1940s) and Ethiopia (1930s).[36]

The education ministry of SIM in Nigeria was the means by which thousands started to read and write. In cooperation with the government, SIM schools did a tremendous work and the quality of education in primary, secondary, and teacher training was of a high standard. Titcombe College ranked above average among other secondary schools.

Photo 4.6. *Ben Aidoo, William Ofori-Atta, and W. Harold Fuller, 1975.*

Mr. William Ofori-Atta signed the papers that established Challenge Enterprises of Ghana (CGE). He did so in the presence of SIM Director of Ghana and Nigeria W. Harold Fuller, and CGE trustee Mr. Ben Aidoo. The creation of the CGE allowed for the official transfer of SIM Ghana's literature assets including *African Challenge* to CGE on 25 January 1975. Ofori-Atta, who was instrumental in helping bring Ghana to indepencence in 1957, became a Christian many years later after reading *African Challenge* while in prison.[40]

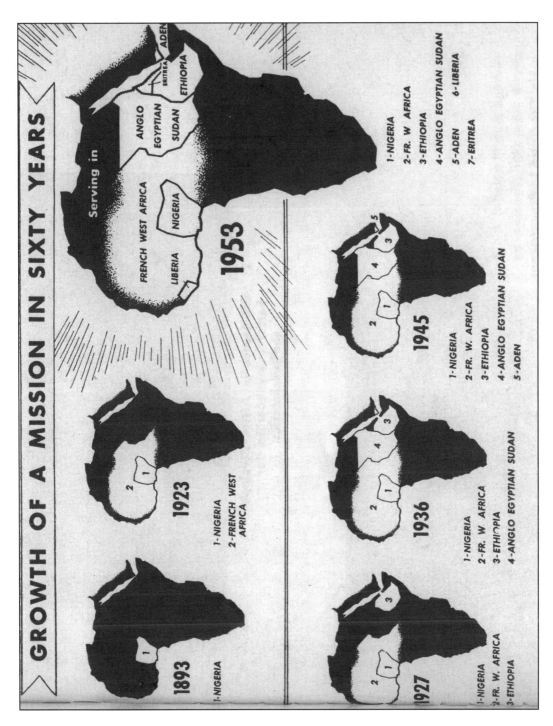

Map 4.2. *"Growth of a Mission in Sixty Years," 1953.*
Source: Sudan Witness *(Jubliee Issue, January 1953): 31.*

In 1959, SIM had 150 junior primary schools, 32 senior primary schools, four third-grade centers and one second-grade center. They also had 216 fourth-grade teachers, 172 third-grade teachers, 68 second-grade teachers, one first-grade teacher, as well as 71 expatriate teachers at various levels.[37]

Teacher colleges subsequently developed as a key strategy of SIM as a result of this educational emphasis and revealed an early willingness on the part of the mission to think outside the box to obtain visas through what today would be called "creative access" means.[38]

Through the years, Niger Press contributed greatly to the printing of the Scriptures in many languages. A major additional success was the printing of Christian literature such as the *African Challenge*. It was well illustrated and the stories were short and the language simple. Under the editorial guidance of the Rev. Harold Fuller it was widely popular.

When Nigeria gained her independence on 1 October 1960, SIM managed 20 bookshops, with 15 Nigerian managers, 90 African salesmen, and 10 missionary staff. They had also distributed in one year 120 tons of literature: 10,000 Bibles in Hausa, 10,000 Bibles in Yoruba, Ibo, and English, and considerable educational material and Christian gospel recordings.[39]

SIM's Expansion from Nigeria to Ethiopia and Beyond[41]

Shifting backward in time, a short explanation is now provided of how SIM expanded from Nigeria into other parts of Africa and the rest of the world.[42] The mission first moved from Nigeria to Niger in 1923, and then to Ethiopia in 1927. SIM's entry into Ethiopia, and hence East Africa, occurred after it merged with the Abyssinian Frontiers Mission (AFM). (Chapter 8 discusses SIM's merger with the AFM.) Dr. Tom Lambie, one of AFM's co-founders, led SIM's first missionaries into Ethiopia.

Photo 4.7. *David Osborne talking to a chief and his elders while Henry Stock and many Africans look on, perhaps in Ouagadougou, Upper Volta, 1930.*
Photo credit: Rowland Bingham.

Bingham traveled to Nigeria in late 1929 to attend an all-missions conference whose members called for the British government to permit mission organizations to expand their work into the north. He then went on an exploratory trip to Haute Volta (Upper Volta, today's Burkina Faso) to secure permission from French authorities to start working among the Gourma; SIM's first missionaries went there in 1930.[43]

In February 1930, Bingham, Guy Playfair, and Bingham's brother-in-law Henry Stock made

Photo 4.8. *"Manpower versus Africa Mud,"* 1930. As Bingham, Playfair, and Stock neared the end of their journey across Africa, they reached Kijabe, Kenya, on 7 March 1930. They hoped to drive Playfair's new Model A Ford to Nairobi, and travel on to Ethiopia. However, Bingham wrote, "We had to leave our car at Kijabi, fifty miles out, because the roads, by the unexpected early rains, had been rendered well-nigh impossible." They ended up taking a train to Nairobi, and then proceeded on to Ethiopia.[45]

a cross-continental journey to Ethiopia to meet Dr. Lambie and other SIM missionaries. From Nigeria, they drove in a southeasterly direction through French Cameroon (today's Cameroon), French Equatorial Africa (present-day Chad and Central African Republic), Belgian Congo (present-day Democratic Republic of Congo), and Uganda, and then headed north to Ethiopia after reaching Nairobi, Kenya.[44]

SIM had only been in Ethiopia for a few years when the Italians invaded in 1935. The mission's last personnel evacuated three years later, with some going to neighboring Anglo-Egyptian Sudan. In 1941, when SIM's missionaries began to filter back to Ethiopia, they were astonished to learn that the number of baptized Wolaitta believers in the south had risen from a few dozen to well over ten thousand. Thousands more had become Christians.[46] (See Supplement 8.2, pages 115-117, titled "Ethiopian Reversals and Church Growth" for more information.) The Anglo-Egyptian Sudan, which became Sudan upon independence in 1956, expulsed all Western missionaries in the south in 1964.[47] Some of SIM's missionaries, however, remained in Khartoum until a few years ago. SIM returned to the south in 1978 to work with refugees, only to be forced out again in 1984 after another civil war started. Its missionaries returned in 2003, though were evacuated in 2009, 2011, 2013, and 2016 due to fighting related to civil war.[48]

Following the close of World War II, which had restricted SIM's travel and expansion, the mission entered several new countries. In 1945, SIM officially began the first of several efforts to evangelize the predominately Muslim Somali in East Africa by placing missionaries in British-governed Aden Colony (part of today's Yemen).

SIM expanded its work to French Somaliland (part of today's Djibouti) in 1948, deployed some of its personnel to eastern Ethiopia in the early 1950s, and entered Italian Somaliland (part of today's Somalia) and Kenya in 1954 and 1977 respectively. In 1974, SIM's missionaries left Somalia due to nationalization. That same year, however, the mission began to produce and air programs in the Somali language in Ethiopia over a local radio station.[49] (See Supplement 17.1, pages 257-259, for more information about SIM's work among the

Somali.) Many also left Ethiopia after the overthrow of Emperor Haile Selassie in 1974.[50]

Another country that SIM entered in East Africa was Eritrea. SIM's first missionaries went there in 1952 to open a home for orphans, but departed in 1975 due to increased risk as Eritrea fought Ethiopia for its independence. SIM's missionaries began to return in 1991 after the war ended, but were forced to leave again in 2006 as the government increasingly restricted all Western missionary activities.[51] SIM's Arabic-speaking workers were forced to leave Aden in 1965 because of heightened terroristic activities. Some moved to Beirut, Lebanon, to assist in the production of Arabic-language programs for Radio ELWA in Liberia. SIM closed its operations in Lebanon in 1975.[52]

In West Africa following the Second World War, SIM entered Dahomey (later Benin) in 1945 to work among the Bariba,[53] Liberia in 1952 to establish a radio station,[54] and the Gold Coast (later Ghana) in 1954 to distribute literature.[55] By 1965,

Photo 4.9. *Reg Pascoe counseling a young man at SIM bookshop, Aden, c. 1965*

SIM's active membership rose to 1318 full-time active missionaries, making it one of the largest Protestant Western mission organizations in Africa.[56] SIM expanded to Côte d'Ivoire (Ivory Coast) in 1968 to publish a magazine in French,[57] the Central African Republic in 1981 to start a medical ministry, Guinea in 1986 to work among the Maninka,[58] Sierra Leone also in 1986 to supply faculty at Fourah Bay College,[59] Togo in 1992 to work among the Kotokoli using radio, and Mali in 2010 for evangelism.[60]

It was with the mergers of major missions that SIM began to spread beyond West and East Africa. Andes Evangelical Mission's merger in 1982 marked SIM's entry into South America in Bolivia and Peru (chapter 10), and later to Paraguay (1987), Chile (1988), Ecuador (1989), Uruguay (1995), and Brazil

Photo 4.10. *"Lebanon: Bud Acord and converted Muslim Arab teacher and priest, Nura Din, preparing Arabic tapes, ELWA Recording Studio, Beirut, 1969"*

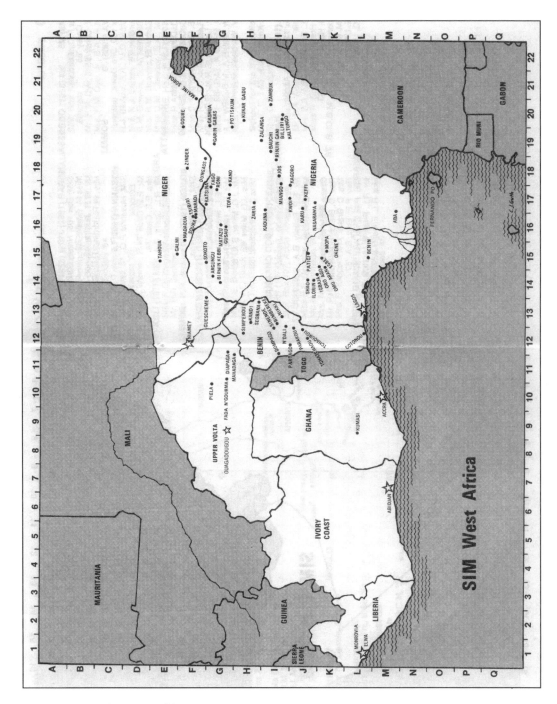

Map 4.3. *SIM in West Africa, 1977.*
Source: SIM 1977 Prayer Guide

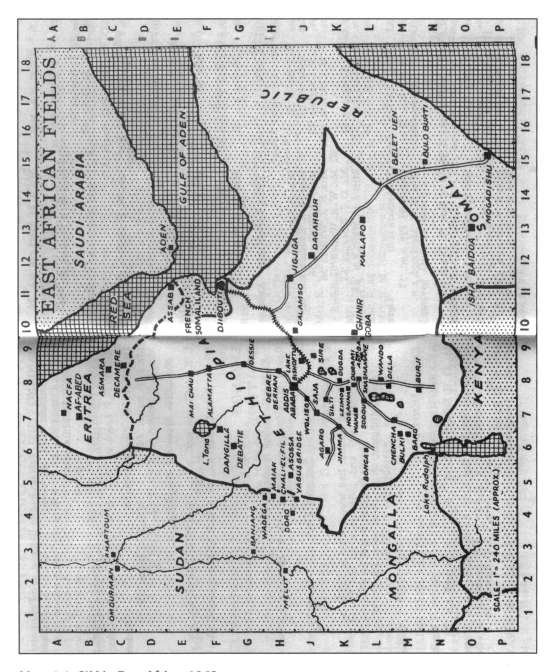

Map 4.4. *SIM in East Africa, 1963.*

Source: SIM 1963 Prayer Guide

(2009). SIM's merger with International Christian Fellowship in 1989 added one more country in Africa—Senegal, and several in Asia: Bangladesh, India, Nepal, Pakistan, Philippines, and Sri Lanka (chapter 12). SIM has since entered Mongolia (1996), China (1997), Japan (2001), Malaysia (2010), Indonesia (2011), and Sri Lanka (2011). SIM's merger with Africa Evangelical Fellowship in 1998 extended its reach into Gabon and a number of countries in Southern Africa: Angola, Botswana, Madagascar, Malawi, Mauritius, Mozambique, Namibia, Réunion, South Africa, Swaziland, Tanzania, Zambia, and Zimbabwe (chapter 13).[61] SIM moved into the Middle Eastern countries of Egypt, Jordan, Lebanon, Iraq and Cyprus when it formed a relationship with the Middle East Christian Outreach in 2016 (chapter 21).

SUPPLEMENT 4.1

Tommy Titcombe[62]

Mr. Thomas Titcombe joined SIM in 1908. After two or three weeks spent at Patigi with Dr. Stirrett, the doctor announced that he felt it was time to open a new station. A tribe several days journey had appealed for help and so Titcombe went to the Yagbas, who were predominantly traditional (non-Muslim), and quite responsive to the gospel. He lived with a Yagba family in a hut for more than a year to learn the language, and then he began to tell the gospel story. Titcombe encountered many remarkable experiences while living with the Yagbas. At that time they were a people in slavery to sin where witchcraft and cannibalism were issues they faced daily. It was a horrendous experience to see the evidence of cannibalism frequently in the village and also the awful suffering caused by witchcraft.

In spite of witnessing these things Titcombe remained with the people and witnessed God changing lives. He related many experiences he had while seeking to present the gospel message. In one encounter he had with traditionalists and Muslims there had been no rain for a long time, the crops were withered, and starvation was a real possibility.

The traditionalists beat their drums, blew their horns, screamed and shouted to their idols for a whole week, and also sacrificed a calf, all in the vain hope to get rain, but nothing came. Then the Muslims said

Photo 4.11. *Tommy Titcombe, "Baptism in Egbe"*

they would bring rain. They also shouted and screamed night and day, fasted and sacrificed a lamb, but there was no rain.

On Sunday the Christians attended church and the pastor went to Titcombe and suggested that the Christians should now pray for rain. After some discussion with the pastor Titcombe turned to the congregation and said, "Tomorrow night we are going to pray for rain. Let none come if they do not believe God hears and answers prayer."

After the Sunday service the pastor and Titcombe were sitting on the veranda when suddenly they heard the sound of drums—it was a message going out to everyone, "Now we shall see who has the God that lives, the believers are going to pray for rain."

The next day it was exceptionally dry and hot with not a cloud in the sky. At 7:00 p.m. the bell rang for church. When Titcombe reached the church, he saw the Muslims were sitting on one side and the traditionalists on the other; but what surprised him most was that the Christians were sitting with big umbrella hats on their heads. When he enquired what the purpose of these was, he was told: "White man, haven't we come to pray for rain, and didn't you tell us that only those who believed God answers prayer were to come?"

Titcombe reminds us that only a few years earlier these people were living as cannibals. Now their lives were changed and they had faith in the Lord Jesus Christ, and were displaying remarkable faith. They had come to pray for rain and were giving evidence of their faith by coming prepared for that rain by bringing their umbrellas.

Titcombe spoke for a few minutes from James 5:17–18 and then they prayed. They prayed for only one thing, "Lord, we need rain." Ten, fifteen, twenty minutes went by and then there was a tapping on the corrugated iron roof of the church that thrilled everyone, the rain had come. It rained so heavily that the people ran in fear to their homes.

The traditionalists said, "We shouted for a week and sacrificed a cow and got no rain." And the Muslims said, "We fasted for a week and sacrificed a lamb, and we got no rain." But the Christians were only praying for a few minutes and God sent a deluge on the earth and has given us all the rain needed. There is only one God and that is the God of the believers." After that encounter many of those traditionalists and Muslims put their faith in the Lord Jesus Christ.

SUPPLEMENT 4.2

"Bob, I am killed!": SIM Missionaries Slain on the Mission Field[63]

Dr. Tim Geysbeek

Many SIM missionaries and their children have died while serving God on the mission field. For example, in the cemetery adjacent to Kirk Chapel in Miango, Nigeria, 56 people had been buried by 1992; 33 were children.[64] Graveyards like this, many of which are often smaller and less cared for, are scattered in every continent where the mission works. The causes of death of SIM's 107 long-term missionaries who died in "active service" from 1940–1990 were, in descending order, cancer, injuries, heart disease, infections, war, and one person each from complications due to a Caeserean section and a dental procedure.[65]

Photo 4.12. *"They Loved Not Their Life Even Unto Death," 1936.*

Photo credit: Esmé Ritchie Rice, Eclipse in Ethiopia and its Corona Glory (London: Marshall, Morgan & Scott Ltd.) c. 1939, iv.

Six individuals have been killed on purpose while working overseas. All were killed in East Africa: three in Ethiopia and three in the Anglo-Egyptian Sudan (today's South Sudan). Except for the grace of God, this number could be much higher given those who have been victims of armed robberies, or who have been wounded or otherwise escaped the ravages of war. Five of the six killed were under the age of 30.

SIM's first missionaries to be killed were G. Clifford Mitchell and Thomas Devers, in Ethiopia, in May 1936.[66] The men, who had been in southern Ethiopia, departed north for Addis Ababa when they heard Italian troops were quickly advancing toward the capital. The Italians had begun their conquest of Ethiopia seven months earlier. Mitchell, a 34-year-old New Zealander, wanted to rejoin his wife, Myrtle, and infant son in Addis. Twenty-six-year-old Devers, a Canadian, hoped to reunite with his fiancé, Gertrude Pogue. Unrest spread south in the wake of the city's fall on the 5th of May. While crossing the Kasse (Kasei) desert, after having left Yerga Alem, the caravan with armed soldiers with whom they were traveling was attacked on the 9th of May by several dozen Arusi bandits. The only survivor, the employee of a Belgian plantation owner, said he saw Mitchell's and Devers' "mutilated bodies" under some bushes. The exact circumstances of their deaths never became public.

The message SIM's office in London sent to their fellow-missionaries in Ethiopia is the same one that Rowland Bingham wrote about his fallen comrades Walter Gowans and Tom Kent years earlier: "Except a corn of wheat fall into the ground and die, it abideth alone; but if it die, it bringeth forth much fruit."

Four years later, an Italian bomber killed Dr. Robert C. Grieve and his pregnant wife Claire in Doro, in the Anglo-Egyptian Sudan. Both were Americans, respectively 27 and 28 years old. The Italians had militarily occupied Ethiopia for over two years by this time and declared war on Great Britain. Neighboring Anglo-Egyptian Sudan was a British colony, hence subject to Italian incursions. In early 1940, the Italians occupied a provincial capital situated about 80 kilometers north of Doro where five SIM missionaries were based.

Photo 4.13. *Bob and Claire Grieve, killed in Doro, Sudan, 1940.*

Photo credit: "Seattleite Killed in Bombing," Seattle Post-Intelligencer, *August 1940.*

On 23 August, two Italian planes made several runs over Doro and dropped over 80 small bombs. One of the first bombs gravely wounded Dr. Grieve and his wife, Claire. After she was thrown to the ground, she turned to her unconscious husband and yelled, "Bob, I am killed!" Shrapnel had hit Dr. Grieve in eight places and crushed his forehead; he died within 90 minutes. His wife bled to death seven hours later after shrapnel had severed her spinal cord and paralyzed her from her waist down. Before she and her unborn child died, Americans Kenneth and Blanche Oglesby, and Australian Zilla Walsh, lay her by her husband in the very clinic where he had just come to work months earlier. With "her face on his," Blanche wrote, she "told him how good and kind he had always been to her."[67] Oglesby was hit in the back and right shoulder in two places. Blanche, who was

Photo 4.14. *Dr. Doug Hill, killed in Markan, Ethiopia, 1975.*

Photo credit: Mary Amalia.

hit by 30 pieces of shrapnel, "had several nasty deep wounds in her leg." Walsh was not physically injured in the attack.

The Italians are thought to have bombed Doro and a nearby town either because they heard British-led African troops had entered the area or because informers had spread rumors that they were aiding the Sudanese against the Italians. Dr. Grieve and Mr. Oglesby's attempt to thwart the bombing by holding up a large American flag only made them prime targets for the attackers.

Thirty-five years later, in 1975, an assailant in Ethiopia stabbed Dr. Doug Hill in the heart. Hill, a 26-year-old "short-term" medical doctor from Australia, was the leader of SIM's Emergency Relief Team in the Ogaden. He, Mary Amalia, Judy Frazer, a Somali translator named Muhammed, and another African went to Markan (Merkan) near Bokh in the eastern part of the country to make inquiries about establishing a nutrition and medical program during the height of the famine. Only a few minutes after they started to introduce the program, a man from the crowd suddenly lunged at Hill and stabbed him on the right side of his chest. After falling to the ground, Hill uttered his last word—"Why?" Onlookers stopped the man from stabbing Amalia and Frazer. The assailant, who some speculate was Somali, escaped and was never apprehended. His motive for wanting to kill the missionaries is not known.[68]

CHAPTER 5

THE ANDES EVANGELICAL MISSION STORY

From New Zealand with Love[1]

George Allan was born in New Zealand of pioneer Scottish stock, the seventh in a family of 10 children. Although he was brought up in a good Presbyterian home, he did not make a commitment to Christ until he went to work on the farm of his oldest brother, James. A joyous and practical Christian, James made an unforgettable impact on George.

At age 22, when he heard a message on John 10:27–28: "My sheep hear my voice . . . and I give unto them eternal life," George was ready. "Why, it's a gift!" he realized, and accepted God's offer of salvation. He soon became active in witness and in his church, where he was attracted to Mary Stirling, daughter of another Scottish pioneer.

Mary had been converted at age 11. During her teens she developed a deep interest in missionary service, a concern that George also shared. They became engaged and went to Adelaide, Australia, to prepare at the Angus Missionary Training College, as no comparable institution existed in New Zealand at that time.

Photo 5.1. *George and Mary Allan, with Margarita and Joe, 1907.*
Photo credit: BIM's News and Report, *1908.*

While at college, Mary and a friend spent much time in prayer for South America's Indian people. On one occasion the Holy Spirit gave them the assurance that great numbers of Indians would be saved. They thanked Him, in faith.

By the time their schooling was finished, George and Mary's correspondence with the Canada-based South American Evangelical Mission was complete and they were accepted as missionaries. In addition, George was commissioned to form an Australasian SAEM Council. They were married at the college and returned to New Zealand to share their concern for the neglected continent.

On 23 April 1899, with two other new recruits, they sailed for Buenos Aires, Argentina.

The year after their arrival, the Allans welcomed their first child, Margarita. At that time, communications with the homeland were slow and undependable. Their funds ran out. It wasn't long before their food supply was exhausted. For three weeks they had very little to eat, and for three days nothing. Mary became unable to nurse her baby.

But they were determined to trust only God. "Borrowing is not faith," they said, "not even from Christian friends." They used their only resource—prayer.

Later that day they heard a knock at the gate. A neighbor stood there with a gift of hot mate, a nourishing drink, and some bread. She knew nothing of the Allans' need and wasn't sure why she had felt impelled to visit them. But the Allans knew.

That same evening a miner, who needed a place to stay when he was in the city, asked to rent a room in their house, which was a large one. He insisted on paying in advance.

Then the long-delayed bank draft arrived from New Zealand. "We learned that no matter how hard the trial might be, our needs would be met," they said. That principle of utter dependence on God characterized not only their own lives, but that of the new mission they would be called upon to form.

In 1906 George led a small party on an extended survey trek into neighboring Bolivia. The next year, when SAEM unexpectedly disbanded, George, inspired by the findings of the survey, founded the Bolivian Indian Mission and pressed on to his goal of establishing a witness among the Quechua and Aymara Indians.

Home base for the new mission was New Zealand; field base was the town of San Pedro, high in Bolivia's mountains.

Photo 5.2. *Central plaza in San Pedro, c. 1923.*
Photo credit: H. E. Vroman.

Not many welcomed the nine BIM missionaries who arrived in 1909. Catholicism was strongly opposed to Protestant influences, and hard times faced missionaries and Indian converts alike. A recurring problem was finding suitable places to live. The Allans' friend, Verne Roberts, rented a house for his family, but upon arrival was refused entrance. The owner had been put under pressure not to rent to "devils" whose money was bewitched and would contaminate other money if mingled with it.

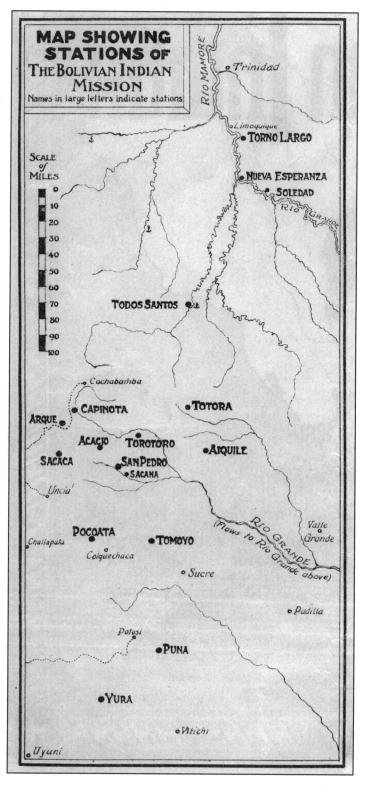

Map 5.1. *The Bolivian Indian Mission, 1932*

When the Roberts' family put up in a local hotel, angered leaders organized a demonstration. "All the town was to be mobilized in one great parade," Roberts related. "They were to tar and feather us and run us out of town." The crisis, however, was defused when the fanatics were reminded that the missionaries had the protection of their home government as well as Bolivia. On another occasion the Allans' home was attacked by a mob that destroyed their furniture and threatened their lives.

Missionaries also had to get used to being shouted at in the streets, called devils, and spat upon. Sometimes they were drenched with dirty water as they passed out tracts. Market women refused to sell them vegetables and meat. During open-air meetings, hostile villagers would drown out their voices by incessantly ringing the church bells.

The missionaries' trials, however, were nothing compared to the persecution received by Bolivians who dared to take a stand for Christ. "The priests sent spies to our services to take names and report anyone who attended, including children," reported Roberts, who later succeeded Allan as general director. "Then the fanatics would threaten them. Young people who ignored the threats and continued to attend services were locked in their rooms at meeting times. Bible burnings were the order of the day. Evangelicals were forbidden to bury their dead in public cemeteries."

One poor, uneducated Indian faced strong opposition from his own villagers. They moved into his fields and harvested his crops for themselves. They took away his water rights to the little irrigation stream and confiscated his land. Granted no legal protection, he was compelled to leave his home and was reduced to doing the most menial labor.

The marvelous thing to the missionaries was his lack of bitterness. "They have taken my land and my home," he told them, "but I am still richer than they are."

Ill health and other hardships gradually reduced the original nine workers to three. Others took their place, however, and by the end of the first decade there were 11 BIM missionaries in Bolivia.

There were neither schools nor doctors for the country people in those days, so the missionaries opened schools and clinics which helped gain the confidence of the Indians.

George Allan's stress on prayer and fellowship, and his unswerving confidence in God's supply, were major forces that bound the young mission together. He was hardworking, compassionate, and undaunted by what appeared to be insurmountable barriers. Much of his leadership quality lay in the fact that he was a humble man who tackled whatever needed to be done. Not only was he a preacher, he was a typist, carpenter, sheepshearer, and linguist.

He learned Greek on his own, and read his Greek New Testament every day—a discipline designed to help fulfill the goals he had set for BIM, which included Scripture translation as one of its main thrusts. (For a story of Allan's co-translator, Crisólogo Barrón, see Supplement 5.1, pages 74-75.)

In 1914 he began translation of the New Testament into Quechua, a project that changed the face of Indian work in Bolivia when it was published in 1920.

Photo 5.3. *BIM missionaries at the Webendorfers house near the Roman Catholic cathedral, San Pedro de Charcas, 24 December 1920.* (L-R): Charles and Ella Mae Larson and Betty, Ruth McCahan, Mildred Lee, Margarita Allan, Henry and Helen Webendorfer and Ellen Grace, Mary and George Allan, Miss Slack, Miss White, Fred Legant, child, and first wife.

Photo credit: Harry Vroman.

The Allans did not live to see the church blossom in Bolivia. They sowed the seed, watered it, and saw it germinate. Others saw it mature and multiply. Today there are hundreds of churches in Bolivia that are the legacy of their vision and labors.

Mary died in 1939, and George in 1941. Twenty-four years after his death, BIM expanded its ministry into the neighboring country of Peru and changed its name to Andes Evangelical Mission. AEM became part of SIM in 1982.

A Broadening Participation and Outreach[2]

In the early decades of the Bolivian Indian Mission, evangelism was the main thrust, coupled with translation of Scripture into Quechua, the largest language group. Missionaries and local believers struggled continually to gain a foothold. Opposition was strong, sometimes harsh. Devotion to the prevailing religious system was intense, and the intolerance of some led to persecution and even bloodshed.

Despite the hardships there were those who took a bold stand for the Lord. One by one little churches sprang up, many of them exclusively Quechua. As rural populations began their shift to the towns and cities, the mission extended its work to other groups. Medical and educational ministries were instrumental in opening up new areas. In 1930 the mission headquarters was moved to Cochabamba and the work broadened to reach Spanish-speaking Bolivians.

On another front, BIM became a pioneer in mission aviation. There were only two planes used in Protestant missionary service in any country in 1941 when BIM missionary Walter (Wally) Herron, from Australia, made his first flight in a Piper Cub he had purchased in the US.

Photo 5.4. *The Missionary Childrens' School in San Pedro, c. 1931–1932.* Pictured are Vi Upton with her students George Legant, Howard Powlison, Lloyd Powlison, Mary Ekdabe, Betty Larson, Homer Larson, Evelyn Shakeshaft, and Paul Powlison (order of students not given).

The Bolivian Indian Mission established this school for its "missionary kids," "mish kids," or "MKs" (now often called "third culture kids" or "TCKs") in 1926. BIM later moved the school to Cochabamba where it was eventually named Carachipampa Christian School. Examples of other schools like this around the world, that often provided boarding accommodations for the children of AEF, ICF, SIM, and MECO missionaries, are (or were) the English School or School for Missionaries' Children in Eritrea, the English School in Lebanon, Bingham Academy in Ethiopia, Dakar Christian Academy in Senegal, ELWA Academy in Liberia, Faith Christian Academy in the Philippines, Farfield Missionary Children's Home in South Africa, Hebron School in India, Hillcrest School in Nigeria, International Christian Academy in Côte d'Ivoire, Kent Academy in Nigeria, Metro Delhi International School in India, Murree Christian School in Pakistan, Rift Valley Academy in Kenya, Sakeji Mission School in South Africa, and the West African High School in Liberia.[3] MKs also lived with their families or in hostels and attended nearby schools, were home schooled, went to small satellite schools, or attended boarding schools like Gowans' Home in Canada while their parents served overseas on the "mission field." MKs such as Tim Bascom, Dan Coleman, Karen Keegan and Minna Kayser, Joy Loewen, Murgatroyd Mitchell, Ruth Van Reken, and Julene (Hodges) Schroeder have written about their childhoods and explained how their experiences affected the rest of their lives (see Asia, Ethiopia, Nigeria, Somalia, and Zambia in the bibliography for these and related books). These MKs talk about the challenges of identity due to the sharp dislocations they faced when moving to places that were often quite different culturally. MKs' experiences ranged from being very positive to those who suffered emotional, physical, and sexual abuse. For a rich source of information written mostly by MKs, see the magazine *SIMRoots* (http://simroots.org/).

The vision for missionary aviation came about as the result of a tragedy in Wally's life. He had taken his bride, Violet, to live in San Ramon, a little town in the vast Beni region of northern Bolivia. Totally cut off from modernity in the tropical lowlands of the Amazon basin, there was no competent medical help to assist Violet when she went into a long difficult labor. Ten minutes after the birth of their son, she entered into the presence of the Lord.

Wally quickly concluded that it would not be possible to care adequately for a baby in the primitive conditions at San Ramon. He accepted the offer of Violet's parents in New Zealand to care for little Robert. For five days and nights he bounced on an oxcart through mosquito infested areas just to get out of the Beni lowlands.

Photo 5.5. *Wally Herron and his plane*

One day a small plane flew overhead. "That's it!" Wally decided. "If I had had a plane like that, I could have taken Violet out for help in no time. That's what we need for the Beni."

Two years later Wally was a licensed pilot, assembling the Piper Cub at the airport on the edge of Cochabamba. A new era of outreach began when he took CB-BIM-1 up for its maiden flight to the Beni. (See Supplement 5.2, page 77, for more about Walter Herron.)

As the work grew, outreach spread to the non-Indian population, as well as spilling over into Peru. In the process many additional avenues of ministry developed. Training believers, the natural offspring of evangelism, is carried out by theological education in seminaries, two Bible institutes, and through theological education by extension (TEE) and correspondence courses. This training goes hand in hand with church planting in both rural and urban areas, and among all social classes.

Outreach to young people through Christian youth centers, a camp and retreat, Bible clubs, and itinerant ministries are other means of evangelism, which remained central to AEM ministry overall. This expanded to include Christian television, Christian films in schools and military facilities, citywide crusades, river launch outreach, literature, radio, home Bible classes, and regular church and personal efforts.

As South America, like much of the majority world, was experiencing rapid growth in literacy, AEM made a priority of producing and distributing evangelical literature. The mission was instrumental in establishing a wholesale supply of Christian literature, as well as numerous outlets, in Bolivia.

A Church Is Born and a Vision Grows[4]

By 1950, the work of the mission had become established in several areas. The mission headquarters had moved from a village in the mountains to the city of Cochabamba. Several churches had been organized. A night school was beginning to train national leaders. The Unión Christiana Evangélica or Evangelical Christian Union (UCE) was born in 1950 with four churches. The Quechua Bible Institute was functioning for a few months each year. (See Supplement 5.3, pages 78-79, for stories about how Arturo and Hilda Arana encouraged the growth of the church.)

During the decades of the 1950s and 1960s, the addition of new missionaries enabled the work to expand. The local political situation lessened Roman Catholic influence, and several Roman Catholic priests were converted. The government recognized Indians as "people" and gave them legal status not previously known. Use of the term "Indians," in fact, became generally disapproved.

Work of the mission expanded in several cities with Christian bookstores, youth centers, and the planting of new churches. Some of the new churches were among Quechuas and Aymaras who were being attracted to the cities by industrialization. A camp property was also purchased and developed for youth and children's camps. A second Bible institute for Quechua believers was opened in Sucre.

In 1956, churches of the Evangelical Union of South America joined the UCE, bringing another ethnic group (the Guarani) into its membership. The UCE is divided into 18 districts called sub-directavas, each with its own local committee with a president and other offices. The UCE as a whole holds a national convention every two years and elects a board of directors.

By 1985 the UCE had grown into a dynamic denomination of approximately five hundred churches and congregations in eight of the nine geographical departments of Bolivia, with strong national leadership in place and with three Bible institutes and a Bible seminary under Bolivian leadership.

Religious liberty in Bolivia during these years meant there were no restrictions on missionary activity, and there were no special requirements to obtain visas for entry into the country. As a result there are many groups working there today, including large numbers of Mormons. The Roman Catholic Church has little political influence currently, but still dominates as a religious force in the country through special feast days or fiestas.

In 1966 the Bolivian Indian Mission name was changed to Andes Evangelical Mission, in part in response to changes in the use of the term "Indian," but also to accommodate new opportunities for ministry. An invitation had come from the Evangelical Peruvian Church (IEP) to assist them, particularly with leadership training (through both Theological Education by Extension and by contributing teachers to the Evangelical Lima Seminary). The IEP had grown out of the work of the Evangelical Union of South America, and numbered more than eight hundred churches by 1985.

SUPPLEMENT 5.1

Crisólogo and Dõna Felicidad Barrón[5]

Crisólogo Barrón was born in Argentina of Bolivian parents. While he was yet very young his parents returned to their own land and took up residence in the city of Potosi. Later he went to Aiquile where he was married. It was there that he first heard of the Bible, but under the influence of the priest he considered it worthy only of flames. When a box of Scriptures, which a colporteur had left in Aiquile, fell into his hands, it was with real satisfaction that he consigned them to the fire.

After fighting in the Acre Campaign on the northern border of Bolivia against Brazil, he and his wife Dõna Felicidad came to reside in Yolala, a small village about nine miles from the old capital city of Sucre. Here they were innkeepers, and prided themselves on making good chicha (an intoxicating local favorite).

Photo 5.6. *Don Crisólogo and Felicidad Barrón*

It was to this very inn that their itinerating brought two colporteurs, R. Rowdon and Horace Grocott, for a meal. The missionaries offered Sr. Barrón a Bible, which he refused. He said that he knew all about the book, had already burned many copies, and besides, it was a prohibited book. As they were leaving, Grocott was inspired to try once more, this time speaking in Quechua, whereas all their prior conversation had been in Spanish. He had remembered that these folk learned Quechua at their mother's knee, that they are generally very proud of its beauty, and that they found particular delight in hearing it spoken by foreigners. Grocott was surprised but thrilled to hear "Certainly!" in reply to his inquiry whether he wouldn't buy a Spanish New Testament.

After this contact, Senor Barrón twice again was in touch with missionaries, but his final breakthrough into the assurance of salvation occurred when no missionary was present, through a pattern of early morning prayer from the heart (rather than the customary rote prayers), and reading from the Bible. It was not long before his wife asked to join him that they both committed their lives to Christ. Barrón summarized the impact this way:

> Before I knew what was taking place, I was a new man, and had begun to walk "in newness of life" and in the consciousness of sins forgiven and cleansed away in the blood of Christ. This was impossible to me while I held to the

dogmas of Rome. The many confessions made at the feet of the priest brought no change in my life, no cessation of the habit of drink, nor of my ill-treatment of my wife which always accompanied my frequent bouts of drunkenness, and scandalized the neighborhood. But what man could not do, God did; and, these things, thank God, are now of the past.

After our conversion, we broke the idols we had in our home into pieces, and I carried them outside the town and burned them, and scattered the ashes to the winds. We believed, from the reading of the Bible, that this was the best thing to do with them.

After a period of unsettledness the conviction grew in the couple that Yotala was not God's place for them. After several moves, including a time of study in the Scriptures helped by Brethren missionaries, they arrived in Cochabamba and once again encountered Mr. Grocott. He in turn contacted George Allan and posed the question, "Is not this man the answer to our prayers for a translator?" The answer as things turned out happened to be yes. BIM's Prayer Book entry for May 1914 records, "Sr. Barrón has come to San Pedro, having agreed to help us in translation work."

Things proceeded well, so that by the latter months of 1916 George Allan was in New York City supervising the publication of the Four Gospels in Quechua by the American Bible Society. An entry in the Prayer Book for June 1920 records, "A few weeks over six years from the date of the coming of Sr. Barrón . . . the task of translating the New Testament into Quechua was finished. It was an arduous task, but a very happy and profitable one to those of us who took part in it." Finally, all obstacles in printing and publishing were overcome, and the first completed Quechua New Testament was introduced in Bolivia in 1923.

And what became of Don Crisólogo after he finished his part of the translation work? On 15 July 1920, a man came to the house where he lived leading a horse, which he had brought from Oruro. With it he handed him a note: "This is a gift to you that you may be able to get out to the villages round about San Pedro, and preach the Gospel to the Indians." Having completed the translation on the 28th of the same month, Don concluded that the finished translation work together with the gift of the horse and the message of the note constituted the Lord's leading of him. He therefore took up the task of itinerant work among the Indians of the area, vaccinating children against small pox, and telling the story of God's love and grace.

Photo 5.7. *Crisólogo Barrón and George Allan, translators of the Quechua New Testament.* The following is a partial list of the Bible, or portions thereof, that missionaries with SIM, AEM, ICF, and AEF; their African, South American, and Asian colleagues; and members of other organizations such as the United Bible Society and the Summer Institute of Linguistics,

have translated (or are translating): *Angola*—Luchzai, Lomhuila, Mbunda; *Benin*—Bariba, Boko, Bakuura Fulfulde, Ditammari, Dompago, Fulfulde Burgo, Lokpa, Monkole, Samba, Sola, Yom; *Bolivia*—Quechua; *Botswana*—!Xoo; *Burkina Faso*—Fulfulde Burkina, Gourma (Gulmancema); *Guinea*—Maninkakã; *Ethiopia*—Aari, Amharic, Banna, Chaha Gurage, Kafa, Kambatta, Me'en, Mursi, Wolaitta; *Liberia*—Gbandi, Gola, Manyakã; *Malawi*—Yao Chiyao; *Mozambique*—Lomwe Bible; *Niger*—Fulfulde Western Niger, Fulfulde Eastern Niger, Kanuri, Manga, Kyanga, Busa, Shanga, Tamaceq; *Nigeria*—Bisã, Bokobaru, Bura, Gbari-Gayegi, Gbari-Gengeyi, Gbari-Mattai, Gbari-Pariko, Gbari-Yamma, Hausa, Igbo, Irigwe, Nupe, Tangale, Waja, Yoruba; *Philippines*—Magindanaon; *Somalia*—Somali; *Sudan*—Arabic (colloquial), Dinka Padaang, Mabaan, Uduk; *Tanzania*—Yao; *Zambia*—Kikanode; *Zimbabwe*—Ndau.[6] Missionaries and their local counterparts also produced literacy materials, dictionaries, grammars, language-learning materials, and Bible commentaries and lessons. The list could go on. With regard to the significance of translations of the scriptures into vernacular languages in the African context (but which apply worldwide), Yale University professor Lamin Sanneh wrote in his landmark book *Translating the Message: The Missionary Impact on Culture*:

> African converts resolved to repudiate Western impositions [of colonialism] . . . in acts of local commitment to the new religion . . . and at the level of indigenous participation in Christianity where local converts engaged in mutual criticism and in competition and debate about what is appropriately indigenous and authentic. The flowering of Christian activity in Africa took place in ground suitably worked by vernacular translation. . . . Behind the backs of imperial masters came the momentous outpouring of Christian conversion throughout the continent, suggesting that missionaries were effective in fertilizing the vernacular environment rather than in making Christianity a sterile copy of its Victorian version.[7]

SUPPLEMENT 5.2

Walter (Wally) Herron: "The King of the Beni"[8]

Wally Heron went from an Australian bush farm in Queensland to Bolivia to preach the gospel. The year was 1933. Wally traveled back and forth throughout the country by horse, mule, canoe, ox cart and on foot, preaching to everyone with whom he could connect.

A young missionary lady from New Zealand caught his eye, and in 1938, Wally and Violet Dunn were married. But great sadness came when Violet died the next year during the birth of their first child—Robert. As Wally traveled out of the Bolivian jungle

 by ox cart with his infant son, he thought about how his wife might have survived if an airplane had been available to take her to medical help. Just then an airplane soared overhead and his vision for missionary aviation was born.

After leaving his baby son safely in the care of Violet's parents in New Zealand, Wally began to raise money to support this innovative, pioneer ministry. After spending some time in the USA, he returned to Bolivia with a pilot's license and a Piper J-5 Cub which had to be assembled in Bolivia.

The plane expanded Wally's ministry tremendously. He was able to establish six or seven churches, start a Christian leprosarium, and save many lives with emergency medical flights. He became known as "The King of the Beni," and could walk into the office of the Bolivian president at any

Photo 5.8. *Wally Herron and his son Robert*

time. In 1944 the Lord provided another partner, and he and Emily Cemak, a Bolivian Indian Mission missionary from the USA, were married. The newlyweds settled at Magdalena and from there were accessible to many areas by air.

Meanwhile, the young son, Robert, was being raised by godly grandparents in New Zealand. As he grew up, Robert also felt called to Bolivia. After Bible training, flight training, and Spanish study, Robert arrived in Bolivia to work alongside his dad. For six months they enjoyed sweet fellowship. And then on 7 March 1964, a tragic airplane crash took the life of Wally Herron. By God's wonderful timing, Wally's replacement, his own son, was able to continue his father's ministry for a time.

In 1961, the Bolivian government awarded its highest honor to Wally Herron: "The Condor of the Andes." With a gold medal and certificate, it publicly acknowledged Wally's incredible contribution to the nation. Wally's life proved that "people that do know their God shall be strong, and do exploits" (Daniel 11:32).

SUPPLEMENT 5.3

Arturo Arana[9]

Arturo Arana was one of a number of Roman Catholic leaders starting in the 1940s who discovered the truth of God's Word and came to saving faith in Christ. He was a wealthy man living in the city of Sucre, and could trace his ancestry back to some of the kings and princes of Spain. He had studied to become a priest at a Jesuit school, and although he did not become a priest he was very religious. He was also a very capable sculptor who made thousands of religious images and made a very good living in the process.

Photo 5.9. *Hilda and Arturo Arana*

While listening to a Roman Catholic conference on the radio Arturo Arana heard a priest talk about the Bible. The priest said it was a wonderful book and told of the prophecies about Jesus that were given hundreds of years before Christ came. This awakened in him a great curiosity to read the Bible. He borrowed a Bible from another priest and began to study it. However, as soon as he began to read the Bible, he became filled with many doubts about the traditions and beliefs that he had been taught. When he sought counsel from the priests about these doubts, he discovered that they had many of the same doubts and were not able to help him. Eventually he returned the Bible, but he bought his own and continued to study it. For three dark years he struggled with his doubts as he continued to read it. Finally, at the end of that time, he surrendered to Christ, putting his trust in him as his only Savior.

At about the same time he met Pastor Turner, a missionary who served in the city of Sucre. He soon discovered that he had found someone who believed the Bible just as he did. He also found himself faced with a dilemma. While studying the book of Exodus, he had discovered the third commandment (Exodus 20:4) which forbids the making of images. This was one of the passages that so disturbed him during his years of struggle. Because making religious images was his trade, he hardly knew what to do. Given the clarity of the Bible on the subject, however, he soon decided that he could not go on making images. But that left him with a big problem—he had a room full of two hundred beautifully carved pieces of work worth thousands of dollars, and he just didn't know what to do with them.

Finally, he decided to add an inscription to each one: "I am an image without a soul, a piece created by men's hands; therefore I do not deserve any adoration or worship." He soon discovered, however, that no one would buy the images with this inscription. His own conviction that he had been making idols was confirmed. At this point, and in obedience to God's Word (Isaiah 30:21–22), he broke them into pieces with the help of a missionary and loaded what was left into a pickup truck. He then hauled it all away and dumped it over a precipice.

When the people of the town learned of this they came in a great mob. Arturo was staying at his father's house at the time and he could hear the mob yelling and talking. He understood what their purpose was and decided to go out and talk to them. Other members of the family tried to dissuade him because they knew his life was in danger, but he finally went out the door to talk to the people. Miraculously he was able to calm them down and they left.

Arturo could see, however, that his life was in danger and shortly after that he and his wife, Hilda, left the city of Sucre. They eventually came to Cochabamba where they joined the Bolivian Indian Mission. During the next 40 years Arturo Arana became one of the greatest evangelists in Bolivian history.

CHAPTER 6

THE INTERNATIONAL CHRISTIAN FELLOWSHIP STORY[1]

The ICF story is really the story of two missions that began their work among the peoples of India and Ceylon at roughly the same time. The first workers of the Ceylon and Indian General Mission, led by Benjamin Davidson, departed from Liverpool, England, on 8 October 1893 and arrived in Ceylon nearly a month later on November 3. (One day after they arrived in Ceylon, SIM co-founders Walter Gowans, Thomas Kent, and Rowland Bingham embarked from Liverpool for Nigeria.)

Charles Reeve and Mr. E. W. McGavin went from Australia to Poona in West India in February 1893 to found and begin the work of the Poona and Indian Village Mission.[2] We shall look at the founding and early work of these two missions individually before looking at their union and subsequent work under the banner of International Christian Fellowship.

Ceylon and India(n)[3] General Mission

Photo 6.1. *Benjamin Davidson, founder and first director of the Ceylon and India General Mission, 1908*

The founding of the Ceylon and Indian General Mission was the result of divine stirrings in the lives of a number of people, not just the vision and purpose of a particularly devout and entrepreneurial individual. That group response and awareness produced a sense of togetherness that became an important characteristic of the mission's movements going forward.

The initial party sailing for Ceylon on board the SS *Clan MacArthur* was all from Great Britain (including Scots, Irish, and English). They included Benjamin Davidson (Director), David and Jessie Gardiner and three children, and six other men and women. Their plan, clear from the outset, was to establish an interdenominational, evangelical, and international work absolutely dependent on the guidance and provision of God. Their purpose, equally clear, was to see many come to faith in the Savior

Mr. HETTIARCHY,   Mr. W. MALLIS.   *Mr. V. D. DAVID.
Colombo,   (Coonoor.)   (Tamil Evangelist.)
(Singalese   Mr. DRUMMOND.   Miss H. TRAIL.   Mr. H. DAVIDSON. Miss NICOLL. Mr. BASS   Mr. WINSLOW.
Evangelist.) (Bangalore)   (Not located.)   (Director.)   (Coimbatore.) (Coonoor.) Tamil worker.

DAVEYSAGIAMU Mr. TEBBS.   DAVID GARDINER.   Mrs. GARDINER. Mrs. GRACIE   Mr. T. GRACIE.
(Tamil worker.) (Colombo.)   KATIE (with Jesus.) (Urugala.)   (Urugala, Ceylon.)
Bangalore.   Miss M. TRAIL. Mr. GARDINER. ANDREW GARDINER. *Mr. WADSWORTH.
                             (Coimbatore.)   (Colombo.)   (Tamil worker.)

—:—o THE FIRST PARTY. o—:—
* Those marked with a star are not members of the Mission.

Photo 6.2. _CIGM, "The First Party," 1894._
The Gardiner's toddler Katie, pictured here, died in Ceylon, weeks after this photo was taken. She was perhaps the first "missionary kid" of all the missions to have passed away while their parents were serving on the field. She would be the first of many. Source: "News From South India," _Darkness and Light_ 8 (August 1894): 89

and many churches established. In spite of various hardships and challenges, they experienced the Lord's blessing in both endeavors.

At the same time that things were getting underway in South Asia, an office was opened in London under the leadership of Charles Ewbank. Upon his death two years later, Mr. Gardiner returned to take over this important position. Councils were formed in Chicago and Toronto in 1915 and in London in 1918.[4]

Meanwhile, back in South Asia in 1894, Tamil evangelist V. D. David led some of the original Ceylon party into India, which was to become the focus of labor for many years. (See Supplement 6.1, pages 89-90, for more about V. D. David.) The mission was committed to the villages of India and almost immediately stations were opened in the vast districts of Anantapur in the Telugu area and Coimbatore among the Tamil. Bangalore was selected as a suitable base of operations, and six stations opened in quick succession to reach the Telugus and Tamils of South India. From these main centers the message spread. Many other stations and outstations were opened, and many new churches, orphanages, Bible schools, and dispensaries were spawned. A number of schools were likewise opened, some that were run by local churches. As late as 1950, additional _taluks_ (roughly equivalent to counties) were being entered in distant hill areas of this region.

Until 1930 the efforts of the CIGM, like almost all missions in India, were directed toward Hindus. But in that year Mr. Silsbee felt the challenge of the six million Muslims in South India, so the mission decided to make provision for qualified missionaries to

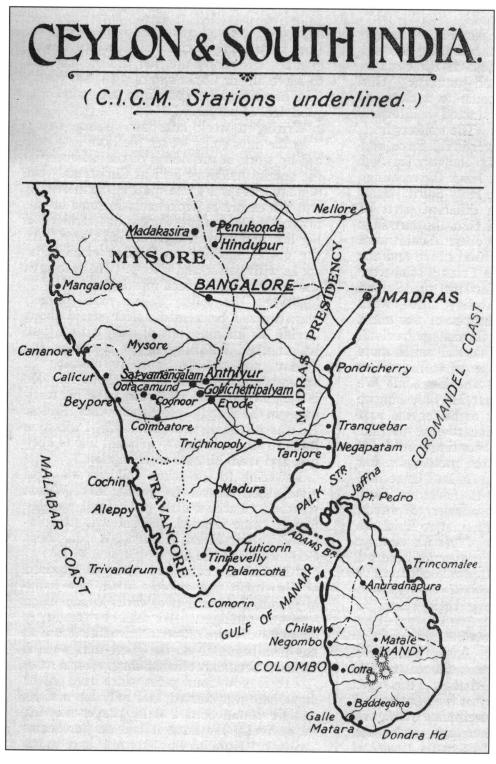

Map 6.1. *Ceylon and India General Mission, 1938.*
Credit: Darkness and Light 45, no. 3 (May–June 1938): 9.

Photo 6.3. *CIGM's annual conference in Bangalore, India, 1937.*
Front row (L–R): Mr. and Mrs. Lubbers, Mr. Paget with Ruth Reynhout, Mrs. Paget with Joyce Paget, Mr. Scott, Mrs. Scott, Emma Lou Henning, Mr. Johnson, Mrs. Johnson and Jean Johnson, Mrs. Henning, and Andrew Henning. Second row: Mr. Worling, Miss Casley, Mr. Sherwood, Miss Ellwood, Mr. Nelson, Miss Dace, Mr. Heslop, Miss Andrews, Mr. Henning, and Miss Dickson. Third Row: Mr. Russell, Mrs. Reynhout, Mr. Reynhout, Miss Rea. Back row: Mr. Jones, Miss Spearman.

study Islamics. The work began in Bangalore and later, under Mr. William Nelson and Mr. H. Reynhout, took root in Mysore. It was slow and painfully difficult, but may have been God's preparation for the later work in North India and Pakistan. One of the most encouraging features of the effort in Bangalore was a large girls school operated by CIGM on behalf of the Church of England Zenana Missionary Society. Attended daily by over two hundred Muslim girls from prominent and wealthy Muslim families, this opened avenues of friendship and witness that would otherwise have been hard to find.

The year 1938 brought a new call to the vast unevangelized areas in the United Provinces.[5] By the end of that year eight missionaries were deployed there. They were led by Thomas Thomson who died during his first year of service. Those who remained, including his widow, Eunice Thomson, carried on in the face of much discouragement and hardship. May Dace, a veteran missionary from the Telegu area, carried the brunt of the leadership responsibilities. Though no work of the mission had presented a more formidable challenge, the patient labors of the small team saw scores confess faith in Christ, many of whom had been Muslims. The formation of sustainable churches among these peoples remains an ongoing challenge, however.

In 1950 William Paget was released from the work in South Asia to help reorganize and strengthen the mission's representation in North America. A home was purchased in Wheaton, Illinois, where a candidate school for outgoing missionaries was held each year.

A new outreach to the Muslims of West Pakistan began in 1954 under the leadership of Keith Jones. Progress was encouraging with the opening of three stations, and the formation of two indigenous churches. Many came to faith, and the gospel was attractively represented for the first time in the state of Bahawalpur, which prior to 1947 had never known a missionary. Special emphasis was focused on Bible teaching, and with the opening of the Hindustani Bible Institute many fine evangelists and pastors received training.

The entry of CIGM into East Pakistan (present-day Bangladesh) in 1957 owed much to two women, Edith Casley, an experienced missionary nurse from the Tamil area, who did the initial survey, and Mary MacDonald, a young recruit from England. They, along with the Laurences, a couple who had also previously worked in South

Photo 6.4. *Dr. Aletta Bell*

India, began work in Sirajganj.[6] Thus began a significant process to put a dent in the lack of evangelical witness in one of the most heavily populated areas of the world. In 1959 another important step was taken when a Bible correspondence school was begun in Manikganj, which served all of East Pakistan with Light of Life courses.

The school was moved to Dacca in 1967 by Phil Parshall when a regional headquarters was also established there. In spite of riots, much violence, tornadoes, and floods, there was great encouragement in the evangelization of that area, as well as increasing cooperation and mutual assistance by the missions working there.

In 1959 a radio ministry began in the Telugu area. Because no religious programming was permitted over the Indian Broadcasting System, tapes were prepared in Telugu, sent to Manila, and then beamed back into India by Far East Broadcasting Company.

A leprosy clinic was built in Utraula, North India, in 1960. Thousands of patients have been treated here and in the Ikauna clinic that was opened shortly thereafter. In 1964 Dr. Aletta Bell joined this work, and a hospital was opened in 1966. This work has had a significant impact for the gospel in both North India and neighboring Nepal.

Cooperative church and mission efforts were expanding during this period. The mission contributed an artist to a Christian publishing house in Lahore in 1963, and shortly thereafter, Lova Bush was loaned to the Christian Education Evangelical Fellowship of India operating in Hyderabad and Secunderabad.

Poona and Indian Village Mission

Charles Reeve and Mr. E. W. Gavin went to Poona in West India to found the Poona and Indian Village Mission (PIVM) in 1893, the same year that the CIGM began work in South India and SIM's co-founders went to Nigeria. The impetus for this work was a "Eurasian"[7] Christian who went to Australia from India to seek missionaries for his home city of Poona.

Photo 6.5. *Charles Reeve, co-founder of the Poona and Indian Village Mission, c. 1880.*
Photo coutesy: Gillian Whittall.

Poona, like Bangalore, was a cantonment, a very large concentration of British military personnel with their families. Work started among the educated classes, both European and Indian. The main thrust of the work, however, was the plan to open a chain of centers along the great pilgrim route from Poona to Pandharpur, the largest festival center in West India.

Because pilgrims are a moving population, much of the result of the work done was seen in the strengthening of the church in other parts of India. This being the case, together with Western India being notoriously resistant to the gospel, the forming of indigenous churches was never easy. But churches were established and mission personnel encouraged them to make their own decisions, to manage their own affairs, but also to remain faithful to the evangelical tenets of the faith.

The work went forward in other areas as well. In 1904 land was secured outside of Pandharpur, where in 1906 a work was begun among women. In addition to three expatriate PIVM missionaries—Miss Tilley, Kitty Steele, and Marion Steele—Pandita Ramabai, founder of Mukti Mission in Kedgaon, responded to a request for help by sending 12 Indian "Biblewomen" to help. In 1910, Australian missionary Dr. Ethel Ambrose opened a dispensary in Pandharpur where she labored until her death in 1934. A hospital was added in 1917.[8] Dr. David Abraham Bidari joined the staff in 1931. He was an outstanding Christian and physician, who eventually purchased the hospital with his physician sons.

Photo 6.6. *"The Hospital Group," c. 1933.* In 1933, "Nurse Gray" wrote this of Dr. Bidari's contribution to the hospital: "This year we have had seventeen thousand, four hundred and thirty-three attendances, out of which Dr. Bidari's patients number five thousand, one hundred and sixteen. An average of sixty-nine per working day. . . . Sometimes we find twenty patients waiting when we get to the dispensary at 6:30 a.m."

Photo and story credit: W. H. Hinton, compiler, Ethel Ambrose: Pioneer Medical Missionary *(London and Edinburgh: Marshall, Morgan & Scott, Ltd., c. 1937), 176, 195.*

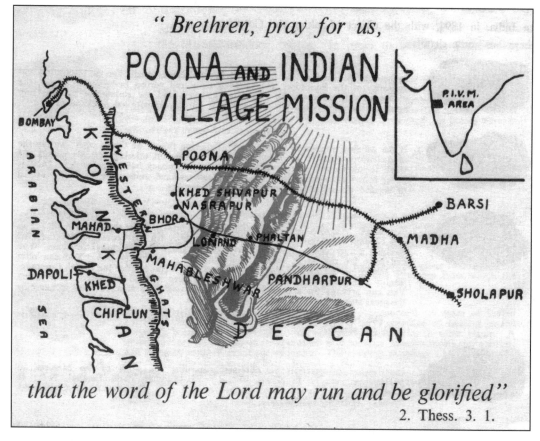

" Brethren, pray for us,
POONA AND INDIAN VILLAGE MISSION
that the word of the Lord may run and be glorified"
2. Thess. 3. 1.

Map 6.2. *Poona and Indian Village Mission, c. 1909*

Along the pilgrim route the work went on in many centers. Gradually churches were established, and many little congregations appeared: Shirwal, Bhor, Lonand, Barsi and Phaltan are some of these.

Although the hospital had been established in the early years of the mission, little work here, as in the rest of India, had been done among the thousands suffering from leprosy or Hansen's disease. This changed in 1952 when political decisions in China compelled Beth Albert to leave China that year. She had been doing medical work there under the International Christian Leprosy Mission, and now began a similar work based in Pandharpur reaching out to many roadside clinics. In 1965 the mission also opened a center in Madha, in cooperation with a government program.

Like the CIGM, the PIVM became involved with literature and radio work in the 1960s. A radio studio was opened in Nasrapur where tapes were made and sent to Manila for broadcasting back to India. Literature ministry was carried on from Poona where the mission cooperated in producing Light of Life Publications; from Barsi, which had become a base for Bible correspondence course distribution and grading; and from Pandharpur, which operated an extensive literature ministry with a mobile unit.

International Christian Fellowship

In July 1968, after 75 years of service in India, CIGM and PIVM merged and became the International Christian Fellowship, believing they could expand their ministry horizons and function more effectively together than either could independently.

In 1969, General Director Keith Jones made a survey of many Asian countries to explore possible new fields of service.

One of those fields was Nepal. In 1974 there were three ICF missionaries working with Nepal Christian Fellowship. In time the Nepal government granted ICF permission to set up leprosy work in western Nepal.

Photo 6.7. *Keith Jones, General Director, 1968–1974*

Recording facilities in Poona and Bangalore studios were greatly improved. The many programs that were recorded each month were also being heard increasingly well, as Far East Broadcasting Company had developed a new and powerful station for transmission to the region.

Work with Indian youth expanded steadily under the new ICF. Three missionaries graded Sunday school lessons with Christian Evangelical Fellowship in Madras, Secunderabad, and Jhansi. One studied Hindi in Allahabad as she worked with the youth there. Another was working in the schools with Christian Union in North India, while still another was on loan to Child Evangelism in Delhi.

In South India, Committees of Indian Christian leaders were now exercising leadership over schools, orphanages, and churches, as well as sending missionaries of their own to work in difficult locations in North India and the Andaman Islands.

Also during this period after the merger, both the hospital and the leprosy clinic in Utraula in North India were enlarged, and the hospital joined the government approved Evangelical Hospital Association.

Interesting developments were taking place in Pakistan as well. Theological education by extension centers and short-term Bible schools proved exceedingly helpful to enable many to get trained who would not otherwise be able to attend the existing Bible school. At the same time, an effective work among the Marwaris, a tribal people of central Pakistan, was proceeding well.

In Bangladesh (formerly East Pakistan) things were moving as well. Enrollment in the Bible Correspondence School had grown so much that the work involved was taxing personnel almost to the limit. A large Christian Center was set up in Dacca to assist with the follow-up work. In the remote town of Manikganj a small medical work was added to the evangelistic work in the area.

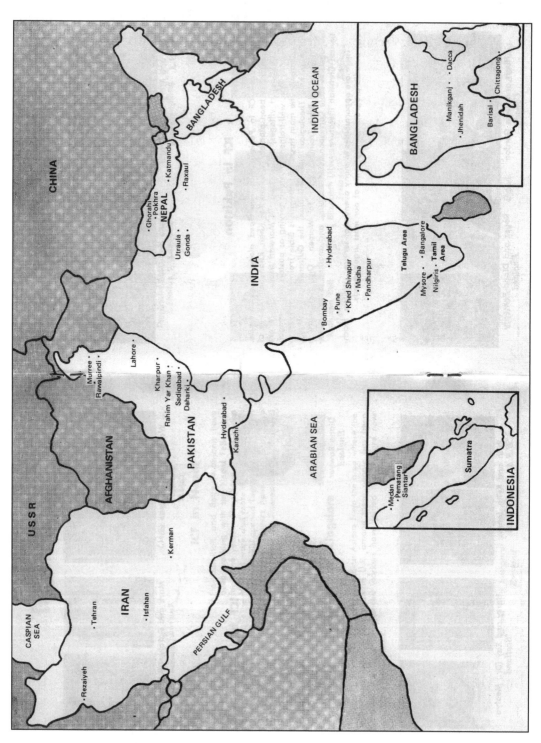

Map 6.3. *International Christian Fellowship, 1978*

Reflection during this period by Phil Parshall, Ed Welch, and others on the slow progress of evangelistic outreach to Muslims in Bangladesh led ultimately to a revolution of sorts in thinking about Muslim outreach that has since impacted mission work all over the world. See Supplement 17.2, pages 259-260, on the work and writings of Phil Parshall for more on this important story.

ICF entered Iran in 1969, when Keith Jones settled in Tehran and began to help with the Bible school there. Before too long ICF personnel in the country numbered five, with one couple stationed in a new area, Kermanshah. This work was cut short with the national changes brought about by the Iranian revolution of 1979.

ICF merged with SIM in 1989 following a thorough process described in the section on mergers.

SUPPLEMENT 6.1

V. D. David

A famous and greatly effective evangelist and preacher in India and many other countries is reputed to have been described by D. L. Moody this way: "He is one of the four men who have done the most to move India. He is marvelous." He was also a great friend of the Ceylon and India General Mission (CIGM). CIGM founder Benjamin Davidson met V. D. David or "David, the Tamil" (1853–1923), when the latter was "itinerating about" in England in 1892. David returned to Ceylon several months later and met the first party of CIGM missionaries who landed in Colombo, Ceylon, in what is today's Sri Lanka, on 3 November 1893.

Photo 6.8. *V. D. David*
Photo credit: "News From South Asia," 8 Darkness and Light (August 1894): 89.

Two days after their arrival, William Mallis preached through a translator in "a native open-air meeting" that David organized. Minnie Nicoll, one of the original 12 CIGM missionaries, wrote on 20 November 1893, that "David is very helpful to us—before he left [the UK] he taught us some Tamil words—he himself is a Tamil evangelist: he is also bright and makes everyone feel happy in his company because Jesus reigns in his soul and lives His life through Him." On 25 January 1894, David, Davidson, and Mallis departed for Madras which is situated east of Cochin in southern India. By April, Davidson and the other missionaries had moved up to Bangalore where they established their base. Over the course of the next year, missionaries joined David at open-air meetings, funerals, services at David's house, and at a conference.[9] Through the course of his life, David worked with CIGM and several other organizations to spread the gospel.

CIGM remembered David in this way in the March–April 1924 issue of *Darkness and Light*:

> In the last issue of our Magazine we referred to the visit of the Rev. V. D. David (better known as Tamil David) to our Penukonda Station in November last, and of the blessing which rested upon the meetings he held. This appears to have been the last special service rendered by our dear old friend, for on 30th November he passed away to be with the Lord. A Memorial Service, in which our Missionary, Mr. N. F. Silsbee, and others took part, was held in Bethesda Hall, Fraser Town, Bangalore, on 15th December. Tamil David was closely associated with the Rev. George C. Grubb's mission party in their tours in Ceylon, Australia, &c., and so he became known to many Christian people in this country, as well as in the Colonies. He showed the deepest interest in our Mission when it began work in Ceylon thirty years ago, and as his home then was in Columbo, he helped us in many ways. In more recent years his home was in India, and he conducted special missions in various parts of the country. He attended several Conferences of our Indian Helpers, and was made a great blessing to many of our Workers. In his wider ministry many received deep spiritual benefit from his addresses and booklets.[10]

CHAPTER 7

THE AFRICA EVANGELICAL FELLOWSHIP STORY[1]

Ron Genheimer
AEF International Director (1988–1994)

In the Beginning

The story of the beginning of the Africa Evangelical Fellowship is not the story of one man, but a pattern designed and worked by God in many lives. It began with God, and His preeminence in the affairs of the mission was stated in its motto—"God First."

In 1882 a young man, Spencer Walton, devoted himself to preaching the gospel in England. That year at the Keswick Convention, Walton, who would later become a hymn writer and evangelist, met Rev. Andrew Murray, a pastor of the Dutch Reformed Church in South Africa.

Photo 7.1. *Rev. and Mrs. Andrew and Emma Murray*

They discussed the needs of South Africa, and Murray told Walton he was welcome at any time.

Meanwhile, in Africa too, God was preparing the way. In Cape Town, where there were many British troops, George Howe opened a house into which he invited soldiers, where they could hear the gospel.

Martha Osborn, widow of a British army officer, heard from Howe about the needs and sailed to the Cape. She partnered with Howe in establishing two soldiers' homes and a sailors' rest, and they were later married in 1891. Mrs. Osborn started a quarterly magazine, first published in October 1886, which later became *The South African Pioneer*, to interest people in the work and to invite prayer. (For more information about Martha Osborn, see Supplement 7.1, pages 106-107.)

In 1888, encouraged by Andrew Murray, Mrs. Osborn invited Spencer Walton to South Africa for evangelistic meetings among the Europeans. He was welcomed by Andrew Murray, George Howe, and local ministers. Everywhere meetings were

Photo 7.2. *Soldiers' Home*

held, the Spirit of God moved. During the tour, the conviction grew that a South Africa mission—"the child of no denomination, and the ally of all"—was God's plan. Mrs. Osborn and Mr. Howe offered Walton the control of the work they had begun. On his return to England, Spencer Walton spent much

Photo 7.3. *George Howe and Martha Osborn-Howe*

time in the prayerful study of the map of Africa. With his finger on the map, he claimed "Swaziland for Christ." So, at the very conception of the mission, work among Africans was included.

Photo 7.4. *"Early Workers," Cape General Mission's first missionaries, 1889.*
Seated L–R: Albert E. Walkett, Wilfred Malcomson, Kathleen Walton, Spencer Walton; Standing L–R: Daniel Jackson, Dudley Kidd, Michael Coates.

The Mission

In England, Walton consulted with godly men including Hudson Taylor and F. B. Meyer, and found leading Christians willing to serve on a council. So it was on 12 March 1889, that Cape General Mission was established, with a council in London and Cape Town. Mr. Spencer Walton was director in South Africa, and Dr. Andrew Murray the first president.

In 1891, now married, Mr. and Mrs. George Osborn-Howe felt God's call to work among the Zulus. They moved up the coast to Durban and established a new work called the South East Africa Evangelistic Mission (SEAEM). The first three members of the work were Otto Witt from

Photo 7.5. *"On trek, Freyling and W. A. Genheimers," Mseleni, c. 1924.*
Ludwig Olsen-Freyling of Norway joined SAGM in 1890. William and Lucina Genheimer (seated) became members in 1922.

Sweden, Fred Suter from Yorkshire, England, and Ludwig Olsen-Freyling from Norway. All three had left their homelands for South Africa to take up secular jobs in order to engage in missionary work. That year in Durban the first Zulu church came into being, and the three men trekked further north into Zululand. By 1893, 36 Zulu men had been baptised and one set aside for evangelistic work among his own people.

In the meantime, back in Cape Town, Walton's wife, Kathleen, died after childbirth. Walton penned the following words:

My Saviour—I will never doubt
His tender, loving will.
That heart of love would ne'er conceive
To do His children ill.
He tells me of His changeless love,
A love that knows no ill;
What can I do but stoop and kiss
His sweet and sacred will.

Kathleen's friends, knowing of her prayer for Swaziland, started a fund to commence work there. So in 1891, on behalf of the Cape General Mission, Walton visited the Queen Mother in Swaziland to obtain permission to open a work. Later that year, a Scot named John Baillie and his wife, Annie, living a few miles outside of Swaziland, felt God's call to the Swazi people and opened the first station near the Royal Kraal at Bethany. Baillie's grandfather, a Scottish shepherd, had prayed years before that the gospel would enter Swaziland.

By 1893 Walton had traveled to what is known today as the Transkei, the land of the Xhosa clans, and opened the door for Cape General Mission missionaries. Before the end of the year four missionaries had entered the area, welcomed by the Wesleyan Mission, but by 1894 only one was left. God sent others, however, and by 1900 there were six main stations and several outstations. Even today, some older believers in the Transkei call the mission "The Cape"!

Go Forward

At the instigation of the Osborn-Howes, the SEAEM was united in 1894 with the Cape General Mission under the name "The South Africa General Mission" (SAGM). At the time of the amalgamation a new watchword was added to the original, "God First." Now the missionaries, serving Europeans, Zulus, Swazis, and Xhosas, marched under the banner "God First—Go Forward."

Gradually the work among the Europeans was taken over by other organisations, and the focus of the SAGM shifted to the African population. Spencer Walton had remarried in 1893 and visited North America to make the work of the mission known there. In 1895 he and his wife moved to Durban to superintend the work of the mission.

In Durban, Walton met many Indians, immigrants brought over from India beginning in 1860, to work on the sugar and tea estates of Natal. In 1896 he commenced a work among these people, many of whom spoke Tamil or Telegu. When Mahatma Ghandi visited South Africa he became a friend of the Waltons, and later wrote:

> . . . when I was in Durban, Mr. Walton, the head of the South Africa General Mission found me out. I became almost a member of his family. Mr. Walton had a manner all of his own. I do not ever recollect his ever having invited me to embrace Christianity, but he placed his life as an open book before me and let me watch all his movements. I liked Mr. Walton's humility, perseverance, and devotion to work and we met frequently. This friendship kept alive my interest in religion.

Before 1900 the first two workers among the Indians had to leave a work that was showing great promise, especially after a school was opened for Indian children. However, because the South African War between Britain and the Dutch settlers required the evacuation of missionaries from Swaziland, others came to fill in.

Photo 7.6. *"Coupland and Raney in the long grass,"* *c. 1897.*

John Coupland died of fever at Dzingire, Southern Rhodesia (today's Zimbabwe). Coupland and his colleagues did not take quinine because they believed in divine healing. As one African church leader wrote, "They did not believe a Christian who has faith in God could at the same time depend on medicine. . . . It would be a lack of faith and sin if he took medicine." Coupland's death caused those in SAGM who believed in this doctrine to reconsider their position.[2]

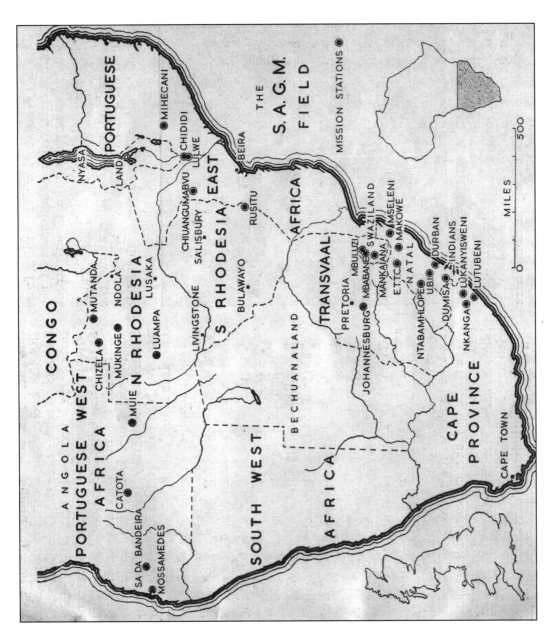

Map 7.1. *South Africa General Mission, 1954*

The "God First—Go Forward" motto meant SAGM was not content to serve only Europeans, indigenous tribes, and immigrant Indians in South Africa. In 1897 three men, Dudley Kidd, Harry Raney, and John Coupland (see Photo 7.6) traveled to the southeast border of Southern Rhodesia (Zimbabwe today). They hoped to reach the colony of Portuguese East Africa (Mozambique today), closed to missionaries, from across the border. Not long after their arrival John Coupland died of malaria. Fifty years later Chief Dzingire testified, "With these hands I helped to bury the first missionary and I could never forget it. I've been a hard stubborn man, but always in my heart was the thought that Christianity must be a great thing when a man was willing to die for the sake of telling it to others."

1900—1910

Nyasaland, now known as Malawi, was the next advance. In 1900 Kidd, Raney, and Edgar Faithful chugged up the mighty Zambezi, following the route taken by David Livingstone, opening a station in the south at Lulwe. Again this was seen as a good place from which to evangelise the closed colony of Portuguese East Africa. It seemed impossible to get a permanent missionary staff as one after the other left because of illness. God enabled, however, and Chididi was opened in 1909.

By 1906 the work was headed by a general superintendent in Cape Town and the work on the field was divided into districts, each with its own superintendent. The first General Conference of the mission was convened in that year. Both Spencer Walton and Albert Head from Britain visited the US in 1905, and an American Council of the mission was formed in 1906. At the same time a committee was formed in Canada, which was later to become a council. Records show that there were 90 missionaries in South Africa and Swaziland by 1910.

1910—1920

During this time the SAGM turned over all of its work among Europeans in South Africa to other ministries. At the same time God used his special servants to deepen the work, first in Southern Rhodesia at Rusitu. Mr. and Mrs. Rees Howells arrived there in 1915 after the people had been studying the book of Acts and were hungry for revival. Howells describes, "I shall never forget the sound in the district that night—praying in every home. The next day the Holy Spirit came again, and people were on their knees until 6 p.m. This went on for six days and people began to confess their sins and meet the Saviour as only the Holy Spirit can reveal Him." Invited to Swaziland and Zululand in 1918, Howells was again used of God and revival broke out there.

Missionary pioneer Fred Arnot of the Christian Missions in Many Lands Mission Society realised that Northern Rhodesia (Zambia today) was ripe for the gospel, and asked Dr. Andrew Murray to send SAGM missionaries to that land. [It was after Rowland Bingham listened to Margaret Gowans tell him about her son back in 1893, and listening to Arnot talk about "his arduous effort to open up . . . the Garanganzee region of South

Africa" in a church service, that Bingham decided to join Walter Gowans and go to the "Sudan."]³ In 1910 Arnot and A. W. Bailey trekked 250 miles from the railhead, stopping only 25 miles from the Congo border to open a work among the Kaonde people. By 1917, missionary Harris reported that village people were at last receiving Christ and taking a stand against evil customs.

Like the one from Macedonia, a man from Portuguese West Africa (later Angola) came to see Bailey in 1915 to tell him that the Ovimbundu there were still in darkness. Bailey had already been deeply concerned for Portuguese West Africa and needed no urging. When a Luchazi man accepted Christ in June 1916, he was the first of many to become a member of the family of God in Angola. Though Bailey almost died of malaria while alone at Muie, the work continued and reinforcements arrived to open other stations.

Dr. Andrew Murray, whose wise prayers and counsel had shaped the Mission as President from 1889, died in 1917.

1920—1940

By God's grace the work had spread to the Cape, Zululand, Transkei, and Natal (all in South Africa), Swaziland, Southern Rhodesia (Zimbabwe), Nyasaland (Malawi), Northern Rhodesia (Zambia), and Portuguese West Africa (Angola). But that elusive country Portuguese East Africa (PEA, later Mozambique) had remained closed. National evangelists had made long preaching trips into PEA, especially after the revival at Rusitu on the border. It was not until Arthur Brown heard the call, and studied Portuguese in Portugal, that the door for SAGM opened in 1936. Jack and Minnie Proctor applied for visas for Angola and were surprised to receive them for PEA as well, so they believed God had opened the door. The work prospered until the Portuguese government ordered the work closed and all missionaries left in 1959.

The chairman of the 1922 General Conference noted:

Regarding workers accepted at the home bases in England and America, the same should have qualifications to train natives to carry forward the winning of fellows to Christ, as it is recognised now in all missionary lands that the work of evangelisation must, in the main, be done by the native agency.

The term "native" was commonly thought to have no derogatory connotation at that time. From this time on, efforts were made to establish indigenous churches and fellowships of churches that could thrive without mission support.

During the Great Depression missionaries received only what came into the sending offices, and many supporters of the work lost jobs and money. Half allowances were not uncommon—sometimes they were even delayed for a month or two. Missionaries learned practically what it was to be a "faith" mission. Some stations closed, and lives

Photo 7.7. *"Members of General Conference, 1931, Cape Town."* Back row (L-R): L. Priestman, C. S. Green, H. G. Pirouet, E. P. Oliver, R. E. Medill, W. A. Genheimer, A. E. Peaston, N. Rowland. Front row: E. Boyce, C. S. Foster, G. F. Gale, E. A. M. Harris, N. E. Tomlinson.

were lost in pioneering efforts in Angola and Mozambique. Yet new stations were opened, translation work was begun, Bible schools founded, and educational work organised and strengthened. In 1920 the Mbuluzi Girls' School became a reality in Swaziland. In 1924 the South African Makhowe Bible School was transferred to Dumisa under the leadership of Fred Suter, a linguist who wrote a grammar of the Zulu language. Later, in 1926, at Muie in Portuguese Angola, a printing press turned out Gospels in the Mbunda language. The Indians of South Africa were not left out, and a Bible school for them opened at Park Rynie in 1929. The Canadian Committee became a fully fledged Council in 1930. The Second World War prevented the convening of general conferences for some time.

1940—1950

Until this time much of the decision making in the SAGM had rested with the Cape Town executive and the home councils. The Rev. Wilfred Green, a son of pioneer missionaries in the Transkei of South Africa, and himself a missionary in Malawi, was appointed general superintendent in 1943.

Photo 7.8. *Wilfred Green, General Superintendent of SAGM*

Three years later a conference of the councils convened in Brooklyn, New York, and restructured the mission, appointing a field council as the "highest executive authority and court of appeal to exercise final control over all personnel of the field staff." For the first time, the fields became autonomous with home councils only responsible for home constituencies. In 1947, the Home Council of the SAGM in South Africa was formally inaugurated.

Progress in administrative matters did not guarantee similar progress in every field. After trial, sickness, and heartbreak, the Chiuangumabvu station in Mozambique (affectionately prayed for as "chewing-gum-avenue") was closed in 1946. The work continued, however, at Mihecani and elsewhere.

Meanwhile, on the fields, there was progress in new ways. One was the cooperation of evangelical mission societies. In South Africa, the SAGM Bible School at Dumisa became the Union Bible Institute at Sweetwaters, under a council composed of six groups. And later an intermission Evangelical Teacher Training College was opened in Vryheid, South Africa, to train Christian teachers for mission and other schools.

A new opportunity was afforded missionaries and national workers when thousands of Africans migrated to the cities in search of work. Believers from rural churches gathered in the cities, and these were soon the focus of evangelism, church planting, and discipleship. A further step forward was the founding of vernacular Bible institutes such as the one at Chizela in Northern Rhodesia, where from its beginning in 1949 national staff were on board. Mr. Emil Pearson's translation of the whole Bible in Angolan Luchazi was published in 1949.

1950—1960

Further changes were instituted to enhance the effectiveness of the mission. The field headquarters was moved to Johannesburg to be more central to all of the fields, and by 1958 Mr. Green was known as the general director. In 1960 a "Directorate" of three men was appointed—Wilfred Green as General Director, Don Genheimer as Executive Director, and H. Gordon Legg as Assistant Director.

At the 1953 Inter-Council Conference the "Unfinished Task" was discussed. Attention was given to medical and educational work, the needs of the indigenous church, and the desperate need for aggressive evangelism. In conclusion, the conference insisted that the emphasis in the future should be on (1) Bible teaching, (2) leadership training, (3) prayer, (4) holiness of heart and life, and (5) evangelism. On the fields, a greater number of postwar veterans began to arrive, many of them specializing in various tasks. In 1953, responding to a request by the church, Dr. Robert Foster established the Mukinge Hospital in Zambia.

The Indian work, begun first on the east coast of South Africa, branched out to the Johannesburg area in 1957. In 1960 the desperate needs of urban youth led Al and Lorry Lutz, and their colleague Jerry Nkosi, to found "Youth Alive" ministering

Photo 7.9. *"Capping ceremony at nurses' graduation at Mukingi Hospital, Zambia, Miss Spahr officiating, 1957"*

Photo 7.10. *"Africa Evangelical Church, first meeting of the Board, Durban, January 7 to 9, 1963."* Front row (L–R): J. D. Fatsha (Transkei Vice-Secretary). P. Magwaza (Treasurer — Johannesburg), G. R. Dlamini (Swaziland), E. J. B. Mdodana (Transkei); Back row (L–R): L. T. J. Magewu (Swaziland Vice-President), E. J. Mfeka (Natal President), Wilfred Green (SAGM Secretary for Church Affairs), P. S. B. Mkhize (Natal Secretary), S. Mawasa (Transkei). Absent: S. E. M. Pheko (Johannesburg, Publicity Secretary).

to youth in the townships of Johannesburg. In the same year, also responding to the needs of the cities, Dr. Terry Hulbert opened the Bible College of Central Africa in Ndola, Zambia. In Malawi, Robert Craille opened the first SAGM School for the Blind at Lulwe. In Johannesburg, the Roodepoort Mission Press (RMP), with workers from New Zealand and Australia, became a part of the SAGM. Significantly, this opened the door to the mission's presence in those countries and led to the eventual opening of sending councils there.

On the other side of the ledger, in 1959, the work in Portuguese East Africa (Mozambique) was ordered closed by the Portuguese government and the missionaries expelled. Believers collected the equivalent of $500 and sent it to the mission as a thanksgiving offering. In South Africa the government took over the mission schools and placed them under local community supervision. But new and unprecedented opportunities opened for Bible teaching in the schools.

African nationalism became a powerful force on the continent, and colonial rule began to give way to independent political entities. The mission Directorate, under the leadership of Wilfred Green, believed that the various church groups associated with the SAGM should be offered their independence. Deliberations began, first with home councils and field councils, and then with national church leaders. National churches were encouraged to request independence, agree on a constitution, and finally develop a structure that would be both biblical and compatible with the social structure of the people.

1960—1970

During this decade, further advances took place in the administration of the work. In 1963, an Australian Home Council was recognised, with oversight over the home functions in New Zealand. South Africa was now notorious worldwide for its "apartheid" stance, and the mission work covered southern Africa as far as the Congo. To avoid misunderstanding, the mission was to be known as the SAGM (Africa Evangelical Fellowship), with the ultimate intention of dropping the "SAGM." In January 1969, a Field Council was instituted to coordinate the work. It was to be composed of the general director and his assistant, all field directors and their assistants where needed, and advisors in specialized fields such as medicine, education, and church affairs. Fields met together in field conferences, and the field council members met in a field council conference. Fields were to be autonomous in local and internal matters.

Translation work continued. Examples were efforts by Willy and Regina Brandle in the Lomhuila language of Angola, and C. S. Foster, Ernie Frost, and John Wright in the Kikaonde language of Zambia. In addition to the printing ministry of RMP, the mission added specialized ministries in several fields. Broadcasting (Christian Radio Fellowship in South Africa and Swaziland) and aviation (in South Africa and Zambia) became means of reaching out further and quicker. Don and Faye Smith envisioned Africa Christian Literature Advance (ACLA) and the *Our Africa* magazine.

ACLA continued mostly as a wholesale literature ministry, and *Our Africa* was distributed widely throughout southern Africa until its closure to accommodate government authorities.

Ray and Rona Oosthuis' vision to reach the 380,000 miners from all over Southern Africa, living in 80 mine compounds on the gold reef in South Africa, resulted in the Christian Ministry to Miners.

In response to repeated pleas from the church, David Barnes built, and Dick and Francie Smith opened, the Mankayane High School for boys in Swaziland.

Photo 7.11. AEF's "hostel" in Lukasa, Zambia, with dorm parent and students, 26 March 1966.
(L-R): Sharon Foster, Joy Huntingford, Mark Hockersmith, David Hockersmith, Shelia Foster, Paul Fields, Paul Hockersmith, "Aunty" Barbara Hockersmith, and Stephen Fields. These students variously attended a local government and private school
Photo credit: "Uncle" Darrell Hockersmith.[4]

Photo 7.12. *Distribution of* Our Africa.
SAGM shut down *Our Africa* in 1963 having started publishing five years earlier. The magazine, which was popular with many church groups, was discontinued because of "financing, staffing, and the political content of certain articles." *Our Africa*'s managing editor at the time, Salzwedel Ernest Motsoko Pheko, had fled into exile because he feared South Africa's secret police would arrest him.

Many of the former colonial countries were granted their independence, and names were changed—among them, Northern Rhodesia became Zambia and Nyasaland became Malawi. In most fields, the national church became independent from the mission, though the actual nature of the independence could vary from field to field. Some fields chose a relationship where mission and church were each autonomous and acted as equal partners. Others chose a relationship in which all missionaries were under the control of church leadership while on the field.

1970—1980

During this decade the mission expanded into new and needy countries—South West Africa (Namibia), Botswana, and the islands of Mauritius and Reunion. David Evans, who joined the Director team in Johannesburg in 1969, remembers vividly the General Conference of 1968 when "without direction from the chair, there was a clatter as our pens were laid down and we fell on our knees to seek God's direction for new ministries." Christian refugees from the Angolan churches, residing then in northern South West Africa, wrote the mission for assistance. Jackson Mmolawa of Botswana, won to Christ through the mission in Johannesburg, urged it to come and help him reach his people. In response, the Southern Field was challenged to

Photo 7.13. *Christian Ministry to Miners*

Photo 7.14. *Jeff Morcum distributing literature to miners*

send survey teams and then workers into these two countries. Two lady missionaries in Mauritius requested that AEF come and take over their work as they were growing too old to continue it. Similarly a door opened in Reunion to assist with church work there. God providentially matched the prayers of the general conference with calls from needy countries.

Further administrative changes resulted in the Rev. Arthur Deane of Australia replacing the retiring Wilfred Green and becoming the "International Secretary" (later to be "International Director").

Michael Warburton, after many years in Zambia, became assistant to the international secretary.

Headquarters was moved from Johannesburg to Reading, England, and the first "International Council" meeting was convened in 1975. It was composed of a chairman, the international secretary, and representatives of each home council and field. Home councils were also allowed "consultants." The fields continued as autonomous entities, each with its own field director and field executive committee.

1980—1990

Dr. Robert Foster served as international director from 1981 through 1988.

He had founded hospitals in Zambia and Angola before becoming the Chief Executive Officer for the American Council. Dr. Foster headed a team in the International Office composed of an assistant to the director (Michael Warburton), a personnel coordinator (Keith Donald), a projects coordinator (Warren Paddon), and a communications coordinator (Will Walker). The Communications Department published a new magazine, *Action Africa*, edited by Will Walker, replacing for the first time the various magazines previously published by individual home councils. Dr. Foster's vision for reaching out led to AEF responding positively to an invitation from the Evangelical Church in Gabon to commence a medical ministry there with Dr. David and Jane Mann. When church leadership changed, it was necessary for the mission to withdraw. In response to a

Photo 7.15. *Arthur Deane, International Secretary/Director, 1974–1981*

Photo 7.16. *Dr. Robert Foster, International Director, 1981–1988*

request from the Baptist Bible Church of Madagascar, Dr. Mann accepted the challenge again to pioneer a new medical work in the north of that country.

In Namibia, the Africa Inland Mission joined forces with the AEF, sending missionaries into that country under an agreement giving them status and responsibility equal to that of AEF missionaries. Though occurring much later than mission/church agreements in other fields, the church and the mission in Zimbabwe finally integrated and properties were turned over to the church.

In 1986 AEF requested the Christian Service Fellowship (CSF) to evaluate whether the mission and the Africa Inland Mission would be better served through a merger. The two missions served in adjacent countries of Africa and sought resources of personnel and finances from the same countries and often the same churches. CSF made a thorough study, querying leaders and missionaries of both organisations before advising against a merger. AEF accepted their recommendation to call "home" councils by the new term "sending" councils.

Though both Angola and Mozambique were still embroiled in civil wars, new medical and Bible training ministries opened up in Angola, and missionaries were allowed to reenter Mozambique only to find that the church there had grown under persecution. In South Africa, the Evangelical Church of South Africa (ECSA) had won converts from Hinduism among the Indians, and the burden to reach Muslims increased.

Realising that Muslim converts would not normally feel comfortable in the culture of the ECSA, the field executive set a goal for workers to be called especially to Muslim work. David and Cathy Foster arrived in Durban in 1985, and eventually established a large and effective network of people from different races and

Photo 7.17. *"Baptismal Service in Outdoor Baptistry, Berachah Evangelical Church, Park Ryne, Natal."* "36 candidates baptized 4th May. This one in [the] picture is a young man, Peter, recently converted from Hinduism through visits to his home by believers from the Evangelical Church. Pastor John Peter Baptizing."

churches whose efforts to reach Muslims have reached far beyond the Durban area.

After the retirement of Dr. Bob and Belva Foster in 1988, the Rev. Ron Genheimer became the third international director. Like "Dr. Bob," he, too, was the child of SAGM/AEF missionaries, and had been a field leader, having served on the Southern Field with his wife, Myrna.

One of Ron's first tasks, ably assisted by AID Michael Warburton, was to celebrate the centennial of the mission in 1989, under the motto, "God First — Go Forward." A significant celebration was held in Dr. Andrew Murray's former church in Cape Town. After one hundred years it was still true that the mission "is not the story of one man, but a pattern designed and worked by God in many lives. It began with God . . ." and it was continuing with His blessing and guidance.

Photo 7.18. *Ron Genheimer, International Director, 1988–1994*

1990—1997

For a number of years, AEF had been concerned for the unreached tribes on the border between Mozambique and Tanzania. After successful negotiations with the German headquarters of Christian Missions to Many Lands in Wiedenest, the mission sent missionaries to Southern Tanzania to assist with their ministry. At about the same time, the last two AEF workers in Reunion felt that the time had come for the mission to leave the work in the hands of local church leaders and other missions. The countries in which the mission continued to serve were Angola, Botswana, Malawi, Madagascar, Mauritius, Mozambique, Namibia, South Africa, Swaziland, Tanzania, Zambia, and Zimbabwe.

As AEF approached the new millennium, the international council executive felt that its administrative structure was too cumbersome to meet the fast-changing pace of the day. The international council was composed of up to 40 representatives and met every three years. After full consultation, the international council approved a smaller policy-making international board of 11 members who would meet annually. Inter-council and inter-field committees would still cater for "home" and "field" needs respectively, while every three years an international consultation was to be held composed of sending, field, and national church representatives. The board commissioned an Investigative Committee that recommended an

Photo 7.19. *Tim Kopp, International Director, 1995–1998*

improved set of objectives, evaluation, pastoral care, and communication, praying that internal renewal would give new vigour to the work.

In 1995, the Rev. Tim Kopp became the fourth international director. His parents, too, had been SAGM/AEF missionaries, and he and his wife Carol had served in Zambia before taking a position teaching missions in the US.

In that year the inter-council committee noted that some of the five sending councils were struggling to represent the work adequately with fewer missionaries applying and increased numbers retiring. They recommended that the board research "the advantages and disadvantages of closer relationships with other like-minded missions, and also the possibility of entering strategic partnerships . . . ." The International Board agreed that internal renewal had still left the mission with needs that might better be met through partnership with another mission. It called the mission to a Day of Prayer.

That Day of Prayer and a lot of hard work led to a merger with SIM in 1998.

SUPPLEMENT 7.1

Martha Storr Osborn-Howe[5]
Dr. James Kallam

Photo 7.20. *Martha Storr Osborn-Howe, co-founder of Cape General Mission and the Southeast Africa Evangelistic Mission*

In a day that is stressing women's right for involvement and leadership, there is a tendency to feel that women were so restricted in the past that they did very little. Not so with Africa Evangelical Fellowship (AEF). In fact, we owe as much to the dynamic creative activity of Martha Storr Osborn-Howe as we do to Andrew Murray or Spencer Walton. As the young widow of a British general she could have enjoyed a life of ease. Instead, because of her Christian experience and commitment, she gave her life over to aggressively seeking the lost; first in England and later in her homeland of South Africa. In England she founded the *Drunkard's Church*, a type of rescue mission. She was an effective speaker in the open air.

Concern for British servicemen brought her home to Cape Town in 1880. Her energy and zeal led to many activities including the founding of the first YWCA in Cape Town, the Sailors' Rest, two Soldiers' Houses and a quarterly paper—*The*

Pioneer—which later became the official organ of AEF. Shortly after her return to Cape Town in 1880 she became associated with George Howe in work with soldiers and railroad men. Later they married and together established the Southeast Africa Evangelistic Mission which eventually amalgamated with the Cape General Mission to form the South Africa General Mission.

While visiting England in 1887, Mrs. Osborne and Mr. Howe met Spencer Walton and invited him to South Africa for a series of meetings throughout the Colony. By this time Mr. Walton was established as an effective evangelist and Bible teacher. He had been converted in 1872 at the age of 22. The years that followed his conversion found him active in lay ministries until he finally gave up his secular position to devote himself full time to evangelism. He regularly spoke at Keswick and other conferences throughout England. It was these conference ministries that the Lord used to bring Spencer Walton, Mrs. Osborn, and George Howe together. At an earlier date Walton had met Andrew Murray at Keswick as well.

Walton accepted the invitation to come to South Africa for a period of ministry among Europeans. The meetings at Cape Town were eminently successful. Beginning in a small hall, the crowds increased until the meetings had to be moved to the Metropolitan Wesleyan Methodist Church, and finally to the Exhibition Building. Special trains were run from the suburbs for these meetings with crowds of two thousand in attendance. Over five hundred conversions were recorded. From Cape Town, Walton moved on to most of the large population centers of the Cape Colony. The planning and conduct of these campaigns was in the hands of Andrew Murray, Martha Osborn, and George Howe.

During this time the Lord was at work. Mrs. Osborn was finding that all the activities she had begun were taxing her health. She could not take the climate without returning to England from time to time. She needed someone to whom she could entrust these works. At the same time, Spencer Walton was being burdened about the need in South Africa and excited about the opportunities. As he traveled throughout the colony he was impressed not only with work to be done among Europeans but also among the "coloured" and black populations. The potential of the mine work at Kimberly especially gripped him. If these Africans who came from points all over southern Africa could be reached and trained, they would in turn become missionaries when they returned home.

The part played by Andrew Murray should not be overlooked in the chain of events leading to the beginning of AEF. Murray had suggested to Walton some years prior to Mrs. Osborn's invitation, that he should come to South Africa. His association and friendship with Spencer Walton and his assurance of continued support helped Walton decide that he should accept her invitation. During the time Walton was touring South Africa and while Mrs. Osborn was weighing whether she should give the work over to him, Murray was acting as advisor and confidant of both. He clearly favored the move and lent his influence to it.

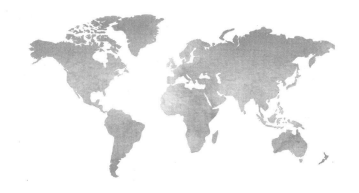

PART II
THE MERGERS INTO SIM

CHAPTER 8

THE ABYSSINIAN FRONTIERS MISSION MERGER (1927)[1]

The year 1927 marked an important milestone in the history of the Sudan Interior Mission. In the providence of God, the practical outworking of commitments to several foundational principles became interwoven in a remarkable way.

The story actually begins in 1926 when Rowland Bingham began a "journey round the world," as he called it. He had a number of purposes for the trip. Foremost was to establish new councils for SIM in Australia and New Zealand. These were needed to serve an increasing number of missionaries coming from the "antipodes," that is "opposite points on the globe."

Writing immediately upon his return under the title, "The Objective Realized," Bingham spoke about the councils formed:

It is not easy in a short time to select and appoint suitable men: and in no sphere does one need the guidance of the Holy Spirit more than in the choice of those already chosen of God to such a sacred task.

We believe that He has led so that in Melbourne, Sydney, and Auckland we now have a group of men, with cooperating committees in Brisbane and Adelaide, who will in future aid very definitely in the awakening of interest in the great Sudan and in the sending forth of workers from those great lands to the South of the Sudan.[2]

Bingham went on in his article to discuss the possibility of opening up a new SIM field in East Africa, which is half the explanation of why Abyssinia or Ethiopia became a strategic new focus for SIM at about the same time. Like many other areas it was in great need of the gospel. Unlike many other areas, however, it was positioned geographically to solve a very practical mission problem. In 1936 Bingham wrote:

While forming our new Councils of the Mission in Australia and New Zealand, we could not but face the difficulties that confronted our friends over there in sending and sustaining their missionaries on our old field in the Central Sudan or Nigeria.

At that time there was no steamboat service between Australia and West Africa. It was necessary to send their workers half round the world to England and then send them by another boat five thousand miles to Lagos. Then come nearly another thousand miles up into the interior.

In as much as the unhealthy nature of the country made frequent furloughs necessary, the transportation problem was tremendous, the cost enormous.[3]

Bingham went on to recount the providential work of God in two events that pointed the way to a solution to this problem. While in Australia he had made the acquaintance of a veteran missionary to Kenya by the name of Canon Burns. Their conversation led him to reflect on the relative ease of access to the eastern side of Africa from this part of the world, and caused him to wonder if a new work could not be undertaken in the Anglo-Egyptian Sudan.

Then upon returning home he found that Mrs. Helen Bingham had inserted a news note in *The Evangelical Christian* that told about the formation of a new society for the purpose of aggressive evangelism in the ancient kingdom of Ethiopia. (This small event provides the other half of the explanation as to why SIM became involved in Ethiopia at this time.) The group was to be known as the Abyssinian Frontiers Mission founded by Dr. Thomas A. Lambie, Rev. George Rhoad, and Mr. Alfred Buxton.

Photo 8.1. *George Rhoad, Alfred Buxton, and Thomas Lambie and families*

Upon reading the item, Bingham immediately wondered if this were not precisely the thing they were especially seeking for SIM's new missionaries from Australia and New Zealand, and proceeded to make contact with the leaders of the new group.

The upshot was two meetings in the summer of 1927, the first of which took place at the Stoneybrook Conference in New York, and the second at Canadian Keswick. From the beginning of those meetings, the feeling was strong that much could be gained if the complementary purposes of the two missions could be unified. The times of discussion and prayer were described as having "so brought the leaders together" that the decision to unite was announced before their departure from Keswick.[4]

Resulting gains were both immediate and significant. Typical of other mergers since, the well-functioning of SIM in the home countries became a real plus for the merging group. Bingham writes:

> All the machinery of the Sudan Interior Mission at the home end was immediately available, and a constituency of praying people already prepared to take the new work upon their hearts.
>
> This was best evidenced in that during the summer, funds had been very short, but the fall announcement of an advance into this new field instead of creating greater financial difficulties immediately drew forth the strongest cooperation from our praying friends; so that by November the full amount was on hand for the launching of the new party into Ethiopia and at the end of December the allowances for the missionaries in the older Nigeria field were met in full.[5]

And what of the benefits to the work in Ethiopia? It is almost inestimable to calculate the importance of having Dr. Lambie from the Abyssinian Frontiers Mission lead the first wave in this new outreach. The fact that Dr. Lambie had served in the Anglo-Egyptian Sudan and Ethiopia for years, and was already a friend of Ras Tafari (Haile Selassie), proved an important lever in the hands of God to enable SIM to gain a foothold and to prosper in the face of serious and prolonged challenges, particularly from the Ethiopian Orthodox Church. Humanly speaking, only this fact and the unwavering heart commitment of Emperor Haile Selassie to use his influence for the enlightenment and advancement of his people stood in those early days between the mission and the intrigues of the orthodox hierarchy, which desired to see the mission removed.

The work developed rapidly. By Christmas of 1927 the party of eight new workers led by Lambie had reached Addis Ababa. Immediately plans were made to go south and begin work among the peoples of the region. By 1930, the year of Haile Selassie's crowning as Emperor, SIM had 24 workers in the country, a large proportion of whom hailed from Australia and New Zealand. By 1935, the year of the Italian take-over of Ethiopia, the number of SIM missionaries had grown to 74, the number of stations had grown from four to fourteen, four little churches had been formed, and two hospitals had been erected.[6]

A small but solid foundation for the gospel had been laid. The proof is seen in that even without significant missionary presence, exponential church growth took place during the succeeding difficult years of Italian occupation. For an extensive treatment of this remarkable story see Ray Davis' book, *Fire on the Mountains*. A more abbreviated version can be found in Supplement 8.2, pages 115-117.

With regard to the bigger picture, establishing a base into Ethiopia in 1927 was part of Bingham's vision to "get a line across the Continent from our present work to East Africa."[7] Bingham even reportedly wanted to "form a chain of stations across Africa, east to west, and north to south."[8] This idea became more realized with the expansion of the mission southward with the merger of Africa Evangelical Fellowship in 1998, and advance into North Africa in the last decade. Indeed, likely in ways that he never anticipated, SIM is now ministering in nearly half of the countries in the world.

In conclusion, it is clear to see that the events of this period were most significant: internationalness expanded and evangelical cooperation grew deeper and wider, leading to the first of SIM's long list of successor mergers. And perhaps most important, the first two missions combined with an enduring burden for the least reached, to open up a new field of service.

The work in Ethiopia would ultimately be rivaled only by Nigeria in terms of its numerical fruitfulness with regard to believers and churches.

SUPPLEMENT 8.1

Baloté Amalo

Dr. E. Paul Balisky[9]

Photo 8.2 *Dästa and Baloté, Soddo, 1964.*
Photo credit: Raymond J. Davis, Fire on the Mountains *(Grand Rapids, MI: Zondervan, 1966), 203.*

Baloté Amalo was born in 1917 in Wolaitta, Koysha, in southern Ethiopia, and was converted in 1944 through the songs her father sang while performing chores around his farmstead. Baloté was one of many believers who attended Toro Dubosho's local church at Gärära, Koysha. She also attended the literacy classes that Toro was teaching several afternoons a week at the Gärära church.

In 1946 Selma Bergsten, fluent in the Wolaitta language because of her 1930–1937 pre-Italian experience in southern Ethiopia, began discussions with the Wolaitta Kale Heywet Church Council about a special teaching program for young Wolaitta women. Baloté, along with 20 other young Christian women, was selected for this initial two-month learning program that convened at the Wanché local church in 1947. After this first course hosted at Wanché, the 21 ladies returned to their local districts to begin teaching what they had learned. Baloté returned to her local church at Gärära in the Koysha district. By 1950, Baloté and other trainees assisted in organizing the Wolaitta Christian Women's Association. Their function was to provide teaching and fellowship, training in crafts, and to collect funds for the evangelists. Through the missionary challenge to bring the gospel to the unreached at the annual Bible conferences held at the SIM center at Soddo and throughout the Wolaitta districts, many women volunteered to evangelize outside of Wolaitta.

In 1954 Baloté, her husband, Amoché, and their son, Dästa, traveled by donkey to Yala, Gofa, a two-day trek from Soddo, to begin evangelistic work. They opened a literacy school and Baloté also taught handcrafts to the young ladies. Within a year the new converts built a small prayer house. In January 1955 Amoché returned to Wolaitta, Soddo, for the annual Bible conference to report on the evangelistic advances in Gofa. Before returning to his missionary ministry in Gofa, he made a business trip by foot to Yirga Aläm in Sidamo Province. While crossing the Bilaté River, Amoché was murdered by Arsi bandits.

When a messenger from Baloté's home church in Koysha brought her the news of Amoché's death, Baloté had to decide whether to remain true to her missionary calling in Gofa or to return to Wolaitta. She reacted by saying, "I have been called of God not by man. I am going to stay." Baloté and her son remained in Gofa for seven additional years teaching children and women. She itinerated throughout Zalla district, teaching courses in literacy, handcrafts, and Bible texts for up to two months at a time. She had no home of her own but depended on the hospitality of the wives of the other evangelists and of Gofa believers during her travels.

In 1962 Baloté returned to Wolaitta when the Wolaitta Church Council assigned her to assist in coordinating the women's ministry within the Wolaitta Kale Heywet Church. Baloté's faithful years of service in Gofa and Wolaitta have been recognized by the Wolaitta Church Council. Many continue to rise up and call her blessed.

SUPPLEMENT 8.2

Ethiopian Reversals and Church Growth

On two separate occasions God did amazing things to achieve his purposes and to grow his church in Ethiopia under what can only be described as most trying circumstances. The first occasion was during the war years of the late 1930s and the Italian occupation of Ethiopia that accompanied it.

The southern provinces of Ethiopia had been opened up to SIM under the leadership of Dr. Thomas Lambie, who had moved into the province of Wolaitta to undertake medical and evangelistic work. Joined by other SIMers in the work, they had seen relatively few results from it. When in 1935 the Italian military moved against Ethiopia, the situation became even more difficult.

Photo 8.3. *"The Sadness of Farewell," 1938.*
The last SIMers to leave Ethiopia were Clarence and Doris Duff, Selma Bergsten, Ruth Brat, and Fiona McLuckie.

They were advised by the British and American embassies to leave immediately, but they decided to stay on. Rowland Bingham as general director had put the decision squarely in their hands: "You are under higher orders than those of the King of England or the President of the United States. Get your instructions from Him and we are one with you."[10]

Knowing that their remaining time in Ethiopia would no doubt be short, and that the state of the work was feeble at best, the missionaries worked tirelessly "to teach the Christians and to get the gospel out."[11] In 1938 the remaining SIM missionaries were forced to leave.

The additional two years had seen fruit, but the tiny Wolaitta church was still very small, numbering only 48. As the missionaries left feeling great sadness, they also wondered: "Would these young Christians, with no more of the Word of God in their own language than the Gospel of Mark and a few small booklets of selected Scripture portions to guide and teach them, be able to stand under the persecution that would inevitably come?"[12]

And come it did, including the imprisonment and flogging of most of its leaders and the maryterdom of some. That the motivation for the persecution was more religious than political became clear when a priest offered them instant freedom if they would kiss the crucifix. They were firm, however, that they would rather die than deny their faith.[13]

That the church grew remarkably during these difficult years can be attributed to several things: the church has always had strong Ethiopian leadership—"common, ordinary men with an uncommon, extraordinary faith in Christ"; the willingness of both leaders and the rank and file of the believers to suffer both cruelties and privations courageously and joyfully, often to pass on the good news of Christ to distant areas; a passion for evangelistic witness; and the warm love displayed by the believers toward one another and toward others in prisons or in other great need. The latter especially made a great impression on unbelievers.[14] By 1941 when the war in Ethiopia was over and the missionaries were allowed to return, the four dozen Christians in one small church that they had left five years earlier had grown to some ten thousand in over one hundred congregations.[15]

The second occasion when God did amazing things to achieve his purposes and grow his church in Ethiopia were through the very trying circumstances that took place between 1974 and 1991. When the Provisional Military Government of Ethiopia seized control from Emperor Haile Selassie in 1974, many were happy, including Christians, that the years of feudal domination had ended. It was only months later that the military administration would reveal itself as being Marxist-Leninist and extremely cruel. During the next 17 years many evangelical Christians were imprisoned, beaten, or killed for their faith.

Only after 1991, when the Communist rule of Lt. Col. Mengistu Hailemarian was itself overthrown, could the full impact of what God was doing be fully appreciated. Ato Shiferaw Wolde Michael, president of the Kale Heywet Church, speaking in 1995 summarized it well:

> Living through the persecution was no joke. It meant losing life. It meant losing jobs. It also meant imprisonment, and living in constant fear, harassment and insecurity. The plowing (cf. Ezek. 36:9–10) was very painful—physically and psychologically. But in retrospect, every evangelical denomination learned through it the truth of Romans 8:28, "And we know that in all things God works for the good of those who love him, who have been called according to his purpose." Our evolutionary growth was changed into revolutionary growth. Praise and glory be to Him. Our God is really a wise businessman. He enabled the Church, His body, to have a beautiful harvest out of the "suffering investment" of His servants.[16]

SUPPLEMENT 8.3

Mulu Meja
Dr. E. Paul Balisky[17]

Mulu Meja was born in 1934 in the subdistrict of Wanche, Wolaitta, some 350 km south of Addis Ababa. His father, Meja Madaro, was a prominent figure in his community and a respected land owner, and because of his bravery in killing a local bandit, he was awarded the title of *danya* (judge).

Through SIM missionaries, the gospel was planted in Wolaitta from 1928 to 1937. Mulu's father and his older brother, Markina, came to faith in 1937 followed eventually by the entire Meja family of fourteen children.

Mulu Meja attended primary and junior high at the SIM center at Soddo from 1948 to 1954. Subsequent to that he joined the Soddo Dresser Training Programme, directed by Dr. Nathan Barlow and graduated in 1956 with an advanced diploma in preventive medicine. He was hired by the Ministry of Education and served in the Ligaba Beyene

School in Wolaitta as a health assistant. Later he was transferred to the Yirga Alem Ras Desta school as coordinator for health services among the schools in Sidamo Province until 1965.

Mulu Meja married Shitaye Galore in 1958 and together they had seven sons and three daughters—all presently residing in Canada except for one who is in the USA. All ten children are active members of Ethiopian Diaspora churches.

The Haile Sellassie government initiated the all-Ethiopia Parliament soon after the Emperor returned from his self-imposed exile in England in 1941. Mulu Meja was elected to the Ethiopian Parliament in 1966. As a parliamentarian, he successfully fought for freedom of worship for the growing number of non-Orthodox evangelicals who were persecuted and harassed by Ethiopian officialdom in Southern Ethiopia. During his years in Parliament, he attended the Law School of the Addis Ababa University and graduated in 1972.

A new opportunity for Mulu Meja came in 1973 when he was appointed to serve in the Ethiopian High Court. He held this position throughout the Marxist regime of Mengistu Haile Mariam and was even promoted in 1979 as Supreme Court Judge. He served on the Judicial Bench until 1991. This was a fitting tribute to the integrity of Mulu Meja's Christian character as many former judges were imprisoned on charges of corruption.

In 1991, when the Ethiopian People's Revolutionary Democratic Front (EPRDF) government came to power, Mulu Meja was one of the founders of the Southern Nations and Nationalities Democratic Union, the official party in opposition to the EPRDF government. In this position as the vice-president, he believed this was a strategic opportunity to assist the country in its journey into democracy. He fearlessly challenged the Meles Zenawi government on several issues regarding the constitution, rule of law, and the democratic transition of the country. His voice was often heard on public radio and television and was regularly quoted in the Addis Ababa press.

Because of his broad previous experience in law and in parliamentary procedures in two former regimes, his advice was sought after by a new generation of politicians. Highly respected for his Christian character and uncompromising stand on human rights, he was a firm believer that Christians must involve themselves in the political life of their respective nations. And Mulu Meja affirmed that because Christians are the salt and the light of the earth they must have a presence in the political realm.

Throughout his life he was an active member of Kale Heywet local churches in Soddo, Arba Minch, Jimma, and Addis Ababa. While he was posted in Yirga Alem from 1958 to 1965, he regularly attended the Ethiopian Evangelical Church Mekane Yesus. During regular visits to his children residing in North America (mainly Toronto), he attended the Ethiopian Evangelical Church. Mulu Meja is lauded by his family as being an upright follower of Jesus, kind, gracious, generous, wise, and an able provider for their educational and spiritual well-being.

During his lengthy government service for his country during three different regimes, and under varying political philosophies, he served with integrity and respect for those of different views. In his retirement he continued to offer legal advice freely to those who were unable to defend themselves for various reasons including financial constraints. And until his death he relentlessly championed the rule of law, justice, and freedom for his beloved country of Ethiopia.

CHAPTER 9

THE WEST AFRICAN BROADCASTING MERGER (1952)

Three mission students from Wheaton College formed the West African Broadcasting Association in April 1950. The students—William Watkins, Merle Steely, and Ernest P. Howard—shared a common vision to see radio play a major part in the evangelization of Africa from a radio station set up in Liberia.

Watkins, a "missionary kid" who had grown up in Guinea, in French West Africa, graduated from Wheaton in 1948 and stayed on to work on the campus as an electrician while he nurtured his vision.[1] He was the original source of the vision, and as Jos M. Strengholt points out, was not above sharing it:

> Merle A. Steely came to study at Wheaton College, and lived in a mobile home in Watkins' backyard. According to Steely, "for a year and a half, [Watkins] unburdened his heart to me about a radio station for Africa." In February 1950, during a week of special revival meetings in Wheaton College, Steely felt compelled to speak to Watkins. "I told him he had been talking about the radio station for Africa for a year and a half and now I felt we ought to do something about it. . . . I said we ought to meet one night a week in special prayer for the station." That night they prayed together. A third Wheaton student who participated was Ernest P. Howard who had also been a *Mission Kid* in Africa.

Photo 9.1. *William "Bill" A. and Sandy Watkins, with Sandy and Bruce, c. 1951*

Next day the three young men went to Raymond Edman, the president of Wheaton College, as they felt they needed advise [sic] for this overwhelming project. Edman suggested they should start a formal group, choose a name, apply for non-profit status, get a bank account and interest some "big people" on campus with their plans. The three immediately began to do as suggested.

In April 1950, the West African Broadcasting Association (WABA) was incorporated. Watkins became president, Steely its secretary, and Howard the treasurer. Some Wheaton College staff joined the board. On 14 August 1950, the constitution, the by-laws and the doctrinal statement were adopted. Abe Thiessen, the future president of the organization, was invited to join WABA later that month and he began in November of that same year.[2]

It would be four years of navigating difficult challenges related to funding, government permissions, securing a site, and leadership issues before Radio ELWA ("Eternal Love Winning Africa") would go on the air. Dr. Timothy Stoneman provides sobering insight into just how challenging even the broader context for radio in Africa could be:

Liberia provided an extremely challenging platform for private American missionary broadcasting on the continent of Africa during the postwar period. To begin with, African countries lacked radio facilities; in 1950 the continent had only 140 transmitters and only 1,100 kilowatts of total transmitter power— the second lowest totals in the world. Furthermore, the meager facilities that existed in Africa were government-run. Broadcasting in Africa in the mid-1950s was under the tight control of French and British colonial authorities—a pattern of public ownership that would be carried over by postcolonial African governments.[3]

During 1951 those involved with WABA became somewhat dissatisfied with the way Watkins was handling the top leadership position, so that in the second annual meeting in August, Thiessen became president, Watkins became vice-president, and Steely continued on as secretary. Nevertheless, in October 1951 it was Watkins who went back to Liberia to buy land for the radio station. Also, by this time, SIM had begun to take an interest in WABA, and sent Hilmer Lindahl, a radio engineer with SIM in Ethiopia, to assist him.[4]

According to Strengholt's compilation from several sources, SIM's early involvement and God's ultimate provision went something like this:

Lindahl had spent the previous four years waiting for the chance to build a radio station for SIM in Ethiopia. During those years, SIM had bought airtime on Radio Addis Ababa and had been involved in some limited Gospel broadcasts, but this had not been very satisfying and had ceased. SIM had therefore hoped to build its own station in Ethiopia and had some money in reserve for that but [sic] however, in 1951 SIM's request for a license was turned down. SIM therefore asked Lindahl, on his way back to the USA, to spend some time in Liberia to help WABA to find the right plot of land. SIM's field director for Nigeria, C. Gordon Beacham, who had been with SIM in Nigeria since 1916, joined them and together they found 180 acres of jungle southwest of Monrovia, bordering on the coast.

WABA's lack of money was made up for by their measure of faith. According to Thiessen, they "prayed that God would move upon the Liberian government officials causing them to give us this property as a land grant. God answered prayer and this was exactly the action taken by the Liberian legislature." They also received a duty-free concession from the Liberian government, making it possible to take radio equipment in the country without paying any duties.[5]

In January 1952 WABA officially became part of SIM. For the next two years periodic shipments of new equipment and crews arrived in Liberia to advance the construction of the radio station. There were some missteps along the way—a serious one being an arrangement that Watkins made with some Liberian government-related construction workers to deliver necessary materials to repair some roads. The upshot was a fine of about US$800 being levied, in addition to threats of deportation. This resulted ultimately in Guy W. Playfair, SIM general director, visiting Liberia and sending SIM's former acting general director, C. Gordon Beacham, to manage ELWA.[6]

On a happier note, Dr. Raymond Edman visited the site in Monrovia to see the construction going on. This was two years after his students had shared their vision. Concerning the visit he wrote:

I have seen it with my own eyes. Last month I visited the ELWA missionaries who are pioneering for Christ in radio for West Africa. I was with them in their homes. I traveled over the road which they had cut through the jungle to the site of ELWA; I saw the completed generator building and the foundation for the control room as well as many other details of the program. While there I remembered the day when ELWA was just a dream, rather a vision, and a burden shared by a few undergraduates on Wheaton campus. I remember the afternoon they came into my office for a conference and prayer on the subject. How impossible, even preposterous it seemed at that moment and already it is a reality![7]

Broadcasting at ELWA began on 18 January 1954. The brief English language program included an introduction to Handel's *Hallelujah Chorus* by Dick Reed (another Wheaton

Photo 9.2. *The official opening of Radio ELWA, 6 May 1954.* (L-R): unidentified, SIM General Director Guy Playfair, William Watkins, Liberian President William V.S. Tubman, SIM Liberia Director C. Gordon Beacham, and unidentified government officials.

grad who, with his wife Jane, had joined WABA in early 1951 when Watkins had returned from Liberia with the broadcasting permit). In addition there were introductions by Bill Thompson, who would later become director of ELWA, scripture readings by Steely, a dedicatory prayer by Beacham, and some remarks by Watkins. The program concluded with Reed singing *Great Is Thy Faithfulness*. A subsequent dedication service of ELWA took place on 6 May 1954. President Tubman was present for the ceremonies.[8]

SUPPLEMENT 9.1

Radio Missions: Station ELWA in West Africa[9]

Dr. Timothy Stoneman

Launched in January 1954, ELWA rapidly increased its transmitter power and expanded its language programs, acquiring worldwide audience. Before long, the "Radio Voice of the Sudan Interior Mission" reached deep into Liberia, a thousand miles along the West African coast, and across the African continent on long wave, medium wave, and shortwave transmitters.[10] Liberia's official use of the English language facilitated ELWA's early growth, providing an immediate market in Monrovia for prerecorded religious programs from the United States. The station aired nearly thirty different sponsored Gospel programs each week, featuring prominent American radio preachers such as Charles Fuller, Billy Graham, and Theodore Epp. ELWA also produced its own studio programs, employing local Liberian musicians and announcers, as well as broadcasting Liberian government material. In 1955, only its second year of operation, ELWA received more than 11,000 letters from forty-four different countries, including twenty-one countries in Africa, various European nations, and the United States, attesting to the new station's strong presence on the continent and the global reach of its transmitters.[11]

Producing Regional Vernacular Programs

Missionaries at ELWA rapidly specialized in regional and vernacular broadcasting. Shortly after adding its first shortwave transmitter in March 1955, ELWA launched its first programs in French, Arabic, and the Nigerian tongues of Hausa and Yoruba.[12] Soon listeners could hear over 100 programs per week on each of ELWA's long wave and shortwave services in twenty different languages overall, mostly tribal dialects from Liberia and Nigeria.[13] By the mid-1960s, ELWA was broadcasting in an astonishing forty-nine regional languages, including the principal tongues of Liberia, Guinea, Mali, Ivory Coast, Nigeria, Ethiopia, Congo, East Africa, North Africa, and the Middle East.[14]

To produce regional material, North American missionaries at ELWA relied on an extensive network of mission groups and workers across Africa. To meet the demand for local Liberian programs, ELWA trained its own local announcers, recruiting candidates from Bible schools in the country's interior. By 1964 the station had ten full-time Liberian "dialect broadcasters" who translated daily news, produced regular programming, and interpreted biblical texts from English, since their native tribes rarely had complete translations of the Bible in their own tongues.[15]

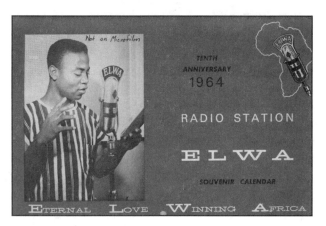

Photo 9.3. *Dã (Gio) broadcaster Edwin Kayea*

Vernacular programming incorporated earlier, face-to-face, evangelistic methods. "Dialect broadcasters" frequently visited their language areas to meet radio listeners and new converts, attend church conferences, conduct evangelistic campaigns, and record popular materials for retransmission on the air.[16] By the start of its third decade in 1970, ELWA had significantly indigenized its operations in order to meet the demand for local material. The station employed more than three times as many local workers and technicians as Western missionaries—200 Africans, mostly from Liberia, compared with 60 expatriates from North America.[17]

Accommodating Liberia's Political Elite

ELWA's success depended on its highly favorable political relations with Liberia's governing elite, the minority Americo-Liberians. Descendants of the former American slaves who originally settled in Liberia in 1822 and later organized the Liberian Republic in 1847, pro-Western Americo-Liberians monopolized political power in the country through the True Whig Party. The small elite imposed centralized governmental rule from Monrovia over Liberia's tribal interior, where 90 percent of the population lived. Through their broadcast operations, ELWA's organizers helped to consolidate the cultural hegemony and political control of Liberia's leaders. In its original license, ELWA's founders agreed to distribute free radios in Liberia's hinterland and to evangelize the populace there, which overwhelmingly practiced African traditional religion. ELWA contracted to air government programs regularly including a variety of "public service" broadcasts, and to publicize the Tubman administration's two economic development plans—the Open Door policy and the National Development Campaign—in the country's rural regions.[18] Finally, ELWA promised to promote the public image of Liberia abroad; by 1958 the station had provided broadcasting services to a lengthy list of the country's government departments and agencies.[19] In return, Liberia's Protestant elite provided ELWA with "an open door for Gospel radio," as the station's first director boasted to supporters.[20] High-ranking members of the Liberian government, including President William Tubman himself, attended ELWA's inaugural ceremony and frequently participated in the station's prayer services and anniversary celebrations. Tubman pronounced ELWA to be his favorite radio station, calling it "a vital part of the nation's religious, educational, social, and cultural progress," and commonly sang its praises in public declarations and speeches.[21] Political accommodation with Liberia's leaders allowed ELWA to survive periodic political unrest in the country and to continue broadcasting continuously for over thirty-five years until the outbreak of Civil War in 1990.[22]

CHAPTER 10

THE ANDES EVANGELICAL MISSION MERGER (1982)[1]

Andes Evangelical Mission (AEM) had four general directors. Upon the death of mission founder George Allan in 1941, Mr. Verne Roberts became general director. He continued in this capacity until 1956 when Rev. Joseph McCullough took office. Upon his retirement from office in 1974, Ronald Wiebe became general director.

Photos 10.1–3. *Directors of the Bolivian Indian Mission and Andes Evangelical Mission.* Vern Roberts (1941-1956), Joseph McCullough (1956-1974), and Ronald Wiebe (1974-1982).

At the time of the merger in 1982, AEM had 66 missionaries working out of 10 centers in Bolivia and Peru. Its members came from seven home countries: Australia, Canada, Germany, Jamaica, New Zealand, the UK, and the USA. The mission headquarters was in Cochabamba, in the vicinity where roughly one-third of Bolivia's population resides. (See Supplement 10.1, pages 129-131, "The Mechanics of Merger.")

Photo 10.4. *AEM and SIM officials sign merger agreement, 1981.*
"AEM General Council Chairman Mr. Albie of New Zealand (seated, left) and SIM General Director Dr. Ian Hay sign the August 5 agreement in Cochabamba." Standing (L-R): Rev. Ron Wiebe, AEM General Director; Mr. Ken Fowler, AEM U.S.A. Representative; Mr. Eldon Howard, SIM International Treasurer.
Source: SIMNOW 1 (January–February 1982): 2.

SIM published the following at the time of the merger:

On 5 August 1981, an agreement was signed in Cochabamba, Bolivia that would make Andes Evangelical Mission a part of SIM as of 1 January 1982—an event that expanded SIM ministry beyond Africa in a major way for the first time. There were interesting anecdotes, however, combined with a remarkable spirit of warmth and compatibility, that made the coming together of AEM and SIM seem more like a marriage than an acquisition or a merger. For example, brothers Arden Steele with AEM in Bolivia, and Roger Steele with SIM in Nigeria, found themselves in the same mission on New Year's Day, 1982. Likewise, SIM's northwestern USA representative, Dick Fuller, and his wife, Muriel, joked that the mission had finally caught up with them—as AEM and SIM had merged, in a sense, back in 1962 when the couple had joined SIM. Muriel had been born and raised in Bolivia as a third generation AEMer. Her grandfather, George Allan, was the founder of AEM. "I am convinced that this is indeed the will of God for us," SIM General Director Hay told the SIM family of missionaries at the time the agreement was made:

In the discussions that I have had with the missionary family of AEM I have discovered a group of people who are unbelievably like SIMers. In discussions with church leaders I found the same kinds of needs and concerns that we have. I threw roadblocks in the way, to test the situation; in each case those obstacles were overcome. The AEM General Council unanimously recommended joining with SIM, and the missionaries gave unanimous endorsement to the Council's recommendation.

Ron Wiebe, formerly known as AEM General Director, and subsequently known as SIM Andes Area Director, had a similar message for the AEM constituency:

> Missions can ill afford to remain static in our rapidly changing world. For the past two years, we in AEM have been taking a hard look at ourselves. Due to our small size, we are severely limited in many key areas. Homeland representation, candidate recruitment, office facilities, administrative expertise, furlough assistance, and pastoral care of missionaries are areas of weakness.
>
> In light of these needs, the AEM General Council decided in August 1981 to become part of SIM. Eighteen months of careful and prayerful communication confirmed the wisdom of taking the step, and demonstrated the high degree of compatibility between AEM and SIM. Your prayer interest is sincerely requested, that the consummation of this union will result in unparalleled expansion of the church in Bolivia and Peru.

Bob Olden, who became Deputy Director for the Andes Area, told his supporters: "AEM approached SIM and asked if they would consider helping us with our work in South America. By God's direction and in his timing, everything fell into place. We feel very privileged to be a part of this much larger fellowship, which provides many advantages for us and our work. We are compatible with SIM in every area of importance."

One of the most fundamental similarities was that both missions are church-planting organizations. They devote their energies to the formation of indigenous church bodies through preaching the gospel, teaching, discipling, and leadership training, while loving their neighbors as themselves through many other ministries, from education and medicine to assistance with agricultural improvement.

The result in Bolivia was the Union Cristiana Evangelica (Evangelical Christian Union). UCE was formed in 1950 with 12 congregations. By 1981, with the admission of several congregations that originated through the work of Gospel Missionary Union, UCE churches totaled 385, with more in formation.

In Peru the picture was somewhat different. The church body known as Iglesia Evangelica Peruana (Fellowship of Evangelical Peruvian Churches) is the result of the coming together of congregations that came into being through the ministries of several missions, including AEM. By 1981 IEP churches numbered eight hundred and were growing rapidly.

Leadership training in Bolivia reached seminary level in 1968. In Peru, several missions came together to provide the Evangelical Seminary of Lima, a training center that reached seminary level in 1971. Both seminaries advanced to the graduate level in the early 1980s.

The union with AEM was truly a turning point for SIM. Since its birth in 1893, SIM had been essentially an African mission, working among people whose ethnic and cultural origins are Negroid and Semitic and mixtures of the two, whose religious backgrounds are dominated by Islam and African Traditional Religions, and who are fragmented by a veritable babel of languages.

In joining with AEM they were entering the Latin American arena of Bolivia and Peru, where people are predominantly Amerindian or a mixture of Amerindian and Spanish, where the major religious influence is animism overlaid with Roman Catholicism, and where communication is simplified by the widespread use of Spanish.

The union of AEM and SIM brought no immediate structural change in the administration of the work in South America.[2] All administrative personnel remained in place, and the name Andes Evangelical Mission was retained in the region. Within SIM, the work in Bolivia and Peru became known as the Andes Area, the seventh field administrative division in the mission.

SUPPLEMENT 10.1

Photo 10.5. *"Expression of unity," 1981. Ron Wiebe of AEM and Ian Hay of SIM.*
Photo credit: SIMNOW 1 (January–February 1982): 3.

The Mechanics of Merger[3]
Dr. Ian Hay
SIM General Director (1979–1993)

"General Director Ian Hay answers your questions" [regarding SIM's first merger outside Africa]

Does entering South America mean that SIM has accomplished its goals in Africa?
There's no way we can say that SIM has accomplished all of its goals in Africa. We have accomplished some of them, and others are within reach, but there are vast areas that still are untouched. The decision to join hands with AEM has nothing to do with the total achievement of tasks in Africa.

The challenge is to "lengthen our cords"—that's evangelism—and "strengthen our stakes"—that's discipling. These are the total goals of SIM. As we expand, we dare not neglect the needs of teaching and discipling in those areas already reached.

Why did AEM choose to merge with SIM rather than with a South American mission?
That's the first question I asked too. They selected SIM because of research they had done into the character and structure of the Mission. AEM is an international organization, with councils in New Zealand, Australia, Britain, Canada, and the U.S.A. SIM has a similar structure, with councils in the same countries. The missions in South America with which AEM found doctrinal compatibility, however, were not international. They were U.S.A.-based, which would have made things difficult for the non-U.S.A. element.

In addition, the financial policies of SIM were very close to those of AEM. This made integration much simpler.

Did AEM want to merge with SIM because it was in trouble?
Two years ago, the Executive Director of the 47-member Interdenominational Foreign Mission Association (IFMA) made the statement that missions with fewer than 200 missionaries were unlikely to survive the 1980s, if only for financial reasons. AEM, with less than 100 missionaries, has done a good work through the years, and God has blessed them, but because of the Mission's smallness, it has been unable to build up a strong home base, which is essential to the recruitment of new workers and provision of funds to expand and develop their ministries. For this reason they sought the help of SIM. AEM is financially viable. There are no liabilities. What they wanted to do is find a way to ensure the continuing viability of their work in South America.

What happens to AEM administration?
In South America, everything stays in place. Only the labels are changed. Bolivia and Peru become known as the Andes Area of SIM, and Ronald Wiebe, formerly known as AEM General Director, becomes known as SIM Area Director.

In the homelands, AEM offices will be absorbed into the SIM home office structure. The home councils of both Missions have worked out arrangements that are best suited to their situations, the end result being one SIM council in each country, with each one having representation from the former AEM council. The AEM General Council has been dissolved, having fulfilled its mandate.

Will SIM now start recruiting missionaries for South America?
Yes. We have already started.

Will this detract from recruitment for Africa?
Some of our missionaries in Africa have also asked this question. There are lots of places there where there's an obvious need for more workers and seemingly none to be found. I feel, however, that God is sovereign in the placement of His people. I don't think that those whom the Lord is directing to Africa will go to South America or vice versa.

Most of the SIM Regional Directors I've talked to feel that recruiting for two continents will be an asset rather than a drawback. They often have students with Spanish-speaking backgrounds asking them if SIM has Latin American ministries. Now we do.

Will SIMers who are now serving in Africa be eligible for service in South America and vice versa?
Yes. But we don't expect much interchange of staff, because of the differences in language and culture and so on. There will be a lot of sharing of expertise, though, such as the seminars on cross-cultural communication that Bill Kornfield, who earned his doctorate in Ethnology in Peru, has just conducted with SIM missionaries in Africa. Similarly, staff people from our International Department have given some significant help to the work in South America.

Can we expect SIM to merge with more missions in the future?
I don't know how to answer that one. We have no way of knowing what the future may hold. But we want to be open to God's leading, so SIM General Council in 1980 made provision for mergers or acquisitions as and if God so directs. If anyone else approaches us, we would follow the same guidelines as we did with AEM.

Will you change the name of the Mission now that you are also working in South America?
We've been struggling for some years with the name "Sudan Interior Mission." Sudan is a valid geographic term referring to the area right across Africa south of the Sahara, but most people don't understand it that way and consider it a misnomer. Also, it's just not appropriate to be known as "Sudan" in some African countries. In fact, even the government of Sudan, which is predominantly Islamic, once asked us to change our name.

On the other hand, the name and initials of our Mission mean a great deal to our members and supporters. So we have not made a major change, but we are working toward the designation "SIM International," with the initials standing for "Society for International Ministry."

CHAPTER 11

THE LIFE CHALLENGE MERGER (1986)[1]

Life Challenge merged with SIM International on 1 January 1986. A South African mission, it had started 10 years earlier under the leadership of Gerhard Nehls, a German missionary who had become burdened to reach the increasing number of Muslims in the Cape Town area. Nehls had relocated from Johannesburg where he had engaged in a Bible club and camp ministry for 13 years with young people of mixed race.

Life Challenge was well-known for direct outreach to Muslims, but perhaps even more so for their training seminars held at Bible colleges and with churches. They aimed to equip Christians to reach out to their neighbours. The ministry also produced various outreach and training publications as well as videos. They also accepted invitations for training seminars in more distance countries, such as Malawi.

Photo 11.1. *"Gerhard Nehls (L) of Life Challenge, and SIM Secretary for South Africa Harald Froise signing the agreement merging the two missions,"* 1986.
Photo credit: SIMNOW 26 (March–April 1986): 12.

By 1985 SIM South Africa had made the decision for South Africa to be a field in addition to its traditional role of sending. They identified Muslims, particularly of Indian descent living in Natal and what was then the Transvaal. Sylvia Ruiters joined the team. In that same year the first South African missionaries, Jurie Goosen and Sandy Willcox, joined the predominantly German Life Challenge team.

Life Challenge saw the need for an administrative structure that would allow for a more international team and began negotiations with SIM with a view of helping to fulfill the vision for sharing their gained experience and work strategy in South Africa and other parts of Africa. Life Challenge had worked in close association with SIM for a few years. Each group could see that a merger would strengthen the work of both in their outreach to Muslims. In 1985 General Director Hay visited the Life Challenge team and came to the same conclusion regarding the value of a merger.

The merger firmly established SIM South Africa as a field office that placed South African missionaries in their own country with the proviso that they would work cross-culturally. This shift in emphasis from "sending" to "field" contributed to some significant tensions between what had been a "sending / home" office and the members of the Muslim outreach "field" team. The result was that SIM South Africa changed its administrative structure from that of a sending office to that of a field office with a sending function. This made it easier for the Life Challenge team to work. Other differences were also worked out and harmony was restored. Reflecting on the tensions Dr. Hay mentioned some time later that, "There's no such thing as a small merger." He went on to reflect that owing to the small number of members (16) in Life Challenge all the pre-merger processes had not been followed.

Following the completion of the merger further expansion soon came into view. In April of 1986, a scouting journey was undertaken to Tanzania to explore additional ministry opportunities. This pattern of expanding usefulness in spurring outreach to Muslims, throughout Africa, has continued ever since.

CHAPTER 12

THE INTERNATIONAL CHRISTIAN FELLOWSHIP MERGER (1989)

The January 1988 issue of *Intercom* (an internal publication for SIM members) provided a kind of "half-time report" to a process that began in January 1987 and would find consummation in the merger of ICF with SIM in January 1989. In it SIM General Director Dr. Ian Hay answered questions under the heading "SIM and International Christian Fellowship Update: Dr. Hay Answers Questions."[1]

Here are some key parts of what he said:

What stage are we at in discussions with ICF?
Last April our Board of Governors approved entering into discussions with ICF, to gather the preliminary information needed to decide whether we should consider a merger. Both missions set up subcommittees to do this.

Photo 12.1. *SIM Deputy General Director W. Harold Fuller and SIM Canada Director Jack Phillips meet with ICF General Director Bruce Sinclair and ICF Canada Director Merle Inniger at SIM's office in Toronto, Canada (L-R)*

SIM's subcommittee is made up of John Cumbers, chairman, Eldon Howard, John Pickett, and Gordon Stanley. The subcommittee had a joint meeting in December, at which they reviewed all the information and set up procedures for further discussions and decision making. In December I also met with a subcommittee of the Board of Governors and passed on the reports of findings thus far.

What was the reaction?
They had the same reaction that I had. All of us have been challenged by the enormous task which ICF missionaries have been facing and by their plea for our help.

Has any SIMer visited the ICF fields?

Gordon Stanley and John Cumbers made a quick trip in November to two of the seven countries where ICF works. In Bangladesh they met with two groups of Christians who had come out of Islam and visited the Bible correspondence school in Dhakar. They also met with all the available ICF missionaries for a time of questions and answers. Then they went on to Pakistan where they had fellowship in different towns with believers who had a Hindu background. At the annual field conference the two men interacted for more than four hours with most of the members of ICF in Pakistan. John and Gordon received a very warm welcome from the missionaries and were greatly impressed with the work they saw.

Is a merger in the offing?

We aren't ready to make a decision yet. The next step is to share the information with our respective mission members, and to get their reaction to the possibility of a merger. I'm asking each SIM director to make sure there is opportunity for discussion with our missionaries, and the directors will share their findings with me and our international council.

Who initiated the discussions, and why?

ICF did. One of their missionaries, Phil Parshall, was a resource person at SIM's consultation on Islam last January. He told me he was impressed with SIM's vision for reaching Muslims and with the strengths he saw in the mission. Subsequently he recommended to ICF leaders that some relationship be explored. ICF general director Rev. Merle Inniger and his executive had been concerned with their need to strengthen ICF's representation, administration, and personnel care. They approached SIM with the suggestion of a merger.

Are the two missions compatible?

Yes. All of us who've been involved in the discussions have been impressed with the basic similarity in objectives, doctrinal position, and attitudes. Both missions belong to the same association of missions in Australia, Britain, New Zealand, and North America.

Are there any dissimilarities which would need attention?

ICF's method of appointing leadership is somewhat different. Also their support system is not pooled mission wide, and support doesn't cover all that SIM support covers. ICF has essentially the same policy as SIM on divisive doctrines and divorce, although both missions would need to examine the wording of their respective statements to bring them into line with each other. ICF leaders and missionaries are very open to adapting to the positions spelled out in the *SIM Manual*, if the missions should merge.

What advantages does ICF see in a merger?

1. Expanded representation, with increased prayer, recruitment, and support.
2. Stronger home offices as sending bases.
3. An office in Singapore, adjacent to their Asian fields.
4. An administrative base and fellowship in West Africa for their Senegal field.
5. Strengthening of the leadership team.
6. Better cost effectiveness, as part of a larger organization.

What advantages does SIM see?

1. Expanding our awareness and skills concerning outreach to Muslims.
2. Providing fields more accessible for missionaries from Australia, East Asia, and New Zealand.
3. Participation in ICF's ministries among new immigrants in Europe, North America, and elsewhere.
4. Enlargement of vision and of constituency.

If the two missions should merge, what merging pains would you foresee?
Obviously we'd need time to get used to an increased number of administrative units. Our Board of Governors is examining that whole question. No General Director would be able to cope without a capable International staff to carry out many of the functions of his office.

A subcommittee of the Board of Governors is currently working on proposals concerning the General Director's workload. When agreed upon, that revision will take place anyway, but the possibility of our incorporating ICF in the future makes it more urgent.

An official announcement of the pending merger which was to take place on 1 January 1989 appeared in the September–October 1988 issue of *SIMNOW*.[2] It summarized plans this way:

After 18 months of consultation, SIM International and International Christian Fellowship have announced the merger of their missions, effective January 1, 1989.

Under the name SIM International, the merger will add ICF ministries in Pakistan, India, Nepal, Bangladesh, Phillipines, Indonesia, and Senegal to those of SIM in Africa and South America.

"We believe this merger is something that God wants us to do," said SIM General Director Dr. Ian Hay in announcing the merger. "All of us who have been involved in the study that has gone into this decision are impressed with the compatibility of the two missions. We share the same basic objectives, doctrinal positions and attitudes, and are members of the same associations of missions in North America, Great Britain, New Zealand and Australia."

Speaking for ICF, General Director Rev. Merle Inniger said, "We believe that in view of the challenges which face missions today, Christ's commission can more fully be obeyed by combining our spiritual, intellectual, and material resources. The ethos and practice of the two missions are remarkably compatible.

The five Home Councils of ICF gave unanimous support to the merger, and ICF missionaries expressed their approval by 'an overwhelming majority,'" Inniger stated.

According to Hay, ICF can expect few if any changes in their ministries. With the exception of Senegal, which will be administered as part of SIM's Western Africa Area, most ICF fields will become SIM's Southern Asia administrative area with Inniger continuing as director, and with all missionaries and leaders remaining in place.

Advantages to SIM include "enlargement of vision and constituency, and fields more accessible to missionaries from East Asia, Australia, and New Zealand," Hay said.

"We believe the merger will strengthen the ministries and outreach of ICF by providing new doors for service, recruitment, and candidate orientation," Inniger commented. "It will also provide a broader structure to accommodate the growing potential of candidates from Latin American, African, and Asian countries; and facilities for more effective presentation of the work in sending countries."

ICF brings 115 missionaries to the merger, of whom 54 are from U.K., 27 from U.S.A., and the balance from Australia, Canada, New Zealand, Switzerland and Japan. SIM membership as of July was 1535.

Finally, in the January-February 1989 issue of *SIMNOW*, Dr. Hay wrote in an article entitled "SIM in Asia: Facing New Challenges":[3]

Some may wonder why SIM, with its emphasis already spread over two continents, would expand to another continent through merger. Perhaps a reminder of SIM's Purpose Statement is in order. Here it is:

"The Purpose of SIM is to glorify God by evangelizing the unreached and ministering to man's needs, discipling believers into churches equipped to fulfill Christ's Commission."

The outworking of that statement means that the missionaries of SIM seek to reach unreached people with the good news of Jesus Christ. Their purpose knows no geographic boundary.

Others may wonder if SIM is in danger of becoming too large. Recently, while driving along a motorway in England, we saw an advertisement on a lorry: "We're big enough to cope," we read, "and small enough to care." We are convinced that both missions will now be stronger, and thus be better able to meet the challenges of our times. The combined forces of our two missions will reduce overhead, expand our mutual recruitment capabilities, and streamline administration.

CHAPTER 13

THE AFRICA EVANGELICAL FELLOWSHIP MERGER (1998)

In the run up to the actual merger of Africa Evangelical Fellowship (AEF) with SIM on 1 October 1998, Graeme Kent, as chairman of the AEF International Board, wrote an "An Open Letter to All *Action Africa* Readers."[1] The following is adapted slightly, but represents the bulk of that letter:

> This was a momentous decision and one not taken quickly or lightly. In fact, it is the culmination of several years' work by the International Board of AEF. . . .
>
> **Why did AEF see the need of a merger?**
> Right from its inception as the Cape General Mission back in 1889, the primary objective of what is now the Africa Evangelical Fellowship has been to glorify God by preaching of the gospel of Christ and assisting the growth to maturity of individual believers and the national churches they form.
>
> We are greatly encouraged (and humbled) as we look back over 110 years of ministry in southern Africa and the Islands to see how the Lord has used AEF and its personnel. Our history in pioneer evangelism, church planting, and ministering to a wide range of needs is, in human terms, quite impressive.
>
> For some years there has been a growing realization that some aspects of the Fellowship needed to be improved significantly if we are to honour properly the aspirations of our motto, "God First—Go Forward." As the International Board considered AEF's ministries, organizational structures, and operational procedures, it has not been satisfied we are in optimum shape to make the most of new opportunities to serve Christ and His church.
>
> Despite a series of changes in recent years to strengthen AEF, we eventually concluded some form of strategic partnership or alliance with a like-minded mission might well provide greater ministry impact and better stewardship of resources as we enter the next century. Even though it would mean major change, we knew we must be ready to "meet the needs of the hour."

Why SIM?

The International Board is delighted the Lord led us to approach SIM. We are both international and interdenominational missions with conservative, evangelical heritage and commitment, and share much in common including:

- Almost identical doctrinal and purpose statements
- Very similar ministry profiles
- Ministry in Africa since inception

Through detailed investigation and discussion at international leadership level over the past 18 months, a mutually acceptable basis had been established for a merger of the two missions.

At its meeting in June 1998, the AEF International Board gave detailed consideration to the relative merits of a merger with SIM or remaining as an independent organization. Noting the unanimous recommendation of its Merger Investigation Committee to proceed with a merger and the wide support throughout AEF for this recommendation, the board concluded that merger was the direction of God's choice.

Photo 13.1. *AEF-SIM merger talks in Waverly, England, 16 June 1998.* Front row (L–R): Tim Kopp, Jim Kallam, Jim Kraakevik, Jim Plueddemann; Back row (L–R): Graeme Kent, Marilyn Barr, Aletta Bell, Hudson Deane.

The SIM Board of Governors, meeting at the same time, reached the same conclusion. An Integration Agreement was duly signed by representatives of both missions.

What benefits are expected from the merger?

The Board believes a merger with SIM will enable AEF and SIM to achieve significantly increased effectiveness at international, sending country and field levels. A wide range of potential benefits becomes available as a result of the merger, including:

- More complete achievement of the ministry objectives of our purpose statements
- Stronger relationships with our partner churches
- Greater strategic direction and expansion of our range of ministries
- Better stewardship of shared resources

We see these benefits being achieved through a combination of factors, especially through a greater sense of vision, motivation, and increased overall capacity. We envisage:

- Increased capacity to recruit, develop, and support missionary personnel
- Synergies from amalgamating sending councils / offices and international administrations
- Stimulus through wider contact with others engaged in similar ministries
- Better use of resources (strategic leadership, leadership training, support of personnel, publicity, promotion, financial administration, crisis management, etc.)
- Involvement of AEF-related national churches with like-minded churches through participation in the "Evangel Fellowship" of SIM-related churches
- Involvement in well-developed SIM ministries such as Tentmaking, Ethnic Focus and Muslim outreach programmes

What are the main implications of the merger for AEF?
When the two missions integrate on 1 October 1998, there will be a number of important changes:

- Organizationally, AEF will join Andes Evangelical Mission, International Christian Fellowship and Sudan Interior Mission as part of an expanded SIM (Society of International Ministries). The name of the new mission will be SIM.
- The current AEF ministries in Africa and the Islands will continue. The name "AEF" will be retained in most field areas and its existing partnerships with national churches will remain in force.
- AEF sending councils and offices in Australia, America, Britain, Canada, and South Africa will be combined with their SIM counterparts.
- The AEF International Office will be closed. International Director, Tim Kopp will move to SIM international headquarters in Charlotte, North Carolina, USA as the SIM Deputy General Director responsible for current AEF field operations. Personnel Co-ordiantor Dorothy Haile will also move to Charlotte to take up a senior personnel post in SIM International.

- AEF missionaries will become missionaries of SIM. They will still require a full team of "partnership" supporters providing prayer and financial support.
- Publication of *Action Africa* will cease. All those currently receiving it will receive the equivalent SIM publication (*SIMNOW* in most countries).

Our deep desire is that *Action Africa* readers will continue to be involved. Our name and organizational structure will change but our commitment to the work of Christ remains strong. We remain dependent upon God and the prayers and practical support of our many supporters and friends around the world. . . .

After the merger actually took place on 1 October 1998 the following report and reactions were recorded in an *Intercom* article entitled "AEF and SIM Join Hands":[2]

These have been momentous days in the life and history of AEF and SIM. After long, intense and prayerful investigation, the decision to merge AEF and SIM took place on June 16, 1998 in Waverly, England.

AEF's International Director, Tim Kopp, wrote,

> When the final vote by both missions showed an overwhelming majority in favour of merger, there was an incredible hush in the room. Tears were shed as the magnitude of the decision and its implications caused each individual to be lost in thought. Four of us in the room were AEF MKs (one a third generation MK) and our hearts were full of emotion as we considered the impact this would have on the organization that we have known all of our lives. But though there was a sense of reluctance and perhaps even grief, we knew that God was in this decision. There was no regret. A feeling of anticipation and excitement for the future was also very real. This was the beginning of a new chapter for all of us. We were stepping out, by faith, in a new direction and His peace was undergirding us.

The merger decision has great implications for SIM as well as AEF. Jim Plueddemann, General Director of SIM says,

> The integration of the two missions will take a lot of hard work. We are sobered by the new responsibilities we face, but are convinced it will be worth every effort if our outreach to those who need Jesus will be enhanced. May God help us to make a beautiful and strong union for the glory of His name.

PART III

THE ONGOING STORY

CHAPTER 14

MAJOR DEVELOPMENTS AND TRENDS[1]

As the important developments of the earlier period were covered in the stories of the "Major Pre-Merger Missions" (Part I), we shall only record the most basic information for that period. In this section, we also add the key dates of the missions that eventually merged to become Middle East Christian Outreach.

Founding Period, 1860–1909

1860
- The Ladies Association for the Social and Religious Improvement of Syrian Females in Beirut, Syria, is founded. (Lebanon was then part of Syria.)

1876
- The name of the Ladies Association for the Social and Religious Improvement of Syrian Females is changed to the British Syrian Schools and Bible Mission.

1889
- Cape General Mission (CGM) is established in South Africa.

1890
- Cape General Mission enters Swaziland.

1891
- South East Africa Evangelistic Mission is founded.

1892
- By this date the British Syrian Schools and Bible Mission's name had been shortened to the British Syrian Mission.
- Ceylon and Indian General Mission (CIGM) is founded.
- Sarah Ann Bennetts is the first Australian to join Cape General Mission.

1893

- CIGM enters Ceylon (Sri Lanka today).
- Poona and Indian Village Mission (PIVM) is founded and enters India.
- Soudan Interior Mission (SIM) is founded and enters the country known today as Nigeria (this is the first of several names of the mission). Walter Gowans is SIM's first "leader."

1894

- Walter Gowans and Thomas Kent die in Nigeria.
- Rowland Victor Bingham effectively succeeds Gowans as SIM's leader.
- V. D. David leads CIGM missionaries into India.
- CGM becomes South Africa General Mission (SAGM) following a merger with South East Africa Evangelistic Mission. Spencer Walton becomes SAGM's first director (1894–1903).
- SAGM by this time has work among Europeans, Zulus, Swazis and Xhosas. The work among Europeans is now being gradually shifted over to other organizations so that focus can be concentrated on African populations.

Photo 14.1. "Bro T. Kent's Grave, Bida," c. 1902.
Photo credit: Alexander Banfield

1897

- SAGM enters Southern Rhodesia (Zimbabwe today).

1898

- SIM changes its name to Africa Industrial Mission and forms a Canadian council.
- Seven men go to Cairo and formed what officially became known as the Egypt Mission Band two years later.

1899

- Belle Hay, of Scot and British Guianan (today's Guyana) descent, becomes a member of SAGM and joins her sister Marion in South Africa. The Hay sisters are the first "coloured" people to join SAGM.

1900

- SAGM enters Nyasaland (Malawi today).

1903

- The Egypt Mission Band's name changes to Egypt General Mission.
- Frank Huskisson becomes the general superintendent of SAGM (1903–1906).

1904

- A "colored couple" from Chicago named Mr. and Mrs. J. Ulysis Turner apply for membership to SIM. They do not join the mission because Mr. Turner is not able to leave the "good position" that he holds in the city.

1905

- SIM changes its name to Africa Evangelistic Mission.
- Nile Mission Press is founded in Cairo, Egypt.

1906

- Following the merger with SUM, SIM changes its name to Sudan United Mission.

1907

- SIM returns to its roots and changes its name to Sudan Interior Mission.
- Bolivian Indian Mission (BIM) is founded.
- James Middlemiss replaces Frank Huskisson as the general superintendent of SAGM until about 1920.

1908

- Africa Inland Mission establishes Rift Valley Academy in Kijabe, Kenya. Many SIM "missionary kids" have attended this boarding school.

1909

- BIM enters Bolivia.
- SIM establishes its first church in Ogga, near Egbe, Nigeria, after it baptizes 13 people.

Early Expansion, 1910–1929

1910

- CIGM opens a training home for converted Indians to provide more missionaries for the work.
- Dr. Ethel Ambrose establishes PIVM's first dispensary in Pandharpur, India.
- SAGM enters Northern Rhodesia (Zambia today).
- The first BIM outstations open in Bolivia—a school for boys in Choquipampa and a girls school in San Pedro. The first BIM missionaries from Australia arrive.
- The Kwoi station opens Nigeria, "a daring advance into the interior." The district is declared by British authorities to be unsafe for white travelers.

- Niger Press is a combined effort of SIM, the Church Missionary Society, and Alex Banfield's Mennonite Church. Publishing efforts included the production of dictionaries, grammars, and other general works significant for local peoples in addition to meeting the needs for specifically Christian literature.

1911

- Daisy Wakefield joins SIM as its first medical doctor and works in Nigeria.

1912

- First evangelical/civil marriage is conducted in Bolivia in November (Annie Cresswell and John Starnes of BIM-NZ). Prior to 1912 only Catholic priests could perform marriages.
- BIM welcomes their first known converts—a widow and son.

1913

- Miango Rest Home opens in Nigeria. Miango, also the site of work among the Irigwe, is centrally located on the plateau. Nearby Jos will become the hub of mission work in Nigeria and headquarters for SIM in West Africa.
- BIM sets up the first provincial field committee to assist the director.

1914

- BIM founder and director George Allan (1907–1941) and Crisólogo Barrón begin translating the New Testament into Bolivian Quechua.
- BIM becomes incorporated in Bolivia.
- SAGM enters Portugese West Africa (Angola today) with the arrival of Albert W. Bailey.
- Among the Yagba (Yoruba) people in Nigeria, 22 churches are planted. Their first Bible conference is held in Egbe.

1915

- SIM co-founder Rowland Bingham visits Tommy Titcombe at Egbe; over one hundred converts are baptized.
- Rowland Bingham and Andrew Stirrett visit Girku, Nigeria, where Walter Gowans died. The woman living in the house where Gowans died gives Bingham her ring to take to Walter's mother Margaret.
- Guy Playfair is appointed field director. This is a significant step, as previously Bingham had direct control of all operations. This appointment made the field director responsible for local operations. This set SIM's policy that decisions should be made as close as possible to those affected.
- CIGM forms a council in the USA.

- A German U-boat sinks the Lusitania. Casualties on the British liner included Rowland Bingham's sister Alice (b. 1880), and David Loynd (b. 1862), along with his wife, Alice. Loynd was one of SIM's first missionaries, having gone to Nigeria in late 1894 to travel with Bingham for several months.
- BIM changes the name of its magazine to *Bolivian Indian*.

1916

- Two women in San Pedro become the first to be baptized by BIM in Bolivia.
- BIM holds its first council meeting in New York.
- First SIM work among Tangale people begins in Kaltungo, Nigeria.

1917

- PIVM builds its first hospital. Missionaries want to build in the city, but can't get permission so they build on the mission compound. The city is later torn by riots and plague, scattering the people. God's sovereignty is noted.
- Dr. Andrew Murray, president of SAGM since 1894, dies.

1918

- First American missionaries join BIM.
- Bingham becomes SIM's general director after having held the positions of treasurer, general secretary, and financial secretary.
- Charles Inwood becomes home director for CIGM UK.
- John and Sadie Hay marry and establish pioneer work in Kuta, Nigeria. Their firstborn son, Ian, born ten years later, becomes SIM's general director in 1975.

1919

- Indian children's homes are established in the Tamil and Telegu areas.
- The first BIM MK returns as a missionary—Margarita Allan.
- SIM's first press, Niger Press, moves to Jos.
- A second Kuta station opens in Nigeria, opening a new area to SIM in the northern section of the Gbagyi region.
- A girls' school opens in San Pedro with 18 students.

1920

- BIM women members are allowed to vote on mission business for the first time, and the first woman becomes a member of the mission council.
- Quechua translation of the New Testament is completed.
- J. G. Gibson becomes SAGM's general superintendent (c. 1920–c.1922).

1921

- Mrs. Fred Legant is the first BIM worker to die in Bolivia.
- The first BIM church is formed in San Pedro.

1922

- George Allan and Ken Powlison are imprisoned in San Pedro. BIM claims that the charges against them were trumped-up.
- John and Edith Hall opens SIM's first school in Kaltungo, Nigeria.
- SIM British and Scottish Councils are formed.
- George Frederick Gale becomes SAGM's general superintendent.

Photo 14.2. *"The Kaltungo school at work: the regular school, with 'irregulars' excluded from the picture. Sept. 20, 1922."*
Edith Hall teaching students how to read and write Tangale, with her daughters Agnes and Margaret (L–R) in the foreground. *Photo credit: John Hall.*

1923

- SIM opens work in Niger (part of French West Africa until 1960) at Zinder.
- BIM's first outstation away from San Pedro area is established at Aiquile.
- George Allan and Henry Webendorfer leave Cochabamba to explore the Beni region of Bolivia. Both become ill on the return trip. Webendorfer sets off for the coast and a furlough in the USA. He dies at sea from malaria. Allan's wife nurses her husband to health in La Paz.
- The first 12 people are baptized in San Pedro, Bolivia.
- The first ten thousand Quechua New Testaments are received from the Bible Society, reported as being "the one outstanding event in the history of evangelical missions in Bolivia." The Old Testament is not completed until the 1980s.
- Jos station opens in Nigeria to become the headquarters for SIM.

Photo 14.3 *Gowans' Home, Collingwood, Ontario*

- SIM opens "Gowans' Home for Missionaries' Children" in Canada. The home closes 65 years later.
- V. D. David, better known as Tamil David, dies. David helped CIGM get established in Ceylon and India.

1924
- The SIM bookstore opens in Jos, beginning a chain of bookstores that will become ubiquitous in Nigeria.

1925
- The first SIM New Zealander, Jack Nicholson, leaves for Nigeria.
- The Plymouth Brethren's Christian Mission in Many Lands establishes Sakeji Mission School about 25 kilometers from Kalene that overlooks the Sakeji River. Many South Africa General Mission (later, Africa Evangelical Fellowship) missionaries sent their children to this school.

1926
- Sudan Interior Mission is incorporated in the USA, with its first office in New York City.
- MK school opens in San Pedro, Bolivia, with four boys.
- Mrs. Merriweather (CIGM) begins works with Muslims near Saty, India.
- The Bolivian Indian Mission establishes what is now known as Carachipampa Christian School in 1926. It moved from its initial location in San Pedro to Capinota in 1935, and then to its present location near Cochabamba ten years later.

1927
- SIM merges with Abyssinian Frontiers Mission, which opens the door for SIM in Ethiopia. The first two stations are Garbitcho and Soddu.
- Work is established in the Beni region of Bolivia. BIM missionaries number 43.
- Jack and Vera Nicholson open a leprosarium in Gelengu, Nigeria.
- Finances are very short. Bingham cables Nigeria to ask if he should send 30 new missionaries who are ready to leave. Missionaries reply: "Send them." SIM ends year rejoicing in funds provided for all 30 and enough to make up shortages of 1926.
- Tom Archibald becomes the first missionary to Kagoro, Nigeria, when he pulls a tooth for the local shaman or "witch doctor." That gains him acceptance. Before that, foreigners were advised not to go there without a gun.

1928

- The CIGM begins work among Muslims in Bangalore, India.

1929

- Kagoro Bible College opens in Nigeria.
- Meeting at Miango, Nigeria, SIM missionaries confirm their decision to expand to reach Northern Nigeria's Hausa people despite financial difficulties and opposition of British colonial policy. Bingham protests to British Colonial Secretary and speaks publicly against policies that prevent missionaries from going north.

Depression and War, 1930–1949

1930

- Work begins in Burkina Faso (then Upper Volta, part of French West Africa) at Fada N'Gourma among Gourma people.
- BIM is incorporated in the USA and moves Bolivian headquarters from San Pedro to Cochabamba.
- Telegu Home Mission, supported by local Indian churches, reports several baptisms.
- Dorothy "Queenie" Howe, who goes to Miango, Nigeria, is perhaps the first South African to join SIM.
- Rowland Bingham, Guy Playfair, and Henry Stock make SIM's first cross-continental trip from west to east Africa.

Photo 14.4. *"Messrs. Rhoad, Bingham, and Lambie, our three beloved leaders, in front of the Mission Home, Addis Ababa, May 20/30"*

1931

- PIVM opens Pandharpur hospital in India.

1932

- Work begins in Igbaja, Nigeria, which becomes the site of SIM's first seminary two decades later.
- SIM establishes the London Council. Robert Lee, one of SIM's first members, is chairman.

- The first Hausa Bible is published with the help of Dr. Walter Miller of the Church Missionary Society, SIM's Andrew Stirrett, and several Africans such as Malam Tafida (John Tafida Omaru) and Barau (Dr. Russell Aliyu Barau Dikko).

1933
- The Kano station opens in Northern Nigeria in fulfillment of SIM's co-founders' dreams to reach the Muslim North.
- CIGM changes policy for teachers' pay. Mission is to pay half salary and the Indian government the other half prior to turning its schools over to the government in 1934.
- Herbert Pirouet replaces George Gale as the general superintendent of SAGM (c. 1933–1938).

1934
- Walter (Wally) Herron and Alex Clark join the BIM team in the Beni Region of Bolivia.
- BIM buys property for headquarters and guesthouse in Cochabamba.

1935
- Work among nomadic Tuaregs begins with a station at Tahoua, Niger.
- King George V awards Ethel Titcombe a medal for the medical work she did serving the women and children of Egbe, Nigeria.
- SIM begins to publicly use "By Prayer" as its motto.

1936
- SAGM enters Mozambique.
- Sixty-two are baptized in Ethiopia.
- Arussi Galla bandits spear Cliff Mitchell and Tom Devers to death in Ethiopia. These were the first members of SIM who are killed while actively serving as missionaries.
- CIGM leaves Ceylon to focus on work in India.

1937
- SIM takes over leprosaria from Nigerian colonial government at Sokoto, Katsina, and Kano, effectively opening mission outreach in the formerly closed north of Nigeria.
- SIM opens 16 centers in Ethiopia from 1927–1937. Most missionaries are expelled by Italian conquest of the country. Italians take over leprosarium built by SIM.
- SIM missionaries expelled from Ethiopia enter Sudan to work with Mabaan, Uduk, Dinka, Jum Jum, and Koma people.

- The first Bible institute for Indians opens in San Pedro, Bolivia, with five students. The next year, with 30 students, the school moves to Sacana.
- CIGM opens Mysore Reading Room (India).

1938

- CIGM enters Basti, Utraula, and Gonda, India, on the border of Nepal. These are the most densely populated areas of India and mostly Muslim with some Hindu.
- Last SIM missionaries leave Ethiopia after the Italian conquest.
- Seven believers from seven districts meet for a one-month Bible study in Spanish outside Cochabamba.
- Percy Victor Watson becomes the general superintendent of SAGM (1938–1942).

1939

- SIM Northern Ireland Committee is established.
- Kagoro Training Center (now College) opens, expanding work in Nigeria's "Bible Belt."
- CIGM opens Muslim work in Coimbatore, India.
- Wally Herron's wife, Violet, dies in childbirth, inspiring Wally to get his pilot's license.

1940

- Wally Herron returns to Bolivia where he will become one of the first pilots in the world to establish a permanent missionary aviation service.
- BIM launches boat work on the Beni River in Bolivia.
- Italians drop 89 bombs on clearly marked mission hospital at Doro, Sudan, killing Dr. Robert Grieve and his wife, Claire. Two Maban girls, along with Kenneth and Blanche Oglesby, are wounded in the attack.
- Eight missionaries, including four SIMers, board the SS *Apapa* in Lagos, Nigeria, for England. November 15, after 27 days at sea, the ship is bombed. The missionaries had just read, "He led them on safely" (Psalm 78:53 KJV) and "Behold, I send an Angel before thee, to keep thee in the way" (Exodus 23:20 KJV). The missionaries and all but 36 passengers and crew were rescued.

1941

- First PIVM church baptizes 20 in Nandeshwar, India. A son of one of the first Christians later becomes a pastor in Pandharpur.
- George Allan dies. Verne D. Roberts is appointed BIM director (1941–1956).
- Wally Herron's first plane—a two-seat Piper Cub—arrives in Bolivia dismantled. Its arrival in crates causes much excitement. It takes a month to assemble.

- In September, the first flight takes place in Cochabamba. In October Herron undertakes the first missionary flight to the lowlands of Bolivia to start aviation evangelism.
- Igbaja Theological College opens in Nigeria as SIM's first formal training institution.
- Two CIGM missionaries join the Indian army. Both die in service outside of India.

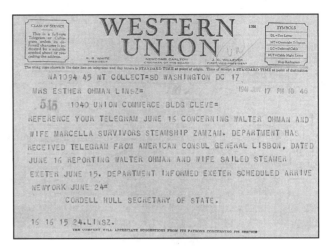

Photo 14.5. *Zamzam telegram, 1941*

- Seventy people are baptized in a joint service at Kaltungo, Nigeria—39 from Billiri and 31 from Kaltungo, the firstfruits from the outstations of Kaltungo.
- An epidemic of measles and poor harvest are blamed on the coming of the gospel to Dadiya, Nigeria.
- Thirty-seven new missionaries are sent to Africa in the midst of World War II.
- A German warship sinks the Zamzam, a passenger liner. Many missionaries survive, including SIM's Mary Beam, Walter Ohman, and his wife, Marcellla.

1942

- Rowland Bingham dies just months before Sudan Interior Mission reaches its Jubilee year and 48 years to the day after his colleague Tom Kent died. Charles Gordon Beacham becomes SIM's acting director / deputy general director (1942–1944).
- SAGM missionary Rev. F. Suter works with members of other evangelical organizations to establish the Union Bible Institute.
- SIM returns to Ethiopia to find thousands of new believers and over one hundred congregations instead of the handful of believers they left in 1938.
- CIGM opens work in Bahraich, India.
- A report from Nigeria reads: "Through the years we have sought to give our Christian people a sound Bible teaching and have been slow to respond to their strong appeals to give them education on other subjects. . . . Hundreds of Africans have left us to secure training elsewhere. . . . We are now trying to undo a wrong we have done these people." There are already 31 schools with applications pending for seven others. These are apart from the four thousand students enrolled in religious knowledge classes.

- Kano Eye Hospital in Nigeria opens under the leadership of Dr. Douglas Hursh. Many hundreds suffer from severe eye disease and travel miles to the hospital.
- The Church of Brethren Mission establishes Hillcrest School in Jos, Nigeria, in 1942. A few hundred SIM MKs have attended this school over the decades.

1943

- Rev. Wilfred Green is appointed general superintendent of SAGM (1943-1968).

1944

- Guy Playfair is appointed SIM's second general director (1944-1957).

1945

- Property is bought for missionary kid (MK) school near Cochabamba, which later becomes Carachipampa Christian School.
- Kwoi Girls School opens in Nigeria.
- SIM outreach to Somali people starts when Warren and Dorothy Modricker go to Aden to learn the Somali language. World War II prevents them from entering Somalia. Dorothy and her African colleagues later translate the entire Bible into Somali.
- In light of subsequent mergers in SIM history, it is interesting to note that general director Guy Playfair wants the mission to enter Japan in 1945–46, but is turned down by national councils not wanting to dissipate SIM's current efforts. Playfair has even raised money for this venture. He subsequently contacts Oswald Sanders of China Inland Mission, which had been largely kicked out of China and is struggling with where to go. Playfair's letter encouraging them to go to Japan and the offer of the money is an important part of their decision to enter Japan.

1946

- Work begins among Bariba people in Benin (then Dahomey).
- Wally Herron organizes the building of a ranch as a leprosy clinic in Tane, Bolivia, with a gift from the governor.

Photo 14.6. *"'Evangel' S.I.M. Plane with Pilot Soderberg & G. W. Playfair. Carries 2 passengers & Pilot. A Gift from Evangel Baptist Church. Newark, N.J."*

- Clarence Soderberg begins to pilot "The Evangel," a three-seater Cessna 170 that the mission "wonderfully used in carrying missionaries to and from their stations, and transporting sick and emergency cases to our hospitals."[2] The aviation ministry of SIM later came to be known as SIMAIR.

- SIM founds Bingham Academy in Addis, Ababa, for the children of its missionaries.

- Property is bought for an Indian Bible Institute in Bolivia.

- The first Somali convert is baptized in Addis Ababa, Ethiopia.

- SAGM is restructured, and for the first time, the fields became autonomous with home councils only responsible for home constituencies.

Photo 14.7. *Students in the dining room, Bingham Academy.*
(L–R): Sharon Coleman, Doug Koop, Loren Kliwer, and Paul Craig.

1947

- Kagoro Bible Training School opens in Nigeria.

- Bingham Memorial Nursing Home, the first SIM nursing home/hospital, opens in Jos, Nigeria.

- SIM opens Kent Academy, a school for its MKs, in Miango, Nigeria.

Photo 14.8. *Missionary kids playing in the school yard, Kent Academy.*
(L–R): Jim Goertz (?), Ralph Olson, and John Willie.

1948

- Arturo and Hilda Arana become Christians in Bolivia, and later become BIM's first Bolivian missionaries as associates. Arturo "had perhaps the greatest soul-winning ministry of any man in Bolivia," writes M. A. Hudspith in *Ripening Fruit*, 1958.

- *West African Christian*, forerunner of *African Challenge*, is first published.

- African Missionary Society (AMS) is formed by a committee of SIM missionaries and Nigerian pastors. Later it becomes Evangelical Missionary

Society (EMS). It is significant that this occurred even before the formal organization of the church denomination (ECWA) and is reflective of their priority concern for the unreached.

- Dr. Andrew Stirrett dies.
- SIM's West Africa Field Council passes a resolution urging its missionaries to avoid "race discrimination."

1949

- SIM's first International Council is formed. It meets until 1957.

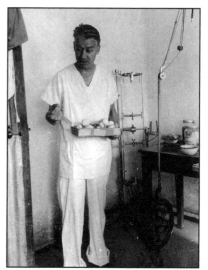

Post War Explosion 1950–1969
1950

- Evangelical Christian Union (UCE) is organized with four churches in Bolivia.
- AMS supports 27 Nigerian missionaries and continues to grow.
- First mission hospital in Niger opens at Galmi. Nearest hospital is seven hundred miles away. Niger has one doctor per one hundred thousand

Photo 14.9. *Dr. Burt Long at Galmi Hospital*

people. Government later decorates founder Dr. Burt Long and several missionary nurses.

- Joan Jackson goes to Niger.
- Bible school opens at Fada N'Gourma, Upper Volta (now Burkina Faso). Sleeping rooms are built on stilts because of the lions.

Photo 14.10. *Joan Jackson*
Miss Jackson was born in Gravelbourg, Saskatchehewan, on 1 February 1916. She became a Christian when she was 13 years old, went to nursing school and seminary, and traveled to Niger, West Africa, in 1950. Miss Jackson worked as a nurse, accountant, and evangelist at Guescheme, Tsibiri, and Galmi, and received the Merit of Niger for the medical services that she rendered to the country. Joan returned to Canada after she retired in 1984 and, among other things, took care of two elderly retired missionaries.

- *African Challenge*, a popular-style magazine, moves to Lagos, Nigeria, where it grows to have the second-largest circulation of any magazine on the continent.
- Titcombe College, a secondary school, opens in Egbe, Nigeria.

1952

- Work opens in Ghana through distribution of *African Challenge*. SIM will go on to open Maranatha Bible College, extensive prison work, "cinevan" outreach, and a church planting ministry.
- West African Broadcasting Association, formed to develop radio ministry in Liberia, joins SIM.
- SIM's South Africa Council is established in Cape Town.

1953

- Egbe Hospital opens and becomes SIM's first training hospital.
- Spanish Day Bible Institute is inaugurated near Cochabamba. It later moves to Calle Bolivar Church.
- In response to a request by the church, Dr. Robert Foster of AEF opens Mukinge Hospital in Zambia.
- Rhodesian H. Stephen Sitole and his African-American wife Priscilla join SAGM and serve in Southern Rhodesia (modern-day Zimbabwe) for a few years. They are the first persons of color to become members of SAGM in a quarter century.

Photo 14.11. *"Vender selling African Challenge at a book stall in Accra, Ghana,"* 1956. Credit: Niger-Challenge Press.

1954

- Radio ELWA begins broadcasting in Liberia.
- SIM ordains Revs. David Kayode, Clyde Jamus, and Samuel Afolabi in Nigeria. Their ordination sets the basis for the establishment of the Association of the Evangelical Churches of West Africa (ECWA) with four hundred churches.
- CIGM is started in Multan, West Pakistan (Pakistan today). Bahawalpur area's population of two million is solidly Muslim.
- SIM enters Somalia as the country is opened by the UN.

1955

- The Bolivian government asks BIM to care for all leprosy patients in Trinidad area.

1956

- ECWA is recognized by the Nigerian government.
- SIM congregations in Ethiopia organize the Wongel Amagnyoch Andenet Mahiber (the Association of Evangelical Believers), which later becomes part of the Kale Heywet Church (Word of Life Church).
- SIM opens a literature center in Accra, Ghana.

Photo 14.12. *Bus trip to Rawalpindi Lake, West Pakistan, Spring 1972*

- Jose Marig Rico is one of dozens of Bolivian Catholic priests who are converted, which leads to national revival.
- Vern Roberts concludes his term as BIM director; Joseph S. McCullough is appointed general director (1956–1974).
- Pakistan Christian Fellowship is formed as part of CIGM.
- The United Presbyterian Mission establishes Murree Christian School for missionary children in Murree, Pakistan. The children of CIGM and ICF missionaries attended this boarding school.
- SIM starts to partner with Deutsche Missionsgemeinschaft (DMG).
- SIM establishes ELWA Academy for missionary children in Monrovia, Liberia.

1957

- Egypt General Mission's name changes to Middle East General Mission after some of its members go to Cyprus, Lebanon, and Eritrea to do missionary work.
- BIM missionary nurse Mary Cermak is awarded the International Red Cross Florence Nightingale Award for meritorious service to leprosy patients in Bolivia. Red Cross and government officials including President Herman Siles attend the ceremony.
- BIM begins Christian day schools in the Beni region.
- SIM's first Memorandum of Agreement: General Council (1957–1985) succeeds International Council. This change ends a dispute that might have split the mission as a result of there being no clear mechanism to appoint a successor. Dr. Albert D. Helser is appointed third general director (1957–1962).

- SIM's General Council cracks the mission's de facto half-century old color bar allowing "non-white married couples qualified for specialized work" to apply for membership.
- Faith Christian Academy is established in Manila, Philippines. Many children of SIM missionaries have attended Faith over the years.

1958

- Outreach to Bengali Muslims begins at Mankgant, East Pakistan (Bangladesh today).
- SIM is incorporated in Australia and UK.
- BIM is instrumental in getting InterVarsity started in Bolivia.
- CIGM has 16 missionaries in West Pakistan (Pakistan today) and enters East Pakistan (Bangladesh today) with two missionaries.
- The field headquarters of SAGM moves to Johannesburg to be more central to all fields.
- Mr. Wilfred Green becomes General Director of SAGM (1958-1968).
- SIM's USA council accepts Rev. Howard O. and Mrs. Wanda Jones as associate members. They are the first people who are not white to join SIM. They go to Liberia one year later.

1959

- The British Syrian Mission leaves Damascus after Syria is divided into the separate nations of Syria and Lebanon after World War II. After the missionaries move to Lebanon, the mission changes its name to the Lebanon Evangelical Mission.
- In Bolivia, Evangelical Union of South America churches merge with churches started by Bolivian Indian Mission to form twelve Evangelical Christian Union churches. Later this grows to 780 congregations with 250 pastors and evangelists.
- Bible correspondence school opens in East Pakistan (Bangladesh today).
- Telegu radio programs are beamed to South India.
- Medical Auxilliary Training School opens in Jos as a branch of SIM's Bingham Memorial Hospital.
- First Northern Europe missionaries are seconded or loaned to SIM for ministry.

1960

- Socio-political revolution in Bolivia brings Indians greater freedom and results in a large movement toward Protestant missions.
- SAGM appoints a three person "Directorate" to run the mission. It is comprised of a general director (Wilfred Green), executive director (Don Genheimer), and an assistant director (H. Gordon Legg).

- Leprosy work starts in Utraula, India.
- SIM has 8 leprosy hospitals, 28 segregation villages, and 130 leprosy outpatient clinics in West Africa.
- Leaders of l'Eglise Evangélique de la Republique du Niger (EERN) sign its constitution. In doing so it becomes formally autonomous from SIM.
- Due to the relocation of the press from Cairo to Beirut, the name of the Nile Mission Press is changed to the Arabic Literature Mission.
- The United World Mission founds Dakar Christian Academy in Dakar, Senegal. Several SIM children have attended this school.

1961

- Bembereke Hospital, the first mission hospital in the country, opens in Benin with President Maga attending the ceremony. In the north where the hospital is located, there are only six doctors for eight hundred thousand people.
- Camp outreach program begins in Bolivia.
- Wally Herron receives the Bolivian government's highest award—The Condor of the Andes—from President Victor Paz Estenssoro. Heron dies three years later when his newly purchased plane crashes enroute to Cochabamba.

1962

- SIM Swiss Council is created for French-speaking Europe.
- A national church is organized in Upper Volta (Burkina Faso today) as Eglise Evangélique Gourmantché en Haute Volta (EEGHV).
- Dr. Raymond J. Davis becomes fourth general director of SIM (1962–1975).
- The Conservative Baptist Foreign Mission Society founds the International Christian Academy in Bouake, Côte d'Ivoire (Ivory Coast). Numerous SIM MKs attend this school until it was forced to close in 2002 due to civil war.

1963

- Work begins among the Marwari people of West Pakistan.
- Property is bought so Beni Bible Institute can be started in Bolivia.
- New Life for All begins in Nigeria. Program systematically mobilizes Christians for evangelistic outreach. Converts are channeled into churches nationwide. Program spreads to other African nations and to South America.

Photo 14.13. *Salim Tannous, SIM's first Arab missionary*

- Oika, the first Quara convert, helps start 20 churches in southern Ethiopia.
- Salim Tannous, from Lebanon, becomes SIM's first Arab missionary. He serves at Radio ELWA as an Arabic broadcaster from 1963–1966.
- SAGM closes *Our Africa* magazine that it launched in 1958 due to pressure from the government.

1964

- All missionaries are expelled from the south of Sudan as civil war escalates. SIM work moves to Khartoum. Sudanese soldiers mistakenly think Pastor Gideon Adwok is a rebel and kill him.
- Sucre Bible Institute for Indians opens in the south of Bolivia.
- AEF missionaries Bill and Margaret Patterson start Johannesburg Correspondence Bible School.

Photo 14.14. *Gideon Adwok, Sudanese pastor killed by rebels in 1964*

1965

- Leprosy work gets underway in Madha, India. Two to three thousand patients are treated.
- ELWA Hospital opens in Liberia with 45 beds. Dr. Robert Schindler is the hospital's first doctor and administrator. The first directors of nursing are Mary Hollingshead, Karen McLain, and Priscilla Payne (the first Liberian).
- South Africa General Mission changes its name to Africa Evangelical Fellowship (AEF) to convey that its work in the

Photo 14.15 *Tom Lowe showing hospital blueprints to Dr. Schindler as Liberians lay the foundation, 1963*

southern cone of Africa extends north all the way to the Democratic Republic of Congo, and to avoid being unfairly tainted by association with South Africa's notorious apartheid policies.

- The Middle East General Mission establishes the multi-mission English School or School for Missionaries' Children in Asmara, Eritrea. The school is forced to close ten years later due to war.

1966

- Bolivian Indian Mission changes its name to Andes Evangelical Mission (AEM) and enters Peru.
- CIGM opens Prem Sewa Hospital in Utraula, India.
- SIM states that "candidates are considered without regard to race or nationality."

1967

- An "audit" of SIM is conducted by the Christian Service Fellowship. Spencer Bower and George Thomas develop questionnaires and spend one year analyzing the findings.

Photo 14.16. *Michika Aoba, SIM's first Asian missionary*

Their recommendations ultimately lead to the creation of SIM International. Without this structure, mergers would not be possible. Thomas subsequently joins SIM and later becomes director in Liberia. Later still he becomes administrative assistant to the general director.
- Michika Aoba, from Japan, goes to Nigeria. She is SIM's first Asian missionary.
- The Evangelical Church in South Africa (ECSA) becomes formally independent from Africa Evangelical Fellowship (AEF). Its first president is Mr. Andrew Kodi. ECSA is a denomination of Indian churches that traces its founding to 1904.

1968

- SIM enters Côte d'Ivoire.
- AEM associates with the Peruvian Evangelical Church or Iglesia Evangélica Peruana (IEP) when the church asks AEM to help develop leadership.
- PIVM and CIGM merge, taking on CIGM's new name of International Christian Fellowship (ICF). Keith Jones becomes ICF's first director (1968–1974).
- Theological Education by Extension (TEE) work begins in Bolivia.
- Camp Candelaria opens in Bolivia.
- Leprosy treatment center opens in Madha, India.
- The Evangelical Christian Union (UCE) in Bolivia becomes autonomous.

- Africa Evangelical Fellowship establishes Farfield Missionary Children's Home in Pietermaritzburg, South Africa, to service the educational needs of their missionaries' children.

1969

- The first AEM missionary moves to Peru.
- ICF seconds missionaries to International Nepal Fellowship.
- ICF begins work in Iran.
- H. Gordon Legg becomes AEF's general director (1969–1974).
- AEF enters Mauritius.
- AEM purchases property for the George Allan Seminary in Cochabamba, which ultimately becomes the Bible Seminary of the Evangelical Christian Union.

Photo 14.17. *Ken and Mervina Sharpe, SIM's first full-fledged members of African descent.* Also pictured are their children Samuel, Helen, and Joseph (L-R)

- Lassa fever is diagnosed in Jos. All who travel in and out of the city are discouraged. SIM nurse Lily "Penny" Pinneo evacuates to the US with the virus. SIM missionary nurse Charlotte Shaw dies. Pinneo returns to Nigeria in a year carrying her own blood plasma with antibodies.
- Ken and Mervina Sharpe from Jamaica become the first persons of African descent to join SIM as "career" missionaries. The Sharpes become members through the Canadian office and serve in Nigeria.
- The Africa Evangelical Church (AEC) in Zimbabwe adopts its first constitution. The AEC is an outgrowth of the work that SAGM started in 1897.
- George Beckford, from Jamaica, becomes the Andes Evangelical Mission's only missionary of African descent. He goes to Bolivia as an associate. He is killed in a vehicle accident in 1992, leaving behind his children and Bolivian wife, Fidelia.

Photo 14.18. *George Beckford*

Late Twentieth Century, 1970–1999

1970

Photo 14.19. *Dr. Jeanette Troup*

- Dr. Jeanette Troup dies of Lassa fever in Jos, Nigeria.
- The Nigerian Civil War (1967–1970), better known as the Biafran War, is fought to counter the secession of Biafra from Nigeria. Both during the war, with refugees, and in the aftermath of the war, SIM combines relief efforts such as "Operation Good Shepherd" and "Operation Dorcas" with the return of many ECWA people to the eastern region to greatly foster church growth. These relief efforts become a blueprint in subsequent years for relief ministries in Sudan with Action of Christian Resource Organizations Serving Sudan (ACROSS) and later still in Ethiopia.
- AEF enters Namibia and Reunion.

1971

- SIM is incorporated in New Zealand.
- The churches associated with SIM in Ethiopia form an association called the Kale Heywet Church (Word of Life Church).

1972

- SIM is instrumental in starting Maranatha Bible College, Ghana.
- ACROSS is established for relief purposes in the Sudan. SIM is a major contributor and partner.
- AEM forms its first general council.

1973

- AEF enters Botswana.
- Television programs begin in La Paz, Bolivia.
- AEM restructures into three divisions: church-related ministries, theological education and Christian service, and support services.

1974

- ECWA Productions Ltd. begins in Nigeria, taking over SIM's literature work which includes *African Challenge*, SIM's literature and publishing department, and SIM bookshops.

- Marxist dictator Mengistu Haile Mariam overthrows Emperor Haile Selassie in Ethiopia. This leads to a reduction of SIM's missionaries there from over 320 missionaries to about 30 within a half-dozen years.
- Ron Wiebe becomes the fourth general director of AEM, leading the mission until its merger with SIM in 1982.
- George Hemming succeeds Keith Jones as the director of ICF (1974–1982).
- Arthur Deane becomes the international secretary of AEF, with his title changing to international director in 1977 (1974-1981).

1975

- Ian M. Hay is appointed as the fifth general director of SIM (1975–1993).
- ECWA doubles the wages of EMS missionaries because of general wage increases in Nigeria. They double again in 1978, but are still only about two-thirds of the government minimum.
- Short-term SIM missionary Dr. Doug Hill is killed by a Somali while doing famine relief work in Ethiopia.
- SIM General Council takes on the challenge of searching out African people groups who have been bypassed by evangelical witness. This coincides with a similar emphasis coming out of Lausanne I (1974) that captivates the imagination of many inside and outside of SIM.
- The Union des Eglises Evangéliques du Bénin (UEEB) is established. Rev. Gabriel Doko becomes its first president.
- Byang Kato, one of Africa's premiere theologians who received his initial theological training at the SIM-related ECWA Theological Seminary in Nigeria, drowns. Kato is the secretary general of the Association of Evangelicals of Africa and Madagascar at the time of his death.

Photo 14.20. *SIM-ECWA turnover ceremony in Nigeria, 1976.*
"ECWA President Rev. David M. Olusiyi accepts transfer of responsibility from SIM Area Director Rev. W. Harold Fuller, Jos, Nigeria, November 19, 1976."
Photo credit: Africa Now *91 (April 1978): 8.*

1976

- Middle East Christian Outreach is formed as a result of the merger of the Arabic Literature Mission, the Lebanon Evangelical Mission, and the Middle East General Mission.

- Work among Fulani people begins in Mahadaga, Upper Volta (now Burkina Faso).
- ECWA assumes responsibility for all SIM work in Nigeria. Missionaries report to ECWA. Harold Fuller's book *Mission-Church Dynamics* (1980) documents how the "increase of ECWA and decrease of SIM" liberates both of them from the tensions of nationalism and calls for a moratorium against foreign missions. Church members triple between then and 2002.
- Reports on the Mandingo (Maniya, Konya, Maninka, Bamana, Jula, etc.) of Liberia, Guinea, Mali, and Côte d'Ivoire as an "unreached Muslim people" lead to the start of broadcasts to them in Maniyakan dialect on Radio ELWA.

1977

- Africa Inland Mission and its related church (Africa Inland Church) invite SIM to work with them to reach Somalis in northern Kenya. Because of revolution in Ethiopia, SIM is no longer able to effectively reach Somalis there.
- SIM is incorporated in Switzerland, which becomes headquarters for SIM in southern Europe.
- Dr. Andrew and Belinda Ng from Singapore begin service with SIM, assigned to Galmi Hospital in Niger.
- Les and Verla Unruh, working with the Gola, become the first full-time church planting missionaries in Liberia.
- Twenty-three-year-old Elsbeth Lenherr, of Switzerland, dies of Lassa fever at Evangel Hospital in Jos, Nigeria. Lenherr contracts Lassa while working as a lab technician at Bembereke Hospital in Benin. She is evacuated to Evangel Hospital after falling into a coma in Benin, and never regains consciousness.

1978

- General Director Ian Hay and Eldon Howard call the first conference on the use of computers in SIM.
- Two SIM-related Sudanese denominations establish Gideon Theological College in Melut, Sudan.

1979

- *Challenge Cinema Today* program begins in Ghana.
- Village Health Project starts in Niger.
- ICF missionaries evacuate from Iran.
- Africans such as Rev. Sule Garko and missionaries from SIM, the Sudan United Mission, and the Church Missionary Society finish translating the second edition of the Hausa Bible. SIMers involved are Ray de la Haye, Helen Watkins, and Ruth Warfield.

Photo 14.21. *Rev. Hsueh Yu Kwong and Lily, 1986.*
"In SIM's Singapore office, East Asia representatives Yu Kwong Hsueh, formerly principal of a Malaysian Bible School, and his wife Lily, typeset *SIMNOW* in Chinese."
Source: SIMNOW *(Australian edition)* *(March-April 1986): 13.*

1980

- Amharic (for Ethiopia) and Somali radio programs are produced in Kenya and beamed into Africa from the Seychelles by Far East Broadcasting Association.
- First SIMers go to Italy to work with Africans.
- Following two years of interaction spurred by North Africa Mission's proposal to SIM concerning the possibility of a merger, the idea is scrapped due to resistance from certain NAM quarters.
- SIM changes its name to SIM International, with its byline being "Society for International Ministry."
- SIM's East Asia Council is registered with Mr. Tony A. Lee as its chairman. The East Asia Council reports to the Australian office until 1992.

1981

- SIM and leaders of SIM-related churches establish Evangel Fellowship.
- Dr. Robert Foster becomes international director of AEF (1981–1988).
- SIM's first Asian missionaries go to Nigeria; these are Rev. Sam and Sarah Kang from Korea, and Rev. Hsueh Yu Kwong and his wife Lily from Malaysia.
- Curtis and Opal Hayes are the first US citizens of African descent to become career members of SIM. They serve in Liberia.

Photo 14.22. *Opal, Collin, and Curtis Hayes*

Photos 14.23 and 14.24. *Pastors' Book Set conference, Bamako, 2011.*
Photo credits: Jamie Geysbeek.

1982

- Merle Inniger replaces George Hemming as the director of ICF (1982–1989).
- Andes Evangelical Mission merges with SIM.
- A partner mission agreement is formulated between SIM and DMG in Germany; this becomes the forerunner of similar agreements with other organizations in Europe.
- SIM International Resource Center (IRC) is established under the leadership of Dr. James Kraakevik (1982–1984) to research and disseminate essential information to assist SIM ministries. Kraakevik is succeeded as director by Gary Corwin (1984–1994), upon his departure to head the Billy Graham Center at Wheaton College. The IRC is phased out in the late-1990s as the widening global availability of the internet made much of its work redundant.
- First edition of *SIMNOW* is published, formerly titled *Africa Now*.
- The first conference where Pastors' Book Sets (PBS) are distributed takes place in Ghana under the direction of Jim Mason. As of 2013, dozens of PBS conferences have been held in 31 countries. Book sets are also sent to 10 other countries where the books are not formally distributed through a conference.

1983

- *Unity and Purity: Keeping the Balance* by General Director Ian Hay is published. The book is, in many ways, the culmination of an SIM response to almost a century of tension. Rowland Bingham and SIM were right in the middle of the modernist/fundamentalist controversy in the early twentieth century. This carried over into midcentury and morphed into the fundamentalist/evangelical controversies in which SIM also found itself in the middle. Dr. Hay writes in an email to this author (13 April 2015), "I don't know how many times I was asked what SIM policy was about Billy Graham. I always wanted to say the proper question is, what think ye of Christ?—not, what do we think of Billy?" He went on the say,

> These controversies in North America transferred to Africa. The World Council of Churches was extremely active trying to recruit leaders from ECWA and other denominations. We did our best to warn the leaders that their young men going to liberal seminaries would do the church damage. Then along came representatives of the International Council of Churches with their extreme separatist emphasis, offering the same things to the African churches. We warned about that, too, and were faced with the charge that we didn't want them to get help from anybody. So in November 1964, Harold Fuller, Howard Dowdell, and I drafted a statement which was reviewed by the West Africa Council and approved. Later the General Council approved it as well. We publicized in *Africa Now* under the heading "Where we Stand."

> I worried about that a bit since it was well worded, but in my mind not adequately based. So I wrote this book to give the biblically balanced perspective to our policy.

> This whole affair was of MAJOR importance to our getting beyond the 1960s as a viable mission.

1984

- SIM begins a major famine relief program for Ethiopia, running through 1986.
- A consortium made up of ICF, OMF, and SEND International begins work among Maguindanao Muslims in the Philippines.
- ICF enters Senegal to work among Wolof people, who make up one-third of their population. Wolof is the dominant ethnic group, with more than 80 percent of Senegal's population speaking the Wolof language. There are fewer than twelve known converts among two million Wolof.

Photo 14.25. *Percy Valiente, SIM's first South American missionary.*
Ministry of Commerce inspecting radio station's license with Valiente (center) and staff looking on.

- SIM begins an outreach to over 350,000 Muslims in South Africa.
- SIM signs a partnership agreement with the General Assembly of the Presbyterian Church in Korea (Hap Dong).
- AEF enters Gabon.
- Percy Valiente of Peru becomes the first South American to become a "career" member of SIM.

1985

- SIM holds a mission-wide Consultation on Church Planting in Monrovia, Liberia, to envision priority efforts for the next decade.
- SIM's Radio ELWA joins HCJB World Radio, Far East Broadcasting Corporation (FEBC), and Trans World Radio (TWR) in "World by 2000" commitment to broadcast the gospel in every language of more than 1 million speakers by A.D. 2000. SIM's point person for this is Stan Bruning.
- SIM Board of Governors replaces General Council.

1986

- The Gourma translation of the New Testament that Eleanor Beckett and her African colleagues worked on in Burkina Faso for years is published.

Photo 14.26. *Eleanor Beckett and colleague translating the Bible into Gourma, pre-1986*

- SIM's Board of Governors establishes International Council, mostly comprised of missionaries, as an advisory group to the general director.
- SIM holds its first Consultation on Muslim Evangelism in Monrovia, Liberia. Gerhard Nehls of Life Challenge in South Africa and Phil Parshall of ICF attend. Side discussions of these resource participants with SIM leaders play a key role leading to the Life Challenge merger later this year, and to the ICF merger in 1989.
- SIM enters Guinea and starts work among Muslim Maninka people in Kankan.
- SIM enters Sierra Leone to teach theology at Fourah Bay College in Freetown. The college, established in 1827, was for many years the only English-speaking, European-style college in black Africa.
- South Africa's Life Challenge, a 16-member outreach to Muslims in Cape Town and Johannesburg areas, joins SIM.
- SIM establishes Sahel Academy in Niamey, Niger, for missionary children.

1987

- SIM enters Paraguay. The country is 96 percent Roman Catholic.
- AEF enters Madagascar.
- In Sudan, the SIM-related Sudan Interior Church totals 38 congregations.
- Civil war in Sudan affects church areas. Many church members are killed, others flee to refugee camps in Ethiopia and other places. Barbara Harper and other SIM missionaries later work with refugees.
- Guerillas kill an Angolan medical worker named Alfonso Daniel who runs a leprosarium in Kalukembe. Daniel was associated with Africa Evangelical Fellowship's work there.

1988

- SIM enters Chile to provide theological education, plant churches, and offer social aid.
- Rev. Ron Genheimer becomes the third international director of AEF (1988-1994).
- ICF missionaries help victims of massive flooding in Bangladesh.

1989

- Work starts in Ecuador with emphasis on church planting.
- International Christian Fellowship merges with SIM.
- Carachipampa Christian School in Bolivia graduates its first high school class.

1990

- SIM missionaries evacuate from Liberia due to civil war. All SIM work is shut down with churches, clinics and schools throughout the country, and Radio ELWA and ELWA Hospital in Monrovia.
- An SIM network of partner missions and committees is strengthened throughout East Asia. Dr. Andrew Ng leads the effort.
- Ecuador Regional Council is established.
- AEF enters Tanzania.
- SIM enters Central African Republic.
- Evangel Fellowship consists of national church associations representing eight thousand churches in Africa, South America, and Asia. This is the first time representatives from former ICF countries can attend (three did not get visas). The fellowship represents 167 ethnic groups. Dr. Panya Baba (Nigeria) encourages delegates to celebrate SIM's centennial as a year to "declare the glory of the Lord."
- SIM International changes its name to SIM, with its trade name meaning "Society for International Ministries."

1991

- Africa Evangelical Fellowship (AEF) establishes the "French Committee" in Paris, with a view to making AEF known and attracting French speakers as members.
- Mengistu Haile Mariam flees Addis Ababa, marking the return of more missionaries to Ethiopia in the years that follow.

1992

- SIM's Radio ELWA in Monrovia, Liberia, resumes broadcasting. Most missionaries evacuate later this year after Charles Taylor's National Patriotic Front of Liberia attacks Monrovia in "Operation Octopus."
- The East Asia Council becomes autonomous from the Australian Council when it becomes the eighth cosignatory of the Joint Venture Agreement. Dr. Andrew Ng continues to serve as director.
- Gloria Cube becomes the first black missionary from South Africa to join AEF in modern times. She goes to Mozambique.

1993

- *Celebrate the God Who Loves!* is published to commemorate the first century of SIM. It combines graphic photographs portraying the exciting world of SIM together with captions and powerful essays by author W. Harold Fuller.
- Dr. James E. Plueddemann becomes the sixth general director of SIM (1993–2003).
- The Christian Community Prince of Peace Church opens in Santiago, Chile. This is the first church SIM plants in Chile.
- The Evangelical Church of West Africa commissions Mrs. Grace and Rev. Sunday Bwanhot, Mrs. Ruth and Rev. Simon Tako, and Dr. Joshua and Dr. Joanna Bogunjoko to serve as missionaries. General Director Jim Plueddemann and other SIM missionaries take part in this event. Their first fields of assignment are—respectively, for the Bwanhots, Takos, and Bogunjokos—the USA, Togo, and Niger.

1994

- From an exclusively white Anglo start, SIM membership now includes 36 nationalities.

1995

- SIM enters Uruguay. Myron Loss is the first director.
- SIM sends its first team into Nepal. Nepalese evangelist Rishi Acharya, based out of Duncan Hospital in India, leads Flo Hamilton, Neal and Lisa Johnson and others across the border.

- Rev. Tim Kopp becomes the fourth international director of AEF (1995–1998).
- Rev. Sam Kasonso dies in Lukasa, Zambia. He was the first general secretary of the Evangelical Church of Zambia that grew out of the work AEF and African believers started decades earlier.

1996

- SIM enters Mongolia.
- Fifty-six SIM missionaries (including 27 children) evacuate from Liberia one week after horrific fighting breaks out yet again in Monrovia.
- SIM International sends its first prayer bulletin by email to each of the mission's sending offices.

1997

- SIM enters Togo and China.
- SIM Korea Council is established.
- The Evangelical Church Union of Liberia is established. The denomination later changes its name to Evangelical Church of Liberia.

Photo 14.27. *Eldon Howard, 28 February 1978.* Following service in Nigeria with SIM (1966–1973) with his wife, Elizabeth, and children, Eldon Howard served as SIM's international treasurer and chief financial officer from 1973–1991, and deputy international director responsible for corporate affairs and finances from 1991 until months before his death in 2002. Among his numerous finance-related contributions to the cause of missions through SIM and others were the following: He wrote SIM's first Finance Manual, enabling a worldwide consolidation, uniform accounting practices throughout SIM, and an internal audit function. He was a visionary who helped establish the Evangelical Council for Financial Accountability (ECFA) and the Evangelical Joint Accounting Committee (EJAC) to promote accountability and accounting principles for evangelical organizations. He created the SIM Trust Interoffice Banking and Accounting System that enabled cost efficient and timely financial transactions throughout SIM, which has remained in place for decades. He facilitated a new pooling system through 2005 to address the diverse needs of sending and field locations with "equal earning power" contributions to the support pool and salary benefits paid out of the pool using "equal purchasing power."

- Support Task Force is set up by General Director Jim Plueddemann to review missionary financial support policy. David Dryer chairs the task force, which is commissioned to review the current support system and to recommend any necessary changes. The board, primarily through the initiative of Eldon Howard, the international director of corporate affairs, has begun to see that the "pooling" support system would not be appropriate for missionaries from newer sending countries. The Support Task Force works for nearly three years and reports to International Council and Board of Governors in 2000. Its recommendations are basically rejected and replaced by a compromise plan in 2000, and then by further compromises until, from about 2005, something resembling the original recommendation becomes accepted and is implemented in around 2006. The whole process of dismantling the cherished "pooling" support system and replacing it with something far more flexible takes almost 10 years.

1998

- Africa Evangelical Fellowship merges with SIM.
- The Bible Church of Africa (BCA) and SIM Ghana hold a seminar on "forgiveness and reconciliation" that is designed to bring all Christians together. BCA leader Stephen Aputara writes that "Unity of the body of Christ to do God's work successfully occurs when we forgive the present, forget the past and are reconciled together no matter what our race." Dr. Allison Howell leads SIM's role in this process.
- Missionaries return to Liberia in full capacity.
- UEEB/SIM Christian Literature Centre opens in Bochicon, Benin. The goal of the center is to spread the gospel among the Fon.

1999

- Radio Mosoj Chaski (New Messenger Radio) starts to broadcast in Abaroa, Bolivia. Its purpose is to "see a solid church planted among the Quechuas of Bolivia."
- SIM Korea, International, registers with the nation's revenue office.

A New Millennium, 2000–2017

2000

- SIM leaves Gabon.
- SIM's name explanation becomes "Serving in Mission." Philippines, China, and Mongolia Area (PCM) created.

- General Director Jim Plueddemann articulates a list of SIM core values that first appear in the 2000 SIM Manual as a front piece along with the purpose statement and a new vision statement based on it. Neither the vision statement nor core values are to be found in the approved text until the 2004 revision. The set of core values have served to reinforce an enduring quality to our identity and have required only minor improvement in succeeding years.

Photo 14.28. *Sports Friend's coach Kurr Japoo playing football with two youth in Thailand, 2011.*
Photo Credit: Austin Mann.

Photo 14.29. *Coach and player reading the Bible in Kenya, 2014.*
Photo credit: Hunter Buchanan.

Sports Friends' nine thousand trained coaches were ministering to over two hundred thousand youth in 13 countries by 2016. These coaches meet with youth several times a week on an ongoing basis throughout the year—building relationships through which they can share their faith in Jesus through both word and deed. They are essentially "life coaches" to young people who are looking for hope and direction. Each year thousands are coming to faith in Christ and tens of thousands are being discipled to live out their faith in Christ in a very practical and real way. As of 2016 the 13 countries where they were working included Ethiopia, Kenya, Malawi, Tanzania, Nigeria, Niger, Ghana, Senegal, Thailand, Laos, Vietnam, India, and Peru. Key leaders come from the USA, UK, Australia, Austria, Ethiopia, Kenya, Malawi, Nigeria, Ghana, Senegal, Thailand, Laos, Vietnam, and India. These leaders are not all missionaries— they are a mix of missionaries, and local SIM employees and volunteers committed to the effort by our various ministry partners.

2001

- Dr. Paul Hudson and others form "Windows of Hope" in South Africa. The name later changes to "Hope for AIDS."

2002

- General Director designation changes to International Director.
- Bryan Davidson and Tripp Johnston found Sports Friends in the USA.
- SIM independently registers in Malawi. Here, and with later registrations like this, SIM works independently in a country while at the same time seeking to strengthen, equip, and support primary church partners in ministry.
- Representatives of SIM and the Ethiopia Kale Heywet Church meet for a Celebration of Unity and sign a Memorandum of Agreement in Addis Ababa. The memorandum markes the culmination of over two years of discussions about "long-standing tensions" that existed between SIM and EKHC, and mark the beginning of a new era of unity as the mission and church work together to meet the challenges and opportunities of the twenty-first century.
- Christar spearheads the formation of Metro Delhi International School in Delhi, India. The missionary children of SIM, Christar, and several other missions have attended MDIS since its founding.

2003

- Malcolm McGregor becomes international director (2003–2013), the first European to hold the position.
- SIM Latino is officially established in Guatemala as a hub for sending Latinos around the world to do cross-cultural ministry. The idea begins with Giovanni Pienda in the late 1990s. Obed Cruz becomes the first director in 2004.
- SIM reenters Sudan.

2004

- C-SEA (Central/Southeast Asia Area) established, separated from the Philippines.
- New SIM Korea office opens.
- The Seize the Day review starts a process the impacts of which are apparent under the succeeding 10-year leadership of International Director Malcolm McGregor. These include a significant broadening of the internationalness of SIM, visible in several ways: (1) SIM's international leadership (international director and his deputies) are no longer exclusively Western; (2) new policies make membership from "anywhere to everywhere" much more the norm; (3) new sending office functions are set up to facilitate member intake from former

"field" regions; and (4) SIM governance broadens the base of "ownership" with a new mission agreement (January 2014) that technically takes effect six months following the conclusion of Malcolm McGregor's term of service.

2004/2005

- Beginning in July 2004 and concluding on 8 January 2005, the Seize the Day review wanted to place SIM in the position of the men of Issachar "who understood the times and knew what Israel should do" (1 Chronicles 12:32). An exhaustive process takes place to achieve that purpose including vast amounts of input both from within and outside of SIM. About 80 recommendations emerge from that process addressing issues from 10 major change areas: sacrificial lifestyle, discipling and mentoring, sharpened focus, emerging missions, redefinition of ministry, stimulating partnerships, short-term ministries, children and youth, simplification of SIM, and celebration of diversity. The implementation process which follows is based on 2 Peter 1:3–11 and is called "Faith Effects." It encapsulated the agenda for action that needed to follow. [3]

2005

- SIM enters Thailand.
- SIM closes Johannesburg Correspondence Bible School.
- SIM holds a continental conference on Muslim ministry in Africa near Nairobi, Kenya.

2006

- SIM adopts a new pooling system that facilitates missionaries from new sending contexts to be full members of SIM.

Photo 14.30. *Bill and Lorraine Foute with some parents of the young women that Boko Haram kidnapped from Chibok, Nigeria, 2015*

Photo 14.31. SIM Trauma Healing Coordinator Stacey Conard facilitating a discussion with South Sudanese in Kenya, 2011.
Photo credit: Tohru Inoue.

2007

- Bill and Lorraine Foute hold SIM's first trauma-healing workshop that the American Bible Society runs in Nigeria. SIM is now conducting, or has conducted, training and healing groups in Bolivia, Ecuador, Nepal, Kenya, Nigeria, Niger, North Africa, South Sudan, Liberia, Nepal, Sri Lanka, Ukraine, and the USA.
- As follow-up to Seize the Day, the first "country review" takes place (in Bolivia).
- In a context of increasing friction in mission circles over contextualization issues and "insider movements," SIM International Director Malcolm McGregor commissions a select team to propose appropriate guidelines. The team's work, which takes over a year, is received and approved in 2008, with one item being amended in 2012 to improve clarity.

2008

- SIM's North East India Council is established.
- Steve Strauss, director of SIM USA, apologizes to the "African-American evangelical community in the United States" for "the sinful exclusion of our African-American brothers and sisters from a potential avenue of ministry. We confess that sin to God, and we ask the forgiveness of Christ's church here on earth."

2009

- Missionaries temporarily evacuate from Sudan.

2010

- Dr. Siegfried Ngubane becomes SIM's South Africa director. Ngubane is the first black African to hold this position.
- The West Africa Office is established in Abidjan, Côte d'Ivoire, to make it easier for Africans to become members of SIM. The office approves its first member, Michael Mensah, in 2011.

- The primary name of SIM Latino becomes Oficiana de Conexión de Latina America (OCLA). The English name is Latin America Service Center.
- SIM Australia accepts Mathew Hongai, of Melanesian background, as its first missionary from Papau New Guinea. He later serves in his own country.

2011

- SIM's five missionaries are evacuated from Doro and Yabus, South Sudan, as fighting intensifies in the region.

Photo 14.32. *Mathew Hongai, SIM Australia's first Melanesian missionary.*
Source: Omar Djoeandy, "Confidence, Unity and Synergy," Mission Together (Australian edition) 128 (Winter 2010): 15.

2012

- SIM establishes the East Africa Service Center in Nairobi to provide leadership and financial services for Kenya, Sudan, South Sudan, Eritrea, Uganda, and Tanzania. The first director is Worku Haile Mariam.
- Asian Access and SIM sign a memorandum of understanding that enables SIM to help Asian Access recruit, care for, and logistically support missionaries who minister in Japan.
- The last International Council, which met every three years, is held in Lima, Peru. The new administrative structure will begin officially with the first General Assembly in 2015.

2013

- Dr. Joshua Bogunjoko becomes international director, the first African and person of color to hold the position (2013–Present).
- The International Conference on SIM History in Africa is held in Addis Ababa, Ethiopia.
- Missionaries are again evacuated from South Sudan after civil war starts.

2014

- Ebola epidemic reaches Liberia, killing well over ten thousand people in West Africa. SIM's ELWA hospital sets up two Ebola Treatment Units (ETU) to treat patients.
- A SIM Strategic Consultation is held in February in Kuala Lumpur that results in what becomes the "Malaysia Initiative" and sets the direction as Dr. Joshua Bogunjoko's tenure as international director is beginning. The framework for

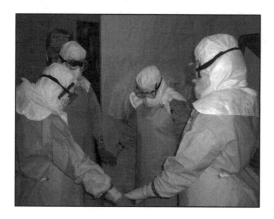

Photo 14.33. *Health-care workers suited up in full protective equipment, praying at ELWA Hospital, before going into the ETU to treat patients.*
Photo credit: Dr. Debbie Eisenhut.
(See Supplement 19.1, pages 292-299.)

the initiative is built on "The Big Why"—We exist to worship Christ in heart, word, and deed. We strive to make him known and make his disciples where he is not known, irrespective of barriers, and compelled by his great love. This leads to "The Big What"—We will place a pioneering focus on those who live and die without hearing the gospel. This in turn leads to "The Big How" that has five priority focus areas: (1) outreach development in the darkest places; (2) ministry training with an emphasis on diverse teams working in tough contexts; (3) focused mobilization and communication of ministry opportunities where Christ is not known; (4) resource development so that necessary finances enable people from everywhere to serve where Christ is not known; and (5) spiritual vitality of a prayerful, resilient workforce for challenging environments.

2014/2015

• SIM adopts a new governance structure that changes from a shareholder model controlled by sending countries able to meet the standards of the Joint Ministry Agreement (operational from 1957 to 2013) to a stakeholder model that shares decision making evenly among all participating entities. The process that led to this change took place over an extended period of years. Malcolm McGregor initiated the process, with Alistair Hornal of the board of governors chairing the working group. The 2015 Global Assembly approves the final implementation and acceptance of the new governance structure, and marks a major change, becoming one of the foundations for the twenty-first century SIM.

2015

• SIM convenes the first Global Assembly under the new stakeholder model in Chiang Mai, Thailand, with approximately 145 participants present. Under this new governance model every SIM country is treated the same (no more home/sending and field distinctions). Each SIM entity can sign the Mission

Agreement and send people to the Global Assembly as well as have its board/ council members eligible for selection to the board of governors. Global Assembly's purpose is to "provide a forum for missiological reflection on the direction and strategy of the mission."

- SIM's Spanish-speaking e-magazine *Vamos*, led by Chris Conti, is read by over fifteen thousand people.

2016

- Middle East Christian Outreach "joins hands" with SIM.
- As a foundational step toward establishing improved policies on the subject of risk, SIM International Director Joshua Bogunjoko commissions a very diverse international team (including members from Australia, Ethiopia, Kenya, Nigeria, Peru, Romania, South Sudan, the UK, and US) to reflect on what a proper theological understanding of the subject might look like. Their labors produce a paper, "Reflecting on a Theology of Risk," which is received as a good concensus statement of SIM's understanding of the subject, and is made available to SIM constituencies and others as requested.
- A new ELWA hospital is dedicated in Monrovia, Liberia. The hospital is built by Samaritan's Purse and operated by SIM.
- All missionaries from South Sudan flee Doro due to a sudden resurgence in fighting.
- Some missionaries from southern Ethiopia are evacuated due to unrest.

SUPPLEMENT 14.1

The Intrepid Women of SIM[4]

They've climbed mountains, driven trucks, explored rivers, and have been known to stride off overland when others preferred to stay on the roads. Here are some vignettes of SIM's women pioneers:

- In 1897, after reading a book titled *The Neglected Continent*, **Mary Allan** received a vision for reaching Quechua Indians of Bolivia. Mary and her husband, George, began what was called Bolivian Indian Mission (later Andes Evangelical Mission) to reach the Quechuas in 1907. AEM became part of SIM in 1982.
- For 36 years, beginning in 1930, **Minnie Myers** also worked among the Quechuas. "Mother Myers" planted over a dozen churches on the high plateau of Bolivia and helped develop leadership within the local population.

- **Margaret Searle** and her husband, Will, traveled the backwaters of the Amazon during the '30s and '40s in a houseboat. During their trips, they planted churches, distributed literature, and helped start schools. Even late into her 52-year career, Margaret continued her trips deep into the Amazon rain forests.

Photo 14.34. *Margaret Cuthbertson (Searle)*

- **Helen Watkins**, who went out in 1927, was a teacher, but after she got leprosy, she had to quit teaching. **Ruth Warfield** lived with her, and the two became known as the Watkins Warfield translators. They were instrumental in translating a Bible commentary into the Hausa language of Nigeria, opening up a language group of 30 million people to the gospel.

- **Effie Varley** arrived in Nigeria in the early 1920s and served eight terms among the Iregwe people. Her work in the village of Miango is legendary. She was renowned for making her ministry rounds by foot, often going a distance of many miles through the jungle bush.

- In 1945, **Lova Bush** began reaching out to the children of India. Her special ministry was Christian art for children, which she used to evangelize children through posters, pictures, and even comic books in Hindi. She began a special Christian art center in Hyderabad and was active in training other women how to teach children.

- **Aletta Bell** began her ministry as a medical doctor in North India in 1965. Her ministry also led to evangelistic opportunities, and she is credited with helping to start some 30 churches in Nepal. She subsequently served as the SIM area director for India/Nepal.

These missionaries—and hundreds like them—provide vivid testimonies of what God can do through dedicated lives.

Look What We Missed! (1984)[5]

It wouldn't happen today, of course, but more than half a century ago SIM rejected 32-year-old Claudie Peyton of West Virginia because "it is our unanimous considered opinion that the woman cannot possibly live for more than one year in the African climate."

Undaunted, Claudie paid her own way to Zambia where she founded an orphanage and adopted 18 children as her own. Last year Claudie, who was "a true legend in Zambia," was awarded the Zambian Medal of Honor by President Kenneth Kaunda.

On March 26th [1984], after 54 years in Zambia, Claudie died at the age of 89 and was buried on the mission compound.

SUPPLEMENT 14.2

It's Dangerous Near the Edge (1996)[6]
Jon Shea

SIM missionaries have been taking substantial risks since 1893. Back then, it was a killer disease called malaria, and the chances were good that a missionary might die. Then road accidents became the primary cause of a missionary's death. Today the kind of risk causing the most anxiety, though rarely death, is being in harm's way, the risk of being under personal attack or caught in civil unrest, terrorism, or war.

Dozens of SIM's members, including short-term associates, have gone rather "near the edge"—being exposed to the dangers of the brutal civil war in Liberia. This past April, for the third time, SIMers were again evacuated from Liberia when fighting endangered their lives. In 1990 most were evacuated by commercial flights, while 10 were escorted overland by one of the fighting factions. In 1992, when a major attack threatened the city of Monrovia, though maintained as a "safe haven" by West African peacekeepers, the US State Department again arranged flights for its citizens and, by prior agreement, other expatriates. In 1996, on April 12, some 56 SIM persons, including 26 children, were evacuated by US military helicopters and transports when Monrovia descended into total anarchy. Looting and killing were rampant throughout the city as three evacuations took place. Three men stayed behind until they, too, had to evacuate three weeks later.[7]

Imagine the pathos among the missionaries, not to mention the panic and death among the people of Monrovia. A few of the most courageous might wonder why we all left, but for most the reaction is a more incredulous, "Why on earth would SIM expose its people to such danger?" The answer is simply to minister to people who have never before been in such dire need of care: medical assistance, encouragement, and

Photo 14.35. *Rebel fighters of the National Patriotic Front of Liberia on the outskirts of ELWA campus, 1990.*
Photo credit: Dr. Bill Ardill.

the gospel. But beyond that, we went back to Liberia in obedience to what we believe is the Lord's call to serve in a dangerous world. Jesus did it. "As the Father has sent me, I am sending you" (John 20:21 NIV).

It takes a lot of trust in God and a certain amount of "nerve" to live so "near the edge" in places such as Liberia. Throughout the war, God has given some the courage to use these opportunities to serve when the people of Liberia have needed them the most. When

Photo 14.36. *The Liberia evacuation, Monrovia, 1996.*
Photo credit: David Decker. Published in SIMNOW 76 (1996): 1.

the risks are high, we can be timid and hold back, or we can be brave and walk through the doors we have asked God to open. The premise has been that he ought to know when to shut them.

By our willingness to take risks, many lives have been touched by Jesus' care. If we had been so timid as to insist that the war be over before we returned to Liberia, four years of broadcasting and five years of medical service, leadership development, Bible training, and more wouldn't have happened. Moreover, the plant and infrastructure of ELWA would have been completely damaged, making it nearly impossible to begin again and broadcast for those additional years.

While warlords, fighters, and opportunists were exploiting the helpless civilians of Liberia—the poorest of the poor—and the world had largely lost interest, Christians were there to minister, not to take. (Even on the refugee ship that made such news, the crew charged destitute, parched passengers $1 per gallon for water: ELWA gave it away free for 40 years, along with the Word of life.)

Wasn't God pleased? Jesus commended Mary's expensive gift to him. Judas thought it a waste. Maybe that's what the investments of the war years were: a sacrifice and an anointing of Jesus as his church in Liberia suffers. God's economy is different than ours. We are grateful for those who have helped us for five more years to make ELWA a lighthouse of God's message to a country in darkness, a touch of his hand for the sick, and an encouragement for church leaders, seeing them become confident in their God and no longer terrified of war.

For some, the expenditures in recent years in Liberia may seem a waste. As we gazed at the world's largest basilica in Côte d'Ivoire not long ago, we wondered about the millions of dollars spent on a fabulous building "to the glory of God." Beautiful buildings may show a little of God's glory. But if God's eternal building is people, then people and ministry to people in Jesus' name are God's real treasures.

So we have no regrets regarding the expenditure of money, emotional energy, and time that went into the ministry of SIM in Liberia over the past six years. Every minute we were on the air, every patient we cared for, every church leader we helped train and encourage is worth what we put into them. We have God's promise, "It will not return to me empty" (Isaiah 55:11 NIV).

A Christian Nigerian businessman on the flight from Dakar to Abidjan said to one of the three SIM wives whose husbands had remained in Liberia, "Now you have done what you could and you are leaving in tears. It's God's time to work. You will see! For in his time when he brings you back, you will have tears of joy to see what God has done in Liberia. I'm telling you, 'God is faithful!'" Ecclesiastes 3:11 (NIV 1984) reminds us, "He has made everything beautiful in its time. He has also set eternity in the hearts of men; yet they cannot fathom what God has done from beginning to end."

Maybe being "near the edge" is worth the risk.

CHAPTER 15

THE EMERGENCE OF DENOMINATIONS AND RELATED ENDEAVOURS

Dr. Tim Geysbeek

One of SIM's important goals has been to establish churches. Indeed, hundreds of churches were established during the first decades of SIM's ministry in Afica. But paternalism led most SIM missionaries to believe it would take years, if not decades, for Africans to independently govern their own churches because they felt Africans did not have the capacity to fully administer their own organizations.[1] Mid-nineteenth- to early-twentieth-century mission theorists postulated versions of the "Three-Self" principles that urged missionaries to encourage local congregations to become independent by promoting "self-supporting, self-propagating, and self-governing" churches.[2] By the end of the nineteenth century, however, such ideas were on the decline in mission circles due to the rise of racial discrimination (see Chapter 16). Well into the 1930s, with its focus on evangelism and baptism, most SIM missionaries only observed self-support and self-propagation.[3] SIM as an institution only began to encourage the emergence of fully self-governing churches in the 1950s.

Walter Gowans, the leader of SIM's first pioneering party that went to Africa, only acknowledged the first two principles in his writings that are extant. In a letter that he sent to his mother after he, Thomas Kent, and Rowland Bingham docked in Lagos in 1893, he wrote: "It is only about 40 years since the first missionary work was started here and already many of the churches are not only self-supporting but missionary"; by "missionary" he meant self-propagating.[4] He did not mention Rev. Mojola Agbebi's indigenous Native Baptist Church that had broken away from the mainline American Southern Baptist Mission (its members finished constructing a new edifice in Lagos earlier that year), or refer to the self-governing process that led the Anglican church to name an African bishop, Samuel Ajayi Crowther, to oversee the Church Missionary Society's work along the Niger River decades earlier. Neither did he comment on the "crisis" that occurred just months before they arrived after the Anglicans replaced Crowther with a white bishop (this was Joseph Hill who Gowans admired and who prayed for Bingham when he was dying of fever) and two assistant bishops (Charles Phillips and Isaac Oluwole) who were Africans.[5]

Bingham also never wrote about the crisis over the Anglican church's investing of Joseph Hill as the Anglican church's bishop, and only focused on the first two principles for most of his career. In 1908, he published a speech Bishop Alfred Tucker of the Church Missionary Society delivered in England in 1901 titled "Self-Extension, Self-Support and Self-Government in Missionary Churches."[6] Tucker, who worked in Uganda, believed there should be an "equality of all workers," and that no distinction between European and African Christians should be made on the basis of race.[7] He said Ugandans should administer the church through local leaders and councils that operated under the control of the bishop (Tucker, in this instance). "Outside support," Tucker explained, "means outside control which means the death of self-government." Bingham only elaborated on Tucker's theory of self-support in his introduction to Tucker's speech.[8] He did believe churches should eventually become self-governing, and in this regard felt Tucker's writings about autonomous churches were instructive. He touted the work of Rev. Mojola Agbebi who, he wrote, was the "pastor of an independent church in Lagos, which has been built up largely by his pastoral and evangelistic labors."[9]

Bingham and some of SIM's other leaders' disbelief in the ability of Africans to fully govern churches that emerged as a result of SIM's ministries is revealed in an exchange he had with West Africa Field Director C. Gordon Beacham in 1932. That year, when SIM's missionaries in Ethiopia were having a dispute about baptism which, by its very nature, implied that a church would be established,[10] Beacham published "Self-Propagation of the Gospel" in the *Sudan Witness*.[11] According to Beacham: "The Sudan Interior Mission from its inception has believed in a self-supporting and self-propagating native church," but "so far as Africa is concerned, I think experience has shown us the third article [self-government] is impractical for the first generation of converts." Bingham challenged Beacham, stating that one of the "healthiest churches" in Lagos was pastored by an African; here, Bingham was likely referring to Rev. Agbebi. But he hedged:

> The earlier that you can put the little trusts into their hands the better for them. I think we can well follow the apostolic model and ordain elders in every church, giving them responsibilities of government. . . . Missionaries should retain a relationship of apostolic authority and leadership to meet such emergencies and mistakes and to invoke all needed discipline.[12]

Beacham exposed the loop-hole in Bingham's argument when he asked, "If the missionary is to retain the apostolic authority and invoke all needed discipline, can we call that self-government?"[13]

Bingham began to question his, and the mission's, lack of vision for developing autonomous churches in 1938. His hope to see self-governing churches was in line with his understanding that "there seems to have been no race line" in the church in Antioch. His ultimate desire was "that all racial lines . . .be eliminated to-day."[14]

Perhaps SIM's most visible protagonist for creating self-governing churches was Alfred Roke who served in Ethiopia and the Anglo-Egyptian Sudan for nearly two decades.

Photo 15.1. *Alf Roke Photo*   **15.2.** *"Alf Roke baptizing, Australia."*
"This photo taken '36 Mid June, Addis Ababa. The Italians had occupied it at end of April, raised their flag over Ethiopia May 15th '36." This photo shows some of the "first converts" being baptized who came "down south of Kanbatta, Durami, & Wallamo Prov." The missionaries (L–R): Gertrude Pogue, Dore Koener (Duff), Zillah Walsh, Marcella Ohman, Glen Cain, Walter Ohman, Alf Roke, Blanche Oglesby; photographer, C. Kenneth Oglesby.

In 1938, Roke published *An Indigenous Church in Action*. He argued that local churches should become "free in every possible way" and not be "dependent upon men and money from foreign sources."[15] Following his discussions with Roke and reading his book, Bingham encouraged SIM's missionaries "to give Mr. Roke's book a prayerful reading, and it may lead to heart-searching as to whether or not our talk about our natives being like babies and their continuing as babies may not be due to our own being unwilling to let them stand on their own two feet." Many SIM missionaries criticized Roke and Bingham's support of Roke's pamphlet.[16] Bingham published Bishop Tucker's speech in pamphlet form in 1939.[17]

Likely due to Bingham's direction, SIM strengthened the self-governing provision in its 1939 manual to read that the mission should "look forward to the time" when "the native churches" would "bear the full responsibility of their own work" without missionary involvement. The previous manual focused on the "self-supporting" and "self-extending" of churches, while only vaguely envisioning the establishment of independent churches.[18]

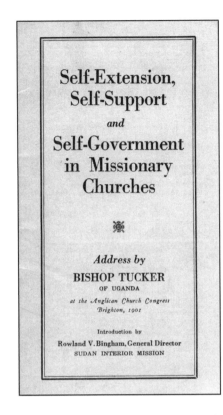

Photo 15.3. *Self-Extension, Self-Support, and Self-Government in Missionary Churches, 1939*

As Dr. Yusufu Turaki explains, while "the classical indigenization principles had a profound effect on SIM," the mission's "only difficulty lay in the actual application of the principles in practical mission work in Africa."[19] A tangible result of the mission's recognition that churches would eventually become self-governing was that SIM licensed its first pastors in 1939, in Nigeria.

Licensed pastors had the authority to baptize, hold communion, administer church discipline, recognize marriages, and establish new churches. Councils of elders were also established in several districts in Nigeria.[21] Essential in establishing self-governing churches was the development of African leaders. SIM did not emphasize seminary-level training of pastors and church administration before World War II because, as Turaki argues, they "felt that these two areas should not be introduced to Africans too soon,"[22] and because of "the lack of missionary understanding of African culture, values, and personality."[23]

The balance of power between the colonizers and Africans started to shift throughout most of the continent by 1949, weakening the link between Christianity and Empire and affecting mission-church relations.[24] "Within the SIM family," Turaki writes with regard to the situation in Nigeria, "some Africans became quite vocal and radical and thereby demanded advanced training and greater participation in the running of the Mission . . . in the late 1940s."[25] Due to pressure from African church leaders to license more pastors and to begin ordaining some, the mission's leaders started to make provisions for churches to become self-governing.

In Nigeria, SIM convened several conferences from 1949–1954 "aimed at developing national church leaders, defining the indigenization process and the form of the national Church."[26] These

Photo 15.4. *Rev. Weyi Zamfara, a former chief of Miango who became one of the first licensed pastors in Nigeria*[20]

THREE S. I. M. PASTORS ORDAINED

Photo 15.5. *The first pastors ordained in Nigeria, 24 January 1954*

Photo 15.6. *First ECWA General Assembly, Egbe, Nigeria, 18 May 1954.*
Some of the attendees were President Pastor David Ishola Olatayo, Vice-President Mr. Douglas Blunt, Treasurer Pastor Bagaiya Nwaya, Secretary Mr. Peter Koledade, and future SIM General Director Ray Davis.[28]

conferences in 1954 led to the ordination of three pastors and establishment of the Evangelical Churches of West Africa (ECWA) by an assembly consisting of Nigerians and missionaries.[27]

ECWA did not become fully independent until after SIM transferred its mission stations, Bible schools, academic schools, and medical programs to ECWA in 1976.[29] In becoming autonomous, Africans gained the ecclesiastical power they needed to begin shifting Christianity from primarily being a foreign creation of missions to becoming an authentic indigenous religion.

To enhance the educational standards of African pastors in the process that led to independence, SIM established post-primary Igbaja Bible College in 1941— which became a post-secondary diploma and degree-granting seminary in 1956, and Kagoro Bible Institute in 1955.[30] The first high-level institution that SIM established in Ethiopia was Grace Bible Institute in 1965; it became a seminary a decade later.[31] The establishment of a scholarship program in 1970 was key in seeking to provide opportunities for African leaders to acquire advanced training.[32] Several church leaders, like Byang Kato, benefitted from this program. (For more about Dr. Kato, see Supplement 15.1, pages 194-195.)

As SIM started to turn the control of churches over to African leaders, some of its leaders acknowledged that their thinking had been misguided. General Director Albert

Helser (1957–1962) said, in the framework of a rapidly changing Africa, that there was no place for a missionary to assume a notion of superiority and be a "little king." African churches could finish the task of evangelization that the mission had started.[33] The mission, he added, was beginning to see that "the African can do anything that any man can do," including "governing himself," if "given the chance to do so."[34] While Helser was still general director, three more denominations were formed: the Église Évangélique de la République du Niger in 1960,[35] and the Sudan Interior Church[36] and Eglise Evangélique Gourmantché en Haute Volta[37] in 1962.

Helser's successor, Raymond Davis (1962–1975), wrote in 1969 that "Christianity does not belong to any one people, race, or color," and that "in many cases" it was best to leave the "indigenous church" alone rather than to try to "structure" it from the outside.[38] The Kale Heywet Church (Word of Life Church) was established in Ethiopia in 1971.[39] In reflecting on the rapid expansion of churches in Africa, Davis admitted that year that

> the abrupt appearance of the church in Africa has caught the church in western lands unprepared. . . . [The church] has blossomed before our very eyes, this living, vibrant reality has surprised us. We were conditioned to filling a funnel. If only we could find enough missionaries . . .and enough money to support them . . .then, someday, maybe, the goal would be won. Faced with the real thing, we are embarrassed . . .[and] surprised, too. Strange, isn't it, that we really didn't expect God to do what He did quite so quickly. . . . I was present when ECWA was born [in 1954]. . . . It is almost impossible to believe the great strides in spiritual maturity and influence that the church has made since then. . . . The leaders of the young church in Africa seem to have sprung all at once.[40]

Perhaps Davis, his missionary colleagues, and their supporters in the western world would not have been taken by surprise if SIM had proactively moved well before World War II to champion the independent self-governance of the churches. Yet, this was not to be because, as is shown in chapter 16, most SIM missionaries up through the end of World War II only gave scant thought of Africans being fully capable of self-government. Denominations that were formed in the years that followed Davis' article were the Eritrean Kale Heywet Church[41] and Union des Eglises Evangéliques du Bénin in 1975,[42] the Eglise Evangélique Indépendente du Togo in 1995,[43] and the Evangelical Church Union of Liberia (later, Evangelical Church of Liberia) in 1997.[44]

Within a decade after the first denominations were established, SIM started several initiatives to strengthen African leaders and their churches. The first, under the leadership of General Director Davis, was granting scholarships to promising African church leaders so they could further their education. A short story of Dr. Byang Kato, who was awarded SIM scholarships in the late 1960s and early 1970s, is told in Supplement 15.1, pages 194-195. Next, with the encouragement of Ian Hay who became general director in 1975, SIM was instrumental in establishing two accrediting agencies to help ensure high standards of seminary-level education. A synopsis of those stories appears in Supplement 15.2, pages 195-197. Last in terms of chronology, but certainly not least, was the formation of Evangel Fellowship in 1981. It brought the denominations that developed out of SIM together, and itself gave birth to the Evangel Fellowship Missions Association in 1996. A summary of how these were founded is provided in Supplement 15.3, pages 197-201.

SUPPLEMENT 15.1

Dr. Byang Kato

Photo 15.7. *Dr. Byang Kato, one of Africa's leading theologians*

Byang Kato became one of Africa's premier theologians before he tragically drowned in 1976. Born near Kwoi, Nigeria, in 1936, he was converted as a result of attending a Sunday School class in Kwoi where SIM had worked for several years. After passing seventh grade, he attended Igbaja Bible College and married Jummai in 1957 while he was still a student there. Upon graduating from the college he taught at Kwoi Bible Training School, Zabolo Bible School, and Igbaja Seminary; worked in the counseling department of Niger Challenge Press; and became general secretary of ECWA. Then, with the benefit of scholarships from SIM, he earned a bachelor of divinity degree at London Bible College, and master of sacred theology and doctor of theology degrees at Dallas Theological Seminary. At the time of his death, he was the general secretary of the Association of Evangelicals of Africa and Madagascar.[45]

One of Kato's most significant writings was his 1975 *Theological Pitfalls in Africa*. According to Cambridge University-trained Dr. Paul Bowers, Kato's *Pitfall*'s was significant because it was

a "maiden effort" in the theological activity of African evangelical Christianity. One may of course find earlier contributions from various African evangelicals, but as often as not these were addressed to the issues preoccupying western missionary forces within Africa. *Pitfalls* represents the first sustained effort by an African evangelical to engage in the theological issues being debated in Africa by African theologians.

Many think indeed that Kato's significant contribution to evangelical Christianity in Africa was his effort to awaken it to the necessity of becoming involved in the theological debate within Africa. He repeatedly charged African evangelicalism with "theological anemia," and energetically exploited his position as general secretary of the Association of Evangelicals of Africa and Madagascar to try to change the pattern. He travelled and wrote and spoke constantly in the interest of an accelerated development of evangelical theological involvement among all evangelicals in their studies and work. He dreamed up programmes to stimulate greater theological involvement among evangelicals, programmes which are still emerging. And he undertook himself an opening step in direct evangelical theological engagement in Africa with the publication of *Pitfalls*. *Pitfalls* thus represents a substantive personal contribution to Kato's larger initiative to rouse evangelical African Christianity toward greater theological responsibility and involvement. This summons and vision may well prove Kato's most abiding legacy to evangelical Christianity on the continent.[46]

SUPPLEMENT 15.2

Advancing Theological Education in Africa and Beyond

Before he died in 1975, General Secretary Byang Kato of the Association of Evangelicals of Africa and Madagascar (AEAM) committed his association to support evangelical schools on the continent and in Madagascar.[47] Larry Fehl, who was principal of ECWA Theological Seminary (ETS) in Igbaja, Nigeria, at the time, assigned one of his lecturers, Paul Bowers, to undertake such an initiative. Back in the USA, SIM General Director Ian Hay provided encouragement and mission funds to begin this project. Bowers started his work in 1976, with the end result being the formation of the Accrediting Council for Theological Education in Africa (ACTEA). ACTEA was formed to set standards to accredit evangelical post-secondary schools and provide accreditation when schools met those standards.

Dr. Paul Bowers has been one of the SIM missionaries who has most consistently championed high standards of evangelical seminary-level education around the world, and served as ACTEA's first coordinator. One of the first schools that ACTEA accredited was ETS. Fehl assigned George Foxall to work with Bowers in 1979, with Foxall becoming ACTEA's coordinating secretary. Dr. Tite Tiénou became ACTEA's chair two years later. He, Foxall, and Bowers worked together as a team until the early 1990s. Dr. Cornelius Olowola, who had since become principal of ETS, replaced Tiénou as chair. One of the

Photo 15.8. *Leadership of the Accrediting Council for Theological Education in Africa, Limuru, Kenya, 1990.*
Photo courtesy: Paul Bowers.
(L–R): Paul Bowers, Cornelius Olowola, Titus Kivunzi, Scott Moreau (back to camera), George Foxall, and Tite Tiénou. The photo was taken during ACTEA's All-Africa Conference of Theological Educators. Tiénou was ACTEA's chair and president of the Faculté de Théologie Evangélique de l'Alliance Chrétienne in Abidjan, Côte d'Ivoire. He later became dean of Trinity Evangelical Divinity School in the USA. Kivunzi was a deputy chair and former principal of Scott Theological College in Machakos, Kenya. He later became bishop of the African Inland Church in Kenya (related to the Africa Inland Mission). Olowola, also a deputy chair, was principal of ECWA Theological Seminary Igbaja, Nigeria. He later became president of the Evangelical Church of West Africa in Nigeria. Moreau was the conference director. He became, and still is, Professor of Intercultural Studies at Wheaton Graduate School and Editor of *Evangelical Mission Quarterly*. Foxall was ACTEA's administrator and Bowers his deputy. Both were, and continue to be, members of SIM.

people who worked closely with Tiénou was SIM missionary Dr. Scott Cunningham. Today, ACTEA's mission is to "promote quality evangelical education in Africa by providing support services, facilitating academic recognition, and fostering continental and intercontinental cooperation."

Not long after ACTEA was founded, the World Evangelical Alliance's Theological Commission sponsored an initiative to establish a network of evangelical theological schools on a global scale. Then in 1980, the International Council for Evangelical Theological Education (ICETE) was founded. Dr. Bowers helped found ICETE, and became its first general secretary. Nine regional associations like ACTEA now sponsor ICETE. Its purpose is to "enable international interaction and collaboration among all those concerned for the enhancement of evangelical theological education worldwide." ICETE is now the voice of evangelical theological education for the World Evangelical Alliance and the Lausanne Movement. Bowers has remained actively involved with ACTEA and ICETE since their inception.

Six years later, Bowers spearheaded the SIM Theological Initiative (SIMTIA) that General Director Hay initiated to "make theological ministries available to God's work wherever needed" throughout Africa. The mission established SIMTIA to respond to the late Dr. Byang Kato's warning that errant doctrines were weakening evangelical Christianity in Africa. SIMTIA helped publish books and a periodical that church leaders could use, assisted ACTEA and related ministries, and organized consultations for evangelical leaders.[48]

SUPPLEMENT 15.3

Evangel Fellowship and the Evangel Fellowship Missions Association

In 1981, SIM invited leaders from the denominations in Nigeria, Niger, Ethiopia, Upper Volta, Sudan, and Benin to attend the Pan-Africa Consultation in Miango, Nigeria. The denomination's leaders collectively represented over four thousand churches, 1.3 million members, and six hundred missionaries. At the conclusion of this consultation, the delegates formed Fraternité Evangélique or Evangel Fellowship. Its goal was "to provide SIM-related churches in Africa with a channel for mutual communications, communion, sharing of resources, and edification—to the glory of God and the fulfillment of the Great Commission of Jesus Christ."[50] The formation of Evangel Fellowship was sparked to a large extent by the embarrassment felt by leaders of the rapidly growing SIM-related

Photo 15.9. *"Pan-Africa Consultation—SIM-Related Churches," 19 June 1981.* Front row (L–R): John Cumbers (Ethiopia), Atchade Y. O. David (Benin), Ian Hay (SIM Intl.), M. Mamane Kouloungou (Niger), M. Ouboba Lamoudi (Upper Volta), David M. Olusiyi (Nigeria), David Hajor (Sudan), Ajuot Alony Akol (Sudan). Back row (L–R): Merle Dye (Sudan), Howard Brant (Ghana), Simon Ibrahim (Nigeria), Jean Klophenstein (Francophone), Gabriel Doko (Benin), Howard Dowdell (Liberia), M. Abba Moussa Moustapha (Niger), M. Madiega Bougandidio (Upper Volta), Larry Fehl (Nigeria), Harold Fuller (SIM Intl.). The Nigerian government did not grant visas to the Ethiopian church representatives to attend the consultation.[49]

denominations (particularly EKHC in Ethiopia and ECWA in Nigeria). They did not have a good answer to the question of who they were related to internationally. Their colleagues from other denominations, returning from global denominational conferences, were a constant reminder of this lack. This event marked a major turning point in helping SIM understand how important connectional relationships are to the long-term health and maturity of the churches being formed.

By 1993, 13 bodies representing eight thousand churches had joined together in this worldwide fellowship. In 2017 it consists of about two dozen national bodies representing tens of thousands of churches, several million members, and many more attendees.[51] Evangel Fellowship now comprises the denominations that are historically related to SIM in Africa, South America, and Asia.[52] These include:

- Africa Evangelical Church of Botswana (AEC-B)
- Africa Evangelical Church of Malawi (AEC-M)
- Africa Evangelical Church of South Africa (AEC-SA)
- Bible Church of Africa (BCA) (Ghana)
- Église Evangélique (EE-BF) (Burkina Faso)
- L'église Évangélique Indépendante du Togo (EEIT)
- Église Évangelique de la République du Niger (EERN)
- Église Évangélique Salama du Niger (EESN)
- Ethiopia Kale Heywet Church (EKHC)
- Evangelical Church of Liberia (ECOL)
- Evangelical Church of South Africa (ECSA)
- Evangelical Church Winning All (ECWA)
- Evangelical Church of Zambia (ECZ)
- Pakistan Christian Fellowship of Churches (PCFC)
- Sudan Interior Church (SIC)
- Unión Christiana Evangélica (UCE) (Bolivia)
- Union des Eglises Évangélique du Bénin (UEEB)
- Union des Église Évangéliques Protestants du Niger (UEEPN)
- União de Igiejas Evangelicas de Angola (Union of the Evangelical Church of Angola) (UIEA)
- United Baptist Church (UBC) (Zimbabwe)

As one reviews some of the reports coming out of the biennial meetings of Evangel Fellowship, it is impossible to miss the strong recurring theme of missions outreach and the need for the various national church bodies to do their part in carrying the gospel where it is not yet known. But other common concerns have always been discussed as well. A report on the December 1988 meeting by W. Harold Fuller, for example, provides a helpful glimpse into what these meetings are all about:[53]

The need for churches to reach out to the unevangelized was one of the major emphases which highlighted the meeting of Evangel Fellowship (EF) in Ethiopia last December. . . .

"If our churches aren't missionary minded, we leaders should blame ourselves," stated Panya Baba, President of Nigeria's Evangelical Churches of West Africa. "SIM's goal has always been to reach the unreached."

There were 22 delegates representing nine countries (Benin, Bolivia, Burkina Faso, Ethiopia, Ghana, Liberia, Niger, Nigeria, Sudan), plus Ian Hay and Harold Fuller from SIM's International offices. Josianne Waridel, Niger, translated for the French speakers, and Arden Steele, Bolivia, for the Spanish-speaking delegate. At times local Ethiopian church leaders attended as observers.

Fellowship was strengthened as delegates studied the Bible, led by Ian Hay, prayed, played games, and ate together.

There were times of humor—as when Ian Hay and Panya Baba sang a duet in Gbari. It was great to see these two men, both born in the same part of Nigeria, singing a duet. But the fun came when Ian introduced the song by speaking in Gbari, then turned and asked Panya, "Aren't you going to interpret?" Panya had been listening to Ian's introduction, without thinking that others couldn't understand it. The thought of Ian speaking in his language, and Panya interpreting into Ian's language suddenly struck him as funny. He stood there rocking with laughter, and we all joined in.

We also had songs in Arabic, French, English, Amharic, Twi, and Dinka. The latter was the most lively, as Dinka pastor Abraham clapped his hands and jigged to the rhythm of a chorus about Daniel in the lions' den.

There were also times of serious discussion, as the leaders from areas of persecution and tension shared with us. It was strengthening for them to realize they are not alone—others in the body of Christ also face problems. We can bear one another's burdens in prayer. After hearing a report from one country about Muslims, a delegate from another nation said, "Evangelize Muslims while you can. In our nation it is not legal to do so."

This was the first time Evangel Fellowship had met in Ethiopia. "This is an answer to prayer," said Dr. Mulatu Baffa, *Kale Hiywet* Church (KHC) General Secretary, who hosted the conference. "This is my first time to take part in a Fellowship conference, and I can see how useful EF is."

It was also the first time a delegate from South America had been able to attend. Gabriel Cruz of Bolivia's Evangelical Christian Union (UCE) joined with an Ethiopian elder to serve the communion elements in the closing session.

The need for a sense of identity came through in several sessions. Obviously, the heady days following national independence have passed, and most churches now value their relationship with SIM in a new way.

"Sometimes a government official asks who we are," one delegation said. "When we tell them we're related to SIM, they accept us."

Several delegates emphasized their desire for closer ties with SIM, and a committee will discuss ways in which the Mission and churches can relate more effectively.

"In a number of countries, we've arrived at the post-independence stage," Ian Hay commented afterward. "We must be sensitive to the churches' need to be identified with believers in other lands and around the world. Perhaps SIM can help provide that identity more widely than in the past."

. . . Participants testified how God had met them during the four days. "We've been encouraged by being here," Liberian William McGee said. "Jon Shea and I were very discouraged by some of the problems we've been facing in the churches. We felt like giving up. But our vision has been renewed, and we're going back to see what the Lord will do."

The 1992 Evangel Fellowship gathering exhibited increasing levels of cooperation between the national church bodies in a number of areas:[54]

During the conference, resolutions were passed for coordinating mission efforts, sharing educational resources, establishing associations for women and young people, and encouraging churches to establish their own style of worship within the framework of their language and culture.

In other action, Dr. Panya Baba, president of the Evangelical Church of West Africa (Nigeria), was appointed to spearhead the mobilization of the churches for missionary outreach. Dr. Yusufu Turaki, also of Nigeria, was appointed to analyze the urgent needs for theological training and Christian education among Evangel Fellowship churches.

The big event regarding cooperative missions efforts, however, came in 1996. Howard Brant describes the event, and with this we will close:[55]

SIM representatives and mission leaders from related church fellowships around the world met in Otford, England, the first week of February, 1996. Following a week of prayer and frank exchange of ideas, they unanimously recommended formation of an association for cross-cultural outreach. In a moving ceremony on the closing night, all of the delegates from twelve countries, followed by SIM's representatives, verbally expressed their commitment to the new mission vision and then added their signatures to the joint document.

. . . The proposed name for the new organization is Evangel Fellowship Missions Association. Its purpose is to stimulate and encourage the missionary initiatives of each of its members and to provide for better communication and coordination. . . . [When approved at the next EF regular meeting] SIM will have the opportunity to take its place as one of the thirteen founding missions in the association.

Evangel Fellowship Missions Association is not a new mission society, but rather an association of existing mission efforts which have been developing for several decades. It has grown out of the need for an organizational framework for voluntary cooperation.

CHAPTER 16

ISSUES OF RACE AND DIVERSITY

Dr. Tim Geysbeek

Note from the general author/editor: Issues of race are not something that missions in general, and evangelical faith missions in particular, have historically been particularly good at addressing head on. Many scholars would go on to point out that missions have a hard time even using the term "racism," when they do address such failings in their own history. While the scholars are no doubt right in pointing out this fact as they address the issue of "racism" academically, there is a reason that I would offer for this reluctance, and why "issues of race" is the term used often but not exclusively here. The reason is that "racism" as commonly used today implies not only serious failings in relating to those of other races, but also communicates malevolent intent, even hatred, which is a very hard case to make with regard to the missionary enterprise.

A difficulty that confronts one when attempting to discuss an issue as important as this, that has been neglected too long, is that there is too much background and lived history to address the subject even cursorily in a "short history" such as this. The attempt, while preliminary and incomplete, still needs to be made. It is our good fortune in this volume to draw on research done by Dr. Tim Geysbeek who served with SIM International for many years as its archivist, and is now its resident historian. What follows is developed from initial research he conducted a few years ago.

Introduction[1]

In 1946, Wilber Harr of the University of Chicago completed his Ph.D. dissertation titled "The Negro as an American Protestant Missionary in Africa."[2] Harr sent a questionnaire to SIM as part of his research, and these are some of the answers SIM Canadian Secretary Graham Hay provided:

Q: Do you have a policy relating to the sending of American-born Negroes to your field?

A: It has not been our custom to send such.

Q: If a promising Negro candidate from your own or from another denomination volunteered for service in Africa, what would be the attitude of your office?

A: I cannot answer this.

Q: Is indigeneity a goal of your mission?

A: Yes.

Q: Has your mission ordained Africans?

A: I am not sure.

Q: What standards of preparation are you expecting of African candidates for orientation?

A: It is an open question.

Q: To what extent do Africans participate in the formulation of your mission policy?

A: Very little.

Hay's view of SIM's work in the mid-1940s was essentially correct. SIM, however, started to change within a decade: its missionaries in West Africa would admit to "race discrimination," ordain its first African pastors, and create a semiautonomous African denomination. SIM's top policy-making body would be on the verge of permitting persons of African heritage to become members. Six decades later, the mission would state that one of its "core values" was to be "Strengthened Through Diversity." Yet racism, that is evil, divisive, and dehumanizing, continues in some places, in part, because of an institutional amnesia that denies today's missionaries' the historical background needed to learn from the past, to put present-day attitudes and behavior into perspective.

I argue that race, in addition to class, ethnicity, gender, nationality, education, theological orientation, personality, and other factors affected missionaries' ideas and behavior. Race influenced the mission's architecture, aesthetics, education, evangelism, fund-raising, gender roles, labor practices, language policies, leadership choices, medical work, politics, promotional work, recreation, recruitment, residential patterns, social life, definition of family, relations with churches, and writing of history. Harr's study exposed the underlying impact race had on SIM's identity, constituency, relation to churches, and policies. He demonstrated that race was one of the most dominating elements up to that time in SIM's history. In this chapter I identify overall shifts in many missionaries' attitudes about race since the mission was founded, and examine how notions of race affected just one aspect of the mission's practice—membership. In doing so, I overview how race has slowly gone from marking difference and separation to being a factor that SIM officially celebrates.

Discussions of race and racism are often difficult. They can create tension and are thus easy to avoid. An immediate problem is how to define these emotionally charged words. Their definitions are ambiguous and arbitrary, and vary according to person, situation, culture, time, and place. Rice University and University of North Carolina–Chapel Hill sociologists Michael Emerson and Christian Smith use the following definition of racism that seems flexible enough to account for most of its different forms around the world and changes over time: "Racism is not mere individual, overt prejudice or the free-floating irrational driver of race problems, but the collective misuse of power that results in diminished life opportunities for some racial groups."[3]

Up through the early 1980s, nearly all SIM missionaries were white. More particularly, the clear majority were Anglo–North Americans from the United States and Canada. Most of the others came from Britain and its settlement colonies of Australia, New Zealand, and South Africa.[4] Correspondingly, for most of the twentieth century, most SIM missionaries used race as a central way to categorize people, often using physical characteristics—primarily colour—as the most important criteria. (When terms such as "race," "white" or "black" are used in this chapter, whether or not in quotes, they are used in ways people socially construct them, not as "objective descriptors of physical or 'racial' difference.")[5] Most discrimination was directed by white missionaries against darker-skinned persons since SIM mainly worked in Africa. Given that SIM primarily worked with black Africans for most of its history, most of this chapter focuses on white people, Africans, and the descendants of Africans. The last section examines how SIM started to become less North American and white in the mid-1980s as it slowly began to become more diverse and move into South America and Asia. Unfortunately, it is beyond the scope of this chapter to deal with the mission's issues of race in South America and Asia where the racial environments and histories are different from Africa, although the human issues are still the same.

Due to the lack of time and space, this chapter only provides a mission-centric, top-down discussion of race as evidenced in SIM International's archives, and privileges the views of missionaries, especially its leaders. It also does little to appreciate the ideas and actions of individual missionaries and the views of people to whom they went.[6] Nonetheless, the author hopes that this chapter offers a preliminary explanation of how attitudes and policies broadly changed over time. (SIM's and AEF's engagement with racism in southern Africa is treated in Supplements 16.1 and 16.2, pages 229-239.) To decolonize this discussion, to make it more authentic, relevant, and nuanced, it would be essential to hear the unfiltered voices of the missionaries' African, Asian, North American, and South American neighbors who were often the "objects" of missionary discrimination.

The chapter is divided into four periods that mark overall shifts in the history of race in SIM. While dates are ascribed for each period based on key events, all but the first date are in a sense arbitrary. None of the events that signify the transition from one period to the next occurred without significant underlying changes having first been made. Within each period, some missionaries exhibited a profound closeness with their neighbors or showed disdain that marked them decades ahead or behind most others in their thinking.

1893—1917: Years of Measured Equality[7]
Introduction
Walter Gowans, Tom Kent, and Rowland Bingham traveled to Nigeria in 1893 only a few years after European countries started to conquer Africa. The British had just asserted their authority 150 miles inland from Lagos, where they landed, and would not finish

conquering what is now Nigeria for 11 years.[8] Racial differences were not as pronounced in Gowans', Kent's, and Bingham's writings of the 1890s as they were in the publications of Bingham and some of SIM's missionaries of the first half of the twentieth century. They seem to have, like most Westerners until the mid-nineteenth century, categorized people more on the basis of class and religion than race. By the late-nineteenth century, egalitarian ideas were on the decline in the church and eliminated in politics because race became so prominent. This was due to the influence of scientific racism and social Darwinism which postulated that white people were morally and intellectually superior to everyone else.[9]

Attitudes

Social Darwinists believed that the key difference between races was biological and that races evolved separately. They believed differences were inherent and therefore permanent, so people could not move beyond the boundaries prescribed by the biology of each race. Skin color and other physical characteristics were the key to understanding peoples' history, civilization, and culture.[10]

Most white evangelical Christians in North America and the British Empire believed God created human beings spiritually equal given that God created all people in his image. In the hierarchy of social, cultural, and political order, however, most of them felt they were superior because of their long association with Christianity. Differences primarily had to do with religion, environment, and social organization, not biology. Even those they considered the "lowest" could eventually rise to the level of white people if they converted and, in the process of changing, also became more "civilized" as they adopted trappings of Western language, food, clothes, and customs.[11] Racism became entrenched as missions became more professionalized due to the need to staff institutions with well-trained people. White missionaries, who filled most senior positions, were at the top of racial hierarchies due to education and experience. Many also felt they were intrinsically superior to, and more advanced than, Africans.[12]

Part of a letter Australian missionary Effie Varley wrote about an encounter she had with a British official in Nigeria in the 1920s reveals how missionaries' "soft" racism differed markedly from that of overt racists.[13] In a letter describing her work among the Irigwe who live on the Jos plateau, she wrote:

> The District Officer had tea with us on Monday evening. He was quite pleasant, but spoke about these pagans being more like animals than humans. He doesn't know some of our church friends, or he shouldn't talk like that. I'm sure they mean as much to us as many of our friends at home. It rubs me the wrong way to hear it said they are more like animals than human beings. All the praise must go to God for our love to them for it is, I believe, the love of God shed abroad in our hearts.[14]

Photo 16.1. *A British official and Africans in southern Nigeria.*

Photo credit: likely Tommy Titcombe.

In addition to having degrading views of some ethnic groups, most British authorities in early colonial Nigeria felt most missionaries were "'an embarrassment to the white race'" because missionaries ignored the "fundamental laws of race difference," considered themselves to be "tribunes of the oppressed," lacked social graces, and despaired about being forced to live separately from Africans.[15] Varley wrote that the Irigwe were "a proud, independent, warlike race," "a negro tribe, primitive, living very close to nature," yet mentioned local methods of architecture, dress, agriculture, and pottery making which indicated her appreciation for their culture.[16] If, as the late church historian Adrian Hastings wrote, one can at times judge an organization based on "the finest it can produce" as long as what was written symbolizes a "wider achievement," Varley may represent many of SIM's missionaries who worked in Africa during the first half of the twentieth century.[17]

In the writings of SIM's co-founders who went to Nigeria in 1893, the language of race is present but not central. Gowans' and his mother's descriptions of the Sudanese ("black people") who lived in spiritual "darkness," or the trio's reference to the "dark Sudan" in their "little Sudan battle song," are examples.[18] Dark (or black) in this context was the antithesis of white or light and represented spiritual blindness, the lack of morals, superstition, evil practices, and inferiority.[19] Gowans' claim that the Sudan was "Satan's stronghold" lent itself to a popular theory of the time, which had racist underpinnings, that divided the world into "Christendom" and "heathendom."[20]

Gowans either called Africans by their names or positions, or used ethnic labels or words like "enemy" (Muslims), "natives," "souls," or "heathens" for groups. He referred to Africans on one occasion as having "dusky faces."[21] Anglo–North American Christians of the time commonly used "heathen" to describe people of any race who they thought were ignorant of God, poor and utterly immoral, and engaged in awful practices.[22] Gowans called their Liberian employee "Thomas." Bingham identified people similarly, but called Thomas "our colored boy" or Gowans' "faithful Kroo boy." ("Thomas" wrote his name "Tom Coffee.")[23]

After Gowans and Kent departed for the interior in 1894, they decided to establish a business. Essential to their planning was Tom Coffee. Coffee was a Western-educated Christian of the Kru ethnic group from Liberia who they envisioned would facilitate the trade of cattle and palm products between Lagos and his hometown of Sasstown to sustain their work. Gowans, who was helped by Coffee during his travels in innumerable ways, wrote that Coffee had been "very faithful" to him. Gowans, on the other hand, developed strained relations with his Nigerian porters who delayed his trip and caused him great anxiety by wanting to earn more money or barter goods than what he was prepared to pay.[24] While economics and cultural tensions rather than race seem to have been the source of this friction, Coffee's Western education, religion (Christianity), and adoption of Western clothes cannot but have helped endear him to Gowans. That Gowans was willing to grant significant responsibility to Coffee is indicative of the capacity he felt Africans had—if even from a limited framework—if they were faithful Christians whom he felt had become partly civilized.

Membership

SIM's co-founders' sense of some practical equality with people who were not white is reflected in the fact that SIM considered allowing persons of African heritage to become members during its early years. In doing so, SIM was following the practice of some white-dominated North American and European missions.[25] The Christian and Missionary Alliance, Sudan United Mission (SUM), and Southern Baptist Foreign Mission Board, for instance, recruited well-educated persons of African descent whom they felt could communicate the gospel well with their African kin and help them become good "civilizing leaven" as craft persons, educators, and evangelists. Western missionaries and colonial administrators also believed people of African heritage were more immune to "fever" than whites, who experienced high death rates in the tropics, and could, therefore, augment their staffing needs.[26]

In 1904, a "colored couple" named Mr. and Mrs. J. Ulysis Turner from Chicago applied for membership. While the Turners were not able to travel to the mission's office in Toronto to be interviewed because Mr. Turner held a "good position" that prohibited them from traveling at a designated time, the council stated it would consider the Turner's application "when the circumstances seem more propitious." The situation never became favourable for the Turners to be interviewed because of Turner's work, not SIM's disinterest, so they never became members.[27]

After SIM merged with SUM in 1906, a Jamaican, Joseph W. Baker, joined SUM and went to Nigeria where he served from 1907 to 1909.[28]

Photo 16.2. *Joseph W. Baker, a Jamaican who joined SUM in 1907.*

Photo credit: "Bound for Africa," The Missionary Witness 2, no. 10 (23 October 1906): 156.

Bingham, who became SUM's director of North America after the merger, published a short write-up of him in *The Missionary Witness* that he edited.[29]

In March 1907, Bingham told SUM's Canadian Council about two trips he made to the historically black Lincoln University in Pennsylvania.[30] On one trip he interviewed an "American negro" who had applied for membership. The council instructed Bingham to "write the authorities at Lincoln expressing the sympathy of this Board with the proposal to utilize the Afro-American in Nigeria and assure them that any application will receive careful consideration."[31] While SIM never claimed Baker as one of its missionaries, Bingham's involvement in publicizing Baker's departure for Nigeria and visits to Lincoln University were in keeping with the earlier attempt he and SIM's Toronto council had made to recruit the Turners.

1918—1947: The High Tide of "Race Discrimination"
Introduction
In 1907, Bingham and his original board that had joined SUM's Canadian Council broke away from SUM and reestablished themselves as the Sudan Interior Mission. From that time until the mid-1950s, there is no evidence that SIM considered accepting people who they did not think were "white."[32] Widespread prejudice of white English-speakers against Asians, Catholics, Jews, people who were not white, whites who did not speak English, and others existed in one or more countries where SIM's missionaries originated.[33] In the United States, whose council and missionaries had gained considerable influence in the mission by midcentury, black Americans had become subject to lynching and other forms of violence. "Jim Crow" laws separated them from white people in public spaces particularly in the south, and states used measures such as poll taxes to deprive black people the opportunity to vote.[34] Whether out of conviction or fear of what their home-based constituencies might think, most SIM missionaries were imbibed with enough of the era's prevailing prejudice to preclude them from thinking about accepting individuals from these minorities who became evangelical Protestants. The exceptions were white non-English speakers and individuals who they singled out as being Jewish.[35]

Attitudes
Social Darwinist thinking powerfully influenced Protestant missionaries from the late nineteenth century to the mid-1930s.[36] According to Professor Yusufu Turaki of Jos ECWA Theological Seminary:[37]

> Racial theories have had profound influence on both colonialists and missionaries. . . . It is not necessary to ask whether a European missionary in Africa ever felt that he had "a superior superiority" over the African to whom he ministered. In Africa, enormous barriers existed "between Europeans and Africans in terms of color, habit, industrial achievement and social organization, as well as religion."

These social facts tended, however, to give a European missionary a feeling of "superiority." Although a missionary draws his missionary ideals from the principles of the Gospel of Christ, he might, nonetheless, have been profoundly influenced by the socio-political values of his society.[38]

SIM missionaries were not immune from developing superiority complexes. Evident in some of their writing is a propensity to use racialized language, cast races in evolutionary scales, and the making of defamatory statements about Africans in ways that were not common in Gowans' and Bingham's writings of the 1890s.

Some of SIM's most educated and influential missionaries ranked civilizations and races in hierarchies during the interwar period. Anglo–North Americans based their rankings on the complexity or lack thereof of a group's religion, political system, social organization, material advancement, language, writing systems, association with people from higher races, sense of civility, and other factors.[39]

Bingham's consistent reference to Tom Coffee as being "black" in his later writings, rather than being "colored" or Gowans' employee as in his earlier writings, is one example of how his ideas became racialized over time.[40] Bingham classified races in descending order from "white" people, to "yellow" Asians, and finally to "negroes" or Africans and their descendants. Asians, he wrote, were quickly becoming equal to whites. He believed, or was at least sympathetic to, the idea that black people were "the sons of Ham."[41] According to the popular fiction of the time, when God cursed Ham, he made his descendants dark-skinned and second-class people (or worse, nonhumans) who were subject to slavery and other forms of oppression by those who were lighter skinned than themselves. This "Hamitic myth," that provided a religious justification for thinking some people were superior to others, developed from a misreading of Genesis 9 where God cursed Canaan because his father, Ham, saw his (Ham's) father Noah naked.[42] Nonetheless, Bingham believed black people could become equal with whites. Asians and Africans, he wrote, had established renowned civilizations in the past and were capable of achieving the same again. Bingham felt the grace that "colored men" exhibited in their religion eclipsed that of white people, and noted that Africans or their descendants who had become bishops, military leaders, lawyers, doctors, and merchants demonstrated that they could someday become equal with whites.[43]

Within Nigeria, some SIM missionaries—like many British officials and European travelers—ranked Africans into three or four groups.[44] Bingham placed the Hausa at the top because he considered them to be "the most enterprising" and "strongest race of the Sudan."[45] He went on to rank the Yagba-Yoruba and Gbagyi after the Hausa, then the Jaba, Irigwe, Rukuba, and Tangale, and finally lepers.[46] Andrew Stirrett wrote that the Fulani were "always so friendly with the white men. They always recognize in him somebody nearer to themselves than the ordinary native." Yet the British race, "whiter than they," conquered them.[47]

John Hall, one of SIM's pioneer missionaries to the Tangale in Nigeria, used a "scale of civilization" to categorize people. He wrote that one of the "superior races"—meaning the Fulani—forced Islam and hence a degree of civilization on one of the country's largest ethnic groups—referring to the Hausa.[48] According to Hall, one "tribe" had not even risen to the lowest rung of civilization because they were lazy, carnal, superstitious, not intelligent, and illiterate, and because they had been dragged down even lower by white men's vices. Reflecting Social Darwinist thought that only the fittest survive, he said they would become extinct if Christianity and "the superior white" did not shield them. Hall distanced himself from blatant racists such as the district officer referenced above who compared some Africans to animals by recognizing that "if these folks are pagan they are also human. How like us after all they are in many essentials."[49] Yes, they were human, but not in all essentials, in all its complexities, nor as fully human as white people or lighter-skinned "civilized" Africans.

Hall and his contemporaries' belief that their white race and culture was superior did not likely seem offensive or unusual to most white Anglo–North American evangelicals of the time. The times, in the white milieu from which most of SIM's missionaries originated, blinded them to their discrimination and to the fact that they were as flawed as everyone else.[50]

Colonial administrators and the mission's intellegencia were probably more likely than most field missionaries to rank people in such carefully constructed hierarchies. Even so, many missionaries contrasted black and white, the colours that represented what many felt were the opposite ends of the scale of civilization, in their stories, drawings, maps, illustrations, and photographs. In doing so, they often used colours or imagery to mark or imply moral or racial superiority and inferiority. Examples are illustrations of white men picking sheaves with the caption of "White Unto Harvest," the juxtaposing of scantily clothed or masked sinners in photographs with dressed converts sometimes holding Bibles, or the contrasting of neatly clad missionaries with negatively stereotyped images of Africans.[51]

Turaki writes, based on his extensive reading of sources in the SIM International Archives and Records, that SIM's missionaries generally had negative views of African culture, introduced Western values in their teaching, presented Africans as backward to raise funds for the mission without according the love and respect due all human beings, believed Western achievements were a blessing of Christianity, and held that Christianity and Western civilization could cure Africa's medical and social ills that were intrinsic to the continent's people.[52] The idea that some Africans were cursed or innately more degenerate than white people was evidenced by one leader who instructed his missionaries to tell their African employees not to teach their "white child[ren] anything about sex" because Africans were immoral; "their pagan minds are corrupted from infancy."[53] Some missionaries felt they were so much better than Africans that they could strike them with, seemingly, no thought of reprisal.[54]

Photo 16.3. *SIM calendar, April 1954*

Some missionaries struggled with the inconsistency that existed between racial hierarchy and equality, although evidence for this in the pre–World War II period in the material thus far examined is slim. One example, seen when reading between the lines, comes from an article that SIM published in its flagship magazine the *Sudan Witness* in 1925. The author, Albert Bailey of the South Africa General Mission, wrote that new missionaries who developed high regard for the potential of African converts should expect them to backslide because the "untruthfulness, dishonesty, and impurity that inhere in the character of the native Christian" would eventually surface. Their sure backsliding, Bailey believed, was due to the "millenniums" that they spent in the "black abyss of heathenism."[55]

Membership

By the end of World War I if not a few years earlier, SIM established a *de facto* policy of only accepting white people as members. Most white-dominated missions began to discourage the acceptance of persons of colour by the 1910s. The Christian and

Missionary Alliance, which did more than most white Protestant missions to use black American missionaries, decided by 1930 to accept only whites.[56]

According to University of London emeritus historian David Killingray:

> Christian missionaries and their supporters were no more immune than other sections of the white population from the current ideas of scientific racism. Predictably, the more rigid racial lines drawn by American white agencies reflected the discriminatory social divisions of the U.S. White colonialism with its overt racial agenda steadily determined that African Americans were unsuitable for missionary work.[57]

White missions also stopped recruiting African-Americans because they could more easily draw from the white American population given that medical advances dramatically reduced the risk of death. In the late 1890s, scientists discovered quinine could prevent and cure malaria, hence markedly lengthening the life-spans of people who lived in the tropics if used.[58] In acting on these discoveries and moderating his earlier view of divine healing, Bingham started to encourage SIM's missionaries to take quinine and other medicines in 1901. Only one missionary died of malaria in Nigeria in the next four decades.[59]

At the end of World War I, Bingham published an open letter to the United States government that provides additional evidence of his evolving racialized thinking. He urged the government to become the "protectorate" of Germany's former colonies. The United States government, that he said "has a colored problem," should encourage large numbers of the "best" of its "colored population" to "return to the land of their fathers" to help Africans develop their resources and educate "the less fortunate people of their race." Bingham implied that the migration of black Americans to Africa would help solve the United States' "colored problem."[60] He did not suggest the problem was white—of white superiority or supremacy[61]—or try to recruit the best African-Americans to engage in the transformative work of missions as he had done a dozen years earlier. It was at this same time that Pan-Africanists like Marcus Garvey were advocating that the descendants of Africans should return to Africa because he felt they had no hope of being justly treated in the United States.[62]

1948—1965: SIM's "Principle" and "Practice" of Discrimination Challenged

Introduction

The years 1948–1965 mark an important transitional period when SIM mission leaders began to recognize that at least some missionaries were discriminating against Africans. Nigerian Christians who resented missionaries' discriminatory attitudes, actions, and policies confronted SIM's leaders and demanded church autonomy. Their outspokenness reflected the sentiments of African nationalists who wanted to gain independence from their colonial masters who had sought to control the lives of Africans for decades.[63] SIM and church leaders in Nigeria eventually established the semiautonomous Association of the Evangelical Churches of West Africa (ECWA) in 1954 that officially became independent two decades later.[64] The formation of ECWA, State University of New York–Stony Brook historian Shobana Shankar notes, "helped foster a more equal relationship between black and white Christians."[65] The mission allowed African-Americans to become members in the late 1950s due to rising pressure from the civil rights movement in the United States that challenged racial injustice. SIM did not recognize its abhorrant sin of racism in response to new revelatory readings of the Bible. Rather, "the mighty wind of change," to use the title of a celebrated speech British Prime Minister Harold Macmillan gave in South Africa in 1960, that blew in the forces of African nationalism, and also the civil rights movement, and grass-roots missionaries' questions that challenged its all-white policy, forced SIM's leaders to reexamine its "principle" and "practice" of white superiority and discrimination.

During this period, SIM accepted a trickle of people who most of its missionaries did not think were "white." Attitudes of racial supremacy stubbornly persisted among some missionaries well into the 1990s and beyond. Africans, persons of color, and liberal white Christians were more sensitive to issues of racial injustice.[66] Fortunately, enough missionaries who went to Africa after World War II had more informed ideas about race and hence had more progressive attitudes about Africans than many of their predecessors.[67] In addition, by midcentury, most social scientists had determined race was fiction, that there was no scientific basis to the idea of biological racism. Race is a social construct.[68]

Attitudes

The first governing body in SIM that officially challenged racism was the West Africa Field Council. The council, based in Jos, Nigeria, had responsibility for overseeing the mission's work in Nigeria, Dahomey (Benin), Haute Volta (Upper Volta), and Niger where about three-quarters of SIM's roughly five hundred missionaries worked.[69] In 1948, the council officially acknowledged that some of its members were guilty of "race discrimination."[70] The council's statement reads:

RACE DISCRIMINATION: In view of the surge of nationalism now sweeping this country the question of race distinction was discussed by the Council. It was agreed that we use the utmost care in the attitude we show toward all Africans. English and French-speaking Africans are particularly sensitive to any evidence of superiority on the part of Europeans, but it is also advisable not to evince anything in the nature of a "High Hat" attitude toward any of the people of this land. They are usually extremely polite. We should be at least equally polite. It is not Christ-like nor Scriptural to assume a superior attitude toward any individual or race, and, although some have asserted to the contrary, this never, in any real way, advances our position or work for God. We should meet and treat all African clerks and all Africans in authority as equals. This does not mean undue familiarity, but it does mean courtesy, a quality valued very highly by all easterners, including Africans. This class is particularly sensitive to any show of superiority, or of condescension on our part. Of all people, missionaries should be careful not to offend in these things. We must rid our minds and hearts of all superiority complex, for if it is there it will show itself in looks, words and conducts, and offend when we are unconscious of it. The following quotation is from an African's letter received by a member of the Council during the time of the Council meeting:

> Some missionaries at times fail to understand that people nowadays do not seriously listen to their preachings but have a very close watch on their behaviours, and with what spirit they impart the Gospel to us. Some discriminate, forgetting that there is "no discrimination in Christ." We should studiously avoid the words "natives," and "blacks" or "black people," using instead the words "'Africans," "Hausas," "Yorubas," and "the people of this land," etc.

This acknowledgement and denunciation of racism occurred one year after Nigeria established its first constitution that marked its initial move toward independence.[71] Though SIM's statement evidenced classism, elitism, and aloofness, it provides a glimpse into the frustration and anger of many Africans, and marked SIM's first official step toward recognizing Africans as equals.

In polished magazines that SIM published for the public to read, however, the mission was never as forthright. Being that the mission mostly used its magazines, films, filmstrips, slide presentations, brochures, and news releases to recruit, raise money, solicit prayer, and craft a positive image of itself, its writers only used euphemisms like "colonial mentality" and "superiority." (One would be hard-pressed to find any direct acknowledgement of "racism," "race discrimination," or an equivalent term, by any individual or office, in media that SIM has ever produced for the public.) The mission's most important concerns at midcentury were the external threats of communism, Islam, modernism, cults, secularism, and nationalism, not racism.[72]

SIM's leaders in West Africa periodically warned its missionaries to guard against feelings of superiority and discriminatory behavior for the next quarter century. In 1952 for instance, three years after the mission established the African Missionary Society to begin replacing SIM missionaries in cross-cultural evangelism and church work, the society's missionaries informed the council about the offensive behavior of SIM's missionaries working with them.[73] According to the West Africa Field Council, the African missionaries "complain[ed] of the lack of real fellowship with their missionary co-workers, lack of love and sympathy, and ruling with force." They gave "example after example of the domineering attitude of the missionary toward pastors, evangelists, and teachers." Giving orders without African input, taking the advice of domestic employees rather than pastors or evangelists, and making society members wait to see missionaries when summoned until missionaries finished their meals were examples.

The council condemned these missionaries' "superior attitude" and "racial discrimination." The council noted that while there are two sides to every story and "the African workers are not without fault," SIM's missionaries often fail to show true love. "We work hard <u>for</u> them and have so little time to spend with them."

Some missionaries sympathized with their African friends. One man, for instance, wrote in about 1953: "My wife and I have been deeply hurt in our hearts by the attitude of many of our S.I.M. missionaries toward the Africans, an attitude combining impatience, condescension, a little cynicism," and "belittling and much suspicion of them."[74]

In 1959, Gerald Swank, who had lived for many years in Nigeria, presented an insightful paper to missionaries from two districts that met for a conference in Miango. "Colonialism," he wrote, where "white people were regarded with awe" and "black people felt themselves inferior to the white," was being quickly swept away by "this New Africa, politically, educationally, socially and religiously." One agenda item was driven by a series of articles in the press that accused SIM of "discrimination." The articles "brought out some very humiliating examples, and also some helpful suggestions emphasizing that it would be much better if we would serve 'with' the Nationals rather than 'over' them." Swank restated African claims that the missionaries were proud, that they felt their cultures were better, and that they considered themselves to be superior, and more intelligent and flexible than Africans. Swank urged his fellow missionaries to treat Africans as equals, take their advice, deal with them more honestly, not treat them paternalistically, be more intentional in preparing Africans to take their jobs, and exhibit more humility, grace, and love.[75] According to Turaki, "SIM made tremendous efforts to ensure her good relationship with the African Church" beginning in the early 1960s, but that "policies and missionary attitudes had a long way to go in pleasing Africans."[76]

The extant minutes of the East Africa Council rarely mention missionaries' relations with Africans, let alone struggle with race prejudice in the manner that one finds in the minutes of the parallel council in West Africa. Even so, there is evidence that some SIM missionaries in East Africa discriminated on the basis of race and class.

Girma Bekele, for instance, uses his personal knowledge of Ethiopia and some examples SIM missionaries have published to argue that the "legacy of SIM in Ethiopia" was characterized by power rather than mission.[77] He cites elitist-minded missionaries living in "ghettoes" who were separated from Ethiopians by language and culture. Some missionaries, working from self-assumed positions of superiority and privilege, expected Ethiopians to call them *Getoch* or "master"; this term harked back to feudal times when serfs and commoners

Photo: 16.4. *Ethiopia cartoon.*

Photo credit: Ethiopia Contact *(August 1973)*

called their "lordly oppressors" *Getoch.* Such a perspective lent itself to paternalism, with some missionaries, Bekele writes, doing things "*for* them, rather than *with* them."

The substance of some of the internal discussions SIM's missionaries were having about improving their relationships with Africans appeared in tempered ways in SIM's *Africa Now* which overlapped with, and eventually replaced, the *Sudan Witness.* W. Harold Fuller began editing and publishing *Africa Now* in 1958 only months after Dr. Albert Helser (1957–1962) became general director. The magazine began at the height of the independence movement as colonial powers and foreign missions were repositioning themselves to be in the best place possible before colonies and churches became independent. British businessman and later SIM associate missionary A. T. de B. Wilmont, who wrote the first article in the first issue, explained that Africans did not want to be controlled by the "dominating foreign race." Missionaries, he said, should view all people as being equal in the manner of Christ and Paul, identify with local churches, and work to provide high education for its leaders.[78] Fuller acknowledged that expatriate missionaries had "never really understood Africa" and did not know what to expect from nationalists who were freeing the continent of "white control." Missionaries had "often worked under the protection of colonial powers and at times unconsciously depended on this position;" many continued to be imperialistic in their thinking, causing them to perceive themselves as being "superior people assisting their inferior peoples." To correct this situation, he urged missionaries to reexamine their "principles and practices," discard their "white master" attitudes, and encourage the growth of biblically-based local churches that would work out their own roles in the new Africa that was evolving.[79] Douglas Blunt explained that there was no place in the missionaries' vocabulary for words like "native," "nigger," "black man," and possibly "national" that reflected white peoples' deeply entrenched sense of "superiority."[80]

Ray Davis (1962–1975), who succeeded Helser as general director, sought to reform SIM's colonialist culture. Davis acknowledged, in an internal report in 1965, the mission's complicity in working with colonial governments. "Very often," he explained, missionaries and "the mission organization were given certain privileges by the government and of necessity a certain amount of respect" by the Africans who lived there. Because of missionaries' association with, and confidence in, colonial governments, those powers protected them and tended to prioritize their requests.[81]

During Davis' tenure, SIM gave Africans a few opportunities to express their opinions about expatriate missionaries in *Africa Now*. In doing so, SIM educated the magazine's readers — primarily its missionaries and the mission's most ardent followers — about the pernicious effects of racial superiority and segregation. While F. I. D. Konotey-Ahulu absolved missionaries of any complicity in European imperialism saying such arguments were Satanic in origin, the others offered criticism and suggestions for reform. Ato Abbeba Retta, Haruna Dandura, Moses Adekoyejo Majekodunmi, Aston S. King, Rae Gourlay, O. O. Sofunde, Paul Thahal, Emmanuel Urhobo, G. A. Ademola, Samuel Abogunrin, Grace Kuboye, Handon Maigida, David Olatayo, and Yohanna Gamba collectively used words such as "conceit," "prejudice," and "superiority" to describe missionaries' attitudes.[82] Francis Ibiam, the governor of Eastern Nigeria, said, "It is wrong for a missionary to play big and assume an air of superiority just because the colour of his skin happens to be different from that of the people amongst whom he works. We Africans note and resent such carrying on."[83] Such attitudes, they observed, led missionaries to portray Africans negatively in stories they told, retain control of institutions as long as possible, treat Africans as servants, and make "sweeping" generalizations about them.

To resolve these problems, many of the writers called on missionaries to love Africans as human beings, as equals, regardless of race or class. As Ibiam noted: "It is very essential that he *love* the *people* to whom he is sent . . . . The missionary must be prepared to work alongside the local people on equal terms . . . and mix freely with people." Missionaries could show their love by being more tolerant and respectful of Africans, learning local languages, working with Africans on equal terms, training and mentoring Africans with a view toward turning their work over to them, identifying with Africans, mixing with Africans in social settings, living among Africans, and working for God's glory rather than the advancement of their own careers.[84] One author identified Tommie Titcombe, who pioneered SIM's work in Egbe, Nigeria, as being a missionary who developed close relationships with Africans.[85]

Membership

SIM, like other faith missions, started to remove racial restrictions from membership in the mid-1950s.[86] SIM's missionaries originated from countries where deep social and racial divisions existed.[87] The drive for change came from the United States that was the source of most of the mission's income and members. In 1957, for instance, 71.6 percent of the mission's revenue and 56.7 percent (732 of the total 1,275) missionaries originated from the United States.[88] Missionaries from the United States were compelled to lead SIM toward greater racial equanimity due to pressure that came from the civil rights movement. Not only were the members of SIM's councils and their constituents in the United States living through changing times, Africans were asking American missionaries challenging questions about the civil rights movement and the brutal way white people were treating black Americans.[89]

In 1949, SIM established an International Council comprised of the general director and directors of West Africa, East Africa, Britain, Australasia, and North America. The council's task was to help the general director manage and connect the mission's work in western and eastern Africa.[90] That same year, West Africa Field Director C. Gordon Beacham asked SIM's home secretarial staff in Toronto not to accept persons of colour given SIM's policy to establish churches that were financially independent. If, he explained, "colored people from America" went as financially supported missionaries, African church workers would ask the mission to pay them as well.[91] In 1952, Toronto's staff passed a resolution based on Beacham's recommendation stating the Canadian office should, "for the present at least, . . .not consider coloured people as candidates." The reason was "not with any thought of racial prejudice," but "to safeguard the principle of self-support of the native church in Africa."[92] While Toronto's council did not have authority over SIM's other councils, the fact that the meeting was chaired by North America Director M. A. Darroch who had oversight of the councils in Toronto and New York made their decision noteworthy.

International Council's records for 1954–1955[93] include an extraordinary exchange of letters that discuss whether SIM should accept "nationals of one type or another" who were not "Americans and Europeans"—people who were not white.[94] Their deliberations reveal how some council members began to question their own views, and challenged the mission's racial hierarchy and understanding of what SIM should become. The council members from the United States were the most sensitive to issues of race. The civil rights movement had culminated, by that time, in the Supreme Court's landmark May 1954 decision which declared that segregating public schools by race was unconstitutional.[95] That October, Darroch told Playfair that an Arab couple had applied for membership, and that John Herr, who was in Hawaii with his wife, Beulah, had asked if SIM would accept "Oriental families."[96] United States Secretary Jack Percy said the council should "take extreme care" in whatever decision they made about this "ticklish" matter.[97] Playfair wrote, concerning the acceptance of "Orientals," that "up to the present time this has not been looked upon with favor."[98] No Asians applied, temporarily putting an end to the Asian question.

United Kingdom representative G. Richie Rice wrote that if SIM accepted "Arabs," in this case a Jordanian pharmacist and his wife in the United States who had applied for membership, "this opening of 'a chink in the door' might be followed by 'a push' from colored folk from South Africa or America." Yet, he added, the mission should not fear "if this Arab pair are clearly called by the Lord for the work."[99]

Percy noted that several missions were "now accepting nationals trained in America." One example he gave was the South Africa General Mission that accepted a Southern Rhodesian who had attended Moody Bible Institute and married an "American colored woman." (These were H. Stephen and Priscilla Sitole discussed in Supplement 16.2, pages 233-235.) Trying to find a way out of this predicament, Percy suggested the council "set our standards of training and spirituality high enough" so they would not qualify. He then reconsidered, saying he was "rapidly coming to the place of believing that if these folks meet our educational and spiritual standards, then we might have to give consideration to them, or run the grave risk . . . [of] racial or color discrimination."[100]

In the end, most of the council members agreed with Playfair's recommendation that SIM's New York council should send the Arab couple to the Anglo-Egyptian Sudan or Eritrea on a test basis if they got some Bible training.[101] While the couple never joined SIM, this discussion seems to have laid the groundwork for General Council, the mission's governing body that succeeded International Council in 1957, to open a crack in the door of racial exclusion.

General Council started to break the color barrier in 1957 after Wanda and Rev. Howard O. Jones, the "noted negro pastor" with the Billy Graham Evangelistic Association, inquired about working at Radio ELWA in Liberia.[102] That July, Ray Davis informed General Council that the West Africa Field Council had "an 'unwritten law' . . . prohibiting American Negroes from entering the S.I.M." General Council tabled the discussion because it remained a "very stormy subject" in certain parts of the United States.[103] In September, President Dwight Eisenhower sent federal troops to Little

Rock, Arkansas, to fend off the state's governor and angry white segregationists who were preventing black American students from attending an all-white high school.[104] One month later, just days before Helser succeeded Playfair as general director, General Council passed a resolution allowing "American Negroes" to become missionaries.[105] The council prefaced its decision by stating that "in principle, 'we are all one in Christ Jesus,' but in practice many problems might arise if this door were opened for missionary candidates." The resolution read:

> AS AN EXPERIMENT, ON A ONE-TERM BASIS OF FOUR OR FIVE YEARS ACCORDING TO THE AREA SELECTED, UP TO SIX NON-WHITE MARRIED COUPLES QUALIFIED FOR SPECIALIZED WORK, AND OTHERWISE SUITABLE ACCORDING TO ALL EXISTING SAFEGUARDS FOR CANDIDATES, SHALL BE ELIGIBLE FOR ADMISSION TO THE MISSION.[106]

As one reader of this chapter asked, did SIM tell the "couples of color that they were being used on an experimental basis to see if they could perform DESPITE their racial handicap?"[107]

Early the following year, in 1958, the London Council questioned General Council's decision to accept nonwhite members, even on an experimental basis. Its secretary interpreted verses like Galatians 3:28 which stated there was "neither Jew nor Greek" to mean that all believers are spiritually united in Christ. But, he emphasized, such verses did not "remove from human society the divisions of race or nationality . . . ." Verses like this, he continued, "can scarcely be interpreted as envisaging 'full equality' with the normal framework of human society."[108] The council's belief that not all peoples were fully equal was reminiscent of John Hall's statement 37 years earlier that the Africans who he regarded as the "lowest" were not as human as white people in all "essentials."[109]

At the same time, in the throes of diminishing racism, General Council declared that "interracial marriages within the S.I.M. are not permitted," and decided to include this provision in the next revision of its *Principles and Practices*.[110] Did SIM oppose interracial couples because people would not be comfortable around them, or was "this just more subtle protection against" what they felt was "the sin of mixed race marriage?"[111] When the council began to backtrack, to consider not putting this proviso in its manual, the London Council expressed its "apprehension." Noting the incident that occurred in Little Rock, it stated that while the "racial . . . problem is possibly more acute in America" than Britain, it hoped General Council would give "*all* the Home Councils" the opportunity to express their opinions so "the Mission may not become involved in grave difficulties."[112] Even though General Council ended up not including the anti-interracial marriage statement in *Principles and Practices* in 1958, the mission still enforced this rule for a few years.[113]

Photo 16.5. *Rev. Howard and Wanda Jones, who broke SIM's color barrier*

Yet SIM did start to change, however slowly, during this period. The United States Council accepted the Joneses in a status that was later defined as "associate" in 1958; they went to Liberia one year later.[114]

Five years later, Salim Tannous, SIM's first Arab member, joined the Joneses in Liberia.[115]

1966—Present: Moving toward the "Principle" and "Practice" of Equality

Introduction

In 1966, SIM declared it would accept all people regardless of race or nationality. In doing so, the mission officially viewed all people as being equal, and soon thereafter began to intensify its effort to diversify its membership. As SIM started to accept more people who were not white, its overall sense of race started to shift from colour to culture, ethnicity, and nationality. This change corresponded to a "new racism" or "cultural racism" which has emerged since the Second World War that takes culture, ethnicity, and nationality into greater consideration than genetics. Even here, biology is often important in the way people define themselves and others, so it is not helpful to exaggerate the difference between the two racisms. Notions of biological racism can disguise itself in these and other social categories, and continues to predominate in many places.[116] Since sin, that can be subtle and subversive in ways that are not readily obvious to some people, is at the heart of racism, all people, everywhere, can discriminate if they think their race, ethnic group, or nationality is superior.[117]

While serving as a deputy international director during the administration of Jim Plueddemann (1993–2003), Howard Brant aptly explained how modern racism works institutionally and in peoples' unconscious biases in a manuscript he wrote in 1998 titled "Breakdown in the Body: Racism in Church and Mission." Missionaries, he wrote,

> don't think we have vestiges of racism lingering in our actions and attitudes, but they [those who were colonized by western powers] perceive it in us still. . . . Western missions and western missionaries have often adopted systems of thinking and operating that are racially loaded. We are often caught in a confluence of unseen forces and unspoken motives that keep us from uniting in the way God intended the church to be.[118]

Brant defined "racism" as "racial, ethnic, social, cultural and economic barriers that divide Christians of different races and strata in society."[119] Brant's explanation speaks to the situation in North America and Western Europe where most white people, who do not understand the pervasiveness of their own "white privilege" because they do not experience how minority populations are unfairly treated, believe they can solve racial problems individually.

Most African-Americans, Latinos, Arabs, and other minorities in this part of the world believe social structures heavily influence choices and opportunity. They tend to see institutional and personal discrimination more easily and through the long view of history, and more readily see racism as being prevalent in the structures of power that influence life. They are also far more likely to personally experience exclusion, violence, and prejudice than white people.[120]

Attitudes

Photo 16.6. *Rev. Simon A. Ibrahim.*
Rev. Ibrahim was trained at SIM's Bible schools in Kagoro and Igbaja. He went on to earn a B.A. degree at Ahmadu Bello University in Nigeria, and a M.A. at Wheaton College in the USA. Source: Ibrahim, "Learning to be on your own," *Africa Now* 87 (July-August 1976): 6.

SIM's West Africa Council continued to admonish its missionaries to treat Africans as equals during this period. In 1971, for example, the council said some missionaries continued to engage in "improper actions indicating an attitude of racism," and identified, by name, missionaries who would not be allowed to return to Africa if they did not change.[121] *Africa Now* continued to publish articles up through the mid-1970s that warned missionaries about the dangers of paternalism, class, supremacy, and residential and social segregation. Mr. Oumarou Youssouf mentioned Andrew Stirrett and Albert Helser as having developed close relationships with Africans. Rev. Simon Ibrahim singled out Charles Frame, Susan Hodge, Margaret Kirk, and Miss Thompson (Elizabeth or Bernice) who positively influenced his life.[122]

SIM's heyday for publicly engaging in some relatively candid self-criticism began in 1958 when *Africa Now* first started being published, when African nationalists were challenging the essence of colonialism and foreign institutions (like Western mission organizations), to the mid-1970s after most African colonies had become independent. In the immediate years that followed, the articles' emphasis shifted more to mission-church relations as SIM and denominations like ECWA went through the difficult process of establishing good working relationships with each other.[123] Since the mid-1970s, SIM has only published a handful of articles in its major periodicals that hint at racial discrimination.[124] It would be comforting to think, given the relatively stark decline in articles that deal with this topic, that the vast majority of SIM's missionaries have overcome most of their prejudices. Evidence in the years that have followed, however, suggests this would be fanciful thinking.

Ian Hay (1975–1993), who succeeded Ray Davis as general director, wrote in 1981 in the mission's in-house periodical *Intercom* that there was "still within our hearts attitudes of colonialism and pride."[125] Seven years later he published a letter from a veteran missionary who expressed her concern that "most missionaries" had attitudes of superiority that lead them to dominate, mistrust, have contempt for, and not listen to the host peoples with whom they live. Her alarm and prescription to accept "nationals" as equals and to serve them was reminiscent of many things some missionaries and many Africans had been saying for decades. Hay introduced her letter by stating that "her deep concern about our relationships with nationals . . .is very real, and we want to be of help to our Mission family to avoid harmful attitudes."[126]

In 1993, SIM held a Community Service Ministry Consultation in Nairobi, Kenya. The African attendees from partner churches voiced their deep concerns about missionaries' attitudes and actions that included pushiness, attitudes of superiority, lack of financial disclosure, divide and rule tactics, cultural arrogance, higher pay, colonialist attitudes, the perpetuation of master-servant relationships, failure to listen, lack of openness, and respect for culture.[127]

In 1998, Howard Brant "confessed the racial sins of our mission" that had occurred several years earlier on behalf of the mission to church elders in Wando, Ethiopia, "and humbly asked the church leaders to forgive us."[128] According to him, the unbecoming behavior of at least some of the missionaries in Wando was symptomatic of the great "challenge" SIM had "to bridge" the evils of "separate development," "apartheid," "nationalism," "racism," and "racial profiling . . .that keep us from becoming a fully integrated mission."[129]

Also in the late 1990s, Dr. Joshua Bogunjoko, who is presently SIM's international director, conducted research among missionaries and Africans in northern Nigeria and southern Niger. His study revealed the tenacious legacy of difference, similar to the actions of missionaries who lived in the region a half-century earlier. In his master's thesis, he wrote that Africans' perceptions of missionaries are often quite different from what missionaries think about themselves. He observed that missionaries often lived separate from or around Africans, but not with them. "The [African] people," he explained, "are their work, . . .not necessarily those that they love." Many missionaries had poor relationships with Africans, in part, because they did not identify with them or understand their culture.[130] During the time he and his wife Joanna worked at Galmi Hospital in Niger in the mid-to-late 1990s and early 2000s, they were instrumental in encouraging the SIM and African staff to break long-held "attitudes of paternalism" by forging closer relationships.[131]

Membership

In 1966, after the United States government passed the Civil Rights and Voting Rights Acts that legally empowered African-Americans and other minorities, SIM declared in its *Principles and Practice* that "Candidates are considered without regard to race or nationality."[132] One caveat that the general council added one year later was that "National Christians" could not join SIM and serve in their countries of origin; rather, they would best be placed working with the church or employed by the mission in non-church roles.[133]

In 1967, Japanese Michika Aoba became SIM's first Asian missionary.[134] Two years later, Ken and Mervina Sharp from Jamaica became the missions' first persons of African descent to become full members. They joined SIM through the Canadian office and went to Nigeria.[135] In 1971, less than one percent of SIM's 1,225 missionaries "disagreed" with the mission's "policy of accepting black missionaries"; three-quarters "suggested SIM should more actively work to get more black missionaries to join SIM."[136]

Two years before Aoba became a member, a Singaporean medical student named Andrew Ng inquired if the mission would accept Asians. Australian director John Neal replied in the affirmative, saying that "SIM would gladly welcome an

Photo 16.7. *Patricia Kim, a Korean, the first SIM majority world member to appear on the front cover of its magazine, 1986.*
Photo credit: SIMNOW 27 (May–June 1986): cover.

Asian missionary."[137] Neal's enthusiastic statement symbolized a break in the mission's long-standing barrier against incorporating Asians that led to the acceptance of Aoba in 1967, Japanese nurse Eiko Kanaoka in 1970, Chinese Dr. Peter and Sylvia Pan in 1975, Dr. Andrew and Belinda Ng in 1976, Koreans Sarah and Sam Kang in 1981, Malaysians Hsueh Yu Kwong and his wife Lily also in 1981, and others.[138] Their memberships paved the way for what is now the fastest-growing segment of people in SIM.[139] After the Ngs went to language school in France and served at Galmi Hospital in Niger, they returned to Singapore where SIM established an East Asia Council in 1980 under Dr. Ng's directorship.[140] (For a short story about the Ngs, see chapter 20, page 308). The number of Asians progressively rose from 10 in 1983 (nearly 1 percent of the mission's "active" membership of 987), to 42 in 1989 (3.3 percent of the mission's membership of 1,260), to 197 in 2016 (12.7 percent of its 1,537 missionaries).[141]

SIM began to recruit more missionaries who were not Anglo–North Americans in the mid-1980s. It had become apparent that North American and Western European recruitment for missions was declining by that time, while the dramatic growth of Christianity in the southern hemisphere provided a great opportunity to gain new recruits. The mission's awareness of these changes prompted General Director Ian Hay to begin "rearranging our thinking" and intentionally integrating "all nationalities" into SIM. (To read more about this shift in the mission's thinking, see chapter 20, pages 301-302.)[142] In doing so, SIM began to publicize that some of its members were not Anglo–North Americans, and that the mission was seeking to recruit more people like them.[143] It was also during this decade that the first persons of African descent became full members under the auspices of SIM USA; these were Rev. Curtis Hayes and his wife, Opal, who went to Liberia in 1981.[144]

At the turn of the millennium, SIM started to facilitate the movement of people "from anywhere to anywhere." Brant, who adopted this term for the SIM context in 2002 in a paper he wrote for SIM titled "A Highway For All Nations," sought to use SIM to help "prepare a highway for people from all nations to become involved in world missions." This meant shifting SIM from being a "'western only' [a relatively rich, predominately white] mission to a 'global mission,'" and changing structures and policies to allow people from less wealthy countries to more easily join the mission.[145] (For some of Brant's writing on this topic, see Appendix F.) This perspective undermined General Council's 1967 policy of not allowing "National Christians" to work in their homelands, and placed a greater emphasis on developing a more diverse missionary force.[146]

Jim Plueddeman's successor, Malcolm McGregor (2003–2013), made diversity a hallmark of his administration, and led SIM to being "Strengthened Through Diversity" as one of its key distinctions.[147] This "core value" now reads:

> We are intentionally interdenominational, international, and multiethnic. We believe this expresses the unity of the body of Christ in the world. We believe we will be more effective in ministry as we incorporate the richness of cultural diversity in SIM and celebrate our oneness in Christ.[148]

SIM now interprets Galatians 3:28, "There is neither Jew nor Gentile, neither slave nor free, nor is there male and female, for you are all one in Christ Jesus," to mean that differences can enrich; they are not inherent markers of difference and levels of humanity. The Holy Spirit can help SIM's missionaries overcome human-made barriers (Ephesians 4:1–6). The Great Commission applies to peoples of all classes, races, and ethnicities.[149] McGregor included an ethnic Cuban (US citizen), a Singaporean, and a Nigerian on his eight-person leadership team; these were the first non-Anglo–North Americans to hold executive positions in SIM.[150] The Nigerian, Joshua Bogunjoko, succeeded McGregor as international director in 2013.[151]

In recent years SIM has opened offices in Guatemala, Côte d'Ivoire, Kenya, Northeast India, and other places to increase opportunities for Latinos, Africans, Asians, and others to become members.[152] Today, SIM has a membership that has far more shades of colour than in 1966 when the mission officially decided not to discriminate on the basis of race. The number of SIM missionaries representing various "ethnic groups" or "nations" has roughly doubled since 1990 from over 30 to about 70.[153] SIM has become progressively less North American in the last three decades, although nearly 80 percent of the mission's 1,537 members still originate from countries that are overwhelmingly white.[154] While diversity introduces new challenges for people with different languages, histories, and traditions to negotiate as they work together, it also provides SIM with broader perspectives and internal mechanisms for correcting and challenging attitudes and behaviors that betray oneness in the body of Christ.[155]

Within the setting of the positive changes that have occurred in the last four decades, it is important to remember the Nigerian proverb—"When you follow in the path of your father, you learn to walk like him."[156] Simply put, it is difficult to change deeply entrenched ideas and behaviors. One example of the complexities and challenges facing racism at an institutional level became apparent in 2007 when SIM USA's board apologized to leaders of black American churches for not having accepted "Africa-American candidates." SIM International archivist Bob Arnold sent the board documentation to provide historical background for their study.[157] The apology, that was the result of two decades of effort to form closer relationships with predominately black churches in the United States,[158] was needed, timely, and appreciated, with SIM USA director Steve Strauss washing the feet of three African-American pastors.[159] According to the official statement,

> the SIM North America Council, did not accept African American candidates as missionaries...to comply with the wishes of the colonial governments which then controlled the African countries where SIM worked. . . . The practice was an unwritten policy, but was ended by a formal Council vote in 1957.

Strauss explained that "during the early twentieth century the colonial governments in parts of Africa did not want African-American missionaries in the countries they controlled."

The board blamed its predecessors' discrimination on colonial policy; previous councils merely acceded to the "wishes" of colonial governments that did not want mission orgainzations to employ dark-skinned people. The problem with the board's apology is twofold. The apology did not acknowledge that its predecessors' decisions were rooted in personal or institutional discrimination as Arnold's document indicated. By not admitting that some of the earlier boards' decisions were inherently racist, the board simply talked around this painful aspect of its past.[160] In addition, while it is conceivable that colonial administrators in the British colonies where SIM worked could have conveyed such sentiments to missionaries in the early colonial period (but not in the later years of colonialism)[161] even though documentary evidence of this having happened has yet to surface, the author has yet to see historical evidence which suggests that officials in French colonies expressed such ideas. The apology did not apply to Ethiopia, SIM's second largest "field," because Ethiopia was independent.

Yet, SIM USA's board is to be commended for having forthrightly acknowledged that its predecessors did discriminate and did ask for forgiveness. To the writer's knowledge, no other entity in SIM has specifically acknowledged in print, for the wider public to read, that some of its missionaries discriminated on the basis of race.[162]

It would be simplistic, irresponsible, and naïve to argue that racial prejudice is the only cause of attitudes of superiority and discrimination. Class, professionalism, ethnicity, nationality, personality, education levels, cultural differences, gender, and other factors, or some combination thereof, are oftentimes more influential. Nonetheless, the question of whether or not racial discrimination is a factor in trying to understand the nature of some problems must always be seriously asked.

Conclusion

Categorizing people on the basis of physical characteristics is part of SIM's history. Creating racial divisons was fundamental to SIM's identity and work throughout most of the twentieth century, and continues to affect missionaries when not checked. SIM's first missionaries do not seem to have viewed race as the key factor when they viewed other people. By World War I however, many had internalized the influences of social Darwinism, developed more racialized views of people, and come to think more highly of their race than their founding predecessors. Missionaries' discriminatory views of Africans and their descendants who lived in the Americas precluded the mission from accepting any people of colour as missionaries by the end of the war. SIM started to change after World War II, leading the mission to accept its first persons of color in 1958. In the 1980s, as more people who were not Anglo–North Americans started to become members, SIM slowly started to move from seeing racial difference as a problem to viewing diversity as a means to strengthen the mission. This meant—at least officially—viewing all human beings as being equal in all "essentials," and in doing so shedding the racial hierarchy, domination, and exclusion that was systemic. The forces for change were African nationalism, the civil rights movement in the United States, the anti-colonial backlash following independence, the rapid growth of Christianity in the global south, and a few missionaries on the ground who asked questions that challenged the establishment.

The mission started to break racial barriers in some countries when individuals or organizational entities courageously confronted racism in their fields of work and countries of origin; recognized that past wrongs influenced the present; and confessed sin, repented, and asked for forgiveness in private (and occasionally in the public media). At the international level, SIM started to change structures so people from all social, economic, and national backgrounds could become missionaries.

SIM has done many things to become more inclusive in recent decades that are laudable. Stories, for instance, of the Joneses and Ngs are inspiring. Yet the legacy of discrimination is far-reaching. For instance, the West Africa Field Council's observation in 1952 that "We work *hard* for them, but have so little time to spend with them" is eerily replicated in Girma Bekele's statement that some SIM missionaries in Ethiopia did things "*for* them, rather than *with* them," and Joshua Bogunjoko's findings in Nigeria and Niger that "the people simply are their work . . . [and] not necessarily those that they love."

In some places today, some missionaries still typecast peoples' work ethic, intelligence, and morality; use stereotypical images in their media; usually only gather for prayer meetings, spiritual life conferences, and entertainment in settings that are primarily inclusive of mission members and other expatriates who are mostly white when meeting as a "missionary" group; live on compounds where indigenes use race-based names (e.g., "black town") to designate where they reside in contrast to missionary areas that are less congested and with bigger and much nicer homes; discriminate in the work place; ban certain hairstyles; or never marry local peoples.[163] Such actions cry out, or at least raise questions of, discrimination, difference, mistrust, and "us" versus "them" attitudes.

On a personal note, as a white guy who was born in the United States, I have thought, said, and done things that were clearly racist. I know of situations where I have discriminated against individuals or whole groups of people on the basis of race, class, and other categories, worked in settings in SIM that reinforced institutional racism without objecting, and been blinded to discriminatory practices because I was functioning in structures that historically and operationally privileged white people like me. I am aware of some of my prejudices thanks at times to people who have challenged me about what I have or have not done or said. I am naturally inclined to view the world through the privilege of my white experience, and am often (usually?) not cognizant of injustice due in part to unconscious bias.

Each generation has its own strengths and weaknesses. It is important to recall the great sacrifice, sometimes even unto death, that many SIM missionaries made. Nonetheless, racial superiority was a particularly grave weakness of many of SIM's first generations of missionaries. This was easy for many SIM missionaries to see by the late 1960s and glaringly so by most revisiting this history today. Yet, what blind spots would SIM's long-departed predecessors, or future generations of missionaries, point out about many of today's missionaries or this chapter? How much more are SIM's present-day missionaries able to avoid being blinded by the times than those who came before them?

At least in the United States, which still constitutes the largest percentage of SIM's work force, race-related problems continue to be very real.[164] Missionaries who do not believe the long reach of racism affects the present need to listen to, try to empathise with, and have thoughtful conversations with their neighbors and fellow missionaries who are not like them. In 1998, SIM missionary Dr. Allison Howell wrote that today's descendants of the white people who enslaved, colonized, and oppressed generations of Africans have, "instead of healing the wound" that their predecessors made, covered it up or ignored it. Unless we allow God to heal the wound, the infection will be passed on to our children and their children and their children. . . . This wound is deep and is oozing with infection. . . . We need to take off the cloth of silence and start to apply the healing oil of Jesus Christ to heal the wound.[165]

Read in the framework of race discrimination in the mission, where has SIM "covered up" or "ignored" problems? Where is the "wound deep and . . . oozing with infection?" Where do SIM missionaries need to "apply the healing oil of Jesus Christ to heal the wound"? The Angolan proverb that Howell applied to the Ghana situation is equally applicable for SIM today: "The one who throws the stone forgets; the one who is hit remembers forever."[166]

Racism is an ugly part of SIM's history that the mission must know and recall to have any chance of overcoming. Present-day prejudice wounds people regardless of missionaries' knowledge of the past and hinders the mission's aim to be "Strengthened Through Diversity." Racial problems will never be solved if the actions of past actors are not part of the discussion. History can serve as a starting-point for informed dialogue. It is through the honest telling of what happened in the past and present that the multiplicity of voices can be heard and wounds can be brought to the surface for all to hear and feel. Only by confronting discrimination which obscures Christianity can the balm of truth heal wounds.

SUPPLEMENT 16.1

Racism and Missions in South Africa

Dr. Siegfried Ngubane
SIM South Africa Director

David Bosch, in his book *Transforming Missions*, stated clearly that during the high imperial era (1880–1920), government spokespersons praised the work of missions or missionaries as a great vehicle to propagate colonial policies, and that missionaries were great allies for executing the government political blue print. This not only happened in South Africa but in many other countries that were opening to missions and missionaries; the colonial power saw them as a great tool to ride on. Bosch directly quoted a member of parliament in South Africa saying: "One of the reasons why still many people are so indifferent to mission was their inability to grasp the political significance of mission work. Only if and when we succeed in incorporating blacks into the Protestant churches, will the white nation and all other population groups in South Africa have a hope for the future."[167] They (the missionaries) were children of their time who "were brought up in consciousness of the superiority of the white race in general since blacks were descendants of the accursed Ham, equality with them was out of the question. It was colonial domination that activated the missionaries' latent racism and made them extremely skeptical of the aptitude of blacks."[168]

But they were not all the same. Some gave in to the temptation of superiority, while some were under the pressure of colonial masters and local governments of their time. And yet there were those who had great respect for the indigenous peoples, treating them with exceptional respect and dignity. John Colenso (24 January 1814 to 20 June 1883) was an example of one who loved the people he was serving, defended them against the harsh treatment people received from either missionaries or white settlers in South Africa. Colenso lived among the Zulus, learned their language and culture, and translated the New Testament to isiZulu.

There are many such examples in different parts of the world. Even today there are so many missionaries who have truly identified themselves with the people they serve. Victor and Rachel Fredlund in South Africa are good examples of those who have made huge sacrifices for the sake of the gospel. They didn't just end up planting a Zulu church (of the AEC) and learning the Zulu culture, but they also have black in-laws, speak isiZulu very well, are fully integrated into the Zulu culture, and have adopted many young Zulu people as their own children.

As a result of SIM's promotion of theological education at an advanced level in Nigeria and elsewhere, many very able African leaders, scholars and theologians were and are being trained. Their influence is felt throughout the continent. Among them is the renowned Dr. Byang Kato. His passion was to see both academics in theological schools writing from the African Christian perspective, as well as the formation of associations and fora where Africans would find a platform to meet and discuss important issues, thereby encouraging and spurring each other on. This vision has resulted in the birth of many theological colleges in Africa and the African Evangelical Associations (members of the Association of Evangelicals of Africa) found in most countries on the continent.

In South Africa, as elsewhere in the world, missionary schools produced well-educated leaders who in turn stood up against colonial powers. They produced health facilities and schools where lives were improved.

On the whole, most evangelical missions and white evangelical churches in South Africa did not take a stand against the atrocities that were being carried out on other races.

It must also be put on record that in South Africa, during Apartheid rule, people (including missionaries) who were seen as being too friendly with black people, were under the very close eye of the Apartheid South African security police. Any missionary who did take a stand was not necessarily looked upon with favour by the leadership of those missions.

It is also noted that during the Apartheid years, most African countries did not grant visas to white South African missionaries, and in fact, the South African government itself prohibited its citizens from entering certain countries.

In some cases, the very presence of these missionaries in certain African countries was perceived as an embarrassment to SIM, even if those governments would have granted them a visa.

SUPPLEMENT 16.2

Africa Evangelical Fellowship and SIM's Engagement with Racism in Southern Africa: a Preliminary Survey

Dr. Tim Geysbeek

Introduction

The history of Africa Evangelical Fellowship (AEF) and SIM in Southern Africa merits special attention given the region's complicated history of racial segregation especially in white settler colonies. With regard to South Africa, in particular, the ideological basis of racism was rooted, in part, on a twisted version of Christianity that justified white supremacy. This theology, mirroring the role of the Israelites in the Old Testament, stated that God chose white people, in particular Afrikaners primarily of Dutch descent, to Christianize, civilize, and rule the supposedly downtrodden black people who lived there in the "promise land."[169] These ideas led to apartheid era (1948–1994) policies that sought to establish total political, economic, and social segregation among South Africa's "races"; the government classified these as "Black," "White," "Coloured," and "Indian" in 1950. Consequently, as the late theologian Steve De Gruchy wrote, "The history of the church in South Africa *is* fundamentally the history of the relationship between Christianity and racism."[170] Another colony that is part of this story was Southern Rhodesia (later Rhodesia, now Zimbabwe) where white power brokers used racism to justify white minority rule and maintain economic and political ascendency at the expense of the overwhelmingly black majority. Not surprisingly, issues of race are intertwined in the histories of AEF and SIM in this region.

Africa Evangelical Fellowship

This story begins with AEF which was established as a white British mission. AEF started its work in Southern Africa as Cape General Mission (CGM) in 1889, and then became South Africa General Mission (SAGM) in 1894 after CGM merged with the South East Africa Evangelistic Mission. The president of CGM, and then SAGM until he died in 1917, was the great theologian and evangelist of the Dutch Reformed Church (DRC), Andrew Murray Jr.

Notable in the battle over racial segregation in the DRC was the resolution that Murray's brother William submitted to its synod in 1857 that the synod passed, and that Andrew Jr. supported. The resolution stated that while it was "desirable and scriptural" that "the Heathen . . . be taken up and incorporated in our existing congregations," "because of the weakness of some"—referring to white people—"Heathen congregations shall enjoy their Christian rights in a separate building or institution." The synod, which officially authorized a common practice and did not believe it was sanctioning racism, hoped "the wall of segregation would fall." With evangelizing the "heathen" taking precedence over advancing the cause of racial equality that Dutch settlers feared, culture trumped Scripture. The "weakness of some" eventually became the will of most. The concession that the ruling granted also led to the formation of black churches that could not become independent within the DRC, and set the overall tone for race relations within churches in the twentieth century.[171]

When CGM was established in 1889, all of its missionaries were white. White missionaries taking the lead in spreading the gospel to black Africans was the DRC's practice, and was common for the times. So, AEF's acceptance of three women who they did not think were white during the 1890s challenged its identity and the pattern of white missions more generally in South Africa. While these women became missionaries during this period when the government was passing laws that were sharpening divisions between people, these years also represented a time when black Africans still had limited political, economic, and social choices. White-dominated Western mission organizations were also accepting persons of color as members into the early twentieth century.

Photo 16.8. *"Mrs. Holt, women & girls at church, Mt. Packard," Transkei, 31 August 1914, 10:00 a.m. Sunday morning*

The first nonwhite member of AEF was Rosabianca Fasulo. She was the daughter of an Italian man and an unmarried woman. Rosabianca was abandoned by her family, rescued from the streets of Rome, and became a Christian. Most western and northern Europeans at this time viewed Italians and other southern Europeans as not being "white," with associative racial aspersions—like ones cast against Rosabianca—which stated they were weak, immoral, animal-like, and not intelligent. Rosabianca went to South Africa with the mission in 1892, married SAGM missionary Samuel Holt two years later, and served until 1927 when she retired. Her marriage to a white man who sired a son, her donning of European clothes, and the mission's commendations of her work provided visible signs of respectability and led the mission to largely remove her race in its literature.[172]

More problematic for SAGM was its acceptance of two "coloured" Scottish-Guyanan sisters, Marion and Bell Hay. When the British council notified the South African council of Marion's candidacy in 1897, they did not mention her physical appearance. When one of the men on the South African council was informed that

Photo 16.9. *Belle Hay, South Africa, 1899.*

Source: Diamonds *2, no. 6 (June 1899): 3.*

she was "coloured," he protested, saying people would "show intense feeling against her" and stop financially supporting the mission. Questions about her membership highlighted the tension between universal humanity and race discrimination in SAGM. Marion steamed to South Africa later that year, and her sister Belle was accepted as a SAGM missionary in 1898. They left the mission in 1899, went to Cairo, and returned to South Africa in 1900. Belle married SAGM missionary Palmer Jones and was reinstated as a member. The mission denied her sister's application. Belle and her husband served with SAGM until at least 1912. Marion returned to London in 1934.

While none of these women, including Rosabianca, were seen by the mission as honorable and lily white like their white British counterparts, each nonetheless "became a particular kind of white" Christian woman in their capacity as expatriate missionaries. It would be three decades after Rosabianca retired before the mission would accept another South African who authorities did not consider was white.

Southern Rhodesia became a British colony in 1923 several years after Cecil Rhodes and his British South Africa Company used deception and force to colonize what later became known as Zimbabwe, and apportion the best land to whites. In doing so, the government instituted a "'structural racism' of the social and political system" that advantaged most white people at the expense of black Africans. By 1950, 120,000 white colonists lived in Southern Rhodesia, with 10,000 new immigrants arriving every year. While white people only represented about six percent of the colony's population, they were politically and economically ascendant. The missionary-turned-politician Garfield Todd, who became prime minister in 1953, pushed through modest reforms to improve the education and working conditions of the colony's black population. However, powerful white elites representing businesses, large-scale farmers, and city workers who sought to retain white rule bitterly opposed his plans and eventually ousted him from power. In 1964, the extremist right-wing settler party, the Rhodesia Front led by Ian Smith, won national elections and instituted policies that further divided the races.[173]

It was during this time in Southern Rhodesia's history that the next persons of color joined SAGM. These were Rev. H. Stephen and Priscilla Sitole.[174] Rev. Sitole, of Venda heritage, was born in Southern Rhodesia in 1916 and attended Moody Bible Institute in Chicago. In 1952 he married a 30-year-old African-American from Oklahoma named

Priscilla James who had attended Wheaton College. When it became known to SAGM's missionaries in Southern Rhodesia that the mission was thinking of assigning the Sitole's to their station in Rusitu, they said this would be a "grave mistake" because their presence would result in "all kinds of complications and untold difficulties." SAGM's missionaries felt European settlers living around them would not accept the Sitoles "on the same footing" as them, and it would hinder their efforts to evangelize local Africans. They also felt the mission's acceptance of missionaries who were not white would set a "doubtful precedent": were "all the Home Councils prepared to adopt Africans, Coloureds, or Indians as full workers?"

SAGM's Canadian and American councils dismissed Rusitu's missionaries' concerns in 1952.[175] With regard to the "colour bar," they said Scriptures like Galatians 3:26–29 are "100% clear . . . [that] race is specifically named as the ground upon which no distinction is allowed." On the point of precedent, the councils said SAGM would be in "infinitely greater danger" if they did not accept them. The fact, the councils added, that donors in the USA were sending the Sitoles to go to Africa testified that SAGM "acknowledge[s] . . . a fellowship in service which transcends consideration of race or color." The American Council accepted the Sitoles as missionaries one year later. It would take SIM's Canadian and USA councils a few years to come to the conclusion of their SAGM counterparts, and then not in such unequivocal terms.

SAGM's leaders in Southern Rhodesia supported the American council's decision to accept the Sitoles as missionaries, but acknowledged that the Sitoles would face many difficulties at the beginning. Indeed, after the Sitoles arrived in Rusitu, they reported that SAGM's missionaries discriminated against them. When, for instance, they were in the home of fellow missionaries, they were asked to "sneak out the back door" if unsaved white visitors arrived. When Priscilla reported that the missionaries were "colour conscious," one leader wrote that "there is a colour-bar in her own mind."

Photo 16.10. *Rev. H. Stephen and Priscilla Sitole, Southern Rhodesia, 1959.*

Photo credit: South Africa Pioneer *111 (1959): 2.*

By 1960, SAGM, or at least some of its leadership, started to change in response to the "winds of change" that were sweeping the continent. Rev. Sitole attended the Congress on World Missions that the Interdenominational Foreign Mission Association convened in Chicago in 1960. He gave two presentations that were later published, and was one of SAGM's representatives on a panel that included SIM General Director Albert Helser.[176] That same year the editor of SAGM's *The South African Pioneer*, Arthur Brown, openly challenged, as unbiblical, several "typical" comments about Africans that people had expressed when writing to the mission. These are a few that he addressed:

- "I suppose they [Africans] have rights, but it makes things very awkward."
- Africans "have not developed morally and spiritually as they have intellectually."
- "The majority of the population is quite happy," so the "only possible course in this land seems definitely to be neutrality [sic.] in anything that is political."
- "Any government which is going to wait for the natives to be 'reasonable' about their subordination to the white man is waiting for the moon."

Brown rebutted, making several points: "It is not reasonable to equate (as so many Christians do) 'ordained of God' with 'approved of God'"; "His Church in the world, is accomplished . . .*through* and not *by* missionaries and ministers of all races"; and "Church or Mission forms of government valid and good in the 1950s require considerable changes in 1960."[177] Attitudes such as these, that explain the disgraceful behavior of some SAGM missionaries toward the Sitloes, were rooted in ideas that were decades old.[178]

The Sitloes left SAGM in 1964. Stephen died in Rhodesia in 1970, and Priscilla in Oklahoma in 1987. Even with the mission's acceptance of the Sitoles as missionaries and resistance to the status quo from leaders like Brown, it would take years before AEF would accept another person who was not white; this might have been Gloria Cube, a South African who joined the mission in about 1992.[179]

In 1948, five years before the Sitoles joined SAGM, the National Party in South Africa won the country's national elections. Its victory marked the beginning of the apartheid era that sought to reconstruct society on the basis of race to keep white people in power. The period officially ended when Nelson Mandela's African National Congress won national elections in 1994. AEF adopted a position common among conservative evangelicals who did not resist apartheid because of biblical injunctions to submit to current governing authorities and to protect the mission's interests. Conservative evangelicals, however, were not the only evangelicals or Christians in South Africa. Many Christians, even white ones mainly of English background, had more progressive views. Some worked in ecumenical forums to address apartheid.[180] Yet, as former AEF missionary Tom Kopp has written, AEF and the Africa Evangelical Church of South Africa (AEC-SA) which originated out of AEF's work had "little or no involvement in the events surrounding the drafting of certain key declarations" such as the Kairos Document (1985) and Rustenburg Declaration (1990); these respectively stated the government was illegitimate and needed to be resisted by means of civil disobedience, and that apartheid was a sin. Neither, Kopp added, had AEF-SA or the

AEC, "like many other conservative groups, officially studied or interacted" with these documents after they were published.[181]

AEF began to change in the late 1980s, shifting from not speaking about politics to encouraging the teaching of biblical principles within the context of present-day conditions. But little of this teaching and application thereof was done because the legacy of the mission's long-standing policy—to not challenge the state and other institutions—was so entrenched. Kopp credits Hugh Wetmore of the Evangelical Fellowship of South Africa (EFSA) for encouraging AEF to engage with the ideas and actions emanating from ecumenical circles and exposing the mission to its blind spots.[182] Kopp also observed that neither AEF-SA nor the AEC had ever "called a meeting for the sole purpose of discussing the past and looking at the options regarding the matter of reconciliation" probably because they did not see any reason to do this.[183]

SIM

SIM's story in Southern Africa begins in the 1930s when the mission started sending white South Africans to West Africa through its UK council. The first South African may have been British-born Dorothy "Queenie" Howe who went to Nigeria in 1930 and served there for four decades.[184]

The mission formed a committee and then a council, in 1943 and 1952 respectively, to give people local opportunities to become members. In 1945, the committee labeled one item of discussion "Colour Bar."[185] Realizing that a "coloured" person might apply for membership, the committee asked London for its advice. As this issue was not raised again in the minutes, perhaps no "coloured" persons applied at this time. In using the term "Colour Bar," SIM was continuing the normal practice of racial discrimination with no thought of questioning its morality. Maintaining the bar, not breaking it, was the norm. By not including "Black" people or "Indians" in their inquiry, the council was apparently precluding the notion that they could become members.

Photo 16.11. *Dorothy "Queenie" Howe*

"Coloured African Christians" applied to SIM in 1960, though none were accepted. Discussions about their application centered around General Council's 1957 resolution which stated that the mission would only accept six couples who had "specific training" like medical personnel or teachers. Persons of colour who had no highly specialized training should not apply as "general missionaries"; this category was reserved for white people. The council also told prospective "coloured candidates" that persons interested in joining the mission should only be "married to persons of their own race and colour." "It is not thought advisable," the council added, in keeping with discussions in the general council, to ban interracial marriages or "to have this in actual writing at this time in view of the attitude of certain governments."[186]

SIM's position in South Africa needs to be interpreted in the context of the "Prohibition of Mixed Marriages Act" and "Immorality Act" that the government respectively passed in 1949 and 1950. These laws made it illegal for persons who the government classified as being members of different "races" from marrying or having sexual relations, with the goal of keeping the "white" race pure and ascendant politically and economically. In 1957, when SIM's General Council was pressured into accepting "American Negroes" on an experimental basis, it also unanimously resolved that "interracial marriages within the S.I.M. are not permitted." SIM did not end up including its ban on interracial marriages in its manual for all to read, unlike what the apartheid government victoriously (to itself) did when it passed their acts. SIM restationed members who became "too friendly with Africans" of the opposite gender.[187]

Two years later, in 1962, SIM's South Africa council wrote: "Strengthened by the peculiar circumstances obtaining in South Africa—that in this non-White world vast opportunities were open to the Mission through the acceptance of non-white candidates." Black members of the mission could teach "African and Coloured brethren" in places like SAGM's Johannesburg Bible School. If the council's statement widened the door for nonwhite missionaries to serve in South Africa, it also just maintained the status quo. SIM's policy reflected the government's notion of separate development which held that persons of the country's various "races" should "develop" separately in their own ways to achieve their full potential.[188] It was theoretically fine, for instance, for SIM missionaries who were not white to work with South Africa's population who the government did not classify as white. But, could they work as equals with whites in all phases of ministry?

When Rev. S. Makakase applied for membership in 1973, SIM declined to accept him because he would not complete his "studies" for three more years; "his educational qualifications were not adequate." Because information about Rev. Makakase's application is incomplete, it is not possible to adequately compare his situation with white persons who applied. At first glance, however, it is legitimate to ask if the council would have accepted a white missionary with his level of education. The council did not strive to get him into

Photo 16.12. *Dianne Guta*

the mission as it did with a white couple a few years earlier who was just advised to "take a regular Bible school training course" before applying.[189] In 1984, SIM accepted Dianne Guta as the first long-term South African who was not white to join SIM; she served in Bolivia for several years and recently passed away.[190]

In 1988, Deputy General Director W. Harold Fuller went to South Africa and published a short report about the head of the EFSA, Hugh Wetmore, who was also the brother of SIM missionary Ruth Craill. Wetmore, he wrote, was working to find a "scriptural balance" between persons who compromised with and strongly opposed apartheid. The EFSA, Fuller noted, "believes in opposition to evil by every legitimate and peaceful means."[191] Two years later, a council member got "in trouble for opposing apartheid." In response, SIM's Board of Governors passed the following resolution that it added to the mission's revised manual in 1991:

> Members should carefully exercise their civic responsibilities in their home country in accordance with the teaching of Scripture and their Christian conscience. They should carefully avoid any actions which may compromise the work and witness of the Mission and Church in any way. They should consult with their National Director on sensitive issues before taking any public action.[192]

The board's cautious statement, that erred on the side of protecting the mission, was rooted in the mission's long-held position of political neutrality, of not taking political positions in the countries where it works and often not adequately exploring how its ministries are connected to politics.[193] Cumulative evidence suggests that SIM's overall response to apartheid was essentially similar to AEF's.

Photo 16.13. *Dr. Siegfried Ngubane's commissioning, 2010.*
Photo credit: Rene Palacio.

It is significant, given AEF and SIM's complicity in racism in South Africa, that Dr. Siegfried Ngubane became the mission's first black South Africa director in 2010.[194] His ascendency as director is evidence of the fact that peoples' attitudes are changing. Yet SIM's missionaries should not be complacent and think racism is an idea of the past given personal sin and the powerful influence of systemic structural racism in the subregion. Being sensitive to racism, and confronting it where it exists, is crucial for Christians who adhere to a gospel that intrinsically proclaims the equality of all humanity, and for SIM missionaries who assert the belief that being "Strengthened Through Diversity" is important and not just a feel-good slogan.

CHAPTER 17

ENCOUNTERING ISLAM¹

SIM General Director Dr. Ian Hay gave the keynote address to SIM's January 1987 Consultation on Islam in Monrovia, Liberia. The title of his address was "SIM, Islam—and a Glimpse of God." It included an overview of the state of Islam in the world, an overview of SIM's history of seeking to introduce Muslims to the Christ of the Bible, and a Scripture-drenched reflection on the task remaining. It is a worthy place to begin our review of SIM's encounter with Islam:²

Islam is on the march in every part of our SIM world. The *UN Yearbook* lists Christianity and Islam as roughly equal in numbers—one billion each. Those figures are inflated from both sides. Christians optimistically call Africa an emerging Christian continent. Muslims also claim it. Even the more realistic number of 800 million Muslims, however, shows a dramatic increase of over 200 percent in the last 50 years.

Ralph Winter of the U.S. Center for World Mission says that "the Muslim group is growing at a biological rate almost double that of Chinese. . . . If present rates continue there will be more Muslims than Chinese within about 10 years."

The resurgence of Islam is unmatched since the conquest of North Africa and the Near East in the seventh and eighth centuries. It has been able to do that because of its near monopoly of the world's oil.

The green tide of Islam, however, has its ebb and flow. Just now traditionalists are striving to turn their nations from materialism and secular philosophies.

What does all this mean to us? If nothing else, it means that all of Christ's servants—missionaries and local believers alike—can expect increasing resistance from leading elements in Islamic communities and a harder line from Islamic officialdom. Entry visas may be harder to get, and restrictions on missionary activity tightened.

On the other hand, in sub-Saharan Africa, Islam has good reason to be concerned. The "Muslim line" runs across Africa about 100–200 miles south of the Sahara. Above this line there are 200 tribes in 109 countries that are 70 percent or more Islamized.

This line advanced slowly from the seventh century down from North Africa, across the desert and into the animistic regions below it. That advance was brought to a standstill in the middle of this century by the explosive six percent growth of Christianity. Some of the strategic thinking of SIM pioneers had something to do with that, by God's good grace.

Not long ago someone asked me about SIM's sudden new preoccupation with evangelizing the Islamic world. The question took me by surprise. It is not a new interest; it is a renewed one.

As you know, our pioneers' original goal was to get to the Muslim population in the heart of Africa's interior, specifically the Hausa-speaking people of northern Nigeria. Many of them never reached that goal. They were forbidden by the colonial government.

Our first field superintendent, Dr. Andrew Stirrett, pointed out, however, that in response to what he called an "urgent appeal which we believe was of God," the Mission turned to the animistic tribes which had not yet been swallowed up by Islam.

We now see with much better perspective what God was doing. Under the Divine Strategist, SIM goals were altered. As a result, God raised up a body of believers now close to two million strong across Africa south of the Sahara. The Holy Spirit has created His church where He planned it—a much more effective tool than any expatriate mission.

This outreach to the Hausas illustrates how strategic they are and how dynamic was the thinking of our pioneers. Politically and economically, the influence of the Hausa is felt all over the western hump of Africa. Their traders are in every major center.

Depending on which census figures are accepted, there are between six and ten million Hausas. The total number of Hausa-speaking people, however, is probably closer to thirty million.

Legend portrays the Hausas as always being Muslim. The facts indicate otherwise. The *Kano Chronicle* says that it wasn't until about 1600 that Muslim Malinke missionaries arrived in Kano.

Firm conversion to Islam did not come until the early part of the nineteenth century, during the Fulani *jihad* led by Othman Dan Fodio. By 1800 [1815] his empire included all of northern Nigeria, a great part of Niger Republic, and parts of Cameroon and Benin.

For years SIM missionaries prayed for these people. Dr. Stirrett spent his lifetime burdened for them. His heart cry was, "Oh Lord, remember the Hausas!" On one occasion he said to a young missionary, "Son, my ear is to the ground, but my eye is on God. I can hear the walls of Mohammedanism crumbling."

Eventually, SIM missionaries were allowed into the northern emirates. This came about when key leaders, backed by prevailing prayer, decided to confront British colonial officers and Muslim emirs.

SIM founder Rowland Bingham tells of a strategic meeting of all SIM missionaries in 1929. "They determined that with or without government consent," he wrote, "we are entering those great provinces of the north."

He tells of his subsequent journey to England and of discussions with the British Foreign Office. The result? The governor general of Nigeria gave assurance that the government would "take steps to inculcate in the minds of the Muslim emirs the British principle of religious toleration which would ensure to the missionaries freedom and liberty for the peaceable propagation of the gospel."

Bingham's successor, Guy

These are two photographs of the Emir of Gwandu, which were taken by Dr. Lambie. The first one shows the Emir seated on his throne in his palace at Birnin Kebbi. In the other one he is accompanied by the District Officer, Mr. Pitcairn, and Dr. Bingham and Dr. Helser.

The Emir of Gwandu is very friendly, and it was he who said: "You may select a site for a mission station anywhere in my territory, and those who wish to follow your faith will not be hindered."

Photo 17.1. "Peaceful Invasion of the Northern Emirates of Nigeria."
Source: Sudan Witness 14, no. 1 (January-February 1938): between pages 12 and 13.

W. Playfair, points out the influence of the Word of God in the hands of a Muslim emir opening the door. The emir, after reading the Bible, noted that Jesus told His disciples to cleanse the leper. Thousands of people in those emirates suffered with that disease. He emphasized that this was something Christian missionaries ought to do and was therefore open to having the Mission in his emirate.

As a result, at one stage SIM operated for the government of Nigeria seven leprosaria with over sixty thousand patients under care. That love shown in meeting human physical need coupled with the verbal witness to the power of the living Christ (see Photo 17.2).

In the meantime, the Holy Spirit opened doors to more responsive people groups throughout the middle belt of Nigeria. Significant movements took place among the Kagoros, the Jabas, the Tangales, the Gbagyis, the Yorubas, and many others. There is no question but that the Holy Spirit directed this.

Among other things, the Evangelical Missionary Society of ECWA has grown out of this work. EMS is a significant force for God.

We meet now at this Consultation to reemphasize this important and historic aspect of SIM ministry. The task is enormous. Our major task is in Africa, although increasingly we are concerned in our sending countries as well. Note how closely areas in Africa where there is a Muslim majority parallel the areas of SIM responsibility. God has placed us in a strategic place. Involvement is mandatory.

In the old days, the shadow of the minaret was long. The task seemed formidable, the results minimal. There came a decline in evangelistic emphasis to Islam. This was true even in SIM, for a time. Perhaps this decline was

Photo 17.2. Emma Snyder playing a record at SIM's leprosarium in Kano, Nigeria, c. 1950

due in part to the strong emphasis of the last decades of reaching "winnable" people. During this time large sections of the church apparently forgot that our mandate is to go everywhere and reach everybody.

Perhaps we also forgot the biblical truth that while some messengers of the gospel are chosen to be the "fragrance of life unto life" to those who are saved, others are chosen to be the "smell of death unto death" to those who reject the truth (2 Corinthians 2:16).

It takes a particular type of person to do this. We need messengers today who have strength of character, tenacity of purpose, and stick-to-it-iveness.

Nowhere in the Scriptures is it promised that all will respond. It is promised, however, that there will be a remnant. Isaiah showed his understanding of this truth when he said: "My word . . . shall not return to me empty without accomplishing what I desire, and without succeeding in the matter for which I sent it" (Isaiah 55:10–11).

The Islamic monolith is a myth. The example of the Hausas proves it. For two centuries Islam dominated all aspects of their lives. There have been many failures in SIM's outreach to the Hausas and they have been a truly resistant people. But by God's grace the monolith is no more.

We can learn from this history. It will help in our plans for reaching the Fulanis, the Mandingos, the Swahili-speaking peoples of East Africa, the urban educated Muslims in London, South Africa, or Chicago, and others.

The indispensable condition for our endeavor, of course, is spelled out plainly in our motto—"By Prayer." A whole new generation of committed, praying people is needed—people who know that the weapons of our warfare are not of the flesh, but powerful for the destruction of fortresses (2 Corinthians 10:4).

May God give us the wisdom, the vision, the strength, and the courage to move forward.

Later in 1987, Howard Brant, the international outreach coordinator for SIM, wrote a short article entitled "SIM's Commitment," further outlining the challenges that lay ahead and reporting on some of the outcomes of the consultation. Here is what he had to say:[3]

"Africa will become the first Muslim continent."

That is what Muslims are predicting in publications like *Arabia* magazine. Their claim is striking in light of the oft-quoted statement by Christian scholars that Africa will become the first Christian continent. David Maranz of Wycliffe rightly asks in the November 1986 issue of *Pulse*, "Is Christianity really winning Africa?"

The truth is that both groups have been making numerous converts from Africa's animists, who no longer wish to be categorized as idolaters, pagans, or fetish worshipers. Furthermore, it is predictable that as the number of convertible animists decline, Islam and Christianity will be on a collision course with each other.

The battle has already begun. A political map of Africa shows tensions right along the sub-Saharan line where Islam and Christianity have historically confronted each other. Countries like Nigeria, Chad, Sudan and Ethiopia are presently embroiled in conflicts which have deep roots in the resurgence of Islam.

At another level, one only needs [sic] visit cities like Mombasa and Abidjan to see the rapid construction of new mosques fueled by Islamic petro dollars.

In the ideological battle, Ahmed Deedat of South Africa is making blasphemous videotapes which strike at the core doctrines of our faith. These are being shown in places like Abidjan and Kano.

When SIM was founded almost one hundred years ago, its pioneers had a vision for sub-Saharan Africa. They were well aware that much of that vast interior was already Islamized. They, along with other mission leaders, spoke of forming a line running across the sub-Sahara which would halt the advance of Islam southward into black Africa. As late as 1978 missiologists were claiming that this line had, in fact, stemmed the tide of advancing Islam.

But that is no longer true. Of the world's 890 million Muslims, 250 million live in Africa. As we in SIM take stock of the countries in which we have (or will have) ministry, we note that there are 93 million Muslims for whom we are potentially responsible. These would include huge people groups like the Hausa (17 million), Oromo (about 15 M.), Yoruba (14.7 M.), Fulani (14.5 M.), Ibo (14 M.), Mandingo (11.1 M.), Somali (7.5 M.), and Manga/Kanuri (4.5 M.). . . .

By the same token we look at SIM's missionary force engaged in this conflict. We have 133 SIMers who have direct contact with Muslims in their ministry. Of these, 61 can be said to be engaged in full-time Muslim evangelism. Though we acknowledge that God has given us related churches with some vision for Muslim outreach, we feel just like the disciples who looked at five loaves and two small fishes and despaired. "What are these among so many?"

In light of this, our General Director, Dr. Ian Hay, recently called together 22 of SIM's missionaries who have had long-standing experience with Muslim outreach. They, together with seven consultants, met to reaffirm our commitments to Muslim evangelism. In his charge, Dr. Hay stated:

Photo 17.3. "Phil Short, Niger: Sharing the Word with Muslims."
Source: SIMNOW 17 (September-October 1984): front cover.

"Our pioneers' original goal was to get to the Muslim population in the heart of Africa's interior. . . . This generation of SIM and her supporting partners need to feel again the burning passion of our forbears to reach the unreached, and in this case, specifically, the world of Islam. . . ."

At this consultation we drafted a thirteen-page document full of recommendations which outline both our policy and strategy in Muslim evangelism. When these recommendations are ratified, they will be implemented right across our fields.

Several other missions asked us if they could attend the SIM Consultation on Muslim Evangelism (SIMCOME). We suggested that this was our attempt to get our own house in order. Now we feel that we are not only ready, but anxious to talk with other like-minded Christian agencies. Definite plans for such a consultation will be submitted to the Joint Committee on Africa at the EFMA/IFMA Conference in Orlando, Florida, next September.

It is interesting to note that participants at SIMCOME included resource persons from two entities that would be key participants in SIM outreach to Muslims in the years going forward. Gerhard Nehls, leader of Life Challenge, which had important direct outreach and church mobilization ministry in South Africa—and would have a much more extensive mobilization ministry across Africa in coming years—was one of them. Life Challenge merged with SIM in 1986 and is discussed more thoroughly in the section discussing mergers.

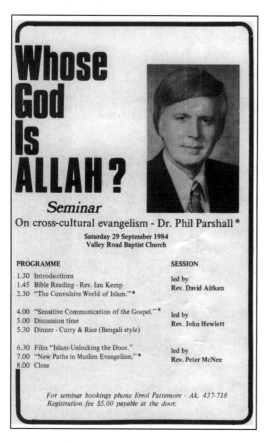

Photo 17.4. *Phil Parshall, "Whose God is Allah?" 1984*

The other resource person was Phil Parshall, a longtime ICF missionary working in Bangladesh, who is perhaps best known today as an early key catalyst (through his extensive writings) for more thoughtful and appropriate contextualization in Muslim ministry. He had recently visited a number of SIM Muslim ministry sites in West Africa with international director of research Gary Corwin conducting workshops on Muslim ministry along the way. He attributes his exposure to SIM leaders and key Muslim ministry personnel at SIMCOME as the key factor in his recommendation to ICF leadership that they explore a possible merger with SIM.[4] This did, in fact, happen, which led ultimately to the merger that occurred in 1989. (See Supplement 17.2, pages 259-260, for more on Dr. Parshall.)

As anyone who has worked in ministry to Muslims knows well, worldview assumptions are often the toughest hurdles to overcome. A 1994 *Intercom* article[5] describes one of the toughest:

Sickness, sorrow and suffering are a normal part of life for Joe and Linda. . . . "Arriving home from a trip to a camp last week, I dropped off one of the families who had hitched a ride back into town with me," says Linda. "When I opened the door, a woman with a crying child got out. The boy, Chef, squatted and screamed.

"As he urinated, his intestines came out about six inches. For three months, Chef had been going through this ordeal every time he would urinate. My heart went out with compassion."

Since then Linda has repeatedly taken the boy and his mother to the hospital for tests and medicines. But though the parents are appreciative, Linda perceives that the attitude of *incha Allah* (the will of God) still prevails in their Muslim thoughts.

Linda says that attitude leads the parents to believe there's no sense in trying to make a difference in the youngster's life. If the boy lives, he lives (by the will of God). If he dies, he dies (by the will of God).

Helping Chef shows Christlike love and compassion. But this help alone does not deal with the root problem of a skewed world view. . . .

"The real medicine for this child, his parents, and his people is the transforming power of the gospel," she explains. "Jesus actively sought to reverse the effects of sin. In doing so, he purchased our salvation on the cross.

"I am constantly reminded that we can not passively say '*incha Allah*' when many people in Africa go without knowledge of Jesus or when they suffer. Active compassion coupled with active proclamation of the gospel is the Biblical response to a sin-sick world."

In a follow-up article in a subsequent *Intercom*,[6] Joe Gallop shares both the sad and hopeful outcomes of this story:

We received several letters from SIMers, mostly doctors and nurses, who were concerned and offered suggestions and help for the treatment of Chef. . . . Some said they hoped to read in the next issue [of *Intercom*] about him being well and whole.

We, too, had hoped to be able to share such good news. However, as we have experienced here so many times, another young African boy passed into eternity. We had taken him to [the] hospital, where he was treated for bladder stones. He passed several stones and was released after 10 days. During those 10 days I had some very good opportunities to share with his father about the Lord.

About a month later, Chef fell gravely ill again. Once more we made the trip to [the] hospital, but this time he died there. Chef's father and I buried him in a shallow rocky grave near the hospital, and although a Muslim, he asked me to pray at the funeral.

Since then he has said that the news he heard from me about the prophets has touched him. He says his "head is soft" and he looks forward to hearing more. Please pray for Chef's father and mother, that they will be drawn to faith in Christ. Perhaps by prayer, new life may come out of this tragic death.

On a more macro level, international director Dr. Jim Plueddemann shared in a 2003 *Intercom* article "Why We Witness to Muslims":[7]

In today's pluralistic world, missionaries are often criticized by unbelievers and even by believers for witnessing to Muslims. At a recent meeting of mission directors, we articulated the reasons for why we are compelled to tell the Good News to Muslims. May we be humble, yet bold as we serve as Christ's ambassadors and as ministers of reconciliation (2 Corinthians 5).

Why Do Evangelical Missionaries Share the Good News with Muslims?
By CEOs of Evangelical Missions, March 2003

1. We love and submit to God with all our hearts.
2. We are disciples of the living Word of God, Jesus Christ.
3. We seek to obey the written Word of God, the Bible.
4. The Bible tells us that God created the people of all nations. He made us to worship and love Him, but all people rejected Him and rebelled against His love.
5. God has given us wonderful Good News. He loved us so much that He came in the person of Jesus to die in our place for our sins so we can be forgiven, adopted into His family and live with Him forever.
6. The Good News is good for the world. The Spirit of God gives us the power to live holy lives. People who live holy lives will love God, love all people and influence society for good.
7. The Bible commands all Christians to go and share the Good News with all nations. Missionaries can't make converts, only God brings people to Himself.
8. God longs for all people to know Him but has given freedom to accept or reject His free gift of eternal life through forgiveness of sins.
9. Missionaries share the Good News with respect. We do not coerce or trick people into believing the Good News. We love Muslims and share the Good News with deep humility and with respect for their culture.
10. Because we love God and love Muslims, we warmly invite Muslims to accept God's love and forgiveness through Jesus Christ.

Also from 2003 came a report concerning Life Challenge Africa and "New Opportunities for Outreach to Muslims," which also provided an update on the scope of SIM outreach to Muslims:[8]

SIM is engaged in a strategic plan to mobilize Anglophone West African Christians for outreach to their Muslim neighbours. Islam consultant Walter Eric, along with his wife, Christel, will be based in Accra, Ghana, for 12 months to assist in training and equipping God's people in the crucial task of Muslim evangelism. They have served in Southern and East Africa over the last 22 years with Life Challenge Africa and are happy to assist the mission family and churches on request.

Resources are available in several languages and include training materials, evangelistic literature, and teaching videos. The "Battle for the Hearts" video series will soon be available in French.

Worldwide, SIM missionaries serve Muslims in 29 countries, reaching 25 different ethnic groups.

A report from another West African country tells the story of a vital aspect in outreach to Muslims that is too often overlooked—how to assist Muslim background believers both to make a living and to grow in their new life as believers in Jesus. The 2004 *Intercom* article is entitled, "Co-ops Help Muslim Background Believers":[9]

Give a man a fish and feed him for a day. Teach a man to fish and you feed him for a lifetime.

In the spirit of this old proverb the Self-Help project for Muslim converts was born. Farmers [where we work] face many challenges just to survive. Dry ground depends on scarce rain for any sort of harvest. Droughts are common, leaving people to merciless loan sharks. Those who leave Islam face even tougher circumstances because help from their Muslim neighbors is often withheld.

The Self-Help project sets up practical assistance for Christian farmers by organizing them into a co-operative. A thresher, mill, and planting machines to use and rent out; and a building to store their goods will help these men avoid the cycle of poverty. (Without this infrastructure, one bad harvest or a medical emergency can force them to sell their equipment, then buy it back from a loan shark when planting season arrives.) We also hope that these machines will ease the workload of women in the society.

We praise God that this project is already fully funded. We pray that these farmers will bond together and support one another as Christians should. This aspect of the project is perhaps the most critical because these men have left behind the security of their larger community. Now they have a good chance to find something far better.

Each successive international director in the last 30 years has underscored both SIM's history of commitment to Muslim outreach, and the need to humbly and courageously continue and expand that good work. In 2005, following the exhaustive "Seize the Day" review, the recently installed international director Malcolm McGregor wrote in part the following under the title, "Our Response to World Disorder":[10]

Sharing the Gospel with Muslims and seeing the church established among them is a strategic priority for SIM. The importance of this priority is demonstrated in . . . three contexts:

Our current organizational context:

As an organization we have devoted a significant amount of time and effort in our recent *Seize the Day* Review, based on 1 Chronicles 12:32, to look at what we are doing and to set priorities for the future. There are still millions of Muslims in African and Asian countries where we currently work who have never heard the Gospel and therefore it is vital that this be a priority for us. This means that we need to continue to strategically invest in outreach to Muslims by mobilizing more prayer, more people and more financial resources.

Our historical context:

Sharing the Gospel and planting the Church among Muslims is at the very roots of SIM. In fact Rowland Bingham took on the colonial government of Nigeria to gain permission to preach the Gospel in the northern Nigerian city of Kano. He refused to accept that he could not share the Gospel in this city. Eventually, after much lobbying and much prayer, he obtained permission to do so.

The work of ICF in Pakistan, India, Bangladesh, Philippines and Iran was motivated by a desire to take the Gospel to Muslim peoples. AEF also had a historic commitment to the coastal Muslim people of Tanzania and South Africa.

Ministry to Muslims is in the DNA of SIM. Many of our missionaries have written extensively on this subject and have been a great influence on other organizations and churches, encouraging them to give energy and resources to this huge unreached group of people. Some have given their lives and the lives of their children because of their passion to meet this great need.

The current world context:

After the fall of Communism in the early 1990s, George Bush Sr. talked about a "new world order" coming into being. [The reality that has emerged] is very different I am sure from what the former President had in mind. It is an order, or perhaps we could call it a "disorder" where:

- The world of politics is now dominated by religious beliefs, not political ideologies.
- Societies of mixed ethnic and religious background clash violently.
- Oil is the economic engine, and most of these resources are held by Middle Eastern countries.
- Christianity as expressed in the West is seen as a failed belief system by many in the world.

This is a world context in which the Gospel needs to be heard, explained and lived. What is our response to this reality? Here are some suggestions:

1. **Dependence on God.** Even though much of what we see, hear and read causes fear and concern, we need to remember what God said to Isaiah, "I am God, and there is no other; . . . my purposes will stand and I will do all that I please" (Isaiah 46:9–10 NIV).

2. **Sensitivity.** We need to listen to all that God is saying to us at this unique time in history and respond with boldness.

3. **Flexibility and harmony.** We need flexibility and harmony in our approach to reaching Muslims. There is no one way to do this, as some may indicate. God needs to guide in each context and we need to be willing to follow.

4. **Courage and perseverance.** This work demands great strength of character in order to keep going in the midst of great fear and discouragement. This is truly "long term" work.

5. **Love and compassion.** These are two attributes that we do not readily associate with Islam. They need to be seen in our lives and they will open doors for the Gospel.

6. **Faithfulness to our witness imperative.** It is not politically correct to share the Gospel with Muslims, but we believe this is good news they need to hear and we need to keep sharing it. The Lord Himself will determine the harvest—we need to be faithful in our calling.

7. **Humility.** As we share what we believe, we need to do it with "gentleness and respect" (1 Peter 3:15–17). We must empty ourselves of superior attitudes and pride.

Items that Malcolm McGregor mentioned in his article include a missiological review by Dr. Ben Hegeman of the book *Why the Rest Hates the West*, by Meic Pearce (IVP, 2004); an article by Gary Corwin republished from the *Evangelical Missions Quarterly* (October 2004) entitled "Ten Things Worth Knowing About Islam"; and an article by Jo-Ann Brant entitled "Five Days in September."[11] Brant's article is a brief reflection on the then just completed 2005 consultation on reaching Muslims in Africa, and follows below:

SIM's consultation for workers involved with Africa's Muslims gathered in Nairobi, Kenya, this past September. We prayed, planned and focused on one of our *Faith Effects* priorities: "As Islam grows and takes on a strong profile in the world, it is a priority that we continue to share Christ with 'gentleness and respect, keeping a clear conscience.'" This is the third such meeting since 1987. We chose the Africa regional focus, with another gathering in Asia planned for the near future. We appreciated the cross-fertilization of ideas from participants who were a mixture of SIM members, fellow-workers from many African nations and several working with other groups.

The days were filled with presentations, panels, resource sharing, meditations and testimonies, and provided thought-provoking opportunities for serious discussions, resulting in future-oriented recommendations. As we gathered, leaders prayed that a team/community be developed that reflects our focused action and solidarity in purpose. Delegates prepared assignments and are now expected to share broadly what they have learned. Each delegate became well informed as to what SIM is already doing and where he or she fits into the larger picture. In addition, a number of recommendations came out of our days together. I will mention just two: we recommended that a consultation such as [a] SIM Consultation on Muslim Evangelism be held every five years, and that it should be regionally based, including representatives from other regions and sending offices.

Secondly, we recommended greater clarity with regard to our approaches to Muslim evangelism. While we encourage the removal of unnecessary barriers from the messenger's culture in our ministry to Muslims, we do not support a strategy where MBBs [Muslim Background Believers] are encouraged to continue practices that are against biblical principles. The deity and uniqueness of Christ is a difficult issue in Muslim evangelism, but we do not believe this crucial tenet of faith can be sidestepped as an essential of faith or a prerequisite for baptism. We oppose efforts to replace almost universally accepted translations of titles of "Christ" in the Bible.

We acknowledge that syncretism is an ever-present threat to our ministry. We are dependent on [the] Holy Spirit to transform all of our worldviews and assumptions as we become more like Jesus. It is not enough simply to teach Christian truth without addressing the underlying belief system and the daily life practices that it fosters.

A number of other key events and "divine encounters" have occurred in the last decade. We will close this section by highlighting just a few.

In 2006 SIM leadership created and filled a crucial new role with the appointment of Franz Nelson as Champion for Muslim Ministries, which he would undertake while continuing his ongoing strategic work with Life Challenge Africa. Writing under the title "That All Muslims May Hear,"[12] he invited other SIMers involved in Muslim ministry to join him in sharing "our wisdom and looking for ways to mentor one another. Let us be open to the Holy Spirit for guidance into creative ways to fulfill our calling." The creation of an internal Muslim Ministry Newsletter has been one of the key ways that has been taking place ever since.

SIM has made every effort through the years to connect with available networks for ministry among Muslims. An upshot of active participation in one such network resulted in significant SIM representation at an important 2007 consultation:[13]

Almost 500 men and women from around the world attended a consultation in Southeast Asia, focusing on developments in church planting among unreached Muslim groups, particularly on what practices are most effective in seeing Muslims come to Christ and which people groups are still beyond the reach of any church planting effort. This was a historic event called together by a strategic partnership of agencies, of which SIM is a member.

Participants were from 46 nationalities and have experience living among 149 Muslim peoples. More than three-quarters of the group were affiliated with just 14 organisations, but a total of 78 organizations and affiliations were represented at the consultation. SIM sent 34 representatives. Thirteen came from Africa, 12 from Asia, and nine from the U.S. Our 12 SIM ladies represented the importance of reaching Muslim women.

Each organization brought its unique characteristics with strengths and weaknesses to the event. Some excel at fundraising, others at research, others at resource development or training. All were keen to bring their gifts to the table and to receive from others in order to see the glory of the Father revealed among the Muslim people they love.

It was refreshing to observe how our own efforts at church planting among Muslims fit into the global picture the Master is making and encouraging to note how much progress has been made in the massive bloc of people who have not yet been introduced to Jesus.

A scholar recalled a similar historic event in 1978 when those who cared about Muslims were asking, "How do we take the Gospel to Muslims?" At this consultation, he noticed, the question has changed: "How do we become more effective at planting churches and discipling Muslim background believers?" A huge move forward!

Researchers were on hand to take advantage of this unique gathering and collect data on the state of the Gospel among Muslim peoples and on the practices being used today in church planting which are seeing fruit. This information will impact SIM's own training and strategies.

Our participants were excited and challenged to trumpet the call for more people in our mission to follow Jesus' call to bring his love to Muslim people. A great strength of the time was the opportunity to network and learn from people who had much to share. One participant said, "For me the highlight of the conference was seeing so many workers among Muslims—a real contrast to 45 years ago when we began our ministry." It was encouraging for everyone there to know that they are in a large fraternity. So many work alone or with just a few other people in the country of their ministry. Now they know there are others dealing with the same challenges—lack of fruit, struggles with language, problems with coworkers, and discouragement. It was good to hear testimonies of those who are seeing results and to be helped in finding new ways to do ministry. We all had a glimpse of what the Father is doing!

One of the outcomes of participation in this event was the commissioning by the international director Malcolm McGregor of a working group to study contextualization issues and draft guidelines for workers among Muslims for submission to the board of governors. A representative group of broadly experienced Muslim workers and missiologists was assembled for the task and worked diligently together (by email as well as by face-to-face meetings) for over a year. The final product entitled "A Discussion Of Contextualization Issues For Personnel Working Among Muslim Peoples" was approved by the board of governors. It was later amended on one of the 16 issues discussed for the sake of clarity, and was again affirmed in its April 2012 version by the board. It now serves as the primary policy statement and training source for SIM regarding the divisive issues it addresses.[14]

Somali news took center stage in 2009. Stan Bruning tells the story:[15]

Good news concerning the nation of Somalia is very difficult to find these days. However, SIM has great news for the Somali people as two major milestones have been reached with the publication of the revised Somali language Bible and the availability of downloads of that Bible on the Somali "New Life" ("Nolosha Cusub") website. The website provides Somalis a link to download the Bible onto their computers and cell phones, plus obtain podcasts of Somali Christian radio programs.

Pioneer SIM missionary Dorothy Modricker [famous in SIM with her husband Warren for their beginning of, energy in, and longevity of outreach to Somalis] directed the initial translation of the Bible into Somali, which was published in 1979. With worldwide supplies of the original Somali Bible nearly exhausted, a decade of revision work took place involving nine SIM missionaries, a colleague with Frontiers, and members of the Somali Christian communities in Nairobi, Kenya, and Addis Ababa, Ethiopia. The revision was printed in cooperation with the United Bible Society, and shipments were made in late November 2008.

The distribution of the revised Somali Bible to the Somali diaspora began in December. The Bible Societies of Kenya and Ethiopia will be responsible for distribution of the Bible on the Horn of Africa.

Each book of the revised Somali Bible can be read or printed from the site. Also, in partnership with Go Bible, website visitors can download the

Photo 17.5. "On the edge of the Sahara in Niger Republic, 'Zeb' Zabriskie witnesses to veiled Tuareg, desert nomads of unknown origin."
Photo credit: W. Harold Fuller, Run While the Sun is Hot *(Aylesbury, Bucks, England: Hazell Watson and Viney Ltd., 1967): between page 24 and 25.*

entire Somali Bible to their computers and cell phones. Within six weeks of posting, the new Somali Bible was downloaded 44 times by website visitors in Somalia, Djibouti, Kenya, Pakistan, the UK, Norway, Sweden, Germany, the Netherlands, Canada, and the USA. On the website, visitors also have access to programs of the SIM Somali language radio ministry.

On another front at the cutting edge of outreach to Muslims, Dr. Malcolm Hunter—arguably the leading missions advocate for nomadic peoples—provided an announcement to others in SIM regarding an upcoming Nomadic Gathering:[16]

Every three years some of those who are trying to show God's love by word and deed to Nomadic Peoples around the world meet together to share what they have learned from God about this specialized ministry. They have formed the Nomadic Peoples Network comprised of Christian workers from many different nationalities and organizations with the common unifying goal of learning how to be more effective in meeting the physical and spiritual needs of that stratum of human society which have a significantly different worldview from settled people. These Gatherings offer a welcome opportunity for those who are usually living in difficult and isolated places to enjoy fellowship with like-minded workers who understand the common issues but have also found no other course or curriculum that provides training for this sort of work.

At the next gathering they are adding a new component by inviting key representatives from the agencies with whom the field workers are associated, to come and hear what ministry to nomads is all about. They are also encouraged to bring along some likely potential recruits.

Finally, we conclude by sharing the recent story of a very low tech, but proven method of outreach that has been around since the beginning of time, and the encouraging results that it engendered. The title of this short piece is "Jesus Calling":[17]

Walking along a dusty road in Mali, an SIM missionary and his Malian colleague arrive at a divine appointment under a shade tree.

Two people walking together down a dusty dirt road encounter a friendly stranger resting beneath a shade tree.

Sound familiar?

How many stories from the Bible start with a similar image? Two walking on the road to Emmaus encounter a stranger who unfolds prophecy concerning the Christ for them. Nathaniel sits peacefully in the shade of a fig tree in the moments just before Philip calls him to meet Jesus, and his life radically changes.

As Joshua and Yacouba made their way home from the Bible study they led . . . they had no idea that a divine appointment was waiting for them.

As they approached a tree, they stopped to exchange a greeting with the stranger sitting there. He replied in English, and he was curious to know where they were from and what brought them to Mali. They shared with him that they are followers of Jesus and that he (Joshua) had come from the US to teach people about The Way.

As they explained to him what it means to follow The Way, he began to respond with amazement and interest. He exclaimed at how this teaching was so different from what the imams teach and lamented that even the imams do not live according to their words.

The conversation progressed, and the two men were able to help him understand that Christianity is not just a religious practice like Buddhism or Hinduism—that it is a way of life, walking in the footsteps of Jesus.

It was clear that the Lord had already been at work in the stranger's heart, for he expressed great interest in Jesus. As a Muslim he had learned about Jesus as a prophet and loved him. Now he asked Joshua and Yacouba if they could have studies because he was hungry to learn more about Jesus and The Way.

The two gave him their phone numbers so that in the future he can call when he is in town and schedule a time to gather for study and fellowship.

As the men prepared to leave, the stranger programmed their number into his phone.

He saved it under the name Jesus.

SUPPLEMENT 17.1

The History of Somali Outreach: Flexibility, Caring, and Sharing
Ben I. Aram

Church history in Somalia parallels that of North Africa. The fledgling church established in Somalia over a millennium ago dwindled away largely because the Ethiopian Orthodox Church retained Old Testament dietary taboos against the camel, along with demanding more than two hundred fast days that forbade consumption of milk or meat. By 1500 the Somali had become 100 percent Muslim.

French Roman Catholic missionaries began their efforts among Somalis in the 1880s in Djibouti and Somaliland. The Swedish Evangelical Mission came to southern Somalia in 1898, and established four mission stations with schools and an orphanage. When they were ejected by Mussolini in 1935, they had made over three hundred converts.

SIM became the second Protestant mission to the Somalis in 1943, when independent missionaries Warren and Dorothy Modricker joined the mission.

Their own work among the Somali had begun in 1933.[18] They ministered in Aden [what is now Yemen], since British colonial authorities had refused them entry to Somaliland. Significantly, the first field location for SIM outside of Africa was in this

Photo 17.6. *"Mr. and Mrs. Modricker, SIM headquarters in Aden. Working on Somali translation of Proverbs and Acts. Somali man is Yusuf Hassan"*

pioneering work among the oldest portion of the now global Somali Diaspora. Between 1947 and 1957, SIM opened stations in the Somali populated region in eastern Ethiopia. In 1954, the Modrickers realized their dream and moved to Somalia itself, opening the SIM station in the capital Muqdisho [Mogadishu]. During this decade Somalia was under a special UN mandate government in preparation for independence, and missionaries had considerable freedom of operation. Working in close coordination and cooperation with SIM, the Eastern Mennonite Mission (EMM) had entered Somalia a year earlier.[19]

Warren Modricker and other missionaries developed good relationships with secular Somali nationalists who dominated the post-independence government after 1960. They valued Christian missionaries as beneficial for providing development help, especially in providing high quality medical and educational facilities. SIM established three other stations in the central and southern regions. The murder of EMM missionary

Merlin Groves by Muslim fanatics in 1962 led to an overall backlash against mission work.[20] The Somali government forbade propagation of religions other than Islam but did allow limited room for both missions to operate.

In 1969, a military coup rebaptized as a Marxist revolution brought General Siyaad Barre into power. Initially, his regime promoted "Scientific Socialism" and firmly aligned Somalia with Communist countries. Mission properties were nationalized. The last SIM workers left in 1974. They were not deported, but elected to leave, since any contact missionaries had with Somali Christians left converts vulnerable to being imprisoned by the Soviet-trained secret police. The EMM left in 1976. The total number of converts from both missions in their two decades was estimated to be approximately 350.[21] A positive legacy of the Barre regime was his decision to forcefully end decades of debate over which alphabet should be used for the Somali language. In 1972, he chose the Latin script and mandated a massive literacy campaign that made over a quarter of the population literate in their mother tongue.

Many SIM missionaries relocated to Ethiopia with hopes of joining colleagues working among Somalis in the eastern provinces of the country. Unfortunately, the outbreak of the Ogaden War between Ethiopia and Somalia in 1977 resulted in the closing of all SIM mission stations among Somalis in eastern Ethiopia.

In Addis Ababa, two significant events took place: in 1974 Warren Modricker began production of "The Voice of New Life" (VNL), a shortwave radio broadcast in Somali on Radio Feba. Dorothy Modricker had also completed the translation of the Bible into Somali in 1977. In the aftermath of Ethiopia's war with Somalia, it became impossible to continue the VNL production in Addis Ababa. Meanwhile, Africa Inland Mission had invited SIM to come to Kenya to work with Somalis there. In 1978, a core group of veteran missionaries who had served in Somalia, then in Ethiopia, moved to Kenya, beginning work in Nairobi, Wajir, and Mombasa. The VNL team moved to Nairobi.

Beginning in Muqdisho in the 1950s, SIM had established a standard of robust language learning for its missionaries, extending this service to the EMM as well. In Nairobi, the SIM Somali language school existed periodically during the 1980s and 1990s, dependent on having qualified teachers. A large number of missionaries and relief/development workers from other organizations studied Somali along with SIM personnel; globally there were very few alternatives, if any, to the SIM language school.

Also in the 1980s and 1990s the VNL began producing a series of Bible correspondence courses, literature, and hymn cassettes. In 1997 a committee was formed [including Somali Christians] to revise the 1979 Bible translation. Work was completed in 2008 with the publication of the revised translation. Due to an influx of Somali refugees after 1991, SIM missionaries in Nairobi began the Somali Discipleship Training Center in close cooperation with four other mission agencies. This operated from 1993 to 1996. The Nairobi team was also involved in facilitating a Somali house church, providing medical assistance, English as a Second Language (ESL), and sports ministry to refugees.[22]

Meanwhile, in Wajir (Kenya's Somali-populated northeastern province), a SIM team gave gospel witness from a platform of agricultural development, education, and health. This was interrupted in 1983 due to false charges by Islamist elements. Later, in 2006, work in Wajir was closed due to security concerns.

In 1990, veteran John Miller began pioneering work with the sizable Somali community in Toronto. This work has continued since his retirement by a couple from Africa Inland Mission.

In 1995, SIM Ethiopia resumed work among Somalis. The initial personnel were all couples who had worked among Somalis in Kenya. The southern province team used adult education, agriculture, and health development as platforms, while in Addis Ababa, the team helped facilitate a fledgling Somali house church. They were also involved in ESL and sports ministry among the large refugee population. The VNL ministry moved back to Addis Ababa in 1998.

At present, SIM's Somali work consists of a team in Kenya, the VNL work in Addis Ababa, personnel seconded to a sister mission in Djibouti, and a team in Seattle, USA. The VNL developed a website and social media ministry in 2006 with a global impact for Somalis both in their global Diaspora and the Horn of Africa.

SUPPLEMENT 17.2

Dr. Phil Parshall

Photo 17.7. *Phil Parshall in his reading room near the Muslim center in Manila, Philippines*

Dr. Phil Parshall is one of the leading evangelical authorities on ministry to Muslims. He served as a missionary with his wife, Julie, sharing the love of Christ with Muslims in Bangladesh for 21 years. He served as field director for most of those years. In addition, he was founder of the Bangladesh Bible Correspondence School; founder of an annual spiritual life conference for missionaries in Bangladesh; vice-president of the Bangladesh Bible Society; member of the international council and executive committee of International Christian Fellowship; and interim home director of ICF (1979–1980). Long before the C1 to C6 spectrum became a common way to discuss contextualization methods for work among Muslims,[23] Parshall was applying to the mission field what would later be known as the C4 perspective. Following the SIM/ICF merger in 1989 he served among Muslims in the Philippines for almost 20 years, as director of the Asian Research Center.

Parshall completed graduate studies at Trinity Evangelical Divinity School (M.A.), Wheaton Graduate School (M.A.), Fuller Theological Seminary (D.Miss.), and Fellowships at Harvard and Yale Divinity School. He has authored nine books on Islam:

1. *The Fortress and the Fire*, Gospel Literature Service, Bombay, 1974 (Spanish and Chinese edition).

2. *New Paths in Muslim Evangelism*, Baker Book House, 1980 (reprinted by Authentic Publishing, 2003 as **Muslim Evangelism**; Chinese, Korean and Romanian editions).

3. *Bridges to Islam*, Baker Book House, 1983 (reprinted by Authentic Publishing, 2007; Indonesian translation).

4. *Beyond the Mosque*, Baker Book House, 1985.

5. *The Cross and the Crescent*, Tyndale House, 1989 (reprinted by Gabriel Publishing, 2002; French and Korean editions).

6. *Inside the Community*, Baker Book House, 1994 (reprinted as **Understanding Muslim Teachings and Traditions**, Baker Book House, 2002).

7. *The Last Great Frontier*, Open Doors, 2000.

8. *Divine Threads within a Human Tapestry*, William Carey, 2000 (Parshall's memoirs, also published in Korean).

9. *Lifting the Veil: The World of Muslim Women*, Gabriel Publishing, 2003 (German edition).

Four of these books are now published by InterVarsity Press.

Since finishing their ministry in the Philippines, the Parshalls have represented SIM and God's heart for the Muslim world in numerous locations where Phil has taught on Islam and reached Muslims with the love of Christ.

CHAPTER 18

SIM AND URBAN MISSIONS

Dr. Tim Geysbeek[1]

Introduction

SIM's International Leadership Team decided, after it concluded its "Seize the Day" review of the mission in January 2005, that one of SIM's "top ten" priorities was to reach urban centers.[2] International Director Malcolm McGregor explained that:

> Historically, urban centers have always been places of influence and innovation. The major cities in the countries where SIM works have exploded over the past 50 years. . . . SIM has historically been a rural-focused organization. That is changing and needs to continue changing as more and more people, in the countries where we work, move into urban centres.[3]

In 2007, roughly two-thirds of SIM's missionary force, or approximately 887 of its 1325 personnel, lived in cities."[4] At that time, SIM hoped—by 2025—to increase the number of people who work in these areas by 30 percent.[5] Seven years later, the United Nations estimated that 54 percent of the world's 7.24 billion people lived in urban areas. Calculating that the world's population will move into urban centers at an annual rate of 0.94 percent for the next few years, the United Nations projects that 60 percent of the world's estimated population of 8.42 billion people will be living in cities by 2030.[6]

Although most of the roots of the pre-merger missions are rural in orientation, these missions developed some remarkable ministries in cities in the past, and its current focus on reaching urban areas with the Christian gospel is not new. A cursory look at the founding of SIM and the missions that merged with SIM point to some rich history that dates back to the founding of Cape General Mission in 1889.

In this chapter we survey the urban origins of SIM and the missions that merged with SIM, fast-forward to the 1950s and beyond when SIM started to become actively involved in urban ministry, and conclude with some thoughts about the future.

The second half of the paper focuses more on what was happening with the Sudan Interior Mission after 1980, when SIM officially lost its "Sudan" identity and was renamed SIM International, and two years later when SIM began to shed its Africa image after its merger with Andes Evangelical Mission (AEM). The discussion is skewed toward SIM before the mergers of AEM, International Christian Fellowship, and Africa Evangelical

Fellowship in the 1980s and 1990s because the author, who was raised in SIM (Liberia, Nigeria) and is thus more familiar with its history, has only had scant opportunity to study the broader history of the missions that merged with SIM. Lastly, most of the scholarly research and publication about the mission has been conducted about the Sudan Interior Mission.[7]

Early Urban Histories
Africa Evangelical Fellowship

One of the oldest parts of today's SIM are the progenitors of Africa Evangelical Fellowship (AEF) which began in some of the major urban centers in today's South Africa, and which represent the most urbanized origins of the pre-merger missions.[8] AEF traced its history to the Cape General Mission (CGM) that Martha Osborn, Andrew Murray, Spencer Walton, and George Howe founded in Cape Town, on 12 March 1889.[9] CGM missionaries expanded into Kimberly and the Transkei along the coast. Martha Osborn-Howe, along with George Howe whom she married, founded the South East Africa Evangelistic Mission (SEAEM) in 1891, and based their operations in Durban. CGM and

Photo 18.1. *SAGM's Hall, Cape Town*

SEAEM merged to form the South Africa General Mission in 1894 (SAGM); SAGM mainly worked in Cape Town, Durban, Johannesburg, and Swaziland during its formative years. SAGM was renamed Africa Evangelical Fellowship (AEF) in 1965. AEF merged with SIM in 1998.[10]

Cape Town, which was the capital of Cape Colony, had an estimated population of 78,000 in 1904.[11] Given that only 50 cities had populations over 50,000 in Africa in 1950, any city with

a population more than 50,000 at the turn of the century was especially large.[12] The missionaries in Cape Town ministered among soldiers, sailors, women, the sick, and railway workers, and built a hall that they used to lead services, sell books, and hold Bible studies and open-air meetings.

Most of their target audience was the white population, but they did reach out to Malay migrants and others when they conducted open-air meetings. The Hall became a model for the work that expanded into Johannesburg and beyond. Missionaries conducted short-lived work among the Africans who labored in the gold fields of Johannesburg (est. pop. 102,000 in 1896).[13] SAGM moved its headquarters to Kimberly (est. pop. 43,000 in 1874)[14] in 1897. In the 1890s, missionaries went to Durban to reach out to Indian migrants and Africans.[15]

In the 1890s and on into the next century, SAGM missionaries moved from Durban into Nyasaland (Malawai), Angola, Mozambique, and Southern (Zimbabwe) and Northern (Zambia) Rhodesia, and they mostly developed rural-based ministries.[16] At midcentury, SAGM's leaders acknowledged that "little spiritual work is done" in the "great

Photo 18.2. *"Mr. Tomlinson baptizing an Indian convert in Durban"*

towns" where thousands of Africans lived. They noted that SAGM was preparing to send two men to minister among the Africans who worked in the Johannesburg mines and in Windermere near Cape Town.[17]

One example of an important urban-based ministry that AEF started after World War II was "Youth Alive." Al and Lorry Lutz and Jerry Mavis Nkosi started to work among the youth of Johannesburg in 1960, and in 1964 named the ministry Youth Alive.

Youth Alive's members led Bible studies, organized prayer meetings during lunch hours in schools, established clubs, and staged evangelistic rallys that often attracted hundreds of youth. Youth Alive later became independent from AEF and continued to do important work among the city's young black population.[18]

Photo 18.3. *Youth Alive staff.*
(L-R): Jerry Mavis Nkosi (white jacket), Lorry and Al Lutz

International Christian Fellowship

The next oldest pre-merger missions are the Ceylon and Indian General Mission (CIGM) and the Poona and Indian Village Mission (PIVM) that centered most of their work in the villages of southern India. Benjamin Davidson founded CIGM on 15 December 1892, and Charles Reeve and E. W. McGavin founded PIVM in February 1893.

CIGM began its first ministry in Colombo, Ceylon (today's Sri Lanka), where its missionaries studied Tamil, visited homes, and conducted outdoor meetings. Colombo was a harbor town with a population of approximately 155,000 in 1900.[19] India's population was 234 million in 1900, as opposed to 133 million for Africa and 74 million in South America, so the average size of cities in parts of the world where the pre-merger missions worked was the highest in south Asia.[20]

CIGM's work at Colombo was sporadic and sometimes nonexistent. One must look, rather, to CIGM's activities in India for a better understanding of the direction of their work. CIGM established its headquarters in Bangalore. Bangalore had a population of 185,000 in 1901 and was used by CIGM as a base to send out and supply missionaries who worked in smaller towns farther north like Hindupur to reach the Telugu, and towns to the southwest like Coimbatore and Coonor to reach the Tamil. Most CIGM missionaries branched out from these centers to market towns and villages to establish churches, orphanages, Bible schools, dispensaries, and boarding homes for boys and girls.[21]

The names "Poona" and "Village" in PIVM indicate the centre and thrust of this mission's early work. Poona, with an estimated population of 153,320 in 1901, was the headquarters of the British army's Southern Command in southwest India.[22] PIVM missionaries opened coffee shops and held services to reach the British troops—similar to what CGM and SAGM did in South Africa.[23] More importantly, PIVM used Poona as a base to send workers out to establish stations along the route that led to the sacred Hindi city of Pandharpur. The missionaries and their Indian

Photo 18.4. *Indian woman leading a Bible study in Pandharpur, early 1900s*

colleagues preached and sold Scriptures along the route. In Pandharpur, they seconded Indian "Bible women" from another mission to help them teach women.

PIVM also built a dispensary and hospital in Pandharpur in 1910 and 1917 respectively, opened two orphanages, and later a hospital in Nasrapur and a clinic in Mahud.[24]

CIGM and PIVM merged to become the International Christian Fellowship (ICF) in 1968, and the ICF united with SIM in 1989. One type of institution that ICF used in its early years to reach people who lived in large cities was Bible schools that prepared men and women to evangelize and become leaders in their churches. There was, for example, the Bible Training School in Hindupur, India; the Bible Training Institute in Hyderabad, Pakistan; and the Bible Correspondence School that moved from Manikganj to Dhaka in Bangladesh.[25] In addition, there was the bookroom that was set up in Manila,

Philippines; ICF's partnership with Scripture Union that was based in Allahabad, India; and the joint ICF–Child Evangelism Fellowship venture in Delhi, India, that prepared lessons and provided instruction for children.[26] ICF was forced to shift its focus from rural to more urban-based ministries in 1967 after India stopped granting missionary visas. Thereafter, for example, a number of ICF personnel undertook graduate studies at universities that were located in the cities, and used their presence there as a platform to engage with university students.[27]

Sudan Interior Mission

The Sudan Interior Mission was founded on 4 December 1893, the date Walter Gowans, Thomas Kent, and Rowland Bingham landed in Lagos, in today's Nigeria. Gowans and Kent headed for the interior in February 1894, leaving Bingham behind because of illness. SIM literature is fond of stating things such as "SIM is historically a rural-oriented mission agency, since our founders opted for the interior."[28] The overall premises that "SIM is historically a rural-oriented mission agency" is correct, but the reason is not because SIM's founders "opted for the interior"; large trade cities existed in the interior when Gowans and Kent trekked northeast in 1894, and they were heading toward one of the most populous—Kano. Kano was one of the most highly populated cities in precolonial and colonial Africa with a population of at least thirty thousand at the turn of the century. It was the commercial capital and largest of the walled Hausa cities that existed in the Sokoto Caliphate.[29]

Gowans and Kent reached the caliphate, but not Kano, and died there in the last weeks of 1894. SIM established its first mission stations in Patigi, Bida, and Wushishi in 1902, 1903, and 1904 respectively. These were predominately Muslim merchant towns situated along important trade routes in the southern reaches of the caliphate. The British conquered the Sokoto Caliphate in 1903, but SIM's anticipation that they could follow the troops turned to disappointment when the British forbade most missionaries

Photo 18.5. *"A Soudanese City."*
Source: "The Soudan," Regions Beyond New Series 75 (September-October 1894): 331.

Photo 18.6. *"Kano city from minaret of Mosque,"*
c. 1940.

Photo credit: Harry Cox

from working in the north. By 1910, SIM shifted its strategy from evangelizing the Muslims in the north to reaching what they called "pagan tribes" like the Yoruba further south. This shift in strategy came about for three reasons: the non-Muslim peoples were less resistant to the gospel; the British permitted SIM to establish ministries in the south; and SIM's leaders felt they should establish churches in the south so Muslims would not win over the predominately non-Muslim peoples who lived there.[30]

SIM returned to its original strategy of reaching the Muslims by the mid-1920s as the missionary presence intensified in the south and SIM's leaders decided that translating the Bible into the very widely spoken Hausa language would be a key means to reach the Hausa. Furthermore, SIM's leaders never abandoned their long-term plan to reach Muslims living in the north—many who lived in cities. SIM and several other mission organizations held a conference in London in 1927 to voice their opposition against the British government that restricted missionary movements in northern Nigeria. Two years later, the leaders of several missions, including SIM's Bingham, held a conference in Miango, Nigeria, and expressed their resolve to move north. In 1933, SIM established a work in Garko just 40 miles south of Kano. SIM's first missionaries moved to Kano in 1936 and eventually established a dispensary, school for the blind, elementary and Hausa language school, leprosy clinic, and eye hospital. From Kano, SIM sent missionaries to several other Hausa cities including Katsina where the British government turned over its large leprosarium to SIM in 1937.[31]

After World War II, SIM used literature and youth centers to reach youth and young adults, many of whom lived in cities.[32] SIM started publishing *African Challenge* in Lagos, Nigeria, in 1946, targeting students who were under 21 years of age. By 1961, nearly 250,000 copies were being sold per month in Nigeria and Ghana. The mission

Photo 18.7. *Albert Brant with students at the Addis Youth Center, 1960s*

estimated that its potential readership was at least 10 times the number of magazines that were sold.[33]

Missionaries established SIM's first youth center in Addis Ababa, Ethiopia, in 1962. The center provided a place of community, religious instruction, and evangelism for secondary and university students, and emerged to be a learning ground for the development of indigenous leaders. The Ethiopian leaders of the youth center later founded the vibrant *Hebret Amba* ("citadel of fellowship"), which eventually joined the Kale Heywet Church.[34]

Andes Evangelical Mission

The Bolivian Indian Mission (BIM) that George and Mary Allan founded in 1907 was the most rural oriented of all the missions that now comprise SIM. The Allans first went to Argentina with the South American Evangelical Mission in 1899.[35] While in Argentina, the Allans formed their own short-lived Australasian South American Mission in 1902 due to "some difficulties" with their mission and its merger with another mission. They moved to Bolivia the following year where they and their small team worked among the Quechua and Aymara-speaking Indians, and started to translate the New Testament into Quechua. While there, they learned that San Pedro de Buena Vista would be a good place to work among the Quechua.[36]

The Allans founded BIM after they left Bolivia and arrived in London in November 1907. They then sailed to New Zealand early the next year, and returned to Bolivia with the first party of BIM missionaries in May 1909.[37]

The political and commercial center of Bolivia was La Paz which had an estimated population of 62,320 in 1893. Cochabama was the second largest city in Bolivia with 20,530 inhabitants. Four other cities registered more than 10,000 residents in 1893.[38] The Allans moved to San Pedro where barely 2,000 people lived. In San Pedro, BIM missionaries held gospel meetings, taught Quechua to new missionaries, translated the New Testament into Quechua, and started a school for missionary children. More missionaries arrived on the field within the next 10 years, and moved into towns that do not seem to have been any larger than San Pedro. BIM only started to become involved in urban ministry in 1937 after it relocated its headquarters to Cochabamba.

Photo 18.8. *Preaching in the market in Cochabamba*

BIM's urban work began in earnest several years later under the direction of Vern Roberts who succeeded George Allan as BIM's director in 1941. In 1950, BIM purchased some property in Cochabamba and built a "meeting hall" and a three-story building that the missionaries used to open a Bible institute and evening school, set up a bookstore, and establish a church.[39]

Renewed Vision for Urban Missions in the 1950s and Beyond

The world's population started a trend toward becoming more urban after World War II. According to the United Nations, the percentage of the world's population that was urban shifted from 28.4 percent in 1950, to 41.3 percent in 1980, to 50 percent in 2007. SIM and the missions that merged with it started to meet some of the challenges of urbanization in the 1950s, but not, however, in a vacuum. The World Council of Churches formed the Urban Rural Mission in the early 1960s to promote strategies for reaching cities.[40] In April 1966, the much more conservative Interdenominational Foreign Mission Association (IFMA) and Evangelical Foreign Mission Association (EFMA) held a Congress on the Church's World Mission (CCWM) at Wheaton College that brought together over 900 delegates from 71 countries which represented nearly 250 mission organizations, churches, and "special interest groups."

Photo 18.9. *Congress on the Church's World Mission, 1966.*

Photo credit: Sudan Witness *(2nd quarter, 1966): cover.*

The CCWM dealt with a wide range of issues such as communism, nationalism, social problems, syncretism, and urbanization. AEF, AEM, CIGM, and SIM sent delegates to the CCWM.[41] CIGM's *Darkness and Light* did not mention the congress, and AEF's *African Evangel* only gave a brief notice in December 1966. BIM's *The Andean Outlook* published an article about two representatives of its related Bolivian church, the Unión Christiana Evangélica or Evangelical Christian Union (UCE), who attended the congress. One of the UCE's attendees was Ezequiel Torres, UCE's executive secretary, who stated that the congress was "one of the greatest events since the Reformation took place."[42] The next issue of the *Outlook* published an article titled "Mission in the Cities" that David Hoffner wrote. Hoffner argued that "In our day of urban explosion . . .the crowded city streets should be just as much a symbol of foreign missions as the thatched-roof huts." He encouraged home churches to consider ministry in cities and rural areas equally viable, and listed several ministries that AEM missionaries were doing in Cochabamba:

> teaching in a missionary children's school, operating a printing press, repairing vehicles, serving as a hostess, treasurer, or secretary, buying endless supplies, [and] working in a bookstore or visiting municipal authorities. . . . In the midst of these more routine and mundane tasks, the universal challenge of evangelism and church planting operates on every level of society, from the filthy slums to the aristocratic suburbs. Opportunities for presenting Christ to thousands of civilized heathen are virtually unlimited.[43]

SIM helped plan the congress and gave it significant coverage in the *Sudan Witnes.*[44] One of the issues that the delegates addressed—and that challenged SIM's leaders—was the "complex problems of urban communities."[45] Before this congress, however, SIM had already started to focus on youth—many who lived in cities—and featured urban missions in the fourth quarter issue of the *Sudan Witness* in 1965.[46] SIM had already started to target students through literature and youth centers in the 1950s and 1960s.

After the CCWM convened in 1966, several other meetings, some of which were more ecumenical in orientation, met to discuss pertinent issues over the next quarter century. Key meetings that dealt with urbanization were the Lausanne Congress on World Evangelization (LCWE) (1974); the LCWE Conference that met in Pattaya, Thailand (1980); the Study Conference on the Evangelism of World-Class Cities in Chicago (1986); the eighth Theological Consultation of the Asian Theological Association in Singapore (1987), the Latin American Theological Fraternity that met in Bravo, Mexico (1988); the Lausanne II meetings that were held in Manila (1989); and the Global Consultation on World Evangelization in Seoul, Korea (1995). Some of the individuals who emerged as leaders of urban missiology were Dr. Timothy Monsma, Dr. Ray Bakke, Dr. Roger Greenway, and Dr. Sam Wilson.[47] SIM worked with these men and participated in some of the above-named meetings.

SIM started to make urban centers a high priority in the 1980s when Ian Hay was SIM's general director. In 1980, General Council, which is the predecessor of today's Global Assembly and Board of Governors, instructed SIM's directors and councils to "develop strategies to cities within their areas of responsibility." They noted the rapid pace of urbanization, the fact that reaching urban dwellers had the potential to influence whole nations, and suggested several strategies: training local pastors and evangelists, assigning missionaries to work with city pastors; teaching Bible knowledge classes in city schools; organizing evangelistic campaigns; establishing reading rooms; being creative in using music and drama; developing contacts with professional and social groups; exploring ways that sports could be used; being hospitable; and showing films to small groups of educated peoples that would appeal to them intellectually and spiritually.[48]

General Council's mandate generated a series of workshops, seminars, and initiatives that Gerald Swank, Jim Kraakevik, Gary Corwin, and others led or encouraged to further SIM's capability to reach cities. In February 1981, Swank, who had worked in Nigeria for several years, drafted a memo that outlined a five-year plan to research the cities and hold seminars. Hay circulated Swank's findings to the mission's leadership.[49] In May 1983, Dr. Raymond J. Bakke led the "Latfricasian Urban Evangelism / Church Planting Seminar" at SIM International's headquarters in Cedar Grove, New Jersey, which included 18 participants from several missions and churches.[50] In 1984, General Council directed SIM to identify key people to conduct research, develop strategies, and mobilize missionaries and nationals to implement plans.[51] Hay lamented at these council meetings that "It's past time for SIM to forge a new plan for tackling the problems of urbanization," and noted that "though perhaps not as romantic, are as great or greater than those of primitive jungles."[52]

Gary Corwin followed Jim Kraakevik as SIM's director of the International Resource Center and director of research in 1984. Corwin added coordinator of urban ministries to

his portfolio two years later, being given responsibility to stimulate, equip, and build networks to expand SIM's work in urban ministries. He and others did this by publishing the *Urban Ministries Log* (1987–1989); contributing to *Africa Report*, *Africa Urban Ministries Review*, and *City Watch*; holding consultations for SIM missionaries in Africa and South America; and conducting workshops in colleges, seminaries, and churches. The first and most inclusive consultation, which included SIMers from Africa and South America, was held in Monrovia, Liberia, in January

Photo 18.10. *SIM missionaries discussing urban ministry, Abidjan, 1987.*
(L-R): Gary Corwin, Hans Mueller, Bob Arnold, Marcia Arnold, Steve Sorensen, and Ron Sonius.

1985.[53] Corwin and Panya Baba, general secretary of the Evangelical Missionary Society, then attended the Trinity Consultation for Evangelizing World-Class Cities in Chicago in 1986 and conducted strategy sessions with specialists in the field.[54]

Several conferences followed the Trinity Consultation that SIM missionaries and church leaders attended: a meeting in Cochabamba for those working with urban professionals (April 1987); "listening groups" that Corwin and Ray Bakke held in Accra, Ghana, and Abidjan, Côte d'Ivoire (July and August 1987); a church planting seminar in Cochabamba with Christian and Missionary Alliance's Rev. Alfredo Smith (April 1988); a workshop which Sam Wilson led in Lima, Peru (April 1988); an urban research workshop that Timothy Monsma and Corwin led for SIM and EMS in Yola, Nigeria (July 1988); urban sessions at Lausanne II that Corwin helped plan and teach (1989); meetings that Roger Greenway led in Ecuador (1990); and a consultation that Monsma organized in Addis Ababa (1991).[55]

SIMNOW drew attention to the needs of cities in the early 1980s[56] and published a special issue on urban missions in 1988. The lead article stated: "No doubt you're aware of the current emphasis on the 'new urgency' to reach city dwellers with the gospel. . . . Without neglecting the rural areas, SIM is laying increasing emphasis on strengthening its present urban ministries and establishing new ones."[57] Stories were written about SIM's work in Abidjan (Côte d'Ivoire), Accra (Ghana), Addis Ababa (Ethiopia), Arequipa (Peru), Kankan (Guinea), Khartoum (Sudan), Lima (Peru), and Monrovia (Liberia). At this time, SIM missionaries were also engaged in urban ministry in Asuncion (Paraguay), Cape Town, Claremont Clareinch (South Africa), Cochabamba (Bolivia), Cotonu (Benin), Huancayo (Peru), Ilorin, Jos (Nigeria), Kumasi (Ghana), Nairobi (Kenya), Niamey (Niger), La Paz (Bolivia), Roma (Italy), and Santiago (Chile).[58] Yet, given increased awareness about the needs in cities, only about 5 percent (52 of 996) of SIM's active missionaries were serving in urban-related ministries in 1988.[59]

Photo 18.11. *"Witness in the City,"* 1988.

Source: SIMNOW 42 (November–December 1988): cover.

Also, by the 1980s, Africa Evangelical Fellowship had come to understand the importance of reaching people who lived in cities. For instance, the main focus of the January–March 1988 issue of AEF's *Action Africa* was urban missions. Editor William Walker noted that "the phenomenal growth of cities . . .has become the greatest challenge ever faced by the church." Although many of the fields had started to "develop strategies for the city and urban areas," Walker noted that AEF needed to give outreach to cities "serious consideration" for the mission to be effective. This issue of *Action Africa* also discussed urban work that AEF was conducting in South Africa, Malawi, and Mozambique.[60] When AEF merged with SIM in 1998, AEF missionaries were ministering in Lubango (Angola), Windhoek (Namibia), Gaborone (Botswana), Harare (Zimbabwe), Lusaka (Zambia), Mupato (Mozambique), Lilongwe (Malawi), Cape Town, Durban, Pietermaritzburg, and Johannesburg (South Africa).[61]

When International Christian Fellowship merged with SIM in 1989, ICF missionaries were living in cities such as Thies (Senegal), Karachi, Lahore, Rahim Yar Khan, Islamabad (Pakistan), Dhaka, Kushtia, Rajshahi (Bangladesh), Manila, and Cotabato City (Philippines).[62]

A reassignment of duties with greater emphasis on theological education took Corwin out of the urban ministry coordinator position in 1991, and added this task to Howard Brant's already crowded portfolio.[63]

SIM reorganized the way it conducted its ministries after Jim Plueddemann became international director in 1993, decentering its emphasis on urban work to focus more on specialized ministries such as children's schooling, education, medicine, AIDS, children, human needs, radio, and church planting. While many of these ministries crosscut urban and rural settings, they were not all necessarily part of a larger integrated strategy to reach cities. This is not to say, however, that SIM stopped being interested in

Photo 18.12. "The Greatest Challenge," 1988.

Source: Action Africa 2, no. 1 *(January-March 1988).*

reaching city dwellers. SIM had appointed John Shane to become SIM's Urban Ministries Consultant in Africa in 1989 (loaned from Mission to the World). Shane continued his work through the Urban Ministries Support Group (UMSG). The UMSG sought to "become a resource for African urban ministry by learning as much as possible about African urbanization and then facilitating or encouraging those involved in reaching African towns and cities for Christ." UMSG staff conducted workshops, taught university courses, took part in programs, organized symposiums for educators, collected and distributed relevant syllabi, published a reader for students, gave presentations, established the Nairobi Urban Ministries Fellowship, published articles and a newsletter. John Koski, who joined UMSG in 1995, became UMSG's director in 1999 after Shane left. Koski worked with UMSG until 2005.[64]

In addition to reaffirming John Shane as the mission's urban specialist for Africa, SIM during Plueddemann's years also held a Vision Consultation on Urban Ministries in 1996. The international council urged SIM's area councils to write vision and strategy statements to explain how they would develop ministries in urban areas in 1997.[65] One would need to conduct research to determine the practical results of the consultations and conferences that the mission became engaged in since the mid-1980s. As stated at the beginning, SIM International Director Malcolm McGregor and his leadership team determined SIM should give "new or greater importance for the years ahead" to working in "Urban centers after the mission evaluated itself in 2005."[66]

CHAPTER 19

MINISTRIES OF COMPASSION

Paul J. Hudson, MD, MPH, FACP

When the Sudan Interior Mission founders first stepped foot on African soil, tropical West Africa was considered the "white man's grave." Sixteen percent of the white people who lived in Lagos in 1894 died mostly of "fever" (malaria, yellow fever, blackwater fever) and dysentery.[1] Our founders embraced both suffering and death for the sake of the gospel. SIM's ministries of compassion are rooted in the love of Christ. This chapter will look at the early roots of care for the sick and suffering, and trace some of the fruit of these efforts in the form of hospital ministries after the Second World War. After 1970 SIM began to focus on community health, development, and relief. This expanded community focus allowed agriculturalists, veterinarians, relief workers, and those caring for HIV/AIDS to join medical missionaries to alleviate and prevent human suffering as part of the ministry of the gospel. However, this same focus also challenges us to examine our theological vision of ministries of compassion, and gives SIM fresh opportunity to integrate institutional and community ministries, in partnership with believers from multiple cultures around the world.

> "We humbly acknowledge that the ultimate human need is to know God. **We also believe that he has called us to compassionate, holistic service** in this broken world by alleviating suffering, fostering development, and effecting change in society."
>
> —*SIM Core Values, 2015*

Roots: Compassionate Care of the Sick, 1893–1945

One of our first missionary doctors was both an evangelist and a physician. Dr. Andrew Stirrett arrived in Nigeria in 1902. Dr. Rowland Bingham, director of the Sudan Interior Mission, said of Dr. Stirrett,

> Over thirty-seven years ago when the Sudan was looked upon as virtually a closed field, when our third expedition had just left, after two attempts had ended in seeming death and disaster, a good brother called upon us and said

that he had read our "Plea for the Central Sudan," and that he felt that the work must be done. If we thought that he was not the man to go, he desired us to sell all his property and to see that someone else was sent. He made over all his property to the Mission and went out to the field. For thirty-seven years and more he has been the beloved physician not only to all our missionaries, but to thousands of natives. And no one ever comes under his hand who does not hear the story of redeeming love.[2]

Photo 19.1. *Dr. Stirrett preaching after having treated wounds*

Dr. Stirrett ministered to body and soul and to missionary and Nigerian alike. In 1931 he wrote and dedicated to missionaries his *Medical Book for The Treatment of Diseases in West Africa; also Pharmacy Notes, dispensary Recipes and Health Hints — Written in Non-Technical Language.*[3]

Rowland Bingham speaks of his "unsparing efforts for the physical and spiritual welfare of the whole staff," as evidenced by only 12 missionary deaths over 40 years of ministry, despite deadly conditions in West Africa and over three hundred white workers. At the same time it was estimated by Rev. G. W. Playfair, who became general director of the SIM in 1944, that the doctor had preached to no less than one and a half million people in Africa, "a somewhat conservative estimate when one knows the congested crowds of the native markets."[4]

In 1905, three years after Dr. Stirrett arrived in West Africa, Dr. Ethel Ambrose landed in India from Australia, part of the Poona and Indian Village Mission (which eventually became part of SIM). She immediately got to work with language learning and meeting medical needs.

One of her fellow workers wrote of her, "Doctor's thoroughness and faithfulness begat the same in all who worked under her. Whatever had to be done was undertaken in a calm and thorough way. The harder she was pressed the calmer she became—it was not that she did not feel things, for she had a fine sensitive nature, but God so ruled in her life that His grace was magnified in her. She was always, first a missionary, then a doctor."[5]

Photo 19.2. *Dispensary in Pandharpur, 1910.*
Dr. Ethel Ambrose, her sister Nurse Lily, and "Miss Gray" established this dispensary over a grain store. They treated 2,342 patients during their first six months of work.[6]

Photo 19.3. *Ethel Titcombe with twins*

Compassion did not flow from professionals alone. Wives often cared for the sick. As a newly arrived bride in Egbe, Nigeria in 1915, Ethel Titcombe had no medical training. A messenger came running from the town. "Can you come quickly?" he asked Ethel. "There is a woman who needs you."

There was a woman who had just given birth to twins. She had had four babies and all had died. The family and friends were waiting for the medicine man to come to take the twins away. She herself would be driven to the bush. At that time the Yagbas believed that a woman who gave birth to twins was something less than human and they wouldn't let her live any longer in the village. Believing one of the twins must be an evil spirit, the medicine man killed both to make sure.

Imagine the bravery of that mother! She held to the beliefs of her people but something gave her the courage to go against custom, so she'd sent for Ethel. She looked up at Ethel from the dirt floor on which she lay and reaching out her arms imploringly, she asked, "White woman, help me. All my babies have died. I do not want to lose these. Please help me!"

Ethel realized that if they were to do anything at all they'd have to do it at once. She put the babies in a large calabash [carrier], covered them with a cloth, and urged the mother to her feet. With a woman carrying the calabash on her head, they made their way home. It was still early, and they were safely away from the town before the medicine man arrived. But the woman was in great danger, and so were they.[7]

Despite the danger, there were no reprisals. The twins thrived (after Ethel coaxed the mother to go against yet another tradition which withheld nursing for the first nine days of a baby's life). Ethel's husband Tommy said, "I had tried for seven years to break this [twins] custom, only to fail. But my wife was in Egbe only two days and the Lord already had begun to use her presence to help her Yagba sisters."

The Sudan Interior Mission's ministry to both body and soul together was shaped in these early decades by good theology. In 1921, SIM General Director Rowland Bingham wrote about bodily healing in the Scriptures in his book, *The Bible and the Body*. He was responding to "our friends in the Christian and Missionary Alliance who believe that God's methods of healing for His people are only through supernatural means." He first tells of his own illness during his first entry to Africa with Gowans and Kent:

> Many years ago the writer was given up to die in a Government hospital in West Africa. The doctor said there was no hope. At that very time he was visited by the saintly Bishop Hill, of the Church Missionary Society, who, on returning from the hospital, called the whole missionary force together for a special prayer meeting on his behalf. At the conclusion of a season of earnest intercession, Bishop Hill turned to one of those taking part, and said, "Miss Maxwell, do you believe we are going to have the thing we ask?" He continued, "I do; I am sure that young man is going to be raised up." To his prayer of faith the writer owes his life today; but before he was raised up, both Bishop Hill and his beloved wife were in their graves, dying less than a week afterwards. . . . We trust we have demonstrated that the Scriptures set forth God as the Healer of His people: that he heals both by natural means and by supernatural quickening: that inasmuch as He is the author of both, they are not antagonistic the one to the other, but supernatural healing supplements the natural: that the Scriptures themselves lay down the basic laws of health and clearly show that all truly natural means of healing are in harmony with the divine will and in accord with the divine law: that God has encouraged us to believe that, he is able and, where it is for His glory, is willing to intervene supernaturally for the healing of His own people.[8]

Founded on these roots of love for body and soul, SIM's ministry to human need over the first half of the twentieth century grew side by side with evangelism and church-planting. Almost every SIM mission station had a dispensary, well over 150 dispensaries on the field. Nigerian Yusufu Turaki wrote, "The contribution of the SIM medical work in Northern Nigeria was quite substantial and was the largest of all Christian missions. SIM was also the largest contributor in Northern Nigeria towards leprosy work and fighting eye diseases and blindness." He continues, "This ministry of mercy and caring was also a ministry of soul winning and evangelism. It would be difficult to quantify the impact of medical work and services in establishing Christianity in the Sudan. However its influence and impact are observable facts."[9]

Ministry to human need is born out of compassion, which literally means "coming alongside in someone else's suffering." Over the decades SIM missionaries have journeyed with individuals affected by disease (from leprosy to Ebola), disaster (from famine to earthquake relief) and dysfunction (alcohol abuse to human trafficking).

This was a bad beginning. To stand there staring was to reveal my horror. To speak seemed to be worse. How would I ever be able to work among these people? I would go back to Kano—to Wushishi. I could not work here! To my inexpressible relief, Sue Hooge came out of the ulcer station carrying a sheaf of records.

"I thought," I said in English, "that leper's hands just get white, and then the fingers fall off! That's what it always sounds like when people talk about it at home!"

"It's not as simple as that," said Sue.

I was seeing the most repulsive aspect of leprosy, bared to view because all the patients had removed their dressings for inspection and treatment. Never had I seen such deep ulceration. Never had I dreamed that any disease could maim and disfigure so cruelly without bringing a speedy end. I shuddered.

I scolded myself mentally as I restrained myself, by sheer determination, from fleeing the station then and there.

Perk up, hard-boiled nurse! This is what you came out to Africa for—remember? And don't feel sorry for yourself! You're just looking at it! These people live with it all the time!

I pondered that thought. These people could smell the rotting of their own tissues and were watching, in their own bodies, what Dr. Jotcham had aptly described as "the remorseless nibblings of unhurried death."

—*missionary nurse Martha Wall*[10]

Bearing Fruit: Growth of Hospitals, 1945–1970

The most unreached areas of the world often experience a disproportionate amount of human suffering. Acts of mercy growing out of homes and then dispensaries in the early decades eventually resulted in the building of hospitals, which became long-term institutionalized strategies for SIM. Egbe Hospital in Nigeria was established by Dr. Campion in 1952, out of the Maternity Center which grew up from Ethel and Tommy Titcombe's ministry in 1928;[11] this was followed by Bingham Memorial Nursing Home in Jos to care for the medical needs of missionaries (1946), Kano Eye Hospital (1943), and Jos Hospital (1959). Meanwhile, beyond Nigeria, SIM was founding hospitals and often involved in leprosy work in Niger, Burkina Faso, Liberia, and Benin, as well as Ethiopia, Sudan, Zambia, and India.

Doro Station, Upper Nile, Sudan

Dr. Bob and Claire Grieve prepared long and well for missionary service, graduating with the class of '39 from medical school and Bible school in Oregon, unaware they would become Multnomah School of the Bible's first missionary martyrs. They left friends and family with these words of conviction from Acts 20:24: "I do not consider my life of any account as dear to myself, so that I may finish my course and the ministry which I received from the Lord Jesus, to testify solemnly of the gospel of the grace of God" (NASB).

The sea journey itself was treacherous, in those early days of World War II. They finally passed through the Suez, disembarking into the vast heat wave of Sudan for an arduous journey up the Nile into the trackless flatlands of the Upper Nile region. The three Doro missionaries welcomed Bob and Claire warmly in early 1940, and they set to work meeting health needs and learning the Mabaan language.

Meanwhile, the Italians extended their tenuous hold on Ethiopia and took Sudan border towns not far from SIM's bases. America was a neutral party to the conflict in those early days of the War, but on a deadly day in August 1940, Italian planes suddenly appeared over the tin roofs of Doro Mission Station, disgorging more than 80 bombs and mortally wounding Bob (buried that evening) and Claire (who died in the night and was interred next to her husband the next morning). Claire Oblesby, despite her own grief and serious shrapnel injuries, sang the old hymn "Face to Face, with Christ my Savior" at the graveside on both occasions, not knowing that she herself would follow them into the Lord's presence just six months later.

Back home, the Grieve's pastor reminded family and friends that "their labor is not in vain, in the Lord". Within a year, the gospel bore fruit among the Mabaan, and the church continues to grow. Claire's little brother Lin (McClenny) committed his life to Christ's service, completed medical training, and two decades later was serving with his own young family in Doro, near the very grove of trees shading the grave site of Bob and Claire (McClenny) Grieve.

Forty-three years after Dr. McClenny's 1964 eviction from Sudan (as the country lapsed into an abyss of devastating conflict) SIM missionaries recently returned to help the Sudanese church return home and begin rebuilding their lives. The first Mabaan Church Conference was announced by a joyous procession of banner-waving, singing believers who ran two miles from the central market to Doro in order to circle the missionary grave site three times, stopping to bow reverently and give thanks to God for the sacrifice which bore such a harvest for Christ, and his Kingdom.

—As told by Dr. Rob Congdon, SIM missionary to South Sudan[12]

In 1946 Dr. Nathan Barlow reopened a medical work in Soddo, Ethiopia, which had begun before World War II, when SIM missionaries, including a Dr. Thomas Lambie, were evicted by the Italians. His story is told by Ethiopian church leader Ato Markina Meja, whom Dr. Barlow called his best friend:

> Soon after Dr. Barlow arrived in Wolaitta, he saw the need for an expanded rural medical programme. He began discussions with the Ethiopian Ministry of Health (MoH) about the possibility of opening a training center for rural medics. He then called the Wolaitta Kale Heywet Church (WKHC) leaders together and proposed his plan. . . . When full permission for such a programme was granted by the MoH, the first class was admitted for a two-year training period. These graduates were assigned back to their respective districts, and they operated rural clinics fully approved by the Ethiopian MoH. The local Wolaitta population was able to receive adequate help for chronic illnesses such as malaria, TB, dysentery, typhus, etc. The health assistants were able to refer severe medical cases to the Soddo SIM hospital. . . . These MoH-approved rural health medics made a significant contribution to the work of the Gospel through Southern Ethiopia.[13]

Many of these health assistants eventually also became trusted leaders in the growing church, giving evidence that the fruit of a hospital institutional ministry could be an ongoing ministry of gospel word and deed.

In 1950 Dr. Bob Foster and family left America with a dream to build a hospital in Zambia; he was the son of missionary parents who had come to the interior of Africa to work on a mission station 300 miles from any medical help. He arrived without adequate money for the hospital, yet by faith Mukinge Hospital was built, as detailed in Lorry Lutz's book, *The Sword and the Scalpel*.[14]

Photo 19.4. *Dr. Robert Foster, Mukinge Hospital, Zambia*

In 1956 Ceylon and India General Mission workers opened a small dispensary in Utraula, a rural north India town with endemic leprosy. The dispensary was expanded to Prem Sewa Hospital for leprosy patients, women, and children by Canadian Dr. Aletta Bell in 1966. In 1974 the hospital was incorporated into the Emmanuel Hospital Association, a network of former foreign mission hospitals and clinics across north India which was turned over to Indian leadership.[15]

Famate Jackson was a Liberian mother of four, educated to the third grade, who lived across the street from SIM's ELWA Hospital in Liberia. She volunteered her time to pray with patients in the hospital. She prayed every day for SIM missionary Bob Blees when he was burned in 1981; Bob and his wife, Gracia, became friends with Famate and her family. During her fifth pregnancy Famate became very ill; she was dying at home because her family couldn't afford hospital treatment. Bob was able to arrange care for her through our Dr. Frank Young, a general surgeon. She was so ill her husband brought her to the hospital in a wheelbarrow! After her recovery, family asked Bob and Gracia to transport her back to her home village and then honored them with presents. Later during the Liberian civil war Bob encouraged her family to return to that same bush village; the devastation of war never touched that family. A ministry of love and prayer became the means God used to save a family for his purposes.[16]

SIM General Director Ian Hay wrote (1982) about the blending of ministry to the whole man in SIM's history:

One of the strong points of SIM throughout its history has been the concern it has shown for the many needs of people in Africa and South America. Those needs relate to the whole man—his spiritual needs as well as his human and physical ones.

This "whole-man," or holistic approach is currently receiving special emphasis, but certainly is not a new one. The words and works of Jesus show clearly His compassion for the total needs of mankind. Not only did He teach and preach, but He fed the hungry, gave sight to the blind, comforted the sorrowing, and dispensed hope and forgiveness. Physical, social and spiritual needs were all of concern to Him.

In some circles today, evangelicals are charged with ignoring human need. SIM is not guilty. We cannot and do not ignore pain, hunger and suffering. . . . To those who express concern about the opposite danger— ignoring the spiritual dimension—again, the Mission is not guilty. SIM General Director Emeritus, Dr. Raymond J. Davis said:

As Christians we must not dismiss man's human need in our concentration on his spiritual need. Not only are they intertwined far more intricately than we can comprehend, but each is a channel to the other. As servants of Jesus Christ, we must be aware that our ministry, like His when He was here upon the earth, must be in consideration of both eternal and temporal values. . . .

This balance is not only a scriptural concept, but one which is consistent with the world view of most cultures. While Western cultures tend to make a sharp distinction between that which is sacred and that which is secular, African cultures decidedly do not. In fact, the spiritual dimension cannot be touched without also touching every other dimension of life. When one tries to separate the two, there is little hope of success in missionary endeavor.[17]

Pruning to Bear More Fruit: Shift of Focus to Community Health, Development and Relief Ministries, 1970–1990

The rise of anti-colonial nationalism in Africa and Asia during the 1960s and 1970s resulted in the handover of many of SIM's medical institutions to governments or churches. SIM continued to supply medical personnel to hospitals where possible. In Africa we continued to serve in many church-based hospitals, whereas in India we worked in partnership with the Indian-led Emmanuel Hospital Association. In the 1970s and 1980s this shift from an institutional focus (especially hospitals) was accompanied by a corresponding shift in emphasis to community health, rural development, famine relief, agriculture, and veterinary work. This shift was made primarily for good practical reasons, rather than theological ones.

Photo 19.5. *Don Stilwell and Daniel W. Giorgis, Durami, Ethiopia, 1982*

Beginning in the 1970s there was increasing emphasis on short-term projects. Many of these were creative development ministries that depended on individuals, not necessarily on long-range strategies; over this time there was an increasing effort to professionalize these new ministries, yet to keep development integrated with other SIM ministries. "Sustainability" and "measuring results" were popular concepts, although the definitions of these noble goals were not always clear. Would sacrifice, the essential hallmark of compassion, be lost? Would the SIM missionary become a good manager but poor servant? Would the gospel itself be lost in our efforts to professionalize?

Don Stilwell was a pharmacist who had served as coordinator for a large SIM relief project in Ethiopia, where two famines in the 1970s resulted in an estimated 250,000 deaths. While Ethiopia was emerging from the famine and SIM's response was shifting to agricultural assistance there, in Nigeria SIM was undertaking a somewhat similar rural development program, directed by Ken Kastner. The concept included a chicken hatchery and feed mill to introduce more productive chickens and better poultry nutrition to benefit subsistence farmers. This, along with the rather large program in Ethiopia, was requiring more and more time and attention from SIM General Director Ian Hay. He saw the need for someone on his staff to coordinate such ministries throughout the mission and appointed Don Stilwell his first coordinator of Physical Ministries in 1978 (later called Community Services). He told Don, "I've got Ken Kastner's chicks running all over my desk."[18]

"Historic perspective: Good Works and Good Intentions" (1995), by Don Stilwell

Twenty years ago this month, while I was managing the SIM Pharmacy in Addis Ababa, the SIM Ethiopia Field Council met and among other things moved to appoint me head of SIM's response to the great famine of 1973. I asked my secretary to get out a new file hanger and mark it "famine." I still remember the documents which went into that hanger. It included the papers for the purchase and transport of 22 tons of corn from Asmara to Alamata, the temporary assignment of one missionary and the temporary hiring of one Ethiopian to help distribute the corn.

Two degrees in Pharmacy and 12 years work in various medical delivery systems hardly prepared me for this assignment as it unfolded. Over the next months this relief work expanded to help many thousands of people in dozens of locations. The death toll is thought to have been about 250,000. But we saved many from that fate. The rains were finally returning, and the survivors needed to farm, but most of their oxen had died and their plows and hoes had been sold. So we launched into a big rehabilitation effort.

While all this was going on, I was starting to hear references to something called *community development*. It sounded like a good idea in which communities would be helped in a variety of ways to make life better for their people. We were especially hopeful that community development would greatly reduce the incidence of epidemics and hunger. Accordingly, we bravely launched into community development as we understood it. What we learned was that this charming idea is not so easily achieved.[19]

Over the next two decades Don Stilwell offered wisdom as he helped SIM critically assess these new ministries, ensuring that our new "community service ministries," alongside existing long-term medical ministries, continued to be related to our basic mission purpose. Don created the first "SIM Physical Ministries Manual"; the title was changed in 1991 to the "Community Services Ministries (CSM) Manual." The manual outlined the purpose, principles, nature, and processes of CSM ministries. He promoted networking, training, and conferences on these ministries throughout SIM. Don Stilwell helped provide the leadership that encouraged integration of physical and spiritual ministries.

Photo 19.6. *Maradi Integrated Development Project*

Some of the language about gospel and ministries of compassion was formalized in corporate SIM documents during this period. The earliest reference in these documents was the 1972 SIM manual, which stated, "Medical work provides opportunity to minister to people in a manner that is universally understood. It enables the Mission to assist its host countries by providing an important service, and establishes an image that is a good testimony of Jesus Christ, and is a basis for good rapport with governments." By 1984 the SIM Manual Health Care Policy stated, "A Christian health care ministry is a valid expression of the gospel, and historically has played a vital part in SIM strategy. It should be recognized that SIM is not a medical mission but a mission with concern for the whole person, a concern in which health care has a contributing role."[20]

Pocketknife Evangelism—The Ministry of Tony Rinaudo[21]

Tony Rinaudo, currently the chief food security advisor for World Vision Australia, served with SIM's Maradi Integrated Development Project (MIDP) from 1980 to 1999. His vision, as team leader, was to serve the lost in an integrated and holistic manner. The MIDP was a multifaceted ministry involving evangelism, church planting, agriculture, and health services.

Believing "the secret to evangelism in Niger [was] in building relationships,"[22] Tony spent years coming alongside those in spiritual and physical need. Helping the lost and impoverished through agriculture, something Tony believed to be his life calling, became his key ministry.

In Niger at that time, farmers routinely cleared their land of all vegetation through burning which led to its desertification. Farmers also tended to overgraze and cultivate every inch of their land. To help improve the farmland the MIDP's goals were to: (1) leave Gao trees to develop and multiply, (2) encourage farmers not to cut down or burn all of their trees, (3) plant and protect Australian acacia trees, (4) reclaim hardpan soils by making catchment basins to hold rain water, and (5) start compost piles to increase crop production.

After planting trees for over two and half years and watching them die under the harsh near-desert conditions, Tony was close to giving up. One day, as the team was taking seedlings to nearby farmers, he stopped to let air out of the trucks' tires to better navigate the roads. As Tony looked out at the practically desert landscape he realized the methods they were using would never work. It was then he prayed a "desperate prayer" that the Lord would give him wisdom and guidance as to what to do. Not long after that, while walking through the fields he noticed the tree stumps which had been there all along. He realized it wasn't really a desert—that a forest had been there. The trees had been cut down, but many of the stumps, roots and even seeds in the ground were still there. On the stumps he noticed many sprouts growing. It was then he realized if he could change the mindset of the farmers, this underground forest could come alive again. If he could get farmers to simply prune back the branches sprouting from each stump, using something as simple as a pocketknife, the forest's regrowth would be rapid. With a new mindscape a new landscape would emerge. Over the next 10 years as he worked and built relationships with the people, Tony's idea of managing regrowth began to gain momentum as it was spread from farmer to farmer.[23]

This technique of rapid reforestation, called Farmer-Managed Natural Regeneration, was introduced by MIDP in Niger under Tony's leadership. Often described as "the Tree Whisperer," Tony Rinaudo spent those years reforesting degraded and ravaged lands bringing hope to impoverished communities through the regeneration program.

John Ockers notes in his paper "History of SIM Work in Niger, 1923–2000":

> This method continues to expand so that today over two million, once barren hectares of land, stretching from Dosso in the west to Zinder in the east, once again have some tree cover. The project worked alongside Église Évangelique de la République du Niger (Evangelical Church of the Republic of Niger) evangelists and saw the growth of bush churches at Batafaduw and Garin Sale.[24]

Three questions arose out of a formal evaluation of SIM's famine relief efforts from 1983–1987, done under Don Stilwell's leadership with the help of Roger Steele. These contributed to the ongoing conversation about the gospel and deeds of compassion.[25]

- **Q: Has the desired balance in SIM ministries been maintained?**

  A: "The dichotomy issue is a difficult one to address because of the scriptural evidence pointing toward the need for the body of Christ to be engaged in holistic ministry addressing all of man's needs. Data collected as part of this evaluation process seems to indicate that SIM is not really in any imminent danger of becoming overly involved in physical ministry. SIM leadership and membership is committed to a balanced ministry. Many feel that if any shift in the balance has occurred at all, the increased famine relief activity has created new opportunities and added vitality to aspects of existing SIM spiritual ministries."

- **Q: What was the impact upon church growth and what new opportunities for outreach resulted?**

  A: "The impact upon church growth is impossible to measure immediately after the completion of a famine relief activity. Most would agree that to have encouraged conversion during the implementation of famine programs would have been a suspect strategy. The impact on church growth can only be measured over long periods of time. The primary motivation of SIM's famine relief involvement was to carry on a ministry of compassion to those in need and to be an encouragement to needy Christian brothers and sisters."

- **Q: What effect did famine relief have upon thinking regarding physical and spiritual outreach?**

  A: "There is uniform support for involvement in short-term emergency relief activities as long as a proper balance, in relation to overall SIM outreach, is maintained. On the other hand, there is a noticeable difference among SIM missionaries regarding the role of more long-term, development-type ministries such as primary health care, rural development, agroforestry, etc. Some SIMers see development ministries as being outside of the scope of the SIM spiritual mandate and best left to other organizations. Other SIMers see implementation of the physical development ministries as being integral to the overall programming and outreach that should occur in SIM. Described in another manner, many SIM field missionaries find themselves in a situation where they regularly observe chronic physical need, see the necessity for long-term development-oriented solutions, but don't know if SIM can become involved in addressing the needs without compromising the SIM purpose and goals."[26]

In 1984 our basic mission purpose was formulated and has lasted in similar form until now: "The purpose of SIM is to glorify God by evangelizing the unreached and ministering to man's needs, discipling believers into churches equipped to fulfill Christ's commission (Matthew 28:19–20)." This was in line with the 1974 Lausanne covenant adopted by evangelicals worldwide describing Christian social responsibility.[27]

At that time Howard Brant, SIM deputy international director, wrote the following:

Recently in memos and writings we have been seeing the phrase, "development has value of its own." This is true in the sense that Christian compassion should be demonstrated whether or not there is an overt opportunity to share the Gospel message. . . . But if this is used to mean that development can stand on its own—that we can choose between either evangelism or development, both are valid in their own right—this strikes a blow to our philosophy of intentional integration. Its value is in its being connected to the rest of what SIM is doing.[28]

SIM also continued to have a hand in hospital ministries. But the long-term vision and strategic role of institutions (expensive and demanding as they are) was not apparent. For example some asked, "Why do we continue to minister in institutions after they have been effective in evangelism and planting the church?" Or, "How might God use long-range endeavors to plant mission enterprises, not only churches?" Furthermore, it was not always clear how institutions and community ministries were related; the challenge was building an integrated long-term strategy. This concern was articulated clearly for CSM ministries by 1997 in a report to SIM's International Council, which stated,

The CSM manual and the 1996 Study Group on CSM have certainly provided a solid framework for CSM, but when one looks at "country strategies," CSM lacks a clear description, vision, and strategy. As our involvement in CSM is on the rise, there needs to be an overall philosophy of CSM, a guiding strategy and means for monitoring its implementation on the field. The foundation for that work, and the missiological dialogue about this vision, would need to wait for some fresh eyes in the 1990s.

Fruit That Abides: Fresh Opportunities for Cross-Cultural Partnership, 1990–2015

SIM missionary Dr. David Van Reken wrote a monograph in 1987 identifying trends occurring in missionary medicine. "The three phases of medical missions can be summarized using a familiar analogy. Giving a man a fish is <u>doing</u>. Showing him how to fish is <u>teaching</u>. Working with him to devise, build, and manage a fish pond is <u>enabling</u>." He continues, "Today, the doing and the teaching continue. But we are confronted with conditions around the globe which call for a shift to a third phase in medical missions: the <u>enabling</u> phase. "Instead of a teacher-student relationship, the association between missionary and national is one of colleagues working together with mutual trust and respect."[29]

In 1993 Dr. Phil Andrew shared SIM Nigeria's experience in residency training of Nigerian physicians and urged the mission to make such training a priority or "neglect the training of national health workers to the peril of the emerging church." Dr. Andrew described the program and listed the graduates until 1992, which included our current international director, Dr. Joshua Bogunjoko:

This programme has revolutionised the work we do as SIM missionaries. Whereas in the past it was mainly a matter of keeping the hospital adequately staffed and equipped and waiting for Nigerians to come so that we could hand over to them, maybe pushing for financial backing to send some of them to England for post graduate training, now the picture has changed. Our task now is training, and not just in the technical area. These committed [Nigerian] Christian doctors live with us on the compound and we are involved with them as colleagues day in and day out. We are now in a mentoring or disciple-making role and this is a major switch. The type of [SIM] people we now need in our hospitals are doctors with firstly a solid academic and professional background to enable them to teach effectively and secondly a commitment to making disciples. People with these interests, combined of course with the usual requirements among SIM missionaries to Nigeria, namely flexibility, patience, sense of humour, willingness to work under the church etc., are finding great fulfillment in their ministries in the medical department of ECWA.[30]

SIM India partner Emmanuel Hospital Association (EHA) is an indigenous mission agency which grew out of the work of traditional missions. One of the EHA leaders wrote in 1994, "Looking back we can see that the crisis of 1950–1970 was part of God's plan. With much prayer and effort the vacuum of leadership left by European missionaries began to be filled by new competent and highly qualified Indian Christian medical leaders. . . . Over its 25-year existence, EHA has been evolving as a medical mission. A medical mission needs to be complemented by church planting teams. I believe that the lack of specialized church planters is the main reason why most Western medical missions have failed to plant churches outside the compound walls. If it is to prove more effective than Western medical missions, EHA needs to forge substantial partnership links with Indian mission agencies which can provide the specialized church-planting thrust."[31]

Although genuine collaboration between SIM and related churches and ministry partners was beginning, it meant the discovery of some of our cultural blind spots. A consultation on Community Services Ministries was held in Nairobi in 1993. "The Africans present were encouraged to speak about ways in which SIM people sometimes hinder good partnership. This revealed an unfortunate level of unworthy attitudes and behaviors on the part of some of our missionaries." (See the following sidebar.) Since some of them had observed succeeding generations of missionaries making the same mistakes, it was suggested that "maybe SIM has some old secret manual which instruct the new missionaries before they come!"[32]

This resulted in a recommendation to our International Council in 1997 that "SIM's church partners should have representation on SIM boards and councils and institutional committees from the Board of Governors down to country-level ministries and institutions."[33] There were further recommendations that SIM organize training in cross-cultural relationship development and conflict management, and invest in developing leadership and management skills among partners. These humble beginnings out of ministries of compassion became the directions the mission eventually took at top levels of leadership.

"The Secret Manual" Uncovered in Nairobi at the Community Services Ministry Consultation

When the time came for the discussion groups to report, the church partner participants listed a number of behaviors of SIM missionaries which they considered a hindrance to good church/mission partnerships. Following is the list they presented, roughly in order of significance:

- Superior attitude
- Lack of openness
- Lack of respect for culture
- Favoritism
- No recognition of nationals (avoiding African doctors in hospitals)
- No financial disclosure
- Hiding experiences
- Using an old manual
- Pushiness
- Divide and rule system
- Carry over culture
- Being higher paid
- Not calling people in low work positions by name

In addition, one African participant, in his plenary presentation, mentioned:

- Bad missionary attitudes (not corresponding to sacrifices made)
- Colonialist attitudes
- Master-servant relationships
- Hands in pockets while worshiping or praying
- Not taking time to greet, befriend, sleep, and eat with partners
- Not sharing one's own time, life, and family
- Selling used articles which might be given
- Not giving in keeping with their level of income
- Not listening (except to favorites and friends)[34]

An SIM evaluation of Galmi Hospital, Niger, in 1993 by Dr. Findlay MacDonald and Dr. Paul Hudson independently arrived at similar conclusions; attitudes of paternalism distorted the gospel of grace, and kept us from finding effective long-term solutions. In an effort to address some of these weaknesses, the decision was made not to close Galmi Hospital, but to seek ways of addressing patterns of prejudice; the Lord brought leadership to the hospital through Drs. Joshua and Joanna Bogunjoko, SIM members from Nigeria. By 2002 they wrote: "Relationships have been good, and for the first time in more than 50 years, we are actually working together (missionaries and Nigeriens) on strategic praying and planning for the hospital."[35]

By 1998 this kind of thinking led to a consultation between SIM Ghana and the Bible Church of Africa in Accra, called "The Slave Trade and Reconciliation: A Northern Ghanaian Perspective." A very significant service of foot washing was begun by one of our SIM leaders on the field who said:

> Today, I want to take off the cover of denial and confess the sins of my forefathers. It was my people that sinned against your people and because of that, we have a wound today. I am deeply sorry for the pain that you have suffered. When you talk behind my back, I know it is because of the wound. I ask for your forgiveness, and I would like to wash the feet of our chairman today Stephen Aputara. I am not going to ask you to formally respond because I do not want to force that. But I would like to start to heal the wound and I want to say, "Yes, I am going to take off the old rag of denial that has covered up the wound of slavery and throw it away. I confess the sins of my people and ask your forgiveness, in Jesus' name." As we do this, we can start to heal the wound that has been passed on and on." [The footwashing began].[36]

Pastor Jose Abias, head of the Alliance of Evangelicals in Angola, reflected on how much he appreciated not only the help that SIM had been able to give for a relief effort in 2000, but especially the trust that SIM had demonstrated in the church by a heavy training component which enabled the Angolan believers to mature as partners of SIM and other evangelical agencies.[37]

Dr. Paul Hudson had replaced Don Stilwell after he retired in 1997. With a small CSM team he helped give birth to SIM's Hope for AIDS ministry in 2001, focused on enabling local believers and churches to live out the gospel in the context of HIV/AIDS, "a disease of broken relationships." Among SIM's ministries of compassion, it was one attempt to provide a mission-wide framework for genuine collaboration and partnership across multiple countries. (See sidebar.)

"Lessons Learned from the Experiences of HOPE for AIDS" (2015), Marcus Bader, SIM HOPE for AIDS Project Director

HOPE for AIDS was created as a coordinated multicountry response to the AIDS pandemic, as it has affected many countries where SIM is active. The response centered on the acronym "HOPE," standing for Home-based care, Orphan care, Prevention, and Enablement. Begun in 2001, it has been geared to encouragement, mutual exchange of expertise, and centralized fundraising. As a group of different SIM projects in more than 12 countries, with over seven thousand local partners, mostly churches, Hope for AIDS is run as an international master project with a common approach to AIDS ministry in order that lessons learned could be shared between countries and local stakeholders given voice. Here are three key lessons learned:

1. Intentional networking provides benefits far beyond AIDS ministries and has strengthened cross-border relationships, encouraged project leaders—both missionaries and local believers—through biannual workshops and has increased the sense of SIM as a global community.
2. HIV and AIDS ministry is a great "entry tool" into other areas of life that churches (particularly in Africa) have traditionally struggled to address, such as sexuality, family life, role of husbands and wives, counselling, and even financial management. Through the sharing of experiences across the variety of HOPE for AIDS projects, new ideas and solutions to provide comprehensive and holistic ministry to those infected or affected by HIV emerged and by extension, these efforts strengthened the church in its social concern and in its teachings around family, sexuality, and care for the sick.
3. A master project can be of use when looking at common fundraising strategies, but unless there is commitment to fundraising (either through a professional or someone who has the time to do it), the benefits of a master project in fundraising are limited. [38]

SIM USA Director Steve Strauss wrote in 2005:

For years Christians have argued over the relationship between the Great Commission and the Great Commandment. My studies of Scripture convince me that as soon as we pit the Great Commission against the Great Commandment, we are off track. Scripture is clear that the believer's responsibility is not simply to witness or meet human need. In fact, if we're asking which is more important, social action or evangelism, our focus is wrong altogether. Our responsibility as New Testament believers is to live as complete kingdom people; we must live with the gospel of the kingdom on our lips and in our lives all the time.[39]

We have discovered that our own programs and efforts have cultural biases which, despite our best intentions, can interfere with what we communicate about God and Christ. Our biblical foundation, embracing both word and deeds of compassion, is sound. Yet the ongoing global reality of human suffering, combined with the limitations of our Western perspective, calls us to a renewed theological vision, grounded in Scripture, created by voices from multiple cultures, reflecting gifts and perspectives of the global body of Christ. As we join in obedience to God's Word in genuine cross-cultural partnership, we can trust the Lord for even more fruitful ministries of compassion, glorifying God by demonstrating his love and transforming lives by the power of the gospel.

SUPPLEMENT 19.1

Lassa Fever . . . and Ebola

SIM nurse Lily Lyman Pinneo, also known as "Penny," is best known for being the first confirmed case of Lassa fever, a viral hemorrhagic illness discovered in 1969. What ultimately became known as the "Pinneo" or "LP" strain of the Lassa virus was isolated from her blood after she acquired the illness caring for others in Nigeria.[40]

Photo 19.7. *Penny Pinneo, early survivor of Lassa fever, 1969*

The unfolding of events began in January 1969, when a missionary nurse working in northern Nigeria in the village of Lassa contracted a previously unrecognized form of hemorrhagic fever. She was then flown four hundred miles to the city of Jos, where Bingham Memorial Hospital had been established by SIM. Unfortunately, there was little the staff there could do and she died within a day of her arrival. Within a week the virus had also claimed the life of one of the nurses at Bingham. Both these women had been cared for by a third nurse, a veteran of missionary work in Nigeria since 1946, Penny Pinneo, who also came down with the fever, but survived it.[41]

She spent her recuperation at Columbia Presbyterian Hospital in New York City under the care of Dr. John Frame, who had arranged for this one surviving but critically ill nurse to be returned to America for treatment. Frame, himself, had served in medical missions in Iran. Upon returning to the USA to commence private practice, he continued to work with several interdenominational mission societies, including SIM, and frequently traveled to Africa on medical business. Frame is credited with being the first to recognize that the hemorrhagic symptoms that had killed several missionary nurses were manifestations of a disease not previously known. In tribute to his labors, he was named Clinical Professor Emeritus when he retired from the Tropical Medicine Division at Columbia University's School of Public Health.[42]

While Pinneo was in New York, Frame sent a sample of her blood to Yale University virologist Jordi Casals-Ariet. He was the first to isolate what would become known as the Lassa fever virus. Unfortunately, both he and one of his technicians, Juan Roman, also became infected. Roman died, but Casals-Ariet survived, having been saved by the use of antibody-laden serum from Penny Pinneo.

> Yale subsequently stopped all research on the samples and sent them to the Centers for Disease Control and Prevention in Atlanta, effectively beginning the era of Biosafety Level 4 precautions in the handling of virulent viruses such as Lassa, Ebola, and hantavirus, and promoting CDC's predominance in this field. The story became world news.[43]

Just before Pinneo was scheduled to return to Nigeria, a further outbreak of Lassa fever emerged near Jos. The director of SIM's Bingham Memorial Hospital (later, Evangel Hospital) in Jos, Dr. Jeanette Troup, whom Penny knew, had come down with the virus. She carried her own plasma to help Dr. Troup when she returned in 1970, but was unfortunately too late, as Dr. Troup had already died.

Penny Pinneo continued to work as a nurse in Africa for many years, at the same time contributing to a number of published works on Lassa fever, and continuing to donate her blood for treatment with convalescent plasma. She retired in 1985, first in Rochester, New York, with her sister, and later at the SIM Retirement Center in Sebring, Florida, USA. She died 17 August 2012 at the age of 95.

The American Society of Tropical Medicine and Hygiene (ASTMH) blog of 2 October 2012 summarized her story this way:

> Penny's story was dramatically told in newspapers of the time and in the 1974 novel, *Fever!* by John G. Fuller. The pain and suffering Penny experienced at the hands of this new and fearful agent might have driven persons of lesser fortitude into retirement, or at least to a career change. Not Penny. In contrast, she won her personal battle with Lassa fever, surviving after a severe and prolonged illness, and then dedicated much of her life's work to combating Lassa virus that threatened populations in West Africa.[44]

Writing now post-2014/2015, at a time when the Ebola virus and SIM were recently very much in the news, it is a bit surreal to juxtapose the seriousness of these two viral diseases and how they are being responded to.[45] An online *Bulletin of the World Health Organization* article entitled "Time to Put Ebola in Context," said the following in 2014 in response to the question, "Why does Ebola attract so much attention when Lassa fever kills more people?" Here is their response:

> Ebola and Lassa fever are part of a larger group of viral haemorrhagic fevers and are the two most important ones epidemiologically in the tropical African context. In the case of Ebola haemorrhagic fever, we are dealing with a very fierce, rapidly lethal filoviral disease that causes death in 50–90% of clinically diagnosed cases. So far there is no antiviral or vaccine available against Ebola haemorrhagic fever—it is a disease with no cure. But when we look at African outbreaks, we notice that, despite their increasing frequency, the overall numbers of deaths are relatively small. The dramatic fear and perception of the global spread of Ebola virus has motivated international and some national health and government officials to develop policies based on this vision. Meanwhile, media coverage has increased public interest and support for tackling this disease. In this respect, Ebola haemorrhagic fever is kind of an "exceptional" or "master status" disease.
>
> Lassa fever is another haemorrhagic disease, but much more endemic across many areas in western Africa. Infection occurs through direct exposure to excreta of infected rats, or less often, person-to-person via bodily fluids. The case fatality rate of Lassa fever is only around 1%, but the disease claims more lives than Ebola fever because its incidence is much higher. It is estimated that there are 300,000 infections and 5,000 deaths per year.

What sort of dilemmas do these kinds of diseases pose?

> This contrast has led some commentators to suggest that Ebola fever is perhaps "much ado about nothing." It is locally devastating but has little international importance. Lassa fever, on the other hand, seems to be an unheralded problem. The number of deaths and of infected cases is high and disproportional with the disease's international profile and the scale of western media attention. Lassa fever requires more sustained engagement of health teams and measures to deal with its more endemic character.[46]

While the relatively greater attention paid to Ebola as compared to Lassa fever may be a relevant subject for informed discussion and planning by global medical experts, it misses the very tangible and human story that was the Ebola crisis in Liberia in 2014/2015.

To that, we now turn with a piece produced by Deborah Sacra, who lived for several years in Liberia and had the frightening experience of her husband, Dr. Rick Sacra, being infected with Ebola. What follows to the end of this supplement is her summary:[47]

Photo 19.8. *Dr. Eisenhut conducting training for some of ELWA Hospital's staff.* To Dr. Eisenhut's right is one of the hospital's nurses, Barbara Bono, who contracted Ebola a few weeks later in July 2014. She thankfully survived.[48] Photo used with permission.

In the early months of 2014, reports began to circulate of an outbreak of the highly contagious Ebola Virus Disease (EVD) in Guinea. In spite of the fact that Ebola had never been endemic to West Africa, physicians at ELWA Hospital in Monrovia, Liberia, just a day's journey from the Guinea border, took them seriously. Dr. Debbie Eisenhut developed a plan for the safe treatment of patients with symptoms of Ebola. An isolation ward that could accommodate six patients was established in the chapel building of the hospital; this became known as ELWA 1. When there were no reported cases in May 2014, they breathed a little easier, hoping that this outbreak, like most others, had been self-contained. But they knew the potential for a major epidemic still existed.

The first patients came in June. In the first month, only a few survived, partly because they came when their infection was far advanced. Most people did not seek treatment early because the first symptoms of Ebola are similar to other common ailments in West Africa such as malaria or measles. Furthermore, in spite of media broadcasts and community-level awareness campaigns to educate people about Ebola, acceptance of the imminent danger was slow to grow.[49]

The hospital was receiving Ebola patients almost daily by mid-July, so with the help

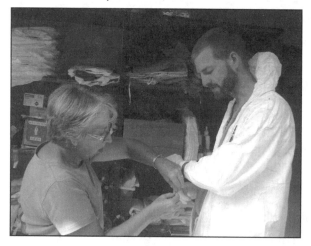

Photo 19.9. *Nancy Writebol suiting up Dr. Brantly.*
Photo credit: Dr. Debbie Eisenhut.

Photo 19.10. *Ebola survivor William Pewee, 12 June 2015.*

Mr. Pewee, who contracted Ebola while working as a file clerk at ELWA Hospital, is pictured in the chapel (ELWA 1) that was converted into an Ebola Treatment Unit (ETU) at the beginning of the crisis. Hospital staff admitted its first Ebola patient into the unit on 12 June 2014, exactly one year earlier. Here, during a trauma-healing session that he was taking, Mr. Pewee is explaining how God permitted him to get Ebola so he could give the patients in ELWA 2's ETU where he was being treated the "hope" they could find in Jesus. While being cared for in the ETU, he saw 19 people die and taken out in body bags. One was his friend, Dr. John Dada, who had once worked at the hospital.[50] Photo used with permission.

of Samaritan's Purse, the isolation ward was expanded to a larger space in the new hospital complex under construction. In the midst of the move, on July 26, two ELWA missionaries, Nancy Writebol from SIM and Dr. Kent Brantly with Samaritan's Purse, became sick with Ebola.

They were able to be evacuated to an isolation treatment unit at Emory Hospital in Atlanta and survived. The rest of the SIM missionaries evacuated soon after.

In Liberia, the ELWA Hospital closed for complete decontamination. SIM missionary Dr. Rick Sacra arrived to help Dr. Jerry Brown reopen the hospital for services, primarily to maternity patients. By this time, nearly all the hospitals in Monrovia had closed for normal services. In the first week after reopening on August 6, nearly all of the women who came for an emergency delivery lost their infants, but thankfully, most of the women's lives were saved. The hospital continued to care for maternity patients in the height of the epidemic from August to November 2014, but could not expand to other areas due to a shortage of staff and personal protection supplies.

Dr. Brown became the director of the ELWA 2 Ebola Unit, which eventually could care for around 80 patients, plus triage and recovery. Because of the power and water utilities that ELWA could provide, Médecins Sans Frontières/Doctors Without Borders (MSF) asked ELWA to host their unit as well, which could accommodate over 150 patients. ELWA's services department was heavily taxed by the two units with the load on its utilities, but the Lord kept the pumps and generators operating with ELWA staff working many long hours.

In the first week of September, Dr. John Fankhauser returned when Dr. Sacra contracted Ebola and was evacuated to the USA. Under his direction, the hospital tightened their anti-infection protocols beyond the recommended World Health Organization (WHO) guidelines to prevent any additional infections. Besides the three Americans, four other ELWA staff became sick: a nurse and a file clerk who survived, and a hygienist and physician's assistant who passed away.

None of those who worked in the Ebola 2 unit contracted the virus. Dr. Brown and the dedicated staff of the Ebola unit rejoiced when they began to release survivors, infusing some degree of hope into the situation.

The media attention created by the evacuation of the missionaries necessitated the creation of a strategic communication response from SIM-USA. Nancy Writebol and Dr. Rick Sacra were able to use their stories to raise awareness of the Ebola epidemic in West Africa and the need for a global humanitarian response. In December 2014, "The Ebola Fighters" were *Time* magazine's Persons of the Year, and Dr. Jerry Brown and Dr. Kent Brantly from ELWA were featured on the cover.[51]

Photo 19.11. *Dr. Jerry Brown on the front cover of* Time *magazine, 2014*

The ELWA 1 and 2 units treated 506 patients from June 2014 to January 2015, with 230 survivors.[52] By the end of 2014, the epidemic in Liberia finally began to subside. Flare-ups occurred over the following 18 months as Sierra Leone and Guinea continued to battle to contain the disease. The World Health Organization declared the epidemic to be over in June 2016.[53]

However, the needs of families impacted by Ebola were still acute. When Ebola hit a household, it could take the lives of most of the adults as they cared for the sick. Those who survived often found they had been evicted from their rented home or were stigmatized by their neighbors when they returned from the treatment center. The SIM-related church in Liberia, the Evangelical Church of Liberia (ECOL), reached out to families affected by Ebola in their church communities to provide help with food and household needs. They provided spiritual support, but the pain was very deep.

To respond to these spiritual needs more intentionally, SIM asked the American Bible Society to adapt their trauma healing materials for Liberia. In July 2015, Liberian church and community leaders learned about the

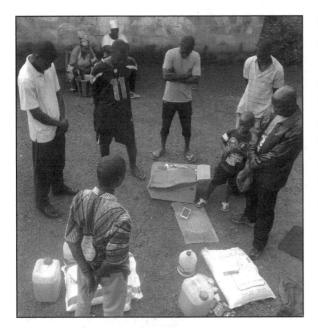

Photo 19.12. *Evangelical Church of Liberia (ECOL) leaders distributing food, hygiene products, and other relief goods to Ebola survivors, Paynesville, 11 June 2015.* (L–R): Pastor Moses Gwole (bottom left), ECOL President Pastor Moses Paye, Solomon King Jr., Reuben Harris, Lawrence King, child, and Pastor Albert Lloyd in the circle. Martha King covering her face with her hand behind Mr. King as she prays. Mr. King Jr. survived Ebola, but his parents, sister, and two of their caregivers did not. Mr. Harris, his son, and one of his daughters survived. From mid-September to mid-November 2015, 36 persons who attended ECOL churches contracted Ebola. Twenty-three died (eight of them children), resulting in a 64 percent mortality rate. Photo used with permission.

stages of grief and symptoms of posttraumatic stress and prepared to lead workshops with those who had been affected by Ebola and other traumas. Many participants found healing in the Lord through the workshops. Radio programs based on the workshops were also broadcast over ELWA Radio. Ebola survivors experienced many physical symptoms after their recovery, including sight and hearing damage, arthritis and general fatigue and pain. Funds raised for the Ebola crisis allowed ELWA Hospital to provide ongoing services to these survivors free of charge in the aftermath of the epidemic.

CHAPTER 20

THE GLOBALIZATION OF MISSIONS

One of the most exciting developments in missions in the last 30 years has been the rapid globalization of the harvest force—no longer from the West to the rest, but from anywhere to everywhere. Cape Town 2010 (Lausanne III, October 17–24) was a vivid reminder of this as probably the broadest expression of the world's nations and Christian leaders came together to reflect on the continued call to take the message of Jesus to all peoples. Coming from over 190 nations, the over four thousand delegates worshiped God together, studied his Word, reflected on and debated issues, and planned means that God might use to carry forward his commission to disciple the nations. Clearly, the whole church has been mobilized in all of its splendid variety to carry the glorious gospel of Christ to the whole world.

Photo 20.1. *Malcolm McGregor*

SIM International Director Malcolm McGregor, in summing up his own thoughts on Cape Town 2010, said this:[1]

> It has been good to reflect on these issues and others since the Congress. How do they relate to SIM? All seven issues I've discussed above [The Diversity of the Church in the 21st Century; The Great Need for Discipleship; Islam; The Challenge of Cities and Urbanization; Living out an Integral Gospel; The Importance of Partnership in the Mission Task; and The Reality of the Suffering Church] are part of SIM's current agenda that came out of our Seize the Day Review in 2004. This is a real encouragement for us. What we are hearing from God inside SIM, others are talking about in the wider church.

Earlier in his article, in discussing "The Importance of Partnership in the Mission Task," he focused in on things of vital importance to SIM as it seeks to fully participate in and promote the globalization of missions. He wrote the following:

Dr. Patrick Fung, the International Director of OMF [Overseas Missionary Fellowship], spoke powerfully on the subject of partnership in the body of Christ. He said, "The foundation of all Christian partnerships is reconciliation. People who were once enemies because of political or racial conflicts, can now work shoulder-to-shoulder to proclaim the message of reconciliation. This message is to be lived out by God's new community, and the fragmented world needs to see it."

The world is longing to see a community of people who work across racial, ethnic, gender and social divides to achieve their purpose, and the Church of Jesus Christ is that community. Jesus said, "All men will know that you are my disciples if you love one another" (John 13:35). The need for reconciliation in the body of Christ is so important if we long to be this kind of partnership community.[2]

In addition to the need for reconciliation, there has also long existed the need to correct flawed thinking. Back in 1986, at a time when there was much rejoicing in the evangelical churches of the West that Christ's church had become a global reality, there was also a mistaken impression taking hold that the need for missions from the West no longer existed. SIM General Director, Ian Hay, addressed both the joyous new reality of expanding non-Western missions and some of the flawed thinking that had accompanied it in an article entitled "Rearranging Our Thinking":[3]

"Behold, how good and how pleasant it is for brethren to dwell together in unity," said the Psalmist. May it be so.

For 200 years the modern missionary movement has been a phenomenal success. The church of our Lord Jesus Christ has become a worldwide reality.

Twenty years ago, however, that movement almost came to a standstill. As news of dynamic church growth in the Third World swept through Western churches, many came to the conclusion that the task was accomplished. Churches were told that missions from the West were a thing of the past. Recruitment sagged. Some mission societies closed their doors.

That philosophy did not prevail. To the contrary, over the last decade a fresh breath of concern to reach the 2.8 billion people who have not yet heard the claims of Christ has swept the church.

With that concern has come the realization that God is doing some startling things—things that are distinct from traditional patterns. They relate to the role that non-Western churches are assuming in world evangelism.

Recently I participated in a consultation in England on the theme "emerging missions" and their relationship to Western mission societies. One of the major addresses was delivered by Rev. Panya Baba, Director of the

Evangelical Missionary Society of Nigeria. It seemed strange to call EMS an emerging mission. Beginning 40 years ago as an outgrowth of SIM work, and now having 622 missionaries, it is larger and older than a majority of Western societies. [See Supplement 20.1, pages 315-317, for part of Rev. Baba's story.]

Then I went to a consultation in U.S.A. to discuss "Third World missions." That term also has problems. With Western Christians now in the minority, someone suggested the term "Two-Thirds World." [The preferred term today seems to be "Majority World."]

Call them what you will, however, non-Western churches are a powerful new factor in reaching the world for Christ. The 200-year-old pattern of Western dominance, it seems, is about to be broken. If present trends continue, the majority of Christian missionaries will soon be from non-Western countries. Already there are an estimated 20,000 of them. At the present growth rate there will be well over 100,000 by the year 2000. (Western missionaries are currently estimated at 60,000.)

This presents missionary societies like SIM with the need to rearrange their thinking and adapt to what is happening. Most international missions are really confederations of various nationalities, each segregated to its own area of work. SIM seeks to integrate all nationalities into a common work force. We have Asians, Europeans, North Americans, and Australasians working together in their assignments.

Tensions aren't unknown when language, social perspectives, and cultural behavior patterns don't jibe. There can be a tendency to feel that one's own ways are somehow superior. Grace is needed for each to understand and accept the other, and thereby enjoy true harmony.

This grace of acceptance is needed throughout the entire body of Christ. Western churches, which have long enjoyed the "prestige" of being the leaders in world evangelism, must come to grips with the fact that God uses whom He will to achieve His goals.

The only way that the unreached of the world will be reached is for the total church to be mobilized. The beauty of it is that we now have a worldwide community through which it can be done.

We must be careful, however, not to come to the same kind of mistaken conclusion that was made in the sixties. We must not infer that since God is raising up non-Western missionaries that we aren't needed in the task. Our Lord wills to use *all* parts of His body in taking the gospel to every creature.

SIM is seeking to honor God in this unique international mix. We ask for your prayers that the unity of the Spirit will continue to make our work effective.

Dr. Hay took the discussion further for mission members in the membership-oriented periodical, *Intercom*, in 1986, focusing particularly on the question of "How We Relate" to non-Western missions. Following a more general introduction focusing on the projected rapid growth of such missions, he said the following:[4]

> We in SIM must be aware of this and of the part God wants us to play in helping these new dynamic groups to move forward.
>
> So, the topic is strategic. If we can learn how to mobilize the enormous potential now available around the world, we have within our grasp the means to reach our generation. The unreached will be reached; the task will be accomplished. But to do this it is imperative that all of the church's resources be utilized, regardless of national or racial origin.
>
> This leads to some very serious considerations. How, exactly, are we to relate to non-Western missions?

Partners

In SIM, we have tried to do this through several different patterns of partnerships. One example is our relationship with EMS. To my knowledge, there really is nothing quite like it anywhere else in the world. EMS is a viable society in its own right, indigenous, responsible, and mature. We are not in any kind of a father-to-son relationship. Rather, our discussions are always on a brother-to-brother level. Within Nigeria we assist in whatever way we can, but the entire responsibility is all in the hands of EMS leadership—not SIM.

Outside Nigeria we have been able to help in practical ways, as was done when EMS sent a missionary to Ghana. EMS supports the missionary by prayer and finance. SIM assists in transportation costs and provides liaison in Ghana. SIM missionaries work together with the EMS missionary in a happy working relationship, but the complete responsibility and authority for the missionary is retained by EMS. We have a true partnership.

The problems become more complicated, however, when a non-Western church or mission wishes to send its missionaries to areas more remote. It is also more complicated when their missionaries have the same basic educational and economic background as do SIM missionaries. In such cases, SIM has entered into some kind of mutual agreements, which keep the integrity of both groups viable, but establishes means whereby the task can be done effectively.

An example of this is in the 40-year-old model of relationship between SIM and *Deutsche Missionsgemeinschaft* (DMG) of Germany, which of course is neither an "emerging" nor a "Third-World" mission.

Photo 20.2. *DMG missionary Eva Liebanau, c. 1956 Photo 20.3.*
Gottfried Liebenau, c. 1956.
Gottfried and Eva Liebenau joined DMG in 1953 and went to
Ethiopia under the auspices of the Swiss and German Committee
of the Falasha Mission in Ethiopia. They then left the Falasha
mission and joined SIM while they were in Ethiopia in March 1956.
The Liebenaus left Ethiopia in 1957 for health reasons and took a
leave of absence from SIM in 1959.

These missionaries are members of SIM and qualify as do all SIM
missionaries. In Germany, however, they are members of and are supported
by DMG and represent DMG in deputation ministries. This has created no
problems either in Germany or in our fields. As with EMS, we have a true
partnership.

Since then, similar partner agreements have been established with
other groups around the world. The latest is the agreement with the General
Assembly of the Presbyterian Church in Korea. Our Korean missionaries are
full members of SIM working in Nigeria and Liberia, but in Korea they are
under the care and discipline of their home denomination.

We anticipate a steady influx of Koreans under this arrangement. Even
while I am writing this, Harold Fuller and Gordon Stanley are in Korea at the
request of church leaders, helping in pastors' conferences, seeking to stimulate
missionary interest.

We have yet another pattern established in regard to our Chinese
members. We have set up an indigenous council and office in Singapore which
is integrated into the SIM family like any other home office. This pattern
seemed best in that situation, whereas it seemed inappropriate in Korea.

SIM has the flexibility to have varied relationships. Serious discussions are going on now with EMS and ECWA leaders to try to establish which of these latter patterns can best be used to assist them in fulfilling their desire for missionary endeavors beyond Nigeria and its environs.

All of these relationships are premised on a basic missiological principle: "It's surprising what can be accomplished if you don't care who gets the credit."

SIM is a unique kind of international mission. Most other international missions are really confederations of various nationalities, each segregated to its own area of work. SIM has sought to integrate all nationalities as a common work force. God has honored that. Our Mission has been strengthened. We currently have Asians, Europeans, North Americans, and Australasians all working together in their assignments.

Photo 20.4. *Sarah and Sam Kang went to Nigeria in 1981 as SIM's first Korean missionaries.* Pictured with them are their children Esther and David. They have continued as longtime mobilizers of missions from Korea.

Culture and Tension

This leads me to share with you again some thoughts about getting along together in a multicultural mission. I have written about this in *Intercom* as far back as 1977. Much has happened since then, and the topic bears repeating.

At times, tensions are evident in our mission family because of our various ethnocentricities, which make it difficult for us to understand each other. Each of us tends to think that it is the other person who is biased. We fail to see the mote that is in our own eye.

These tensions will not go away, nor will they be lessened as we become more cosmopolitan. The contrary is true. We each must, therefore, sit down now and again and think through the implications of being international.

In reading Marvin Mayer's *Christianity Confronts Culture*, I came across some comments on culture shock which I think can also be applied in principle to relationships between missionaries who come from different cultures:

Culture shock has been described as that emotional disturbance which results from adjustments to a new cultural environment. The person in culture shock takes flight in one of two directions: Either he clings blindly or immoveably to his original ways, or he blindly and indiscriminately renounces his former ways and values in favor of the ways and values that are responsible for the culture shock to which he has fallen prey.

Those who cling to their original ways and values become more and more aggressively anti-native, while those caught in the second current "go native."

An anti-nativist tends more and more to pull himself back into his shell of culturally acquired beliefs, attitudes, and behavior. Thus in his view, the local people must become like him rather than he become like them.

Going native, on the other hand, is a neurotic longing for security and an exaggerated longing for belonging. This unbalanced craving for acceptance drives the unwary individual to approve and to accept as his own, indiscriminately and blindly, any and all local ways and values.

Understanding Needed

In our cross-cultural encounters with Africans or South Americans, we would be first to admit that we have made mistakes. We have offended our brethren unwittingly. But relationships will improve with God's help if we sincerely try to understand one another's behavioral patterns. This same sincere effort will work within our multinational mission if we are alert to the dangers and sensitive to each other's needs.

Remember the statement in our Manual:

SIM is international. Contact with missionaries from other countries and cultures provides opportunity to develop an international outlook and to see the viewpoints of others. Sometimes, however, there is a tendency to feel that one's own background, manner of speech, dress, and other cultural things are superior. Missionaries must be careful to avoid comments and conversation that may give offense to others and not to take offense at remarks and actions which are made innocently.

David summed it up nicely for us in Psalm 133: "Behold, how good and how pleasant it is," he said, "for brethren to dwell together in unity!"

Let us continue to strive together for the kind of interpersonal understanding and harmony that will radiate the fragrance of our Lord Jesus Christ.

Since the late 1980s, significant strides have been made in orienting missionaries, both new and old, to the broadening internationalness and multicultural nature of SIM's

Photo 20.5. *"You Are Worthy," painted by Chuck Guth, 1993.* Perhaps the most recognized piece of art associated with SIM in recent years is "You Are Worthy," a painting that Chuck Guth produced in 1993 for SIM's centennial. Guth ministered with his family among the Koma and others in Sudan from 1948–1962, and then worked in SIM's publication department in Canada until he and his wife Betty retired in 1988. At the time of its painting, SIM was serving in Africa, South America, and Asia. One of the historical persons in the painting is the Italian Sam Panoessa, the man with black hair without a hat under South America, who represents the variety of Europeans who live in South America. Another historical person is just to his left in the white shirt and bowtie near the center of the painting—Emmanuel Ampansa-Kuffour. He is a Ghanaian who leads a Bible school and denomination of churches in Ghana. All of the other people are composites from pictures that missionaries took or photos that *National Geographic* published. From left to right facing the picture are the Andes, with perhaps a Roman Catholic church in the foreground; Yabus River in Sudan where the Guths lived for five years; Niamey, Niger, with Tamajaq (Tuareg) camel riders; and a rear view of the Taj Mahal in India.[5]

membership. This writer took part in helping to organize some early pilot courses known as SIMIOC (SIM International Orientation Course). "Orientation" was soon changed to "Outlook" to emphasize that the change in thinking wasn't just for newcomers. These have been followed through the years by many more regular courses or training on the subject organized at both the international level and as components in broader orientation programs conducted at regional and national office levels. Under the early leadership of Brian and Maureen Butler, and others since, these courses were significant in bringing about many of the advances in diversity now celebrated.

The breadth of participation in, or in partnership with, SIM in globalized mission has also increased dramatically over the years, so that today SIM members come from more than 65 countries and include members from every region of the world. Together they work in over 70 countries. Significant in this process was the decision, by 2007, that

Photo 20.6. *Dr. Andrew and Belinda Ng, with their children Joel and Nathanial (oldest).*
Andrew Ng, a Singaporean by nationality, was born in Malaysia. He attended the University of Singapore where he became a medical doctor, and married Belinda in 1973. After Andrew completed his FRCS (Edinburgh), the Ngs joined SIM in 1976 and went to Galmi Hospital in Niger the following year where he worked as a surgeon for 12 years. The Ngs returned to Singapore in 1989, and a month later became SIM's sending director for East Asia; he held this position until 2005. While serving in this capacity he successfully encouraged SIM to enter China as a new field and did considerable work to expand SIM East Asia into several other countries in Asia. In 2006, Andrew and Belinda moved to the US where he served as the deputy international director for Asia and the Pacific until 2011 when he "retired." Belinda became an integral part of the International Personnel Department during that time. Andrew and Belinda continue to serve the Lord through SIM in Asia and elsewhere.

offices would no longer be thought of in terms of either sending or receiving, but that all offices would function to carry out both roles.[6]

This evolution of inclusion in SIM as a movement and not just as an organization, has also led to new committees and councils being formed in far-flung parts of Asia, Africa, Latin America, and Europe. Most recently, it has led to an organizational restructuring of SIM internationally in 2014 to better reflect this new reality (Photo 20.7).

Before closing this section we shall highlight just two examples of the rich fruit that has been borne through SIM's participation in, and encouragement of, the globalization of mission. The first is from the 1980s, and the second is from the last decade. The first features the movement to Christ of the Maguzawa people of Nigeria spearheaded by the Evangelical Missionary Society (EMS) of ECWA, and the second involves the impact that Ethiopian missionaries in SIM are having among the Marwari people of Pakistan.

The story of the Maguzawa as told by Kerry Lovering in 1985 in an article entitled "The People Who Fled":[7]

The people of Tamarke village had never seen a celebration like it. People came from miles around. They sat under the trees, singing and laughing. There was a loudspeaker, and benches for special guests.

Photo 20.7. *SIM Board of Governors, Sucre, Bolivia, 2017.* Front row (L–R): Ryan Hannah, Helen Ko, JaeOK Lee, Bev Howell, Joshua Bogunjoko, Steve Hawthrone, Gillian Phillips, Daniel Salinas. Back row (L–R): Ben Pillay, Stephen Roy, Ron Williams, Chris Seddon, Rod Russell.

Called a "feast of repentance," the event was designed to introduce to the predominantly Islamic community 60 Maguzawa people who had decided to follow Jesus Christ.

The feast was instituted by a Nigerian missionary, and patterned after the celebration that Muslims of that area hold when initiating a convert into Islam.

For the new Christians, the event was a springboard into a new standing in the community. "Persecution will come," the Nigerian missionary explained, "but these converts are not afraid. They do not stand as individuals, but as a group. They have community recognition."

The feast not only strengthened the new Christians, it made an impact upon the Muslims who heard their testimonies. Many indicated a sincere desire to know more about Christ.

The feast of repentance at Tamarke was one of the first in what has become the accepted way for believers from among the Maguzawa people to take their stand for Christ.

The Maguzawa movement began early in 1977. Within five years, trained converts were beginning to replace the Nigerian missionaries who had introduced the gospel to their areas. Within six years there were 200 churches, an effective Bible teaching program, and a Maguzawa Bible School offering a three-year diploma course.

Truly indigenous

Perhaps the greatest significance of the movement is that it is truly indigenous, carried out under the guidance of the Holy Spirit by the Evangelical Missionary Society (EMS), missionary arm of the SIM-related Evangelical Churches of West Africa (ECWA).

For generations the Maguzawas have resisted Islam. Their name means "the runners," referring to their ancestors' flight from the Islamic conquest of northern Nigeria early in the nineteenth century. They remained [followers of African traditional religions] surrounded by a sea of Islam.

Half a million in number, they are Hausa-speaking farmers with a reputation for hard work and honesty. They do not live in exclusive tribal districts, but are scattered in large groups throughout three states.

SIM missionaries had exposed several Maguzawa communities to the gospel years ago, but with very little response. "The runners" were resistant to any kind of change, and looked upon Christianity as the white man's religion.

That attitude began to soften in the 1970s as increasing numbers of their children started school under a nationwide education program. Animism was not considered progressive. Reacting to pressure to accept Islam, many Maguzawas became open to the gospel.

In 1976 SIM's Jerry Swank conducted a survey of central Nigeria for the Nigerian Evangelical Fellowship. NEF listed the Maguzawas as a major, unreached group with potential for ready response, and called for an immediate, large-scale effort to reach them for Christ. Because the family unit is very strong, the report recommended that missionaries seek household conversions through approaches to fathers and sons.

Photo 20.8. *Jerry Swank leading a New Life For All seminar, Nigeria, 1974.* On 1 August 1963, SIM missionary Jerry Swank, then principal of the Bible college in Kagoro, Nigeria, helped organize "New Life For All" which sought to bring Christians "together to evangelize their country for Christ." Members of New Life For All played an important role in evangelizing thousands of Nigerians and many across the continent and beyond in the years that followed. By 1989 the movement, which mobilized the total church for outreach to every person in its community, had spread to 20 countries in Africa, and had taken hold as far afield as Bolivia, Papua New Guinea, and Australia. Handbooks and other NLFA materials had been translated into 70 languages. In 1988 tens of thousands of people thronged to the Jos (Nigeria) Polo Grounds to praise God and thank SIM missionary Jerry Swank who founded NLFA "to help the church accomplish its God-given task of reaching every person with the gospel." Much of the growth of the Evangelical Church Winning All (ECWA) is attributed to NLFA. Swank traveled from his home in California, USA, at the invitation of NLFA to address the Silver Jubilee Rally and to be interviewed on TV.[8]

In view of politico-religious sensitivities, ECWA and SIM agreed that SIM missionaries should stay out of this one. It would be a totally EMS venture.

Immediate Response

It was a wise decision. Fluent in Hausa and equipped with the Hausa Bible, EMS missionaries found immediate response. In the first few weeks of 1977, about 200 Maguzawas chose the Christian way.

ECWA then called upon its churches to release 100 Hausa-speaking pastors to serve among the Maguzawas for one year. Conversion figures soared to 700, then 1,300. EMS gave up counting.

By March 1979, 52 permanent EMS families had settled in Maguzawa villages, and 25 short-term Bible schools were in operation. As the volunteer ECWA pastors completed their year of ministry, ECWA turned its attention to Bible Training School (BTS) graduates, encouraging them to spend their first year of ministry with EMS.

That idea, too, took hold. In 1982, 99 BTS grads, including the complete graduating classes of two schools, headed off to Maguzawa areas. The practice has become widely accepted and has contributed greatly to ECWA's missionary vision.

How EMS began

Photo 20.9. *African Missionary Society*

By the end of the second World War, a large number of independent SIM churches had been established in Nigeria. In 1949, before these churches were formed into an organization, SIM launched the African Missionary Society (AMS). The goal was to send national missionaries across ethnic and cultural boundaries, as distinct from "evangelists" who worked out from their local churches.

The principles laid down concerning AMS included instructing SIM churches in the concept of foreign missions; encouragement to all churches to set aside one Sunday a month for missions and missionary offerings; administration by African church leaders in partnership with SIM; financial support to be entirely African; and the formulation of principles and practices by AMS's own council, as approved by SIM.

"The need for an African missionary society has been sensed for a long time," an SIM field letter said. "No church which does not have a missionary vision will continue to be a strong, virile church. This is just as true in Africa as in the homelands."

As times changed, the paternal aspects of the founding years changed with them. But the original goal was maintained—a sending society to cross ethnic and cultural lines.

AMS was three years old when SIM churches were organized as ECWA in 1952 [1954]. Two years later ECWA was registered with [the] government as an autonomous organization, and AMS became the Evangelical Missionary Society.

The growth of ECWA churches since 1954 (from 400 to over 1,500) has been more than matched by the growth of EMS: 54 missionaries then, 565 now.

EMS faces the same kind of cultural clashes that expatriate missionaries face. When EMS missionaries from animistic backgrounds cross ethnic lines to Islamic areas, their dress, eating habits, accent, and other customs can be barriers to acceptance.

Financially self-reliant

Since its founding, EMS has been financially independent. That has not been easy. The support figure has always been minimal, so low, in fact, that for the first 20 years EMS missionaries could not support their families without farming. That picture has improved, but the EMS calling is still one of sacrifice. Salary fluctuates monthly, dependent on ECWA church offerings.

Church leadership is the key to adequate funding, explains EMS General Secretary Panya Baba. He tells of a church whose missionary vision dropped off because of a building program. Then a new pastor came. He told the congregation that not another concrete block would be laid until they paid what they owed to EMS. It was hard, but they did it. Then they started building again, this time with a policy that nothing would take away from their missionary giving.

"It is the policy of both ECWA and SIM that EMS should be self-reliant," Panya explains. "However, in our Maguzawa outreach we jumped from adding 10 missionary couples each year to 68. The churches weren't ready."

"SIM realized the need, and helped build the Bible School. It also helped, with other agencies, to build dormitories. It is very encouraging to know that when we are pushed to the wall, SIM will stand with us."

As members of ECWA congregations, SIM missionaries contribute to EMS through church offerings. They also rally to special needs. One Christmas they gave 5,500 naira ($8,250) to help pay transportation costs for the soaring number of EMS missionaries. The following Christmas they gave a similar sum toward the purchase of a vehicle.

Fully committed

The task facing EMS and other indigenous evangelical mission societies is formidable. In Nigeria alone there are not less than 25 million unevangelized people. In neighboring nations, there are millions more. The new aggressiveness of Islam, the resurgence of traditional religions, and the political uncertainty that shrouds so much of Africa, require a deeply rooted commitment.

EMS is endowed with just that. "Evangelism is at the heart of our church," says one ECWA leader. "When we stop evangelizing, ECWA will be dead."

The second, but far from the only other example of the increased fruitfulness that the globalization of mission has brought to SIM is the impact that Ethiopian missionaries are having among the Marwari people of Pakistan. Their story, published in 2011 and edited slightly for the purposes of this book, follows:[9]

The field was struggling. To many, it seemed as if the SIM mission in Pakistan might be on its last legs. But while men despaired at what looked like the closing gambit of a lost chess game, God was behind the scenes, subtly arranging pieces for a new play.

In the Pakistan field, SIM had merged with International Christian Fellowship. Still, there were only seven struggling SIM-related churches, and the missionaries working that field were discouraged. In the few years following the merger, seeing little fruit and wondering if God might not be calling them elsewhere, many packed up and left the field. At the SIM International office the question was tentatively raised: Should we close the field?

With faith that God still had plans for Pakistan, especially among a special group of forgotten people, the Marwari, SIM decided to keep the field open and see what God would do. It quickly became clear that, while the future was veiled, He had exciting things planned.

God had raised up a new leader named Clive Barker, a man with bold vision. When the field was dwindling at its lowest ebb, Clive was sending out the call, believing that God was going to double his field.

Meanwhile, Howard and Jo-Ann Brant were serving with SIM in Ethiopia—an SIM mission with a long history. Around the same time that Clive was beginning his new work, they were busy leading a team of Ethiopian missionaries into India. There, God awakened the hearts of the Ethiopian team and the very next year the Ethiopians decided to go on a longer trip to Pakistan. During their six months there, they were an encouragement to the struggling churches, and saw about 200 of the local people embrace Christ.

One of these unique Ethiopian individuals was a woman named Desta. When she returned from her mission in Pakistan, she met and married a wonderful Ethiopian evangelist named Abera. And those whom God brought together, He called. As a couple, they went off to Singapore for training and then they became the first long-term missionaries out of Ethiopia to work in a foreign country—in Pakistan.

There they found their assignment to be a difficult one. They were tasked with teaching the Marwari—an isolated group of low-caste Hindu people living in a society dominated by others. When India and Pakistan divided in 1948, many of these landless peasants decided to remain in Pakistan instead of going to India with the rest of the Hindu population. This remnant remained to be day laborers to the rich local landowners. Since that time the remnant has grown.

But despite their growing numbers, the Marwari have no rights. The majority people look down on them, often forbidding their children to attend school, and allowing them to marry only their own kind. They are castigated their entire lives, subsisting on the fringes of society.

In working with the Marwari, Desta and Abera found that there were incredibly few believers—and that they were so distant from each other that churches were impossible. But the Ethiopian missionaries got to work. Abera searched diligently and chose twenty young men to train as house leaders. They would conduct worship in their homes for their immediate family and anyone else who happened to drop by, and of these twenty he chose a small handful to disciple personally.

Soon the idea of discipleship took off among the people. As this model grew, another of God's key pieces fell into place: a different mission withdrew from Pakistan, abandoning to the care of SIM a large training center with the only stipulation that it continue to be used for discipleship.

With this foothold, Abera dug in with the Marwari, teaching short courses and discipling them. When the SIM missionaries, the Brants, visited Desta and Abera's work in Pakistan, they were encouraged to find that things with the Marwari had really progressed! But even more, Abera had been able to reach the mainline, traditional churches all across Pakistan—challenging them in their own mission work.

The Brants found that Abera—with his unique gifts of powerful preaching and fluent Urdu—was being heard all through the nation! With their experience and insight, they encouraged Abera and Desta to begin forming house churches among the Marwari, where Christianity had begun to take root. They suggested they hold periodic celebrations to bring the house churches together, and even proposed they hold an annual celebration at the new discipleship center.

Abera did just that. About two hundred people came to the first conference, giving all involved a reason to rejoice. But God was planning something even greater than SIM, Clive Barker, the Brants, or Desta and Abera could have ever dreamed.

This year, invitations began pouring in from every quarter of the Marwari's isolated communities asking Abera and his Ethiopian colleague to come and share the Gospel. People everywhere began believing, and at the most recent conference nearly 5,000 people were in attendance!

Many who attended the conference were not yet believers, but these downtrodden people came with hope after seeing their neighbors find a new identity in Christ. The meetings were packed as speaker after speaker shared the Gospel, challenging their lost and disconsolate people to follow the Lord.

Through this traditionally Hindu people group, isolated in a country that is 97% of another religion, God is doing something amazing—uplifting the oppressed and forgotten and claiming them for Himself. There, in the heart of Pakistan, He is preparing to reach a wayward majority through a faithful remnant.

SUPPLEMENT 20.1

Panya Dabo Baba[10]
Dr. Musa A. B. Gaiya

Panya Dabo Baba, a resident of the Overseas Ministry Study Center from 1996 to 1997, has been described as the greatest missiologist of the ECWA (Evangelical Church of West Africa founded by Sudan Interior Mission).[11] His tenure as director of the Evangelical Missionary Society (EMS) was outstanding and he raised the mission to an international level. The growth of the ECWA in Nigeria and abroad was mainly due to his ingenious mission strategy.

Panya was born in Karu on January 20, 1932 to Baba and Gnubwanyi, both of them Gbagyi of Nasarawa State in Nigeria. Panya's parents were Christians, so he grew up in a Christian family.[12] Baba was the chief of the Karu or the Estu Karu. At his birth Panya was named Panyadabo, which means

Photo 20.10. *Rev. Panya Baba*

"remember God the owner"—advice to Panya to remember God who made him. Panya did. When Panya sustained an injury that broke his skull as a toddler, his parents thought he would never survive. He survived but still carries a visible scar—a recovery which Panya considers miraculous. Later in his life, God also healed him of a very serious stomach ailment that almost killed him when he was working as a missionary.

He began his early education by enrolling in the Karu SIM Primary School where he studied from 1942 to 1945. Panya heard the gospel from SIM missionary Mrs. H. W. Caster but did not understand it initially. In 1945, though, Panya clearly heard the gospel and received Christ as his personal Savior through Malam Sabuda, a student at the Karu Bible School who hailed from Kaltungo, in northeastern Nigeria. As Panya testified, "Kneeling to God in my small room, I told Him I was sorry for my sins and asked for His forgiveness. I told God I wanted to be one of His children. The moment I finished that prayer, I felt different. . . . that was the day and time Jesus came into my life." Panya was baptized in 1946.

Having heard the call of God to go into full-time Christian service, Panya studied at the Karu Vernacular Bible Training School from 1946 to 1947. In 1949 he accepted the challenge to become a missionary among his people, the Gbagyi, in Sarkin Pawa (Niger Province) in northern Nigeria to teach them the Bible. His desire to do mission work continued to grow. He returned to Karu in 1951 and was admitted to Karu Bible Training School for additional training in 1952. In 1954 he was called by the ECWA church in Karu to be a pastor starting in 1957 and was licensed and ordained in 1960. In 1961 Panya went to Kagoro Bible College where he earned a certificate in Bible. He returned to Karu in 1963 to continue as pastor of the Evangelical Church of West Africa (ECWA) church there. But Panya's heart was more in missions. While Panya was pastoring this church he was appointed director of the Evangelical Missionary Society, where he made his most significant contribution to the course of evangelization of Africa.

Panya married Tayado Dokwadayi in February of 1951. Tayado means "Never depart"—perhaps a prayer that she not die. They had six children—three girls and three boys. They adopted an orphan boy named Ishaya at the age of six. Tayado died in childbirth on April 23, 1963.

Afterward Panya married Ruth Lami Ataku on February 22, 1964. She gave birth to seven children, two of whom died. All together Panya had fourteen children including one adopted son. One of his sons, Luka, is now (2006) the Estu Karu or paramount chief of Karu.

Panya's growing interest in missions led him to apply to All Nations Christian College in England where he was accepted and studied from 1969 to 1970. When he returned to Nigeria he was the best person to take charge of the Evangelical Missionary Society (EMS)—at that time the only indigenous mission organization in Nigeria. His training at Fuller Theological Seminary in Pasadena, USA, further enriched his understanding of missions and evangelism. He brought his knowledge, experience, leadership abilities, and zeal to EMS. He encouraged young graduates from Bible colleges and seminaries to join the mission, and as a result the number of missionaries increased from 194 in 1970 when he took over to 750 in 1988 when he left office as director.

He also believed in sending missionaries abroad as he felt Nigeria had come to that stage. As a result, EMS missionaries were sent out from two West African countries to five other countries including the United Kingdom and the United States of America. Panya believed in the interdependence between the developed world and the underdeveloped world in mission. He believed the developed West had a lot to give Africa in terms of finances, specialized personnel, and technical assistance, and Africa had a lot to give the West in terms of evangelism and mission. That is why when he stepped down as ECWA president in 1994, he started the Foreign Mission of EMS.

Panya personally founded the Nigeria Evangelical Mission Association (NEMA) that brought together all evangelical mission bodies. Out of NEMA the Nigeria Evangelical Missionary Institute was created to train young men and women for crosscultural mission work and the NEMA Searchlight Project designed to research unreached peoples groups. Through the Searchlight Project Panya discovered a number of ethnic groups in Nigeria that had not heard the gospel. These were the Koma, the Boko, the Dakawa, the Kambari, the Undir, the Dirim, and the Bolewa.

Panya was not only a missionary administrator and a strategist; he was also a missionary advocate. Everywhere he went he spoke on missions. At all the international conferences he attended, any papers he gave were on the topic of mission. Panya was a member of several international missionary organizations and associations. Ruth Cox, his secretary while he was director of EMS, said of him, "He is always looking for ways to spread the gospel, looking for areas where it has not been preached. He doesn't know the difference between work and pleasure. . . . to him they are the same. He has put missions and the gospel first. . . . This is his life."

When Panya was elected president of the ECWA in 1988 it meant he would have to leave EMS, the place he loved so much. He served as president of ECWA for six years, but although he did his work well he did not love it as much as being a missions' administrator. Also, it was very difficult to find someone to fill the vacuum created after Panya left EMS.

As a result of Panya's immense service in the ECWA, especially as EMS director, the governing council and faculty of the ECWA Seminary, Igbaja, awarded him a doctorate of divinity honoraris causa on May 18, 1991. In addition, the West African Theological Seminary gave Panya the Akanu Ibiam Award "for excellence in cross-cultural mission."[13]

Panya Baba retired from active service in the ECWA in 1998. He returned home to Karu and has been preoccupied with writing his thoughts about mission, giving lectures at mission conferences, preaching, offering counseling and helping in any way he can in the local ECWA church in Karu.

CHAPTER 2 I

MIDDLE EAST CHRISTIAN OUTREACH

IM "joined hands" with Middle East Christian Outreach (MECO) in 2016.[1] In doing so, SIM reentered the Middle East region that it had left decades earlier. The mission's earlier work had been in Aden in today's Yemen (1945–1965) and Lebanon (1965–1975).[2] When the two missions made this arrangement in 2016, MECO had colleagues working in Egypt, Jordan, Lebanon, Iraq Kurdistan, and Cyprus.[3] Its missionaries had partnered and worked with "Christian schools, churches, medical and rehabilitation centers, orphanages, children's homes, Bible Colleges and in the publishing and distribution of Christian literature in Arabic and other Middle Eastern languages."

Photo 21.1. *International Director's Mike Parker (MECO) and Joshua Bogunjoko (SIM) "joining hands"*

Previously their work included production of significant evangelistic videos in Arabic.[4]

MECO's strategy in the region has always been to work alongside local Christians, churches, and agencies. Despite the confusions of Middle East life and politics, those groups have grown in their leadership. Their boldness in witnessing to Christ under increasing pressure from the majority around them has been impressive and moving and is a story MECO has learned from and been pleased to tell in Western countries.[5]

A number of trends led MECO to join with SIM. Among the attractors were SIM's global reach—which would open the Middle East up to people from Asia, Africa, and South America—and the revised and sharpened vision of SIM International, under the leadership of Dr. Joshua Bogunjoko. MECO found SIM's capacity among its people particularly attractive. The combination of an increasingly aging profile and a steady decline in numbers led MECO to

pray and reflect on what the Lord was saying and eventually to approach SIM. MECO's approach coincided with SIM's desire to be present again in the Middle East. It proved to be a powerful example of the Lord's timing and providence for both groups, who are now eagerly engaged in developing relationships and anticipating bringing new people in to grow the team in the region.

What follows is the story of MECO's origins that MECO published a few years ago. MECO came into being in 1976 as the result of the merger of Lebanon Evangelical Mission, the Middle East General Mission, and the Arabic Literature Mission.

Lebanon Evangelical Mission[6]
formerly the British Syrian Mission

The British Syrian Mission (BSM) was founded in 1860 as *The Society for the Social and Religious Improvement of Syrian Females*. Mrs. Bowen-Thompson had gone to Beirut in October 1860 with the *Syrian Temporal Relief Fund*, part of an international effort to aid victims of the massacres in Syria earlier that year. Soon after her arrival she recognized the need for a more permanent, specifically Christian work, independent of the relief fund. One of her great concerns was the education of women and girls.

The following is an excerpt from her biography titled *Daughters of Syria:*[7]

Photo 21.2. Elizabeth Maria Bowen, founder of the Society for the Social and Religious Improvement of Syrian Females.

Source: H. B. Tristram, editor, The Daughters of Syria: A narrative of efforts by the late Mrs. Bowen Thompson, for the evangelization of the Syrian females, *2nd ed. (London: Seeley, Jackson & Halliday, 1872), frontispiece.*

> The first evening I came here, I asked the Arab waiter, "Did he speak any English?" "Could he read Arabic?" "No." "Why don't you learn?" I asked. "I have nobody to teach me." I then asked to see the maid and she no sooner came than she exclaimed in Arabic, "Oh, lady, I want to learn to read." I took out pen and ink and wrote the first six letters of the Arabic. They repeated these letters till they knew them and then they both tried to copy them; every day they learnt a little. Yesterday I went to the Arab printing press and bought some alphabet cards. These were at once put into requisition and the waiter brought four women, relations of his, who also wanted to learn. This morning the cook of the motel made his appearance and said, "Lady, will you teach me?" I proposed an evening school and the master of the hotel, who speaks English, came to me and said, "If you will open a school here, I will give you a room—I will be the first pupil."

Why was Mrs. Thompson able to make such an impact on the community? The introduction to her biography explains:

> The fact that a lone English lady, who worked single-handed, commenced in 1860 a work entirely new, amidst the ruins and devastation of a civil war of extermination, left behind her after nine years, twenty-three firmly established schools, containing about 1,700 pupils under fifty-six teachers, is enough to arrest attention. What was the key of her success? Firm consistency and a single eye. She had but one object—to bring souls to Christ. Her aim was far higher than the desire to promote secular or intellectual improvement. From the determination to make known the Word of God, she never flinched.

By her death in 1869 she had established 23 schools in nine centres, including Hasbaiya, Tyre, Beirut, Baalbek, and Damascus. These came to be known as the *British Syrian Schools*. Of central importance in her strategy was the Institute (later called the Training College) in Beirut. Here female teachers were trained for both the *British Syrian Schools* and other Christian schools in Syria and Egypt. For more than a century the Institute had a significant influence on the development of female education in the region.

Although the immediate need for relief work soon passed, care for the needy continued through schools for the blind established in Beirut (1868), Damascus and Tyre (1872), and a school for the crippled in Beirut (approx. 1868). But Mrs. Bowen-Thompson was not only concerned for the physical and social well-being of Syrian women, but also that they might come to faith in Christ. From the outset evangelism was a key component of her work. In association with the schools, women were trained to visit homes and share the gospel. These "Bible women" became known as the Bible Mission. From 1876 the title British Syrian Schools and Bible Mission was used. By 1892 this had been shortened to British Syrian Mission. Although the focus was largely on the schools and their potential as centres for evangelism, the BSM ever had an eye to new opportunities as and when they arose. The most significant of these developments were the introduction of small-scale medical work in 1885, evangelistic work among the Bedouin in the 1890s, the Weaving School in Beirut, the evangelistic work of Miss Paludan amongst the Alawites (Nusairya) in North West Syria and the Bible School in Shemlan, 1938.

The emergence of Lebanon and Syria as separate independent nations after the Second World War brought considerable changes to the mission. In 1958 they withdrew from Damascus. With the work now concentrated in Lebanon the name Lebanon Evangelical Mission (LEM) was adopted (1959). These changing circumstances led to a broadening of vision rather than simple retrenchment. The Bible School was reopened in 1952, and continued to train evangelists and pastors until 1971. After its closure LEM continued to take an active interest in Bible teaching through its participation in a Theological Education by Extension programme established in 1970. In 1965 a literature department was established which, in 1967, became part of an intermission venture know as the Christian Arabic Literature League (CALL). In 1971 CALL was reorganized and registered as a Lebanese organization, Clarion Publishing House, under the direction of Hanna Bassous. It was during this period that LEM also became involved for a time in radio ministry, preparing tapes for a number of Christian radio stations. But perhaps the most significant development period was passing control of the work to Lebanese Christians, resulting in the formation of the Lebanese Evangelical Society (LES) in 1967 under the leadership of David Tleel. LEM became a partner with the LES seeking to build on the past and expand into new avenues of service. The LES began to look seriously at sending workers to other parts of the Middle East. As well as continuing to be involved in witness within Lebanon, LES started to have a wider vision and sent a number of workers to other parts of the Middle East.

Middle East General Mission[8]
formerly the Egypt General Mission
The Egypt General Mission (EGM) came into being in part through God's call to a group of seven young men at the YMCA in Belfast, and in part through the vision of a remarkable Victorian lady, Annie Van Sommer.

Photo 21.3. *"Egypt Mission Band. The First Seven," 1899.*
Photo credit: George Swan, Lacked Ye Anything?: A Brief Story of the Egypt General Mission *(London: Egypt General Mission, 1923), 17.*

Annie Van Sommer had gone to Egypt in the 1880s in response to an appeal for Christian work among British troops stationed in Egypt. While there, she became increasingly concerned for the Egyptian people themselves. On her return to England in 1896 she formed the Prayer Union for Egypt, to promote prayer for that land.

While speaking at a student conference in Curbar, Derbyshire, in 1897 she met four of the group from the YMCA in

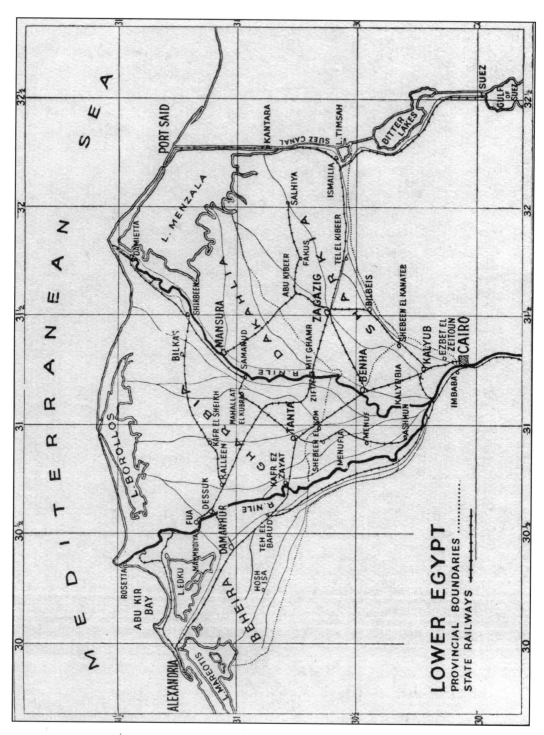

Map 21.1. *Lower Egypt.*

Source: George Swan, Lacked Ye Anything?: A Brief Story of the Egypt General Mission *(London: Egypt General Mission, 1923), 21.*

Belfast. Because of that meeting their thoughts were directed toward Egypt. The seven, William Bradley, Martin Cleaver, Fred Cooney, Gordon Logan, George Swan, Edward Swan, and Elias Thompson sailed for Egypt in 1898. Initially they set themselves the task of learning Arabic, visiting various parts of the Middle East to see where they could best be of service. Eventually they decided to focus on the villages of the Eastern Nile Delta, establishing schools and clinics and engaging in church planting as the opportunity arose.

It was not until 1900 that they formally established a society, the Egypt Mission Band (EMB). In 1903 the name was changed to the Egypt General Mission (EGM). The ministry in Egypt gradually expanded around a dozen or more "stations" in the Eastern Delta. The field headquarters were moved to Izbat al-Zaitûn (Cairo) in 1907. The dispensary in Shibîn al-Qanâtir became a hospital. Book depots and schools were opened in a number of other locations. But after the Second World War the changing political climate forced the mission to withdraw from Egypt in 1956. Some workers were relocated in Cyprus and Lebanon, seconded to other missions.

In April 1957 two members of the mission visited Eritrea with the view to opening a new work there. Following the advice of other missions, a headquarters was established in Asmara as a base for work in the northwestern lowlands. The name of the mission was changed to the Middle East General Mission (MEGM). The pattern of work was similar to Egypt, combining medical work, schools, and evangelism in village centres strung out along the Asmara-Tessenei road.

A Bible School was established in Keren and a hospital in Haicota in 1964. Although MEGM had no permission to work among Eritreans in Asmara itself, it opened a school for missionary children there in 1966. But eventually in 1977 the civil war in Eritrea forced the missionaries to leave. At this time MECO began working with Eritrean refugees in East Sudan.

Arabic Literature Mission[9]
formerly the Nile Mission Press

The Nile Mission Press (NMP), formed in 1905, was from the outset a joint venture between a number of mission agencies. The emergence of a growing literate class in Egypt at the turn of the century, and the increased demand for literature in Arabic, had convinced Annie Van Sommer of the need for a Christian press in Egypt. She canvassed the various groups working in Egypt, but none of the groups were willing to take responsibility for financing such a work on their own. In 1902 an inter-mission committee, with representatives from five missions, was formed in Egypt. The same year Miss Van Sommer asked Arthur Upson (North Africa Mission) to become superintendent of the

Press. In May he sailed to Beirut to see the operations of the American Mission Press, and then to England to raise support. Percy Allen became the UK treasurer and the following year committees were established in UK and USA.

At this point (1903) the project almost failed, but a large donation from New Zealand persuaded the committee to go ahead. Upson returned to Cairo in January 1905 as manager of the Publications Department with William Gentles as manager of the Press. They rented rooms in Bulaq and within a few months the Press was operational. From the beginning they printed both material for other groups and their own publications. The NMP also bought stocks of Arabic books from the American Mission Press and the Religious Tract Society, some of which it reprinted. By 1925 they had published over four hundred titles in a variety of languages. By 1956 the number of titles had reached nine hundred, although many were by that time out of print.

From the beginning the NMP engaged in both production and distribution. In 1912 the Nile Valley Joint Colportage Committee was formed to coordinate the colportage work of the different societies.

Photo 21.4. *"Cover of the Arabic Magazine, 'Beshair es Salaam.'"*
Photo credit: George Swan, Lacked Ye Anything?: A Brief Story of the Egypt General Mission *(London: Egypt General Mission, 1923), 52.*

From about 1915 the NMP became actively engaged in "purity" campaigns and produced a large number of tracts highlighting the evils of prostitution, drunkenness, and smoking.

Just before the outbreak of World War I the Press moved into new premises. A department for children's material was created in 1916 under Constance Padwick and Elsie Anna Wood. Miss Van Sommer urged expansion into Palestine and, in 1919, supervised the opening of a bookshop in Jerusalem.

In 1923 the work was reorganized, making Upson overall director. He continued in this post until 1931 when he moved to Jerusalem. In 1938 the Press moved to the Van Sommer Memorial Hall, a dual purpose building that they shared with Ibrahim Sa'id's congregation. John Menzies became director in 1931, and George Wald in 1946. But by this time the NMP was in financial difficulty. The Press was moved to cheaper premises in Zaiton [Cairo] (1948), but the shortage of funds continued. Following George Wald's resignation (1954) it proved difficult to find a new director. The EGM agreed to second workers and Aubrey Whitehouse acted as director for a year. By 1956 there was talk of closing the Press. But in the end God used the political situation to redirect the society.

In the upheavals of the Suez Crisis the printing works was sealed by the police. Through the assistance of the Evangelical Literature Organization in Chicago the bookshop was transferred to the Free Methodist Mission. This continues to operate to this day under Egyptian management as the Nile Christian Bookshops.

The publishing work was relocated in Beirut under the direction of Douglas Howell. The experience in Egypt, and the improving standard of commercial printing, made the establishment of a new press unthinkable. For a number of years they continued to publish new books, developing a new range of Christian fiction. The name was changed to the Arabic Literature Mission (ALM) in 1960. By this time there were a number of evangelical literature agencies working in Beirut. In 1962 the ALM advisory committee in Lebanon suggested setting up a cooperative venture controlled by an intermission committee. At the time the ALM Council in London rejected these proposals as "too nebulous," but in 1971 joined with the Christian Arabic Literature League (CALL) in forming Clarion Publishing House.

Middle East Christian Outreach[10]

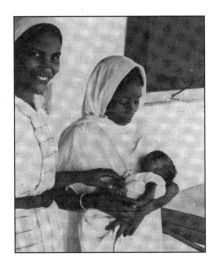

Middle East Christian Outreach (MECO) was formed on 1 September 1976 from the merging of three missions: the *Arabic Literature Mission (ALM)*, the *Lebanon Evangelical Mission (LEM)*, and the *Middle East General Mission (MEGM)*. Throughout its history MECO has combined Christian compassion for the disadvantaged with a desire to share the Good News about Jesus Christ. Evangelism and social concern go hand in hand. The merger of the missions could hardly have come at a more inauspicious time. LEM and MEGM had personnel in Lebanon and Eritrea, but both countries were caught up in long and bitter civil wars. ALM had no staff at all. But the vision for expansion had already been planted some years before the merger. The results of careful planning were ready to bear

Photo 21.5. *"Outside the Women's Ward,"* Eritrea.
Photo credit: Paul Shepherd, Decade in the Desert: The Story of Haicota Hospital *(Kent: Middle East Christian Outreach, 1977), 40.*

Photo 21.6. *SIM and MECO leaders meet in Toronto, Canada, 1978.* (L-R): SIM Deputy General Director W. Harold Fuller, SIM Canada Director Howard Dowdell, and MECO Director Douglas S. Anderson. Anderson showed a film and spoke in chapel.

fruit. The need to relocate some personnel proved to be the catalyst for a much wider ministry.

In February 1976, Douglas Anderson and his sister Loris visited Cyprus from Lebanon, to investigate schooling for missionary children and the establishment of a distribution centre for Publishing House, Beirut. This was the prelude to a long association with the island. At the second International Council meeting (1977) it was decided to establish the international headquarters in Limassol. This moved to Larnaca in 1982.

The ministry quickly expanded into a number of different countries. Language students were sent to a school in Jordan (1976), and in later years personnel were seconded to ministries in that country: the tuberculosis hospital in Mafraq (1985), the Church of the Nazarene in Amman, the Programme for Theological Education by Extension (1984), and the Deaf School in Salt.

In 1977 a nurse was seconded to the Christian hospital in Tanta, Egypt, and a teacher to Ramses Girls College in Cairo (Evangelical Synod of the Nile). The following year a team of teachers were put in the Orouba School, Assiut. Personnel were subsequently seconded to the Coptic Evangelical Organization for Social Services, the Anglican Church, and for a time a Coptic Orthodox school. Others worked in a magazine ministry, amongst the rubbish collectors, and with the blind and deaf.

Personnel were also sent to the United Arab Emirates, again working with existing ministries in Al Ain (1976), and Ajman (1977). In 1981 MECO was asked to take over the running of the Sarah Hosman Hospital in Sharjah (founded in 1941 by the Independent Board for Presbyterian Foreign Mission). In 1994, after a number of fruitful years, this was closed because of a shortage of suitable medical staff.

Relief work among Eritrea refugees in Sudan was started soon after the evacuation from Eritrea. At first this was done under the umbrella of the

Sudanese Council of Churches. In 1990 MECO began work with a primary health care programme run by a relief agency, Christian Outreach.

The literature distribution centre in Cyprus, known today as MECO Literature, began operations in the spring of 1976. It moved to Larnaca with MECO in 1982, but was then still technically part of Clarion Publishing House. From 1977 to 1982 it had been the base for Clarion's operations, but with the resignation of Hanna Bassous in 1981 and the appointment of George Feghali in Beirut the centre of the work returned to Lebanon. In 1983 MECO Literature was separated from Clarion and reorganized into two divisions: *MECO Literature* and MECO Video. Subsequently the video ministry became a separate department operating under the name *Vision Through Vision (VTV)*. By 1997 it had established a considerable reputation for producing culturally sensitive films. The Literature Department continued to fulfill a vital role in distributing books worldwide for a number of Lebanese and Egyptian publishers.

Throughout this period MECO continued to work closely with the LES in Lebanon, recruiting teachers for the schools and work with the blind. It also seconded personnel to other ministries, including a new work amongst Palestinian refugees in Sidon (1983) and the Mediterranean Bible College (1984).

In 1986 MECO was responsible for instigating a ministry to migrants in Australia, opening a Centre of Friendship in Sydney. A second centre was opened in Melbourne shortly after. Both centres were run by Egyptians who had settled in Australia.

With an increasing number of mission groups opening offices in Cyprus, MECO became concerned to foster cooperation among them. To this end it helped set up a number of intermission forums promoting a diversity of activities. These included support for Tent-makers, a forum for publishers and other media organizations to meet (Arab Media Convention), and a group concerned with justice issues. Part of the function of the international office was to serve missionaries located in other parts of the Middle East. Some of its activities were directed toward the training and refreshment of personnel. This was done through organizing conferences and providing facilities for rest and recuperation. In 1982 MECO assumed responsibility for running two adjacent camp sites in Troodos leased to the American Presbyterian Mission in Egypt and the Free Methodist Mission. These are now used by a number of different missions for holidays and conferences.

MECO continued to expand its areas of interest, although the total number of personnel did not rise significantly. Members were located in Turkey from 1985 and Syria from 1990. A ministry among Kurds was established in 1992 in association with Middle Eastern Christians. MECO continued to show interest in other countries in the Middle East, and maintained close contact with a wide circle of evangelical leaders. More recently it has been looking into new service opportunities in Yemen.[11]

SUPPLEMENT 21.1

Sir James Norman Dalrymple Anderson: Missionary and Scholar
Dr. Tim Geysbeek

Professor Sir James Norman Dalrmple Anderson (1908–1994) was the most prominent scholar, renowned worldwide, to be a member of any of the missions that merged with SIM—SIM included.[12] He started his career as a member of Egypt General Mission (EGM), and later became a legal scholar who gained his reputation in British academia and popularized discussions about reforming Islam. He believed evangelical Christianity's evangelistic efforts would gain their "widest influence" by changing individuals and societies. "On any long-term view," he wrote, "it is essential that a few give themselves to scholarship so that they may thereby serve the many whose call is to direct evangelism."[13] Yet, as Baylor University historian Todd Thompson, the leading authority on Anderson writes, "until his death" he "remained first and foremost a missionary."[14]

Norman Anderson was born in England, studied law at Cambridge University's Trinity College, and joined EGM in the early 1930s. He was a member of the EGM in Egypt for 14 years, working full-time with the EGM until the mid-1940s and then as a British intelligence officer until shortly after World War II. Anderson then became a scholar in Islamic law, holding various positions at the University of London until his retirement in 1976. He remained engaged in missions and academia, and as a consultant, until his death in 1994.

Anderson and his wife, Pat (Gavin), were members of EGM in Egypt from 1932–1946. When

Photo 21.7. *James Norman Dalrymple Anderson*
Photo Credit: Norman Anderson, An Adopted Son: The Story of My Life *(Leicester: Inter-Varsity Press, 1985), back cover.*

they joined the mission, EGM's missionaries' and their Egyptian colleagues' most prominent ministries were evangelism, discipleship, the selling and distribution of tracts and books, and educational and medical work. The Andersons started their missionary career by learning Arabic in Cairo at the School of Oriental Studies. As Anderson became proficient in Arabic he started to preach and read Islamic philosophy.

After a short time they moved to Ismailia where he attended (and sometimes led) the Evangelical Church's school's daily prayers, played soccer with the boys at a nearby pitch, continued to improve his aptitude in reading and speaking Arabic, and journeyed with an Egyptian evangelist to visit and preach in a nearby village. While in Ismailia, Sheikh Kamil Mansur guided Anderson through the reading of a text on Islamic law. Mansur, who had studied at Cairo's esteemed El Azhar University, was Egypt's leading Christian convert at the time.

The Andersons returned to Cairo where Anderson did what he felt was his most important work as a missionary—evangelizing and influencing Egypt's up-and-coming educated elite. He enrolled as an "affiliate student" at Fuad I University (Cairo University). While there he attended lectures in Arabic literature and Islamic law hoping to learn more about these disciplines, improve his Arabic, and meet students. He also taught Bible classes and had a Lebanese-designed house built near the university where he could meet students. Anderson felt it was important to work with Egypt's educated elite in Cairo because he believed Cairo "was the intellectual center of the Muslim world."[15] He also felt that its university students would play influential roles as entrepreneurs, health-care workers, lawyers, and politicians in Egypt's future. His work at the center involved inviting students there for tea or coffee, visiting them in their homes, and preaching in local churches. He evangelized as many students as possible and sought to shape their intellectual outlook in the face of materialism and rationalism that was challenging their faith in orthodox Islam. In 1939, Anderson published his first book, titled *Al-ʾaql wa'l-Imam* (*Faith and Reason*), to answer Christian students' questions about Christianity and to "catch the eye of a Muslim reader."[16]

Photo 21.8. *Sheikh Kamil Mansur.*

Photo credit: Aubrey H. Whitehouse, The Complete Circle: A Story of Medical Work in Egypt *(London: Egypt General Mission, 1958), 68.*

In July 1940, one month after Italy declared war on Great Britain, Anderson enlisted in the British army and became an intelligence officer. He was tasked with helping Sayed Idris al-Senussi—who became Libya's king after the war—organize refugees into a guerilla army to revolt against Italy's occupation of Libya. He later engaged in debates that led to the founding of the modern state of Libya and served as a diplomatic aide to Britain's foreign minister. For his service the British government honored him as a member of the Most Excellent Order of the British Empire (MBE) and as an officer of the Order of the British Empire (OBE).

Anderson chose a career in Islamic law rather than biblical studies or returning to missionary work after he concluded his military service in 1946. In the late 1940s he joined the faculty of the University of London where he eventually became the chairperson of the Law Department at the School of Oriental and African Studies and director of the prestigious Institute of Advance Legal Studies. Two of his many major scholarly publications were *Islamic Law in Africa* (1954) and *Law Reform in the Muslim World* (1976). While at the university, Anderson served as a consultant on Islamic law in many capacities and traveled widely in Asia and Africa. The government knighted him and the British Academy elected him as a fellow before he retired in 1976.

Coinciding with his work in law, Anderson sought to transform evangelical thinking about other religions' societies and Islam in particular. He encouraged evangelicals to become actively engaged in social and political issues, become more ecumenical, shun "cultural imperialism," and to participate in dialogue (rather than monologue) with peoples of other faiths. Two of his most significant books in this area were *World Religions* (1975) and *Islam in the Modern World: a Christian Perspective* (1990).

After Anderson resigned from the EGM in 1946, he served as the chairman of its London Council for three decades; EGM was renamed the Middle East General Mission in 1957. He worked with others to unite the Middle East General Mission, the Lebanon Evangelical Mission, and the Arab Literature Mission into one organization known as Middle East Christian Outreach (MECO) in 1976. Anderson did not hold any positions with MECO, but maintained sporadic contact with MECO missionaries in the years that followed. He also served on the boards of other Christian organizations, and came to hold leadership positions in the Church of England, including becoming the lay chairman of its General Synod.

EPILOGUE

INTO THE FUTURE WITH GOD AND THE GOSPEL

THE BIG "WHY" OF SIM'S CONTINUING EXISTENCE

Dr. Joshua Bogunjoko
SIM International Director

The three men who pioneered the Soudan Interior Mission (SIM) set out on their faithful and fateful journey into the heart of Africa not thinking just *what*, or *how*, but *why*? If they had been asking what—that is to say, if they were asking what can we do, what can we bring, and what should our ministry be?—they would have quickly discovered that they did not have to risk their lives in Africa to find something commendable to do. They did not have to go into the disease-infested interior to find people with whom to share the gospel. They did not have to leave the coast to find a worthy ministry to engage in. They did not need to be experts in any ministry area to be able to give themselves to work among the animistic people that they encountered in southwestern Nigeria.

Photo Epilogue.1. *Dr. Joshua Bogunjoko*

If these men were only asking what to do and how to do it, they would have found plenty to occupy them in Lagos or Ibadan before traversing hundreds of miles through pathless jungles to reach the heart of the region then called the Central Soudan where 60 to 90 million people were living and dying without ever hearing the good news of Christ's death, resurrection, and the forgiveness of sin by faith in him. No, these men were not asking what or how, they were asking why. They were focused on why they needed to leave North America in spite of all the opportunities available to them. They were focused on why they needed to push on into the interior in spite of the danger, the warnings, and the obvious needs that surrounded them on the coast. They were navigating by a common northern star. Their conviction to carry on into the interior was rooted in their beliefs. SIM's founding story is that of individual faithfulness and team commitment. It is the story of a community of believers, prayer warriors, and giving partners who came together, believing in the same reason for being and, by faith, making it happen.

Why does SIM continue to exist? What is the bigger picture, the guiding star into the future?

This question lies at the heart of how SIM looks at the future. It is rooted in our convictions and beliefs about what we should do and be doing and not just what we could do. To understand where we are and where we are going, it is essential to refocus on the *why*.

In the days before GPS and radar, shippers learned to navigate by the stars or risk being lost at sea. All ship captains depended on the same source for their bearings and direction—the stars, fixed far above the shifting, treacherous expanse of the open sea. Star maps and simple nautical measuring instruments kept every crew oriented until they reached their destination. Daylight dimmed the stars and storms blocked the view, but even today, many yachtsmen still rely on celestial navigation. In these days of high tech GPS and radar, it is easy to do that. Gadgets fail. If GPS fails to capture satellite signals or radar loses its power source, disorientation sets in and we are cast about in a sea of activities that do not seem to be leading us on a specific course. We as a mission seek to lift our eyes above the waves and fix them once again on our greater purpose.

Our mission history demonstrates that we are not attempting to do any more now than we have always done. SIM's ministries, in all of their variety, have always been an integrated whole. SIM was involved in radio, agriculture, education in both mission-owned and government-run schools, dispensaries and health centers, translation and literacy, printing, publishing, and in the business of bookstores. We were even involved in the abolition of slavery in northern Nigeria, though we were not there specifically to fight slavery. SIM missionaries launched one of the first indigenous mission agencies in Nigeria—the Evangelical Missionary Society (EMS)—and worked side by side with those being sent from that new agency. The founding of this agency arose out of SIM's clear sense of purpose. SIM established a mission agency before it ever established a church denomination.

The answer to the question "why does SIM continue to exist" is rooted in biblical truth, historical facts, and contemporary realities. God often chooses an agent or agents through whom he will bring his plan and purpose to pass. In the Old Testament, God chose Abraham and then his descendants, the people of Israel. Consistent with his unfathomable wisdom, God also choose the church as his agent to make known the good news of redemption through the preaching of the gospel, the good news of the kingdom of God.

The Great Commission was given to the church, the new people of God of the new covenant. In Act 1:8 Christ said, "And you shall be My witnesses both in Jerusalem, and in all Judea and Samaria, and even to the remotest part of the earth" (NASB). In Matthew 28:18–20, he commissioned us to make "learning followers" (disciples) of the nations as we go and to teach them to obey all that he has commanded. The apostle Paul understood clearly what this meant as he declared what Christ himself had said to him, "rescuing you from the Jewish people and from the Gentiles, to whom I am sending you, to open their eyes so that they may turn from darkness to light and from the dominion of Satan to God, that they may receive forgiveness of sins and an inheritance among those who have been sanctified by faith in Me" (Acts 26:17–18 NASB). SIM owes its existence to this same understanding of the need of those who still live in darkness and under the dominion of Satan and die without an opportunity to hear and understand the life-giving news of salvation in Christ.

The critical question that SIM is seeking to answer for itself and for the sake of the church in our day is whether we, like Israel of old, will be so preoccupied with other things that we will forget our reason for being and God's purpose for our existence. Jesus, in the midst of what we would consider a great success in his ministry, replied in response to the crowd that was looking for him, "Let us go somewhere else to the towns nearby, so that I may preach there also; for that is what I came for" (Mark 1:37–38 NASB). He again reiterated his focus on his purpose in Matthew 18:11, when he said "For the Son of Man has come to save that which was lost" (NASB). As God has blessed the labor of generations of SIM workers around the world and as the direction set by our past leaders has enriched us and our ministries, we must now harness the result of that labor in a growing number of churches and growing diversity of workers to focus, laser-like, on the work of the gospel.

To understand our direction for the future, it is essential that we understand our past and our roots. History is essential to SIM. Why did each mission's pioneers set out? They set out because people in the interior of the Soudan, in the mountains of the Andes, in the villages of India and in other corners of Southern Africa were living and dying without ever hearing or understanding the gospel of Christ. Indeed, the beginnings of SIM and each mission that now comprise SIM were only possible because of singleminded commitments to a clear understanding of *why*, and a sense of *why not*? While many were asking our founders *why do it*, they in turn were asking, *why not do it*, and *why not us*? They lived in the consciousness of the reality of Acts 4:12: "And there is salvation in no one else, for there is no other name under heaven given among men by which we must be saved" (NASB). They knew that the reality of darkness and death both physical and spiritual were the lot of the people of the Soudan, the interior of Southern Africa, the interior of the Andes region, and the deep parts of Asia to which they were called. They had an impossible task ahead of them, and an even more improbable job of convincing people in their own home that what they were embarking upon was worth it. Kerry E. Lovering wrote this account of an encounter between Walter Gowans and Kilgour Green:[1]

Walter had it laid on his heart that the heathen millions of the Central Soudan, who never had a missionary, ought to have one. He applied to most of the missionary societies in America to send him out as their missionary, but the bad climate and unpromising country caused each society to refuse him. So he made up his mind to go on his own account. Having made that decision, a determined Walter had lost no time in finalizing plans to set off for Africa by way of Britain, where he hoped to induce some missionary society to send him as their messenger of the gospel to the unreached "heathen millions of the Soudan," to whom he was irrevocably committed.

In Rowland Bingham's book *Seven Sevens of Years and a Jubilee: The Story of the Sudan Interior Mission*, G. Ritchie Rice wrote in the foreword:[2]

I have known Dr. Bingham for many years and we have had many times of sweet communion together. I can recall no occasion when the subject of our conversation has not been the extension of Christ's Kingdom. He was essentially a man of vision, lifting up his eyes and beholding the fields white already to harvest—calling for immediate action in the gathering of more and more of the harvest.

In that book, Dr. Bingham himself wrote:[3]

It was the impassioned pleading of a quiet little Scotch lady that linked up my life with the Sudan. She had invited me to her home for lunch, from a meeting where I had been speaking in the City of Toronto. There, in the quietness of her parlour, she told the story of her home and unburdened her heart . . . . That night I felt God laid His hand on me for the Sudan. There it was, a great, black belt, stretching for twenty-five hundred miles across Africa, steeped in the densest darkness. . . . Whatever I saw that night, I know I heard the voice of the Lord saying, "Whom shall I send, and who will go for us?" And I know, too, that He heard my response, "Here am I, send me!"

God is once again laying the burden for the lost on SIM's heart and renewing our vision of the needs of those in spiritual darkness and great physical, emotional, psychological, and environmental needs. There is still a burden. There are still many who live in the densest of darkness. The call to SIM and to many others—churches and individuals—is still "Whom shall I send, and who will go for us?" The dark belt of Bingham's day has become a beacon of gospel light. However, darkness still reigns in many places. Will SIM and its missionaries, supporters, leaders, board members, local churches, and partner organizations and mission agencies respond like the foreign mission boards of Gowans' day and say we have no means of expansion, or shall we rediscover our reason for being and respond in faith to the billions still in darkness across Asia, North Africa, the Middle East, Europe, the Americas, in cities and villages, and say, "It shall be done." "Here we are, Lord, send us!"

Many experts have painted quite accurately the current reality of the world. The gospel has made significant impact in the densest of darkness that captured Gowans' and then Bingham's heart. The question is, what are we going to do about those places where the presence of that darkness has continued? This is not to imply that work is finished in Africa or Latin America; in fact, there are still large swaths of populations in these places who still live and die without hearing or understanding the gospel. Many have not experienced the gospel lived out in heart, word, and deed. Many of those are in seemingly closed regions (Gowans said, no place is closed to the gospel); some are hidden in cities where the church seems to be thriving, while others are in rural and/or less accessible areas. The motivation of SIM's founders was their love for Christ and their love for the lost. This ought to be our motivation as well.

The starting assumption in SIM is the gospel of Christ that is proclaimed and lived out in teams around the world. In order for us to continue to be effective in living out that gospel in a changing world, we have to refocus on our reason for being. To answer the question of why SIM still exists, we took our bearings from our existing mission statement:

> The mission of SIM is to plant, strengthen, and partner with churches around
> the world, as we evangelize the unreached, minister to human need, disciple
> believers into churches and equip churches to fulfill Christ's Commission.

In refocusing therefore, SIM is simply reemphasizing what has always been in its DNA. For an interagency leadership consultation in the Netherlands in 2014, Keith Walker, SIM's international director for strategic development, had this to say when summarizing the current focus of SIM as he traced its 10 years' missiological journey:[4]

> Dr. Joshua Bogunjoko, one of the Deputies whom Malcolm McGregor
> appointed early in his drive for diversity, was appointed as his successor in
> 2013. He made an early commitment [Strategic Consultation, Kuala Lumpur,
> Malaysia, 16–21 February 2014] to refocus SIM toward contexts where people
> live and die without hearing of Jesus. This language though simple is quite
> deliberate. It is intended both to offer clarity and to avoid words which carry
> unfortunate missiological baggage. It reflects a move from thinking simply in
> geographical terms to an understanding that the social spaces which people
> inhabit may be defined in terms of culture and subculture, demographics,
> social groups, ethnicities, and so on. Each of these realities may offer either
> avenues for or barriers to the Gospel.

Photo Epilogue 2. *Drs. Joshua and Joanna Bogunjoko*

In bringing this emphasis on the lost, Joshua has drawn on his personal heritage and on Scripture. He is a Nigerian converted through SIM-planted ministry and a member of the denomination which flowed out of the pioneering work of Bingham, Kent, and Gowans (Kent and Gowans being SIM's first short-term missionaries—albeit unintentionally short-term!). Joshua's and Joanna's home context is one where in 1893 people lived and died without hearing of Jesus. They have a sense of indebtedness which echoes that of the Apostle Paul (Romans 1:8–15).

The argument of Romans in this respect runs through to 15:20 where Paul declares his "ambition to preach the gospel where Christ is not known" [NIV]. Despite the desire expressed in Romans 1, Paul had been prevented from visiting Rome because of his singleminded commitment to this cause. This fits the trajectory of Acts as expounded by Howie Brant at the Malaysia Consultation, and discussed by others in preparatory papers. The notion of living in Acts 29—in continuity with Luke's story of Apostolic mission which breaks through barriers of all kinds—geographical, social, and religious—resonates with our mission force as we encourage our teams to stretch toward those living in contexts where Christ is not known.

Malcolm McGregor's leadership moving into Seize the Day made it clear that diversity and discipleship were our set direction. Those coming to Malaysia were equally clear that contexts where people live and die without hearing of Jesus are to be our focus. The question for Malaysia was what this would mean in terms of priorities in ministry and in terms of deployment and redeployment of resources.

It would certainly not mean any withdrawal from the diversity and discipleship agenda. Indeed, the consultation acknowledged the need for us to repent of past practices which excluded the less powerful voices. Diversity needs to be pressed though, for the needs of the unreached will demand the formation of multicultural, multiethnic and multiskilled teams. Likewise, discipleship which integrates faith and life was seen to be critical to the kind of gospel progress for which we pray. Whole life discipleship and mission are inseparable if we are to reach those who live without the knowledge of Christ.

Thus the current phase of SIM's journey is one in which we are equipping ourselves to refocus on the lost. Outreach will touch on the "everydayness" of life—poverty, injustice, sin—and will proclaim Christ and his love for all. It is one in which prayer and the cultivation of spiritual vitality is critical. If we are to reach the hard places, the cultivation of resilience, not least spiritual resilience, is a critical factor.

Indeed in response to the critical questions of *why*, *what*, and *where*, we have arrived at conclusions for our future that the above statement described. But first, we asked the following questions:

Why?

Why has God strategically placed SIM where we are—organizationally, geographically, theologically, etc.? Why has God opened the door of mission and ministry in diverse cross-cultural settings to SIM? Why has God preserved SIM over 120 years of ministry? Why has God kept SIM together, still growing us and still providing for us? What is the primary expected outcome of the sum of SIM's ministries around the world?

What?

What is at the heart of SIM's calling? What is God's priority for us at this time in history? What is the heartbeat of God with which our hearts have to beat in rhythm?

Where?

Where is God leading us locally, regionally, and internationally? Where is God directing our ministries?

In answering these questions we came up with a renewed focus and direction for SIM as follows:

WE ANSWERED OUR BIG *WHY*:
We exist to worship Christ in heart, word and deed.

Thus, SIM will strive to make Christ known and make His disciples where He is not known, irrespective of barriers and compelled by His great love; we would serve His churches in fulfilling His mission across cultures and we would enable those whom He is calling to participate in His harvest irrespective of where they come from or where they go.[5]

As a result of this focus on the worship of Christ in heart, word, and deed, we would invest in seeking to bring others into that worship through the proclamation of the gospel and living out the gospel as we serve as loving neighbors in all kinds of ministries that address various needs around us. We expressed this as follows:

> We will place a pioneering focus on those who live and die without hearing or understanding the gospel, through collaborative and effective outreach, disciple-making, compassion and equipping ministries, by wholesomely resilient personnel who are motivated by the love of Christ and served by courageous leaders.

WE RENWED OUR PURPOSE, MISSION, AND VISION:
In doing this we expressed our conviction of what God has called us to do based on our big *why*:

> **Purpose and Mission:** Convinced that no one should live and die without hearing God's good news, we believe that He has called us to make disciples of the Lord Jesus Christ in communities where He is least known. Therefore, compelled by God's great love and empowered by the Holy Spirit … *we* cross barriers to proclaim the crucified and risen Christ, expressing His love and compassion among those who live and die without Him. We make disciples who will trust and obey Jesus, and become part of Christ-centred churches. We work together with churches to fulfil God's mission across cultures locally and globally. We facilitate the participation in cross-cultural ministry of those whom God is calling.

> **Vision:** The vision of SIM is to see a witness to Christ's love where He is least known, disciples of Jesus expressing God's love in their communities, and Christ-centered churches among all peoples.

> *By faith we see in the world:* A vibrant testimony to the gospel through character, word and action among communities where currently Jesus is least known. Followers of Jesus living out the gospel in unity and in the power of the Holy Spirit, making disciples who trust Him, obey Him, and play a full part in church life. Churches serving their communities and reaching out with the gospel locally and globally.

> *By faith we see in SIM:* A community growing in faith, in obedience to Jesus, and in ministry competence. Workers crossing barriers with the gospel, being and making disciples of Jesus, expressing His love and compassion. Multiethnic

and multiskilled teams serving together in love and harmony. Courageous leaders investing in the development of others for life transforming ministries. Effective partnerships with Christ-centered churches and organisations facilitating the spread of the gospel.

By faith we see in eternity: The redeemed from all tribes, languages, peoples, and nations worshiping the living God.

FOCUSED OUTCOMES

The initiative arising from this process is about outreach development—that is, in contexts where Christ is not known we will take ministries to those who are living and dying without the gospel. We will investigate new opportunities (including opportunities for collaboration and partnership) where SIM does not currently work and where Christ is not known in order to initiate engagement. We will encourage and enable SIM country/context leaders to identify and lead engagement with specific unreached peoples or groups in their contexts or to identify strategies for reengaging with already identified groups. We will assist and guide SIM teams in evaluating new outreach and disciple-making opportunities and the impact of each existing SIM ministry.

An implementation task force for this Malaysia Initiative has been formed to carry forward priorities in areas of outreach development, ministry training, focused mobilization, resource development, and investment in the spiritual vitality of SIM workers around the world. This task force will be advancing mission-changing initiatives which will have impact on the whole of SIM. It will have an especial (but not exclusive) focus on contexts where Christ is not known. Each area will be led by a facilitator.

Keith Walker has helpfully identified a number of foreseeable challenges relating to this Initiative which those in governance and executive leadership need to embrace:[6]

- Our intention to focus on contexts where Christ is not known will mean that more of our people will work in contexts of increased risk. Some may expect to experience greater hostility to Christ and his people, whether open or passive. The spiritual battle will become more intense.
- In the contexts which we desire to engage more fully, it is likely that our teams will benefit by having more missionaries from newer sending contexts. We need to pray and work to break down the barriers which continue to slow down effective mobilization and resourcing of workers from these contexts.
- Our new focus will likely mean that we need to look freshly at how we engage with other agencies. It is predictable that some smaller agencies working in contexts that we desire to enter may look to us as larger resourceful partners or even to merge. We need to be wise how we handle

these possibilities. They may on the one hand open up new and highly valuable avenues for ministry, on the other, issues of merger and the like could become organizational distractions.

- The (gradual) redirection of resources from well-served areas to those in greatest need will demand leadership solidarity and skill in explaining to missionaries and partners why we are refocusing, in order to enable them not only to embrace change but actively join us in reaching the lost.
- Our historic systems and structures, which tend to favor ministry where we are strong rather than where we are weak, will need to be reworked so that they present as priorities those contexts and ministries which fit our new focus. This will demand a significant cultural change within the mission in which voices from the fringe and those who speak on behalf of the lost are listened to with increased attention.

SIM stands at a very exciting juncture in its history. The challenges of our strategic developments may be significant, and may turn out to be ones we had not anticipated at all. Yet the strategic goals are biblically formed and, we believe, God-honoring.

In addition to the work of the Malaysia Initiative, international leaders within SIM have been assigned responsibility for five specific priority areas that the mission needs in order to fulfil its reason for being. These Five Priority Focuses for leadership are as follows:

Flourishing Personnel are those who have been called by God, commissioned by churches, and sent by the Holy Spirit through SIM to fulfill His Great Commission and His Great Commandment among the nations. They are sent to be His witnesses among those who still live and die without ever hearing or understanding the gospel of Christ. It is a must if SIM is to fulfill the vision that God has given to her that we care well for those whom God is calling to serve in His harvest.

Flourishing Leaders are those whom the Lord has chosen and gifted to shepherd, serve, and steward the individuals and teams that God is drawing together to declare His glory among the nations. Without effective leadership, teams flounder, people are hurt, and ministry effectiveness diminishes. People suffer in a vacuum of coordination, synergy, and support.

Outreach and Disciple Making is the core of what we do. The vision that gave birth to SIM is that of proclaiming Christ where darkness still reigns. We continue to carry that banner high. We open our eyes, looking up to see the harvest wherever it may be, and to work in collaboration and partnership to bring the good news of Christ's death and resurrection to those people. Only with flourishing and well-led personnel and teams will this be possible, for none can do it alone.

Compassion and Equipping is the life of a disciple. Every disciple of Christ is commanded to love their neighbor and to disciple others. Our witness to the world is made real as we show the love of Christ in small and great things. Our ministry of sharing the gospel will be incomplete without our love in action through acts of kindness and our love in equipping for godliness and service those who come to faith. In a world where theological compromise is threatening the very existence of the church, we cannot underestimate the importance of equipping in theological rootedness. We are commanded to love the Lord our God with all our heart, soul, mind, and strength and to love our neighbors as ourselves. As those who have been called cross-culturally to proclaim Christ, we must live among others just as the Word became flesh and dwelt among us.

Partnering and Mobilization are key to the fulfillment of our purpose. The great commission was given to Christ's new community of the redeemed. Jesus demonstrated the importance of teams, collaboration, and partnership as He sent out groups of two for every purpose that He delegated to individuals. The Great Commission is the center of the church's ministry and the Great Commandment is the true expression of the life of that community. Responsibility for sharing the gospel is both personal and cooperate. While individuals were called for Christ's purpose in Acts 13, it was the whole church that was called to obedience in commissioning and sending those people forth to what God had already assigned for them, the proclamation of the gospel. In other words, the mobilization of the global church for God's global mission is an urgent task if those who still live and die without ever hearing the good news of redemption in Christ would ever have a chance. The church is the center of God's mission.

This, in brief, is how all of these responsibility areas that we will be examining tie together. These five areas of responsibility are different sides of a five-sided prism which, when struck with a beam of white light, divide into a spectrum of distinct colors. Each of these five is a component functioning together to enable SIM to live up to its *why*; its *raison d'être*.

Losing our sense of why we exist would mean that each SIM entity and office defines that for itself and, in these days of hyperindividualism, each individual would also do the same. The result invariably would be a seascape of ships busily turning about—uncoordinated, unrelated, and disjointed, at times even demonstrating a subtle sense of working at cross purposes between countries and ministries or between sending and receiving functions.

In the past, SIM did not experience disorientation while reaching an unreached ethnic group, operating medical centers, schools, radio, or even launching a missionary sending agency because every activity took its positioning coordinates from the same purpose. SIM is returning to that again. Indeed, we must. Like a fleet of ships fanned out across the globe with prows pointing in the same direction, we would remain a truly general mission, celebrating a variety of ministries in a variety of contexts by a variety of teams but united around a common purpose.

Finally, in the words of Walter Gowans, one of our founders:

> It is said that God closed the door to the Soudan. Beloved! God closes no door to the Gospel. It is not God, it is the enemy who closes the door. With God no door is closed. We have simply to march forward in the name of Jesus, and in the faith of God, and the doors must and will fly open every time. Hallelujah![7]

And in the words of the psalmist:

> God be gracious to us and bless us, and cause His face to shine upon us— Selah. That Your way may be known on the earth, Your salvation among all nations. Let the peoples praise You, O God; let all the peoples praise You. Let the nations be glad and sing for joy; for You will judge the peoples with uprightness and guide the nations on the earth. Selah. Let the peoples praise You, O God; let all the peoples praise You. The earth has yielded its produce; God, our God, blesses us. God blesses us, that all the ends of the earth may fear Him. (Psalm 67:1–7 NASB)

APPENDIX A

SIM STATEMENT OF FAITH[1]

Those who serve with SIM are committed to the essential truths of biblical Christianity. These include the following:

God

There is one God who exists eternally in three persons: Father, Son, and Holy Spirit. God is the almighty Creator, Saviour, and Judge who governs all things according to His sovereign will and is accomplishing His purposes in creation and in the Church to His glory.

The Father

God the Father is the source of all that is good. He initiates creation and redemption which He accomplishes through His Son and the Holy Spirit.

God's Written Word

The Bible, consisting of the Old and New Testaments, is God's written Word, revealing for all peoples His character and purposes. It is the final authority in all matters relating to belief and behaviour. The Holy Spirit moved the human authors of the Bible so that what they wrote is inspired, fully reliable, and without error in all it affirms.

The Human Race

Humanity is the climax of God's earthly creation, bearing His image, designed for relationship with Him, and being the object of His redeeming love. All people have sinned. This results in guilt, death, and alienation from God as well as the defacing of every aspect of human nature. People are unable to save themselves from sin's penalty and power and from Satan's dominion.

Jesus Christ

Jesus Christ, both fully God and fully man, entered history as Saviour of the world. He was conceived of the Holy Spirit, born of a virgin, and lived an exemplary, sinless life in perfect submission to the Father and in loving relationships with others. He died on a cross, rose bodily, and ascended to heaven where He is an advocate for His people and is exalted as Lord of all.

Salvation

Christ's sacrificial death, in which He bore the punishment due to sinners, is the only and all-sufficient basis of God's provision of salvation for all people of every culture and age, expressing His love and satisfying His justice. By God's grace the repentant sinner, through trusting alone in the Lord Jesus Christ as Saviour, is put right with God, adopted by the Father into His family and receives eternal life.

The Holy Spirit

The Holy Spirit makes the work of Christ effective to sinners, giving spiritual life and placing them into the Church. He indwells all believers, empowers them to love, serve, witness, and obey God, equips them with gifts, and transforms them to be increasingly like Christ.

The Church

The universal Church is made up of all who have been born of the Spirit. It finds local expression in communities of believers called by God to worship, fellowship, proclaim the Gospel, and make disciples among all peoples, reflect God's character, engage in works of compassion, contend for truth and justice, and celebrate baptism and communion.

The Spirit World

The holy angels are personal spirit beings who glorify God, serve Him, and minister to His people. Satan is a spiritual being who was created by God but fell through sin. He, along with other evil spirits, is the enemy of God and humanity, has been defeated by the work of Christ, is subject to God's authority, and faces eternal condemnation.

The Future

The Lord Jesus Christ will visibly return to the earth in glory and accomplish the final triumph over evil. God will make everything new. The dead will be raised and judged. Unbelievers will suffer eternal punishment in separation from God; believers will enter into a life of eternal joy in fellowship with God, glorifying Him forever.

APPENDIX B

PURPOSE AND MISSION, CORE VALUES, AND VISION OF SIM

Purpose and Mission Statement[1]

Convinced that no one should live and die without hearing God's good news, we believe that He has called us to make disciples of the Lord Jesus Christ in communities where He is least known.

Therefore, compelled by God's great love and empowered by the Holy Spirit . . .

- We cross barriers to proclaim the crucified and risen Christ, expressing His love and compassion among those who live and die without Him.
- We make disciples who will trust and obey Jesus, and become part of Christ-centered churches.
- We work together with churches to fulfil God's mission across cultures locally and globally.
- We facilitate the participation in cross-cultural ministry of those whom God is calling.

Core Values[2]
SIM Is a "Gospel Community" That Is:
- **Committed to Biblical Truth**
  We are committed to biblical truth and joyfully affirm historic, evangelical Christianity. With courage, we declare to the nations the good news of new life in Jesus Christ.

- **Dependent on God**
  "By Prayer" and in faith we depend on God for the provision of all our needs. We will demonstrate diligence, integrity, sharing, and accountability in cultivating and using the resources God provides.

- **A People of Prayer**
  Prayer is foundational in our life and ministry. "By Prayer" we praise God, seek his direction, request resources, and call upon the Holy Spirit to empower our ministries.

- **Mission-Focused**
  We are committed to the urgent and unfinished task of making disciples of Jesus Christ in all nations. In doing this we desire to work in loving, trusting, interdependent relationships with churches and other partners who share our vision.

- **Church-Centered**
  We are committed to being a mission that begins, nurtures, and equips churches to be the expression of Christ in their communities and to reach out with cross-cultural missionary vision and action.

- **Concerned about Human Needs**
  We humbly acknowledge that the ultimate human need is to know God. We also believe that He has called us to compassionate, holistic service in this broken world by alleviating suffering, fostering development, and effecting change in society.

- **A Christlike Community**
  We desire to be a transforming community dedicated to becoming like Christ in love, servanthood, holiness, and obedience to the Father. We believe that following Christ's example means sacrifice, sometimes hardship, and perhaps even death.

- **A Learning, Growing Community**
  We believe in the worth and giftedness of each person in SIM and of those we seek to serve. We practise the giving and receiving of discipleship, lifelong learning, consultative leadership, mutual development, and training as enduring disciplines.

- **Strengthened Through Diversity**
  We are intentionally interdenominational, international, and multiethnic. We believe this expresses the unity of the body of Christ in the world. We believe we will be more effective in ministry as we incorporate the richness of cultural diversity in SIM and celebrate our oneness in Christ.

- **Responsive to Our Times**
  We will respond with creativity and courage to evolving needs and opportunities under the guidance of the Holy Spirit. To be effective and relevant, our ministries, priorities, and structures are subject to ongoing evaluation and adaptation.

Vision Statement[3]

The vision of SIM is to see a witness to Christ's love where He is least known, disciples of Jesus expressing God's love in their communities, and Christ-centered churches among all peoples.

By faith we see in the world:

A vibrant testimony to the gospel through character, word, and action among communities where currently Jesus is least known. Followers of Jesus living out the gospel in unity and in the power of the Holy Spirit, making disciples who trust Him, obey Him, and play a full part in church life. Churches serving their communities and reaching out with the gospel locally and globally.

By faith we see in SIM:

A community growing in faith, in obedience to Jesus, and in ministry competence. Workers crossing barriers with the gospel, being and making disciples of Jesus, expressing His love and compassion. Multi-ethnic and multi-skilled teams serving together in love and harmony. Courageous leaders investing in the development of others for life-transforming ministries. Effective partnerships with Christ-centered churches and organisations facilitating the spread of the gospel.

By faith we see in eternity:

The redeemed from all tribes, languages, peoples, and nations worshiping the Living God.

APPENDIX C

DIRECTORS OF MISSIONS

issions are presented in the order that they merged with SIM. Considerable work needs to be done to identify the leaders of the Ceylon and Indian General Mission, the Poona and Indian Village Mission, the Lebanon Evangelical Mission, the Middle East General Mission, and the Arabic Literature Mission past their founders, and the dates they served. In addition, more research needs to be conducted to determine the precise dates of when many of the directors of the South Africa General Mission and Africa Evangelical Fellowship served.

SIM

Soudan Interior Mission (1893–1895)
1.   Walter Gowans: 1893–1894, "leader"
2.   Rowland Bingham: (1894–1942)—1894–1895, defacto leader after Gowans died; 1898–1918, treasurer and other titles; 1918–8 December 1942, General Director

Africa Industrial Mission (1898–1905)

Africa Evangelistic Mission (1905–1906)

Sudan United Mission (1906–1907)

Sudan Interior Mission (1907–1980)
3.   Charles Gordon Beacham Sr.: 8 December 1942-1 May 1944, Acting/Deputy General Director
4.   Guy William Playfair: 1 May 1944–14 October 1957, General Director
5.   Albert D. Helser: 14 October 1957–6 November 1962, General Director
6.   Raymond J. Davis: 6 November 1962–22 November 1975, General Director
7.   Ian M. Hay: 22 November 1975–19 December 1993, General Director

SIM INTERNATIONAL (Society for International Ministry *became the trade name)* (1980–1990)

SIM (Society for International Ministries *became the trade name)* (1990–2000)
8.   Jim Plueddemann: 19 December 1993–20 December 2003, General Director (International Director, 2000)

SIM (Serving in Mission *became the trade name)* (2000–Present)
9.   Malcolm McGregor: 20 December 2003–1 June 2013, International Director
10.   Joshua Bogunjoko: 1 June 2013–Present, International Director

Andes Evangelical Mission (formerly the Bolivian Indian Mission)
Bolivian Indian Mission (1907–1966)
1. George Allan, 1907–1941, Director
2. Verne D. Roberts, 1941–1956, Director
3. Joseph McCullough, 1956–1974, Director (continuation of leadership after name change)

Andes Evangelical Mission (1966–1982)
4. Ron Wiebe: 1974–1982, Director

International Christian Fellowship (including the merged missions of the Ceylon and Indian General Mission and the Poona and Indian Village Mission)
Ceylon and Indian General Mission
1. Benjamin Davidson: 15 December 1892–3 October 1921, Director

Poona and Indian Village Mission
2. E. McGavin, February 1893–c. 1895, Co-Director with Charles Reeve
3. Charles Reeve, 1895–1921, Director

International Christian Fellowship (1968-1989):
CIGM and PIVM merged to form ICF in 1968
4. Keith Jones: 1968–1974, Director
5. George Hemming: 1974–1982, Director
6. Merle Inniger: 1982–1989, Director

Africa Evangelical Fellowship (formerly known as the South Africa General Mission, including the merged missions of Cape General Mission and the South East Africa Evangelistic Mission)[1]
Cape General Mission (1889–1894)
1. Andrew Murray: 1889–1894, President
2. Spencer Walton: 1889–July 1890, Director
3. Dudley Kidd & Frank Huskisson: July 1890–April 1891, Co-Directors
4. Spencer Walton: April 1891–1894, Director

South East Africa Evangelistic Mission (1891–1894)
1. Martha Osborn-Howe and George Howe: Co-Directors

South Africa General Mission (1894–1965):
formed by merger of CGM and SEAEM
1. Andrew Murray: 1894–1917, President
2. Spencer Walton: 1894–1903, Director
3. Frank Huskisson: 1903–1906, General Superintendent
4. James Middlemiss: 1907–1920?, General Superintendent
5. J. G. Gibson: 1920?–1922?, General Superintendent
6. George Frederick Gale: 1922?–1933?, General Superintendent
7. Herbert Pirouet: 1933?–1938, General Superintendent
8. Percy Victor Watson: 1938–1942, General Superintendent
9. Wilfred P. Green: 1943–1965, General Superintendent; title changed to Field Director (c. 1950–1953), and then General Director (1958).

Africa Evangelical Fellowship (1965–1998)
Wilfred P. Green: 1965–1968, General Director (continuation of leadership after name change)
10. H. Gordon Legg: 1969–1974, General Director
11. Arthur Deane: 1974–1981, International Secretary, title changed to International Director (1977)
12. Robert Foster: 1981–1988, International Director
13. Ron Genheimer: 1988–1994, International Director
14. Tim Kopp: 1995–1998, International Director

Middle East Christian Outreach (1976–2016)[2]
*Note: Some names reflect different leadership positions.
1. David Bentley Taylor, 1976–1977
2. Douglas Anderson, 1977–1991
3. Paul Shepherd, 1977–1980
4. Pat Thurman, 1991–1994
5. Graham Rowe, 1987–1994
6. David Judson, 1992–2006
7. Violet McCombe, 1992–2001
8. Stuart Plowman, 2006–2012
9. John Carrick, 2012–2013
10. Mike Parker, 2013–2016

APPENDIX D

DATES WHEN SIM ENTERED VARIOUS REGIONS AND COUNTRIES[1]

Angola, 1914 (SAGM)

Australia, 1927 (SIM council); 1986, (MECO)

Bangladesh, 1958 (CIGM)

Benin, 1946 (SIM)

Bolivia, 1909 (BIM)

Botswana, 1973 (AEF)

Burkina Faso, 1930 (SIM)

Canada, 1893, 1898 (SIM officially founded here)

Chile, 1988 (SIM)

China, 1997 (SIM)

Côte d'Ivoire (Ivory Coast), 1968 (SIM)

C-SEA (Central and Southeast Asia), 2004 (SIM)

Cyprus, 1976 (MECO)

East Africa Office, 2012 (SIM)

East Asia, 1982, SIM council established

Ecuador, 1989 (SIM)

Egypt, 1898 (MEGM); 1905 (ALM)

Eritrea, 1952–1975, 1991–2006 (SIM); 1957-1977 (MEGM/MECO)

Ethiopia, 1927 (SIM)

France, 1978, SIM council established

Ghana, 1952 (SIM)

Guatemala, 2006 (SIM)

Guinea, 1986 (SIM)

India, 1893 (PIVM), 1894 (CIGM)

Indonesia, 1995, SIM council, fieldwork in 2011

Iran, 1969–1979 (ICF)

Iraq, 1992 (MECO)

Japan, 2001 (SIM council)

Jordan, 1976 (MECO)

Kenya, 1977 (SIM)

Korea, 1997, (SIM council) established

Lebanon, 1943 (LEM), 1965–1975 (SIM)

Liberia, 1952 (SIM)

Madagascar, 1987 (AEF)

Malawi, 1900 (SAGM)

Mali, 2010 (SIM)

Mauritius, 1969 (SAGM)

Mongolia, 1996 (SIM)

Mozambique, 1936 (SAGM)

Namibia, 1970 (AEF)

Nepal, 1969 (ICF)

New Zealand, 1927 (SIM council) established

Niger, 1923 (SIM)

Nigeria, 1893 (SIM)

OCLA (Oficina de Conexión de Latina America), 2006

Pakistan, 1954 (CIGM)

Paraguay, 1987 (SIM)

Peru, 1965 (AEM)

Philippines, 1984 (ICF)

Reunion, 1970 (AEF)

ROSA Office (Region of South Africa), 2006

Senegal, 1984 (ICF)

Somalia, 1954–1974 (SIM)

South Africa, 1889 (SAGM); 1952 (SIM council)

South Sudan (new country), 2011 (SIM)

Sri Lanka (Ceylon), 1893–1936 (CIGM), 2011 (SIM)

Sudan, 1938, 2003 (SIM); 1977 (MECO)

Swaziland, 1890 (SAGM)

Switzerland, 1962 (SIM council)

Syria, 1860-1958 (LEM); 1990 (MECO)

Tanzania, 1990 (AEF)

Thailand, 2005 (SIM)

Togo, 1997 (SIM)

Turkey, 1985 (MECO)

United Arab Emirates, 1976-1994 (MECO)

United Kingdom, 1922 (SIM council)

United States, 1926 (SIM council)

Uruguay, 1995 (SIM)

West African Office (Abidjan), 2009

West Malaysia Office, 2011

Yemen (Aden), 1945-1966 (SIM)

Zambia, 1910 (SAGM)

Zimbabwe, 1897 (SAGM)

APPENDIX E

HOW WE BECAME INTERDENOMINATIONAL[1]

A presentation by Dr. Rowland V. Bingham on how and why SIM was founded as an interdenominational missionary society, working with all God's people, regardless of church affiliation.

In God's providence the three men who were brought together for the pioneer effort in the Sudan were from three denominations—the first, Presbyterian, the second, Congregationalist, while I, the third, had a little while earlier resigned from the Salvation Army and held, in general, the doctrinal position of the Plymouth Brethren. After the death of my two companions, I returned home, and after applying for some months in a Baptist church, was called to its pastorate and ordained to its ministry. When I started out to arouse interest in a new work in the Sudan, I thought at first to interest those of my own church affiliation.

On one memorable occasion while seeking entrance into churches with which I was associated, I reached the last dollar I possessed. I visited at that time a public institution under the direction of a Christian superintendent who later took me into her office to give me a cup of tea. As we sat at the table, she told me how, years before, she had her heart stirred for missions and had offered her services to the Presbyterian Board for China, but was turned down on account of her age.

> "Since then," she said, "I have been living for missions. All my earnings beyond my bare needs have been put into the missionary treasury. Some time ago a friend left me a little legacy of one hundred dollars and I put it in the bank as a reserve. While you spoke today I felt I should give you that to get this work started. I want you to take it to help until the work gets on its feet."

I refused to consider taking her last dollar, but she insisted firmly that God had laid it on her heart, and finally she prevailed and I walked out with a check for her last hundred dollars. I returned to my room and spent a sleepless night. I felt that God was speaking to me. I could not get over the fact that here was a Presbyterian lady giving me everything she possessed to enable me to start a Baptist work, and though I might take her last dollar, if she herself applied she could not be accepted if it were to be a denominational mission.

Here was a Presbyterian, who did not see eye to eye with Baptists in the matter of an ordinance, but was ready to give up for her Lord everything she possessed. All night long my mind wrestled with this problem, until, as morning dawned, I had been brought definitely from my denominational position to an interdenominational ground of fellowship. I had faced in that mental conflict the question of what my church would think, and then of what my denomination might do, but the conviction that minor differences of denominations afforded no basis for separation in our work grew so strong that I settled it definitely that I would operate upon a wider foundation.

It may be well to state my reasons for advocating cooperation and fellowship in as many lines as possible:

1.   Because God's children are scattered throughout the whole of the evangelical denominations.
2.   Because the Great High Priest is ministering to all the children of God. The Holy Spirit, in like manner, refuses to be confined to any one body of believers, but works continuously and graciously in all, and through all to the full extent of their permission and faith.
3.   Because God has ever granted His greatest blessing where believers have gathered for united service, recognizing their common unity in Christ and taking their place as servants under one common Lord.
4.   Because the practicability of union effort in Christian service has been demonstrated in such undertakings as the Bible societies, the tract societies, Bible colleges, union evangelistic campaigns, the Bible Conference and the missionary societies.
5.   Because denominationalism is a serious hindrance on the foreign field. Missionaries of nearly all societies admit that the perpetuation of denominational differences in foreign lands is a stumbling-block and an occasion of advantage to the great adversary, while the practicability of the interdenominational method has been abundantly proven.

As a Mission, we have been insistent that every candidate shall be, without question, loyal to the fundamentals of the faith and the great basic doctrines of the Scriptures. God has given us from almost every evangelical denomination men and women who have come together for one common task—the giving of the gospel to every soul in the Sudan.

When I decided that our platform ought to be one which would include in full fellowship the one who was giving us her all, the question of baptism loomed large in my mental struggle, but scripture came to my mind, written when the Apostle Paul was evidently having trouble in the church over the same matter. With me it was the mode of baptism, but with his converts it was a controversy over the baptizer. Paul raises the question, "Is Christ divided?" Then he says, "I thank God that I baptized none of you, except"—listing then a half-dozen by name, and he affirms, "Christ sent me not to baptize but to preach the gospel." What did Paul mean? I think he meant that if baptism was to become a matter of controversy and strife in the church, it would be better to discard it rather than fight over it.

I preferred not to influence any of our pioneers in the early days. They were accepted without regard to their denomination. But a strange thing happened. The one denomination that was seeking to enter the central Sudan with us was the Church of England. Their custom at home is well known. But on the Sudan field they came to baptize their first band of coverts before we did, and to the astonishment of everyone, they decided to revert to the very early practice of their church—baptism by immersion.

Our senior missionary on the field was Presbyterian, but when it came to the baptism of our first converts he decided to follow the example set by our Anglican friends and immerse that first band of Christians. This became the general practice upon the field, so that we had no baptismal controversy and only one practice in that central Sudan.

Our missionaries have had minor doctrinal differences, but facing millions of people in the darkness of their heathenism there has been a unity in presenting Christ as the Saviour of sinners and "able to save to the uttermost all that come unto God by Him."

APPENDIX F

WHAT'S IN A NAME?[1]

"What's in a name? That which we call a rose. By any other name would smell as sweet."
(Shakespeare, *Romeo & Juliet*, ii, 43)

The history of SIM is replete with name changes and mergers. While the mergers are fairly straightforward, the name changes are not. It is even a little tricky to be sure what one should count. Even the smallest groups that have merged into the mission have a history of their own in this regard.

There have been more than a dozen name changes in the history of the major branches of the mission. Many of these have been the direct result of mergers. Others were the result of updating terminology. But a few of them came about for other, more philosophical reasons. This latter group, which is concentrated in the mission's Africa endeavors between the years 1893 and 1907, is the focus of our attention here.

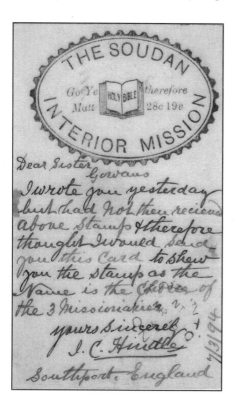

Photo F.1. *SIM's first logo, 1894*

When Gowans, Bingham, and Kent first went to Africa in 1893, the banner under which they went was the Soudan Interior Mission. (Soudan, of course, was the name given at the time to that whole middle belt of Africa just below the Sahara, which runs from Senegal in the west to the Horn of Africa in the east.) The name first appears in the letter Bingham wrote to John Hindle in January 1894 when the three were in Lagos. In that letter, he told Hindle that they had selected SIM for their name. Hindle, in turn, used the name/logo when he wrote Gowans' mother in May 1894.

While the name Soudan Interior Mission was clearly the first name the mission ever had, it had several replacements between 1893 and 1907. In 1907 the original name was reestablished, with the slight difference that the more current spelling "Sudan" replaced the earlier French spelling "Soudan." And thus it remained until 1980 when SIM International went on the letterhead. This was good preparation for the merger with the Andes Evangelical Mission in 1982, which took the mission for the first time into significant ministry outside Africa. This served well not only to accommodate the AEM merger, but also the entrance of SIM into Asia, southern Africa, and the Middle East that accompanied the mergers with International Christian Fellowship, Africa Evangelical Fellowship, and Middle East Christian Outreach in 1989, 1998, and 2016 respectively.

This latter name, of course, was further honed to the simple designation SIM, with "Society for International Ministries" (1990), and later "Serving in Mission" (2000), becoming the defining explanation for the acronym. But this part of the history is pretty well known. The part that is not so well known—and which we believe reveals much about our core beliefs as a mission—is the series of name changes that took place in the Africa sphere between 1893 and 1907.

After the death of Gowans and Kent in 1894 and Bingham's subsequent return to Canada in 1895, the mission entered into a brief cocoon stage in which the ground was laid for a significant new beginning. During the period between 1895 and 1898 several important events left their stamp on Rowland Bingham. First, Bingham undertook formal Bible and missions training at A. B. Simpson's Missionary Training Institute in New York City. Founded in 1884, this was the first of the scores of schools that would ultimately constitute the great Bible college movement in North America. It had also been the school that Gowans and Kent attended.

Second, Bingham gained increased ministry experience by serving for a time as pastor of Peoples Baptist Church in Newburgh, New York. Finally, he met Helen Blair and married her in 1898. She would become his lifelong and effective collaborator in the work of Sudan Interior Mission, *The Evangelical Christian* magazine, and the many other ministries that Bingham was instrumental in founding.

Photo F.2. *African Evangelistic Mission leaflet, cover, 1905*

All of these events helped to prepare Bingham for the next phase of the mission's history, a formal reorganization under the name Africa Industrial Mission on June 3, 1898. How did this come about? Between 1893 and 1904 there were a large number of favorable references in *The Faithful Witness* (the earlier name of the *Evangelical Christian*, which Bingham edited from 1904 until his death in 1942) to the work of the British-based Zambesi Industrial Mission and to the work of industrial missions more generally. Industrial missions were obviously a cutting-edge missions concept at that time, and Bingham was fully prepared to explore it and utilize it in the pursuit of larger evangelistic goals.

The 15 August 1899 issue of *The Faithful Witness* includes an article by Bingham that outlines the reasons why the society was formed and the details of the strategy. [2] Space does not permit a thorough review of those details, but several points are worth noting. Particularly instructive are the three overarching reasons given for the society's formation:

1. The sense of the intense need and destitution of the 150 million heathen in Africa, and the knowledge that present means are totally inadequate to give them the Gospel. *[The priority of evangelism.]*
2. The belief that something more should be done to send out to this needy field the scores of men anxious to go who can find no opening through existing agencies. *[The priority of the task.]*
3. The conviction that more could be done to utilize the wealth of the African soil for its own evangelization by the employment of practical laymen to direct the natives in various remunerative ministries that, through this, the work might early become self-supporting. *[The priority of indigenous mission principles.]*

Bingham went on to distinguish between "Our work—A mission to the heathen," and "Our means of support—industries; the initiatory expense to be provided by voluntary subscriptions." The emphasis was clearly on the "Mission," rather than the "Industrial" part of the name, as shall be seen when we introduce the next name. Before doing that, however, it would be good to mention several other principles and practices which characterized the mission at that time.

One thing was the continuing emphasis on interdenominationalism, a commitment which was reflected in the backgrounds of the three founders, but which here had become stated explicitly as principle.

A second matter, more a reflection of mindset than explicit principle, was the desire to work closely with others, and possession of the necessary humility to learn from them. This was reflected in their having sent two pioneer missionaries, Messrs. Andrew Moline and Herbert Lawrence, to British Central Africa (present-day Malawi) to learn from the successful industrial missions operating there.

A third feature should also be born in mind, however. Linking up with others was always undertaken in the context of a clear and unwavering commitment to channel their energies to least reached areas:

> We have been watching the hand of Providence and weighing the relative needs of the various fields in Africa and with a unity of mind have been directed to the vast Soudan, with its 60 to 90,000,000 of almost totally unevangelized souls. Especially have we been prayerfully led to consider and to direct our energies to aid in giving the Gospel to the Central Soudan, sometimes known as Hausaland.

Bingham went on to describe the more limited dimensions of Hausaland and the plight of those who lived there:

> These fifteen millions of people have at the present time only one missionary with the three or four more under appointment. Where could a more destitute field be found?[3]

As a fourth point, please note that he did not consider them destitute because of poverty or poor living conditions, but destitute because of their lack of access to the gospel. Bingham went on, in fact, to describe Hausaland as a "wonderland" with marvelous walled cities, the mining and smelting of iron ore, the manufacturing of hoes and cutlasses, and other excellent craft works. He spoke also of the Hausa as "this fascinating people," characterized by marvelous business and trading talents, by a widely traveled cosmopolitan worldview and, rare as it was, a great love of reading their own Arabic-script literature. At the same time, he also recognized the awful blight of the slave trade, "the open sore of the world" as Livingstone called it, which was rampant in so much of Hausaland.

The next name change, to Africa Evangelistic Mission, was for the clear purpose of removing any confusion that might exist about the mission's primary purpose. In the 5 October 1905 issue of *The Missionary Witness* (yet another name for *The Evangelical Christian* magazine) we read the following:

> The Africa Industrial Mission, which for some years has been carrying on missionary work in Northern Nigeria, has recently taken a new name. Owing to undue emphasis upon the industrial phase of the work in the minds of the people, many of whom have thought the object of the Mission was to civilize rather than to evangelize, it has been decided to drop the central word from the old name and in future the Society will be known as the Africa Evangelistic Mission.
>
> The primary object of the Mission has ever been to make known the Glad Tidings to the benighted heathen. Industrial, medical and educational operations have simply been an adjunct spiritual work.[4]

If there has been any uncertainty about the Mission's purpose before, there could be none now. And yet, the ongoing commitment to ministry in these "adjunct" areas of industry, medicine, and education make very clear that the mission's approach was holistic from the beginning. It was ever mindful of the primacy of eternal spiritual needs, but equally committed to living out the life-changing effects of the gospel in ministry to human need.

The final name changes we must treat resulted from the amalgamation of AEM into the recently formed Sudan United Mission (SUM) on 1 August 1906. The factors involved are described in the 25 September 1906 issue of *The Missionary Witness*. Owing to the recent British conquest of Northern Nigeria and the consequent open door to ministry there, the SUM had been formed in Britain to address the crying evangelistic needs of that region. Dr. Karl W. Kumm of that group subsequently traveled to North America to enlist the sympathies and involvement of churches there. It was this endeavor which produced the discussions which resulted in the merger and name change.

Here again was a reflection of commitment to the broadest possible interdenominational and international cooperation. Unfortunately, there are at times obstacles too large to overcome in such efforts, and this proved to the case with this union that lasted slightly less than one year. Apparently new organizational arrangements being pursued by the SUM elsewhere were seen as contrary to earlier terms of agreement established between the two groups, so both the Canadian Council (AEM-SUM) and Dr. Kumm of SUM desired release from the earlier agreement. This took place, together with the formal adoption of an earlier name, the Sudan Interior Mission, on 3 June 1907. Bingham explained the change in this way in a subsequent article in *The Missionary Witness*, dated 2 July 1907:

> We return to our former basis with a chastened spirit, humbled with the consciousness that possibly mixed motives may have led us out of the line of God's plan for us. However, we cast ourselves and our work afresh on Him Who first moved us out to attempt the evangelization of the interior of the Sudan when no agency was operating there. . . .
>
> We do not deem it for the best interest of the cause of Christ to make public at this time the matters that have led to this step, but we feel satisfied that were this done, the friends of the mission would approve of the course our Board has taken and continue to give us their confidence and prayers.
>
> In the future our society will be known as the Sudan Interior Mission, the name selected fourteen years ago by Mr. Walter Gowans, the first missionary to reach the far interior of the Sudan. It was from this pioneer effort that our mission sprang, and although Mr. Gowans laid down his life soon after reaching the interior of Nigeria, his devotion to the cause of evangelizing the Sudan has been a constant incentive to those who have succeeded him.[5]

Thus in the span of 14 years the name of the Sudan Interior Mission had come full circle. But along the way several name changes, and the purposes they represented, had articulated in eloquent fashion many of the first principles that have guided SIM to our own day. In conclusion the most important of these are: (1) the priority of evangelism; (2) the priority of the task; (3) the priority of indigenous mission principles; (4) the priority of interdenominational, international, and cooperative mission endeavor, but not at the expense of truth and principle; (5) the priority of the least reached; (6) the priority of appreciating cultures combined with the recognition that even the very best in a culture is really only destitution if the gospel is not there; and (7) the priority of holistic ministry which responds in compassion to human need, but is ever mindful and focused on the greatest of human needs, the need for reconciliation with God.

What's in a name? A great deal more than we usually think!

A TIME LINE DEPICTING CHANGES IN SIM ORGANIZATIONAL STRUCTURE FROM 1893–1993[1]

Dr. Ian M. Hay
International Director Emeritus

Introduction

It was Aristotle who said, "Man cannot live in chaos, he must live in cosmos." He concurred with what is learned from biblical teaching showing the Holy Spirit as the author of order. Both Old and New Testaments bear ample testimony to good organizational principles. It is even seen through the Trinity in the very nature of God.

One of the strengths of SIM throughout its history has been its careful attention to the orderliness of its structure. SIM is made up of people—individuals with a personal calling from God—serving him, in one field or another. Each one joined the mission: What then? Was the mission merely a travel agency or financial manager? No, each of us joins an organization because we realize that our pooled efforts will produce greater returns than would the uncoordinated efforts of separate individuals. The whole biblical principle of body life and the gifts of the Spirit teach this truth.

The late Francis Schaefer once said, "Christianity is an individual religion, but it is not individualistic." The Scriptures teach that there is no such thing as individualism. In the final analysis, then, there is no biblical basis for an independent missionary, although we have all seen plenty of them! In his book *The 17 Indisputable Laws of Teamwork* John Maxwell essentially makes the same point in his first law, the Law of Significance, where he states that "One is too Small a Number to Achieve Greatness."

Early in my leadership role in SIM, I was influenced by two concepts found in Louis Allen's *The Management Profession*. The first was the concept of limits of freedom. He stated that "freedom of action needs to be limited to the extent that the liberty of the individual to act does not encroach upon the rights of others" (p. 17).

This says, when I joined SIM, in doing so, I gained, but I also lost some freedom. Allen goes on to say:

Freedom can continue only in the presence of restrictions, freedom does not simply exist; it must be created. It does not continue as a natural condition; it must be cultivated, pruned and tended. The important requirement is not to want freedom; vital, rather is to know how to discipline ourselves to enjoy it and to educate ourselves and others to share it.

A second concept I learned was that where there is growth there is always change. Most organizations begin with the vision of one person, usually an entrepreneur, a person of great vision and determination. However, as soon as one other person joins him, it is no longer an individual, rather it has become a group. And, if there is not change *with growth*, the organization will die. Many an entrepreneur has lived and maintained control without change long enough to see his vision clouded and his organization doomed.

During its 110-year history, SIM has witnessed much cataclysmic change in our world. It has also lived through much change internally brought about by growth. With those changes has come structural and organizational change within the mission. The following outline is based on the core Sudan Interior Mission branch of what is today called Serving In Mission (SIM).

The Pioneer Days—1893–1915

SIM began with the vision of an entrepreneur. In 1893, three pioneers, Walter Gowans, Thomas Kent, and Rowland Bingham, went to West Africa determined to reach the "Soudan" with its 60 million unreached people. They went on their own without any council or board backing them. Within a year Gowans and Kent died and Bingham, the youngest, was shipped home critically ill. Bingham was a man with dogged determination. He formed a council in Canada to back him, tried again, and again failed because of ill health in what was called "the white man's grave." Still, he made a third attempt, sending a small team who started a work at Patigi on the Niger River in Nigeria. Other pioneers soon followed and the work was begun in different locations in central Nigeria.

From the earliest years, Bingham had formed a council in Canada, which he chaired, and which existed to give him counsel and backing. The Council was composed of interested business people and pastors. The members were drawn from both Canada and the USA.

The organization was all very loose and with minimal structure. Each missionary on the field did his or her own thing and related, when necessary, directly to the general director back in Canada. All of those missionaries, recruited by Bingham, were people like himself, with the same rugged determinism, almost to the point of stubbornness.

This structure continued until 1915. By that time significant church growth had occurred particularly among the Yagba people around Egbe, Nigeria. Bingham, accompanied by a member of the Council, a USA pastor, toured the field. When they returned, Pastor MacKenzie reported to the Council telling of the spectacular growth

Photo G.1. *Rowland Bingham, co-founder and General Director, 1893–1895, 1898–1942*[2]

of the church. He also compared SIM missionaries and their working relationships to the days of the judges with everyone doing what was right in his/her own eyes!

Bingham with the Council's hearty agreement made a decision, which would affect the structure of the mission. In the future, SIM was to be organized so that decisions would be made as close to the action as possible. This followed the pattern for interdenominational missions set earlier by Hudson Taylor of the China Inland Mission. More than that, however, this was based on a biblical pattern, for it must be noted that Paul and his missionary band went about their decision making unencumbered by cables, faxes, or emails. This is seen in Acts 16 when a strategic decision was made to go to Europe in response to God's direction, without any reference to either the Antioch or Jerusalem churches. The missionaries themselves concluded (verse 10) that God had called them to answer the Macedonian call, so they immediately boarded ship and set sail. It was, of necessity, a field-based decision made by men working as a team who determined and followed God's direction.

Based on this decision, Guy Playfair was appointed field superintendent (later called the director) and the field missionaries were to relate to and report to him, not Bingham or the Council in Canada. He was accountable for all the field activities to Dr. Bingham and the Council, but decisions regarding ministry were to be made by him and his council as close to the action as possible.

A Period of Organizational Crisis and Consolidation—1915–1957

During this period the mission grew, slowly at first, but after World War II more rapidly, in both East and West Africa, while it expanded its home base to other English-speaking bases around the world. Dr. Bingham created councils in Canada, the USA, Australia/NZ and in the United Kingdom. On the fields East and West Africa became separate entities, each with its own director.

Dr. Bingham was a member of each council and chaired those councils whenever he was present. Otherwise the respective director chaired the councils. The offices in the sending countries were managed in each case by a secretary/treasurer who reported to the general director.

Note that during this period there was no legal bond between the various councils or with the general director. Bingham was used of God to tie the whole together by virtue of his pioneer status as well as his considerable personal charisma. He demanded and received loyalty. It worked!

In 1942, however, an organizational crisis arose. Bingham had founded the mission and directed it for almost 49 years. On the eve of the Jubilee year, he died shortly after completing his book *Seven Sevens of Years and a Jubilee.*

Since SIM had been structured somewhat after the pattern of Hudson Taylor and the China Inland Mission, it was assumed that somewhere in the safe in Toronto there would be a sacred envelope with Dr. Bingham's choice of his successor—his Elisha. That is what Taylor had done. Alas, no envelope was found. Furthermore, there was no structure to determine how another general director could be appointed, nor was there unanimity about who that person should be.

The mission went two years without a general director, with each of the home offices carrying on as they had and the field missionaries continuing under the direction of the well-established field directors. Finally in 1944, Guy Playfair, who had been the West Africa Field Director since 1915, was appointed by mutual agreement as the second general director of SIM.[3] He held this post until 1957 and the mission continued to function as it had without any structural change.

Photo G.2. *Guy Playfair,*
General Director, 1944–1957

Playfair was a field missionary and he continued to make his base in Nigeria. He appointed a director for North America to whom both the Canada and USA offices reported, while the chairmen of the other home councils functioned as honorary directors relating to the general director.

By 1956, the mission had grown spectacularly through the post–World War II era. It now faced another organizational crisis. Mr. Playfair was aged. It was time for a new leader to be appointed. But once again there was no mechanism through which a new general director could be appointed. Mr. Playfair felt he had the prerogative to anoint his successor and campaigned vigorously amongst the missionaries to do so. However, most of the missionaries and the field leadership did not support his nominee. There was deep tension in the ranks with the possibility of a split in the mission. The crisis was acute.

At that point the councils in Canada, USA, UK, South Africa, Australia, and New Zealand, along with representatives from the East and West Africa councils agreed to meet at the USA headquarters at 164 W. 74th Street, New York. Technically, there was no legal basis for that meeting. But they met by mutual agreement, and in retrospect, it was obviously by the direct leading of our Sovereign Lord.

The Emergence of a General Council, 1957–1972

The gathering in New York City met for two weeks during which time they recommended a new structure which would tie the mission together by means of a Memorandum of Agreement to be entered into by the councils,[4] all legal entities in their own right, and to be approved by the mission family as a whole. Time was given for these councils to consider and approve the new structure and for the mission family to be informed and by means of their representatives give approval. Finally, in July 1957 the documents were approved and a new general director was appointed under the new system.

Prior to this date, the general director had been accountable to no one, but God. Now the third general director would be accountable to a General Council composed of representatives from each sending country and each of the directors.

The general director was given responsibility for the administration of the whole mission under the General Council. International coordination and liaison between all of the offices remained his responsibility. Oversight financially for the whole mission was his responsibility, also, with each home office advising him monthly what funds were available. He could determine, then, what the monthly allowance for the missionaries should be, and which projects should be helped. It was the task of each home office to see to it that all local bills were paid; everything left over was to be made available for the allowance pool.

Photo G.3. *"Formation of First General Council," c. 17 July 1957.*

Front Row (L–R): Unidentified, Ray Davis (Nigeria), Guy Playfair (Nigeria), Ritchie Rice (UK), Glen Cain (Ethiopia), Al Termer (US).
Back row (L–R): Homer Wilson (Ethiopia), Bob Thompson (Ethiopia), John Wiebe (Nigeria), Mr. Simmons (Canada), Mr. Baker (South Africa), Pastor Holbrook (USA), Mr. Quenton (Australia), Stewart Boemer (Canada).

The role of the sending councils was unique in this structure. Each home director and home council had to work within the laws of their country to ensure that all legal requirements were cared for and that the mission was run in each place with integrity. The directors, however, were responsible to the general director to ensure that everything done in their sphere of responsibility was in accordance with the *Principles and Practices* of the mission, which by this time were coordinated mission-wide. Changes in these overall policies were to be made by the General Council under the chairmanship of the general director.

Photo G.4. *Albert Helser,*
General Director, 1957–1962

The process for appointing a general director was also established in this memorandum. The General Council was to nominate a man of their choosing after they had received recommendations from the mission family. This nominee was then approved by each of the councils in the mission, following which, the mission family voted. The nominee had to obtain a 75 percent (later amended to 66 2/3 percent) majority vote by secret ballot of eligible members of the mission. He was then appointed by the General Council for a five-year term and was accountable to it.

Albert D. Helser, longtime missionary in Nigeria, was appointed by this process and became the third general director in 1957.

The memorandum also established age 65 as the mandatory retirement age for all elected officers. Dr. Helser was 60 when he assumed office, which limited his tenure as general director to one five-year term.

In 1962, Raymond J. Davis was appointed as the fourth general director. He lived in Grand Rapids, Michigan, and he used to say his office was in his brief case.

He functioned with the assistance of only a part-time treasurer. The new structure provided a chain of command through which responsibilities were delegated. Each director had a council, which provided counsel and advice.

Photo G.5. *Raymond Davis,*
General Director, 1962–1975

The Period of Decentralization, Phase 1, 1972–1975

By 1972 radical changes were occurring brought about both by expansion in the fields, as well as complex political changes altering the face of Africa. This made centralized administration in East and West Africa more difficult. With the demise of colonialism; crossing national borders was an administrative nightmare. As a result, the one large West Africa administration was divided into three smaller administrations; Ghana/Nigeria, Francophone Africa (including Benin, Niger, and Burkina Faso) and Liberia/Côte d'Ivoire.

Furthermore, full-time directors were appointed in the United Kingdom, Australia, and New Zealand. The North America director role was eliminated in favor of separate administrations in Canada and the United States.

To accommodate this decentralization, which maintained SIM's principle that decisions be made as close to the action as possible, it became necessary to strengthen the central core. Otherwise the mission could well splinter into diverse entities with differing policies. Thus, centralization and decentralization were demanded simultaneously. Two deputies were provided to the general director with increased staff including a full-time treasurer, as well as a personnel and a public relations office both of which were initially cared for by one of the deputies.

Dr. Davis continued as general director during this period with William Crouch (former West Africa director) and Ian Hay (former North America director) as his deputies. It should be noted that this gradual development of an International Department did not come without some strong difference of opinion on the part of some who feared we were creating a hierarchy that would limit the historic strengths of our field administrations.

The Period of Decentralization, Phase 2, 1975–1980

At the 1975 General Council, the mission once again faced a major organizational challenge. The general director Ray Davis and deputy general director Bill Crouch

both retired within a few months of each other. Furthermore, it was obvious that the decentralization of 1972 had worked so well that more of the same was needed. Ghana was separated from Nigeria and Sudan from Ethiopia. Francophone Europe was given separate national division status. The mission now had 12 directors all reporting to the general director.

Ian Hay was nominated and appointed the fifth general director. He assumed the role with only one staff officer—the treasurer.

Recognizing the impossibility of this structure the council strongly encouraged the strengthening of the international office. The purpose of this was to

Photo G.6. *Ian Hay, General Director, 1975–1993*

coordinate the work, in order to strengthen the field workers, enabling the frontline missionaries to better perform their ministries. The international office was to be a servant to the other offices, which in turn were to serve the mission family enabling stronger ministry at the grassroots level.

In an organization like SIM, there is a constant temptation on the part of either field or home offices to strive for efficiency to the point they make the missionaries serve the office, rather than vice versa. The mission is the missionaries; each office exists to serve them. This truth must never be forgotten.

During this five-year period, a new deputy general director was appointed (W. Harold Fuller) with the public relations aspect of the administration delegated to him. Added to the treasurer role, staff officers for personnel, research, and ministry were created. An administrative assistant to the general director was also appointed.

Amalgamations

Any consideration of SIM's expanding roles must recognize the various mergers that took place during its first one hundred years of existence. The recent merger with AEF was an even more significant enlargement of the mission's structure. This paper, however, does not deal with this modern era.

Establishment of Board of Governors, 1980–1990

By 1980, I (Ian Hay) had been general director for five years following three years in the deputy slot. It became increasingly clear to me that radical changes were needed for the good of the mission in the future. I was carrying on the role of general director, with all these organizational changes, but still functioning in the role, as far as accountability was concerned, essentially as my predecessors had functioned. Meanwhile, the world had changed. Scandals in the Christian world made nonprofit organizations, structured like SIM, vulnerable and open to accusations of mismanagement. The potential for misunderstanding by the world at large was very real.

The home councils were structured legally according to their local laws and the composition of those councils was for the most part objective. However, in our SIM culture, the director concerned chaired each council. Furthermore, the General Council, while having representatives from home councils, was composed mostly of the directors and international staff of the mission. In other words, the council to which the general director was accountable was composed mostly of people who were appointed by him to their jobs and who were responsible to him for their work. The potential for a conflict of interest was real. I personally felt that for the protection of the mission and the integrity of the Lord's name, the general director needed to be more accountable. Any human being could be tempted to lead the mission off course without the checks and balances of better accountability.

Consequently, a radical proposal was debated and finally approved, creating a Board of Governors which represents all the legal bodies of the mission with minor representation from the mission family. The general director thus became accountable to a totally objective body.

To ensure that the voices of the missionaries were clearly heard, an International Council was established as advisory to the general director. This is composed entirely within the internal administrative structure including staff and directors. It is an advisory body and that fills the role formerly filled by the General Council.

The national (home) council and the national director were each responsible for all legal and policy matters, which applied to their respective countries. By signing the

Memorandum of Agreement, however, they then delegated to the Board of Governors, through their representative(s), the responsibility and authority to administer the overall mission, which is done through the general director.

Preparation for a New General Director, 1993

At the Board of Governors meeting in 1990, I had been general director for 15 years, but faced mandatory retirement at age 65 in three more years. The Board followed up on discussions its executive committee had been having with me stressing the need for administrative changes at the international level to help the next general director, whoever he might be, to cope with the scope of the organizational structure. I was charged with the responsibility of restructure to that end.

To achieve this goal, four deputy general directors were appointed with the geographic responsibilities divided amongst them. International staff was increased leaving the general director with fewer people reporting directly to him.

By God's grace, this made the transition on 19 December 1993 from Ian Hay to Jim Plueddemann run smoothly. The supportive staff was in place enabling Dr. Plueddemann to begin his tenure with a group of knowledgeable, competent associates. This made possible his ability to quickly assimilate the wide span of control for which he is accountable to the Board of Governors.

Photo G.7. Jim Plueddemann, International Director, 2003–2013

Conclusion

By better understanding the changes that have taken place, and the reasons for them, we hope to display how the mission has been affected over the years by them, the roles that SIM's directors, boards, and councils have taken on and how each role interacts with the other. While this has been mainly a history of the international development of the mission through 1993, I believe that it should help new members of other councils see the overall picture and thus understand the role and function of their council in helping SIM to continue to be a viable organization as it has moved into its second century and into the twenty-first century.

APPENDIX H

REDEEMING MISSION AGENCIES

"A HIGHWAY FOR THE NATIONS"[1]

Dr. Howard Brant

Ponder the question, "What is a mission agency?" Our quick response would be that we are a religious order whose purpose is to plant, strengthen, and partner with churches around the world. We agree that is what we do. Another way to ask the same question is, "What is the function of a mission organization? What are its structures set up to do?" By the same token, we are a channel through which the needs of the world are identified and shared with those who have the ability to respond. So, functionally, we create a mission infrastructure that enables us to *move people, resources, and information* from one part of the world to another. Can we agree on this functional definition? If so, then we are ready to embrace a new analogy that can help us think about how we can do all of this more effectively.

Mission as a Highway for the Nations

Missions started as a trickle and moved in the last century to a mighty river of missionaries flowing from one part of the world to the other. But now the "river" is drying up. The gradation that once caused the missionary river to flow from the West to the Rest has shifted. A river flows "one way," downstream. Now we need a new paradigm that more accurately describes our reality. We need to change the concept of rivers into that of a highway that allows for "two way" traffic.[2] If we do, then we will suddenly see the traffic pick up again for there will always be people called of God from every nation who need to get involved in missions. If we could just change a few things in the system, we would find that traffic flowing from [the] USA to Spain could just as easily flow from Spain to [the] USA—or from Ecuador to Spain.

What keeps this from happening? It is lack of access! In our mission there is a sharp distinction between sending and receiving offices. One will hear the argument, "We are not set up for that." That may be true, but what would really need to change? Are our structures so inviolate? What would it really take for our "field offices" to take on "sending" roles and visa versa? The cost in terms of finance and personnel would be minimal compared to the enormous benefit in kingdom terms.

What would it really take? Transfer of funds from one office to another could work just about the same. It is just as easy to make a deposit in a bank as to draw a check. Visa and immigration services would simply drop off passports at the embassy rather than at the immigration office. It would be possible to set up local Sending Councils in each country to recruit and screen applicants. Orientation could be held once a year and some of our best staff from other countries could come over to help orientate a group that is ready to go to the field. There could even be an international candidate course held in some part of the world that would be more accessible to everyone.

The "Highway" Analogy

This analogy of a mission agency as being a highway is rather intriguing. Recently I traveled from downtown Hong Kong to the new international airport. It took about 20 minutes to traverse one of the most densely populated cities in the world, cross over a bay on a suspension bridge, and then pass freely through a massive mountain tunnel and into the new Hong Kong Airport.

Have you ever thought about how highways are created? A highway usually starts as a tiny footpath to get from one village to another. Over the years, the footpath becomes a trail for the oxcart and eventually for the tractor and truck. The once tiny path becomes more traveled. But then one day, some dreamer gets the idea of building a super highway. For years nobody takes action because the cost and labor are enormous. But at some point the villages get together and say, "We really need a highway that would enable us all to

Photo H.1. *East Africa Office—first director, Worku Haile Mariam*

connect with one another." They see the potential of efficiency and connectivity. They understand that a highway allows for all kinds of new innovation, new business, and new opportunity.

Highways are built to transport people and goods with the least amount of obstacles. They go up over cities, down under water via tunnels, across bridges, through mountains—over or through or under every barrier. It takes enormous coordination, effort, and expense to build a highway. To prepare a highway, deserts and wildernesses must be crossed. Every valley must be filled up. Every mountain must be brought low. Rough places have to be made smooth and even mountain ranges have to be turned into broad valleys. Usually when great highways are completed, there is a day on which the king opens the highway. His glory is revealed and "all flesh" sees it. After the king goes down the highway, anyone can follow. Long after the highway is built, the voice that cried out, "Prepare a highway!" is forgotten. But the highway moves thousands of people for years to come. What a challenge to prepare a highway . . . a highway for all nations!

Some people come onto highways in motor homes or fancy Cadillacs. Formerly, most cars on the missions highway were Jeeps, Chevys, and Fords. Today it is just as likely that you will pass a Hyundai, Volvo, BMW, Ambassador, Fiat, or those new little VW Beetles made in Brazil. But highways are wonderful things. You will see all those fine cars—even a Rolls-Royce or a Mercedes speeding along, but you might also see someone cruising along on their Italian motor scooter, or some brave guy peddling his Chinese bicycle . . . each according to their ability but all going down the same highway.

Progression of an Idea Already There

In my own mission (SIM) I can see that the concept of "missions as a highway" has been developing for a long time. In fact, as I talk about this concept, I find this dream latent in the spirits of many around the world. I believe it is a concept whose time has come. As I look at what God has been doing in our mission over the past 10 to 15 years, I can see the ways He has led us to become the kind of mission that is poised to take on this new challenge:

1. Part of our purpose statement challenges us to "partner with churches around the world to fulfill the Great Commission."

2. One of our SIM Core Values is to be "joyfully international." We say, "We are intentionally international because we believe this best expresses the nature of the body of Christ in the world. We believe we will be more effective as we incorporate the richness of cultural diversity in our membership."

3. God is wonderfully at work in our so-called "mission field" countries. These churches are catching the vision for world missions.

4. Our agency is in great need of many more missionaries (about eight hundred). We are not finding these people in our traditional fishing grounds. Often missionaries from less-developed countries adapt better and identify better with third-world cultures.

5. We are making our support system much more flexible, making it easier for people from less-developed countries to send missionaries.

6. There are hints along the line that our agency is drawing more and more non-Westerners. We have drawn more and more Asians over the past 15 years. Our fastest growing office is Korea. We now have Guatemalans in India, Peruvians in China. Our director for Sudan is from North India. Our sending director in Australia is ethnic Chinese, raised in Indonesia, and his sending church is Nairobi Chapel in Kenya, East Africa.

7. Several of our sending offices are developing partnerships with countries that have no sending office. Canada is working with Brazil. USA is working with

Guatemala and recently set up a branch office in Ecuador so that Ecuadorian applicants to SIM can be handled there and *not* need to come to the USA to join SIM. The number of missionaries applying from countries where there is no SIM sending office (such as Nigeria, Ecuador, or Peru) is growing rapidly.

8.   Through merger and growth, we have already set up an infrastructure that connects over 46 countries of the world. People from many nations of the world could use this same highway to serve the Lord in various parts of the world.

Photo H.2. *Obed Cruz, first OCLA director*

When you put all this together, it becomes clear that missions like ours are well positioned and really do have the capacity to think about becoming a highway for all nations. The network, experience, and infrastructure that we have developed over the years are now being challenged to go to the next level. The critical question is whether we are ready to add this new challenge to our mission agenda. If we rise to the challenge, we could well be a blessing to the nations, not only in taking the gospel to them, but in allowing them to use our infrastructure to take the gospel to others. If we balk at the obstacles, shrink at the challenges, or get caught in the paralysis of analysis, this moment could pass us by. Certainly like Mordecai told Esther, "God will raise up others to do it, but perhaps God has raised us up for such a time as this" (Esther 4:14).

Action Points

In practical terms, what would it mean for a traditional mission to become a Highway for all Nations—to move missionaries "from anywhere to anywhere" or at least to move them from where we have worked to other parts of the world where our mission presently works?

1.   First, we need to make a conscious decision that we will become intentionally international—not just allowing people from other nations to join us—but purposefully seeking ways to make our infrastructures more accommodating and less restrictive for them to use.

2.   Second, to change our policies and systems that tend to exclude others from becoming a part of us. These need to be changed at our top international council and board levels. We need to make sure that our promotional literature states clearly, "All candidates are considered without regard to race or nationality."

3. What we need most is an ethos change that stops us from thinking of "us" and "them," and helps us to see one another as part and parcel of the same kingdom of God.

4. We need to remove obstacles and create systems that ease the movement of missionaries from one part of the world to another. This would include changes in our financial systems, personnel system, language requirements, orientation process, manual translation, etc.

5. We need to start seeing each of our mission offices around the world as having both a "sending" as well as "receiving" function. Every country in the world should potentially have "on ramps" as well as "off ramps." Only then will we have two-way traffic on our highway. In order to do that we may have to intentionally erase the arbitrary distinction between sending and field offices and simply refer to them as our "office in X country."

6. We need to clearly define the rules of the road so that they are well understood by all those who choose to travel this way. This "retooling of mission" would include educating existing members of our agency that "new two-way traffic" will soon be on the road.

7. Finally, we would need to make sure that the King of Glory walks first upon our highway, for unless the Glory of the Lord is revealed, we cannot expect the nations of the earth to benefit.

In order to accomplish all these larger tasks, many minor changes are needed. We can do them if we focus on the larger goal ahead. Our plea, however, would be that we step out in faith and not be paralyzed by trying to analyze every aspect of the whole thing before we do anything. Many of the obstacles to building this highway will not be apparent until we get to them. The paralysis of analysis destroys initiative and growth. Like a person who sets out into the night on a long journey, we can only see a short distance ahead of us. Let us go as far as we can see and believe that the lights will reveal new ways to move ahead when we get there.

Concluding Thoughts

The goal of missions should not be limited to evangelism or church planting. The ultimate goal is not an independent church, but a church enabled to become a full participant in propagating the gospel to the nations of the world. Once we embrace this larger vision, we will have made a radical shift in our missiological thinking. If we do, we will find that new avenues of engagement in mission will open before us.

The bottom line is whether or not we can catch a vision of what God intended His church and mission agencies to look like at the end of the age. God separated the races at Babel so that evil would be restrained from spreading too rapidly. From the many nations, God chose one (Israel) to reveal His purposes and bring forth a Savior. But on the Day of Pentecost, something wonderful happened. The Holy Spirit descended. Certainly there were the tongues of fire, the mighty rushing wind, and the experience of tongues. But what really happened that day is later pinpointed by Paul when he writes to the Corinthians and tells them, "By one Spirit we were all baptized into one body . . . whether Jew or Greek, bond or free" (I Corinthians 12: 13). What Paul is telling us is that the church is something totally unique in God's economy. Here *national barriers are to be shattered* . . . for there is neither Jew nor Greek. But also *economic barriers are to be shattered* . . . for there is neither bond (slave) nor free man.

If we say that the cultural, stylistic, organizational, linguistic, operational, and practical barriers are too great, then we may not have understood what God did when He placed us into the church. To our peril we neglect the ministry of the Holy Spirit within us. We limit the power of God to demonstrate what the church should be. If we as foreign missionaries cannot allow the Holy Spirit to overcome our ethnic as well as class distinctions, then who can? I believe it can be done. It should be done. And by God's grace it will be done—if not by us, by others who are in tune with what the Spirit is saying to the churches of our day. The tide of mission history is pressing hard against us. We need to be like the sons of Issachar "who understood the times and had knowledge of what Israel ought to do."[3] Let those of us who understand our times, and know what to do, do it by faith and for the glory of God's kingdom.

APPENDIX I

SIM INTERNATIONAL ARCHIVES AND RECORDS

I t is because SIM had the foresight several decades ago to establish an archive that the mission now has one of the better collections of primary sources of any nondenominational evangelical mission in North America. The archives, based first in Toronto, then in Charlotte, North Carolina, and now in Fort Mill, South Carolina, have been used by dozens of scholars since the mid-1980s. Hundreds of others, including pastors, missionaries, academics, and family members of missionaries have solicited information, documents, photos, and film from the collection.

The idea for the archive originated in the late 1950s when Ian Hay, while serving in Nigeria as SIM's West Africa Field Secretary, felt it would be prudent to send its most valuable records to Toronto as Nigeria approached independence. Hay collected, culled, and shipped boxes of materials with the help of Vera Batke (Crouch) and Barbara Reeves.

From the mid-1960s to the mid-1980s, Kerry Lovering, Chris Ferrier, Betty Harrison, and others started to collect and organize SIM's archive in Toronto.

The following are the names of some of the others, listed more or less in chronological order, who have worked in the archives since the mid-1970s: Dr. James Kraakevik, Gary Corwin, Anne Parlane, Marj

Photo I.1. *Yusufu Turaki conducting research in Toronto, Canada, with the assistance of Betty Harrison, 1985*

Koop, Joan Wiebe, Alberta Simms, Lucille Anderson, Theresa Anderson, Sara Ely, Lillian Dorer, Tom Fesmire, Glenda Johnson, Jo-Ann Brant (archivist), Dave Christie, John Holmes, Doris Custer, Clarence Ely, Ed Iwan, Eleanor Iwan, Bob Arnold (archivist), Roger Nagel, Rachael Conger, Susan Arnold, Tim Geysbeek (archivist), Adam Geysbeek, Cate O'Brien, Ryan Geysbeek, Judie Fiegel, Natalia Bremner, Muriel Hirons, Shirley Fehl, Pam Dudeck, Don Hall, Betty Hall, Maybeth Henderson, Kelly Grimshaw, Jan Klipowitz,

Photo I. 2. *Chris Ferrier, Chuck Guth, and Kerry Lovering, Toronto, 1977.*
These three formed the International Publications Department. Here, they are designing the January-February 1978 issue of *Africa Now.*[1]

Photo I.3. *Evie Bowers sorting documents in the library, Fort Mill, SC, 2012.*
Evie Bowers organizing Africa Evangelical Fellowship and SIM documents that Ryan Hannah sent from Malawi.

Dr. Joanna Bogunjoko, Evie Bowers, Pat Sutton, Susan McKinney, Kaitlyn McKinney, and Marguerite Malloy. SIM's current international archivist is Susan McKinney.

Every year for the past several years, many people from Ebenezer Mennonite Church in Bluffton, Ohio, have come to the archives to volunteer. These include Ruth Anna Bixel, Rosie Good, Dave Ream, Susan Hawk, Sharon Forrer, Rhody Hartman, Linda Saunders, Joyce Cupples, Wilda Hanthorn, Rev. Dick Tschetter, Ruth Tschetter, Bill Steiner, Ruth Hefner, Diane Sharrock, Kay Spallinger, and Vicki Cartright.

Jackie Fowler and Dr. Jim Kallam respectively provided an invaluable service by ensuring that the records of Andes Evangelical Mission and Africa Evangelical Fellowship were transferred to the SIM International Archives after the mergers of their missions. They worked in the archives for many years to organize the materials. In addition, since the mid-1980s, Paul Ericksen and Robert Schuster of the Billy Graham Center at Wheaton College have graciously provided invaluable professional guidance in numerous ways.

SIM thanks all of these people, and surely many not mentioned, who have devoted seemingly countless hours to the archives so future generations can use them.

SIM International Archives and Records
1838 Gold Hill Rd.
Fort Mill, SC 29708
international.archives@sim.org
https://www.facebook.com/SIMInternationalArchives

ENDNOTES

Preface

1   Credit and with gratitude to SIM International Communication Coordinator Tabitha Plueddemann for suggesting the title.

2   From a descriptive 1935 lapel pin advert held in the SIM International Archives and Records (SIMIAR) (Bingham, to Dear Fellow Workers, 16 December 1935, AM-2, Box 4, File 1). This verse is from the *King James Version* (1935). Unless otherwise indicated, or from quoted material, all other versions are from the *New International Version* (1984).

3   SIM made "By Prayer" its official motto in 1989 (Minutes, Board of Governors, 24-30 April, minute 90/13, p. 30).

4   It is worth noting that there is another book currently in process that contains many of the papers presented at a 2013 conference held in Addis Ababa, Ethiopia, on the history of SIM work in Africa. Its projected title is *Breaking Barriers: The Sudan Interior Mission and African Pioneers Remaking Missions across the Sahel*, and it is to be published by Africa World Press/Red Sea Press.

Chapter 1: The Faith Missions Story

1   Ralph D. Winter, "Four Men, Three Eras, Two Transitions: Modern Missions," in *Perspective on the World Christian Movement: A Reader*, 3rd ed., Ralph D. Winter and Steven C. Hawthorne, eds. (Pasadena: William Carey Library, 1999), 253-261.

2   Klaus Fiedler, *The Story of Faith Missions* (Oxford, England: Regnum Lynx, 1994), 11.

3   Andrew Murray, *Key to the Missionary Problem* (Fort Washington, PA: Christian Literature Crusade, 1979), 130.

4   It is interesting to note the general pattern that has existed throughout the history of faith missions, that approximately one third of the members are men, one third are married women, and one third are single women.

5   G. R. Corwin, "Faith Missions Movement," in *Dictionary of Christianity in America*, Daniel G. Reid, Robert D. Linder, Bruce L. Shelley, and Harry S. Stout, eds. (Downers Grove, IL: InterVarsity Press, 1990), 426.

6   See Joel A. Carpenter, "Propagating the Faith Once Delivered: The Fundamentalist Missionary Enterprise, 1920–1945," in *Earthen Vessels: American Evangelicals and Foreign Missions, 1880–1980*, Joel A. Carpenter and Wilbert R. Shenk, eds. (Grand Rapids: William B. Eerdmans Publishing Company, 1990), 127–128.

7   For the fullest treatment available of all these connections, especially with regard to the Africa-oriented faith missions, see Fiedler, *The Story*.

8   This entire list is gratefully gleaned from Fiedler, *The Story*, 34-50. See also Yusufu Turaki, *Theory and Practice of Christian Missions in Africa: A Century of SIM/ECWA History and Legacy in Nigeria, 1893-1993* (Nairobi, Kenya: International Bible Society Africa, 1999), ch. 3; and Christof Sauer, *Reaching the Unreached Sudan Belt: Guinness, Kumm, and the Sudan-Pionier-Mission* (Nurnberg: VTR, 2005).

9   A. B. Simpson, "My Medicine Chest, or, Helps to Divine Healing," *The Alliance Weekly* 41, no. 2 (11 October 1913): 18–21; Lindsay Reynolds, *Rebirth: The Development of the Christian and Missionary Alliance in Canada, 1919–1983* (Beaverlodge, Alberta: Evangelistic Enterprises, 1992), 9, 12, 15, 21–22; Fiedler, *The Story*, 213–214, 221.

10   J[im] H. Hunter, *A Flame of Fire: The Life and Work of R. V. Bingham, Ll.D.* (Aslesbury and Slough: Hazell Watson & Viney Limited, 1961), 58–60, 64–65, 78–85, 88–90; Yusufu Turaki, *Theory and Practice of Christian Missions in Africa: A Century of SIM/ECWA History and Legacy in Nigeria 1893–1993*, vol. 1 (Nairobi, Kenya: International Bible Society Africa, 1999), 81–93, 102–103, 112–113. After Bingham's fever rose above 105° on Christmas day of 1893, a rift developed between Bingham and Gowans after Bingham called for a doctor and took medicine (Tim Geysbeek and Cate O'Brien, "Walter Gowans, Rowland Bingham, and the Controversy over Divine Healing in the Sudan Interior Mission," paper presented at the Yale-Edinburgh Group Conference on the History of the Missionary Movement and World Christianity, 29 June 2013, Yale Divinity School, New Haven, CT; revised in 2014). Some members of other faith missions at the end of the nineteenth century also believed in various notions of "divine healing" (e.g., Alvyn Austin, *China's Millions: The China Inland Mission and Late Qing Society, 1832–1905* [Grand Rapids: Eerdmans, 2007], 309–311).

11   Walter Gowans, To My Dear Mother, 6 January 1894, SIMIAR, BM-1, Box 10b; "Our English editorial correspondent…." *The Missionary Review of the World* 7, no. 7 (New Series) (July 1894): 540; Rowland Bingham, "The Second Attempt Which Failed," *The Evangelical Christian and Missionary Witness* 29, no. 6 (August 1933): 334-335; Bingham, *Seven Sevens of Years and a Jubilee: The Story of the Sudan Interior Mission*, 5th ed. (New York: Evangelical Publishers, 1957), 25, 31; Hunter, *A Flame of Fire*, 65; Geysbeek and O'Brien, "Walter Gowans."

12   Bingham, *Seven Sevens*, 31; Rowland Bingham, *The Bible and the Body: Healing in the Scriptures*, 4th ed. (Toronto: Evangelical Publishers, 1952); Brian Alexander McKenzie, "Fundamentalism, Christian Unity, and Premillennialism in the Thought of Rowland Victor Bingham (1872–1942): A Study of Anti-Modernism in Canada" (Ph.D. diss., Toronto School of Theology, 1985), 80, fn. 8.

13   For example, see A. B. Simpson, "The Relation of Divine Healing to the Holy Ghost," *Darkness and Light* 7 (July 1894): 74; George Donaldson, "My Testimony," *Darkness and Light* 11 (November 1894): 182; Mr. Gardiner, "Deputation Tour in the United States and Canada," *Darkness and Light* 21, no. 10 (October 1914): 113–116; "News and Notes: 'Heal the Sick,'" *Darkness and Light* 37, no. 4 (July–August 1930): 10–11.

14   James Robinson, *Divine Healing, the Formative Years: 1830–1890* (Eugene, OR: Pickworth Publications), 2011, 218–225; Pamela J. Walker, "Negotiating Britishness: the South Africa General Mission," paper presented at the American Historical Association meeting (Washington, D.C.), 5 January 2014; Joshua Dhube, *The Association of The United Baptist Churches of Zimbabwe Commonly called United Baptist Church of Zimbabwe (UBC) Celebrating 100 years of Gospel Witness, 1897–1997* (Harare: Jongwe Printing, 1997), 4–12.

15   For example, Dr. Wanless, "The Medical Mission," *White Already to Harvest* 6, no. 2 (November 1901): 172–173; J. R. Burrow, "The Touch of His Hand," *Tahuantin Suyu* 1, no. 7 (July 1912): 83–84.

16   Fiedler, *The Story*, 272.

17   Fiedler, *The Story*, 275.

18   Fiedler, *The Story*, 272.

Chapter 2: The Burden of the Least Reached

1   The first published use of this phrase occurred in 1909, in Rowland Bingham, "The Story of the Sudan Interior Mission," *The Missionary Witness* 5, no. 4 (6 April 1909): 62.

2   "Departments of Work," *Christian Alliance and Missionary Weekly* 11, no. 22 (1 December 1893): 367.

3   Rowland Bingham, *Seven Sevens of Years and a Jubilee: The Story of the Sudan Interior Mission*, 5th ed. (New York: Evangelical Publishers, 1957), 9-15.

4   Christof Sauer, *Reaching the Unreached Sudan Belt: Guinness, Kumm, and the Sudan-Pionier-Mission* (Nurnberg: VTR, 2005), 48, 310. The Sudan of those days should not be confused with the Republic of Sudan or South Sudan known today. It was the vast area south of the Sahara and Egypt stretching from Ethiopia on the East, to the hinterlands of the Gambia, Sierra Leone, Liberia, Côte d'Ivoire (Ivory Coast), Ghana (Gold Coast), Republic of Benin (Dahomey), Nigeria, and Cameroon to the west, and to the Democratic Republic of Congo (Congo) in the south. Through the travels of many courageous men, various parts of this land were becoming better known to Westerners, but the interior was still little known and very dangerous for the uninitiated. It was only after 1884 when the Europeans participated in what has been called the "Scramble for Africa" that it was divided out into various colonies with Britain, France, Germany, and Belgium as the chief Protectorates.

5   "Africa," *Christian Alliance Foreign Missionary Weekly*" 14, no. 11 (13 March 1895): 173.

6   T. K. [Thomas Kent], to R. V. Bingham, 8 August 1893, SIMIAR, BM-1, Box 10b; Sauer, *Reaching the Unreached Sudan Belt*, 72–73.

7   Tom Lambie, *A Doctor's Great Commission* (Wheaton, IL: Van Kampen Press, 1954), 167.

8   Both were based in London. Given that the CMS and Wesleyan Methodists had missionaries in Lagos and other parts of Nigeria, and that Gowans and Bingham went to to London, it is plausible that one of them contacted these societies.

9   Walter Gowans, to Rowland Bingham and John Hindle, 23 July 1893, SIMIAR, BM-1, Box 10b.

10   "A Story of Toronto's Missionary Martyrs," *The Saturday Globe* 1 (13 April 1895): 1–2; Rowland V. Bingham, *Seven Sevens of Years and a Jubliee: The Story of the Sudan Interior Mission*, 5th ed. (New York: Evangelical Publishers, 1957), 9–10, 15.

11   Sanneh, Lamin, "The CMS and the African Transformation: Samuel Ajayi Crowther and the Opening of Nigeria," in *The Church Mission Society and World Christianity, 1799–1999*, Kevin Ward and Brian Stanley, eds. (Grand Rapids, Michigan, and Richmond, Surrey, UK: William B. Eerdman's Publishing Company and Curzon Press Ltd., 2000), 173–197.

12   R. V. Bingham, "The Cradle Roll of Our Magazine: A Review of History, Editors And Policy," in *The Evangelical Christian and Missionary Witness*, quoted in Yusufu Turaki, *Theory and Practice of Christian Missions in Africa: A Century of SIM/ECWA History and Legacy in Nigeria 1893–1993*, vol. 1 (International Bible Society Africa, Nairobi, Kenya 1999), 91.

13   Ibid., 91.

14   Rowland Bingham and Kerry Lovering, *Root From Dry Ground: The Story of the Sudan Interior Mission* (SIM, 1966), 13.

15   Together with Gowans, Kent, and Bingham during this period of concerted prayer and decision making were two Brits, David Loynd and Robert Lee. Loynd and Lee did not travel with Gowans, Kent, and Bingham due to the lack of funds. Loynd met up with Bingham in Lagos in November 1894 and traveled with him for five months, but parted ways with Bingham after they returned to England. Lee ended up never going to Africa, but became SIM's "Home Director" in Britain. According to Lee, he and these four other men co-founded SIM in Britain after they could not find any other agencies who would accept them as missionaries ("From the archives: The forgotten pioneers," *Intercom* 35 [March 1977]: 5.

16   Turaki, *Theory and Practice*, 92.

17   On 30 June 1967, SIM's General Council (Item 20) declared 4 December 1893, as "Founders' Day," enhancing this date in SIM's history. Since the mission takes 1893 as the year that the mission was founded, Gowans, Kent, and Bingham are rightly thought of as co-founders. After Bingham died in 1942, however, the mission started to list Bingham as SIM's "Founder" in its general directors' letterheads and other documents. This and similar actions tended to augment Bingham's role in SIM's early history. This misinterpretation of history still seeps into documents, mission displays, and academic literature. SIM could claim Bingham was its founder if it dated its origins to 1898 when Bingham formally organized the mission with a board and constitution. However, 1893 is so embedded in SIM's identity and history that its founding date is not likely to change any time soon. To date the founding of SIM to 1893 and name Bingham as its founder minimizes the more significant initial role Gowans, and even Kent, had in founding the mission. Gowans was the leader and visionary of the three, and he and Kent were the ones who trekked into the interior and died there. By 24 January 1894, Gowans, Kent, and Bingham decided to call their organization the "Soudan Interior Mission" per Gowans' suggestion (Hindle, "The Soudan Interior Mission"; "Important Announcement," *The Missionary Witness* 3, no. 6 [2 July 1907]: 98).

18   Bingham and Lovering, *Root From Dry Ground*, 14. Rowe was the superintendent of the Wesleyan Methodists in Lagos from 1893–1896 (George G. Findlay and William Holdsworth, *The History of the Wesleyan Methodist Missionary Society*, vol. IV [London: Epworth Press, 1922], 211–217).

19   Ibid., 17. This was Bishop Hill and other CMS missionaries.

20   J. H. Hunter, *A Flame of Fire: The Life and Work of R. V. Bingham, Ll. D.* (Aylesbury and Slough: Hazell Watson & Viney Limited, 1961), 8.

21   "The Story of the Sudan Interior Mission," *The Evangelical Christian and Missionary Witness* 5, no. 4 (April 1909): 62.

22   "Faith, mighty faith, the promise sees," http://www.hymnary.org/text/faith_mighty_faith_the_promise_sees, accessed 27 March 2017; Ian M. Hay, "A miraculous way to function," *Africa Now* 89 (November–December 1976): 15; Helen Bingham, *The Irish Saint* (Canada: Evangelical Publishers, [1907] 1927), 65.

23   Walter Gowans, To My Dear Mother, 6 January 1894, BM-1, Box 10b; Bingham, *Seven Sevens*, 27.

24   Walter Gowans' diary, c. 9 August 1894, BM-2, Box 13; Tim Geysbeek, "From Sasstown to Zaria: Tom Coffee and the Kru origins of the Sudan Interior Mission, 1893-1895," paper presented at

the Yale-Edinburgh Group Conference on the History of the Missionary Movement and World Christianity, 30 June 2017, Yale Divinity School, New Haven, CT.

25   Charles H. Robinson, *Hausaland; or, Fifteen Hundred Miles through the Central Soudan* (London: Sampson, Low, Marston, 1896), 75–77; T. J. Tonkin, "A Missionary Martyr in West Africa," *World Wide Magazine* (April 1900): 670–676.

26   Bingham, *Seven Sevens*, 13–30; "A Story of Toronto's Missionary Martyrs," 2.

27   Bingham and Lovering, *Root From Dry Ground*, 19.

28   Turaki, *Theory and Practice*, 10.

29   Adapted from Gary Corwin, "Walter Gowans' Desire to Redeem the Soudan," *Serving in Mission—U.K.* (Summer 2012): 13–14.

Chapter 3: The Common Context, Characteristics, and Challenges

1   Brian Stanley, *The Bible and the Flag: Protestant Missions & British Imperialism in the Nineteenth & Twentieth Centuries* (Trowbridge: Apollos, 1990), 184.

2   Adrian Hastings, "The Clash of Nationalism and Universalism within Twentieth-Century Missionary Christianity," in *Missions, Nationalism, and the End of Empire (Studies in the History of Christian Missions)*, Brian Stanley, ed. (Grand Rapids: Wm. B. Eerdmans Publishing Company, 2003), 18.

3   Ibid., 21.

4   W. Harold Fuller, "Serving in Mission: Linking Hands around the Globe," (2007), 3, SIMIAR.

Chapter 4: The Sudan Interior Mission Story

1   "Mrs. Bingham called home," *Sudan Witness* (January–March 1965): 8; John Hay, interview by Chris Ferrier, 1971, SIMIAR, MM-2, Box 159, File 6; J. H. Hunter, *A Flame of Fire: The Life and Work of R .V. Bingham, Ll. D.* (Aylesbury and Slough, England: Hazell Watson & Viney Limited, 1961), 257; Brian Alexander McKenzie, "Fundamentalism, Christian Unity, and Premillennialism in the Thought of Rowland Victor Bingham (1872–1942): A Study of Anti-Modernism in Canada," Ph.D. diss., Toronto School of Theology, 1985), 61–62.

2   General Council, Resolutions Passed, 3B3, (3–14 March 1980), 49.

3   While the mission started to use "Society for International Ministries" as an acronym in 1990 based on a resolution that the Board of Governors passed, the name did not technically change until SIM's signatories signed the revised Memorandum of Agreement (which updated the Constitution) in 1992 ("Unanimity Marks 1990 Council and Board Meetings," *Intercom* 92 [June–August 1990]: 3; SIM Manual [1991 edition, including 1992 amendments], Constitution 1–5).

4   SIM's Board of Governors changed the mission's name to SIM in 2000, with the byline "Serving in Mission." The official change was made in 2002 after the manual and constitution were revised (Jim Plueddemann, "SIM is 'Serving in Mission," *SIMNOW* 93 [2000]: 7; Board of Governors, 2.3.8 Name of the Mission [10–12 June 2002], 4).

5   Rowland V. Bingham, *Seven Sevens of Years and a Jubliee: The Story of the Sudan Interior Mission*, 5th ed. (New York: Evangelical Publishers, 1957), 31; Hunter, *A Flame of Fire*, 82–94.

6   From an interview with Rev. A. W. Banfield, "The Bible in the World" in 1908, quoted in Jim Mason, *Literature Outreach in Nigeria: A History of SIM Literature Work, 1901–1980* (Breslau, Canada: Denison Print, 2009), 4.

7   "The First Convert," *Sudan Witness*, 2nd Quarter (May 1963): 2.

8   Thomas Dow, "A. W. Banfield: Missionary Pioneer in Nigeria," http://www.bethelcollege.edu/assets/content/mcarchives/pdfs/v2n1p12_15.pdf, accessed 27 July 2016; Hunter, *A Flame of Fire*, 82, 89–92.

9   Dow, "A. W. Banfield."

10   Shobana Shankar, *Who Shall Enter Paradise? Christian Origins in Muslim Northern Nigeria, ca. 1890–1975* (Athens, Ohio: Ohio University Press and Swallow Press, 2014), 52–53, 65; Stella Archer, email to Bob Arnold, 24 February 2003; Bob Arnold, to Stella Archer, 4 March 2003, 31 July 2003.

11   This section about Stirrett is closely adapted from Percy, *Stirrett of the Sudan, the Beloved Physican of the Sudan* (Toronto: Sudan Interior Mission, 1948), 24-27. See also Yusufu Turaki, *Theory and Practice of Christian Missions in Africa: A Century of SIM/ECWA History and Legacy in Nigeria, 1893–1993*, vol. 1 (Nairobi, Kenya: International Bible Society Africa, 1999), 117.

12   Percy, *Stirrett of the Sudan*, 27.

13   Barbara M. Cooper, *Evangelical Christians in the Muslim Sahel* (Bloomington, IN: Indiana University Press, 2006), 150.

14   Hunter, *A Flame of Fire*, 103.

15   For Titcombe's biography, see Sophie de la Haye, *Tread upon the lion: The story of Tommie Titcombe*, 3rd printing (Scarborough, Canada: Sudan Interior Mission, 1980).

16   de la Haye, *Tread upon the lion*, 33; Ian Hay, *The Master Plan* (Canada: SIM USA, Inc., 2000), 55.

17   Bingham, *Seven Sevens*, 47–54.

18   Ibid., 55.

19   Ibid., 56–58.

20   Ibid., 58.

21   Bingham, *Seven Sevens*, 58–64.

22   de la Haye, *Tread upon the Lion*, 73–76, here and the next two paragraphs for the story about about the twins.

23   Mason, *Literature Outreach*, 12–13.

24   Mason, *Literature Outreach*, 12-14.

25   Bingham, *Seven Sevens*, 84-93; Yusufu Turaki, *An Introduction to the History of SIM/ECWA in Nigeria, 1893-1993* (Jos: Challenge Press, 1993), 142-152.

26   Mason, *Literature Outreach*, 16-17.

27   Ethnologue: Languages of the World (Nigeria), https://www.ethnologue.com/country/NG, accessed 7 July 2017.

28   Mason, *Literature Outreach*, 26-32, 144-154.

29   Turaki, *An Introduction*, 146-148; Julius B. Lawal, "The Birth of the Seminary," in *Thus Far the Lord has Helped Us: A Collection of Articles*, Julius B. Lawal, ed. (Ilorin, Nigeria: Awoyemi Press, c. 2001), 1-7.

30   Turaki, *Theory and Practice*, 312–330.

31   S. B. Agaja, *ECWA Hospital Egbe: A Citadel of Blessing* (Ilorin: Fhb/Legacy Print, c. 2007), 14; George and Esther Campion, *The Beginning of Egbe Hospital* (n.p.: Aro Major Press, 2016).

32   de la Haye, *Tread upon the lion*, 111.

33   Hunter, *A Flame of Fire*, 139–140.

34   "An Amazing Egbe Story," http://egbehospital.org/, accessed 27 February 2017.

35   Turaki, *Theory and Practice*, 537, 552, 555, 609; Ralph Madugu, "When ECWA Youths Converged at Egbe," *Today's Challenge* 6, no. 5 (June 2011): 25.

36   Panya Baba, *A Vision Received, A Vision Passed On: The History of EMS of ECWA, 1948–1998* (Bukuru: ACTS, 2009).

37   Hunter, *A Flame of Fire*, 229–230.

38   From an email to the author from Gordon Stanley, dated 17 April 2015.

39   Hunter, *A Flame of Fire*, 93–94.

40   Jim Mason, *God's Challenge in Africa* (Belleville, Ontario, Canada: Essence Publishing), 73, 91-92.

41   This section written by Tim Geysbeek.

42   For more information about SIM's work in each country mentioned in this section, in addition to the references given, see sources cited in the bibliogaphy and "Where You Can Serve," http://www.sim.org/index.php/webregion, accessed 4 March 2017.

43   Bruce E. C. Dipple, "A Missiological Evaluation of the History of the Sudan Interior Mission in French West Africa 1924–1962," (D.Miss. major project, Trinity Evangelical Divinity School, Deerfield, IL), 1994, 26–28; Rowland Bingham, "Through the Jungles of Africa by Motor Car," *The Evangelical Christian and Missionary Witness* 26, no. 3 (March 1930): 141–143; Edward Morrow, to Dear friends, March 1930 (Niger Box 17, Niger History 1924–1985).

44   Rowland Bingham, "From the Niger to the Nile," *The Evangelical Christian and Missionary Witness* 26, no. 5 (May 1930): 273–274, 317; other articles in issues 6–8, 10–11 of this periodical; Guy W. Playfair, *Our Trip across Africa* (Jos, Nigeria: Niger Press, 1930); T. A. Lambie, *Missionary Beginnings in Ethiopia (Abyssinia)* (n.p.: c. 1931), 10–11.

45   Rowland V. Bingham, "Airway or Mudway?: S-k-i-d-d-i-n-g along the Equator," *The Evangelical Christian and Missionary Witness* 26, no. 5 (May 1930): 453; Playfair, *Our Trip across Africa*, 11–13. This was a 1929 or 1930 Ford Model A Woody Station Wagon (Jon Shea email to T. Geysbeek, 25 May 2017).

46   Raymond J. Davis, *Fire on the Mountains* (Grand Rapids: Zondervan, 1966), 105–106, 146; F. Peter Cotterell, *Born at Midnight* (Chicago: Moody Press, 1973), 102.

47   South Sudan declared its independence from Sudan in 2011. At the time this book is being written, SIM's missionaries only work in South Sudan.

48   Lovering, "East Africa's Swinging Doors," *Africa Now* 103 (March–May 1979): 3–4; Patricia Porter, "War . . .and Peace," *Serving in Mission Together* 107 (2004): 14–15; "Evacuation from South Sudan" and "Remaining Team Evacuates from Doro, South Sudan," http://www.sim.org/index.php/content/sudan-prayer, accessed 10 March 2017; "Answering the Call," *SIM Global*, 141 (Winter 2014): 7; "SIM evacuates personnel amidst escalating crisis," https://web.archive.org/web/20140208203029/http://www.sim.org/index.php/content/evacuation-south-sudan-personnel, accessed 5 March 2017; "Entire SIM South Sudan team safely evacuated amidst unrest,"   http://sim.org/index.php/content/entire-sim-south-sudan-team-safely-evacuated-amidst-unrest, accessed 4 March 2017.

49   Hunter, *A Flame of Fire*, 203–204; *Root from Dry Ground: The Story of the Sudan Interior Mission* (Aylesbury, Bucks, England: Hazell Watson & Viney Ltd., c. 1966), 52–57; Fred D. Acord, *God Moves In* (Colorado Springs, CO, USA: Williams & Acord, c. 1972); Kerry Lovering, "'Harambee!' at Work," *SIMNOW* 16 (July–August 1984): 6–8; Helen Miller, *The Hardest Place: The Biography of Warren and Dorothy Modricker* (Belleville, Ontario, Canada: Guardian Books, 2006); Ahmed

Ali Haile, *Teatime in Mogadishu: My Journey as a Peace Ambassador in the World of Islam* (Harrisburg, VA: Herald Press, 2011), 30–40; Ruth Myors, *When the Lights Go Out: Memoir of a Missionary to Somalia* (Moreland, Australia: Acorn Press Ltd., 2016).

50   For example, John Cumbers. *Count It All Joy: Testimonies from a Persecuted Church* (Kearney, NE: Morris Publishing, 1995).

51   "Eritrea: A Nation is Born," *SIMNOW* (New Zealand edition) 63b (September–October 1993): 8–9; "Decamare: Orphanage for Boys!" *SIMNOW* (New Zealand edition) 63b (September–October 1993): 10.

52   Acord, *God Moves In*, 20–33; Jos Strengholt, *Gospel in the Air: 50 Years of Christian Witness through Radio in the Arab World* (Zoetermeer, 2008), 9–30; Len Salisbury, with Helen Salisbury, *War, Typhoons & the Gospel: Life long journey of two people surviving & thriving in Mission* (Sydney: FC Productions, 2016), 34–69.

53   Dipple, "A Missiological Evaluation," 40–42.

54   Major evacuations of SIM's missionaries in Liberia occurred in 1990, 1992, 1996, and 2003 during its civil war, and in 2014 during the Ebola crisis. For the war, see "Refugee Reprise" and other articles in *News & Notes for WAFA Folks* (December 1992): 1–4; Steve Befus, "The Final Days at ELWA," *Harvest* 5, no. 2 (Summer 1996): 1–2; Jon Shea, "Radio ELWA Turns 50: 'To God Be the Glory,'" *Serving in Mission Together* 106 (2004): 6. For Ebola, see Supplement 19.1, pages 296-299, and Kent and Amber Brantly and Nancy Sheppard's books in the bibliography, pages 434-435.

55   W. Harold Fuller, "Pioneer Advance," *SIMNOW* 101 (November–December 1981: 5–7; Leona Mason and Kerry Lovering, "Kingdom of Gold: Saying Yes to the King," *SIMNOW* 113 (March–April 1981): 2–8.

56   Stephen Neill, *A History of Christian Missions*, 2nd ed. (London: Penguin Books, 1991), 421; Edward R. Dayton, ed., *Mission Handbook: North American Protestant Missions Overseas* (Monrovia, CA: Missions Advanced Research and Communication Center, 1973), 84, 89.

57   "Champion moves to Abidjan," *Africa Now* 39 (July–August 1968): 13; "ELWA French department moves to Ivory Coast," *Africa Now* 69 (July–August 1973): 13.

58   "First SIM missionaries arrive in Guinea," *SIMNOW* 30 (November–December 1986): 12.

59   "The Modern World, 1970–1989," *SIMNOW* 61 (Winter 1992–1993): 13. SIM faculty taught at Fourah Bay College until the mid-1990s.

60   "Jesus Calling," *SIM Global* 141 (Winter 2014): 7.

61   For SIM's current work in each of these countries, see http://www.simusa.org/about/where-we-work/ and http://sim.org/where.

62   Closely adapted from James H. Hunter, *A Flame of Fire: The Life and Work of R. V. Bingham, Ll. D.* (Aslesbury and Slough: Hazell Watson & Viney Limited), 153–156. For his biography, see Sophie de la Haye, *Tread upon the Lion: The Story of Tommie Titcombe* (Ontario: Sudan Interior Mission, 1974).

63   Thanks to Don Stilwell who has engaged the author with discussions about the deaths of these missionaries over the years. The author does not regard any of the persons discussed in this supplement to have been "martyrs" in a narrow classical sense, persons who were specifically targeted for their beliefs (in this case, Christianity). Mitchell, Devers, and the Grieves were casualties of war. The motive for Hill's death is uncertain. Did the assassin kill Hill because he was a Christian, or was the killer deranged as some people speculated, or was there another

reason? Decades later we repeat the question that Hill asked - "Why?" Numerous believers who belong to churches related to SIM have been maryrtered because of their faith over the years. For example, Dimi evangelist Tekka Mikael was killed by one or more assailants while on an evangelistic tour near Gura, Ethiopia, in 1977. Rev. Julius Yako, his wife Rhoda, and their daughter Husseina were burned to death in Karshin Daji, Nigeria, in 2014.

64   Charles White, "Small Sacrifices," *Christianity Today* (22 June 1992): 32-33; White, "High Cost, High Privilege: Paying the High Price," *SIMNOW* 97 (2001): 6-7.

65   Paul Hudson, "Mortality Among Active SIMers," *SIM Health Newsnotes* 1,1 (February 1993): 1, and accompanying notes. Thanks to Dr. Hudson for providing this article and background material including a copy of White's article.

66   Stephen Hewlett, "The story of Cliff Mitchell: missionary to Abyssinia," 1994; Esme Ritchie Rice, *Eclipse in Ethiopia and its Corona Glory* (London: Marshall, Morgan & Scott Ltd), c. 1938, 83; Thomas A. Lambie, *A Doctor's Great Commission* (Wheaton, IL: Van Kampen Press), 1954, 246-248; Malcolm Forsberg, *Land Beyond the Nile* (New York: Harper Brothers, 1958), 85; Raymond J. Davis, *Fire on the Mountains* (Grand Rapids: Zondervan, 1966), 88-90; Albert E. Brant, *In the Wake of Martyrs: A Modern Saga in Ancient Ethiopia* (Langley, Canada: Omega Publications), 1992, 29.

67   Dr. Wendy James kindly informed the author of the letter Kenneth Oglesby wrote four days after the attack that provides this and other interesting details. For published accounts, see Mrs. C. K. Oglesby, "The Bombing at Doro," *Sudan Witness* 17, no. 1 (January 1941): 7–10; Thomas Lambie, *A Doctor Carries On* (Philadelphia: The Blakiston Company, 1942), 59–72.

68   Lloyd Stinson, "Report on the death of Dr. Douglas Hill," n.d., one-page typewritten report, SIMIAR, Hill biographical file.

Chapter 5: The Andes Evangelical Mission Story

1   Material in this section is excerpted with only minor changes from Marjory Koop, "George and Mary: Profile in Commitment," *SIMNOW* 25 January–February 1986): 8–10.

2   Material in this section is excerpted with only minor changes from Marjory Koop, "View from the Andes," *AFRICA NOW* 117 (November–December 1981): 8–9.

3   Many thanks to Barb and Darrell Hockersmith, Tim and Carol Kopp, Julie and Phil Parshall, Ed and Irene Welch, and John and Bene Wood for providing information about some of these schools (T. Geysbeek).

4   Material in this section is adapted with only minor changes from a 1985 Andes Area Report, SIM International Archives.

5   Adapted from Margarita Allan Hudspith, *Ripening Fruit* (Harrington Park, New Jersey: The Harrington Press, 1958), 52–55, 67.

6   Harold and Isabelle Walker, "Linguistics, Translation, and Literacy," *Africa Now* 111 (November–December 1980): 4; "Summary of SIM Bible Translation Work," SIMIAR, Box 596, File 11; Bruce Adams email to T.G., 31 August 2015; Bob Hay email to T.G., 4 September 2015.

7   (Maryknoll, NY: Orbis Books, 2009), 4–5.

8   Dotsie Corwin, "The King of the Beni," *Intercom* 130 (November–December 1997): 6, based on "His Life Proved," a pamphlet from the Bolivian Indian Mission on the life of Wally Heron. For a fuller treatment of Herron's life and work see *The Condor of the Andes*, by C. Peter Wagner and Joseph S. McCullough (Andes Evangelical Mission, 1966), and released in several countries in

other editions and years, sometimes under the title, *Condor of the Jungle*. For some of his letters and articles written by and about him, see Robert Herron, compiler, *Walter Herron: Pioneer Missionary to Bolivia* (n.p., c. 2010).

9   Adapted from James L. Hansen, *A Heart to Serve: Ordinary People with an Extraordinary God* (Cochabamba, Bolivia: Mision Andina Evangelica, 2007), 55–56.

Chapter 6: The International Christian Fellowship Story

1   Unless otherwise noted the material in this chapter is adapted from "Workers Together: The Story of the International Christian Fellowship," n.d.; ICF Box 01, CIGM Origin, History, Reports.

2   "The Annual Convention of the Poona and Indian Village Mission," *White Already to Harvest*, 8, no. 3 (March 1903): 36.

3   The name was changed in 1901 from "Indian" to "India" (W. H. Cherry, "A History of CIGM," in *Advancing Together: A Tale of Two Missions*, G. A. Hemming, ed. [London: International Christian Fellowship, c. 1974], 20).

4   *Witnessing . . .Unto this day: Ceylon and India General Mission, 1893–1943* (London, 1943).

5   An Indian administrative division formed by the union of Agra and Oudh that has been called Uttar Pradesh since 1950.

6   Ruth Tozer, "A Brief History of the First 100 Years of Ceylon and India General Mission and Poona and Indian Village Mission," typescript (1997), 9, SIMIAR, ICF Box 103.

7   Eurasian is an equivalent term to Aryan, and in the Indian context also implies a member of the ruling caste or Brahmins. This is a group from which few Christians in India have come, so his plea was most enticing.

8   Basil Tyson and Helen Rosan, "A History of P.I.V.M.," in *Advancing Together: A Tale of Two Missions*, G. A. Hemming, ed. (London: International Christian Fellowship, c. 1974), 38.

9   "Other Difficulties," *Darkness and Light* no. 1 (February 1894): 19; "Notes," *Darkenss and Light* no. 3 (March 1894): 25; "Notes," *Darkness and Light* no. 1 (April 1894): 37; "News from Ceylon," *Darkness and Light* no. 8 (August 1894): 87; V. D. David, "Address on Prayer," *Darkness and Light* no. 8 (August 1894): 96; "Our First Annual Meeting," *Darkness and Light* no. 12 (December 1894): 135.

10   "Rev. V. D. David," *Darkness and Light* 31, no. 2 (March-April 1924): 13. For more information about V. D. David, see Ian Welch, "TAMIL DAVID, The Tamil Evangelist. 'Vathakunu Deresegayam David,' (V. D. 'Eye of faith, God helps')," Working paper, 2014 draft, https://digitalcollections.anu.edu.au/bitstream/1885/11494/1/Welch%20Tamil%20David%202014.pdf, accessed 22 March 2017.

Chapter 7: The Africa Evangelical Fellowship Story

1   This material is adapted with minor changes from a major portion of "The Story Of The South Africa General Mission / Africa Evangelical Fellowship," an unpublished document in the SIMIAR by Ron Genheimer, 2003. It indicates that material for this history has been obtained and sometimes excerpted from the following: Alan Huntingford, *History of the Southern Field*, (n.p., c. 1991); "History of the Fellowship," *Guide to Daily Prayer* (AEF, 1993); Winona Ingles, "Called Into Light," (manuscript, 1966); James G. Kallam, "A History of the Africa Evangelical Fellowship from its Inception to 1917," (Ph.D. diss., New York University, 1978); "The Story of the South Africa General Mission," *On Trek* 19, no. 5, (1945). Photos and captions added.

2 Joshua Dhube, *The Association of United Baptist Churches of Zimbabwe Commonly called United Baptist Church of Zimbabwe (UBC) Celebrating 100 years of Gospel Witness (1897–1997)* (n.p., c. 1997), 5.

3 Rowland Bingham, "The Making of a Mission: The Story of the Sudan Interior Mission," *The Evangelical Christian* 29, no. 1 (January 1933): 36.

4 T. Geysbeek's emails with Tim Kopp, 13 May 2017, and Barbara Hockersmith, 19 May 2017.

5 Dr. Kallam was the chairman of AEF's International Board. He published this under the title "Martha Storr Osborn-Howe: A Life of Energy and Zeal," *Intercom* 135 (September–October, 1998): 4. See also Martha Osborn-Howe, *By Fire and Cloud* (London: Hodder and Stoughton, 1894).

Chapter 8: The Abyssinian Frontiers Mission Merger (1927)

1 Adapted from Gary Corwin, "Abyssinia and the Antipodes," *SIM USA News* (July 1993): 3, 5.

2 Rowland Bingham, "The Objective Realized," *The Evangelical Christian* 23, no. 3 (March 1927): 314.

3 Rowland Bingham, "Entering Ethiopia with Christ," *The Evangelical Christian* 32, no. 6 (June 1936): 226.

4 Ibid.

5 Ibid.

6 Ibid., 227.

7 R. V. Bingham, to Mr. G. Playfair, 8 November 1917, PC-1, Box 169.

8 Chris Ferrier, interview with Kay Herring, Sebring, January 1971 (MM-2, Box 159, File 6.14). See also Albert Helser, "We Must Advance," *Africa Now* 5 (April–June 1960): 15; "Beyond the Vision," *SIMNOW* 61 (Winter 1992): 8.

9 "Baloté Amalo, Ethiopia, Wolaitta Kale Heywet Church," http://www.dacb.org/stories/ethiopia/balote_aymalo.html, accessed 23 May 2017, and reproduced in its entirety from the *Dictionary of African Christian Biography*. Sources: Personal information from Baloté Aymalo; E. Paul Balisky, "Wolaitta Evangelists: A Study in Religious Innovation in Southern Ethiopia, 1937–1975," Ph.D. thesis, University of Aberdeen, 1997, 236–238; Raymond Davis, *Fire on the Mountains* (Chicago: Moody Press, 1966), 196–206. Dr. Paul Balisky is a former lecturer at the Ethiopian Graduate School of Theology, a *DACB* Participating Institution. "The Dictionary stimulates local data gathering and input. As a non-proprietary electronic database, it constitutes a uniquely dynamic way to maintain, amend, expand, access, and disseminate information vital to an understanding of African Christianity. Being non-proprietary, it is possible for material within it to be freely reproduced locally in printed form. Being electronic, the material is simultaneously accessible to readers around the world." Dr. Jonathan Bonk, director, September 2, 2013.

10 Raymond J. Davis, *Fire on the Mountains* (Grand Rapids: Zondervan, 1966), 88.

11 Ibid., 107.

12 Ibid.

13 Ibid., 115–116.

14 Ibid., 245–247.

15 Ruth A. Tucker, *From Jerusalem to Irian Jaya: A Biographical History of Christian Missions*, 2nd ed. (Grand Rapids: Zondervan, 2004), 345.

16 John Cumbers, *Count It All Joy: Testimonies from a Persecuted Church* (Kearney, NE: Morris Publishing, 1995), 251.

17   "Mulu Meja, Kale Heywet Church, Ethiopia," http://www.dacb.org/stories/ethiopia/mulu-meja.
      html, accessed 23 May 2017, and reproduced in its entirety from the *Dictionary of African
      Christian Biography*. Sources: 1) Teshome Amare, son-in-law of Judge Mulu Meja, facilitated
      the collecting of biographical information including a detailed response by Shitaye Galore, wife
      of Judge Mulu Meja; 2) Girum Molla, "Believer and Politician: The Life and Testimony of Mulu
      Meja," a term paper presented to the Ethiopian Graduate School of Theology for the course,
      "Church and State," 2008. This article received in 2013, was written by Dr. Paul Balisky, a former
      lecturer at the Ethiopian Graduate School of Theology, a *DACB* Participating Member.

Chapter 9: The West African Broadcasting Association Merger (1952)

1   Jos M. Strengholt, *Gospel in the Air: 50 Years of Christian Witness through Radio in the Arab
      World* (Zoetermeer: Boekencentrum, 2008), 273, from an unpublished document by Merle A.
      Steely, "The Founding of ELWA in 1950," 2003.
2   Strengholt, *Gospel in the Air*, 274.
3   Timothy Stoneman, "Radio Missions: Station ELWA in West Africa," *International Bulletin of
      Missionary Research* 36, no. 4 (October 2012): 200–201.
4   Steely, "The Founding of ELWA," cited in Strengholt, *Gospel in the Air*, 276.
5   Orbra Bliss in an email to the author [Stoneman], 1 May 2004; Abe Thiessen, "The Beginnings
      of ELWA," 3; Jane Reed and Jim Grant, *Voice Under Every Palm: The Story of Radio Station ELWA*
      (Grand Rapids: Zondervan, 1968), 33–34; cited in Strengholt, *Gospel in the Air*, 236–237.
6   Steely, "The Founding of ELWA," cited in Strengholt, *Gospel in the Air*, 277.
7   Ibid., 277–278.
8   Thiessen, "The Beginnings of ELWA," cited in Strengholt, *Gospel in the Air*, 2.
9   Excerpted from Timothy Stoneman, "Radio Missions," 201–202. Used with permission. All
      of the following endnotes are renumbered from the original document. Photos and captions
      added.
10   Herschel Ries to Abe Thiesen, 1 July 1955, Folder 25, Box 19, Collection 86, and Ries to Hank
      Voss and Tom Gilmer, 28 October 1955, Folder 35, Box 19, Collection 86, BGCA [Billy Graham
      Center Archives]. See also "Review of Technical Department Activities, September 1954–1955,"
      Correspondence (1966–67), Box 23, Engineering and Audience Survey, Liberia Collection, SIM
      (henceforth LC-SIM), Fort Mill, SC.
11   "Statistics—November 1, 1955," Statistical Reports and Correspondence (1955–1972), Box 24,
      Audience Survey, LC-SIM.
12   "First Short Wave Broadcast—March 14, 1955," Fifteenth Anniversary (1969), Box 14,
      Broadcast Division; and "Review of Technical Department Activities, September 1954–1955,"
      Correspondence (1966–1967), Box 23, Engineering and Audience Survey, LC-SIM.
13   R. G. de la Haye to Abe Thiessen, 27 August 1957, Folder 26, Box 33, Collection 86, BGCA.
      Languages included Arabic, Bassa, Belle, English, Fanti, French, Fula, Gio, Konobo, Kpelle, Kru,
      Maninka, Mende, Putu, Sabo, Tchien, Twarbo, Twi, and Vai ("List of Languages Heard over
      ELWA During 1955," Beginnings [1956–1969] Folder, Box 14, Broadcast Division, LC-SIM).
14   "Report on African Languages Department—ELWA," undated, Newspaper Clippings—Press
      Releases (1969--1982) Folder, Box 1, Liberia Information; and Edwin Kayea, "Programming—
      The Station's View," undated, Testimonies Folder, Box 24, Audience Survey, LC-SIM.

15   "Report on African Languages Department—ELWA."

16   "Dialect Broadcasters Visiting Up Country," *Listener*, 24 December 1964; "Mr. Robert Grear, Krahn Broadcaster," *Liberian Age*, 28 December 1964; and "Dialect Broadcasters Tour Listening Posts," 1964, all in Newspaper Clippings—Press Releases (1961–1965) Folder, Box 1, Liberia Information, LC-SIM.

17   Press release, "Radio ELWA Increases Coverage in French-Speaking West Africa," 7 June 1971, Newspaper Clippings—Press Releases (1969–1982) Folder, Box 1, Liberia Information, LC-SIM.

18   John L. Cooper, Commissioner of Communications and Aeronautics, to William Watkins, 14 February 1951, Documents—Correspondence (1951–1994) Folder, Box 4, Important Documents; and Dick Reed, "Report for Mr. Darroch," 30 May 1955, Newspaper Clippings (1951–1960) Folder, Box 1, Liberia Information, LC-SIM. See also Alhaji G. V. Kromah, "The Utilisation of Broadcasting for National Development in Liberia," in *Making Broadcasting Useful: The African Experience*, ed. George Wedell (Manchester: Manchester University Press, 1986), 200.

19   The complete list includes the Booker Washington Institute, Bureau of Fundamental Education, Bureau of Immigration and Naturalization, Bureau of Information, Department of Defense, Department of National Defense, Department of Public Instruction, Department of Public Works and Utilities, Department of State, House of Representatives, Liberian Senate, National Police Force, National Public Health Service, Post Office, Supreme Court, Treasury Department, Customs Office, and University of Liberia ("Here is some interesting information for your files, Ray," 25 February 1958, Newspaper Clippings [1951–1960] Folder, Box 1, Liberia Information, LC-SIM).

20   "Radio Station ELWA Annual Report (1954)," Director's Annual Reports (1960–1980) Folder, Box 15, Broadcasting Division, LC-SIM.

21   William S. Tubman to Ray de la Haye, 18 January 1964, Public Information Office—Publication Reviews (1964–1969) Folder, Box 13, Administration, LC-SIM.

22   The station fell prey to the civil war that broke out in Liberia in 1990, which disrupted its transmission capabilities.

Chapter 10: The Andes Evangelical Mission Merger (1982)

1   This material is adapted with minor changes from Marjory Koop, "View from the Andes," *AFRICA NOW* 117 (November–December 1981), 9; and Koop, "Historic Moment," *SIMNOW* 1 (January–February 1982): 3–4.

2   While the merger produced no immediate change in the administrative structure in South America, it did produce change in the UK. The UK section of AEM opted out of the merger with SIM and merged instead with what became the Latin Link. Mary Evans, who at the time was involved with the Evangelical Union of South America, a significant part of Latin Link, mentioned in an email to the author (13 April 2015) her belief that they thought SIM's lack of experience in Latin America was a key issue.

3   This material is adapted with minor changes from Ian Hay, "The Mechanics of Merger," *SIMNOW* 1 (January–February 1982): 5.

Chapter 11: The Life Challenge Merger

1   The section was originally adapted from material in "South Africa: Life Challenge mission merges with SIM," *SIMNOW* 26 (March–April 1986): 13; and "History and Development of Life Challenge Africa," unpublished manuscript by Walter Eric, 2007. It has benefited greatly, however, from significant editing by Sandy Willcox and Ruth Craill who were actually part of the merger process—Ruth on council before and after the merger, and Sandy, both as part of the merger and a member of council when the changes happened. Note: since this chapter has been written, Gerhard Nehls and Walter Eric published *Life is a Challenge more so in Africa: The Story of Gerhard Nehls and Life Challenge* (Nairobi: Life Challenge, 2016).

Chapter 12: The International Christian Fellowship Merger (1989)

1   *Intercom* 81 (January 1988): 1–3.
2   "International Christian Fellowship to merge with SIM International," *SIMNOW* 41 (September–October 1988): 10.
3   Ian M. Hay, "SIM in Asia: Facing New Challenges," *SIMNOW* 43 (January–February 1989): 3.

Chapter 13: The Africa Evangelical Fellowship Merger (1988)

1   *Action Africa* 12, no. 3 (September–December 1998): 3.
2   "AEF and SIM Join Hands," *Intercom* (September–October 1998): 1.

Chapter 14: Major Developments and Trends

1   Significant additional detail on AEF's expansion is not included here because it is already outlined by decades in chapter 7. Considerable research would need to be done to include all the important things which have happened over the years in all the missions.
2   "Wanted, Wings for the Evangel," *The Sudan Witness Supplement* 2, no. 6 (November 1949): 3.
3   The author wishes to express special thanks to Doug Christensen, David Dryer, and Gordon Stanley for extensive helpful input on this and other SIM governance and corporate issues during the last 25 years.
4   "The Intrepid Women of SIM," *SIMNOW* (Summer 1995): 3. See the related item on Martha Storr Osborn at the end of chapter 7 for the story of another very "intrepid woman."
5   "Look What We Missed!" *Intercom* 62 (May 1984): 6.
6   This material is from Jon Shea, "It's Dangerous Near the Edge," *Intercom* 124 (August–October 1996): 1–2.
7   These three men were Steve Kejr, Dr. Steve Befus, and Randy Wildman. These were the same men who remained on the ELWA campus in 1992 after all of the other missionaries evacuated.

Chapter 15: Debates about "Self-Government" in SIM and the Emergence of Denominations

1   Andrew E. Barnes, *Global Christianity and the Black Atlantic: Tuskegee, Colonialism, and the Shaping of African Industrial Education* (Waco, TX: Baylor University Press, 2017), xi.
2   Bengt Sundkler and Christopher Steed, *A History of the Church in Africa* (Cambridge: Cambridge University Press, 2000), 115–116.

3   Brian L. Fargher, *The Origins of the New Churches Movement in Southern Ethiopia, 1927–1944* (Leiden, Neth.: E. J. Brill, 1996), 32.

4   Gowans (Lagos), to Dear Mother (Toronto), n.d., SIMIAR, BM-1, Box 10a.

5   Andrew Ross, "Christian Missions and the Mid-Nineteenth-Century Change in Attitudes to Race: The African Experience," in *Imperial Horizons of British Protestant Missions, 1880–1914*, Andrew Porter, ed. (Grand Rapids: Eerdmans, 2003), 94–96; Bingham, *Seven Sevens of Years and Jubilee: The Story of the Sudan Interior Mission*, 5th ed. (New York: Evangelical Publishers, 1957), 27. Gowans (Lagos), to My Dear Mother (Toronto), 6 January 1894, SIMIAR, BM-1, Box 10a; E. A. Ayandele, *The Missionary Impact on Northern Nigeria, 1842-1914: A Political and Social Analysis* (London: Longmans, 1966), 194-201; Lamin Sanneh, *West African Christianity: The Religious Impact* (Maryknoll, NY: Orbis Books), 1983, 174-176; C. P. Williams, *The Ideal of the Self-Governing Church: A Study in Victorian Missionary Strategy* (Leiden, Neth.: E. J. Brill, 1990).

6   "Self-Extension, Self-Support and Self-Government in Missionary Churches," *The Missionary Witness* 4, no. 4 (7 April 1908): 54–55.

7   Ross, "Christian Missions," 97–98; Jeffery Cox, *The British Missionary Enterprise since 1700* (New York: Routledge, 2010), 78–79, 166–168, 210–211.

8   "A Revolutionary Article," *The Missionary Witness* 4, no. 4 (7 April 1908): 50.

9   "The Negro," *The Evangelical Christian and Missionary Witness*, 8 no. 3 (March 1911): 65. No author is credited for this article. Bingham was the editor of the periodical when this was published, which minimally means that he agreed the article should be published. (The assumption is that editors are the authors of unauthored articles published in periodicals they edit.) The author mentioned the Church Missionary Society and Rev. Mojola Agbebi, both that were well-known to Bingham. These factors strongly argue for Bingham's authorship, or at least his input, in the article. Agbebi was one of the most important pastors in Lagos who promoted ecclesiastical nationalism. He pastored a church under the auspices of the American Southern Baptists for years, but broke away from the mission church to establish the Native Baptist Church in 1888 (Ayandele, *The Missionary Impact*, 198–201).

10   Clarence Duff, *Cords of Love: A Pioneer Mission to Ethiopia* (Phillipsburg, NJ: Presbyterian and Reformed Publishing Co., 1980), 263–271; Fargher, *Origins*, 44-45.

11   "Self-Propagation of the Gospel," *Sudan Witness* 5, no. 3 (November–December 1932): 3–5.

12   Bingham (Toronto), to Beacham (Jos), 14 December 1932, SIMIAR, CB-3, Box 19, Beacham, C. G., 1922–1935.

13   Beacham (Jos), to Bingham (Toronto), 13 February 1933, SIMIAR, CB-3, Box 19, Beacham, C. G., 1922–1935. Rev. Dr. Barje S. Maigadi of ECWA calls this the "policy of non-self-governing" (*Divisive Ethnicity in the Church in Africa* [Kaduna, Nigeria: Baraka Press and Publishers Ltd., 2006], 117–118).

14   "The Power of the Local Church in World Evangelism," *The Evangelical Christian and Missionary Witness* 17, no. 7 (July 1921): 206–208.

15   Alfred Roke, *An Indigenous Church in Action* (Auckland: Scott & Scott Ltd., 1938), 8–9.

16   Bingham (Toronto), to Dear Fellow-Worker, 15 November 1938, SIMIAR, Bingham Circulars, 1913–1942; AM-2, Box 4b; Roke, *They Went Forth*, 183–192, 258–259, 311–406. Playfair and Beacham said Roke's position was "very extreme." In 1947, Beacham publicly accused Roke of, among other things, being disloyal and overemphasizing indigeneity. Roke eventually resigned,

believing Beacham leveled unjust accusations against him (Roke, *They Went Forth*, 183–188, 258–259, 311–406). For widely differing views that many of SIM's missionaries in Nigeria and Ethiopia had with regard to each other's "church-planting policy," see Fargher (*Origins*, 52) and Roke (*They Went Forth*, 184, 350–351).

17   *Self-Extension, Self-Support and Self-Government in Missionary Churches* (Toronto: Evangelical Publishers, 1939), SIMIAR, BM-1, Box 11.

18   *The S.I.M. Handbook* (Jos: Niger Press, 1939), 40–41; *The Principles and Practice of the Sudan Interior Mission* (Toronto: Evangelical Publishers, c. 1921), 12–13; Fargher, *Origins*, 52–53; Roke, *They Went Forth*, 329–330.

19   Yusufu Turaki, *Theory and Practice of Christian Missions in Africa: A Century of SIM/ECWA History and Legacy in Nigeria, 1893–1993* (Nairobi, Kenya: International Bible Society Africa, 1999), 483. For more information in his *Theory and Practice*, see chapter 15 ("Mission Indigenization Policy") and chapter 16 ("Mission Indigenous Church"), 481–592.

20   For an article about Pastor Zamfara, see "Christian Chief of a Pagan Tribe," *Africa Now* 16 (January–March 1963): 8.

21   Turaki, *Theory and Practice*, 489, 525–526, 614.

22   Turaki, *Theory and Practice*, 490. For discussions of the ways SIM missionaries' paternalistic attitudes stifled higher theological education and limited Africans' role in church governance in the Nigerian, Nigerien, and Ethiopian contexts into the 1950s, see Turaki, *Theory and Practice*, 272–285, 489–490; Barbara M. Cooper, *Evangelical Christians in the Muslim Sahel* (Bloomington: Indiana University Press, 2006), 183–223; and Tibebe Eshete, "The Sudan Interior Mission (SIM) in Ethiopia (1928–1970)," *Northeast African Studies* 6, no. 3 (1999): 47–50.

23   Turaki, *Theory and Practice*, 514.

24   David Maxwell, "Decolonization," in *Missions and Empire*, Norman Etherington, ed. (Oxford: Oxford University Press, 2007), 294–296.

25   Turaki, *Theory and Practice*, 514–515, 526–527.

26   Turaki, *Theory and Practice*, 514–515, 525–526; W. Paul Todd, "The Attitudes of the Evangelical Church of West Africa (ECWA) towards Islam in light of ethnic and religious violence" (Ph.D. diss., Queens University of Belfast, 2010), 181; D. I. Olatayo, *ECWA: The Root, Birth, and Growth* (Ilorin: Ocare Publications, 1993), 21.

27   Turaki, *Theory and Practice*, 490, 537–540. Two years earlier, SIM registered this group of congregations in what was called the "SIM Churches" (Turaki, *Theory and Practice*, 537). SIM's missionaries primarily view ECWA's creation as "part of the natural maturing process" of SIM's long-held beliefs in self-government while recognizing the significance of nationalism (W. Harold Fuller, *Mission-Church Dynamics: How to change bicultural tensions into dynamic missionary outreach* [Pasadena, CA: William Carey Library, 1980], 193–201; Ian M. Hay, "A Study of the Relationship between SIM International and the Evangelical Missionary Society" [D.Miss. diss., Trinity Evangelical Divinity School, Deerfield, IL, 1984], 148–154; Todd, "Attitudes," 181, n. 497). Nigerians put the onus of SIM's indigenization program on its fears about nationalism and the rise of Islam (Todd, "Attitudes," 181, n. 497; Olatayo, *ECWA*, 21.)

28   Turaki, *Theory and Practice*, 556.

29   For example, see Fuller, *Mission-Church Dynamics*, 198–228; Turaki, *Theory and Practice*, 483, 489–490, 514–527, 542–543, 614; Maigadi, *Divisive Ethnicity*, 117–118, 140–145.

30   Turaki, *Theory and Practice*, 282, 285. The school at Igbaja became known as Igbaja Seminary, and, later, ECWA Theological Seminary.

31   "Happy Problem: how to invest $15,000," *Africa Now* 58 (September–October 1971): 4; Fargher, *Origins*, 299.

32   "Scholarship program prepares Church/Mission leaders," *Africa Now* 50 (May–June 1980): 5.

33   "An interview with Dr. Albert D. Helser," *Africa Now* 12 (January–March 1962): 4.

34   Albert Helser, "Calling You!," *Africa Now* 7 (October–December 1960): 15. Helser earned his Ph.D. in education at Columbia University under the tutelage of pioneering anthropologist Franz Boas. Boas taught that differences between peoples were attributed to cultural and social factors, not biological ones. The latter rendering posited that fixed characteristics passed down from one generation to the next in each supposed race. Boaz thus argued against so-called scientific racism that was prevalent in North America and Western Europe at the time (Shobana Shankar, "Race, Ethnicity, and Assimilation: The Influence of American Anthropology on Christian-Muslim Relations in British Northern Nigeria," *Social Sciences and Missions* 29 [2016]: 37-55; James T. Campbell, *Middle Passages: African American Journeys to Africa, 1787-2005* [New York: Penguin Books, 2007], 193). Further research will ascertain if Helser, who joined SIM in 1936 and became its general director twenty-one years later, was a modernizing influence to his missionary colleagues who had imbibed much of Social Darwinism.

35   Bruce E. C. Dipple, "A Missiological Evaluation of the History of the Sudan Interior Mission in French West Africa 1924–1962," (D.Miss. Major Project, Trinity Evangelical Divinity School, Deerfield, IL), 1994, 73–74; Cooper, *Evangelical Christians*, 220–223.

36   Haruun L. Runn, "Paper on the S.I.C. History Presented to the Pan-Africa Fellowship of S.I.M.-Related Churches" (June 1981): 3, SIMIAR, Sudan Box 19, File 4.

37   Dipple, "A Missiological Evaluation," 80.

38   "Christ feels perfectly at home in Africa," *Africa Now* 45 (July–August 1969): 15.

39   John Cumbers, *Count It All Joy: Testimonies from a Persecuted Church* (Kearney, NE: Morris Publishing, 1995), 20; Erik Egeland, *Christianity, Generation and Narrative: Religious Conversion and Change in Sidama, Ethiopia, 1974–2012* (Uppsala, Swed.: Uppsala University, 2016), 46, n. 116.

40   "Funnel fillers—rejoice!" *Africa Now* 58 (September–October 1971): 13. Davis is the person kneeling in the second row on the far left in the photo taken in 1954 when ECWA was founded (Photo 15.5, page 192.)

41   The Eritrean KHC effectively became autonomous in 1975 after SIM's missionaries evacuated ("Kale Kiwot Church of Eritrea," brochure, 1996, SIMIAR, Library, Countries, SIM—Eritrea).

42   Benjamin L. Hegeman, *Between Shame and Glory: A Historical and Systematic Study of Education and Leadership Training Models among the Baatonu in North Benin* (Zoetermeer: Uitgeverij Boekencentrum, 2001), 239; Colin S. McDougall and Edna M. McDougall, *Acceptable Costs: Planting the Church in Dahomey, 1947 to 1975* (Eugene, OR: Wipf & Stock Publishers, 2005), 201.

43   "Country Profiles: Togo," http://sim.org/index.php/country/TG, accessed 5 September 2016.

44   "Welcome to the Evangelical Church of Liberia," http://www.ecoliberia.org/, accessed 6 June 2016.

45   "Byang Kato" obituary, *Africa Now* 85 (March–April 1976): 7; Sophie de la Haye, *Byang Kato: Ambassador for Christ* (Achimota, Ghana: Africa Christian Press), 1986. For a recent overview of Kato's legacy, see Mark Noll and Carolyn Nystrom, *Clouds of Witnesses: Christian Voices from Africa and Asia* (Downers Grove, IL: IVP Books, 2011), 80–96. For a more critical assessment of

Kato, see Kwame Bediako, *Theology and Identity: The Impact of Culture on Christian Thought in the Second Century and Modern Africa* (Oxford: Regnum Books, 1992), chapter 10.

46 "Review Article: Evangelical Theology in Africa: Byang Kato's Legacy," *Trinity Journal* 1, no. 1 (Spring 1980): 33–34.

47 AEAM is now known as the Association of Evangelicals in Africa (AEA).

48 The sources for this supplement are: "Evangelicals Strengthen Theology Base," *Africa Now* 90 (January–February 1977): 11; "African Evangelicals Stress Biblical Base," *Africa Now* 95 (November–December 1977): 10; "ACTEA Accredits 5 Theological Schools," *Africa Now* 103 (March–May 1979): 11; "East Africa Base for Bowers," *Intercom* 49 (September 1981): 5; "Niger: ACTEA Accredits First Francophone School," *Africa Now* 114 (May–June 1981): 11; Paul Bowers, "SIMTIA and All That," *Intercom* 71 (January 1986): 3; Paul Bowers' email correspondence with T. Geysbeek (22 April 2017, 25 April 2017), and http://www.acteaweb.org/ and http://www.icete-edu.org/ (both accessed on 18 May 2017).

49 For more information about this event, see Ian M. Hay, "Report: Pan-Africa consultation," *Intercom* 49 (September 1981): 1.

50 "SIM-related churches form pan-Africa fellowship," *Africa Now* 116 (September–October 1981): 12; Ian Hay, "Report: Pan-Africa consultation," 1–3; Ian Hay, *The Master Plan* (Toronto: SIM USA, Inc., 2000), 115–125.

51 In 2002, SIM reported that there were 14,954 "fully organized churches," 3,893 "developing churches and preaching points," and 4,746 "evangelistic Bible studies" for all of its related churches in Asia, Africa, and South America. This translated into 6,466,189 "baptized members" and 9,237,473 persons who attended services at churches and preaching points (International Resource Center, "SIM Profiles of Ministries, People, Countries, and Bi-Annual Statistics," typescript, 2000, SIMIAR Spec BV 2105 S56 P7 2000). The Ethiopia Kale Heywet Church claims to have over 8,600 churches and a membership of about eight million people ("Ethiopian Kale Heywet Church," http://www.ekhc.net/, accessed 10 June 2017). ECWA, based out of Nigeria, claims to have over 6,000 churches, two and one half million adult members, and nearly five million attendees ("Evangelical Church Winning All [ECWA]," http://www.ecwausa.org/?page_id=28, accessed 10 June 2017).

52 "Evangel Fellowship International Conference," *SIMNOW* 95 (2001): 1–5.

53 W. Harold Fuller, "Evangel Fellowship Emphasizes Missions," *Intercom* 86 (April 1989): 4–5.

54 "Asia and Eritrea Send First Delegates to Evangel Fellowship Meeting in Burkina Faso," *SIMNOW* 63 (Summer 1993): 8.

55 Howard Brant, "SIM and Related Churches Unite for Cross-Cultural Missions," *Intercom* 122 (April–May 1996): 2.

Chapter 16: Issues of Race and Diversity

1 I thank Ken Baker, W. Harold Fuller, Tami Geysbeek, Juan Goodsen, Ian Hay, Don Hall, Carmen Imes, David Park, Ben Pillay, Carol Plueddemann, Jim Plueddemann, Dwight Simmons, Don Stilwell, Tony Weedor, Elizabeth Fahn-Weedor, and especially Gary Corwin and Cate O'Brien for insightful feedback they provided on this and/or an earlier paper that helped me rethink, clarify, and sharpen this chapter. Discussions with Rev. Philip Nelson have also been helpful. The findings and weaknesses of this chapter are mine, and do not represent the official position of SIM.

2   Wilber Harr,"The Negro as an American Protestant Missionary in Africa" (Ph.D. diss., University of Chicago, 1946), 177.

3   *Divided by Faith: Evangelical Religion and the Problem of Race in America* (Oxford: Oxford University Press, 2000), 9.

4   In 1914, 58.1% of SIM's 31 missionaries came from North America: twelve (38.7%) from Canada and six (19.4%) from the United States. Ten (32.3%) British missionaries (eight English, two Scots) represented the next largest block, followed by one (3.2% each) Swiss, Swedish American, and Australian. Hence, all but two of SIM's first generation of missionaries were Anglo-North American (West Africa Yearbook, 1901–1928, 1914, SIMIAR, ME-1, Box 156). In 1933, after writing that he, Walter Gowans, and Tom Kent respectively originated from Scotland, England, and the United States, Rowland Bingham wrote:

> God has kept that principle of "supernationalism," through the power of the Spirit, alive and ever increasingly triumphant in the Spirit of love until this present. This was manifest in the past year, when of the thirty-one missionaries sent to the field, one was born in South Africa and educated in the United States; another was born in Greece; a third an Armenian; a fourth a Swiss lady; the next three from New Zealand and one from Australia; Britain mingled English and Scotch in its quota, and two were added from Ireland; then Canada came with a group of six, while in the record balance from the United States there were blended as great a variety of ancestry from Scandinavia, Germany, and Anglo-Saxondom as ever intermingled. All were welcomed on the field as members of one holy, happy family—all one in Christ Jesus. . . . The ties that bound the first trio together forty years ago in launching the pioneer effort to reach the Sudan have bound all the additions since ("First Lessons in Faith," *The Evangelical Christian* 29, no. 2 [February 1933]: 97–98).

In 1943, 80% of SIM's 426 missionaries came from North America: 230 or 54% were from the United States and 113 or 26.5% from Canada. The others were British (60, 14.8%), Australians (20, 4.7%), New Zealanders (two, .05%), Danes (two, .05%) and South Africans (one, .02%) ("S.I.M. Missionaries as of 31 December 1943, SIMIAR, MM-3,4 Box 162, File 2). Of SIM's 987 active missionaries in 1983, 74% were from the United States (551, or 55.8%) and Canada (178, 18%). The others originated from Australia (73, 7.4%), the United Kingdom (71, 7.2%), New Zealand (43, 4.3%), Switzerland (40, 4%), Northern Europe (18, 1.8%), East Asia (10, 1%), and South Africa (three, .3%) (SIMIAR, SIM International Council 1990, Personnel).

5   Bruce Hall, *A History of Race in Muslim West Africa, 1600–1960* (Cambridge: Cambridge University Press, 2011), 6. For shifting notions of what it has meant to be "white" and markers of other socially defined "races" around the globe, see: Colin Kidd, *The Forging of Races: Race and Scripture in the Protestant Atlantic World, 1600-2000* (Cambridge: Cambridge University Press, 2006); Nell Irvin Painter, *The History of White People* (New York: W.W. Norton & Company, 2010).

6   Many of the archival materials used are council minutes, and then only to the early 1970s. Further work would entail fieldwork, research in records that are closer to where SIM's missionaries originated and went, and in-depth reading in the vast secondary literature on race and identity. (At a future date, the author hopes to develop many of the themes only presented here in a cursory way.) With the exception of some statistics, emails generated in the course of this research, and

an unpublished manuscript, information about the last quarter century with regard to SIM's history only comes from published or publicly available sources. For the modern period, see Allie Schwaar's forthcoming dissertation being written at the University of Edinburgh's Centre for the Study of World Christianity. Her working title is "SIM—Strengthened through Diversity? An examination of the origins and effects of cultural diversity within a multi-national Christian Mission Agency, 1975–2015."

7   This section is a revision of a paper titled "Examining Race in the Sudan Interior Mission: Mr. and Mrs. J. Ulysis Turner and the Years of Toleration, 1893 – c. 1918" that the author presented at the African Studies Association meeting held in San Francisco, CA, on 19 November 2010.

8   Toyin Falola and Matthew Heaton, *A History of Nigeria* (Cambridge: Cambridge University Press, 2008), 93–95.

9   Andrew C. Ross, "Christian Missions and the Mid-Nineteenth Century Change in Attitudes to Race: The African Experience," in *The Imperial Horizons of British Protestant Missions, 1880–1914*, Andrew Porter, ed. (Grand Rapids: Eerdmans, 2003), 86–89, 94; Jennifer Snow, *Protestant Missions, Asian Immigrants, and Ideologies of Race in America, 1850–1924* (New York: Routledge, 2006), 3, 53.

10   Jeffery Cox, *The British Missionary Enterprise since 1700* (New York: Routledge, 2010), 39–41, 120, 175–179; Brian Stanley, "From 'the poor heathen' to 'the glory and honour of all nations': Vocabularies of Race and Custom in Protestant Missions, 1844–1928," *International Bulletin of Missionary Research* 34, no. 1 (January 2010): 3–4; Ross, "Christian Missions," 87–93.

11   Bolivian Indian Mission founder George Allan explained what he felt was the connection between Christianity, civilization, and white superiority this way: "The cleanliness and healthiness of Anglo-Saxon peoples are directly traceable to the propagation of a pure Gospel, which is also a Gospel of purity, among them. The dirt and disease of Roman Catholic lands is traceable as directly to their lack of the Gospel" ("Why Do They Die?" *The Bolivian Indian* 1, 5th year [January 1915]: 9–10).

12   Cox, *The British Missionary*, 198–212, 237.

13   On missionary racism, see Cox, *The British Missionary*, 120; Stanley, "From 'the poor heathen,'" 3–4; and Snow, *Protestant Missionaries*, 18, 24.

14   Effie Varley, "Extracts from Letters," 28 October 1926 or 1927, SIMIAR, Varley biographical file.

15   Andrew E. Barnes, "'Evangelization where it is not wanted': Colonial Administrators and Missionaries in Northern Nigeria During the First Third of the Twentieth Century," *Journal of Religion in Africa* 25 (1995): 423, 412–441; Shobana Shankar, *Who Shall Enter Paradise: Christian Origins in Muslim Northern Nigeria, ca. 1890–1975* (Athens: Ohio University Press, 2014), 32–33.

16   *Stories from Miango* (Belfast: Graham & Heslip, Ltd., c. 1937), 4.

17   Adrian Hastings, *The Church in Africa, 1450–1950* (Oxford: Clarendon Press, 1994), 304–305.

18   Rowland Bingham, *Seven Sevens of Years and a Jubilee: The Story of the Sudan Interior Mission*, 5th ed. (New York: Evangelical Publishers, 1957), 9–13; Bingham, *The Burden of the Sudan: The Story of the Sudan Interior Mission* (Brooklyn, NY: Sudan Interior Mission, 1918), SIMIAR, 5, SD-1, Box 182a; Gowans (Lagos) to Dear Mother (Toronto), 11 or 18 December 1893, SIMIAR, BM-2, Box 13. For the song, see chapter 2, page 32.

19   Hastings, *The Church*, 299.

20   Rowland Bingham, "Except a Corn of Wheat . . .Die," *The Evangelical Christian and Missionary Witness* (*TECMW*) 11, no. 12 (December 1915): 367; Brian Stanley, "Conversion to Christianity:

the colonization of the mind?" *International Review of Mission* 92 (2003): 328–329; Todd Thompson, *Norman Anderson and the Christian Mission to Modernize Islam* (Oxford: Oxford University Press, forthcoming). Such an idea, which includes the sense of rivalry, is a precursor of present-day theories of the "clash of civilizations."

21   Bingham, "Except a Corn of Wheat," 370.

22   Hastings, *The Church in Africa*, 300.

23   Gowans' diary, 3 January 1894, SIMIAR, BM-2, Box 13; Bingham, to John Hindle, 24 January 1894, SIMIAR, BM-1, Box 10; Bingham, "The Story of the Sudan Interior Mission," *The Missionary Witness* 5, no. 4 (6 April 1909): 63; Tom Coffee, to Rowland Bingham, 12 February 1895, SIMIAR, BM-1, Box 10.

24   Walter Gowans diary, c. 9 August 1894; Tim Geysbeek, "From Sasstown to Zaria: Tom Coffee and the Kru origins of the Sudan Interior Mission, 1893-1895," paper presented at the Yale-Edinburgh Group Conference on the History of the Missionary Movement and World Christianity, 30 June 2017, Yale Divinity School, New Haven, CT.

25   David Killingray, "The Black Atlantic Missionary Movement and Africa, 1780s–1920s," *Journal of Religion in Africa* 33, no. 1 (2003): 13–14.

26   Klaus Fiedler, *The Story of Faith Missions* (Oxford: Regnum Book and Lynx Communications, 1994), 138–141; Killingray, "The Black Atlantic," 9, 13–14.

27   Minutes of the Africa Industrial Mission, 25 October 1904, 28 March 1905, SIMIAR, MC-1, Box 147; Fiedler, *The Story*, 139, 162, n. 193.

28   Fiedler, *The Story*, 139–140, 162 n. 185, 186.

29   "Bound for Nigeria," *The Missionary Witness* 2, no. 10 (23 October 1906): 155–156.

30   People from overwhelmingly white organizations went to historically black universities like Lincoln to recruit workers (Killingray, "The Black Atlantic," 15).

31   Minutes of the Sudan United Mission, 14 March 1907, SIMIAR, MC-1, Box 147.

32   For insight into how people construct the notion of what it means to be white, see Ta-Nehisi Coates, *Between the World and Me* (New York, Spiegel & Grau, 2015); Painter, *The History*.

33   Marilyn Lake and Henry Reynolds, *Drawing the Global Color Line: White Men's Countries and the International Challenge of Racial Equality* (Cambridge: Cambridge University Press, 2008).

34   John Hope Franklin and Alfred A. Moss, *From Slavery to Freedom: A History of African Americans* (New York: Alfred A. Knopf, 2007), 281–291, 345–350; Michelle Alexander, *The New Jim Crow: Mass Incarceration in the Age of Colorblindness* (New York: The New Press, 2012).

35   For example, see Minutes of the French West African Associate Council (30-31 May 1955, p. 2, ME-1, Box 155) and the United States Council (14 November 1952, p. 2, Sending Councils Box 10).

36   Shankar, *Who Shall Enter Paradise?* 3–4, 6; Ross, "Christian Missionaries," 91–94, 104; George Fredrickson, *Racism: A Short History* (Princeton: Princeton University Press), 2003, 156; Derek Chang, *Citizens of a Christian Nation: Evangelical Missions and the Problem of Race in the Nineteenth Century* (Philadelphia: University of Pennsylvania Press, 2010), 164-165; Andrew E. Barnes, *Global Christianity and the Black Atlantic: Tuskegee, Colonialism, and the Shaping of African Industrial Education* (Waco, TX: Baylor University Press, 2017), ch. 3.

37   Yusufu Turaki, *Theory and Practice of Christian Missions in Africa: A Century of SIM/ECWA History and Legacy in Nigeria, 1893-1993* (Nairobi, Kenya: International Bible Society Africa, 1999), 51, 54–55.

38 Turaki's citation: Christine Bolt, *Victorian Attitudes to Race* (London: Routledge and Kegan Paul), 1971.

39 For example, Bingham, *Burden*, 17; John Hall, "Exploring in Pioneer Land: the Land and its People," *TECMW* 15, no. 7 (July 1919): 213–214; Andrew Stirrett, "The Black Gypsies of the Sudan," *TECMW* 19, no. 7 (July 1923): 262–263. To set their thinking in context, see Cox, *British Missionaries*, 141–143, 176–177.

40 For example, Bingham, *Seven Sevens*, 31.

41 "The Negro," *TECMW* 7, no. 3 (March 1911): 65.

42 Hall, *A History*, 40, 46–47, 49.

43 "The Negro," 65; "Facts About the Chinese," *The Missionary Witness* 2, no. 12 (18 December 1906): 188; Brian Alexander McKenzie, "Fundamentalism, Christian Unity, and Premillennialism in the thought of Rowland Victor Bingham (1872–1942): A Study of Anti-Modernism in Canada (Ph.D. diss., Toronto School of Theology, 1985), 287–288; Hastings, *The Church*, 299.

44 Andrew Barnes, *Making Headway: The Introduction of Western Civilization in Colonial Northern Nigeria* (New York: University of Rochester Press, 2009), 45–52, 109–115.

45 Bingham, *Burden*, 17.

46 Bingham, "The Story," 6–10; "A Christmas Transformation in the Sudan," *TECMW* 9, no. 12 (December 1913): 368–369; "How It Happened," *TECMW* 18, no. 7 (June 1922): 251; Albert D. Helser, *The Glory of the Impossible* (Toronto and New York: Evangelical Publishers, 1940), 7.

47 "Black Gypsies," 262–263; Shankar, *Who Shall Enter Paradise?*, 4.

48 Hall, "Exploring," 213–214; "Missions in Nigeria," *TECMW* 17, no. 1 (January 1921): 21.

49 For example, "Missions in Nigeria," *TECMW* 17, no. 1 (January 1921): 21–23; "The Tangale and Its Untouched Neighbors," *TECMW* 14, no. 6 (1918): 227.

50 John David Smith, "Confession and Catharsis," *The Charlotte Observer*, 8c (4 September 2016): 1; Alexander, *The New Jim Crow*, 241.

51 "Mastered by the Master," *Sudan Witness* 36, no. 2 (April–June 1960): 1; John Hall, *From Cannibalism to Christ* (Toronto: Evangelical Publishers, 1944), jacket.

52 Turaki, *Theory and Practice*, 594–597.

53 Guy Playfair (Jos), to Parents (West Africa), 18 December 1946, SIMIAR, PC-2, Box 166.

54 Kerry Lovering, "Good News—They're Human," *Africa Now* 57 (July–August 1971): 2.

55 "The Testing Day of the New Missionary," *Sudan Witness* 4, no. 4 (January–March 1925): 6–7. Originally published in the *South African Pioneer* 32, no. 1 (January 1919): 5–6.

56 Fiedler, *The Story*, 139–140.

57 Killingray, "The Black Atlantic," 17, 19.

58 Robert Gordon, "Black Man's Burden," in *African-American Experience in World Mission: A Call Beyond Community*, Vaughn J. Walston and Robert J. Steven, eds. (Pasadena, CA: William Carey Library, 2002), 58.

59 Bingham, *Seven Sevens*, 30–31.

60 Bingham, "Africa at the Peace Table: A Missionary's Suggestion to President Wilson," *TECMW* 14, no. 11 (November 1918): 298–299; "Will the United States Take Up 'The African Burden'?" *TECMW* 14, no. 12 (December 1918): 320; see Chang, *Citizens*, 4–10, 28–29.

61 See Harr, "The Negro," 100; Chang, *Citizens*, 4, 6–11, 48.

62 Cate O'Brien, email to author, 21 July 2016; Franklin and Moss, *From Freedom to Slavery*, 395–397.

63   Turaki, *Theory and Practice*, 597–599. For more discussion of missionary attitudes and African reactions, see Turaki, *Theory and Practice*, 597–605, 627–647.

64   Turaki, *Theory and Practice*, 626–627; Maigadi, *Divisive Ethnicity*, 123–154.

65   "A Fifty-Year Muslim Conversion to Christianity: Religious Ambiguities and Colonial Boundaries in Northern Nigeria, c. 1910–1963," in *Muslim-Christian Encounters in Africa*, Benjamin F. Soares, ed. (Leiden: Brill, 2006), 113.

66   Emerson and Smith, *Divided by Faith*, 45–48; Snow, *Protestant Missions*, 37–41, 48, 144. For instance, SIM representatives actively participated in the Congress on the Church's Worldwide Mission in Wheaton, IL, USA, in 1966, that the Evangelical Foreign Missions Association and Interdenominational Foreign Mission Association convened. SIM's article about the proceedings did not mention racism (Kerry Lovering, "Evangelicals Have Declared Themselves," *Sudan Witness* [Second Quarter 1966]: 2–5). Three years later, the World Council of Churches declared that racism was "the fundamental problem of the twentieth century" (Bengt Sundkler and Christopher Steed, *A History of the Church in Africa* [Cambridge: Cambridge University Press, 2000], 908; this is Sundkler and Steed's quote). While SIM did not engage with ecumenical organizations like the International Missionary Council or the World Council of Churches for profound theological reasons, these groups were ahead in proactively struggling with the problem of race in missions (Ian M. Hay, *Unity & Purity: keeping the balance* [Canada: n.p., 1983]; Elisabeth Engel, *Encountering Empire: African American Missionaries in Colonial Africa, 1900–1939* [Stuttgart: Franz Steiner Verlag, 2015], 146–158, 183–189).

67   Ian Hay, 26 October 2007 interview with the author; 13 May 2010 email to the author.

68   Frederickson, *Racism*, 115–129; "Race: are we so different?" *American Anthropological Association*, http://www.understandingrace.org/home.html, accessed 10 April 2016.

69   *1949 Sudan Interior Mission Prayer Calendar* (Canada: Sudan Interior Mission, n.d.). The council's name changed to West Africa Council in 1966.

70   Turaki, *Theory and Practice*, 597–599; West Africa Field letter, 1 April 1948, SIMIAR, AM-2, Box 13, File 17b. The modern form of "racial prejudice," that is akin to "race discrimination," is "racism" (Fredrickson, *Racism*, 156, 162, 167).

71   Falola and Heaton, *A History of Nigeria*, 148–151.

72   Barbara Cooper, *Evangelical Christians in the Muslim Sahel* (Bloomington: Indiana University Press, 2006), 111–114.

73   West Africa Field Letter, 5 January 1952, no. 5, SIMIAR, AM-2, Box 3, File 18. The African Missionary Society later changed its name to the Evangelical Missionary Society (Turaki, *Theory and Practice*, 491–505).

74   Playfair (Toronto), to Dear Fellow Missionaries, 20 November 1953, SIMIAR, PC-1, PC-2, Box 165, File 5.

75   Turaki, *Theory and Practice*, 599–602; Swank, "Educating Ourselves to a New Africa," SIMIAR, MM-2, Box 159, File: SIM Early Conferences in Africa.

76   Turaki, *Theory and Practice*, 602–604.

77   *The In-Between People: A Reading of David Bosch through the Lens of Mission History and Contemporary Challenges in Ethiopia* (Eugene, Oregon: Pickwick Publications), 2011, 218–221.

78   "Can Missions Survive Nationalism," *Africa Now* 1, no. 1 (1958): 3.

79   "The African Personality and Missions," *Africa Now* 12 (January–March 1962): 15; "Missions and Humility," *Africa Now* 21 (April–June 1964): 15.

80　　"Words that Wound," *Africa Now* 15 (October–December 1962): 13. Blunt noted that while "national" did not appear to offend Africans, one could just say "Africans." Joshua Bogunjoko criticizes using "national" to designate a group because it denotes untrustworthiness and leads to stereotyping ("'Who do you say that I am?' A Comparative Study of How Missionaries Think They are Perceived Compared to How the Host People Perceive Them" (M.A. research project, Briercrest Biblical Seminary, 2001), 82. "Tribe" is another stereotypical term that most Americans use to refer, whether consciously or not, to people who they think are not as civilized or sophisticated as them. (They would not, for instance, typically talk about the "Dutch tribe," but would not give a second thought about referring to the Fulani as a "tribe.") For a discussion about the problematic usage of the word "tribe," see Chris Lowe, "Talking about 'Tribe': Moving from Stereotypes to Analysis," http://web.mnstate.edu/robertsb/313/TalkingaboutTribeFeb2008Update_001.pdf, accessed 24 August 2016.

81　　"S.I.M. Strategy 1965–1970," SIMIAR, MC-1, Box 149, File 5c.

82　　"Missionaries Aren't Imperialist Agents," *Africa Now* 21 (April–June 1964): 8–9; Maigadi, *Divisive Ethnicity*, 101–108; "The Kind of Missionary We Want," *Africa Now* 17 (April–June 1963): 2–3; Rae Gourlay, "How about YOU? ARE YOU AN IMPERIALIST?" *Africa Now* 21 (April–June 1964): 9; "What Africa Thinks," *Africa Now* 23 (October–December 1964): 7.

83　　"The Kind of Missionary," 3.

84　　"The Kind of Missionary," 3.

85　　Maigadi, *Divisive Ethnicity*, 101.

86　　Fiedler, *The Story*, 140–141.

87　　Lake and Reynolds, *Drawing the Global Color Line*.

88　　"Receipts for Each Country for years 1957–1961," SIMIAR, SIM International Administration, Box 565, File 4; "Country of Origin of Missionary Force," SIMIAR, SIM International Administration, Box 565, File 1.

89　　Raymond Davis, "The Church's Mission in Africa," *Africa Now* 29 (April–June 1965): 3.

90　　*The Principles and Practice of the Sudan Interior Mission*, rev. ed. (Canada: n.p., 1951), 1–2.

91　　"Minutes of the Conference of the S.I.M. Home Secretarial Staff," Toronto, 14–17 January 1952, 8–9, SIMIAR, MC-1, Box 149, File 2.

92　　Ibid.

93　　The letters cited in this section are in International Council, 1949–1957, SIMIAR, MC-1, Box 149, Files 3, 4a.

94　　J. O. Percy, to G. W. Playfair, 26 October 1954.

95　　Billy Graham only started to desegregate all of his crusades after the 1954 Supreme Courts' decision in Brown vs. Board of Education (Emerson and Smith, *Divided by Faith*, 46–47).

96　　M. A. Darroch, to G. W. Playfair, 9 October 1954. Darroch did not name the Arab couple. Herr said that some Japanese Christians, who they met in Hawaii, told he and his wife that they wanted to serve as missionaries in the hardest places in Africa like Somalia. On one occasion, after one "oriental" told Herr that they were a mission field, Herr said that they too could be missionaries (T. Geysbeek phone interview with John Herr, 3 June 2010).

97　　J. O. Percy, to G. W. Playfair, 26 October 1954.

98　　G. W. Playfair, to Members of the International Council, 8 November 1954.

99　　G. Richie Rice, to Mr. Playfair, 26 November 1954. Rice did not name the pharmacist and his wife.

100   J. O. Percy, to G. W. Playfair, 26 October 1954.

101   G. W. Playfair, to Members of the International Council, 8 November 1954; G. Richie Rice, to Rev. G. W. Playfair, 26 November 1954; Glen H. Cain, to Dear Mr. Playfair, 2 December 1954; M. A. Darroch, to J. O. Percy and R. B. Oliver, 1 February 1955. International Council's minutes for 17 February 1955 and 8 June 1955 no longer exist, or are at least not filed in the right place, so it is not known if the council acted on Playfair's recommendation and voted to accept the Arab couple on a trial basis.

102   "Prayer," *Sudan Witness* 33, no. 2 (March-April 1957): 2; "American Negroes as S.I.M. Missionaries," S.I.M. General Council minutes, 17 July 1957, p. 8-9, SIMIAR, General Council 1953–1980, MC-1, Box 148, File 5.

103   S.I.M General Council Minutes, 17 July 1957, SIMIAR, General Council 1953–1980, MC-1, Box 149, File 5.

104   Franklin and Moss, *From Slavery to Freedom*, 523.

105   Minutes, 9–11 October 1957, SIMIAR, MC-1, Box 148, File 5.

106   S.I.M. General Council Minutes, Agenda item 17, p. 9, 9-11 October 1957, SIMIA, MC-1, Box 148, Correspondence and Minutes.

107   Cate O'Brien, email to the author, 2 May 2010.

108   E. S. Horn, to Helser, 24 February 1958, SIMIAR, CO-5, 6, Box 44, London 1958.

109   This chapter, page 210.

110   General Council Minutes, 9–11 October 1957, SIMIAR, MC-1, Box 148, File 5.

111   Cate O'Brien, email to author, 2 May 2010.

112   E. S. Horn, to Helser, 24 February 1958, SIMIAR, CO-5, 6, Box 44, London 1958.

113   General Council Minutes, 5 January 1959, SIMIAR, MC-1, Box 148, File 6; West Africa Field Council Minutes, 14–21 November 1962, SIMIAR, ME-1, Box 157b, File 1.

114   Minutes, 9 September 1958, SIMIAR, Sending Councils Box 10, File 7; Davis (Grand Rapids) to Hay (New Jersey), 4 January 1968, SIMIAR, Jones biographical file. For more information, see the books listed in the biography that Howard and Wanda Jones wrote (see page 434).

115   "First Arab Preacher Joins Radio ELWA," *Africa Now* 2 (January–March 1964): 13.

116   Chang, *Citizens*, 9–10; Fredrickson, *Racism*, 141–150; Hall, *A History*, 14–15.

117   Darrell L. Whiteman, "Anthropology and Mission: The Incarnational Connection," *International Journal of Frontier Missions* 21, no. 2 (Summer 2004): 82. Thanks to Dr. Hyung-Jin Park of Torch Trinity Graduate School of Theology (Seoul) for apprising me of this article. Whiteman reminds missionaries from Asia and other parts of the "non-Western world" not to follow the "pattern of confusing the gospel with one's culture" like their American predecessors.

118   Typescript (22 May 1998), 17, 54.

119   "Breakdown," 4.

120   George Yancy, *Beyond Racial Gridlock: Embracing Mutual Responsibility* (Downers Grove, IL: InterVarsity Press, 2006), 20–23; Emerson and Smith, *Divided by Faith*, 9, 76–87, 170; Alexander, *The New Jim Crow*; Coates, *Between the World and Me*; Adelle M. Banks, "Churches hold classes to discuss white privilege," *The Charlotte Observer* (23 April 2016): 2C; Cate O'Brien email to author, 21 July 2016. For a thought-provoking documentary about what it means to be "white" in the United States, see Jose Antonio Vargas' "White People" (https://www.youtube.com/watch?v=_zjj1PmJcRM), accessed 10 June 2017. (O'Brien was an associate archivist of the SIMIAR.)

121 Turaki, *Theory and Practice*, 605; West Africa Council Minutes, 12–20 May 1971, SIMIAR, ME-1, Box 157b. SIM disbanded the West Africa Council in 1972 when it divided its work in the region into three divisions: Nigeria-Ghana, Francophone, and Liberia-Côte d'Ivoire. None of the minutes of these newly-formed councils, or the East African council after this period, were consulted for this study.

122 Bill Crouch, "Shedding the Cocoon," *Africa Now* 41 (November–December 1968): 1–2; Ray Davis, "Missions in Africa—A whole new ball game," *Africa Now* 56 (May–June 1971): 2–5; Byang Kato, "Africa outlines 'new missionary' qualifications," *Africa Now* 55 (March–April 1971): 10; Oumaruo Youssouf, "Come…but live among my people!" *Africa Now* 60 (January–February 1972): 6; Simon Ibrahim, "Learning to be on our own," *Africa Now* 87 (July–August 1976): 7.

123 For example, "The Impossible Church," *Africa Now* 91 (March–April 1977): 2–5.

124 For example, "Picking Up Stones Together," *Serving in Mission Together* 117 (2007): 7; "Healing the Wounds of Slavery," *Serving in Mission Together* 108 (2004): 3–4.

125 "Ian Hay talks about Church-Mission culture shock," *Intercom* 48 (June 1981): 1–2; Maigadi, *Divisive Ethnicity*, 96.

126 "Relationships," *Intercom* 83 (June 1988): 6–7.

127 Chapter 19, pages 289-290.

128 "Breakdown," 67; Brant email to author, 11 March 2016.

129 "Breakdown," 54.

130 "'Who do you say that I am?,'" 11, 26–33, 55–63, 73, 79–89, 93. Given that Bogunjoko worked closely with SIM missionaries in Niger and Nigeria, it is likely that many of the missionaries and Africans who filled out the questionnaire respectively were with SIM or worked for SIM.

131 Joshua and Joanna Bogunjoko," http://www.sim.org/index.php/worker/1202769, accessed 13 March 2017; Hudson, "Ministries of Compassion," chapter 19, pages 290-291.

132 Interim edition, 1966, SIMIAR, Spec BV 2050 S5S8 1967–1977.

133 General Council Minutes, 5 May 1967, SIMIAR, MC-1, Box 149, File 5. Because SIM's missionaries did not consider themselves to be "nationals" (or "others"), they did not think it was hypocritical for them to work in their own home countries as missionaries.

134 Lovering, "Ambassador from Asia," *Africa Now* 38 (May–June 1968): 10.

135 "Bible teachers' influence expanding," *Africa Now* 65 (November–December 1972): 112.

136 Howard Dowdell, "Report on Opinion Poll," *Intercom* 13 (January 1971): 5; see Cooper, *Evangelical Christians*, 87. For the statistic, see Eldon Howard, "Sudan Interior Mission Cumulative Statistics (1893-1983)," SIMIAR, Personnel, SIM Statistics, Box 565.

137 "A Good 'Explosion,'" *Serving in Mission Together* 111 (2005): 6.

138 Leona Choy, "The Testing of Peter Pan," *Africa Now* 100 (September–October 1978): 14–15; Lovering, "The Asians are Coming!" *Africa Now* 110 (August–October 1980): 3; Hsueh Yu Kwong, *You Guided my Life: An Autobiography of Rev. Hsueh Yu Kwong* (Singapore: Caseline Manufacturing Sdn. Bhd., for SIM East Asia Pte. Ltd., 2005).

139 See Joshua Bogunjoko, "35 Years of God's Goodness in East Asia," *SIMNOW* (Korea) 3 (2015): 1.

140 "SIM committee formed in Asia," *Africa Now* 96 (January–February 1978): 10; "SIM East Asia Council," *SIMNOW* (East Asia), (March 1990): 14. The East Asia Council that initially operated under the auspices of of SIM Australia became an independent legal entity of SIM in 1993 ("East Asia Officially Joins SIM Fold," *SIMNOW* 63 [Summer 1993]: 8).

141 "National Office Personnel Recruitment Goals," International Council 1990, Personnel; "International Statistics 2016" (thanks to SIM International personnel statistics administrator Cherry Long Sabathne for providing the current information, 17 August 2016). The statistics for 2016 represent missionaries who serve for more than 10 months (see endnote 154).

142 "Rearranging Our Thinking," 27 *SIMNOW* (May–June 1986): 7.

143 For example, "It's a big family," *Africa Now* 59 (November–December 1971): 8–9; Choy, "The Testing of Peter Pan"; Kerry Lovering, "Who else is in the family?" *Africa Now* 110 (August–October 1980): 4–5; W. Harold Fuller, "'Wonder Woman' Patricia Kim," *SIMNOW* 27 (May–June 1986): 4–6; Lovering, "Global Village, Global Family," *SIMNOW* 33 (May–June 1987): 2–3.

144 Curtis L. Hayes, *Life Still Goes On* (Bloomington: iUniverse, Inc., 2013), 52–75.

145 "Emerging Missions," *Serving in Mission Together* 111 (2005): 2, 4.

146 Brant emails to author, 15, 20 December 2009; Brant, "Emerging Missions," *Serving in Mission Together*, 111 (2005): 2, 4.

147 "A Summary of the Top Ten Areas for Change," *Serving in Mission Together* 110 (2005): 3; McGregor, "SIM's Role in Multidirectional Mission," *Serving in Mission Together* 119 (2007): 2; "The Changing Face of SIM," *Mission Together* (Australia) 124 (2009).

148 Appendix H.

149 Dianne Marshall, "Intentional Diversity," *SIMNOW* (East Asia Edition) 2 (2012): 2.

150 Malcolm McGregor, "Diversity Marks New Leadership Team at SIM International," *Serving in Mission Together* 115 (2006): 2. Rene Palacio was the ethnic Cuban, and Andrew Ng the Singaporean. For the current leaders of SIM, see https://www.sim.org/our-leadership, accessed 12 July 2017.

151 "Dr Bogunjoko Est la Nouveau Directeur International de la SIM," *SIM Actualités* 3 (2013): 2.

152 Jeff Hahn, "Supporting and Sending," *Serving in Mission Together* (New Zealand) 132 (November 2011): 14–15; "Yo Nací par Esto," *Vamos* (Septiembre 2014): 4–5; Ruby Mikulencak, "Encouraging a vision for world vision in Ghana," *Serving in Mission* (UK) (Spring 2011): 18; "Recruiting office opens in East Africa," http://www.sim.org/index.php/content/new-sim-east-africa-recruiting-office, accessed 3 February 2016.

153 Gordon Stanley, "Staffing to Reach a Changing World," *SIMNOW* 51 (May–June 1990): 8; "Who Are We," http://www.sim.org/index.php/content/our-purpose, accessed 3 February 2016.

154 In July 2016, North America accounted for 55.5% of SIM's 1,537 missionaries; 696 (45.2%) from the United States and 158 (10.3%) from Canada. The remaining missionaries were sent by the offices in the United Kingdom (136 missionaries, 8.8%), Australia (125 missionaries, 8.1%), East Asia (116 missionaries, 7.5%), Korea (89 missionaries, 5.8%), South Africa (56 missionaries, 3.6%), New Zealand (43 missionaries, 2.8%), Switzerland (37 missionaries, 2.4%), East Africa (25 missionaries, 1.6%), France (26 missionaries, 1.7%), Guatemala/OCLA (15 missionaries from Latin America, .098%), and West Africa (15 missionaries, .098%) ("International Statistics 2016"). When adding the mission's roughly 2,500 employees worldwide, more than 4,000 people presently work for SIM ("Who We Are," https://www.sim.org/about, accessed 12 July 2017).

155 "Can We Work Together?" *Serving in Mission Together* 119 (2007): 3; David Park, email to author, 1 February 2016.

156 Hay, "Foundation for the Future," *SIMNOW* 61 (Winter 1992–1993): 3.

157 Arnold, "Minutes with regard to the acceptance of non-white missionaries," 2004. All the key points that Arnold compiled are in this chapter.

158   For example, "SIM, black churches get together," *SIMNOW* 45 (May–June 1989): 10; Larry Fehl, "An Introduction and a Greeting to the Family," *U.S. News* (December 1990): 1.

159   "Together as One," 4 February 2008, http://www.sim.org/index.php/content/together-as-one, accessed 14 January 2016.

160   See Douglas R. Sharp, *No Partiality: The Idolotry of Race & The New Humanity* (Downers Grove, IL: InterVarsity Press, 2002), 22.

161   Killingray, "The Black Atlantic," 20–21; Engel, *Encountering Empire*, 184–189, 202–204; Dennis Laumann, *Colonial Africa, 1884–1994* (New York, Oxford University Press), 2013, 38–39.

162   The most clear, extended, and succinct acknowledgement of racism to date occurred when the West Africa Field Council chided its missionaries, internally, for "race discrimination" in 1948 (this chapter, pages 213-214). Brant's apology to church leaders in Ethiopia is reported in his unpublished manuscript. SIM Ethiopia, SIM Ghana, SIM Niger, and their respective related denominations held consultations to reconcile long-standing differences. If racism factored into the discussions—which it may not have, corporate responsibility did not explicitly appear in the published reports. For the Ethiopia case, see chapter 14, page 178. For Ghana, see Allison Howell, ed., *The Slave Trade and Reconciliation: A Northern Ghanaian Perspective* (Accra: Bible Church of Africa and SIM Ghana, Assemblies of God Literature Centre, Ltd., 1998); "Healing the Wounds of Slavery," 3–5; chapter 19, pages 176, 291. For Niger, see Steve Schmidt, "Rebuilding Trust in Niger," *Serving in Mission* (UK edition) (Autumn 2012): 13–14.

163   All of these examples are based on personal observation or credible firsthand accounts.

164   For discussions about racial disparities in education, employment, health care, housing, residential patterns, the justice system, standards of living, and other factors, see Coates, *Between the World and Me*; Alexander, *The New Jim Crow*.

165   Howell, *The Slave Trade*, 55–59.

166   Howell, *The Slave Trade*, 55.

167   David Bosch, *Transforming Mission: Paradigm Shifts in Theology of Mission* (Maryknoll, New York: Orbis Books, [1991] 2006): 304.

168   310.

169   Hendrik Verwoerd, "Verwoerd reaffirms South Africa's commitment to white supremacy (1958)," in *Africa and the West: A Documentary History from Colonialism to Independence, 1875 to the Present*, vol. 2, William H. Worger, Nancy L. Clark, Edward A. Alpers, eds. (Oxford: Oxford University Press, 2010), 129–134.

170   Steve De Gruchy, "Religion and Racism: struggles around segregation, 'Jim Crow,' and apartheid," in *The Cambridge History of Christianity, World Christianities c. 1914–c. 2000*, Hugh McLeod, ed. (Cambridge: Cambridge University Press, 2006), 393. For information about South African history referenced in this supplement, see De Gruchy's chapter and Leonard Thompson, *A History of South Africa* (New Haven and London: Yale University Press, 2001). Time and space do not permit adequate use of the rich scholarship that is available on Christianity in Southern Africa. The author is thankful for the helpful feedback that Ben Pilley and one other person provided for this section. The author alone, however, is solely responsible for this supplement which does not represent the official position of SIM.

171   Richard Elphick, *The Equality of Believers: Protestant Missionaries and the Racial Politics of South Africa* (Charlottesville & London: University of Virginia Press, 2012), 41–45; John W. de Gruchy, with Steve de Gruchy, *The Church Struggle in South Africa* (Minneapolis: Fortress Press, 2005), 7-8.

172 For the story of Rosabianca and the Hay sisters discussed in the next paragraph, see Pamela J. Walker, "Women's Work in the South Africa General Mission" (paper presented at the International Conference on SIM History in Africa, Addis Ababa, July 2013). The author thanks Dr. Walker for allowing her paper to be used for this section.

173 Adrian Hastings, *A History of African Christianity, 1950-1975* (Cambridge: Cambridge University Press, 1979), 15, 99, 131, 138; Bengt Sundkler and Christopher Steed, *A History of the Church in Africa* (Cambridge: Cambridge University Press, 2000), 800–801.

174 Information about the Sitoles can be found in AEF Personnel Records, Box 25, in the SIMIAR. *The South African Pioneer* published a few articles about their work from 1955–1958. Before the Sitoles joined SAGM, B. H. Shadduck published a book about his experiences in Southern Rhodesia titled *H. Stephen Sitole: "A Simple Faith Wrestling with the Obviously Impossible" from the Heart of Africa* (Chicago: Van Kampen Press), 1948.

175 Conjoint Meeting of the Canadian and American Councils of the S.A.G.M, Brooklyn, NY, 12-13 December 1952 (Sitole file).

176 In *Facing the Unfinished Task: Messages Delivered at the Congress on World Missions*, J. O. Percy, ed. (Grand Rapids: Zondervan Publishing, 1961), 17–26, 225–230.

177 "The Powers That Be" 74, nos. 9–10 (September–October 1960): 54–56. Thanks to Cate O'Brien who alerted the author of this and another article, and letters written against and in defense of Brown's article.

178 For example, see reference to the article that SAGM pioneer missionary Albert Bailey published in *The South African Pioneer* in 1919 that SIM republished in 1923 (chapter 16, page 211).

179 Ann Fraser Brown, *Betting on a Certainty* (Sydney?: Birch Island Books, 2014), 124–125.

180 John W. De Gruchy, "Grappling with a Colonial Heritage: The English-Speaking Churches under Imperialism and Apartheid," in *Christianity in South Africa: A Political, Social, and Cultural History*, Richard Elphick and Rodney Davenport, eds. (Claremont, South Africa: David Philip Publishers, 1997), 166.

181 Thomas J. Kopp, "Church and Mission: Decolonizing the Mind," *Evangelical Review of Theology* 28, no. 3 (2004): 260–261; see De Gruchy, "Grappling with a Colonial Heritage," 166–172.

182 Thomas J. Kopp, *God First—Go Forward: The Impact of the South Africa General Mission / Africa Evangelical Fellowship on the Africa Evangelical Church, 1962–1994* (Pasadena, CA: William Carey International University Press, 2011), 88. This is the published version of the dissertation Kopp completed in 2001 for his studies at the University of South Africa.

183 Ibid., 128. By the time of this writing, AEF had merged with SIM. Kopp, then, was at least indirectly addressing SIM.

184 "Miango," SIMIAR, SR-25/A, Miango Miscellaneous; "Called Home," *Intercom* 23 (August 1973): 5.

185 Ruth Craill, "Minutes from Sudan Interior Mission, South African Council Minutes," typewritten, 2004.

186 Perhaps referring to the United States government, some of whose citizens were engaged in the throes of the civil rights movement.

187 For example, see West Africa Field Council Meeting Minutes, 22–23 February 1956, 1, SIMIAR, ME-1, Box 157A, File 6.

188 "Hendrik Verwoerd explains apartheid (1950)," in *Africa and the West*, 101–106.

189 West Africa Field Council Meeting Minutes, 21–28 May 1957, 1, SIMIAR, ME-1, Box 157A.

190   Dianne Guta, "SIM—Retirees," *SIMNOW* (South Africa), 133 (2011): 7.

191   "East Africa Overview: DGD Harold Fuller Reports," *Intercom* 81 (January 1988): 5.

192   SIM Board of Governors Minutes, 29 April–2 May 1990, 90/46 (Political Action), 41–42, SIMIAR, BOG minutes. These two sentences were added to SIM's "noninterference policy" that appeared in a section titled "Relationships with Governments in SIM Areas" which begins with this sentence: "In no circumstances must a missionary interfere in political or administrative affairs" (*SIM Manual*, 1991, Section 3, IX, 3-19, 3-20).

193   For a discussion, see Cooper, *Evangelical Christians*, 87–93.

194   "Introducing Siegfried and Maureen Ngubane," *SIMNOW* (South Africa) 128 (2010): 14.

Chapter 17: Encountering Islam

1   For discussions of how the views of Islam of many SIM missionaries changed in Nigeria and Niger during the twentieth century, see Barbara Cooper, *Evangelical Christian in the Muslim Sahel* (Bloomington: Indiana University Press, 2006), 84–114; Paul Todd, "The Attitudes of the Evangelical Church of West Africa [ECWA] towards Islam in light of ethnic and religious violence" (Ph.D. diss., Queens University of Belfast, 2010).

2   Ian M. Hay, "SIM, Islam—and a Glimpse of God," *Intercom* 76 (March 1987): 1–2.

3   Howard Brant, "SIM's Commitment," *Intercom* 79 (September 1987): 3. Abridged slightly to avoid repeating material from Dr. Hay's address, included above.

4   Expressed on numerous occasions to the author and others.

5   "Wrestling with *Incha Allah*," *Intercom* 112 (March–April 1994): 2.

6   Joe Gallop, "Follow-up to 'Wrestling with *Incha Allah*,'" *Intercom* 115 (November 1994–January 1995): 2.

7   Jim Plueddemann, "Why We Witness to Muslims," *Intercom* 163 (May–June 2003): 12.

8   "New Opportunities for Outreach to Muslims," *Intercom* 166 (November–December 2003): 2.

9   Mark Garrett, "Co-ops Help Muslim Background Believers," *Intercom* 170 (August–October 2004): 6.

10   Malcolm McGregor, "Our Response to World Disorder," *Intercom* 177 (November–December 2005): 1, 5.

11   All of these items are found in *Intercom* 177 (November–December 2005), 6.

12   Franz Nelson, "That All Muslims May Hear," *Intercom* 186 (July–August 2007): 10.

13   "Consultation Gathers Many Organizations Focused on Sharing Jesus with Muslims," *Intercom* 186 (July–August 2007): 12.

14   Based on the author's personal experience as chairman of this working group.

15   Stan Bruning, "Good News for Somalis: New Bibles Now Available," *Intercom* 195 (March–May 2009): 4.

16   "The Nomadic Gathering 2012," *Intercom* 206 (November 2011–January 2012): 10.

17   *SIMGLOBAL* 141 (Winter 2014): 7.

18   Helen Miller, *The Hardest Place. The biography of Warren and Dorothy Modricker* (Belleville, ON, Canada: Guardian Books, 2006), 270. Lest anyone quibble with the title, this memoir by a decidedly secular author echoes Miller's designation: Jim Douglas, *The Toughest Peace Corps Job. Letters from Somalia 1969* (Portland, OR: Inkwater Press, 2016), 323.

19   Obed Eby, *Fifty Years, Fifty Stories: The Mennonite Mission in Somalia: 1953–2003* (Telford, PA: Cascadia Publishing House, 2003), 141.

20   For Muslim Somali perspective on this, see Abdurahman M. Abdullahi, *The Islamic Movement in Somalia: A Study of the Islah Movement, 1950–2000* (London: Adonis & Abbey Publishers Ltd.), 121–131.

21   For an explanation of the complex mission agency–church dynamics at this time, see Ahmed A. Haile and David W. Shenk, *Teatime in Mogadishu: My Journey as a Peace Ambassador in the World of Islam* (Harrisonburg, VA: Herald Press, 2011).

22   See Haile and Shenk for the perspective of the noted church leader Ahmed A. Haile on this work.

23   John Travis, "The C1 to C6 Spectrum," *Evangelical Missions Quarterly* 34, no 4 (1998): 407–408. In the same *EMQ* issue Parshall expressed his own concerns about contextualization approaches that he believed went too far: Phil Parshall, "Danger! New Directions in Contextualization," *Evangelical Missions Quarterly* 34, no. 4 (1998): 404–406, 409–410. For his autobiography, see *Divine Threads within a Human Tapestry: Memoirs of Phil Parshall* (Pasadena, CA: William Carey Library, 2000). For a study of his writings, see Arnold Arredondo, "An Analysis of Missionary Contextualization in the Muslim Evangelism of Phil Parshall" (Ph.D. diss., New Orleans Baptist Theological Seminary, 2009).

Chapter 18: SIM and Urban Missions

1   This survey is adapted, with minor changes and updated information, from a preliminary paper written in 2008. This chapter does not say anything about the urban areas (e.g., Beirut, Cairo) where the Middle East Christian Outreach (MECO) worked because it was written prior to the relationship that SIM and MECO formed in 2016.

2   "Seize the Day," complete version, final report to international director (8 January 2005): 173.

3   McGregor, Malcolm, "Top Ten Ministry Priorities," *Intercom* 175 (July–August 2005): 8.

4   Erin Bergen (International Personnel), personal communication with author, October 2007.

5   *Mission and the City*, SIM's urban newsletter, 1 (July 2007); Brian Seim, "Building Urban Churches beyond the Ordinary," *Intercom* 188 (November–December 2007): 8–9.

6   "World Urbanization Prospects: The 2014 Revision," xxi, 21, 23, https://esa.un.org/unpd/wup/Publications/Files/WUP2014-Report.pdf, accessed 8 March 2017. This report defines an urban center has having more than 300,000 people (xxi).

7   As evidence of this scholarship, SIM International, SIM Ethiopia, and the Ethiopia Kale Heywet Church co-hosted the "International Conference on SIM History in Africa" in Addis Ababa in July 2013. This conference brought twenty-three scholars from Canada, Ethiopia, Niger, Nigeria, the UK, and the USA to present papers.

8   With the joining of MECO with SIM in 2016, the oldest part of SIM is now the British Syrian Mission, founded in 1860. It became the Lebanon Evangelical Mission in 1959 and merged into the newly formed MECO in 1976. (See chapter 21 for more on MECO.)

9   James Gray Kallam, "A History of the Africa Evangelical Fellowship from its inception to 1917" (Ph.D. diss., New York University, 1978); George Howe co-founded CGM as well as Osborn, Murray, and Walton (author's emails with John Freeman [10 March 2013] and Dr. Pamela J. Walker [5 September 2013]).

10   Kallam, "A History"; Alan C. F. Huntingford, *AEF: History of the Southern Field, the first one hundred years* (n.p.: c. 1991).

11   Catherine Coquery-Vidrovitch, *The History of African Cities South of the Sahara: From the Origins to Colonization*, trans. Mary Baker (Princeton: Markus Wiener Publishers, 2005), 316. For the history of CGM and SAGM's growth outlined in this paragraph, see Kallam, "A History," 60-108.

12 Anthony O'Connor, *The African City* (New York, NY: Holmes & Meier, 1983), 43.

13 Bill Freund, *The African City: A History* (Cambridge: Cambridge University Press, 2007), 66. See also Leonard Thompson, *A History of South Africa* (New Haven: Yale University Press, 2000), 120.

14 William Worger, "Workers as Criminals: The Rule of Law in Early Kimberly, 1870-1885," in *Struggle for the City: Migrant Labor, Capital, and the State in Urban Africa*, Frederick Cooper, ed. (Beverly Hills, CA: Sage Publications, 1983), 60.

15 Christopher Saunders, *Historical Dictionary of South Africa* (Lanham, MD: Scarecrow Press, 2000), 84-85.

16 Kallam, "A History"; *Guide for Daily Prayer* (Berks, England: AEF International, c. 1990).

17 *SAGM Prayer Circle* (Northcants, Great Britain: Stanley L. Hunt, 1949), Day 26.

18 Huntingford, *AEF*, 29, 32; Lorry Lutz, "Youth Evangelism in South Africa," *African Evangel* 208 (November 1967).

19 B. R. Mitchell, *International Historical Statistics* (London: MacMillan Reference, 1998), 39.

20 SASO Group (University of Sheffield) and Mark Newman (University of Michigan), "Population 1900," 2006, http://www.worldmapper.org/display.php?selected=9, accessed on 9 October 2007; "The World at Six Billion" (United Nations Population Division, 1999), http://www.un.org/esa/population/publications/sixbillion/sixbilpart1.pdf, accessed 9 October 2007.

21 *Witnessing. . .unto this day* (London: Ceylon and India General Mission, c. 1943); W. H. Cherry, "A History of CIGM," in *Advancing Together: A Tale of Two Missions*, G. A. Hemming ed. (London: International Christian Fellowship, c. 1971), 18–31; Ed Welch, "Workers Together: The Story of the International Christian Fellowship," typescript (1985) (SIMIAR, ICF Box 103); Ruth Tozer, "A Brief History of the first 100 years of CIGM and PIVM, which together became ICF, and then Society for International Ministries in South Asia," typescript (1997) (SIMIAR, ICF Box 103); George and Ina McCormick, "ICF Archives" [History of CIGM], typescript (18 November 2000).

22 "Poona" (1911), http://www.1911encyclopedia.org/Poona, accessed 8 October 2007.

23 C. F. Reeve, "A Retrospect," *White Already to Harvest,*" 3, no. 12 (December 1898): 1–2.

24 Basil Tyson and Helen Rosan, "A History of P.I.V.M.," in *Advancing Together: A Tale of Two Missions*, G. A. Hemming, ed. (London: International Christian Fellowship, c. 1971), 32–49; Welch, "Workers Together"; Tozer, "A Brief History."

25 Merle W. Inniger, "View from West Pakistan," in *Advancing Together: A Tale of Two Missions*, G. A. Hemming, ed. (London: International Christian Fellowship, c. 1971), 79–85; Dorothy McQuaker, "East Pakistan Points," in *Advancing Together: A Tale of Two Missions*, G. A. Hemming, ed. (London: International Christian Fellowship, c. 1971), 87–94.

26 Aletta Bell, two emails with the author, 15 December 2007; Ed Welch, two emails with the author, 14 December 2007.

27 Aletta Bell, two emails with the author, 15 December 2007.

28 For example, Jim Kraakevik, "Evangelism and Church Planting—Urban Ministries," Work Paper (II.A.1.b., Ministries committee, SIM General Council, 1984).

29 Freund, *The African City*, 42, 66; John Iliffe, *Africans: the history of a continent* (Cambridge: Cambridge University Press, 2007), 175.

30 Rowland V. Bingham, *Seven Sevens of Years and Jubliee: The Story of the Sudan Interior Mission*, 5th ed. (New York: Evangelical Publishers, 1957), chs. 1–4; Ian Hay, "A Study of the Relationship between SIM International and the Evangelical Missionary Society" (D.Min. thesis, Trinity

Evangelical Divinity School, 1984), 20–22; Yusufu Turkai, *Theory and Practice of Christian Missions in Africa: A Century of SIM/ECWA History and Legacy in Nigeria, 1893–1993*, vol. 1 (Nairobi, Kenya: International Bible Society Africa, 1999), 156–157, 177–180; Barbara Cooper, *Evangelical Christians in the Muslim Sahel* (Bloomington: Indiana University Press, 2006), 89, 100–101, 118–120.

31   Bingham, *Seven Sevens*, chs. 5–6; Hay, "A Study," 25–33; Turaki, *Theory and Practice*, 131, 184, 188, 220, 259–260; Cooper, *Evangelical Christians*, 9, 101, 120, 150; Shobana Shankar, *Who Shall Enter Paradise? Christian Origins in Muslim Northern Nigeria, c. 1890–1975* (Athens: Ohio University Press and Swallow Press, 2014), 71–93; Andrew Barnes, *Making Headway: The Introduction of Western Civilization in Colonial Northern Nigeria* (Rochester, NY: University of Rochester Press, 2009), 103–167.

32   "Youth Centers," SIM Field Council Minutes, November 30–December 3, 1964, SIMIAR, ME-1/A, no. 157B.

33   W. Harold Fuller, *Run While the Sun is Hot* (Aylesbury, Bucks, England: Hazell Watson and Viney Ltd., 1967), 22, 31–36; Ian Hay, interview with the author (26 October 2007); Jim Mason, *Literature Outreach in Nigeria: A History of SIM Literature Work 1901–1980* (Breslau, Canada: Denison Print, 2009), ch. 9.

34   Ian Hay, "Africa's Cities—Bold New Challenge," *Sudan Witness* (4th Quarter 1965): 11; "Africa's Big-City Youth," *Sudan Witness* (4th Quarter 1965): 8–9; Tibebe Eshete, *The Evangelical Movement in Ethiopia: Resistance and Resilience* (Baylor University Press, 2009), 131–138.

35   This mission's *South American Messenger* (1897–1906) can be found at http://archives.sim.org/.

36   Margarita Allan Hudspith, *Ripening Fruit: A History of the Bolivian Indian Mission* (Harrington Park, NJ: Harrington Press, c. 1958), 31-35.

37   Ibid., 35-42.

38   Charles Edmond Akers, *A History of South America, 1854–1904* (London: John Murray, 1904), 566–567.

39   Allan, *Reminiscences*; Hudspeth, *Ripening Fruit*.

40   Harvie Conn, "Urban Mission," in *Toward the Twenty-first Century in Christian Mission*, James M. Phillips and Robert T. Cole, eds. (Grand Rapids: Eerdmans, 1993), 319, 330.

41   Harold Lindsell, ed., *The Church's Worldwide Mission* (Waco, TX: Word Books, 1966), ch. 2, 283–284.

42   "World Congress on Evangelism," *The Andean Outlook* 57, no. 1 (January–March 1967): 15.

43   David Hoffner, "Mission in the Cities," *The Andean Outlook* 57, no. 2 (April–June 1967): 8–9.

44   Kerry Lovering, "Evangelicals Have Declared Themselves," *Sudan Witness* (2nd Quarter 1966): 3–5.

45   Lindsell, *The Church's Worldwide Mission*; Hay, interview (26 October 2007).

46   "Africa's Big-City Youth"; Hay, "Africa's Cities."

47   Conn, "Urban Mission"; Conn, preface to *Planting and Growing Urban Churches: From Dream to Reality*, Harvie M. Conn, ed. (Grand Rapids: Baker Books, 1997); Conn, introduction to *Planting and Growing Urban Churches: From Dream to Reality*, Harvie M. Conn, ed. (Grand Rapids: Baker Books, 1997).

48   "Urban," in "Suggestions for Ministry Handbook," SIM General Council (1980); *SIM Manual* (1980), 47–48.

49   Gerald O. Swank, "Rough Draft on Urban Evangelism and Church Planting," Memo to African Directors (26 February 1981); Ian Hay, "Urban Evangelism and Church Planting," Memo (6 May 1981).

50   "Seminar on Latfricasian Urban Evangelism / Church Planting," Cedar Grove (20–21 May 1983) (Urban Ministries B).

51   Kraakevik, "Evangelism and Church Planting."

52   Ian Hay, "Reaching our Cities," *Intercom* 64 (September 1984). See also Howard Brant, "'Save the City': An Inquiry into seven factors which retarded urban evangelism in the large Interdenominational faith missions" (D.Miss. 866 paper, Trinity Evangelical Divinity School, 1 December 1984); James H. Kraakevik, "Seminar on Urban Evangelism / Church Planting" (12 January 1984); Kraakevik, "Urban Evangelism, *Intercom* 64 (September 1984): 1–2.

53   "Urban Church Planting—Principles, Proposals, and Guidelines," *SIM Ministries Manual* (February 1986).

54   The Evangelical Missionary Society is the missionary arm of Evangelical Church Winning All, then known as the Evangelical Churches of West Africa.

55   Gary Corwin, "Workshops for Urban Ministry," SIM International Council, Ministries, Agenda Item II.15 (21 March 1986); Corwin, "Review of Urban Ministries Coordination," memo to Howard Brant (6 February 1991).

56   "World city dwellers increase from one percent to 50," *SIMNOW* 1 (January–February 1982): 10; Kerry Lovering, "We've said goodbye to yesterday. Here's why," *SIMNOW* 8 (March–April 1983): 2–5.

57   Lovering, Kerry, "Witness in the City," *SIMNOW* (November–December 1988): 2.

58   Gary Corwin, "Urban Ministries Review", SIM International Council, Ministries, Agenda Item II.22, 3–14 May 1988.

59   Gary Corwin, "SIM Urban Workers," (15 December 1988), SIMIAR, Church Planting Box 531; Gary Corwin, Urban Ministries 8.100; *SIM Prayer Guide 1988* (Canada, 1987); W. Harold Fuller, *Celebrate the God Who Loves!: SIM Pictorial* (Scarborough, Canada: SIM International Media, 1992).

60   William Walker, "The Greatest Challenge," *Action Africa* 2, no. 1 (January–March 1988): 1, 4.

61   Rindi Bowman, discussion with author (18 October 2007).

62   Ed Welch, discussion with the author (19 October 2007).

63   Gary Corwin, "Review of Urban Ministries Coordination," Memo to Howard Brant (6 February 1991), SIMIAR, Gary Corwin Collection; Howard Brant, "Urban Ministries Report," SIMIAR, SIM International Council, Urban Ministry A (70.3), Ref. II.25, no. 94, 34; 27 (8 April 1992).

64   Conn, "Urban Mission," 327; John J. Shane, "Urban Ministries Support Group" June 1988–October 1989 (SIMIAR, Gary Corwin Collection, Urban Box, Urban Ministries Seminar NEGST); Shane, email to author (22 October 2007); Mike Kosi, "Urban Ministries Serving God (formerly Urban Ministries Support Group): A Brief History of a Ministry of SIM" (22 October 2007 email).

65   "Vision Consultation," SIMIAR, SIM International Manual, Urban Ministries Vision Statement (70.3.2) (June 2003).

66   "Seize the Day," 173.

Chapter 19: Ministries of Compassion

1   R. R. Kuczynski, *A Demographic Study of the British Colonial Empire*, vol. 1 (London: Oxford University Press, 1948), 763–766.

2   Rowland V. Bingham, "Luke, the Beloved Physician," in *The Bible and the Body: Or Healing in the Scriptures* (London: Marshall, Morgan & Scott, 1939), 84–85.

3   Andrew Stirrett, *Medical Book for the Treatment of Diseases in West Africa; also Pharmacy Notes, Dispensary Recipes and Health Hints—Written in Non-Technical Language* (Jos, Nigeria: Sudan Interior Mission, 1931).

4   Douglas C. Percy, "Served His Generation," in *Stirrett of the Sudan, the Beloved Physican of the Sudan* (Toronto: Sudan Interior Mission, 1948), 43.

5   W. H. Hinton, "Early Experiences," in *Ethel Ambrose, Pioneer Medical Missionary: Poona and Indian Village Mission, Bombay Presidency, India* (London: Marshall, Morgan & Scott, 1936), 92.

6   Basil Tyson and Helen Rosan, "A History of P.I.V.M.," in *Advancing Together: A Tale of Two Missions*, G. A. Hemming, ed. (London: International Christian Fellowship, c. 1974), 37–38.

7   Haye, Sophie de la Haye, "Angels Guard You," in *Tread upon the lion: The story of Tommie Titcombe* (Scarborough, Ontario: SIM International, 1987), 73–78.

8   Rowland V. Bingham, "Luke, the Beloved Physician," 84-85.

9   Yusufu Turaki,"Mission Medical Services," in *An Introduction to the History of SIM/ECWA in Nigeria, 1893–1993* (Nigeria: Y. Turaki, 1993), 186.

10 Martha Wall, "Leper Village," in *Splinters from an African Log* (Chicago: Moody Press, 1960), 85.

11 Agaja, S. B. *A Citadel of Blessings, ECWA Hospital Egbe* (Nigeria: S. B. Agaja, 2008).

12 Rob Congdon, "Doro Station, Upper Nile, Sudan, 1940," email message to author, 27 May 2015.

13 Lois Barlow Merritt, "A Tribute from a Man Who My Father Called the Best Friend He Ever Had," in *Nathan Barlow MD, Nearest Doctor for a Million People* (Bloomington, MN: Bethany Press International, 2013), 225–228.

14 Lorry Lutz, *Sword and Scalpel: A Surgeon's Story of Faith and Courage* (Orange, CA: Promise Pub., 1990).

15 "General Setting of Prem Sewa Hospital," *Love and Service, An Invitation to Prem Sewa Hospital, India* (Godalming, England: Godalming Baptist Church, 1991), 6–10.

16 Bob Blees, "SIM Medical Ministries at ELWA Hospital in Liberia," interview by the author, 11 May 2015.

17 Ian M. Hay, "SIM: Evangelism or Social Concern, Which?" Report, Deerfield, Illinois, 1982.

18 "Re: Invitation to Become CSM Coordinator," email message to author, 8 May 2015.

19 Don Stilwell, SIM International and Community Service Ministries: Trends and Issues," discussion paper, Issue brief, Vol. 5.3, Charlotte: SIM Ministries Manual, 1995.

20 Jon Shea, "SIM Response to Human Need," email message to author, 21 May 2015. This was research of SIM Manuals, SIM Constitution, and corporate documents including the Community Service Ministries manual for the origins and our mission purpose of "ministering to human needs."

21 Sue McKinney, "Tony Rinaudo Article," email to the author, 1 June 2015.

22 "Tilling the Soil and Tending the Sick, the Maradi Team Is Winning Friends—and Converts," *SIMNOW, Volume 76 (1996): 6.*

23   Jonathan Green and Tony Rinaudo, Regreening Ethiopia—Tony Rinaudo on ABC Radio
      National, November 10, 2014, podcast audio, MP3, 9:39, accessed on 1 June 2015, http://
      mpegmedia.abc.net.au/rn/podcast/2014/11/sra_20141109_0845.mp3.

24   John Ockers, "History of SIM Work in Niger 1923–2000," Report compiled for SIM, 2005, 26.

25   Don Stilwell, ed., "SIM Famine Relief Evaluation Report (Especially Covering the Period 1983–
      1987)," Working paper, Charlotte, SIM, 1989.

26   Jon Shea, "SIM Response to Human Need," email message to author, 21 May 2015.

27   "The Lausanne Covenant." Lausanne Movement, http://www.lausanne.org/content/covenant/
      lausanne-covenant, accessed 1 June 2015.

28   "The Challenge of the Future in SIM Community Service Ministries," MS, SIM Ministries
      Manual, SIM Archives, Charlotte, 1996.

29   David Van Reken, MD, "Introduction," *Mission and Ministry: Christian Medical Practice in
      Today's Changing World Cultures* (Wheaton, IL: Billy Graham Center, 1987), 5–7.

30   Phil Andrew, MD, "Training Health Workers in SIM: The Quiet Revolution in Medical Missions
      Strategy," MS, SIM Archives, Sydney, 1993.

31   *God with Us: The History of EHA—an Indigenous Medical Mission in India* (New Delhi, India:
      Emmanuel Hospital Association, 1994).

32   "Community Services Ministries Consultation Report and Recommendations to International
      Council," MS, SIM Ministries Manual, SIM Archives, Charlotte, NC, 1993.

33   Ibid.

34   Ibid.

35   Hudson, Paul J., MD. "Health Ministry Review A Call for a Strategic Plan for National Leadership
      Development in Medical Missions," MS, SIM Archives, Fort Mill, SC, 2003.

36   Jay Moon, "Forgiveness and Reconciliation," in *The Slave Trade and Reconciliation: A Northern
      Ghana Perspective,* Allison Howell, ed. (Accra, Ghana: Bible Church of Africa and SIM Ghana,
      1998), 66; "Healing the Wounds of Slavery," *Serving in Mission Together* 108 (2004): 3–5.

37   Paul J. Hudson, MD, Report on AERDO and CCC Meetings, MS, Banff, 2000.

38   Marcus Baeder, "Lessons Learned from the Experiences of HOPE for AIDS," email message to
      author, 22 May 2015.

39   Steve Strauss, "Kingdom Living: The Gospel on Our Lips and In Our Lives," *Evangelical Mission
      Quarterly 41, no. 1* (January 2005).

40   Daniel G. Bausch and Hal White, "ASTMH Remembers Penny Pinneo, a Pioneer in Combating
      Lassa Fever (1917–2012)," *ASTMH BLOG* (2 October 2012), http://www.astmh.org/source/
      blog/post.cfm/astmh-remembers-, accessed 5 August 2014. ASTMH is the American Society of
      Tropical Medicine and Hygiene.

41   Geoff Watts, "Lily Lyman Pinneo," *The Lancet*, 380, no. 9853 (3 November 2012): 1552, http://
      www.thelancet.com/journals/lancet/article/PIIS0140-6736, accessed 31 July 2014.

42   Stephen Miller, Staff Reporter of the *Sun*, 22 January 2008, "John Frame, 90, Discovered
      Lassa Fever," http://www.nysun.com/obituaries/john-frame-90-discovered-lassa-fever/69916/,
      accessed 31 July 2014. Additional information from the author's personal acquaintance with
      Dr. Frame.

43   Bausch and White, "ASTMH Remembers."

44   Ibid.

45   For example, David Von Drehle, "The Ones Who Answered the Call," *Time* magazine (22/29 December 2014): 72–107.

46   Melissa Leach, "Time to Put Ebola in Context," *Bulletin of the World Health Organization, 88, no. 7*, http:www.who.int/bulletin/volumes/88/7/10-030710/en/, accessed 29 July 2014.

47   An unpublished manuscript sent to the author by Deborah L. Sacra, via email 14 September 2016. Used with permission. Photos and sidebars added.

48   Barbara K. Bono, "How I Contracted Ebola," http://blog.visiontrust.org/how-i-contracted-ebola/, accessed 15 June 2017.

49   Caelainn Hogan, "'There Is No Such Thing as Ebola'—The Washington Post," *Washington Post*, 18 July 2014, https://www.washingtonpost.com/news/morning-mix/wp/2014/07/18/there-is-no-such-thing-as-ebola.

50   T. Geysbeek's interview with William Pewee, 23 May 2015; "He Never Imagined He'd be the Answer to his own Prayer," *SIM Global* 150 (June 2016), https://www.simusa.org/wp-content/uploads/2016/03/SIM0395-NEWSLETTER_FINAL.pdf , accessed 15 June 2017. The first Ebola patient arrived late in the evening on 11 June and was admitted to ELWA 1 in the early hours of 12 June (D. Eisenhut email to T. Geysbeek, 3 March 2015).

51   Von Drehle, "The Ones Who Answered the Call," 72-107.

52   Dr. John Fankhauser email to Debbie Sacra, 28 March 2017.

53   "WHO declares end of the most recent Ebola virus disease outbreak in Liberia," *WHO*, http://www.who.int/mediacentre/news/releases/2016/ebola-liberia/en/, accessed 14 September 2016.

Chapter 20: The Globalization of Missions

1   "Cape Town 2010: Lausanne III," *Intercom* 102 (November–January 2011): 1–3.

2   Ibid., p. 3.

3   *SIMNOW* 27 (May–June 1986): 7.

4   "Non-Western Missions—How We Relate," *Intercom* 71 (January 1986): 1–2. Photos added to his article.

5   Tim Geysbeek's discussion with Chuck Guth, January 2006.

6   Detlef Bloecher, "Links that Liberate," *Serving in Mission Together* 117 (2007): 4.

7   *SIMNOW* 21 (May–June 1985): 6–7.

8   Eileen Lagger, *New Life for All: Thrilling stories of evangelism in West Africa* (London: Oliphants, 1969.)

9   "The Marwari, *SIMGLOBAL* 132 (Autumn 2011): 4–6.

10   "Panya Dabo Baba, Nigeria, ECWA / Sudan Interior Mission, http://www.dacb.org/stories/nigeria/panya_dabo.html, accessed 12 August 2014, and reproduced in its entirety from the *Dictionary of African Christian Biography*. Sources: Panya Baba, interview by the author at his house in Karu, August 2003; Yusufu Turaki, "Citation given on behalf of Panya Baba," typescript, May 18, 1991; Ian M. Hay, "Baba, Panya (1932–)," in J. D. Douglas, ed., *Twentieth-Century Dictionary of Christian Biography* (Grand Rapids: Baker Books, 1995); Wale Banks and Wale Olaniyan, *Nigerian Indigenous Missions: Pioneers Behind the Scene* (Ibadan: Alliance Research Network International, 2005); Anonymous, "Panya Baba," typescript, n.d.; Anonymous, "Panya Baba: A Committed Life as Leader," typescript, n.d., Panya Baba's curriculum vitae. This article, received in 2006, was researched and written by Dr. Musa A. B. Gaiya, Senior Lecturer in Church

History at the University of Jos Department of Religious Studies, Jos, Nigeria, and Project Luke fellow in Fall 2003 and Fall 2006.

11   Note: ECWA now means Evangelical Church Winning All.

12   The "Gbagyi" are also called the "Gwari." Today the Gbagyi are said to number more than three million, making them one of the largest ethnic groups in central Nigeria. (This and the next one is an original footnote.)

13   Wale Banks and Wale Olaniyan, *Nigerian Indigenous Missions: Pioneers Behind the Scene* (Ibadan: Alliance Research Network International, 2005).

Chapter 21: Middle East Christian Outreach

1   This arrangement included the MECO United Kingdom, Ireland, and South Africa branches. MECO New Zealand partnered with another organization, and MECO Canada decided to remain independent. At the date of this writing, "arrangements" between MECO and SIM Australia are still being discussed. For more information, see: "SIM and MECO International join hands in the Middle East," *Together* (SIM New Zealand) 149 (April 2016): 25; "Special Announcement," *MECO International* 2 (2016): 2; "Coming Together," *MECO International* 2 (2016): 4–5; "MECO Canada not affected by recent decision," Press Release, http://mecocanada.org/press-release-meco-canada/, accessed 16 June 2017.

2   See chapter 4, pages 57-58.

3   "Where We Serve," http://mecoglobal.com/about-us/where-we-serve/, accessed 29 August 2016.

4   "History repeats itself," *MECO International* 2 (2016): 8.

5   Thanks to Mike Parker for writing this and the next paragraph (25 May 2017 email).

6   "Lebanon Evangelical Mission," https://web.archive.org/web/20060505050329/http://www.aboutmeco.org/website/lem.htm (May 2006 posting), accessed 25 March 2017. With gratitude to Phil Bourne, MECO's research officer, and other archives sources for each of these histories. For more information about the histories of these missions, see the Bibliography, pages 422-424.

7   This section that begins with "The following is an excerpt," and ends with "she never flinched" three paragraphs later, is from "MECO celebrates 150 years in the Middle East," *MECO International* 2 (2010): 5.

8   "Middle East General Mission," https://web.archive.org/web/20050413205837/http://www.aboutmeco.org/website/megm.htm (May 2006 posting), accessed 25 March 2017. For scholarly works that set Egypt General Mission's work in more historical context, see Beth Barron, *The Orphan Scandal: Christian Missionaries and the Rise of the Muslim Brotherhood* (Stanford: Stanford University Press, 2014); Heather J. Sharkey, *American Evangelicals in Egypt: Missionary Encounters in an Age of Empire* (Princeton, NJ: Princeton University Press, 2008); Samir Boulos, *European Evangelicals in Egypt (1900-1956): Cultural Entanglements and Missionary Spaces* (Leiden: Brill, 2016).

9   "Arabic Literature Mission," https://web.archive.org/web/20060505050336/http://www.aboutmeco.org/website/alm.htm, (May 2006 posting), accessed 25 March 2017.

10   "Middle East Christian Outreach," https://web.archive.org/web/20060501065157/http://www.aboutmeco.org/website/mecohistory.htm, accessed 25 March 2017.

11   For more recent information about MECO's activities, see back issues of its magazines: https://web.archive.org/web/20030608131809/http://www.aboutmeco.org/crossroads/index.htm and http://mecoglobal.com/magazine/, both accessed on 25 March 2017.

12   Information about Anderson's life in this supplement is based on: Norman Anderson, *An Adopted Son: The Story of My Life* (Leicester: Inter-Varsity Press, 1985); David A. Kerr, "Anderson, James Norman Dalrymple (1908–1994), in *Biographical Dictionary of Christian Missions*, Gerald H. Anderson, ed. (New York: Macmillan Reference USA, 1998), 18; Todd M. Thompson, "Anderson, Sir (James) Norman Dalrymple (1908–1994)," http://www.oxforddnb.com/view/article/54706, accessed 10 September 2016; Thompson, "The King and Anderson," *History Today* 61, no. 12 (December 2011): 49-52; Thompson, *Norman Anderson and the Christian Mission to Modernize Islam* (Oxford, forthcoming). Many thanks to Dr. Thompson for providing a pre-publication draft of his forthcoming book.

13   Cited in Thompson, *Norman Anderson.*

14   Thompson, "Anderson, Sir (James) Norman Dalrymple (1908–1994)."

15   Anderson, *An Adopted Son*, 43.

16   Anderson, *An Adopted Son*, 87.

Epilogue

1   Kerry E. Lovering, "Death Is Not Failure—The Story of Walter H. Gowans," manuscript, 1992, 5.

2   Rowland Bingham, *Seven Sevens of Years and a Jubilee: The Story of the Sudan Interior Mission* (New York: Evangelical Publishers, 1957), 5.

3   Ibid., 9, 11–12.

4   "SIM—A Ten-Year Missiological Trajectory," paper presented at Inter-Agency Leadership Consultation on Collaboration, The Netherlands, 2014.

5   Joshua Bogunjoko, "The Big Why: SIM's Reason for Being," http://www.sim.org/index.php/content/the-big-why-sim-s-reason-for-being, accessed 30 March 2017.

6   Report to the SIM Board of Governors on Refocusing SIM, June 2014.

7   Lovering, "Death Is Not Failure," 19.

Appendix A: SIM Statement of Faith

1   From http://sim.org/index.php/content/statement-of-faith, accessed 24 February 2017.

Appendix B: Purpose and Mission, Core Values, and Vision of SIM

1   From http://sim.org/index.php/content/our-purpose, accessed 24 February 2017.

2   From http://sim.org/index.php/content/core-values, accessed 24 February 2017.

3   From http://sim.org/index.php/content/our-purpose, 24 February 2017.

Appendix C: Directors of Missions

1   Dr. James Kallam compiled this list.

2   "Leading the way," *MECO International* 2 (2016): 8.

Appendix E: How We Became Interdenominational

1   Rowland Bingham and Kerry Lovering, *Root from Dry Ground* (Toronto: SIM International Media, 1991), 64–68.

Appendix F: What's in a Name?

1   Adapted from Gary Corwin, "What's in a Name?" *SIM USA News* (April 1993): 3 and (May 1993): 5–6.
2   "Africa Industrial Mission," *The Faithful Witness* 12, no. 33 (15 August 1899): 7–8. Italicized descriptors are added, not in the original.
3   Ibid.
4   "A New Name for an Established Mission," *The Missionary Witness* 1, no. 10 (17 October 1905): 186–187.
5   "Important Announcement," *The Missionary Witness* 3, no. 6 (2 July 1907): 97–98.

Appendix G: A Time Line Depicting Changes in SIM Organizational Structure from 1893-1993

1   Written originally for the SIM International Archives as an unpublished document by Dr. Hay titled "Musings from an Old Director: A Time Line Depicting Changes in SIM Organizational Structure from 1893–1993" (13 August 2002).
2   Bingham co-founded SIM along with Walter Gowans and Thomas Kent, and became the mission's leader by default after Gowans and Kent died in 1894.
3   Note: C. Gordon Beacham served as acting/deputy director until Playfair became general director.
4   Note: SIM's Canadian and United States corporations, in consultation with its West and East Africa Councils, formed the Memoranda of Agreement. This agreement included the mission's branches that existed in the United Kingdom, Australia, New Zealand, and South Africa (*The Principles and Practice of the Sudan Interior Mission* [N.p.: Sudan Interior Mission, 1958], 3-4).

Appendix H: Redeeming Mission Agencies: "A Highway to the Nations"

1   This material is adapted from a larger unpublished document by Howard Brant, "Redefining Missions for the 21st Century," dated 21 May 2004, 17–23. Endnotes included beyond this one are part of the original document. The original paper, "Highway for the Nations," was written in 2002. Brant was one of SIM's deputy international directors when he wrote this document.
2   This is very much in the spirit of COMIBAM that declared that Latin America is no longer just a mission receiving continent—but a mission sending one as well.
3   1 Chronicles 12:32. The new incoming Director of SIM International, Malcolm McGregor, has taken this verse and adopted the motto, Seize the Day. He calls for not only understanding the times—but taking action accordingly. May it be so.

Appendix I: SIM International Archives and Records

1   For a similar photo and caption, see "Family Album," *Intercom* 39 (August 1978): 5.

SELECT BIBLIOGRAPHY OF SIM-RELATED SOURCES

Dr. Tim Geysbeek, compiler

The following represent some of the key publications, theses, and manuscripts written about the histories of Africa Evangelical Fellowship (formerly the South Africa General Mission, including the merged mission of Cape General Mission); Andes Evangelical Fellowship (formerly the Bolivian Indian Mission); International Christian Fellowship (including the merged missions of the Ceylon and Indian General Mission and Poona and Indian Village Mission); Middle East Christian Outreach (including the merged missions of the Lebanon Evangelical Mission, Middle East General Mission, and Arabic Literature Mission); and SIM, formerly known as the Sudan Interior Mission.

Excluded are hundreds of pamphlets, booklets, and articles that have been published in encyclopedias, popular magazines, mission periodicals, and the Dictionary of African Christian Biography. Also not listed are publications of translations, medicine, missiology, theology and other genres not set in a strong historical context.

The titles of some of each mission's main periodicals are included. (Not noted are instances where countries published separate editions of the same periodical or countries that gave different titles for their editions of the same magazine.) Some of the digital editions can be found at http://archives.sim.org/. Hard copies of the periodicals are in the SIM International Archives and Records located in Fort Mill, South Carolina, USA. For current publications, see https://www.sim.org/.

MISSION HISTORIES

Africa Evangelical Fellowship (formerly the South Africa General Mission, including the merged mission of Cape General Mission)

Periodicals (select)
- *South African Pioneer* (Cape Town, 1885–1945)
- *South African Pioneer* (London, 1896–1964)

- *Diamonds* (1901–1916)
- *South African Pioneer* (New York, 1920–1964)
- *Our Africa* (1958–1963)
- *African Evangel* (1964–1986) (This is a continuation of New York's *South African Pioneer*)
- *Pioneer* (1965–1987)
- *Action Africa* (1986–1998)

Books, theses, manuscripts, and articles

- Hardy, Steve. "Lessons from a Merger." *Evangelical Missions Quarterly* 43, no. 4 (October 2007): 468–473.
- Huntingford, Alan C. F. *History of the Southern Field (C.G.M., S.A.G.M., A.E.F.): The First One Hundred Years.* N.p., c. 1991.
- Ingles, Winona M. "Called into the Light: The Story of the Africa Evangelical Fellowship [and] the South Africa General Mission." Manuscript, c. 1966.
- Kallam, James Gray. "A History of the Africa Evangelical Fellowship from Its Inception to 1917." Ph.D. diss., New York University, 1978.
- Mark, Helen B. *The Wind of His Power: A skeletal sketch of the history of the Africa Evangelical Fellowship (A.E.F.), formerly The South Africa General Mission (S.A.G.M.).* N.p: Africa Evangelical Fellowship, c. 1971.
- Procter, John Craig. "The Cross in Southern Africa: A History of the South Africa General Mission." Manuscript, Brooklyn, NY, 1945.

Andes Evangelical Mission (formerly the Bolivian Indian Mission)

Periodicals

- *News and Report* (1908–1910)
- *Tahuantin Suyu* (1911–1914)
- *Bolivian Indian* (1915–1965)
- *Andean Outlook* (1966–1981)

Books and articles

- Allan, George. *Reminiscences: Being Incidents from Missionary Experience.* Cochamba, Bolivia: Bolivian Indian Mission and Stanton Bros., c. 1936.
- Hansen, Jim, ed. *A Heart to Serve: Ordinary People with an Extraordinary God.* Cochabamba, Bolivia: Mision Andiana Evangelica, 2007. (Centenary publication of AEM and SIM's work in South America.)
- Hudspith, Margaret Allan. *Ripening Fruit: A History of the Bolivian Indian Mission.* Harrington Park, NJ: Harrington Press, c. 1958.

- Lemaitre, Arana Arturo. *Yo Era Fabricante De Dioses*. Cochabamba: Librería Buenas Nuevas, c. 1950. (This is a personal testimony of one of the great mid-twentieth-century evangelists of South America and beyond.)
- Morrison, Hugh. "Negotiated and Mediated Lives: Bolivian Teachers, New Zealand Missionaries and the Bolivian Indian Mission, 1908–1932." *Itinerario* 40, no. 3 (2016): 429–449.
- _____. *Pushing Boundaries: New Zealand Protestants and Overseas Missions 1827–1939*. Dunedin, New Zealand: Otago University Press, 2016. (Chapter 5 is about BIM. The author also writes about the Poona and Indian Village Mission.)
- _____. "Theorizing Missionary Education: The Bolivian Indian Mission, 1908–1920." *History of Education Review* 42, no. 1 (2013): 4–23.
- _____. "'We carry joyous news that has made us free': New Zealand Missionaries, the Bolivian Indian Mission and Global Engagement, 1980–1930." *New Zealand Journal of History* 39, no. 1 (April 2005): 39–56.
- Shereda, Edith. *Among the Bolivian Indians*. Chicago: Moody Church Office, n.d. (The author recounts her work in Bolivia from 1930 to 1933.)

International Christian Fellowship (including the merged missions of Ceylon and Indian General Mission and Poona and Indian Mission)

Periodicals
- *Darkness and Light* (1893–1988; CIGM/ICF)
- *White Already to Harvest* (1893–1968; PIVM)

Books, articles, and papers
- Dover, Irene. *Pathway through India: The Life of Amy Parsons*. N.p.: PIVM, n.d.
- Haggis, Jane, and Margaret Allen. "Imperial Emotions: Affective Communities of Mission in British Protestant Women's Missionary Publications c. 1880–1920." *Journal of Social History* 41, no. 3 (Spring 2008): 691–716. (Focus on women mentioned in PIVM's *White Already to Harvest*.)
- Heming, G. A., ed. *Advancing Together: A Tale of Two Missions*. London: International Christian Fellowship, c. 1974. (Chapters about CIGM, PIVM, and ICF, and their work in Bangladesh, Ceylon [Sri Lanka], India, and Pakistan.)
- Welch, Ian. "Poona (Pune) and Indian Village Mission (PIVM)." Working paper, 2014; (*https://digitalcollections.anu.edu.au/bitstream/1885/13041/1/Welch%20Poona%202014.pdf*), accessed 30 October 2015.
- Whittall, Gillian Watch. *From Gallipoli to the Skies: The Story of a Young Man Who Dreamed of Flying*. Xlibris, 2014. (Chapter 1 includes information about PIVM co-founder Charles Reeve.)

Middle East Christian Outreach (including the merged missions of the Lebanon Evangelical Mission, Middle East General Mission, and Arabic Literature Mission)

Lebanon Evangelical Mission
(Ladies Association for the Social and Religious Improvement of Syrian Females, British Syrian Schools and Bible Mission, British Syrian Mission)

Periodicals
- *Daughters of Syria* (pre–1933) (British Syrian Mission)
- *Under Syrian Skies* (1933–1959) (British Syrian Mission)
- *Light on Lebanon* (1960–1971) (Lebanon Evangelical Mission)
- *Crossroads* (1972–1975) (Lebanon Evangelical Mission)

Books
- H., J. E. *One Hundred Syrian Pictures, Illustrating the Work of the British Syrian Mission*. London, 1903.
- *Lebanon at the Crossroads*. Tunbridge Wells, England: Lebanon Evangelical Mission, c. 1960.
- Maitland-Kirwan, J. D. *Sunrise in Syria: A Short History of the British Syrian Mission from 1860 to 1930*. London: British Syrian Mission, 1930.
- Scott, Frances E. *Dare and Persevere: The Story of One Hundred Years of Evangelism in Syria and Lebanon, 1860–1960*. London: The Camelot Press, Ltd., 1960. (Documenting the history of the Ladies Association for the School and Religious Improvement of Syrian Families [1860], which later became known as the British Syrian Schools and Bible Mission [1873], the British Syrian Mission [1891], and the Lebanon Evangelical Mission [1959].)
- Tristram, H. B, editor. *The Daughters of Syria: A Narrative of Efforts by the Late Mrs. Bowen Thompson, for the Evangelization of the Syrian Females*. 2nd ed. London: Seeley, Jackson & Halliday, 1872. (This work is the story of Elizabeth Maria Bowen Thompson who founded the Ladies Association for the Social & Religious Improvement of Syrian Females in 1860.)

Middle East General Mission
(Egypt Mission Band, Egypt General Mission)

Periodicals
- *Egypt General Mission News* (1901–1957)
- *Vision and Commission* (1957–1976; Middle East General Mission)

Books

- French, Margaret, and Sybil Webb. *Miracles of Mercy*. Tunbridge Wells: Middle East General Mission, c. 1950.
- Hamilton, Kathleen L. *At Thy Disposal: The Beginnings of the Egypt General Mission*. London: Egypt General Mission, 1944.
- Naish, Irene E. *Wonders in Egypt: The Story of the Egypt General Mission*. London: Egypt General Mission, 1951.
- Roome, William John Watterman. *Blessed Be Egypt: A Missionary Story; Being Some Account of Present Missionary Effort in Egypt, and the Story of the Lord's Leading of the Egypt Mission Band*. London: Marshall Brothers, 1898. Reprint, Forgotten Books, 2015.
- Swan, George. *Lacked Ye Anything?: A Brief Story of the Egypt General Mission*. London: Egypt General Mission, 1923.
- Tucker, Lilian M. *Except the Lord . . .* St. Ives, Huntington, UK: The Ridley Press, c. 1970.
- Upson, Arthur T. *High lights in the Near East: Reminiscences of Nearly 40 Years' Service*. London: Marshall, Morgan & Scott, c. 1931.
- _____. *The High Soul Climbs the High Way*. N.p., 1949. (Biography of George Swan of Egypt General Mission.)
- Whitehouse, Aubrey H. *Do You Remember?* Melbourne: Melbourne School of Theology, forthcoming. (This is the author's recollections of his work in Egypt from 1935-1956.)
- _____. *The Complete Circle: A Story of Medical Work in Egypt*. London: Egypt General Mission, 1958.

Arabic Literature Mission
(Nile Mission Press)

Periodicals

- *Blessed Be Egypt* (1906; Nile Mission Press)
- *Nile Mission Press News* (1948–1960)
- *Message* (1960–?; Arabic Literature Mission)

Books

- *Descriptive Guide to the Nile Mission Press and Other Publications, Suitable for Work in Oriental Lands among Moslems, Jews, and Christians*. Cairo: Nile Mission Press, 1914.
- Upson, Arthur T. *The Unfolding of a Vision*. N.p., 1958. (This is a short history of Nile Mission Press.)

Middle East Christian Outreach

Periodicals

- *Crossroads* (1976–2007)
- *MECO International Magazine* (2008–2016)

Books

- Napper, Joyce. *Christianity in the Middle East.* Larnaca, Cyprus: Middle East Christian Outreach, 1992.
- Shepherd, Paul. *Decade in the Desert: The Story of Haicota Hospital.* Kent, England: Middle East Christian Outreach, 1977.

SIM (formerly the Sudan Interior Mission)

Periodicals (select)

- *The Minna Witness* (1919–1922; only one issue is known to exist)
- *The Sudan Witness* (1923–1971; published in Nigeria until 1950, and then Australia, North America [copublished in the United States and Canada], Britain, South Africa, and New Zealand from 1967–1971)
- *The Sudan Witness Supplements* (1948–1954; published in New Zealand, South Africa, Britain, and North America)
- *The West African Christian* (1948–1951)
- *African Challenge* (1951–1973)
- *Labarin Ekklesiya* ("News of the Church" in Hausa; 1953–1957)
- *Yoruba Challenge* (1954–1973)
- *Today's Teacher* (1956–1964)
- *Kakai* ("The Chief's Trumpet," 1957–1958; a continuation of *Labarin Ekklesiya*)
- *Africa Now* (1958–1981)
- *Champion* (1964–1978; in French)
- *Ghana Challenge* (1973–1977)
- *Today's Challenge* (1974–present; a continuation of *African Challenge*, published by SIM until 1977, and thereafter by ECWA)
- *SIMNOW* (1982–2000)
- *Serving in Mission Together* (2001–2011)
- For recent editions of SIM's major periodicals published in different countries around the world with varying titles, see https://www.sim.org/, accessed 13 July 2017.

Founding and General Background

- *Africa Today: The Church's Task in a Developing Continent.* St. Albans: Campfield Press, 1967. (This booklet is comprised of articles originally published in the *Sudan Witness.*)
- Benge, Janet, and Geoff Benge. *Rowland Bingham: Into Africa's Interior.* Seattle, WA: YWAM Publishing, 2003.
- Bingham, Rowland. *Burden of the Sudan.* Brooklyn, NY: Sudan Interior Mission, 1918. (Bingham published eight more editions of this booklet before he died in 1942.)
- _____. *Seven Sevens of Years and a Jubilee: The Story of the Sudan Interior Mission.* 5th ed. New York: Evangelical Publishers, 1957. (First published in 1943).
- Bingham, Rowland, and Kerry Lovering. *Root from Dry Ground: The Birth of the Sudan Interior Mission.* Toronto: SIM International Media, 1991.
- _____. *Root from Dry Ground: The Story of the Sudan Interior Mission.* Aylesbury, England: Hazel Watson & Viney Ltd., 1966.
- Bingham, Rowland, and Douglas Percy. *Burden of the Sudan.* Toronto: Sudan Interior Mission, Rev. ed., 1955.
- _____. *Root from Dry Ground: The story of the Sudan Interior Mission.* Toronto: Sudan Interior Mission, c. 1960.
- Bruning, Stan. "Christian Radio Into the World By 2000." Typescript. [Sebring, FL], 2017. (Bruning tells about SIM and other missions' engagement in the World By 2000 gospel radio initiative.)
- Cooper, Barbara, Gary Corwin, Tibebe Eshete, Musa Gaiya, Tim Geysbeek, Shobana Shankar, eds. *Breaking Barriers: The Sudan Interior Mission and African Pioneers Remaking Missions across the Sahel* (tentative title). Trenton, NJ: Africa World Press/Red Sea Press, forthcoming. (This book will include one or more chapters on Canada, Ethiopia, Ghana, Liberia, Niger, Nigeria, South Sudan, and Sudan.)
- Fuller, W. Harold. "My Pilgrimage in Mission." *International Bulletin of Missionary Research* 34, no. 1 (2010): 37–40.
- Guth, Charles J., complier, edited by Marjory Koop. *Escape to the Jungle . . . and 31 Other Outstanding Missionary Stories.* Cedar Grove, NJ: Sudan Interior Mission, 1981. (The stories were first published in *Africa Now.*)
- Hay, Ian M. *Foundations: Scriptural Principles Undergirding SIM.* Toronto: SIM International, 1988.
- _____. *The Master Plan.* Toronto: SIM USA, Inc., 2000. (Hay writes to help churches understand God's understanding of missions and churches' role in it.)
- _____. *Unity & Purity: Keeping the Balance.* Toronto: SIM International, 1983. (The author explores ecumenism, fellowship, separation, and doctrinal integrity.)

- Hunter, Jim H. *A Flame of Fire: The Life and Work of R. V. Bingham, Ll.D.* Aylesbury: Hazell, Watson & Viney Limited, 1961. (This is a favorable biography of Bingham that includes an overview of SIM's work in Africa.)
- Kato, Byang H. *African Cultural Revolution and the Christian Faith.* Jos: Challenge Pbs., 1976.
- McKenzie, Brian Alexander. "Fundamentalism, Christian Unity, and Premillennialism in the Thought of Rowland Victor Bingham (1872–1942): A Study of Anti-Modernism in Canada." Ph.D. diss., Toronto School of Theology, 1985.
- Plueddemann, Carol, and James Plueddemann. "How I Changed My Mind about Women in Church Leadership: Transforming Moments in our Pilgrimage." In *How I Changed My Mind about Women in Leadership: Compelling Stories from Prominent Evangelicals*, Alan F. Johnson, ed. Grand Rapids: Zondervan, 2010, 197–208.
- Plueddemann, Jim. "SIM's Agenda for a Gracious Revolution." *International Bulletin of Missionary Research* 23, no. 4 (October 1999): 156–160.
- Thiombiano, Oualidia Ezéchiel. "Aperç Historique d'une Mission Evangélique: la SIM, 1893–1993. Typescript, c. 1993.
- _____. "Naissance et Developpement de la SIM Internationale, 1893–1999." Typescript, c. 1999.

AFRICA

Continent
- Fuller, W. Harold. *Run While the Sun Is Hot.* New York: Sudan Interior Mission, 1967.
- _____. *Courez Avant la Nuit* ("*Run While the Sun Is Hot*"), Hélène Cruvellier trans., Vevey, Switzerland: Editions des Groupes Missionaires, 1968.

Angola (Portuguese West Africa)
- Arrington, Andrea L. "Making Sense of Martha: Single Women and Mission Work." *Social Sciences and Missions* 23 (2010): 276–300. (Story of SAGM's Martha Moors who went to Portuguese West Africa in 1920.)
- Calenga, Eduardo. *Historia de UIEA* (Uniaõ de Igrejas Evangélicas de Angola). Londrina, Brazil: Editora Descoberta, 2014.
- Ferguson, James. *The One Thing: The Ron Filby Story.* Cape Town: Southern Africa Youth for Christ, 1965.
- Lutz, Lorry. *Sword & Scalpel: A Surgeon's Story of Faith and Courage.* Orange, CA: Promise Publishing Co., 1997. (Story of Dr. Robert Foster and his wife Belva.)

- Procter, Jack. *Fools for Christ's Sake*. N.p.: Africa Evangelical Fellowship, 1965. (Angola, Mozambique, South Africa, Canada)
- Procter, Minnie. *African Circular Digest*. Toronto: N.p.: Africa Evangelical Digest, c. 1965.

Benin (Dahomey)
- Dipple, Bruce E. "A Missiological Evaluation of the History of the Sudan Interior Mission in French West Africa, 1924–1962." D. Miss. thesis, Trinity Evangelical Divinity School, 1994. (Benin, Burkina Faso, Niger)
- Dufour, Andrée. *Le Pays Que J'ai Aimé: Notes Prises au Cours de 22 Années au Bénin*. Genève: La Maison de la Bible, 1996.
- Fredlund, Alice. *Alice in Africa*. Oxford, England: Friends Print+media, 2007. (An account of Alice and Gus Fredlund's work in Dahomey from the mid-1940s to the mid-1960s.)
- Gaitou, Jeannette. "Christian Faith-Based Organisations and Transformational Development in Togo, Benin, and the Democratic Republic of the Congo." Ph.D. diss., Oxford Centre for Mission Studies and the University of Wales, 2013.
- Hegeman, Benjamin L. *Between Shame and Glory: A Historical and Systematic Study of Education and Leadership Training Models among the Baatonu in North Benin*. Zoetermeer: Uitgeverij Boekencentrum, 2001.
- McDougall, Colin S., and Edna M. McDougall. *Acceptable Costs: Planting the Church in Dahomey, 1947 to 1975*. Eugene, OR: Wipf & Stock Publishers, 2005.
- Pierre, Barassounon, Benjamin Lee Hegeman, David Atchadé, Jacob Ichola, Koma Enée, Kpétéré Bio K. Darius, and Méré Jean-Claude Orou Yorou. *L'UEEB et la DEIF Missionnaire, 1946–1996: Une Introduction à l'Histoire de l'Union des Eglises Evangéliques du Bénin (UEEB)*. Parakou: Centre Informatique (SIM/UEEB), 1996.

Burkina Faso (Haute Volta, Upper Volta)
- Dipple, Bruce E. "A Missiological Evaluation of the History of the Sudan Interior Mission in French West Africa, 1924–1962." D. Miss. thesis, Trinity Evangelical Divinity School, 1994.
- Gray, Joel. "White Hair Is Not Purchased in the Marketplace: A Historical and Comparative Study of Traditional, Islamic, and Secular Models of Education in Burkina Faso, with a Plea for Renewal in Christian Leadership Development." S.T.M. thesis, Boston University School of Theology, 2006.
- Lochstampfor, Ed. *While There's Still Time: A Missionary Journey*. Columbia, SC: Tall Grass Media, 2016. (Ed and Charlotte Lockstampfor served in Burkina Faso and Guinea.)

- Ruten, David Costas. "In Spite of Us: An Evangelical Biographical History of the Gourmantché Church." M.A. thesis, Providence Theological Seminary, 2007.
- Thiombiano, Oualidia Ezéchiel. "Historique de l'Eglise Evangélique SIM (EE/SIM) à Travers des Dates, 1930–2005." Typescript, 2005.

Egypt

For materials published about work in Egypt, see periodicals and books published under the heading Middle East General Mission (pages 422-424).

Ethiopia

- Adolph, Harold. *I Should Have Been Dead: An International Surgeon's Many Narrow Escapes Prove That God Loves Life.* New York: Vantage Press, 1990. (Harold and Bonnie Jo Adolph worked for SIM in Liberia, Niger, and Zambia.)
- Adolph, Harold, with Mark D. Williams. *Today's Decisions, Tomorrow's Destiny.* Spooner, WI: White Birch Printing, Inc., 2000.
- Ali, Wondiye. *Bemekera wist Yabebech Betekristian (Church Out of Tribulation) 1928–1941.* Vol. 1 of *The Story of the Ethiopian Kale Heywet Church in Ethiopia.* Addis Ababa: KHC Literature Department, 1988. (Published in Amharic.)
- _____. *Yekule Lelit Wegeta (Awakening at Midnight) 1942–1973.* Vol. 2 of *The Story of the Kale Heywet Church in Ethiopia.* Addia Ababa: KHC Literature Department, 2000. (Published in Amharic.)
- Balisky, E. Paul. "Wolaitta Evangelists: A Study of Religious Innovation in Southern Ethiopia, 1937–1975." Ph. D. diss., University of Aberdeen, 1997.
- _____. *Wolaitta Evangelists: A Study of Religious Innovation in Southern Ethiopia, 1937–1975.* Eugene, OR: Pickwick Publications, 2009.
- Balisky, E. Paul, and Lila Balisky. *SIM Ethiopia: Stones of Remembrance.* N.p.: E. Paul Balisky and Lila Balisky, 2004.
- Balisky, Lila. "SIM Kamba, Ethiopia: Study of a Mission in NGO Project Implementation." University of Edinburgh, M.Th. diss., 1981.
- _____. "Songs of Ethiopia's Tesfaye Gabbiso: Singing with understanding in Babylon, the Meantime and Zion." D.Miss. diss., Fuller Theological Seminary, 2015.
- _____. *Songs of Ethiopia's Tesfaye Gabbiso: Singing with Understanding in Babylon, the Meantime and in Zion.* Eugene, OR: Pickwick Publications, forthcoming.
- Banks, Donald. *It Won't Work Here.* Tunbridge Wells: Sudan Interior Mission, 1980. (Stories about SIM's work in Canada, Ethiopia, Liberia, Niger, and Nigeria.)
- Bascom, Kay. *Hidden Triumph in Ethiopia.* Pasadena, CA: William Carey Library, 2001.

- Bascom, Tim. *Chameleon Days: An American Boyhood in Ethiopia*. Boston: Houghton Mifflin Company, 2006. (This won the Bakeless Literary Prize in nonfiction.)
- _____. *Running to the Fire: An American Missionary Comes of Age in Revolutionary Ethiopia*. Iowa City: University of Iowa Press, 2015.
- Bond, Bruce, and Norene Bond. *When Spider Webs Unite They Can Tie Up a Lion*. Ackland, New Zealand: Bruce and Norene Bond, 2005.
- Bonk, Jon. "Toward an approach to the Gurage." *Trinity Studies* 2 (1972): 37–47.
- Bowers, Robert. *With Dr. Bob in Ethiopia*. CreateSpace Independent Publishing Platform, 2016. (Dr. Bowers and his wife Marion worked in Liberia, Kenya, Zambia, and Bangladesh, as well as Ethiopia.)
- Brant, Albert E. *In the Wake of Martyrs: A Modern Saga in Ancient Ethiopia*. Langley, Canada: Omega Publications, 1992.
- Chroamo, Mehari. *Ethiopian Revivalist: Autobiography of Evangelist Mehari Choramo*. Annotated by Brian L. Fargher. Edmonton: Enterprise Publications, 1997.
- Coleman, Daniel. *The Scent of Eucalyptus: A Missionary Childhood in Ethiopia*. Fredericton, NB: Goose Land Editions, 2003.
- Cotterell, F. Peter. *Born at Midnight*. Chicago: Moody Bible Institute, 1973. (SIM in Ethiopia from 1927–1970.)
- _____. "The Case of Ethiopia." In *Exploring Church Growth*, edited by Wilbert R. Shenk. Grand Rapids: Eerdmans, 1983, 12–23.
- _____. *Cry Ethiopia: One man's first-hand account of life and death in a war-torn land*. Lottbridge, England: Kingsway Publications, 1988.
- _____. "Dr. T. A. Lambie: some biographical notes." *Journal of Ethiopian Studies* 10 (1972): 3–53.
- _____. "An Indigenous Church in Southern Ethiopia." *The Bulletin for African Church History* 311, nos. 1–2 (1969–1970): 68–104.
- Creighton, Gordon. *Keeping The Woodbox Full: Missionary Adventures in Ethiopia*. Taber, Alberta, n.d. (Leprosy work, relief, and development)
- Cumbers, John. *Count it all joy: testimonies from a persecuted church*. Kearney, NE: Morris Publishers, 1995.
- _____. *Living with the Red Terror: Missionary Experiences in Communist Ethiopia*. Kearney, NE: Morris Publishers, 1996.
- Davis, Raymond J. *Fire on the Mountains*, Grand Rapids: Zondervan, 1966. (Chronicle of the tremendous growth of the Wolaitta church in southern Ethiopia during the Italian occupation.)
- _____. *The Winds of God: how the gospel swept the far corners of southern Ethiopia*. N.p.: SIM Publications, 1984. (Stories of Wolaitta evangelists.)

- Davis, Rebecca. *With Two Hands: Stories of God at Work in Ethiopia*. Ross-shire, Great Britain, 2010. (An account of Dick and Vida McLellan and some of the Africans who worked with them.)
- Dennett, Bill, and Jo Anne Dennett. *Unusual Marriage: The Story of Bill Dennett and Dr. Jo Anne Ader*. Adelaide: SPCK-Australia Publishing, 2006.
- Donham, Donald L. "La dialectique religion et politique dans la révolution éthiopienne: pour une ethnographie historique de la revolution marxiste." *Social Sciences and Missions* 22 (2009): 131–167. (Chapter 5 of Donham's *Marxist Modern*.)
- _____. *Marxist Modern: An Ethnographic History of the Ethiopian Revolution*. Berkeley: University of California Press, 1999.
- Dow, Philip. "Romance in a Marriage of Convenience: The Missionary Factor in Early Cold War U.S.-Ethiopian Relations, 1941–1960." *Diplomatic History* 35, no. 5 (2011): 859–895.
- Duff, Clarence W. *Cords of Love: A Pioneer Mission to Ethiopia*. Phillipsburg, NJ: Presbyterian and Reformed Publishing Co., 1980. (SIM before Italy's invasion of Ethiopia in 1935.)
- Ediger, LaVerna. *Worth It All: A Saga of a Family's Life in East Africa*. Walnut, KS: Ediger Publishing, 2001.
- Egeland, Erik. *Christianity, Generation and Narrative: Religious Conversion and Change in Sidama, Ethiopia, 1974–2012*. Uppsala: Uppsala Universitet, 2016.
- Eshete, Tibebe. "The Early Charismatic Movement in the Ethiopian Kale Heywet Church." *PentecoStudies* 12, no. 2 (2013): 162–182.
- _____. *The Evangelical Movement in Ethiopia: Resistance and Resilience*. Waco, TX: Baylor University Press, 2009. (The editors of the *International Bulletin of Missionary Research* selected this as one of the 15 best books published in 2009 that advanced "scholarship in studies of Christian mission and world Christianity.")
- _____. "Marxism and Religion: The Paradox of Church Growth in Ethiopia, 1974-1991." *In Freedom of Belief and Christian Mission*, Hans Aage Gravaas et. al., eds. Eugene, OR: *Regnum Edinburgh Centenary Series* (Book 26), 2015: 242-258.
- _____. "The Sudan Interior Mission (SIM) in Ethiopia (1928–1970)." *Northeast African Studies* 6, no. 3 (1999): 27–58.
- Fargher, Brian Leslie. *Evangelizing Individuals who Plant Churches: The Biography of Ato Sorsa Sumamo, an Ethiopian Itinerant Preacher*. Edmonton: Enterprise Publications, 2007.
- _____. "The Origins of the New Churches Movement in Ethiopia, 1927-1944." Ph. D., diss., University of Aberdeen, 1988.

- ———. *The Origins of the New Churches Movement in Ethiopia, 1927-1944.* Leiden: E. J. Brill, 1996.
- Forsberg, Malcolm, and Enid Forsberg. *In Famine He Shall Redeem Thee: Famine relief and rehabilitation in Ethiopia.* Summer Hill, Australia: Sudan Interior Mission, 1975.
- ———. *Land Beyond the Nile.* New York: Harper & Brothers, 1958. (Ethiopia and Sudan)
- Getachew, Bellete. *Elohena Halueluya (Agonies and Hallelujahs) 1974–2000.* Vol. 3 of *The Story of the Kale Heywet Church in Ethiopia.* Addis Ababa: KHC Literature Department, 2000. (Published in Amharic.)
- ———. "Intercultural Communication in Missions: With Special Reference to The Ethiopian Kale Heywet Church and the Sudan Interior Mission." M.A. Thesis, Bethel College, 2002.
- Grubb, Norman. *Alfred Buxton of Abyssinia and Congo.* London: Litterworth Press, 1942.
- Harrison, Norm and Betty. *Build a Camp: A pictorial account of building Ethiopia's first Youth Camp & Conference Center at Lake Langano.* Three Hills, AB Canada: Inkkers Fine Printing, 2016.
- Horn, Lucy Winifred. *Hearth and Home in Ethiopia.* Aylesbury, England: Hazell, Watson and Viney Ltd., c. 1960. (Accounts of Horn's work with women in Ethiopia.)
- Hungerford, Sue. *Marching with Joy: The story of Joy Crombie's 45 years serving with SIM in Ethiopia and Liberia.* Auckland, NZ: Outline Print Consultancy, Ltd., 1998.
- Keegan, Karen A., and Minna J. Kayser. *Diamond Fractal: A Story of a Shattered Mind Made Whole.* CreateSpace Independent Publishing Platform, 2014.
- Koop, Marjory. *Bumps on the Trail: Family Memoirs.* Calgary, Alberta: J & J Publishing, 2004.
- Lambie, Tom. *Abayte!: Ethiopia's Plea.* Brooklyn, NY: Sudan Interior Mission, c. 1935.
- ———. *Boot and Saddle in Africa.* Philadelphia: Blakinston Company, 1943.
- ———. *A Bride for His Son.* New York: Loizeaux Brothers, 1957.
- ———. *A Doctor Carries On.* New York: Fleming H. Revell Co., 1942.
- ———. *A Doctor's Great Commission.* Wheaton, IL: Van Kampen Press, 1954.
- McLellan, Richard J. *Messengers of Ethiopia: Extraordinary Stories of Men and Women Who Suffered and Died for the Gospel.* N.p.: Lost Coin Books, 2014.
- ———. *Warriors of Ethiopia: Ethiopian National Missionaries, Heroes of the Gospel in the Omo River Valley.* Kingsgrove, Australia: Kingsgrove Press Pty. Ltd., 2006.

- McLellan, Vida. *A Girl from Wondah Farm: The Life of a Missionary Nurse in Ethiopia*. Eastwood, Australia: Vida McLellan, 2015.
- Meja, Markina. *An Unbroken Covenant with God: An Autobiography in the Context of the Wolaitta Kale Heywet Church*. Ontario: Guardian Books, 2008.
- Merritt, Lois Barlow. *Nathan Barlow, MD: Nearest Doctor For a Million People*. N.p.: Bethany Press International, 2013.
- Metro, Harry J. *Adventures in Ethiopia*. Lapeer, MI: Blue Water Publishing, n.d.
- Middleton, George. *Miracles Do Happen*. Canada: George Middleton, c. 2016.
- Pearce, Ivy. *An Ethiopian Harvest*. Worthing: Churchman Publishing Ltd., 1988. (The author tells of her work in Pakistan and Nigeria before joining SIM to minister in Ethiopia during the 1960s.)
- Playfair, Guy W. *Trials and Triumphs in Ethiopia*. SIM Publications, c. 1943. (Travelogue about the author's five-month journey to Sudan and Ethiopia.)
- Quinton, A. G. H. *Ethiopia and the Evangel*. London: Marshall, Morgan & Scott, 1949. (A record of SIM's work in Ethiopia from 1927 to the 1940s.)
- Ratzliff, Ed and Edna. *Letters from The Uttermost Parts of the Earth*. N.p., 1987. (These letters recount the Ratzliff's work in Ethiopia from 1947–1974.)
- Rice, Esme Ritchie. *Eclipse in Ethiopia and its Corona Glory*. London: Marshall, Morgan & Scott Ltd, c. 1938. (Ethiopia during the Italian occupation [1935–1941].)
- Roke, Alfred G. *An Indigenous Church in Action*. Auckland: Scott & Scott Ltd., 1938.
- _____. *They Went Forth: Trials and Triumphs of a Pioneer SIM Missionary in Ethiopia*. Auckland: Outline Print Consultancy Ltd., 2003. (This is a candid assessment of "Alf Roke's experiences in Ethiopia and the Anglo-Egyptian Sudan during the period 1929–1947.")
- Rowe, Eleanor L. *Incredible Through Insignificance*. Chicago: Adam's Press, 2006.
- Schroeder, Julene Hodges. *Under an African Sky: The Unusual Life of a Missionaries' Kid in Ethiopia*. Agassiz, Canada: Summer Bay Press, 2013.
- Sigg, Michèle Miller. "The Dictionary of African Christian Biography and the Story of Ethiopian Christianity." *International Bulletin of Missionary Research* 39, no. 4 (October 2015): 204–207.
- Steggal, Stephany Evans. *Bingham Academy: Beyond The Gate, 1946-2017*. N.p.: Stephany Evans Steggall, 2017; and Addis Ababa, Ethiopia: SIM Ethiopia, 2017.
- Towes, Laura Jacobson. *Amharic Bible Schools: Celebrating 60 Years of Serving Together (1950–2010)—Ethiopian Kale Heywet Church (EKHC) & Serving in Mission (SIM)*. Canada: Laura Jacobson Towes, c. 2010.
- Wallace, Roy. *Shaping a Saint: A Brief History of the Life of Frances Kerr Wallace*. Ilderton, Ontario: Poplar Hill Printing, c. 1999.

- Willmott, Helen M. *The Doors were Opened: the remarkable advance of the Gospel in Ethiopia*. SIM Publications, n.d. (History of SIM in southern Ethiopia.)
- Wilson, Talmage. *Golden Memories: Doris and Talmage Wilson*. Shelton, WA: Gregg's Graphics and Printing, 2002.

Ghana (Gold Coast)

- Amralo, Titus. "An Assessment of the Commencement and Growth of the Bible Church of Africa in the Greater Accra District Church Council." M. Th. diss., Akrofi-Christaller Institute, Akropong-Akuapem, Ghana, 2006.
- Baumann, Phil. "The Gospel, Culture and the Local Congregation: an Evaluation of SIM Ghana's Mission, Vision, and the Church Planting Philosophy in Partnership with the Bible Church of Africa." M.A. project essay, Akfori-Christaller Institute of Theology, Akropong-Akuapem, Ghana, 2007.
- Bergen, Violet. *Hold Fast Your Ground*. Escondido, CA: Bervine Publishers, 1992. (Bergen details the work of *African Challenge* and founding of Maranatha Bible College.)
- Darteh, Maxwell Y. E. "Resourcing Pastors in Ghana for Holistic Ministry: An Assessment of Challenge National Pastors and Christian Leaders Conferences, 2000–2010." M.Th. thesis, Trinity Theological Seminary, 2012.
- Howell, Allison M. *The Religious Itinerary of a Ghanaian People: The Kasena and the Christian Gospel*. Frankfurt: Peter Lang, 1996.
- _____, editor. *The Slave Trade and Reconciliation: A Northern Ghana Perspective*. Accra: Assemblies of God Literature Distribution Centre, 1998.
- Mason, Jim. *God's Challenge in Ghana*. Belleville, CA: Guardian Books, 2013. (An account of the distribution of *African Challenge* in Ghana and later ministries.)
- McKie, I. J. *The Challenge of People and Places*. Midlothian, UK, n.d.

Guinea

- Lochstampfor, Ed. *While There's Still Time: A Missionary Journey*. Columbia, SC: Tall Grass Media, 2016.

Kenya

- Bowers, Robert. *With Dr. Bob in Ethiopia*. CreateSpace Independent Publishing Platform, 2016.
- Dow, Phil. *"School in the Clouds": The Rift Valley Academy Story*. Pasadena, CA: William Carey Library, 2003.
- McDougall, Rebecca. *Letters from Africa*. Glendora, CA: Rebecca McDougall, 2002.

- Myors, Ruth. *When the Lights Go Out: Memoir of a Missionary to Somalia.* Moreland, Australia: Acorn Press Ltd., 2016. (Myors also worked in Somalia.)

Liberia
- Ardill, William. *Where Elephants Fight: autobiographical account of the Liberian civil war.* Jos, Nigeria: Fab Anieh (Nigeria) Limited, 1997.
- Banks, Donald. *It Won't Work Here.* Tunbridge Wells: Sudan Interior Mission, 1980.
- Brantly, Kent, and Amber Brantley. *Called for Life: How Loving our Neighbor Led Us into the Heart of the Ebola Epidemic.* With David Thomas. Colorado Springs: WaterBrook Press, 2015.
- Corey, John, Jim Morud, and Jeanette Corey. *Any Ol' Bush Will Do: The Life Story of John Corey.* Amazon Digital Services, 2016.
- Dowdell, Howard F. *It Just Happened to Happen.* Stouffville, Ontario, 2002. (Howard and Marion Dowdell served in Nigeria, Niger, Liberia, and Canada.)
- Fahn-Weedor, Elizabeth. *Out of the Ashes: My Journey from Tragedy to Redemption.* Bloomington, IN: WestBow Press, 2014.
- Hayes, L. Curtis. *Life Still Goes On.* Bloomington: iUniverse, 2013.
- Jentzsch, Michael, and Benjamin Kwato Zahn. *Blood Brothers: Our Friendship in Liberia.* Kindle edition, 2013.
- _____. *Blutsbrüder: Unsere Freundschaft in Liberia.* (German edition). Cologne: Bastei Lübbe, 2013.
- Jones, Howard O. *For This Time: A Challenge to Black and White Christians.* Chicago: Moody Press, 1966.
- _____. *Gospel Trailblazer: An African-American Preacher's Historic Journey Across Racial Lines.* Chicago: Moody Publishers, 2003.
- Jones, Wanda. *Living in Two Worlds: The Wanda Jones Story.* With Sandra Picklesimer Aldrich. Grand Rapids: Zondervan Books, 1988.
- Kabakole, Faiyah Awonah. *My Spiritual Journey in War-Torn Liberia: An Autobiography.* Shelbyville, KY: Wasteland Press, 2011.
- Nash, Joseph E. *From Covered Wagon to Covered Head: The Making of and the Life Work of a Missionary.* N.p., 1994. (The author recounts his work, and that of his wife, Wilma, and their family, in Nigeria, Sudan, and Liberia.)
- O'Brien, David. "Fire on their feet: the story of SIM missionaries in the early months of The Liberian Civil War." Manuscript, n.p., 1991.
- Reed, Jane, and Jim Grant. *Voice under every palm: the story of radio station ELWA.* Grand Rapids: Zondervan, 1968.
- Rittenhouse, Flora. *Reaching Beyond Barriers: A Legacy of Hope.* N.p.: Trans World Radio, 2009.

- Sawyer, David G. *Always Faithful Margaret Lacey: A Story of God's Provision*. N.p.: David Sawyer, 2007. (Lacey served in Liberia, Ethiopia, Niger, and Kenya.)
- Schindler, Robert, and Marion Schindler. *Mission Possible*. Wheaton, IL: Victor Books, 1984.
- Schoffstall, Robert O. *No Man Can Shut It*. Ventura, CA: Simpson Publications, 1977. (Medical work in Liberia and Nigeria.)
- Sheppard, Nancy D. *In Harm's Way: A View from the Epicenter of Liberia's Ebola Crisis*. With the assistance of Karen J. Gruver. USA: Sheppard's Books, 2014.
- Shope, Ronald Joseph. "The Patron's Press: An Examination of Broadcast Press Freedom in the Republic of Liberia between 1976 and 1986." Ph.D. diss., Pennsylvania State University, 1995.
- Stoneman, Timothy H. B. "An 'African' Gospel: American Evangelical Radio in West Africa, 1954–1970." *New Global Studies* 1, no. 1 (2007): 1–26.
- _____. "Capturing Believers: American International Radio, Religion and Reception, 1931–1970." Ph.D. diss., Georgia Institute of Technology, May 2006.
- _____. "Radio Missions: Station ELWA in West Africa." *International Bulletin of Missionary Research* 36, no. 4 (October 2014): 200–204.
- Strengholt, Jos M. *Gospel in the Air: 50 Years of Christian Witness through Radio in the Arab World*. Zoetermeer, 2008. (Chapter 7 is about Radio ELWA.)
- Thiessen, Abe. *A Media Pioneer (Radio-Television-Satellite): The Abe Thiessen Story*. Victoria, BC: Trafford Publishing, 2005.

Malawi (Nyasaland)
- Lamport-Stokes, Barbara. "Harry Raney in Nyasaland, July 1900 to September 1901." *The Society of Malawi Journal* 39, no. 2 (1986): 26–36.

Mozambique (Portuguese East Africa)
- Procter, Jack. *Fools for Christ's Sake*. N.p.: Africa Evangelical Fellowship, 1965.
- Thompson, Phyllis. *Life Out of Death in Mozambique*. London: Hodder and Stoughton, 1989.

Niger
- Banks, Donald. *It Won't Work Here*. Tunbridge Wells: Sudan Interior Mission, 1980.
- Cooper, Barbara M. *Evangelical Christians in the Muslim Sahel*. Bloomington: Indiana University Press, 2006. (Melville J. Herskovits Prize of the African Studies Association for the best book published in 2006, and one of the best 15 books published in 2006 to advance "scholarship in studies of Christian mission and world Christianity" listed by the editors of the *International Bulletin of Missionary Research*.)

- Dipple, Bruce E. "A Missiological Evaluation of the History of the Sudan Interior Mission in French West Africa, 1924–1962." D. Miss. thesis, Trinity Evangelical Divinity School, 1994.
- Dowdell, Howard F. *It Just Happened to Happen.* Stouffville, Ontario, 2002.
- Long, Ruth. *A Family Living Under the Sun.* N.p.: Xlibris Corporation, 2011. (Long tells the story of her family, including her husband Burt's founding of Galmi Hospital. The Longs also worked in Nigeria, Liberia, and Chad.)
- Wall, Martha. *Splinters from an African Log,* Chicago: Moody Press, 1960. (Wall tells writes about her work as a nurse.)

Nigeria

- Abbas, Simon Itodo. *ECWA Odogunyan Mission Field & Studies on Practical Church Planting.* Lagos: Soldiers of the Cross, c. 2015.
- Adekeye, S. S., ed. *Evangelical Church Winning All (ECWA), History of Ebute-Metta District Church Council: Past, Present, And Prospect.* Lagos: Fesby Resources Link, 2015.
- Adeniyi, J. O. *Centenary of Christianity in Egbe: Rev. Tommie Titcombe, 1908-2008.* Ibadan: Daybis Limited, 2012.
- Adeyemi, E. A. *From Seven to Seven Thousand: The Story of the Birth and Growth of SIM/ECWA church in Ilorin.* Ilorin: Okinbaloye Commercial Press, 1995.
- Agaja, S.B. *ECWA Hospital Egbe: Citadel of Blessings.* Ilorin: Fhb/Legacy, c. 2007.
- Aka, Ronku. *Rigwe Kingdom: The Story from the Beginning.* Jos: Molkai Services, 2015.
- Aliyu, Hawa'u Lynne M. "The Contribution of Sudan Interior Mission (S.I.M.) on Women's Education in Kano State with Special Reference to Kabo Girls' School." B.A. thesis, Ahmadu Bello University, 1975.
- Ardill, William David. *Journey On A Dusty Road: Memoir of a missionary surgeon's twenty year career in Nigeria.* N.p.: CreateSpace Independent Publishing Platform, 2015.
- Ariyo, Rebecca. *Ralph Balisky: A Pioneer Missionary to the Core-North of Nigeria.* Kaduna: A CLTE Production, Crest Royal Ventures, 2016.
- Asonibare, Stephen. *The Ancient Paths: Christianity and Oro-Ago and Environs (1912–2012).* Ilorin: Hue Illustrations & Media, for the Central Planning Committee of the Centenary Celebration, 2012.
- Audu, Zemo N., ed. *The Advent of Christianity in Ham Land: A Historical Account of God's Grace and Faithfulness in Ham Land (Jaba) and Environs from 1910-2010.* Kaduna: Pyla-mak Services Ltd., 2010.
- Baba, Panya. *A Vision Received, A Vision Passed On: The History of EMS of ECWA, 1948-1998.* Bukuru: ACTS, 2009.

- Banfield, Alex W. *Life Among the Nupe Tribe in West Africa*. Berlin, CA: H.S. Hallman, 1905.
- Banks, Donald. *It Won't Work Here*. Tunbridge Wells: Sudan Interior Mission, 1980.
- Barnes, Andrew. "Evangelization Where It Is Not Wanted: Colonial Administrators and Missionaries in Northern Nigeria during the First Third of the Twentieth Century." *Journal of Religion in Africa* 25, no. 2 (1995): 412–441.
- _____. *Making Headway: The Introduction of Western Civilization in Colonial Northern Nigeria*. Rochester, NY: University of Rochester Press, 2009.
- Beacham, C. Gordon. *New Frontiers in the Central Sudan*. Toronto: Evangelical Publishers, 1928.
- Blench, Roger M., ed. *Out of the Cactus: From Darkness to Light, an Introduction to the History of SIM/ECWA in Rigweland*. Jos: Unimark Limited, 2012. (The growth of Christianity among the Irigwe of Miango, Kwall, and other places in Nigeria.)
- Bowers, Paul. "Evangelical Theology in Africa: Byang Kato's Legacy." *Trinity Journal*, n.s., 1 (1980): 86.
- Brigfield, Charlotte Dale. "To Africa: The Journal of Charlotte Dale Brigfield." N.d., 1990.
- Brown, Estella Grooters. *In His Time: Recollections of the Christian Missionary Estella Grooters Brown*. As told to Jean Lucas. Grapeland, TX: Frontier Publications, 2002.
- Bulifant, Josephine C. *Forty Years in the African Bush*. Grand Rapids: Zondervan, 1950. (Author recounts some of her experiences with Yoruba African women and girls.)
- Bunza, Mukhtar Umar. *Christian Missions Among Muslims: Sokoto Province, Nigeria, 1935–1990*. Trenton, NJ: Africa World Press, Inc., 2007.
- Calenberg, Rick. "Mission and church partnership dynamics: lessons from SIM-ECWA in Nigeria." *Evangelical Missions Quarterly* 41, no. 3 (July 2005): 302–310.
- Campion, George, and Esther Campion. *The Beginning of Egbe Hospital*. N.p.: Aro Major Press, 2016.
- Capill, Wendy, and Julie Belding. *No Turning Back: The Story of Jack and Vera Nicholson, Missionaries in Northern Nigeria*. New Zealand: Outline Print Consultancy Ltd., 1998.
- Collins, Laurie Berg. *Treasures in Clay Jars: A Story of Victory in Disability and Fulfillment of God's Plan in Service*. Bloomington, IN: Xlibris Corporation, 2001.
- Cox, Ruth. "The Lord's Work: Perspectives of Early Leaders of The Evangelical Church of West Africa in Nigeria Regarding the Spread of Christianity." Ph.D. diss., Trinity International University, 2000.

- Dada, James, and Titus Oshagbemi. *Egbe History and Culture.* 2nd ed. Suffolk, England: Arima Publishing, 2008. (Chapter 5, "The Legacy of the Early Missionaries.")
- Davidson, Lena Dorothy. *To God be the Glory.* N.p., n.d. (Story of Arthur and Lena Davidson.)
- Davis, Raymond J. *Swords in the Desert.* Minneapolis: Wilson Press, 1944. Five editions from 1944–1966. (Stories of missionaries working among Muslims in northern Nigeria.)
- de la Haye, Sophie. *Byang Kato: Ambassador for Christ.* Achimota, Ghana: Africa Christian Press, 1986.
- _____. *Tread upon the Lion: The Story of Tommie Titcombe.* Shoals, IN: Kingsley Press, 2014. (This is the most recent of several editions. Tommie Titcombe and his wife, Ethel, served in Egbe from 1908–1928.)
- Diko, Danlami Z. *A Brief Biography of the Late Bmazazhin—Miss Esther H. Anderson (1899–1980).* Suleja: Peak Press Ltd., 2007.
- Dirks, Floreine. *Reflections: The Joys & Trials of Being a Missionary in Nigeria, 1945–1986.* Mountridge, KS: Floreine Dirks, 2006.
- Doerksen, Eva. *Black Nomad: The Story of Adamu Dogon Yaro, messenger to West Africa's Fulani.* Aylesbury, England: Hazell, Watson & Viney Ltd., 1969.
- Dow, Thomas. "A. W. Banfield: Missionary Pioneer in Nigeria." http://www.bethelcollege.edu/assets/content/mcarchives/pdfs/v2n1p12_15.pdf, accessed 27 July 2016.
- Dowdell, Howard F. *It Just Happened to Happen.* Stouffville, Ontario, 2002.
- Dunn, Murray. *Dunn and Dusted: The Autobiography of Murray Dunn.* N.p.: Murray Dunn, c. 2012. (Dunn was the owner of a light aircraft outfit that did crop dusting before he became SIM New Zealand's director.)
- Duya, Andrew A. *ECWA (Evangelical Church Winning All): Compendium and Facts Finder.* Lagos: Victory Signs International, 2013.
- Elliott, Hazel, and Archie Elliott. *This Is Our Story.* Newton, New Zealand: Wentforth Print, c. 2005.
- Ferdinando, Keith. "The Legacy of Byang Kato." *International Bulletin of Missionary Research* 28, no. 4 (2004): 169–174.
- First ECWA, Ilorin, Kwara State. *On Christ the Solid Rock: A Narrative of the Major Milestones of First ECWA, Ilorin.* Ilorin: Carrot Publishers, 2016.
- Foxall, George M. "An Area Study of Nigeria: Guided Research." Th.M. thesis, Canadian Theological College, 1973.
- Foxall, George M., and Zemo N. Audu, compilers. *Kwoi Jubilee Tidings (1910–1960).* Kaduna: Pyla-mak Services Ltd., 2010.
- Fraught, Brad C. "Missionaries, Indirect Rule, and the Changing Mandate of Mission in Colonial Northern Nigeria: the Case of Canada's Rowland Victor

Bingham and the Sudan Interior Mission." *Journal of the Canadian Church Historical Society* 43, no. 2 (2001): 147–169.

- Fuller, Clare. *Banfield, Nupe and the UMCA*. Ilorin: INDEMAC Publishers, Ltd., 2001.

- Fuller, John G. *Fever!: The Hunt for a New Killer Virus*. New York: Reader's Digest, 1974. (Story of the emergence of Lassa Fever in Nigeria which claimed numerous lives including those of SIM missionaries Dr. Jeanette Troup and Charlotte Shaw.)

- Fuller, W. Harold. *Aftermath: the dramatic rebirth of eastern Nigeria*. Canada: Sudan Interior Mission, 1970. (A look at SIM's work in this region after Nigeria's civil war.)

- _____. *Mission-Church Dynamics: How to change bicultural tensions into dynamic missionary outreach*. Pasadena, CA: William Carey Library, 1980.

- Goifa, Nanyak Barko. "A Historical Study of Mission's Approach to Culture and Evangelization of Northern Nigeria: An Evaluation of Religion and Socio-Political Work of the SIM in Southern Zaria (Kaduna State), 1910–1954." M.Phil. thesis, Oxford Centre for Mission Studies, Oxford, 2009.

- Greene, Betty, with Dietrich Buss. *Flying High: The Amazing Story of Betty Greene and the Early Years of Mission Aviation Fellowship*. Camp Hill, PA: Christian Publications Inc., 2002. (Greene piloted a plane for SIM in Nigeria in the early 1950s.)

- Hall, John S. *From Cannibalism to Christ: A Story of the Transforming Power of the Gospel in Darkest Africa* Toronto: Evangelical Publishers, 1944.

- _____. *Religion, Myth and Magic in Tangale*, H. Junghraithmayr and J. Adelberger, eds. Köln: Rüdiger Köppe Verlag, 1994. (An introduction to, and publication of, Hall's M.A. thesis, McMaster University, 1921.)

- Harnischfeger, Johannes. "'Man eaters under new management': Christliche Mission bei den Tangale in Nigeria." *Zeitschrift für Mission* 32, no. 4 (2006): 388–433.

- Harris, Edwin A., with Richard B. Harris Sr. *Munganga: Memoirs of a Country Doctor*. Rev. Ed. Maitland, FL: Xulon Press, 2011.

- Hay, Graham. *"Africa's Open Sore": Satanic Fear, Finding Expression in Mistreatment and Neglect of Children*. Toronto: Sudan Interior Mission, 1945. (The author conveys what he believes are the cultural practices that threaten the well-being of African children.)

- Hay, Ian M.. "A Study of the Relationship between SIM International and the Evangelical Missionary Society." D.Miss. diss., Trinity Evangelical Divinity School, Deerfield, IL, 1984.

- Hay, John. *Along Nigerian Roads*. Lagos: Niger-Challenge Press, 1961.

- _____. *With the Gbaries: Experiences and Impressions of a first term of mission work in Nigeria.* Minna, Nigeria: The Niger Press, 1921.
- Helser, Albert D. *Africa's Bible: The Power of God Unto Salvation.* Chicago: Moody Press, 1951. (A collection of testimonies from African converts.)
- _____. *The Glory of the Impossible: Demonstrations of Divine Power in the Sudan.* Toronto: Evangelical Publishers, 1940. (Helser's account of SIM's work with lepers in Nigeria.)
- _____. *The Hand of God in the Sudan.* New York: Fleming H. Revell Company, 1946. (Missionary stories with a view toward encouraging people to become missionaries.)
- _____. "We Must Advance." *Africa Now* 5 (April–June 1960): 15.
- Hodges, Doreen. *The Way It Really Was: Reflections of a Missionary Wife and Mother.* Victoria, Canada: n.p., 2002.
- Hsueh, Yu Kwong. *Preaching His Word in Africa.* Singapore: Singapore Every Home Crusade Co. Ltd., 2016.
- _____. *You Guided my Life: An Autobiography of Rev. Hsueh Yu Kwong.* Singapore: Caseline Manufacturing Sdn. Bhd., for SIM East Asia Pte. Ltd., 2005.
- Hurlbert, Phyllis. *Whatever happened to Calamity Jane?* N.p.: Phyllis Hurlbert, c. 1994. (The story of Phyllis and Vern Hurlbert who served in Nigeria from 1954-1971.)
- Ijagbemi, E. Adeleye. *Christian Missionary Activity in Colonial Nigeria: The work of the Sudan Interior Mission Among the Yoruba, 1908–1967.* Lagos: Nigeria Magazine, 1986.
- _____. *The Role of M. J. P. Koledade (1902–1973) in Pioneering Nigerian Education.* Lewiston, Queenston, Lampeter: The Edwin Mellen Press, 1992.
- Jacobson, Ruth M. *Queen with a Pure White Heart: The adventuresome biography of Mary M. Haas, the Story-Teller who charmed audiences wherever she went.* Belleville, CA: Essence Publishing, 1998.
- Kastner, Rod. *The Journey so far: Seventy Years of God's Faithfulness at Kagoro ECWA Theological College (KETC).* Kwoi, Nigeria: Personal Touch Publishing, 2000.
- Keegan, Karen A., and Minna J. Kayser. *Diamond Fractal: A Story of a Shattered Mind Made Whole.* CreateSpace Independent Publishing Platform, 2014.
- Koggie, Amos, Zamfara Iveh, Tim Geysbeek. "'That Was the Beginning of Great Things at Miango': Brra Kwẹ Tingwẹ and the Origins of Christianity in Miango, Nigeria, 1913–1936." *International Bulletin of Missionary Research* 39, no. 3 (July 2015): 133–137.
- Lagger, Eileen. *New Life for All: True Accounts of In-Depth Evangelism in West Africa.* Chicago: Moody Press, 1970. (A report about New Life For All founded in 1963 to evangelize Nigeria.)

- Lawal, Julius B., ed. *Thus Far The Lord Has Helped Us: A Collection of Articles.* Ilorin, Nigeria: Awoyemi Press, c. 2001. (Articles written on the occasion of the 60th anniversary of the founding of ECWA Theological Seminary Igbaja.)
- Lawson, Phyllis I. *Take My Life, Lord: Memories of Seventy Years.* Lloydminster, Canada, 1997.
- Long, Ruth. *A Family Living Under the Sun.* N.p.: Xlibris Corporation, 2011.
- Maigadi, Barje S. *Divisive Ethnicity in the Church in Africa.* Kaduna, Nigeria: Baraka Press and Publishers Ltd., 2006.
- Maiture, Reuben. "Contributions of Tangale Missionary Agents in the Christianization of Northern Nigeria, 1917–1976." Ph.D. diss., University of Jos, Nigeria, 2008.
- Mason, Jim. *Literature Outreach in Nigeria: A History of SIM Literature Work, 1901–1980.* Breslau, Canada: Denison Print, 2009.
- McKie, I. J. *The Challenge of People and Places.* Midlothian, UK, n.d.
- Menzies, Edna. *Little Teny of Nigeria.* Grand Rapids, MI: Baker Book House, 1967. (This is the story of an orphan who went to a girl's school.)
- Mitchell, Murgatroyd. *Missionary Makebelieve.* Murgatroyd MK, 2014. (Memories of Floyd and Phyllis's experiences in Nigeria.)
- Myra, Harold. *Elsbeth.* Old Tappan, NJ: Fleming H. Revell Company, 1976. (Medical work in Nigeria, including Lassa fever.)
- Nash, Joseph E. *From Covered Wagon to Covered Head: The Making of and the Life Work of a Missionary.* N.p., 1994.
- Olatayo, D. I. *ECWA: The Root, Birth, and Growth.* Ilorin: Ocare Publications, 1993.
- Olumotanmi, Abiodun Omonie. *Titcombe College, Egbe: A Legacy of Faith.* Ibadan: Feyisetan Press, c. 2007.
- Olutimiyan, Nathaniel L. "A Study of the Evangelical Churches of West Africa." M.S.T. thesis, Dallas Theological Seminary, 1976.
- Oshaboba, Seth A. *SIM and ECWA in Nigeria: The Story of the Beginnings.* Ilorin: Gbenle Press Ltd., 1985.
- _____. *SIM/ECWA Voices and Statistics from the Past.* Jos: Challenge Press, 1994.
- Osundeyi, David Oluwole. *From Valley to Hill Top: a biography of Deacon (Chief) S. A. Sayomi (JP), The Asiwaju of Igosun Land.* Lagos: Dee Sage Nigeria Limited, 2006.
- Paproth, Darrell, and David Turnbull. "Effie Varley: Missiology as Biography." *Australian Journal of Mission Studies* 1, no. 1 (June 2007): 22–29.
- Peevy, Eunice. *Behind the Scenes of the Mission Mailbag.* Delta City, OK: Mission Mailbag, c. 1990.
- Percy, Douglas C. *Doctor to Africa: The Story of Stirrett of the Sudan.* Chicago: Good News Press, 1948.

- _____. *Stirrett of the Sudan: The Beloved Physician of the Sudan*. Toronto: Livingstone Press, 1948.
- Rabe, Dahiru. *The rols [sic.] of Sudan interior mission (S.I.M.) missionary in the British colonial leprosy campaigns in Katsina Emirate*. Munich: GRIN Verlag, 2013.
- Schaffer, Rich. *Just One SIMAIR Story*. Bloomington: iUniverse, Inc., 2012.
- Schalm, Gottfried. *God's Pathways in Africa: Adventures of a Pioneering Family*. Calgary: Gottfried Schalm, 2005.
- Schoffstall, Robert O. *No Man Can Shut It*. Ventura, CA: Simpson Publications, 1977. (Medical work in Liberia and Nigeria.)
- Shankar, Shobana. "A Fifty Year Muslim Conversion to Christianity: Religious Ambiguities and Colonial Boundaries in Northern Nigeria, c. 1910–1963." In *Muslim-Christian Encounters in Africa*, Benjamin F. Soares, ed. Leiden: Brill, 2006, 89–114.
- _____. "Medical Missionaries and Modernizing Emirs in Colonial Hausaland: Leprosy Control and Native Authority in the 1930s." *Journal of African History* 48, no. 1 (March 2007): 45–68.
- _____. "Race, Ethnicity, and Assimilation: The Influence of American Anthropology on Christian-Muslim Relations in British Northern Nigeria." *Social Sciences and Missions* 29 (2016): 37-55.
- _____. "The Social Dimensions of Christian Leprosy Work among Muslims: American Missionaries and Young Patients in Colonial Northern Nigeria, 1920–1940." In *Healing Bodies, Saving Souls: Medical Missions in Asia and Africa*, David Hardiman, ed. Amsterdam: Editions Rodopi B.V.. 2006, 281–305.
- _____. *Who Shall Enter Paradise?: Christian Origins in Muslim Northern Nigeria, c. 1890–1975*. Athens, Ohio: Ohio University Press and Swallow Press, 2014.
- Stromme, Harvey. *From the Dust Bowls of the Canadian Prairies to the Parched Sahara of Africa: The Story of Harvey Stromme, Missionary to Nigeria*. As told to Irene Ward. N.p.: Nallenart, 2015.
- Swank, Gerald O. *Frontier Peoples of Central Nigeria and a strategy for outreach*. South Pasadena, Calif.: William Carey Library, 1977. (Report of a survey of 30 ethnic groups in central Nigeria in 1975.)
- _____. *Labarin Marasa Jin Bishara a chicken Nigeria ta tsakiya Dabarun Hanyoyin Aiki*. South Pasadena, Calif.: William Carey Library, 1977. (Translation of Swank's *Frontier Peoples*.)
- Thamer, Ethel Neal. *Little Is Much: When God Is in It—The Autobiography of Ethel Neal Thamer*. N.p.: Ethel Neal Thamer, 1994.

- Todd, W. Paul. "The Attitudes of the Evangelical Church of West Africa (ECWA) towards Islam in light of ethnic and religious violence." Ph.D. diss., Queens University of Belfast, 2010.
- Turaki, Yusufu. *An Introduction to the History of SIM/ECWA in Nigeria, 1893–1993.* N.p.: Yusufu Turaki, 1993.
- _____. "The Theological Legacy of the Reverend Doctor Byang Kato." *Africa Journal of Evangelical Theology* 20, no. 2 (2001): 133–55.
- _____. *Theory and Practice of Christian Missions in Africa: A Century of SIM/ECWA History and Legacy in Nigeria, 1893–1993,* vol. 1. Nairobi, Kenya: International Bible Society Africa, 1999.
- Tyrrell, Mabel. *A Missionary in the Making.* USA: Xulon Press, 2007. (Tyrrell served in Nigeria from 1950–1984.)
- Ubah, C. N. "Christian Missionary Penetration of the Nigerian Emirates: The Village School Approach." *Transafrican Journal of History* 17 (1988): 108–122.
- _____. "Christian Missionary Penetration of the Nigerian Emirates with Special Reference to the Medical Missions Approach." *The Muslim World* LXXVII, no. 1 (1987): 16–27.
- VanderSchie, Phyllis, and John VanderSchie. *Experiencing God's Faithfulness.* Grand Rapids: Kregel Publications, n.d.
- Van Reken, Ruth E. *Letters Never Sent: A Global Nomad's Journey from Hurt to Healing.* Rev. ed. The Hague: Summertime Publishing, 2012. (The author's thoughts about living at boarding school while attending Kent Academy, and her journey to healing as an adult from the pain she experienced as a child.)
- Waya, Saratu D. B, with Peter D. Sabo. *Concise History of ECWA Women's Fellowship.* Abuja: Impact Media Int'l, 2010.
- White, H[al] A. "Lassa Fever: A Study of 23 Hospital Cases." *Transactions of the Royal Society of Tropical Medicine and Hygiene* 66, no. 3 (1972): 390–401.
- Wooding, Anne, with Dan Wooding. *Blind Faith: The Extraordinary Real-Life Story of a Woman from Liverpool, England, Who Dared to Believe God and Pioneered a Missionary Work among the Blind of Kano, Nigeria.* Garden Grove, CA: Assist Books, 1996.
- Wright, Bill. *A Fire by Night, A Cloud by Day.* Toronto: Britannia Printers Inc., 1988.
- _____. *Fragments that Remain.* Mississagua, Canada: VAZ Publishers and Stationers, 1994.
- Yaro, Labarin Adamu Dogon. *Daga Kiwon Shanu Zuwa Kiwon Ja'amar Allah (From Herding Sheep to Shepherding the People of God).* Lagos: Oluseyi Press Limited, for Challenge Publications, n.d. (The story of Eva Doerksen in Hausa.)

Somalia

- Haile, Ahmed Ali. *Teatime in Mogadishu: My Journey as a Peace Ambassador in the World of Islam*. Harrisburg, VA: Herald Press, 2011. As told to David W. Shenk.
- _____. *Jidkii Nabaddonka*. VA: Herald Press, 2011. (Somali translation of *Teatime.*)
- Loewen, Joy. *Woman to Woman: Sharing Jesus with a Muslim Friend*. Grand Rapids, MI: Chosen, 2010. In chapter two, Loewen shares some of the experiences she had with her parents (Warren and Dorothy Modricker) in Somalia and Ethiopia.
- Miller, Helen. *The Hardest Place: The Biography of Warren and Dorothy Modricker*. Belleville, Canada: Guardian Books, 2006.
- Myors, Ruth. *When the Lights Go Out: Memoir of a Missionary to Somalia*. Moreland, Australia: Acorn Press Ltd., 2016. (This is a candid assessment of the author's, and SIM's, work among the Somali in East Africa.)

South Africa

- Brown, Ann Fraser. *Betting on a Certainty*. Sydney?: Birch Island Books, 2014. (Ann and her husband, Derek, worked in Mseleni, Mtubatuba, Durban, and Pietermaritzburg with AEF and SIM.)
- Green, Emily, and Emily Eldridge. *A Pondoland Hilltop*. London: South Africa General Mission, n.d.
- Hanbury, Charlotte. *Life of Mrs. Albert Head*. Richmond: R. W. Simpson and Co., Ltd., c. 1905.
- Hoyt, Norman A. "Significant Features of Church Growth among the Indians of Natal, South Africa." Ph.D. diss., Dallas Theological Seminary, 1981. (Chapter 2 is about the Evangelical Church of South Africa.)
- Johanson, B. *We Watched It Grow: A story of the Union Bible Institute*. Durban: The Mission Press, 1971.
- Kopp, Thomas J. "Church and Mission: Decolonizing the Mind." *Evangelical Review of Theology* 28, no. 3 (July 2004): 255–269.
- _____. *God First—Go Forward: The Impact of the South Africa General Mission/Africa Evangelical Fellowship on the Africa Evangelical Church, 1962–1994*. Pasadena, CA: William Carey International University Press, 2011.
- Nehls, Gerhard. *Auf den Spuren der Sehnsucht: Aus dem Gulag nach Kapstadt (In the Footsteps of Our Lives: From the Gulag to Cape Town)*. Holzgerlingen: Haenssler-Verlag GmbH, 2008. (A history in German of Life Challenge [Africa] that started in South Africa.)
- Nehls, Gerhard, and Walter Eric. *Life is a Challenge more so in Africa: The Story of Gerhard Nehls and Life Challenge*. Nairobi: Life Challenge, 2016.

- Osborn-Howe, Martha. *By Fire and Cloud*. London: Hodder and Stoughton, 1894.
- Procter, Jack. *Fools for Christ's Sake*. N.p.: Africa Evangelical Fellowship, 1965.
- Scutt, J. F. *The Man Who Loved the Zulus*. Pierermartizburg: Shuter and Shooter, n.d. (Biography of Fred Suter.)
- _____. *The Story of the E.T.T.C.* Pietermarizburg: Natal Witness, Ltd., 1950. (Story of how the Evangelical Teacher Training College was founded in Vryhed, Natal, in 1948.)
- Searle, Walter. *She Loved Much: A Memorial Sketch of Mrs. Walter Searle*. London: Christian Herald Co. Ltd., 1926.
- Shank, Ezra A. *Fervent in Spirit: The Biography of Arthur J. Bowen*. Chicago: Moody Press, 1954.
- Theron, Anita. *Out of the Ditch: The Mseleni Story*. Pretoria: V & R Printers, c. 1975.
- Thompson, Ada. *"Promoted": The Memorials of Charles Dixon Kimber*. South Africa, 1915. (A story of SAGM's work with Soldiers' Homes.)
- Walker, Pamela. "Adoption and Victorian Culture." *The History of the Family* 11 (2006): 211–221.
- Weeks, George E. *W. Spencer Walton*. London: Marshall Brothers, 1897.

Sudan (Anglo-Egyptian Sudan)

- Forsberg, Malcolm. *Dry Season: Today's Church Crisis in the Sudan*. Toronto: Sudan Interior Mission, c. 1964. (The development of the church in Sudan and events that led to the expulsion of SIM's missionaries in southern Sudan in 1964.)
- _____. *Land Beyond the Nile*. New York: Harper Brothers, 1958.
- _____. *Last Days on the Nile*. Philadelphia: J.B. Lippincott Co., 1966. (Personal reflections of SIM's work in southern Sudan from 1937–1964.)
- James, Wendy. `*Kwanim Pa—The Making of the Uduk People: An Ethnographic Study of Survival in the Sudan-Ethiopian Borderlands*. Oxford: Clarendon Press, 1979.
- _____. *The Listening Ebony: Moral Knowledge, Religion, and Power among the Uduk of Sudan*. Oxford: Clarendon Press, 1988. (Chapter 4 includes considerable information about SIM.)
- _____. *War and Survival in Sudan's Frontier Lands: Voices from the Blue Nile*. Oxford: Oxford University Press, 2007. (Chapter 10 focuses on SIM's work.)
- Lambie, Tom. *A Doctor Carries On*. New York: Fleming H. Revell Co., 1942.
- Morrow, George A. *Dawn at Doro*. Melbourne: Sudan Interior Mission in association with S. John Bacon, c. 1945.
- Roke, Alfred G. *They Went Forth: Trials and Triumphs of a Pioneer SIM Missionary in Ethiopia*. Auckland: Outline Print Consultancy Ltd., 2003.

- Sanderson, Lilian. "The Sudan Interior Mission and the Condominium Sudan, 1937–1955." *Journal of Religion in Africa* 8 (1974): 13–40.
- Sanderson, Lilian, and Neville Sanderson. *Education, Religion & Politics in Southern Sudan 1899–1964.* London: Ithaca Press, 1981.
- Stevens, Steve. *Early Wings Over Africa.* West Sussex, United Kingdom, 2010. (Stevens recounts stories of his time as a Missionary Aviation Fellowship aviator based in Doro, Sudan, where he flew Africans and personnel from SIM and other missions during the early-to-mid 1950s.)

Swaziland

- Scutt, J. F. *The Drums are Beating: Missionary Life in Swaziland.* 3rd ed. Worthing: Henry E. Walter, Ltd., 1966.
- Sharp, Phyllis E. *This Pioneering.* Northants, Great Britain: Stanley L. Hunt Ltd., c. post-1965. (Story of the League of Pioneers.)

Zambia (Northern Rhodesia)

- Bowers, Robert. *With Dr. Bob in Ethiopia.* CreateSpace Independent Publishing Platform, 2016.
- Forman, Janetta. *The Light Is Come.* London: South Africa General Mission, n.d.
- Foulkes, James. *To Africa With Love: A Bush Doc's Story.* Nappanee, IN: Francis Asbury Press of Evangel Publishing House, 2005.
- _____. *Hunting Stories: Missionary Doctor.* N.p.: Rafiki Books, 2014.
- Kopp, Dwight Andrew. *Made in Africa.* N.p.: Dwight Andrew Kopp, 2014. (Kopp's book includes information about his parents, Tim and Carol Kopp.)
- Lutz, Lorry. *Sword & Scalpel: A Surgeon's Story of Faith and Courage,* Orange, CA: Promise Publishing Co, 1997. (Story of Dr. Robert Foster and his wife Belva.)
- Warburton, Michael. *A Dedicated Wheelchair.* N.p., c. 1968.

Zimbabwe (Southern Rhodesia)

- Dhube, Joshua. *The Association of The United Baptist Churches of Zimbabwe Commonly called United Baptist Church of Zimbabwe (UBC): Celebrating 100 years of Gospel Witness (1897–1977)—The Highlights.* N.p., 1997.
- Doner, Elmina. *He Called . . . I answered: The Personal Story of Elmina Doner.* Three Hills, Alberta: E.M.F. Press, n.d.
- Merritt, Judson H. *Blow Wind, Burn Candle: True tales from Zimbabwe.* N.p.: John Deyell Company, c. 1986.

ASIA

Continent

- Cherry, W. H. *Outstretched Hands*. London: Ceylon and India General Mission, 1960.
- Fuller, W. Harold. *Sun Like Thunder: Following Jesus on Asia's Spice Road*. 2nd ed. Victoria, Canada: Friesen Press, 2015.
- Hemming, G. A., editor. *Advancing Together: Tale of Two Missions*. London: International Christian Fellowship, c. 1974.
- Ho, Polly C, ed. *Rice, Noodles, Bread, or Chapati: The Untold Stories of Asian MKs*. Singapore: Third Culture Kids Care Fellowship, 2013.
- Hsueh, Lily, ed. *A Word for Preachers*. Singapore: Singapore Every Home Crusade Co. Ltd., 2007. (Writings of Rev. Hsueh Yu Kwong.)
- Hsueh, Yu Kwong. *Preaching His Word in Africa*. Singapore: Singapore Every Home Crusade Co. Ltd., 2016.
- _____. *You Guided my Life: An Autobiography of Rev. Hsueh Yu Kwong*. Singapore: Caseline Manufacturing Sdn. Bhd., for SIM East Asia Pte. Ltd., 2005.

Bangladesh

- Bowers, Robert. *With Dr. Bob in Ethiopia*. CreateSpace Independent Publishing Platform, 2016.
- McQuaker, Dorothy. "East Pakistan Points." In *Advancing Together: A Tale of Two Missions*, G. A. Hemming, ed. London: International Christian Fellowship, c. 1974, 86–94.
- Parshall, Phil. *Divine Threads within a Human Tapestry: Memoirs of Phil Parshall*. Pasadena, CA: William Carey Library, 2000.

India

- Cherry, W. H. *Give Me This Mountain*. London: Ceylon and India General Mission. Guildford: Billing & Sons Ltd., 1956.
- Dawson, Mary. *The Life Story of John Wilfred Dawson: Missionary in the Tamil Field for over 28 Years as a member of the Ceylon and India General Mission*. Bangalore: Christian Literature Society, 1946.
- Dover, Irene. *Path Through India: The Story of Amy Parsons—Pioneer*. N.p.: Poona and Indian Village Mission, c. 1958.
- Fauchai, Laiu. *The Maras: From Warriors to Missionaries*. Mizoram, India: Evangelical Church of Maraland Mission, 1994.

- Haggis, Jane, and Margaret Allen. "Imperial Emotions: Affective Communities of Mission in British Protestant Women's Missionary Publications, c. 1880–1920." *Journal of Social History* 42, no. 3 (Spring 2008): 691–716. (This article includes a few pages about some early PIVM missionaries.)
- Hemming, G. A., ed. *Advancing Together: Tale of Two Missions*. London: International Christian Fellowship, c. 1974.
- ———. *See for Yourself: The Story of a Visit to Western India*. London: Poona and Indian Village Mission, c. 1950.
- Hinton, W. H., compiler. *Ethel Ambrose: Pioneer Medical Missionary*. London: Marshall, Morgan & Scott, Ltd., c. 1937.
- Paget, Kathleen. *Out of the Hand of the Terrible*. Grand Rapids: Wealthy Heights Printing Co., 1949.
- Tozer, Ruth. *Miles to Go . . . and Promises Kept*. Auckland, New Zealand: Wentforth Press, 2009.
- Treasure, Pearl. *Something to Live For*. Lynwood, WA: T. & L. Scotland, n.d.
- Tyson, Basil. *This India*. London: Henry E. Walter Ltd., for the Poona and Indian Village Mission, 1958.
- Welch, Ian. "TAMIL DAVID, The Tamil Evangelist. 'Vathakunu Deresegayam David,' (V.D. 'Eye of faith, God helps')." Working paper, 2014 draft, https://openresearch-repository.anu.edu.au/bitstream/1885/11494/1/Welch%20Tamil%20David%202014.pdf, accessed 14 June 2017.

Nepal

- Brown, Florence, with Valmai Redhead. *Precious Treasure, Clay Pot: A Nurse in Nepal*. N.p.: Castle Publishing Services, 2010.
- Treasure, Pearl. *Something to Live For*. Lynwood, WA: T. & L. Scotland, n.d.

Pakistan

- Inniger, Merle E. "View from West Pakistan." In *Advancing Together: Tale of Two Missions*, G. A. Hemming, ed. London: International Christian Fellowship, c. 1974, 79-85.
- Inniger, Merle, and Gloria Inniger. "Shielded: Memoirs of the Lives and Ministry of Merle and Gloria Inniger," 2001. (The Innigers worked in Pakistan, Iran, England, and the United States.)
- Seaman, Paul Asbury, editor. *Far Above the Plain: Private Profiles and Admissible Evidence from the First Forty Years of Murree Christian School, Pakistan*. Pasadena, CA: William Carey Library, 1996.

Philippines

- Parshall, Phil. *Divine Threads within a Human Tapestry: Memoirs of Phil Parshall*. Pasadena, CA: William Carey Library, 2000.

EUROPE

Ireland

- White, Oliver. *A Century of Service: A history of Irish men and women who have served with SIM*. Belfast: Ulster Services, 1994.

MIDDLE EAST

Aden Colony (part of today's Yemen)

- Acord, Fred D. *God Moves In*. Colorado Springs: Williams & Acord, c. 1972.

Lebanon

*For other sources of work in Lebanon, see the periodicals and books listed in the "Lebanon Evangelical Mission" section (pages 422-424).

- Acord, Fred D. *God Moves In*. Colorado Springs: Williams & Acord, c. 1972.
- Salisbury, Len, with Helen Salisbury. *War, Typhoons & the Gospel: Lifelong journey of two people surviving & thriving in Mission*. Sydney: FC Productions, 2016.
- Strengholt, Jos M. *Gospel in the Air: 50 Years of Christian Witness through Radio in the Arab World*. Zoetermeer, 2008. (Chapter 7 is about Radio ELWA.)

SOUTH AMERICA

Continent

- Fuller, W. Harold. *Tie Down the Sun: Adventure in Latin America*. Scarborough, Canada: SIM International Media, 1990.

Bolivia

- Anonymous. *Unión Christiana Evangélica: Bodas de Oro, 1950–2000*. Cochabamba, c. 2000.

- Collins, Laurie Berg. *To the Next Generation: One family's story of God's call to missions.* Cloverdale, IN: Step by Step Publications, 2001.
- _____. *Treasures in the Clay Jars: The Story of Victory in Disability and Fulfillment of God's Plan in Service.* N.p.: Xlibris Corporation, 2001.
- Hansen, James L., ed. and comp. *A Heart to Serve: Ordinary people with an extraordinary God.* Cochabamba, Bolivia: Mision Andina Evangelica, 2007.
- Hawthorne, Sally Reese. *Cloud Country Sojourn.* London: Marshall, Morgan and Scott Ltd., n.d.
- Herron, Robert, comp. *Walter Herron: Pioneer Missionary to Bolivia.* N.p., c. 2010.
- Hudspith, Margarita Allan. *Ripening Fruit: A History of the Bolivian Indian Mission.* Harrington Park, NJ: Harrington Press, c. 1958.
- Shereda, Edith. *The Indian War Cry,* New York: Loizeaux Brothers Publishers, 1942. (The author tells about her work among the Quechua.)
- Torres, Por Ezequiel G. *Historia de la Union Christiana Evangelica, 1950–1994.* Cochabamba, Bolivia, 1992.
- Wagner, C. Peter, and Joseph S. McCullough. *The Condor of the Andes: Missionary Pilot of Bolivia.* Andes Evangelical Mission, 1966. Reprint, Evangelistic Literature Enterprise, 1987. (Story of AEM pilot Wally Herron.)
- Windle, Jeanette. *Yandicu: From witch doctor to evangelist.* Kansas City, MO: Gospel Missionary Union, 1992. (Yandicu was a great Guarani evangelist with the Union Christiana Evangelica.)

INDEX